Risking
Contact

Risking Contact

Readings to Challenge Our Thinking

W. Royce Adams

Emeritus
Santa Barbara City College

Houghton Mifflin Company
Boston   New York

Senior Sponsoring Editor: Dean Johnson
Senior Associate Editor: Linda Bieze
Editorial Assistant: Mary Healey
Associate Project Editor: Elena Di Cesare
Editorial Assistant: Angela Schoenherr
Production/Design Coordinator: Jennifer Meyer
Director of Manufacturing: Michael O'Dea
Marketing Manager: Nancy Lyman

Cover design by Cathy Hawkes.
Cover image: Vasily Kandinsky, *Capricious,* September 1927. The Solomon R. Guggenheim Museum, New York.
Photograph by David Heald © The Solomon R. Guggenheim Foundation, New York. (FN 38.298)

Acknowledgments appear on pages 592–595, which constitute a continuation of the copyright page.

Printed in the U.S.A.

Library of Congress Catalog Card Number: 96-76853

ISBN: 0-669-39327-4

23456789-QF-00 99 98 97

Contents

❧ *Always Running*   25
LUIS RODRIGUEZ
The Crazy Life in my youth, although devastating, was only the beginning stages in what I believe now is a consistent and growing level of destruction predicated on the premise there are marginalized youth with no jobs or future, and therefore expendable.

❧ *The Content of Our Character*   33
SHELBY STEELE
And simply living as an individual in America—with my racial identity struggle suspended by my subscription to the black power identity—I discovered that American society offered me and blacks in general a remarkable range of opportunity if we were willing to pursue it.

❧ *Then and Now*   40
MARY PIPHER
Our culture has changed from one in which it was hard to get information about sexuality to one in which it's impossible to escape information about sexuality.

❧ *An Outlaw Mom Tells All*   48
MARY KAY BLAKELY
Because most of our work is invisible to the family values crowd, they're probably unaware of what valuable [single mother] worker bees we are in

this society. Take us out, and you need four people to replace each one of us.

Race and Rights   219

Preface

In a publication of the Association of American Colleges, *Integrity in the College Curriculum*, the following point is stressed:

> How do we know? Why do we believe? What is the evidence? Here, whatever the subject matter, we are at the heart of the intellectual process, concerned with the phenomenon of human thinking, the processes whereby they establish a fact, put two or more of them together, come to conclusions as to their meaning, and perhaps even soar with some leap of the imagination to a thought that has never been thought before. To reason well, to recognize when reason and evidence is not enough, to discover the legitimacy of intuition, to subject inert data to the probing analysis of the mind—these are the primary experiences required of the undergraduate course of study. . . . Students possess great untrained and untapped capacities for logical thinking, critical analysis, and inquiry, but these are capacities that are not spontaneous: they grow out of wise instruction, experience, encouragement, correction, and constant use.

The purpose of *Risking Contact* is to provide an instructional tool that helps meet the need to develop students' capacities for critical thinking by providing readings and questions that confront and stimulate students with alternate viewpoints on contemporary controversial issues. Students are asked to analyze an author's position, to examine his or her reasoning, to become aware of fallacious thinking, and to reevaluate their own views and opinions.

The intent is not to provide a "how-to-think" book; rather, the intent is to expose and challenge academically capable students through reading material that stimulates them into actively thinking about issues that challenge our society, issues about which they should and must make choices. But these choices must be based on "the probing analysis of the mind."

The first section, *Reading and Writing Processes,* offers a brief overview of the reading, thinking, and writing processes necessary for approaching the readings in this text. Information on the essay format, proofreading, quoting and documenting sources, and library research sources can be found in the Appendixes. The reading selections are categorized into six units dealing with lifestyles, prejudice, race, religion, responsibility, and the media. Despite these divisions, no borders really exist between units. For example, a reading selection presented in the race section might just as easily cross over into themes presented in the sections on prejudice or social responsibility revealing the interconnection of so many seemingly different issues. In all units more than several viewpoints are presented, always with at least two authors in direct opposition.

Each thematic unit begins with prefatory comments that provide an overview of the problems associated with the topic that need to be resolved. Each essay within a unit is preceded by a brief comment regarding the author and the issue being addressed. Following each reading are three sets of questions designed to get students to think critically about the author's issue and conclusion. The first set asks questions about the content, the second set asks questions about the author's writing techniques, and the third poses questions to use in group discussions and/or possible writing assignments. Together they form the basis for critical thinking: the identification and recall of information, the selection and organization of facts and ideas, the analysis of the whole and its parts, the synthesis of the ideas as a whole, and the evaluation and prioritization of opinions, judgments, and decisions.

Risking Contact calls for just what the title states: risking contact with ideas, beliefs, and opinions of others who may not see things the way we do. Some of the reading selections may unsettle or even offend a few, but at the very least they will be challenging and offer engaging openings for discussion and writing topics.

For their valuable reviews and suggestions, I would like to thank Keith Kroll, Kalamazoo Valley Community College, Michigan; Frances Leonard, West Los Angeles College; Margaret Mahoney, Iowa State University; Robert Miedel, La Salle University, Pennsylvania; and Mary Sue Rickels, Laredo Junior College, Texas.

My appreciation and thanks are extended to editors Dean Johnson, Linda Bieze, and Elena Di Cesare for their invaluable support, guidance, and assistance with this project.

W. Royce Adams

To the Student

As a college student you must leave much of the security of easy answers behind and face the often unfamiliar job of having to make choices and take stands on a variety of perplexing questions to which there are no easy answers. Indeed, the process continues well beyond college. In order to get the most from your education, you must first become aware of yourself by examining the validity of your opinions, how those opinions were formed, how willing you are to hear the views of those in opposition, how willing you are to change, and under what circumstances you are willing to change. You need to examine and test your beliefs by risking contact with the beliefs of others whose ideas may be contrary to your own or ones you've never considered.

In his Foreword to David Schaafsma's *Eating on the Street,* Jay Robinson states:

> Few of us risk contacts with others that will trouble us, that will unsettle our customary ways of seeing and understanding. Untroubled perspectives on the world, clear and clean ones, comfort us, but they don't help us see much that is there; neither do they help us see ourselves in our relations to others.

The reading selections in *Risking Contact* contain "troubled perspectives on the world" and have been selected not only to help you "see much that is there," but to help you see yourself in your relations with others. You will read what others have to say on six general areas: lifestyles, prejudice, race, religion, responsibility, and the media. All of the readings present issues and questions that demand critical evaluation on your part. Since many of the arguments may be in opposition to your own views, or perhaps even offensive in some cases, you will need to approach such positions with an open and analytical attitude. In turn, you will be asked to think through certain issues critically and to write essays presenting your own conclusions.

Dealing with opinions on issues would be easy if thinking were perfectly logical. Our minds would already be open to available evidence, we'd examine it logically, and then we'd form our conclusion. Unfortunately, that's not the way our minds usually work. We human beings are opinionated organisms with convictions on a wide range of topics, such as who will make our best elected officials, what is the funniest show on television, which café has the best espresso, or whether capital punishment is moral. What we need to remember is that such opinions are just that, opinions, not fact, and as such they are subject to argument and change. We need to examine not just evidence that supports our opinions, but evidence that conflicts with our beliefs. *Risking Contact* hopes to challenge many of your formed opinions on a variety of issues by presenting you with alternate and often opposing opinions. If after critically thinking through your beliefs and those of others you still hold your original convictions, you will know they are truly yours, not hand-me-down opinions.

In his book *On Liberty,* the political philosopher John Stuart Mill explains what it takes to obtain wisdom, which he terms a prerequisite for true liberty. It's sound advice to follow.

> In the case of any person whose judgment is really deserving of confidence, how has it become so? Because he has kept his mind open to criticism of his opinions and conduct. Because it has been his practice to listen to all that could be said against him; to profit by it as much of it as was just, and expound to himself, and upon occasion to others, the fallacy of what was fallacious. Because he has felt, that the only way in which a human being can make some approach to knowing the whole subject, is by hearing what can be said about it by persons of every variety of opinion, and studying all modes in which it can be looked at by every character of mind. No wise man ever acquired wisdom in any mode but this; nor is it in the nature of human intellect to become wise in any other manner. [John Stuart Mill, "On Liberty," *The English Philosophers From Bacon to Mill,* New York: Modern Library, 1939, 964]

Risking
Contact

Reading and Writing Processes

Reading Critically

The first step in acquiring wisdom from this book is to learn to read critically. Reading critically not only demands being open-minded and setting aside your own opinions, but being mentally alert as well. Not always easy, reading critically takes practice and concentrated effort. Until you become proficient at it, you may need to read each assigned reading selection at least twice, perhaps more, depending on the difficulty of the material. The more you practice reading critically, the more natural it will become if it isn't already.

First Reading

As part of your first reading, make certain you have read the introduction to the unit in which the assigned reading selection appears. You will gain an overview and a perspective on the range of views on the unit's topic. Also make certain you read the short introduction presented before each reading selection as a way to focus your attention on the author and the content. Then quickly read through the selection to get a general idea of the issue or controversy being discussed and the author's thesis or conclusion regarding the issue. For instance, an author's topic might deal with prayer in the public schools. As you read, you realize the *issue* the author is raising:

Should school prayer be allowed in the public schools?

As you read, you learn the author's thesis or conclusion is:

School prayer should not be permitted in public schools because it goes against the First Amendment's intention to keep church and state separate.

Of course, the author's thesis might also be:

School prayer should be permitted in public schools because the First Amendment guarantees the right of free speech.

At this point, you may not agree with the author's conclusion because it's contrary to your opinion. That's when you need to keep an open mind and put aside your biases so you can examine the author's reasons

1

for his or her conclusions. But even if you agree with the author's conclusion, you still need to carefully examine the reasons given: they may be weak, deceptive, or irrational. On the other hand, the reasons may be valid and provide you with new insights that bolster your own views on the issue.

Sometimes a thesis or conclusion is not obvious on first reading because the author implies rather than states the thesis. A second, more careful reading will help you infer the author's meaning.

Second Reading

Your second reading is done more critically by thoughtfully examining the reasons the author provides for the conclusion. As you identify each of the supporting reasons offered, evaluate its validity. Consider the reasoning used, the connection between the support and the conclusion, the style and ability of the author to persuade, and your personal reactions.

MARKING   The best way to work your way through a second reading is to mark key passages and raise questions as you read. For instance, notice how the following passage has been marked to identify the issue, conclusion, and supporting points.

THE PUSH FOR SCHOOL PRAYER

Adam Ribb

why an
amendment?

any more than
other time?

author's
conclusion

Periodically, there are political attempts by Christian   1
members of Congress to pass a Constitutional amendment to allow prayer in public schools. As one of the
reasons, we are told by those with a religious agenda
that putting prayer back in school would result in a more
moral country. While there is good cause to wonder
about the moral decay in America today, is this the
proper way to do it? I think not. Those who push for
school prayer are going about it the wrong way, because
the real arguments against school prayer are not legal
but theological.

The argument usually put forth that America is at   2
root a religious nation and should be evidenced in our
schools is growing thin as the country enlarges its cultural diversity. According to a recent *Time* magazine

wow! didn't realize that

good question!

look up word

What kind of prayer do they want?

all good questions

like?

Sounds good, but I need to hear a counter argument.

report, there are at least 1,200 organized, distinct religious groups in America, many of them far afield of the Judeo-Christian roots of the founding fathers. What kind of prayers, then, would be held in school? Cultural historian and evangelical author Os Guiness says evangelicals should know better than to demand school prayer. "The same parents who press for prayer in the South would be outraged by Buddhist meditation in Hawaii or reading from the Book of Mormon in Utah. For them to argue like European Anglicans is an exercise in historical amnesia." In other words, we either secularize our faith or we scandalize nonbelievers.

Those pushing for an amendment to allow school 3 prayer are usually conservative Christians. As Joe Loconte, a former senior news writer for *Christianity Today*, points out, "One of the most compelling features of conservative Christianity is belief in a God who is both personal and purposeful. A gray, soulless generic prayer could not include most of the divine attributes considered basic to Christian believers." Because prayer is personal, an attempt to put prayer in schools could not be satisfying on an individual level. Who would say the prayer? What would the prayer contain? What faith's denominational dogma would it contain?

There are better ways to exert moral influence in 4 the schools than prayer over the intercom. Those ways must be found and pursued. But empty prayers will not undo prejudices against faith nor will it strengthen the already faithful.

Notice that the marks and questions are personal in nature. They reflect the thinking of the reader while in communion with the writer. In effect, a type of dialogue has taken place and a record of that dialogue is there for future review or use during class discussions or writing exercises.

READING JOURNALS   You may want (or might be assigned) to keep a reading journal. In addition to what an instructor might want you to keep in your journal, you should use it to record thoughts, ideas, and reactions to each reading selection assigned in *Risking Contact*. In your journal, you don't need to worry about spelling or grammar errors. You can write what you really feel at the moment, capturing thoughts or reactions that might be useful or the basis for a future essay of your own. You can use the journal to write questions you might want to ask in class, to summarize the content of a reading selection, to argue with the author, or to explore your own feelings about the issue or conclusion of an author.

Here is an example of a possible journal entry for "Pushing for School Prayer":

> I've never really given much thought about the prayer in school issue. Ribb raises some interesting questions to consider: Why do people want prayer in school? How would prayers be conducted? Would Muslims bring prayer rugs and stop class to pray at certain times? (I think that's what they do, but I don't know.) Would everyone in class go do their prayer thing? Would there really be prayers over the intercom? Do Christians, who seem to be the ones pushing for school prayer, want to force everyone to believe in their God? Is there a hidden agenda behind the push? Would school prayer really raise the morals of this country? I wonder if the morals of this country are really any worse than any other generation? A political fear tactic maybe? I need to learn more about this issue before I can write anything intelligent about it.

Notice that the entry reflects questions that the reading selection raised and the recognition that the student has not thought much about the issue and needs to find answers to the questions raised before being able to write an essay on the subject. Another student, knowing more about the subject, or having stronger feelings about the issue, might write a rebuttal argument against the conclusion made by the author.

Thinking Critically about What You've Read

Critical thinking involves making a cautious and considered assessment of whether to accept, reject, or hold judgment on a conclusion made by the writer and then making a decision as to what level of trust is appropriate if we accept or reject the conclusion. Once you have identified the issue and the conclusion of an author through critical reading, you are ready to:

1. Examine for accuracy and validity the reasons or logic behind the conclusion;

2. Explore alternative reasons, omitted interpretations, or bias; and

3. Accept, reject, or hold judgment on a conclusion based on your findings.

These steps are not always easy to follow. Sometimes we may not know enough about a subject and need to learn more. Sometimes our opinions, biases, and prejudices interfere, blocking critical thought. And sometimes we just may not be interested or may be too lazy to bother. Thinking critically requires an application of skills that often don't come easily or naturally and must be learned and practiced.

Look for the following as you examine an author's conclusion and reasoning for accuracy and validity.

Examining for Accuracy and Validity

How does one go about examining the reasons or logic behind an author's conclusion for accuracy and validity? As you think through an author's reasoning, always keep in mind the issue raised and the conclusion made by the author. Then look for the following elements in the presentation of the argument.

AMBIGUITY   As you examine each of the reasons given for the conclusion, make certain you understand any ambiguous words or terms. For instance, does *school prayer* mean the same thing to everyone? When you read the phrase, what is your idea of school prayer? Is it the same as the author's, your neighbor's, mine? Without an understanding of an author's use of such ambiguous terms, it is possible to misunderstand an author's reasoning as well as conclusion. When authors use phrases such as *television violence, obscenity in books, graphic sex in movies, feminism,* and so on, it is important to make certain you understand the issue as defined by the author since you may hold a different definition. Good writers will make certain they define or at least make clear their ambiguous terms for the reader.

ASSUMPTIONS   Also look for reasoning based on assumptions, that is, ideas or reasons the author takes for granted everyone would accept. For instance, an author arguing for school prayer may, because of his or her convictions, be convinced that school prayer will help slow society's "rapid moral decaying." Reasoning may then be based on the assumption that society's morality is decaying rapidly and that school prayer will slow or stop the process. Without valid proof there is "rapid moral decaying," such an argument is based on an assumption not verifiable by fact or necessarily even true.

COMMON FALLACIES IN REASONING   Examine statements for fallacies in reasoning. The most common fallacies include:

- **Oversimplifying,** or focusing attention on only one cause or effect,
  ignoring those that might even be more significant
- **Overgeneralizing** by exaggerating a valid idea beyond the limits
  of reasonableness
- **Either/or statements** that mislead one into thinking there are only
  two possible choices to be made
- **Irrational appeal** aims at people's emotions rather than reason
  and attempts to instill fear, appeal to tradition, or to common
  practice regardless of its merits
- **Diverting attention** by making an assumption without proof and
  then charging the opposition to prove it false
- **Avoiding the issue** by deliberately attacking someone to shift attention to another issue
- **Circular reasoning** or begging the question occurs when an author
  tries to support a conclusion by stating another conclusion rather
  than providing a reason of support.

Be on guard for these fallacies. Don't let yourself fall into agreement
with arguments based on fallacious reasoning.

SUPPORTING EVIDENCE   Look carefully at any evidence provided to
bolster an author's conclusion, such as statistics or quotations from
authority figures. Statistics can be deceiving, as witnessed by Leonard
Huff's classic book *How to Lie with Statistics.* To evaluate statistics
critically requires knowing the reliability source of the numbers. Numbers can be inflated or made to look more impressive than they are.
For instance, results of a poll might show there was a 67 percent
increase in bodily assaults on teachers on a particular campus. But
such a figure could mean that the increase was actually small—from
three assaults to five, or quite large—from 300 to 500. Without the
actual figures, the percentages mean little here.

Even with the figures, information can be misleading. Reading
that three out of four hospitals prescribe Tylenol means little. How
many hospitals were involved—four? Were the three hospitals given
the medication as a promotional for the drug company that makes
Tylenol? Was Tylenol the only medication of its type prescribed, or
does it just mean that along with other medications they prescribe
Tylenol? Be wary when you read statistics.

Naturally, you cannot take the time to verify every single statistic. You must consider the source and use common sense in accepting or rejecting numbers. But when you read statements that claim "All of . . . ," or "Most of . . . ," or "Thousands and thousands . . . ," chances are the evidence is being exaggerated. Such hyperbole should cause you to put such statements on hold until they can be verified.

Writers frequently use quotations as a way to support a point being made. When an author uses a quotation from someone who is supposed to be an authority, make certain the quotation is relevant and not diverting your attention away from the issue. Unless the person being quoted is universally known, the author should provide some pertinent information about the person's background or relation to the issue, or perhaps even a footnote with the source so that it can be verified.

FACT VS. OPINION   A *fact* is usually defined as something that can be proven. We accept something as a fact only when many different people come to the same conclusion after many years of observation, research, and experimentation. Evidence that supports a fact is usually arrived at objectively. An *opinion*, on the other hand, is a belief, feeling, or judgment made about something or someone that a person may hold as fact but cannot prove. Evidence that supports an opinion is usually subjective.

Separating fact from opinion is not always easy. One reason is that facts change. At one time in history it was a "fact" that the earth was flat, that the sun circled the earth, that no one could ever walk on the moon, that the atom was the smallest particle, and that getting a tan was healthy. Evidence gathered over time proved these "facts" to be wrong. Facts of today may be laughed at in the future.

Another reason separating fact from opinion is difficult is that statements of opinion can be made to sound factual. We might read one claim that the first inhabitants of North America arrived "around 25,000 years ago." Another source may say, "over 35,000 years ago." Which is correct? Since no one lived back then kept record, we have to be careful of accepting such numbers as "fact." The best we can do is check the dates of publication and lean toward the statement bearing the latest date. Or, we could check other sources to see if there is any agreement on a date.

Our personal bias or prejudice also interferes with the separation of fact and opinion. Frequently, we allow our feelings and beliefs instilled in us as we grew up to override our acceptance of facts. Family, friends, teachers, and people we admire influence our thinking. If someone grows up with a strong belief that the Bible is the literal word of God, that person will probably have difficulty accepting any writer's conclusion that might shatter that belief. Yet, a critical reader and thinker must be open to opposing viewpoints and subject personal beliefs to critical reasoning. What facts are there to support your opinion? Is your viewpoint based only on opinion, especially the opinion of others that you have been accepting without thinking for yourself?

Exploring Alternative Reasons

We may find ourselves resisting certain reasons or conclusions because they are contrary to our own. It is human nature to resist changing our minds or to go against tradition. And, of course, there are times when accepting new ideas merely because they *are* new is a mistake. But it is important to overcome a resistance to changing our minds or to accepting new ideas when that resistance is based on fear or an unwillingness to examine them critically.

To overcome this resistance when it occurs, accept your negative reaction as natural, especially when it offends or goes against your beliefs. But don't stop there. Put aside your negative reaction long enough to examine the issue and conclusion critically. Try to identify with the opposition. Ask yourself if any alternative reasons support or refute the conclusion. Were arguments omitted or ignored? If so, why do you think they were? Are there other interpretations of the reasons given that would lead to a conclusion different from the author's? In other words, make certain you have looked beyond your initial negative reaction and given the opposing ideas careful consideration.

On the other hand, you don't want to be too quick to accept a conclusion simply because you agree with it. Don't fall into a "mine is better" mentality, preferring your own opinions simply because they are yours. Critical thinking requires that you examine your own conclusions as well as other people's. Again, try to see things from an opposing viewpoint. How would they react to the conclusion? What ideas and facts might support the other side? Are there alternate possibilities omitted or neglected that fairly challenge your views? Only after such a critical analysis will you then be in a position to accept, reject, or hold judgment on a conclusion.

Once you have accepted, rejected, or decided to hold judgment on the author's conclusion, write a summary of your reaction to the reading selection in your journal. The summary should include a statement of the author's issue, the author's conclusion, and then reasons you agree, disagree, or need to know more about the issue before you can discuss the topic with knowledge. This enables you to focus your attention on your critical analysis as well as preserve your thoughts for possible use when you select an issue for an essay of your own.

DISCUSSION GROUPS   One of the best ways to seek answers to the questions critical thinking requires is to form a small group with other students and discuss all your various reactions. Some bravery may be required on your part in stating and supporting your views and opinions with others, but it forces you to risk contact with others and to put your beliefs to the test. Discussion affords you the opportunity of hearing why others think and believe the way they do. You discover where you stand among others. Be willing to listen to ideas contrary to yours. Don't keep your thoughts to yourself. As mentioned earlier, when you read critically, you should enter into a dialogue with a writer. That dialogue is extended when you exchange ideas in a discussion group. The issues and conclusions grow in scope beyond that presented by an individual author. In turn, your critical thinking ability is strengthened through discussion and provides you with an intellectual perspective and scope on the issues presented in *Risking Contact*.

Following each reading selection are three sets of questions for you to use as a way to think critically about the author's issue and conclusion. The first set asks you questions about the content, the second set asks questions about the author's writing techniques, and the third poses questions for you to use in group discussions and/or possible writing assignments. Together they form the basis for critical thinking: the identification and recall of information, the selection and organization of facts and ideas, the analysis of the whole and its parts, the synthesis of the ideas as a whole, and the evaluation and prioritization of opinions, judgments, and decisions.

Putting Your Conclusions in Writing

Sometimes a discussion of the writing process makes it sound linear. It isn't. As someone has suggested, writing is an act of chaos, an attempt to give meaning to our interpretations of ideas and events. It may, in fact, be impossible to explain the writing process or present it like a recipe. One step *here* doesn't always mean the next step is *there*. Good writing involves starting and stopping, eagerly writing away and angrily throwing away, moving along and stalling, feeling pleased and feeling frustrated, thinking you've finished and then realizing you need to start again. Sometimes, when you have thoroughly thought about an issue, a writing assignment may come effortlessly, but more often you will have to work hard at it.

If possible, do your work on a word processor. Making changes, doing revisions, and producing neat essays is much easier once you learn word processing. It enables you to make changes without having to retype or recopy your entire essay once a mistake or false start is discovered. But whatever you use for your first drafts—pencil, pen, typewriter, or word processor—don't worry too much about minor mistakes in punctuation, spelling, or word choice. Save that for later. At this point, get your thoughts into words as best you can without losing your train of thought. On the other hand, if you see an error you can quickly fix, do so, but not at the expense of losing your thoughts on the issue.

What follows are suggestions that may help you find your way through the chaos involved in putting ideas into words. Eventually you will find a way to put words on paper that works best for you.

Getting Started

Unless a particular issue and a conclusion has been assigned to you, you will need to decide what your topic will be, what the issue regarding the topic is, and then present your conclusion or thesis backed up with reasonable support. It's critical reading in reverse. Don't even begin an essay until you are fairly certain you know what you want to say and why you have made the conclusion you have on the topic.

SEARCHING YOUR JOURNAL A good place to start searching for a topic is in your journal, provided you have kept one that reflects thoughts you can use as a basis for an essay. Look over your journal entries. You may have already written down some reactions, ideas, or questions that you can use as a starting point. Also look over any textbook markings you made when reading assigned essays. You may see other essay possibilities in your markings or be reminded of issues you feel strongly about. Chances are you won't be given a writing assignment until after you have read some of the readings on a particular issue. If that's the case, you will have gained some background information and critical analyses to draw from.

BRAINSTORMING Another way to decide on a topic or issue is to brainstorm, either alone or in a small group. If, for example, you have been asked to write an essay on the influence of violence depicted in movies and television, turn the topic into an issue, such as: Does violence depicted in movies and on television have an influence on children's behavior? Then start jotting down every idea or thought that pops into your head. Don't be critical about the value of the idea, at least not during your brainstorming. Just let the ideas come and write them down. You can accept and reject various thoughts later. If you find you don't have much to say or think about the issue, form a new one, such as: Does violence depicted in movies and on television reflect society? Or: Should the violence as depicted in movies and on television be censored? Or: Should consumers boycott advertisers who sponsor violent programs on television? The point is, try to make the issue one you know or have strong feelings about.

NUTSHELL STATEMENTS   Once you think you have decided on an issue and drawn a conclusion or thesis, write out a nutshell statement. A *nutshell statement* is a one-paragraph statement of the issue you want to address (best done in the form of a question), your conclusion about the issue (your answer to the question), a summary of the main supporting points, and an acknowledgment of the audience to whom you are directing your essay. A nutshell statement helps you put your ideas into words. It serves as a guide until you have gathered all the evidence you need to support your conclusion. It may be that during the course of gathering and evaluating your supporting evidence that you change direction or even change your mind. That's not unusual; indeed, it's frequently the case. Just pick a different conclusion or start over with a new issue. Better to change your mind now than after you've written a first draft.

Gather Evidence and Support Your Conclusion

Once you have your conclusion or thesis, you need valid evidence to support it. If your essay is to be of any substance, it should contain evidence of critical thinking regarding the issue. Some of your evidence may come from personal experience, some drawn from the reading selections in *Risking Contact,* and some may come from research.

If you need to research your topic, don't limit yourself to library research. Depending on the issue, you may find some experts on campus you can interview: professors, administrators, and other students. Some sources are listed at the end of each unit to help you get started. They can lead to other sources. You can also call upon experts in your community for more information. The point is, deliberately seek out as many views on the issue as you can, not forgetting to get views that oppose your own. The more information you gain, the more you can use as evidence to support your claim. Or, you may even find you change your mind. There's no harm in that.

Once you have collected the evidence, you need to put it into essay form. As you write your first draft, keep in mind that's all it is—a first draft. At this stage, you want to get your issue, conclusion, and evidence down on paper. Once you have it all written out, you will then rearrange, add, delete, and polish it during the revision process.

Your first draft might be ordered something like this:

Opening paragraph establishes the issue and viewpoint

2nd paragraph   Supporting idea #1

3rd paragraph   Perhaps more support for idea #1

4th paragraph   Supporting idea #2

5th paragraph   Perhaps more support for idea #2

6th paragraph   Supporting idea #3

(continuing with as many supporting paragraphs as needed)

Last paragraph offers summary or conclusion

Once you have stated your supporting points, evaluate them just as you did when you read the selections in this book. Look for ambiguity or assumptions you may have made. Check to make sure you have not used any fallacious reasoning. If you are using statistics, present them in a balanced way and cite the source. Any quotations you use should be accompanied by some type of introduction to the person's position or knowledge of the issue. Try, where possible, to use facts, making certain that opinions expressed are reasonable. Toss any evidence that does not meet these criteria.

Patterning Your Paragraphs

THE INTRODUCTION   Once you are satisfied you have critically evaluated your evidence, turn your attention to the essay form itself. As you will see from the variety of ways authors in *Risking Contact* introduce their topics and develop their conclusions, there is no one best way. Length, however, has much to do with how quickly you get to the point or whether or not you can afford to expand your introduction.

Here are some suggestions that may work for you, depending on your essay audience and the way you want to present your conclusion. Many of the essays in this book use these methods.

1. Get right to the point, stating your thesis or conclusion and your reasons in general for believing as you do. One drawback to this approach is that unless your thesis is stated in such a way that your audience will be interested in reading on, it could be a boring opening. See how this technique is done in Camille Paglia's "The Date-Rape Debate" and Leslie Lafayette's "Why Don't You Have Kids?"

2. Use a quotation that relates to your thesis, one by someone respected by most everyone, one that supports your point of view, or one that you disagree with and want to prove wrong in your essay. See a form of this in Vincent Ryan Ruggiero's "The Basic

Problem: Mine Is Better," Jonathan Rauch's "In Defense of Prejudice," and Moorhead Kennedy's "Why Fear Fundamentalism?"

3. Offer a brief anecdote or story that relates in some way to or
   introduces the point of your essay. Notice variants of this technique
   in Joseph Campbell's "The Emergence of Mankind" and Sallie
   Tisdale's "The Myth of Social Consensus."

4. Use one or more questions that cause the reader to think about
   your topic, questions that you intend to answer in the body of
   your essay. See David Moberg's "Suite Crimes" and Cornel West's
   "How Do We Fight Xenophobia?"

5. Provide some startling statistics, information, or descriptive scene
   that will grab your readers' attention and that will appeal to their
   good sense. Notice forms of this technique in Andrew Ferguson's
   "McNamara's Brand" and Luis Rodriguez's "Always Running."

6. Be creative. See how Andrew Klavan's "In Praise of Gore" gets
   your attention.

The introductory paragraph may be your most important one. Without
a good opening, no reader will even want to get involved with your
issue or conclusion.

THE SUPPORT   How you say what you want to say is important, so
make certain your paragraphs of supporting evidence are well developed and varied. How you phrase your topic sentence in a paragraph
determines what rhetorical shape that paragraph will take. Some of
the basic paragraph patterns found in good writing are: comparison-
contrast, narration, description, division-classification, analysis, example or illustration, definition, and cause-effect relationship.

Let's say that you've written the following topic sentence for a
supporting paragraph:

> When one looks closely, the changes in the welfare system
> as proposed by Congress are scarcely different from the present
> system.

Such a statement calls for the **comparison-contrast** pattern. The proposed welfare changes must be compared and contrasted with the
present system.

Here is another possible topic sentence:

> I'll never forget my humiliation the day I had to sign up as
> a welfare recipient.

The use of "I" calls for a first-person **narration,** an account of the humiliating experience that helps the reader understand and feel the embarrassment of the writer.

Another possible topic sentence might begin:

> Just the introduction to the proposed welfare bill is 700
> pages long and weighs 55 pounds.

From such a statement, it appears the author wants to write a **description** of the physical appearance of the welfare package itself. Of course, this is limited in scope and probably would lead to a discussion of the "weighty" components of the welfare bill.

A writer dealing with an evaluation of the welfare proposal and his or her reasons for its predicted failure might write:

> The welfare proposal should not pass Congress for four
> primary reasons.

Each of the four reasons must be presented to the reader, which suggests the use of the **division and classification** pattern.

Another writer may undertake a step-by-step **analysis** of the welfare package and write:

> The first error of many that needs correction in this bill is
> the assumption that huge numbers of teenage girls get
> pregnant in order to collect welfare.

The author must then take each of the "many errors" and show why they need correcting.

Another writer may want to show the reader that the welfare bill is full of discrepancies or contradictions and write:

> Many contradictions exist in the proposed welfare bill.

Such a statement requires **examples or illustrations** of contradictions that exist in the bill.

Perhaps a writer finds fault or the need for further elaboration of words or terms used in the bill:

> The term unable to work as used in the welfare package
> needs elaboration.

Such a sentence requires the writer to follow up with an extended **definition** of those terms found ambiguous.

Or, this sentence:

> Pressure from the liberal left has forced Congress into re-
> vamping the welfare package.

requires dealing with a **cause and effect** pattern: the cause (pressure
from the liberal left) and the effect (forcing Congress to revamp the
package).

This is not to say that other patterns could not be used in addition
to those discussed, but the illustrations should help you to see that
the wording of your topic sentence often requires that you follow a
pattern that allows your reader to follow your reasoning easily. If you
need it, most all college composition handbooks can provide more
detailed information about these patterns than space allows here.

As you read the selections in this book, pay attention to the many
ways authors develop their paragraphs.

THE CLOSING PARAGRAPH   As with introductory paragraphs, there
is no one way to conclude an essay. However, the closing paragraph
of an essay should neither simply duplicate what has already been
said, nor repeat verbatim what was said in the opening paragraph.
Instead, based on how you have presented your evidence, you will
want to do something similar to the following:

1. Draw a conclusion based on the evidence you have presented. This
   method works best when you have been arguing for a particular
   viewpoint and have presented support that needs to be highlighted
   in order to draw a conclusion for the reader. Dinesh D'Souza does
   this in "The End of Racism."

2. Offer a solution, emphasize the need for change, or demand more
   attention be given to the issue you've presented. Stir your readers
   to think more, care more, or act more on the issue because of the
   information you have provided. See forms of this technique in
   Charles Derber's "Civic Responsibility" and Paul Hawken's "A
   Declaration of Sustainability."

3. Summarize the evidence that has led you to your conclusion or
   thesis regarding the issue you've discussed. Make certain you summarize by using different wording to restate the points you've
   made. Don't simply repeat what you have already said. This
   method doesn't work too well in a short essay because you can
   sound redundant. It works best when you have written a longer
   piece with a mixture of evidence that needs to be brought back
   to the readers' attention before you end your essay. Notice how
   Gerald Early does this in "Understanding Afrocentrism."

Studying some of the ways the authors in *Risking Contact* conclude
their essays will be helpful patterns for you to consider.

Remember that your first draft attempts to put into words what you think you mean or know regarding an issue and to organize your evidence in a way that will interest your readers. This does not mean you will necessarily begin writing an introductory paragraph, then paragraphs of support, then your conclusion. That should be the way your essay is finally organized, but our minds don't always let us think in a linear fashion. Your introductory paragraph may be the last paragraph you write, because until you put your ideas together, you may not be able to introduce your reader to what you want to say. A supporting point may turn out to be an issue that needs an essay of its own that you then pursue. You may discover that you can't really support your conclusion and so must find another issue or conclusion. What you never see in a finished piece of writing are all of the changes, deletions, false starts—the chaos—that went into that final draft.

Revising and Editing

While you are writing your first draft, some revision and editing may take place. But major revision and editing should be done once you are satisfied you have finalized your thoughts regarding your conclusion and supporting evidence into the proper essay form. Don't get impatient with revision. It is necessary, expected, and part of the writing process.

REVISING   Use the following questions to revise your first draft:

1. *Have you clearly stated the issue and conclusion?*
   Stated or implied, your purpose and thesis should be clear to the reader. Have someone read your draft and restate for you what the reader thinks your conclusion or thesis is. If it is not clear, rewrite until it becomes clear.

2. *Does your supporting evidence move smoothly from one point to the next?*
   You may need to "cut and paste," or move a sentence or even a paragraph from one place to another. Use scissors and literally cut up your draft, moving parts around so the ideas flow smoothly. If you are working on a word processor, you can easily move parts around to the places where they fit best.

3. *Have you developed each paragraph fully?*
   Find the topic sentence in each of your paragraphs. Do you provide enough support to develop the topic sentence? You may need to rewrite your topic sentence to fit the content of the paragraph.

4. *Will your essay interest your audience?*
   Your opening paragraph should want your reader to read on. Try to picture your audience and talk to them in writing.

5. *Is the tone of your essay consistent and fitting for your audience?*
   Try to maintain the same tone throughout your essay. If you are being sarcastic don't suddenly switch to being funny. If you feel pessimistic about your issue, reflect that pessimism in your tone. If you want to relate things on a personal level, keep it personal. If you feel offended by a writer, be defensive or go on the offense, but stay consistent in tone.

6. *Have you said everything that needs to be said and deleted superfluous material?*
   Make certain you have said everything that needs to be said to support your conclusion and inform your reader, but also make certain you delete material that is not relevant to your thesis.

Other questions and concerns you need to address will occur as you apply this checklist of questions to your first draft.

EDITING   Try to give yourself some time off from your latest draft before editing it. Schedule time so that you have a least a day away from your essay. You need to get away from what you've written so that you can come to it with fresh eyes.

Once you have rewritten or revised your essay into its final stages, you need to edit for minor errors in punctuation and mechanics. As you do this, you may see other problems or errors that need correction or even revision—again. Revision is part of the continual "chaotic" process of composing. But chances are by this stage you have your issue, conclusion and supporting evidence well organized.

Here's one way to begin editing. Begin by reading aloud the last sentence of your essay. Does it say what you intend it to say? Does it say it well? Do you use the best choice of words for your audience? Do you repeat words too often? Then, working your way backward, read the next-to-the-last sentence and look for the same things in that sentence. It sounds odd to work your way a sentence at a time toward the beginning, but doing so forces you to look at each sentence out of context, as a separate piece of writing, not as part of the flow of ideas.

Next, read your essay through from the beginning now checking for proper punctuation, subject and verb agreement, correct pronoun references, and spelling. You may want to buy (or your instructor may require it) a grammar handbook for review and reference. Make certain it is a fairly recent edition that reflects the current usage your instructor expects in your essays.

Your instructor may require that you follow a particular format regarding size of margins, position of name, title, and page numbers, and so on. If not, you will find information on form and style in the Appendix.

A Final Word

Once you begin reading the assigned selections in *Risking Contact*, remember what has been offered here. Feel free to return and reread all or portions of this introduction as often as you need to help you get the maximum possible from each assignment. What value you get from exploring the ideas presented in the reading selections in this book is up to you.

Lifestyles

Life is the continuous adjustment of internal relations to external relations.

—HERBERT SPENCER

The best use of life is to spend it for something that outlasts life.

—WILLIAM JAMES

Life is not lost by dying; life is lost minute by minute, day by dragging day, in all the thousand small uncaring ways.

—STEPHEN VINCENT BENÉT

We are here to add what we can to life, not to get what we can from it.

—WILLIAM OSLER

Let us so live that when we come to die even the undertaker will be sorry.

—MARK TWAIN

There is only one success—to be able to spend your life in your own way.

—CHRISTOPHER MORLEY

I think that, as life is action and passion, it is required of a man that he should share the passion and action of his time at peril of being judged not to have lived.

—OLIVER WENDELL HOLMES

Do not take life too seriously; you will never get out of it alive.

—ELBERT HUBBARD

Life is like a cash register, in that every account, every thought, every deed, like every sale, is registered and recorded.

—FULTON J. SHEEN

Were it offered to my choice, I should have no objection to a repetition of the same life from its beginning, only asking the advantages authors have in a second edition to correct some faults in the first.

—BENJAMIN FRANKLIN

Life is a tragedy for those who feel, and a comedy for those who think.

—JEAN DE LA BRUYÈRE

Life is a dead-end street.

—H. L. MENCKEN

IN THE LAST DECADE MUCH has been written about the breakdown of U.S. society—violence on the streets, family dissolution, chaos in government, moral disintegration—all causing civilized behavior and vital social institutions to languish and perhaps die. We are told that U.S. cities have always been violent places, but now the violence being reported is more in number, more menacing, more bizarre, more meaningless, more random. The message heard by many? Be more vigilant and assume that every fellow citizen is a threat.

To protect themselves, journalist Chris Black writes in the *Boston Globe,* "Citizens have hunkered down with their nuclear families and turned their homes into suburban bunkers against outside threats." Michel Marriott, in her *Newsweek* report, "Living in 'Lockdown,' " revealed that many inner-city parents are keeping their children inside for fear of the violence on the streets. But this "cocooning" has its dark side. Researchers Richard J. Gelles and Murray A. Straus found, "The cruel irony of staying home because one fears violence in the streets is that the real danger of personal attack is *in the home.* Offenders are not strangers climbing through windows, but loved ones, family members." Between 1980 and 1990, a 50 percent increase in family violence was reported. Approximately 5,000 Americans murdered someone in their immediate family in 1990, accounting for almost one-fourth of all the murders in the country.

Other reports support the concern that the nuclear family is clearly becoming a less stable institution or taking on a different shape. More children are being born out of wedlock; child abuse and abandonment are not unusual; though somewhat stabilized, divorce rates are still high with single-parent households on the rise. Even among two-parent, affluent households, families are not always stable. Studies show that many professionals, consumed by their careers, do not invest enough time with their kids, destroying the kindness and care on which loving families depend. Teenagers, it is reported, now spend more time "hanging out" in the mall than anywhere else but home and school. Sociologists warn that the so-called traditional family is coming unglued.

At the same time family unity seems to be falling apart, so political and social structures seem to be in a state of flux. Recognizing that voters are disgruntled at "big government spending and huge deficits," politicians find they can be elected by vowing "no new taxes." Refusing to raise taxes has become an acceptable political theme to lash out and eradicate "wasteful government spending." Ironically, those calling for less government are often the ones also calling for a return to family values. "It should come as no surprise," writes Neal Gabler in the *Los Angeles Times*, "that those targets are invariably the least powerful among us: the poor, the foreign-born, the disadvantaged. They are the ones who suffer when the populace is in a foul mood."

A look at the news almost any day reflects a mean-spirited, intolerant nation. Talk radio and television programs seem to be designed to let angry people lash out at gays, immigrants, welfare recipients, the homeless, the disadvantaged, spouses, their own children.

What effect are these social trends—growing violence, family disorder, chaos in government, intolerance—having on individual lifestyles? Who or what is responsible for violence on the streets and in the home? Why are so many inner-city kids joining gangs? What needs to be done? What role should government play in helping the less fortunate, the needy? How do certain lifestyles create problems for others? Should they? What happens to individual lifestyles when the traditional family unit comes apart? What role does the family play in creating or hindering a "kinder, gentler" nation? What is your role in all of this?

Reading selections in this unit should cause you to reflect on some of these questions.

LUIS RODRIGUEZ

Journalist, publisher, critic, and poet, Luis Rodriguez grew up in the late 1960s and early 1970s in Los Angeles in what he calls "the gang capital of the country." His teen years were one of "drugs, shootings, beatings, and arrests." Rodriguez claims, "By the time I turned eighteen years old, twenty-five of my friends had been killed by rival gangs, police, drugs, car crashes, and suicides."

While Rodriguez survived and has carved out a better lifestyle for himself, his book, *Always Running: la vida loca, gang days in L.A.*, recounts some of his own struggles during ages twelve to eighteen when he was active in *Las Lamos* barrio to show that there are members of a social stratum that includes welfare mothers, housing project residents, immigrant families, the homeless, and the unemployed whose lifestyles reflect their depravation of the basic necessities of life.

The following selection is taken from the Preface to *Always Running*.

☙

Always Running

L ate winter Chicago, early 1991: The once-white snow which fell   1
in December had turned into a dark scum, mixed with ice-melting salt, car oil and decay. Icicles hung from rooftops and windowsills like the whiskers of old men.

For months, the bone-chilling "hawk" swooped down and forced   2
everyone in the family to squeeze into a one-and-a-half bedroom apartment in a gray-stone, three-flat building in the Humboldt Park neighborhood.

Inside tensions built up like fever as we crammed around the TV   3
set or kitchen table, the crowding made more intolerable because of heaps of paper, opened file drawers and shelves packed with books that garnered every section of empty space (a sort of writer's torture chamber). The family included my third wife Trini; our child, Rubén Joaquín, born in 1988; and my 15-year-old son Ramiro (a 13-year-old daughter, Andrea, lived with her mother in East Los Angeles).

We hardly ventured outside. Few things were worth heaving on   4
the layers of clothing and the coats, boots and gloves required to step out the door.

Ramiro had been placed on punishment, but not for an act of disobedience or the usual outburst of teenage anxiety. Ramiro had been on a rapidly declining roller coaster ride into the world of street-gang America, not unexpected for this neighborhood, once designated as one of the 10 poorest in the country and also known as one of the most gang-infested.

Humboldt Park is a predominantly Puerto Rican community with growing numbers of Mexican immigrants and uprooted blacks and sprinklings of Ukrainians and Poles from previous generations. But along with the greater West Town area it was considered a "changing neighborhood," dotted here and there with rehabs, signs of gentrification and for many of us, imminent displacement.

Weeks before, Ramiro had received a 10-day suspension from Roberto Clemente High School, a beleaguered school with a good number of caring personnel, but one which, unfortunately, was an epicenter of gang activity. The suspension came after a school fight which involved a war between "Insanes" and "Maniacs," two factions of the "Folks" ("Folks" are those gangs allied with the Spanish Cobras and Gangster Disciples; the "People" are gangs tied to the Latin Kings and Vice Lords, symbolic of the complicated structures most inner-city gangs had come to establish). There was also an "S.O.S."—a "smash-on-sight"—contract issued on Ramiro. As a result I took him out of Clemente and enrolled him in another school. He lasted less than two weeks before school officials there kicked him out. By then I also had to pick him up from local jails following other fighting incidents—and once from a hospital where I watched a doctor put 11 stitches above his eye.

Following me, Ramiro was a second-generation gang member. My involvement was in the late 1960s and early 1970s in Los Angeles, the so-called gang capital of the country. My teen years were ones of drugs, shootings and beatings, and arrests. I was around when South Central Los Angeles gave birth to the Crips and Bloods. By the time I turned 18 years old, 25 of my friends had been killed by rival gangs, police, drugs, car crashes and suicides.

If I had barely survived all this—to emerge eventually as a journalist, publisher, critic, and poet—it appeared unlikely my own son would make it. I had to cut his blood line to the street early, before it became too late. I had to begin the long, intense struggle to save his life from the gathering storm of street violence sweeping the country—some 20 years after I sneaked out of my 'hood in the dark of night, hid out in an L.A. housing project, and removed myself from the death-fires of *La Vida Loca*.

La Vida Loca or The Crazy Life is what we called the barrio gang   10
experience. This lifestyle originated with the Mexican *Pachuco* gangs
of the 1930s and 1940s, and was later recreated with the *Cholos*. It
became the main model and influence for outlaw bikers of the 1950s
and 1960s, the L.A. punk/rock scene in the 1970s and 1980s, and the
Crips and Bloods of the 1980s and early 1990s. As Leon Bing com-
mented in her 1991 book *Do or Die* (HarperCollins): "It was the *cholo*
homeboy who first walked the walk and talked the talk. It was the
Mexican American *pachuco* who initiated the emblematic tattoos, the
signing with hands, the writing of legends on walls."

One evening that winter, after Ramiro had come in late following   11
weeks of trouble at school, I gave him an ultimatum. Yelling burst
back and forth between the walls of our Humboldt Park flat. Two-
year-old Rubén, confused and afraid, hugged my leg as the shouting
erupted. In moments, Ramiro ran out of the house, entering the cold
Chicago night without a jacket. I went after him, although by my mid-
thirties I had gained enough weight to slow me down considerably.
Still I sprinted down the gangway which led to a debris-strewn alley,
filled with furniture parts and overturned trash cans. I saw Ramiro's
fleeing figure, his breath rising above him in quickly-dissipating clouds.

I followed him toward Augusta Boulevard, the main drag of the   12
neighborhood. People yelled out of windows and doorways: *"¿Qué
pasa, hombre?"* Others offered information on Ramiro's direction. A
father or mother chasing some child down the street is not an unfamiliar
sight around here.

A city like Chicago has so many places in which to hide. The gray   13
and brown brick buildings seem to suck people in. Ramiro would
make a turn and then vanish, only to pop up again. Appearing and
disappearing. He flew over brick walls, scurried down another alley
then veered into a building that swallowed him up and spit him out
the other side.

I kept after Ramiro until, unexpectedly, I found him hiding in   14
some bushes. He stepped out, unaware I was to the side of him.

"Ramiro . . . come home," I gently implored, knowing if I   15
pounced on him there would be little hope he'd come back. He sped
off again.

"Leave me alone!" he yelled.   16

As I watched his escape, it was like looking back into a distant   17
time, back to my own youth, when I ran and ran, when I jumped over
peeling fences, fleeing *vatos locos,* the police or my own shadow in
some drug-induced hysteria.

I saw Ramiro run off and then saw *my* body entering the mouth   18
of darkness, my breath cutting the frigid flesh of night; it was my voice
cracking open the winter sky.

Ramiro was born just prior to my 21st birthday. I had been working   19
in a steel mill in Los Angeles. His mother Camila, not yet 19, was an
East Los Angeles woman who grew up in one of East L.A.'s roughest
barrios: *La Gerahty Loma.* Yet Camila and her five sisters, with the
help of their mother, managed to stave off attempts to pull them into
the street life there—even having battles on their front porch with the
locas who tried to recruit them.

The media likens Los Angeles to a "Beirut by the Beach." For   20
1991, police cited these statistics: 100,000 gang members, 800 gangs,
nearly 600 young people killed. Parts of the city, particularly the public
housing projects, have been called "ungovernable." These stats have
been used to create a hysteria against black and Latino youth. Police
in L.A. have practically instituted martial law in the inner city. Michael
Davis in his book *City of Quartz* (Verso Press, 1991) says that by
1990 the various law enforcement "operations" to destroy gangs (using
helicopters, infra-red lights and made-over armored vehicles—not far
behind what was used in "Desert Storm") detained or arrested 50,000
youth, in South Central alone.

"The Crazy Life" in my youth, although devastating, was only   21
the beginning stages of what I believe is now a consistent and growing
genocidal level of destruction predicated on the premise there are
marginalized youth with no jobs or future, and therefore expendable.

Camila's brothers weren't spared. One of them became active in   22
Gerahty Loma, a witness to a number of killings himself, and later a
heroin addict and a convict. Another brother got jumped and stabbed
seven times—but survived And an older half-brother was killed while
trying to exact some revenge one night near the Mexican border.

Later, her nephews from an older sister got involved in the barrio   23
and one of them, known as Shorty, was murdered outside his home
at the age of 17 (but not before he fathered a baby).

When Ramiro was two years old, and his sister only 10 months,   24
Camila and I broke up. About seven years later, I moved to Chicago.
After being left behind, Ramiro failed miserably in school, although
he had been tested as a gifted child. He ran away from home a number
of times. Once when he was about 10 years old he hopped a train
from L.A. to Chicago, but police pulled him out of a boxcar before
he passed the city limits. When he turned 13 years old, he came to
stay with me. Because of what Camila and I had been through, we

tried everything we could to keep him out of the "life," even after we divorced and lived a couple of thousands of miles apart. But often there was too much against us.

In East L.A. and in schools like Chicago's Clemente were some   25
of the nation's highest drop-out rates. Youth unemployment hovered around 75 percent in the most neglected areas. And what of those who did everything right, got all the good grades and followed the "rules?" Camila, for example, had been an A student at Garfield High School (site of the 1988 movie "Stand and Deliver") and was active in school affairs. But after we married, she applied for work and was told she didn't know enough to get a basic 9 to 5 office job. She even had to go back to some classes to make up for the lack of schooling she received despite being one of the best students at Garfield! The fact the L.A. schools now give "warranties" only underscores the point.

With little productive to do, drug selling becomes a lucrative means   26
of survival. A 10-year-old in Humboldt Park can make $80–$100 a day as a lookout for local dealers. The drug trade is business. It's capitalism: Cutthroat, profit-motivated and expedient. Also, the values which drive gangs are linked to the control of markets, in a way similar to what has created borders between nations. In communities with limited resources like Humboldt Park and East L.A., sophisticated survival structures evolved, including gangs, out of the bone and sinew tossed up by this environment.

After Ramiro ran away, he failed to return home for another two   27
weeks. I was so angry at him for leaving, I bought locks to keep him out. I kept a vigil at home to catch him should he sneak in to eat. But then I remembered what I had been through. I recalled how many institutions and people had failed my son—and now he was expected to rise above all this! Soon I spent every night he was gone driving around the streets, talking to the "boys" in their street-corner domains, making daily calls to the police. I placed handwritten notes in the basement which said it was okay for him to come back. I left food for him to get to. Suddenly every teenage Latino male looked like Ramiro.

With the help of some of his friends, I finally found Ramiro in a   28
rundown barrio hovel and convinced him to come home. He agreed to obtain help in getting through some deep emotional and psychological problems—stemming in large part from an unstable childhood, including abuse he sustained as a kid from his stepfathers, one who was an alcoholic and another who regularly beat him. And I could not remove

myself from being struck by the hammerhead of responsibility. A key factor was my relative lack of involvement in Ramiro's life as I became increasingly active in politics and writing.

Although the best way to deal with one's own children is to help construct the conditions that will ensure the free and healthy development of all, it's also true you can't be for all children if you can't be for your own. 29

By mid-1991, Ramiro had undergone a few months in a psychiatric hospital and various counseling and family sessions that also involved bringing his mother in from L.A. We implemented an educational and employment plan, worked out with school officials, teachers and social workers (everyone who had dealings with him had to be involved, to get them on "our side" so to speak). I also learned a parent cannot just turn over a child to a school, a court, or hospital without stepping in at various times to insure his or her best interests are being met. My aim was to help Ramiro get through his teen-age years with a sense of empowerment and esteem, with what I call complete literacy: The ability to participate competently and confidently in any level of society one chooses. 30

There is an aspect of suicide in young people whose options have been cut off. They stand on street corners, flashing hand signs, inviting the bullets. It's either *la torcida* or death: A warrior's path, when even self-preservation is not at stake. And if they murder, the victims are usually the ones who look like them, the ones closest to who they are—the mirror reflections. They murder and they're killing themselves, over and over. 31

At the same time, individual efforts must be linked with social ones. I tried to get Ramiro to understand the systematic nature of what was happening in the street which in effect made choices for him before he was born. The thing is, no matter what one does individually, in this setting, the dangers keep lurking around every corner. 32

A couple of examples helped Ramiro see the point. Not long ago, a few of his friends were picked up by police, who drove them around in a squad car. The police took them to a rival gang neighborhood. There they forced Ramiro's friends to spray paint over the graffiti with their own insignias—as rival gang members watched—and then left them there to find their way home. It's an old police practice. 33

A second incident involved the shooting death of a Dragon, a Puerto Rican teenager named Efrain, who Ramiro knew. Soon after, we happened to drive through a Latin Kings' territory. The words "Efrain Rots" had been emblazoned on a wall. That night, Ramiro sat alone, intensely quiet, in the backyard, thinking about this for a long time. 34

Things between us, for now, are being dealt with day by day. Although Ramiro has gained a much more viable perspective on his place in the world, there are choices he has to make "not just once, but every time they come up."   35

Meanwhile I've pursued writing this book—after a 10-year lapse. The writing first began when I was 15, but the urgency of the present predicament demands it finally see the light of day. This work is an argument for the reorganization of American society—not where a few benefit at the expense of the many, but where everyone has access to decent health care, clothing, food and housing, based on need, not whether they can afford them. It's an indictment against the use of deadly force which has been the principal means this society uses against those it cannot accommodate (as I write this, Rodney King's beating by the LAPD continues to play itself out throughout the country. And the *Los Angeles Daily News* in late October 1991 reported that the L.A. County Sheriff's Department had shot 57 people since the first of the year—about 80 percent were people of color, and a few were disabled or mentally ill; all of them were unarmed or shot in the back).   36

Criminality in this country is a class issue. Many of those warehoused in overcrowded prisons can be properly called "criminals of want," those who've been deprived of the basic necessities of life and therefore forced into so-called criminal acts to survive. Many of them just don't have the means to buy their "justice." They are members of a social stratum which includes welfare mothers, housing project residents, immigrant families, the homeless and unemployed. This book is part of their story.   37

Although the work begins with my family's trek from Mexico when I was a child and touches on our early years in Watts, it primarily covers the period from ages 12 until 18 when I became active in *Las Lomas* barrio. . . .   38

The more we know, the more we owe. This is a responsibility I take seriously. My hope in producing this work is that perhaps there's a thread to be found, a pattern or connection, a seed of apprehension herein, which can be of some use, no matter how slight, in helping to end the rising casualty count for the Ramiros of this world, as more and more communities come under the death grip of what we called "The Crazy Life."   39

THINKING ABOUT THE CONTENT

1. What, according to Rodriguez, is the history of *La Vida Loca*? Are you aware of any of the "offshoot" gangs? Are there gangs in your area?

2. To what does Rodriguez attribute his son's problems? Who does he imply is to blame? What makes it difficult for youth in the barrios to combat the prevailing gang lifestyle?

3. What does Rodriguez mean by "complete literacy" (30)? How does one learn such literacy? Do you consider yourself "literate" in that respect? Why or why not?

4. What parallels exist in the lifestyle Rodriguez describes here with your own?

Looking at Structure and Style

5. What is the function of the first four paragraphs? How well do they help establish the issue Rodriguez wants to deal with?

6. Rodriguez does not tell his story in a linear fashion. Would it be better if he had? Why or why not?

7. What is the effectiveness of paragraph 18? What purpose does it serve?

8. Describe the selection's tone and attitude. How does Rodriguez develop both?

Exploring Discussion and Writing Topics

9. Have you ever wanted to run away from home? Why? Where did you want to go? Did you do it? If you didn't, but had done so, what difference might it have made in your life today?

10. Rodriguez says in his Preface that his book is "an argument for the reorganization of American society—not where a few benefit at the expense of the many, but where everyone has access to decent health care, clothing, food and housing, based on need, not whether they can afford them" (36). What kind or reorganization would this take? Is it possible?

11. Rodriguez says his book is "an indictment against the use of deadly force which has been the principal means this society uses against those it cannot accommodate" (36). Is this true? Are his statistics correct? If you were a police officer in a community with rival gang activity, how might you answer Rodriguez?

12. At one point of frustration, Rodriguez locked his son out of the house, but later relinquished this idea. In a January 23, 1995, *Newsweek* article, "Living in 'Lockdown,'" it was reported that many inner-city parents out of fear for their children's welfare, are locking their children in the house after they come home from school, or at least limiting the amount of time and places where they can stay outdoors. Is this a good solution to inner-city dangers or does it create dangers of its own? Discuss your views.

SHELBY STEELE

Professor of English at San Jose State University at California, Shelby Steele's writing has appeared in such publications as *Harper's,* the *American Scholar,* the *Washington Post,* the *New Republic,* and the *New York Times Book Review.* He won a National Magazine Award in 1989, and one of his essays was selected for *The Best American Essays 1989.*

With the 1990 publication of his book *The Content of Our Character,* Steele created quite a stir among whites and African Americans with his personal examination of the conflict in race relations today. Using his own life in an integrated society, Steele explores how blacks and whites relate to each other in real-life situations—in the schools, in the office, in social situations, and in politics. Accepting the need, gratitude, and benefits from the civil rights movement and the rise of black power in the 1960s and 1970s, Steele now feels that black leadership must stop making society feel it has not done enough for blacks, although he feels it has not, but instead help blacks understand the freedom and opportunities that do exist.

Following is the Epilogue from his book in which he summarizes his thesis: "I believe it is time for blacks to begin the shift from a wartime to a peacetime identity, from fighting for opportunity to the seizing of it" (15).

❧

The Content of Our Character

I have mentioned in several places in this book that I was caught up in the new spirit of black power and pride that swept over black America in the late sixties like one of those storms that changes the landscape. I will always believe this storm was inevitable and, therefore, positive in many ways. What I gained from it was the power to be racially unapologetic, no mean benefit considering the long trial of patience that the civil rights movement subjected blacks to. But after awhile, by the early seventies, it became clear that black power did not offer much of a blueprint on how to move my life forward. Despite the strong feeling that it had given me a crucial part of myself, it told me virtually nothing about who I was as an individual or how I might live in the world as myself. Of course, it was my mistake to think it could. But in the late sixties, "blackness" was an invasive form of collective identity that cut so deeply into one's individual space that it seemed also to be an individual identity. It came as something of a disappointment to realize that the two could not be the same, that being "black" in no way spared me the necessity of being myself.

In the early seventies, without realizing it, I made a sort of bargain   2 with the prevailing black identity—I subscribed in a general way to its point of view so that I could be free to get on with my life. Many other blacks I knew made this same bargain, got on with their lives and fellow-traveled with black power. I don't believe this subscription was insincere, but it was convenient since it opened the individual space out of which we could make our lives.

And what were we subscribing to? Generally, I think it was a form   3 of black identity grounded in the spirit of black power. It carried a righteous anger at and mistrust of American society. It believed that blacks continued to be the victims of institutional racism, that we would have to maintain an adversarial stance toward society, and that a tight racial unity was necessary both for survival and advancement. This identity was, and is, predicated on the notion that those who burned you once will burn you again, and it presupposes a deep racist reflex in American life that will forever try to limit black possibility.

I think it was the space I cleared for myself by loosely subscribing   4 to this identity that ultimately put me in conflict with it. It is in the day-to-day struggle of living on the floor of a society, so to speak, that one gains a measure of what is possible in that society. And by simply living as an individual in America—with my racial identity struggle suspended by my subscription to the black power identity—I discovered that American society offered me and blacks in general a remarkable range of opportunity if we were willing to pursue it.

In my daily life I continue to experience racial indignities and   5 slights. This morning I was told that blacks had too much musical feeling (soul, I suppose) to be good classical musicians; yesterday I passed two houses with gnomish little black lawn jockeys on the front porch; my children have been called "nigger," not to mention myself; I wear a tie and carry a professorial briefcase so my students on the first day of class will know I'm the teacher; and so on. I also know that actual racial discrimination persists in many areas of American life. I have been the victor in one housing-discrimination suit, as were my parents before me. And, certainly, garden variety racism is still a tonic for the inadequate white. In my daily life I have no immunity from any of this. What is more, I do not like it, nor will I ever endure it with élan. Yet I have also come to realize that in this same society, I have been more in charge of my fate than I always wanted to believe, and that though I have been limited by many things, my race was not foremost among them.

The point is that both realities are true. There is still racial insensitivity and some racial discrimination against blacks in this society, but there is also much opportunity. What brought me into conflict with the prevailing black identity was that it was almost entirely preoccupied with the former to the exclusion of the latter. The black identity I was subscribing to in the seventies—and that still prevails today—was essentially a "wartime" identity shaped in the confrontational sixties. It presumed that black opportunity was sharply limited by racism and that blacks had to "win" more "victories" "against" society before real opportunity would open up. This was an identity that still saw blacks as victims and that kept them at war with society even as new possibilities for advancement opened all around. Worse, by focusing so exclusively on white racism and black victimization, it implied that our fate was in society's control rather than our own, and that opportunity itself was something that was given rather than taken. This identity robs us of the very self-determination we have sought for so long, and deepens our dependency on the benevolence of others.

Why do we cling to an adversarial, victim-focused identity that preoccupies us with white racism? I think because of fear, self-doubt, and simple inexperience. As I've discussed elsewhere in this book, I believe we carry an inferiority anxiety that makes the seizing of opportunity more risky for us, since setbacks and failures may seem to confirm inferiority. To avoid this risk we may hold a victim-focused identity that tells us there is less opportunity than there really is. Our culture was formed in oppression rather than in freedom, which means we are somewhat inexperienced in the full use of freedom, in seeing possibilities and developing them. In oppression we were punished for having initiative and thereby conditioned away from it. Also, our victimization itself has been our primary source of power in society— the basis of our demands for redress—and the paradoxical result of relying on this source of power is that it rewards us for continuing to see ourselves as victims of a racist society. So our victim-focused identity serves us by preserving our main source of power and by shielding us from our fear of inferiority and our relative inexperience with the challenges of freedom.

And yet this leaves us with an identity that is at war with our own best interests, that magnifies our oppression and diminishes our sense of possibility. I think this identity is a weight on blacks because it is built around our collective insecurity rather than our faith in our human capacity to seize opportunity as individuals. It amounts to a self-protective collectivism that obsesses us with black unity instead of individual initiative. To be "black" in this identity, one need only manifest the symbols, postures, and rhetoric of black unity. Not only is personal initiative unnecessary for being "black," but the successful exercise of initiative—working one's way into the middle class, becoming well-off, gaining an important position—may in fact jeopardize one's "blackness," make one somehow less black. The poor black is the true black; the successful black is more marginally black unless he (or she) frequently announces his solidarity with the race in the way politicians declare their patriotism. This sort of identity never works, never translates into the actual uplift of black people. It confuses racial unity with initiative by relying on unity to do what only individual initiative can do. Uplift can only come when many millions of blacks seize the possibilities inside the sphere of their personal lives and use them to take themselves forward. Collectively, we can resist oppression, but racial development will always be, as Ralph Ellison once put it, "the gift of its individuals."

The collective black identity fogs up the sacred line between the ⁹ individual and the collective. To find my own individuality, I had to do what many blacks in fact do—push the collective out of my individual space by subscribing to an identity I wasn't living by. Many blacks maintain their "blackness" as a sort of union card while actually living by principles and values that are classically American and universal to the middle class everywhere: hard work, self-reliance, initiative, property ownership, family ties, and so on. In pushing the collective identity out of our individual space, we are also pushing back the diminished sense of possibility that it carries in order to take advantage of the broader field of possibility that our actual experience shows us is there. To retrieve our individuality and find opportunity, blacks today must—consciously or unconsciously—disregard the prevailing victim-focused black identity. Though it espouses black pride, it is actually a repressive identity that generates a victimized self-image, curbs individualism and initiative, diminishes our sense of possibility, and contributes to our demoralization and inertia. It is a skin that needs shedding.

There are many profound problems facing black America today—a ¹⁰ swelling black underclass, a black middle class that declined slightly in the eighties, a declining number of black college students, an epidemic of teenage pregnancy, drug use, and gang violence, continuing chronic unemployment, astoundingly high college and high school dropout rates, an increasing number of single-parent families, a disproportionately high infant mortality rate, and so on. Against all this it seems almost esoteric to talk about identity and possibility. Yet, in this book, I have tried to look at the underlying network of attitudes, pressures, and anxieties that have deepened our problems even as more opportunity has opened up to us. Without understanding these intangibles, I don't think we can easily know what to do.

Many remedies have been tried. Here and there various social programs, "interventions," have worked. Many more programs and policies have not worked. Clearly we should find the ones that do work and have more of them. But my deepest feeling is that, in a society of increasingly limited resources, there will never be enough programs to meet the need. What I really believe is that we black Americans will never be saved or even assisted terribly much by others, never be repaid for our suffering, and never find that symmetrical, historical justice that we cannot help but long for. These things will never happen. Jean-Paul Sartre once said that we were the true "existential people," and certainly we have always had to create ourselves out of whole cloth and find our own means for survival. Nothing has really changed.

I think the most cursory glance at the list of problems that blacks now face reveals that we are in a kind of despair. The evidence of this is everywhere, from the college campuses—where black students are five times more likely than whites to drop out—to the black underclass where a miasma of drug addiction, violence, and hopelessness has already transformed many inner cities into hearts of darkness. I have written in this book about some of the sources of this despair, but I also believe that they all pressure us into a single overriding mistake: a hesitation before the challenges of self-interested, individual action. It is at the point of taking self-interested action in the American mainstream that all the unresolved wounds of oppression manifest themselves and become a wall. Here is where inferiority anxiety, a victim-focused identity, that peculiar mix of personal and racial self-doubt, fear of failure, and even self-hate all combine to make for a fear of self-interested action. And without such action, there can only be despair and inertia.

There will be no end to despair and no lasting solution to any of our problems until we rely on individual effort within the American mainstream—rather than collective action against the mainstream—as our means of advancement. We need a collective identity that encourages diversity within the race, that does not make black unity a form of repression, that does not imply that the least among us are the most black, and that makes the highest challenge of "blackness" personal development. This identity must be grounded also in the reality that I and many other blacks have discovered in the space of our individual lives: that there is today, despite America's residual racism, an enormous range of opportunity open to blacks in this society. The nexus of this new identity must be a meeting of black individual initiative and American possibility.

I believe black leadership must make this nexus its primary focus. 14 They must preach it, tell it, sell it, and demand it. Our leadership has looked at government and white society very critically. Now they must help us look at ourselves. We need our real problems named and explained; otherwise, we have no chance to overcome them. Their impulse is to be "political," to keep the larger society on edge, to keep them feeling as though they have not done enough for blacks. And, clearly, they have not. But the price they pay for this form of "politics" is to keep blacks focused on an illusion of deliverance by others, and no illusion weakens us more. Our leaders must take a risk. They must tell us the truth, tell us of the freedom and opportunity they have discovered in their own lives. They must tell us what they tell their own children when they go home at night: to study hard, pursue their dreams with discipline and effort, to be responsible for themselves, to have concern for others, to cherish their race and at the same time make their own lives as Americans. When our leaders put a spotlight on our victimization and seize upon our suffering to gain us ineffectual concessions, they inadvertently turn themselves into enemies of the truth, not to mention enemies of their own people.

I believe that black Americans are infinitely freer today than ever 15 before. This is not a hope; this is a reality, an extremely hard-won reality. Many of our great leaders, and countless foot soldiers with them, died for this reality. Racial hatred has not yet left the American landscape. Who knows how or when this deliverance will occur? Yet the American black, supported by a massive body of law and the not inconsiderable goodwill of his fellow citizens, is basically as free as he or she wants to be. For every white I have met who is a racist, I have met twenty more who have seen me as an equal. And of those twenty, ten have wished me only the best as an individual. This I say, as opposed to confessing, has been my actual reality. I believe it is time for blacks to begin the shift from a wartime to a peacetime identity, from fighting for opportunity to the seizing of it. The immutable fact of late twentieth-century life is that it *is* there for blacks to seize. Martin Luther King did not live to experience this. But, of course, on the night before he died he seemed to know he would not. From the mountaintop he had looked over and seen the promised land, but then he said, "I may not get there with you. . . ." I won't say we are snuggled deep in the promised valley he saw beyond the mountain. Every day things remind me that we are not. But I also know that we have it over our greatest leader. We are on the other side of his mountaintop, on the downward slope toward the valley he saw. This is something we ought to know. But what we must know even more than this is that nothing on this earth can be promised but a chance. The promised land guarantees nothing. It is only an opportunity, not a deliverance.

THINKING ABOUT THE CONTENT

1. What does Steele mean by a "wartime identity" (6)? Why did he reject this identity? Are they good reasons? Why or why not?
2. Why, according to Steele, do some African Americans "cling to an adversarial, victim-focused identity that preoccupies us with white racism" (7)? What is wrong with this attitude according to the author? Do you agree? Why or why not?
3. What kind of lifestyle does Steele seem to have made for himself with the attitude he has? Does he serve as a role model for other African Americans? Might some blacks consider Steele a "sellout" of his race?
4. What is your opinion of Steele's thesis?

LOOKING AT STRUCTURE AND STYLE

5. How well does Steele explain his shift from a "wartime" to a "peacetime" identity?
6. To whom is Steele writing? What passages give you that impression?
7. What passages develop the attitude and tone of the essay? Are they appropriate for the topic?

EXPLORING DISCUSSION AND WRITING TOPICS

8. Read more of Steele's book *The Content of Our Character* and respond to some of his reasoning. What is the alternative to his thesis?
9. What does your own lifestyle tell you about your character? Do you know who you are? What social advantages or disadvantages have helped mold your character? What opportunities are open to you?

MARY PIPHER

Mary Pipher is a practicing clinical psychologist who teaches part-time at the University of Nebraska in Lincoln and serves as a commentator on Nebraska Public Radio. She is the author of *Hunger Pains: The American Women's Tragic Quest for Thinness* and *Reviving Ophelia: Saving the Lives of Adolescent Girls.* In *Hunger Pains,* Pipher deals with what she calls the "epidemic of eating disorders" among women and young girls. *Reviving Ophelia,* Pipher says, is her "attempt to understand my experiences in therapy with adolescent girls."

As a therapist, Pipher found she could not draw upon her own experiences as an adolescent to understand the problems of today's young girls and women. Her frustration in treating girls in therapy led her to find answers to such questions as: Why are so many girls in therapy in the 1990s? What is the meaning of lip, nose, and eyebrow piercing? How does one help thirteen-year-old girls deal with herpes or genital warts? Why is alcohol and drug use so common with seventh graders? Why do so many girls hate their parents? Why are girls having more trouble now than previous generations?

Pipher believes that girls today are more oppressed, that they are "coming of age" in a more dangerous, sexualized, and media-saturated culture, a culture than stresses beauty and pseudosophistication. In the following selection from *Reviving Ophelia* (1994), Pipher compares the adolescent life of "Cassie," a case study composite, with her own adolescence to illustrate what many teenage American girls face growing up today.

❧

Then and Now

Cassie attends a high school with 2,300 students. She doesn't know her teachers' children or her neighbors' cousins. When she meets people she doesn't try to establish their place in a complicated kinship network. When she shops for jeans, she doesn't expect the clerk to ask after her family.

Cassie sees her extended family infrequently, particularly since her parents' divorce. They are scattered all over the map. Most of the adults in her neighborhood work. In the evening people no longer sit on their front porches. Instead they prefer the privacy of backyard patios, which keep their doings invisible. Air-conditioning contributes to each family's isolation. On hot summer days and nights people go inside to stay cool. Cassie knows the Cosby family and the people from "Northern Exposure" better than she knows anyone on her block.

Cassie fights with her parents in a more aggressive way than the   3
teens of my youth. She yells, swears, accuses and threatens to run away. Her parents tolerate this open anger much more readily than earlier generations would have. I'm confused about whether I was more repressed as a child or just happier. Sometimes I think all this expression of emotion is good, and sometimes, particularly when I see beleaguered mothers, I wonder if we have made progress.

Cassie is much more politically aware of the world than I was.   4
By the time she was ten she'd been in a protest march in Washington, D.C. She's demonstrated against the death penalty and the Rodney King trial. She writes letters to her congressmen and to the newspapers. She writes letters for Amnesty International to stop torture all over the world. She is part of a larger world than I was and takes her role as an active participant seriously.

Cassie and her friends all tried smoking cigarettes in junior high.   5
Like most teenagers today, Cassie was offered drugs in junior high. She can name more kinds of illegal drugs than the average junkie from the fifties. She knows about local drug-related killings and crack rings. Marijuana, which my father saw once in his lifetime, wafts through the air at her rock concerts and midnight movies.

Alcohol is omnipresent—in bowling alleys, gas stations, grocery   6
stores, skating rinks and Laundromats. Alcohol advertising is rampant, and drinking is associated with wealth, travel, romance and fun. At sixteen, Cassie has friends who have been through treatment for drugs or alcohol. The schools attempt alcohol and drug education, but they are no match for the peer pressure to consume. Cassie knows some Just Say No leaders who get drunk every weekend. By eighth grade, kids who aren't drinking are labeled geeks and left out of the popular scene.

Spending money is a pastime. Cassie wants expensive items—a   7
computer, a racing bike and trips to Costa Rica with her Spanish class and to the ski slopes of Colorado. She takes violin and voice lessons from university professors and attends special camps for musicians.

Cassie's been surrounded by media since birth. Her family owns   8
a VCR, a stereo system, two color televisions and six radios. Cassie wakes to a radio, plays the car stereo on the way to school, sees videos

at school and returns home to a choice of stereo, radio, television or videocassettes. She can choose between forty channels twenty-four hours a day. She plays music while she studies and communicates via computer modem with hackers all over the country in her spare time.

Cassie and her friends have been inundated with advertising since birth and are sophisticated about brand names and commercials. While most of her friends can't identify our state flower, the goldenrod, in a ditch along the highway, they can shout out the brand of a can of soda from a hundred yards away. They can sing commercial jingles endlessly.

Cassie's been exposed to years of sophisticated advertising in which she's heard that happiness comes from consuming the right products. She can catch the small lies and knows that adults tell lies to make money. We do not consider that a sin—we call it marketing. But I'm not sure that she catches the big lie, which is that consumer goods are essential to happiness.

Cassie has more access to books than I had. I was limited to a town library the size of a Quick Stop and a weekly bookmobile. She has a six-branch public library system, a school library as big as a gymnasium and three university libraries. But she reads much less than I did. Particularly the classics that I loved, *Jane Eyre, Moby Dick,* and *Return of the Native* bore her with their loopy, ornamental prose. She has more choices about how to spend her time, and like most teens raised in a media-saturated culture, Cassie does not often choose to read books.

There are more magazines for girls now, but they are relatively unchanged in the thirty years since I bought my copies of *Teen.* The content for girls is makeup, acne products, fashion, thinness and attracting boys. Some of the headlines could be the same: TRUE COLORS QUIZ, GET THE LOOK THAT GETS BOYS, TEN COMMANDMENTS OF HAIR, THE BEST PLACES TO MEET AVAILABLE MEN and TEN WAYS TO TRIM DOWN. Some headlines are updated to pay lip service to the themes of the 1990s: TWO MODELS CHILL OUT AT OXFORD UNIVERSITY IN SEASON'S GREATEST GRAY CLOTHES OR ECO-INSPIRED LOOKS FOR FALL. A few reflect the greater stress that the 1990s offer the young: REV UP YOUR LOOKS WHEN STRESS HAS YOU DOWN, THE STD OF THE MONTH, GENITAL WARTS and SHOULD I GET TESTED FOR AIDS? Some would never have appeared in the 1950s: WHEN YOU'RE HIGHLY SEXED, IS ONE PARTNER ENOUGH? and ADVICE ON ORGASMS.

Cassie listens to music by the Dead Milkmen, 10,000 Maniacs, Nirvana and They Might Be Giants. She dances to Madonna's song

"Erotica," with its sadomasochistic lyrics. The rock-and-roll lyrics by 2 Live Crew that make Tipper Gore cringe don't upset her. Sexist lyrics and the marketing of products with young women's naked bodies are part of the wallpaper of her life.

Cassie's favorite movies are *The Crying Game, Harold and Maude* and *My Own Private Idaho*. None of these movies would have made it past the theater owner of my hometown.   14

Our culture has changed from one in which it was hard to get information about sexuality to one in which it's impossible to escape information about sexuality. Inhibition has quit the scene. In the 1950s a married couple on TV had to be shown sleeping in twin beds because a double bed was too suggestive. Now anything—incest, menstruation, crotch itch or vaginal odors—can be discussed on TV. Television shows invite couples to sell their most private moments for a dishwasher.   15

The plot for romance movies is different. In the fifties people met, argued, fell in love, then kissed. By the seventies, people met, argued, fell in love and then had sex. In the nineties people meet, have sex, argue and then, maybe, fall in love. Hollywood lovers don't discuss birth control, past sexual encounters or how a sexual experience will affect the involved parties; they just do it. The Hollywood model of sexual behavior couldn't be more harmful and misleading if it were trying to be.   16

Cassie has seen *Playboys* and *Penthouses* on the racks at local drugstores and Quick Stops. Our city has adult XXX-rated movie theaters and adult bookstores. She's watched the adult channels in hotel rooms while bouncing on "magic fingers" beds. Advertisements that disturb me with their sexual content don't bother her. When I told her that I first heard the word *"orgasm"* when I was twenty, she looked at me with disbelief.   17

Cassie's world is more tolerant and open about sex. Her friends produced a campy play entitled *Vampire Lesbians of Sodom*. For a joke she displays Kiss of Mint condoms in her room. She's a member of her school's branch of Flag—Friends of Lesbians and Gays—which she joined after one of her male friends "came out" to her. She's nonjudgmental about sexual orientation and outspoken in her defense of gay rights. Her world is a kinder, gentler place for girls who have babies. One-fifth of all babies today are born to single mothers. Some of her schoolmates bring their babies to school.   18

In some ways Cassie is more informed about sex than I was. She's read books on puberty and sexuality and watched films at school. She's seen explicit movies and listened to hours of explicit music. But   19

Cassie still hasn't heard answers to the questions she's most interested in. She hasn't had much help sorting out when to have sex, how to say no or what a good sexual experience would entail.

Cassie is as tongue-tied with boys she likes as I was, and she is even more confused about proper behavior. The values she learned at home and at church are at odds with the values broadcast by the media. She's been raised to love and value herself in a society where an enormous pornography industry reduces women to body parts. She's been taught by movies and television that sophisticated people are sexually free and spontaneous, and at the same time she's been warned that casual sex can kill. And she's been raped.

Cassie knows girls who had sex with boys they hardly knew. She knows a girl whose reason for having sex was "to get it over with." Another classmate had sex because her two best girlfriends had had sex and she didn't want to feel left out. More touching and sexual harassment happens in the halls of her school than did in the halls of mine. Girls are referred to as bitches, whores and sluts.

Cassie has been desensitized to violence. She's watched television specials on incest and sexual assaults and seen thousands of murders on the screen. She's seen *Fatal Attraction* and *Halloween II*. Since Jeffrey Dahmer, she knows what necrophilia is. She wasn't traumatized by *The Diary of Anne Frank*.

Cassie can't walk alone after dark. Her family locks doors and bicycles. She carries Mace in her purse and a whistle on her car keys. She doesn't speak to men she doesn't know. When she is late, her parents are immediately alarmed. Of course there were girls who were traumatized in the fifties, and there are girls who lead protected lives in the 1990s, but the proportions have changed significantly. We feel it in our bones.

I am not claiming that our childhoods are representative of the childhoods of all other females in America. In some ways Cassie and I have both had unusual childhoods. I grew up in a rural, isolated area with much less exposure to television than the average child of the times. My mother was a doctor instead of a homemaker. Compared to other girls, Cassie lives in a city that is safer than most and has a family with more money. Even with the rape, Cassie's situation is by no means a worst-case scenario. She lives in a middle-class environment, not an inner city. Her parents aren't psychotic, abusive or drug-addicted.

Also, I am not claiming that I lived in the good old days and that Cassie lives in the wicked present. I don't want to glorify or to "Donna

Reedify" the fifties, which were not a golden age. They were the years of Joe McCarthy and Jim Crow. How things looked was more important than how things really were. There was a great deal of sexual, religious and racial intolerance. Many families had shameful secrets, and if revealed, they led to public disgrace rather than community help.

I left my town as soon as I could, and as an adult, I have been   26
much happier in a larger, less structured environment. Many of my friends come from small towns, and particularly the smart women among them have horror stories of not fitting in.

What I am claiming is that our stories have something to say   27
about the way the world has stayed the same and the way it has changed for adolescent girls. We had in common that our bodies changed and those changes caused us anxiety. With puberty, we both struggled to relate to girls and boys in new ways. We struggled to be attractive and to understand our own sexual urges. We were awkward around boys and hurt by girls. As we struggled to grow up and define ourselves as adults, we both distanced ourselves from our parents and felt some loneliness as a result. As we searched for our identities, we grew confused and sad. Both of us had times when we were moody, secretive, inarticulate and introspective.

But while some of our experiences are similar, many are radically   28
different. Cassie's community is a global one, mine was a small town. Her parents were divorcing, mine stayed together. She lives in a society more stratified by money and more driven by addictions. She's been exposed to more television, movies and music. She lives in a more sexualized world.

Things that shocked us in the 1950s make us yawn now. The   29
world has changed from one in which people blushed at the term *chicken breast* to one in which a movie such as *Pretty Woman* is not embarrassing. We've gone from a world with no locks on the doors to one of bolt locks and handguns. The issues that I struggled with as a college student—when I should have sex, should I drink, smoke or hang out with bad company—now must be considered in early adolescence.

Neither the 1950s nor the 1990s offered us environments that   30
totally met our needs. My childhood was structured and safe, but the costs of that security were limited tolerance of diversity, rigid rules about proper behavior and lack of privacy. As one man from a small town said, "I don't need to worry about running my own business because there are so many other people who are minding it for me."

Although my community provided many surrogate parents and clear rules about right and wrong, this structure was often used to enforce rigid social and class codes and to keep people in their place.

Cassie lives in a town that's less rigid about roles and more support-   31
ive of autonomy, but she has little protected space. Cassie is freer in some ways than I was. She has more options. But ironically, in some ways, she's less free. She cannot move freely in the halls of her school because of security precautions. Everyone she meets is not part of a community of connected people. She can't walk alone looking at the Milky Way on a summer night.

The ideal community would somehow be able to combine the   32
sense of belonging that small towns offer with the freedom to be oneself that small towns sometimes inhibit. Utopia for teenage girls would be a place in which they are safe and free, able to grow and develop in an atmosphere of tolerance and diversity and protected by adults who have their best interest at heart.

THINKING ABOUT THE CONTENT

1. Pipher discusses social influences Cassie faces that she and her generation never experienced. What are some of those influences? Are all of them negative? Explain.
2. Why does Pipher feel Cassie has more options than she did as a teenager, but in many ways is less free? Do you agree? Explain.
3. According to Pipher, in what ways has the world stayed the same and in what ways has it changed for teenagers? Do you agree? Explain.
4. Are Cassie's lifestyle and experiences similar to your own experiences as a teenager? In what ways are they similar and in what ways different?
5. Do you agree with what Pipher sees as the ideal community in which to raise an adolescent girl? Should it be different for teenage boys? Explain.

LOOKING AT STRUCTURE AND STYLE

6. Pipher begins many of her paragraphs with "Cassie" this and "Cassie" that. Why do you think she does this? Is it appropriate here? Explain.
7. How well does the author compare and contrast the "then" and the "now" of teen years?
8. What, if any, bias does the author reveal? Is any bias justified? Explain.

EXPLORING DISCUSSION AND WRITING TOPICS

9. Use yourself and your friends' experiences as teenagers to create a composite of a sixteen-year-old girl or boy of your generation. Discuss the social forces that influenced your generation.

10. Support or refute Pipher's attack on what she sees as negative media influences on today's teenagers.
11. Describe your ideal community for raising teenagers. How could Cassie benefit from your community?
12. Explain why you think it is or is not more difficult to be a teenager today than it was for past generations.

Mary Kay Blakely is a journalist and the author of *Wake Me When It's Over: A Journey to the Edge and Back* and *American Mom,* an excerpt from which follows. Using personal experiences, Blakely describes the deterioration of her ten-year marriage and the struggle to survive as a single parent. In addition to the hardship and emotional strain involved in the dissolution of a marriage, Blakely felt the additional stigma of being castigated by what she calls "a new breed of motherhood professionals: the family values evangelists." Blakely has an answer to Pat Buchanan's "fever pitch at the 1992 Republican National Convention, damning single, divorced, and working mothers for neglecting their children and loosing 'barbarians out of public schools' on society." In fact, she wishes motherhood had the power he imagines it has.

Blakely's comments offer a look at a not-too-uncommon lifestyle in today's culture.

⚜

An Outlaw Mom Tells All

A candid shot taken in the park across from our house in Fort Wayne, Indiana, circa 1977, shows a young family romping in the fall leaves, looking insanely happy, as we desperately wanted to be. One of my two boys is in the picture, dressed in a tie-dyed T–shirt and overalls (the other is a baby, snug at home in his crib), I am a writer in my late twenties, my husband, Howard, is a professional city planner in his early thirties. The faint shadows under Howard's and my eyes are the only traces of the argument we had the night before, the usual one about money and job prospects and who was more irresponsible, the unpublished writer or the unemployed planner?

The photo shoot took hours—the photographer wanted to pose our spontaneous fun just right. In the last shot, I'm lying on my stomach in the leaves, propped up on my elbows and looking over my shoulder at my son, who is seated on my back and supported from behind by Howard. He is smiling through clenched teeth, since we can hardly afford this professional photographer. I'm straining to hold my grin but thinking, "C'mon . . . click the shutter. My back is killing me."

We kept trying to hold position through our excruciating discom-   3
fort that year—we thought we'd just hit a rough patch, as every family
does sooner or later. We didn't know we were on a long, dangerous
downgrade that would demolish our brakes. Not long after I'd resigned
my position as dean of students at a local high school so I could write,
Howard lost his job. The boys now had two full-time parents but
no one to pay the bills. The brief period of unemployment we were
marginally prepared for stretched into one merciless year after another.
To make ends meet, Howard and I patched together an ever-changing
crazy quilt of part-time jobs, while we alternated shifts as single parents
to save on child care.

I still feel a vague ache in my back whenever I look at those old   4
photographs, an echo of the acute strain I felt playing "let's pretend"
in the park that autumn. I now see the body sculpture of a woman in
deep trouble, twisted into a position the human form was never meant
to hold.

"Each divorce is the death of a small civilization," novelist Pat   5
Conroy once wrote. I may spend the rest of my life trying to figure
out why we could not mend our small civilization. God knows, we
tried desperately to fend off that death. Night after night at the kitchen
table, we argued about money and responsibility, about which of us
needed professional help.

Whenever I read the cold facts about unemployment in newspapers   6
today, I flash back to my own long sentence under that statistic. I
imagine the private stories behind the anonymous numbers, the personal grief and desperation the media mention only in passing. Once
you have lived within those marginal asides about "tensions at home,"
you know there is nothing abstract about numbers. The unemployment
rate, if it happens to apply to you, can become intensely particular in
a hundred mundane details, from anxious moments in the grocery
checkout line to angry outbursts at dinner to silent, brooding nights
in front of the TV.

Yes, we would co-sign another loan. Yes, we would both begin   7
therapy. Yes, after five happy years of "for better" we would honor
our vows through five long years of "for worse." And yes, as Mary
McCarthy wrote in *How I Grew,* we would eventually discover that
someone you love "could exhaust your capacity for suffering." After
Howard and I agreed to separate, he left Fort Wayne to resurrect his
life as a graduate student at the University of Michigan, and I remained
in town with the kids. I worked at home and supported us on my
erratic income as a writer, which sometimes meant drafting fictional
checks at Kroger's supermarket.

Fortunately, my mothering was already rather out of control. First [8] by choice, then by circumstance, we lived like "outlaws from the institution of motherhood," as the poet Adrienne Rich described those who drift—or flee—from traditional rules and expectations. All of my job titles, from Working Mom to Unnatural Mom, were deliberate career moves. Our family values may have looked odd or painful to those who still believed there could be only one kind of family, but once we'd split from the nuclear mold, cooled off, and expanded, squeezing ourselves back in would have been painful.

I prepared for the legal negotiations of divorce by reading every- [9] thing I could find on the topic. I knew we weren't destined to have a "clean break," if there really was such a thing, because Howard and I had a mutual passion for the children. I assumed we'd be parents together for the rest of our lives. More than a decade of my own history had been spent with this man, my best friend and main enthusiast during those first rocky years of adulthood. I wanted to honor the tenderness of those years, hoping we could eventually salvage the friendship that once sustained us.

Nevertheless, Howard and I spent the last year of our marriage [10] preparing for divorce: we assigned blame and listed grievances. Our bursts of rage were necessary, I suppose, the noisy booster rockets lifting us out of a depressed marriage. But in the grip of rage and terror at being single again, people are in no shape to negotiate the tough legal questions of divorce. Yet that's generally the stage when the attorneys are called in to chisel settlement terms into cement. Behind the clinical phrases and seemingly impartial laws, however, it's clear that anger and madness are writing the rules: women's standard of living drops 33 percent after divorce, while men's rises 10 to 15 percent; more than 60 percent of the fathers pay no child support after five years, and the majority exercise visitation rights erratically, if at all.

Since fatherhood is reduced by court orders to a monthly check [11] and two hours a week for a ball game, it isn't amazing that fathers lose track of their children. (What *is* amazing is that fathers' rights groups blame women for the tragedy—do they really think that mothers designed this grand arrangement, plunging ourselves into poverty and single motherhood?)

Since I thought hard-ass attorneys were largely responsible for [12] much of the pain people suffer during divorce, I found a kind of holistic attorney to serve as a mediator for a settlement we could write ourselves. He called the document we created a "dissolution agreement." Before it was written down, I thought he was saying "disillusion agreement" and was impressed with his poetic sensibility.

Divorce exposes absolutely every buried assumption about mar-   13
riage—what we mean by "motherhood" and "fatherhood," who actually owns the joint bank accounts, how a husband's sense of entitlement
and a wife's sense of duty turned the principle of "our money, our
kids" into the reality of "his money, her kids." It had taken Howard
and me only about ten minutes to pronounce the "I do's," but we
would spend the next ten years trying to figure out who, exactly, was
supposed to do what: Who was responsible for providing child care,
finding baby-sitters and tutors, driving car pools, for which periods
and where? Who would pay for the kids' clothing/medical bills/music
lessons/college tuitions?

Because we had made certain amendments to the traditions of   14
marriage—I had retrieved my own name after first taking Howard's;
Howard shared the care of the children—we were under the illusion
we had achieved a marriage of equals. In fact, we were like the hybrid
produce being tested in grocery stores around the U.S. that year. Bright-
red hothouse tomatoes heightened temptations to buy, but when you
took a bite, you discovered the grainy, juiceless pulp of the "concept
tomato." Though Howard and I had customized our marriage to suit
the times, the fundamental attitudes we inherited were still firmly and
invisibly in place. We had achieved only "concept equality."

Still, since we had been striving for a nontraditional marriage, it   15
made sense to end it with a nontraditional divorce. The agreement we
wrote was designed to expire periodically—I imagined we'd need five
or six divorces before we were through with the commitments we'd
initiated by having babies. Because our careers were both in a state
of flux, making it difficult to predict future incomes, I wrote an essay-
divorce, outlining the tenets of my faith: he would resume paying
his financial share when he became gainfully employed; and to keep
monetary obligations fairly balanced against resources, we would rene-
gotiate each time one of us had a change in income.

Leaving the specifics about dental bills and reading tutors to "the   16
parent who could best afford them," I assumed that after ten years of
love and friendship we would not be tempted to screw each other. We
promised instead "to be fair and honest in all the future negotiations."
The judge who had to approve this document took off his glasses after
reading it and studied us curiously, as if we had arrived in his courtroom
directly from Mars. "God bless you," he said, then shook his head. "I
hope to hell it works for you."

The kids were not involved in any of the fractious negotiations   17
Howard and I conducted through those hostile years—at least, not
directly. My own demeanor was aggressively cheerful in their presence.

One month, when a paycheck was late, our electricity and phone were shut off. I acted as if everybody lived in the dark once in a while; the kids, given their strong need to pass for normal, readily accepted my performance. I remember the night I told Ryan and Darren that our life in Camelot, such as it was, had officially come to an end. I imagined they would accept the divorce as I did, a mere formality that simply named the life we were living, since Howard and I were already separated. I imagined too—because divorced mothers also have a huge capacity for denial—they would adjust to the news without much grief.

We were on our way home from visiting my friend Larry, the man   18
who would eventually live with us. It seemed like the right time to introduce them to our new reality. I told them, "We filed for divorce this month. It will be official in a few days." They had known for some time it might happen, but that was the night they had to believe it. The impact was immediate and dramatic. They both wailed loudly, as if they'd taken a bullet in the heart. Flung forcefully into the backseat, they vanished from the rearview mirror. I heard their sobs break open between gasps for air, and felt a dam break inside my chest.

As I drove the car into the night I promised them the moon: they   19
would still see as much of their dad as ever. They weren't getting divorced from him—I was. We would both make sure they had everything they needed to be happy.

I made these midnight promises in good faith, though I was wrong   20
about almost everything. Life would not be almost the same. They would not have the support of both parents. They would not see as much of their dad in the years ahead. The boys intuitively knew how the phantom pains of a missing parent, one or the other, would accompany them for the rest of their childhood. The wounds they sustained that night would reopen again and again before they healed, and expressions of pain too deep for their young faces would sink my heart.

I occupied the witch role that year. Whatever I did, I could never   21
conjure enough magic to relieve all the aches divorce brought into their childhood. While I directed my attention to the kids, who directed their attention to their father, most of the attention directed to me during those rocky transition years came from outside sources.

In addition to the usual scrutiny from sociologists and politicians   22
and editors with a career interest in motherhood, my period as Divorced Mom unfortunately coincided with the rise of a new breed of motherhood professionals: the family values evangelists. When these folks organized a witch hunt, it wasn't hard to form a posse—especially in the Midwest, where the rising divorce rate accompanied a sinking

economy. The same way psychiatrists once blamed our mothers for genetic tragedies like schizophrenia and manic depression, the family values evangelists blame the mothers of my generation for the socially manufactured disaster of adolescents with guns and bad attitudes. Right-wing candidate Pat Buchanan reached fever pitch at the 1992 Republican National Convention, damning single, divorced, and working mothers for neglecting their children and loosing "barbarians out of public schools" on society. I imagine Buchanan felt better afterward. But here in the pews we know that motherhood, as currently framed by the culture, has nowhere near the power he imagines.

My sister Regina recognized the futility of powerless responsibility   23 after teaching in a high school for several years. As Reg began her last term, six of her students did not have desks (not a problem, she was advised, once the drop-out rate kicks in); there were no lights in her classroom for four months (a problem, especially on cloudy days, when she had to move her rowdy troop to the cafeteria without losing any along the way); and she had to buy her own mimeograph paper (big problem, since it coincided with a teacher pay cut). It was clear to Regina that even if every mother quit work and went on welfare so she could be home with her kids, or whatever else an individual mother could do so Buchanan would like her better, she still needed desks and paper and dedicated teachers for her children. Our "education president," George Bush, was reluctant to "throw taxpayer dollars" at these needs—he suggested instead the problems could be solved with voluntary school prayer. Dear God, could we please have some lights?

It has become such a jungle out there, the family values evangelists   24 are making converts of frightened citizens right and left. In an *Atlantic* cover story called "Dan Quayle Was Right," sociologist Barbara Dafoe Whitehead reviewed the theory that the Los Angeles uprising can be traced to *Murphy Brown*—the weekly comedy that exposes TV viewers to the dangerous image of a happy single mother. According to our former vice president, this positive portrayal of an independent, unmarried mother is the reason the American family broke down. Whitehead amassed scientific proof that poverty, urban violence, lousy SAT scores, and the bleak economy can be directly linked to the selfishness of divorced and single mothers. "At some point in the 1970s Americans changed their minds . . . what had once been regarded as hostile to children's best interests was now considered essential to adults' happiness," she wrote. Since two-thirds of all divorces are filed by women, we can assume that it was mostly mothers putting their own needs first.

Whitehead cites numerous studies to prove that children living   25
with two biological parents are better off than children in households
headed by a single parent: they inherit more money, live in nicer homes,
have superior medical care, get better educations, even marry earlier,
for what that's worth. Undisturbed by the possibility that divorce
might be the result rather than the cause of economic instability,
she concludes that the solution to the steady downward mobility of
this country's working classes, to drug abuse/decaying schools/over-
crowded jails, is to "restigmatize" divorce. We can only be grateful
she wasn't among the social scientists studying urban violence in the
early 1960s, when rocks and flames accompanied black families into
white neighborhoods. She might have suggested the solution to racism
was to bring back segregation.

"Stigmatization is a powerful means of regulating behavior, as   26
any smoker or overeater will testify," Whitehead notes, as if the need
for divorce were in the same category with cravings for a hot fudge
sundae. Since divorce has never been fully *de*stigmatized, the family
values evangelists shouldn't have too much trouble restigmatizing it.
Maybe I missed some amnesty period, but it seems that my sons and
I have had to live under labels like "broken home" or "dysfunctional
family" for most of their childhood.

There is always a nod, among the more responsible family experts,   27
that there might be "other factors" besides women's selfishness for the
alarming deterioration of family life: the overwhelming violence in
movies and on television, domestic battery and sexual abuse, rising
unemployment, institutionalized wage discrimination, the disappear-
ance of jobs that can support a family, the redistribution of resources
in the last decade that saw the share of wealth held by the top one
percent of the population increase by 60 percent, increasing homelessness among the poor and mentally ill, the AIDS epidemic, the
growing number of guns in U.S. homes, and the disintegration of good
public education.

Hardly anyone is more alarmed about urban violence and poverty   28
than the mothers of children most vulnerable to them, but nowhere
do the family values preachers acknowledge that my heart might be
breaking too, raising sons in a society where they must pass through
metal detectors before they can study multiplication tables, where it
can be easier and cheaper for a ten-year-old to buy a handgun than a
pair of sneakers.

It's not that I don't believe the grim statistics about female-headed   29
households—I do. I've lived the facts and figures of single motherhood

every day for the last 13 years. The mathematics of my life, translated into a word problem, are these:

Place me in a society where I am encouraged to marry young and have 2.5 children (two sons, one miscarriage); give us a few adjustment problems, because we are human; begin a recession that costs Howard his job; watch him devastated by guilt for not being a "breadwinner"; send me to work but apply a 35 percent discount to my wages because I am female; grant me a no-fault divorce and make me dependent on child support, understanding that there is a less than a 50 percent chance the father will pay; make the odds even slimmer if he's angry, which he is; provide no day care or health insurance; watch me slide below the poverty line, where the vast majority of other residents are women and children; permit public education—the only kind I can afford—to deteriorate so severely that inner-city schools must put armed guards on the regular payroll; acknowledge the fatality of AIDS and the impulsiveness of teenagers, but deny them access to condoms and sex education; declare a "war on drugs," offer a moronic slogan that blames the victim, and arrest the children of the poor. Be mystified when reports of "female voter outrage" start showing up. Decide it's Anita Hill's fault. Blame urban riots on working mothers and the absence of school prayer. Now calculate: if the only recommended solution is to couple every poor mother with a wealthy breadwinner who espouses family values, how many wives would Pat Buchanan have to marry?

If statistics could be set aside for a moment in favor of listening to some of the stories, it would soon be clear that restigmatizing divorce would not only further handicap single mothers; it would have a devastating effect on our married peers as well. By restigmatizing divorce, the message goes out to abusive husbands and fathers: be mean, be brutal, do whatever you want—your wife can't leave you. In a culture where independent mothers were visibly thriving, however, the message would be: better talk, better listen, better not take her for granted—she knows as well as you do she could survive without you.

The problem with the evangelists for "traditional family values" is they are uninterested in learning about anybody else's religion. Their either/or thinking—either you're a good nuclear family or you don't count as a family at all—prohibits recognition that some parts of marriage are bad and some parts of divorce are good. Despite the multiple hazards we face, single mothers often successfully restructure the old hierarchical pattern into a more consensual arrangement. Family therapist Thelma Jean Goodrich reports that in many of these evolved families "conflict is low, closeness is habitual, mothers feel competent and children are responsible, both in tasks and in decision-making." If divorce were destigmatized, all families could experiment with structures that would suit their needs.

Besides creating a more humane environment "for the sake of the   33
children," there is an even more compelling reason to stop stigmatizing working or single mothers. Because most of our work is invisible to the family values crowd, they're probably unaware of what valuable worker bees we are in this society. Take us out, and you need four people to replace each one of us. Hierarchies never get it: If you whip the slaves nearly to death, who's going to bring in the crop?

Early in our postdivorce life, I moved to Ann Arbor for a few years   34
so the boys could be near Howard: my work as a writer was portable and their father's doctoral program was not. Once a month I commuted to New York City to meet with editors and to slip down to Washington, D.C., to spend time with Larry. By the time the Ann Arbor phase of our marital dissolution was scheduled to end, I felt like a marathon runner straining to make it through the twenty-sixth mile. The next phase, as outlined, would offer a much saner pace. The kids would move east with me, where I would be closer to my work and colleagues; Howard would complete his dissertation and focus his job search near the kids' new home, where we would continue our joint custody arrangement; and Larry would move his career from Washington to New York City. We would all live happily ever after.

Almost immediately, a few complications became obvious. How-   35
ard resented Larry mightily. He saw a new "stepfather" not as a parent-ing ally but as a potential competitor. He seemed to think, "My kids, her monied boyfriend." Larry did not actually have any money, but he did earn a regular paycheck, which made him exotic among the group he was joining. Nor was there anything in Larry's history as an only child that prepared him for living with two young jocks. While he'd enjoyed weekends with Ryan and Darren, playing father once a month was hardly a realistic introduction to the actual job. He was still innocent about how completely a man could come undone when he discovered his brand-new electric razor in the driveway after being used to buzz-cut a mohawk on the neighbor's poodle.

As for me, the architect of this plan, I would soon discover that   36
beyond a working mother's "dual careers" I had a third role: diplomat. Before I could live the life I longed for, I had to conduct a tremendous amount of negotiating. I was exhausted. And I was not alone. By the late 1980s, media commentators noticed that more and more women

were exhausted. They interpreted the fall of Superwoman as the end of feminism. Headlines were reporting that professional women were leaving their jobs in droves because a mother "can't do both." A cover story in the *New York Times Magazine* featured a photojournalist identified as "one of the top three or four in the world," explaining why she decided against motherhood. "I don't see how a woman in documentary photography could have children," she said. "I think it's a very difficult thing to raise a family, and I have enormous respect for people who do it. I'd hate to do something like that and not be good at it. It's for a long time."

The news that mothers "can't do both" was happily received by folks who hoped women had finally come to our senses and would soon be resuming our rightful place at the ironing board. It was not so happily received by those who had no choice about doing both—all the mothers in the middle and lower classes of that Kinder, Gentler Nation. If the most well positioned and influential women were either going home or remaining childless, there would be less pressure for the institutional changes the rest of us needed in the echelons below. Even for those lucky few who did have the luxury of choice, being asked to decide between your passion for work and your passion for children was like being told by your doctor: "Something's got to go, ma'am—would you prefer we take your brain or your heart?" 37

A reporter once asked me if women shouldn't limit themselves to either work or family. Weren't women inviting stress by "trying to do too much"? 38

"Women aren't trying to do too much," I said. "Women have too much to do." Most of us are still laboring under the cliché, "A woman has to work twice as hard as any man to be considered half as good." 39

A man in documentary photography faces no dilemma about having children. To put it in a more modern cliché, a father has to work only half as hard as any mother to be considered twice as good. "Though it's very important to men to marry and have a family," Dr. Daniel J. Levinson of Yale University said, "the big difference is that a man feels he is taking care of his family by working." Most women, on the other hand, think that motherhood or any other love relationship involves some element of *being there.* 40

I see no way around the "twice as hard" part of the formula, at least in my lifetime. For all the stridency and hysteria about unequal pay in the last two decades, we've narrowed the 35-cent wage gap—and therefore our working hours—by only a dime. We've won a coffee break, as it were. While we have limited power to change the economic part of the equation, we have some control over the self-esteem part— 41 the "half as good" judgment. What would our lives look like if we needed zero approval?

The anticipation of getting a "C" on life's transcript is worse than   42
the actual fact. My first one arrived that year the kids moved east to live with Larry and me. What with all the worrying, adjusting, accommodating, talking, and listening of those first months, when the kids weren't having a sleepless night, I was. Because then, as now, there was no such thing as nightmare leave, I began work each day with what working mothers I know call "soft brain."

Being slow of mind during those months, I armed one copy edi-   43
tor—an arrogant young man who relished my errors with glee—with this ammunition against my brilliance: in a single essay, I described "a white house with green shudders" inhabited by a person who was "fearful down to the souls of her feet." For the next six months, the copy editor performed a little green shudder and laughed every time I handed in an assignment, as I felt my soul relocating to my feet.

As humiliating as it was to be an imperfect writer, being an imper-   44
fect mother was even worse. One night I returned home two hours later than promised. I found four messages on the answering machine from Darren, reporting that he was in the emergency room of the local hospital with his elder brother. The moment every working mother fears had finally arrived: I was not there for an emergency.

Heart pounding, I barreled into the emergency room, anticipating   45
the horror of finding my elder son on a stretcher. Instead, I found him sitting calmly in the waiting area, holding an ice pack around a swollen hand. Since the minor fracture wasn't life-threatening, the hospital staff couldn't X–ray or set the small bone without parental permission. The major discomfort Ryan felt during the extended wait came from his long distance from the refrigerator. The hospital cafeteria was closed, so he called two friends who brought supplies from McDon-ald's. When I arrived, the four boys were camped out eating burgers and fries, as if a hospital emergency room were a genial place for an impromptu picnic.

Is it heretical for me to admit that, once my heartbeat returned to   46
normal, I was pleased that I had not "been there" for my sons? In the hospital that night I saw two boys, long accustomed to answering ma-chines and pay phones, confidently and ingeniously filling in for me.

"So you finally got here," the resident remarked disdainfully. He   47
looked at the boys with pity, seeing two nearly motherless children. When the young doctor returned his gaze to me I felt the rising tremor of a green shudder, but I didn't apologize. I had to stop regarding my many professional and familial absences as cause for apology. I began

to see them as opportunities for my family and colleagues to exercise compassion. Unfortunately, the resident in the emergency room missed his opportunity.

It is essential to keep offering these opportunities for compassion. 48 Men as well as women must have the courage to become provocatively imperfect. The willingness to risk imperfection, in fact, might ultimately be the most valuable contribution my generation of women can make to the workplace. Our current work habits have become even more stressful than in the unenlightened days of my own young motherhood, since the economy is still largely unrecognized as a family issue.

"Nine P.M. and I'm still at the office," a friend called to say recently, 49 dead tired after her fourth double shift in a row. She still had Easter baskets and a family reunion to prepare when she got home later that night.

"Go home," I advised her. "If you get fired, at least you can put 50 'Easter Bunny' on your next résumé."

If all 54 million working women took the risk and stepped even 51 slightly off the center of prevailing attitudes, the center would move. That enormous tremor might not happen in my lifetime, but I can feel it coming each time I contribute a solitary green shudder. I imagine myself as part of a vast mediocre majority, and it elevates my soul right up to my knees.

It wasn't my mission then, and it's not my mission now, to help anybody 52 adjust to reality. I'm interested in keeping the idea of alternatives alive. I suspect my sons have multiple reactions to the dual worlds they have been navigating. My role is largely a silent one now, dependent on telepathic insights, and most of their future ideas about sexual politics will come from other sources. It grieves me that the culture provides so little reinforcement for what they have learned so far, and I wonder how the lessons of their youth will hold up in the years ahead. The pressures for conformity will be enormous—although they have plenty of experience being the odd men out.

I can't know how my sons will turn out—whether they will become 53 the "feminist men" most of my friends were predicting during their youth. Since children are products of their culture as much as their families, I'm grateful to know my sons love and respect me. They also love the *Sports Illustrated* swimsuit issue.

In the last two decades, millions of American women have changed 54 not only their language and thinking, their professional choices and banking habits, but also the shape of the nonreciprocal gift that goes one way from mothers to children. Without asking anybody's permission, many mothers began teaching new conditions for love: no sexism, no racism, no violence, no gender entitlements. Whether these incremental, daily efforts will amount to the third wave of feminism remains to be seen. Change comes slowly, but a blizzard accumulates one flake at time.

THINKING ABOUT THE CONTENT

1. Why does Blakely call herself an "outlaw mom"? What does she mean when she says, "we lived like 'outlaws from the institution of mother-hood' " (8)? What do people mean by the phrase "the institution of motherhood"?
2. What does Blakely see as the problem with "evangelists for 'traditional family values' " (32)? What are "traditional family values"? What is her answer to sociologist Barbara Dafoe Whitehead's call to "restigmatize divorce" (24)? Do you agree with Blakely or Whitehead? Why?
3. What are some of the problems single, divorced mothers face in our society? Who is responsible for some of these problems, according to Blakely? Do you agree? Why or why not?
4. Reread paragraph 30. Is this a good rebuttal statement to those who share Pat Buchanan's views? Why or why not?
5. What does Blakely men in the last paragraph that a "third wave of feminism remains to be seen"? What were the first and second waves? Is she correct? Why or why not?

LOOKING AT STRUCTURE AND STYLE

6. To whom is Blakely writing? What in her writing makes you think so?
7. What are some passages that develop her attitude and tone toward "evangelists for traditional family values"? toward her own lifestyle? toward her divorce?

EXPLORING DISCUSSION AND WRITING TOPICS

8. Reread paragraph 48. Explain what Blakely means, then defend or refute her statements.
9. Blakely feels that "If divorce were destigmatized, all families could experiment with structures that would suit their need" (32). What does she mean? How might lifestyles change if divorce were destigmatized?
10. Do you feel that a woman's place is "at the ironing board"? Is it more a woman's responsibility to raise a family than a man's? Should the man be the principal breadwinner in a marriage? Is it possible that so-called traditional family values are no longer possible in some cases considering changing economic conditions and lifestyles?

What exactly is the woman's role in regard to "traditional family values"? Is she just naturally expected to want to become a mother? Is there a silent pressure from society for women to feel unfulfilled if they don't produce children? Is there something wrong if a woman decides she doesn't want motherhood? Is such an attitude unnatural? Can women live happy, guilt-free lives when they decide against having children?

The following reading selection from Leslie Lafayette's *Why Don't You Have Kids? Living in Full Without Parenthood,* shows her own personal struggle with such questions that ultimately lead to the formation of the ChildFree Network.

᠁

Why Don't You Have Kids?

On a summer afternoon in Sacramento, weary from listening to 1 speech after speech from both political parties about "family values," of watching children and grandchildren of political candidates paraded out onto the stage as if they were medals of honor, I sat down at my kitchen table and wrote:

"Am I the only person in America who doesn't have kids?" 2

I knew the question was ridiculous. But it really felt that way. The 3 implication of all the "family values" speeches was not so much that those without children were selfish or evil or abnormal or pathetic . . . although all of those criticisms have been aimed at childless adults at one time or another.

No, the implication was something far more disturbing: childless 4 adults didn't fit into the family values picture.

We were invisible. 5

And that was simply not acceptable to me. It was time to 6 speak up.

I didn't set out to be childfree. It wasn't a goal, a decision reached 7 in a blazing Moment of Truth somewhere along the way. Like many of life's most profound outcomes, it came about almost accidentally, the result of a combination of factors. My lack of planning, for one. Marrying when I was 30 years old, recognizing that the marriage was not solid and secure, and divorcing before I was 35. Perhaps most important, never really giving the issue much thought until the times, and my age, conspired to force it upon me.

There was certainly no pressure—perhaps not even any encourage- 8 ment—to have children from my parents. They were married fifteen years before I was born. For the first five years of their marriage they deliberately avoided pregnancy. Then for the next ten, they let nature take its course. Nothing happened. Neither of my parents were particularly distressed about this nonturn of events. My mother told me that at one point they were considering adoption but "never quite got around to it." They had some tests and discovered they were both "capable." By this time, Mother was 36 and Dad 40.

Then one day my mother missed her period, took a rabbit test, 9 and heard from her doctor that she was pregnant. When she told my father, he cut himself shaving. After that, the pregnancy proceeded normally and was taken calmly by both of them.

Probably because my mother was 37 when I was born and my 10 father 41, I remained an only child. My parents' attitude regarding my having children and their becoming grandparents was casual, to say the least. I do not recall either parent ever telling me about the day I would grow up and "have children of my own." I do recall my father telling me that college, a career like teaching, and money of my own was paramount.

"You'll never be dependent on anyone, and teaching is secure," 11 he told me. As a publicist for Fox, RKO, and eventually United Artists, my father knew what it meant to walk into your office in the morning and not take off your hat until you read the mail. He didn't want that for his daughter. He also, apparently, did not want his daughter to be dependent on some man for her financial security.

Mother never talked about babies either. She lived in mortal terror 12 that I would lose my virginity before I was 40. She warned me about men; phrases such as "Any port in a storm," and "Why buy the cow when you can get the milk for free?" peppered many of our discussions about the opposite sex.

She never encouraged me to have children; I suppose that had 13 as much to do with my complete lack of concern over having a family in my early adult years as anything. I don't know what it would have been like to live with parents who encouraged marriage and parenthood as an early, and natural, course of events. Because I wanted to please my parents, and because I saw them as inherently wise and experienced, I probably would have married young and had babies.

This theory seems to make sense to me until I think about my   14
East Coast cousins, whose parents had—to all outside appearances,
anyway—a model marriage. My aunt and uncle had four children and
lived in a wonderful two-story white clapboard house in upstate New
York. I loved visiting them as a child. In fact, the only time I ever
thought about having children was on the rare occasions I visited
them. I wanted a house just like theirs, a collie dog like their "Lady,"
and four kids. Their children are now in their 50s and 40s, and only
one of them married and had children. The other three are single and
childfree. So much for theories.

I went off to the University of California in 1962 at the age of   15
17. And by the time I graduated in 1966, a revolution had begun. My
role as "Woman" was pretty clear to me when I started college. I would
meet Mr. Right and get married, live in a house out in the suburbs,
and greet him with the perfectly chilled cocktail when he came home at
five. An acquisition of "steady boyfriends," pinnings, and engagements
were worthy endeavors and major accomplishments for a young
woman at college in the sixties.

I remember a song of the times by Jack Jones: "Hey little girl,   16
better wear something pretty, something you'd wear to go to the city
in . . . dim all the lights, pour the wine, start the music . . . time to
get ready for love." As stale and offensive as those lyrics and those
times seem now, that song still touches a chord in me. I wanted to be
someone's wife, someone's "little girl." I just never thought about being
someone's mother.

My role as a woman was less clear to me by the end of the sixties.   17
Independence and career were the buzzwords now; the "little girl" was
the object of sneers and derision. And babies? Give me a break. *No
one* was having babies—at least not in my circle. The horror of finding
oneself pregnant could only be compared to having the doctor announce you had terminal cancer. That's why I'm at best surprised and
at worst skeptical about those pregnancy test commercials on TV
today, with the young man and woman looking eagerly for the pink
or blue color that confirms pregnancy and then actually smiling! That's
why the proliferation of 15-year-old girls in this country who are
blossoming proudly into pregnancy sets me back—way back—on my
heels. In the late sixties and through the seventies as well, most people
I knew who had a positive pregnancy test weren't smiling, they were
panicking.

My friends and I used birth control with religious fervor. We did   18
not think accidental pregnancy was "cute," nor did we look on it as

a way to trap men into marriage. In fact, the typical man's attitude about pregnancy was casual, cavalier really: How could you be so stupid? Get an abortion. The men my friends and I knew in the seventies most definitely were not into fatherhood.

Ironically, it was not during my marriage but after my divorce in   19
the early eighties that the first tickings of the "biological clock" began. Friends were having their babies now that we were in our thirties. More importantly, society had done a 180-degree turn. Gone were the independent, confident career women of the seventies. In their place were these newly programmed Stepford Yuppies who carried the leather attaché case in the right hand, wore the wedding ring on the left, and hung a "Baby on Board" sign in the back window of the BMW.

Overnight, babies were the latest sensation, the must-have acces-   20
sory. All the smart, upscale women were shopping for maternity clothes that "went to the office." If you weren't pregnant or trying to get that way, you simply weren't "in."

Suddenly I couldn't navigate an aisle in the Safeway without seeing   21
babies or toddlers in every cart except mine. I couldn't take my mother to the mall without counting all the swollen bellies. I began to feel as if life had most definitely passed me by. It was as bad as being the only girl at the prom without a date; I wanted to hide my head in shame.

Despite the fact that I was unmarried, I considered having a baby   22
anyway. I began to be less religious about the diaphragm, playing "baby roulette." Sometimes I used it, sometimes I didn't. When that didn't work, I became more scientific . . . and more desperate. (I was about 37 then.) I started taking my temperature in the mornings. It dipped! It rose! I was fertile! It dipped again! I was infertile! I didn't know what was going on.

I went to see a doctor in Palo Alto who specialized in artificial   23
insemination. His claim to fame was that his sperm donors were all in med school at Stanford. Who could ask for more? Maybe you couldn't marry a doctor but you could still have his baby. The price was high though: $200 per sperm "introduction" using a device like a turkey baster. Three "introductions" a cycle. And no guarantee that it would work.

It seemed far more cost effective to pick up one of these guys in   24
a bar in Palo Alto. That way, you could get your drinks for free, too. I never went back to the sperm doctor, and I was just too chicken—and too particular—to pick up someone in a bar to make a baby. And then, about 1984, we began hearing about a terrible new sexually

transmitted disease that killed. They called it AIDS. It certainly put a damper on recreational sex and indiscriminate sperm-donor selection.

In 1986, at the age of 41, I became pregnant by my ex-husband. It was as much a surprise to me as it was to him. I was filled with wonder and awe. (He was not.) I couldn't believe it, even after the ob-gyn confirmed it with an examination. I took prenatal vitamins. I started drinking milk. I suppose like every other mother-to-be in the world, my head was filled with thoughts of the pregnancy. I read every book on pregnancy I could get my hands on. I felt as if I were a cargo vessel, carrying a most precious jewel to a distant port through stormy and treacherous seas.

I took long walks and touched my tummy and talked to the baby. It was as if I had left the everyday, mundane world behind and dwelled on a different plane. It was strange and exciting. I surprised myself with my intensity. It was frightening.

And then, nine weeks into my pregnancy, I miscarried. It wasn't simple and neat. I had cramps, staining, bleeding, for over a week. The entire time, the doctor could not tell me whether I would sustain this pregnancy or not. On the eighth day of this I felt the most incredible pain and passed tissue along with blood. The next day I endured a D and C; a week later, the doctor called and insisted on another test because he was concerned it had been an ectopic pregnancy and that I might suffer a hemorrhage. It wasn't, but it terrified me. The entire episode was a nightmare.

But nothing in those two weeks prepared me for the depression and despair I felt for six months after the miscarriage. I remember one afternoon in particular, lying on my bed reading a book about pregnancy loss. I heard sobbing so loud and so wrenching. I could not imagine where it was coming from. Only after a moment or two did I realize it was coming from me. I had not truly realized how badly I had wanted this baby or how broken I was at its loss.

The point to be made here is not that I wanted the baby—I did, desperately—but the reasons why I had wanted it. The issue is pivotal to any decision about whether to be a parent or whether to live childfree. Looking back, I can see now that my desperate desire to have a baby came not from some internal biological drive, nor was it the result of thoughtful introspection and practical planning. It was my response to a hysterical society, a culture that stripped me of my intrinsic worth and told me point-blank that to fail to reproduce was to fail.

After the miscarriage I was more determined than ever that I must have a baby at any cost. I was goaded onward by the women's magazines (even *Cosmo*, the last sanctuary of the working girl, started

in with the baby talk), television talk shows, sitcoms, pregnant an-
chorwomen and celebrities, friends, coworkers, and society in general,
all of whom were whipping up a baby hysteria the likes of which have
never been seen in this country.

Meanwhile there was no opposing view, no voice of reason, no   31
organization or group to provide a dialogue. There was no sanity, no
refuge. Where was Planned Parenthood? Where was Zero Population
Growth? Where was the National Organization for Non-Parents? (This
important forerunner of The ChildFree Network disbanded in 1979,
claiming it had accomplished its work. Ironically, it left the scene just
as it was most desperately needed.) It was as if all of these organizations
had been run out of town on a rail or willingly went underground.
The message was baby all the way.

And there was something else wrong with the whole picture.   32

At least the original baby boom, after World War II, was built on   33
something true, something real: men coming home from war, grateful
to be alive and young; a feeling of hope, optimism, growth . . . a time
to build again. It was a more innocent time; there was less availability of
effective birth control and a more rigidly defined role for women
as mothers and housekeepers. If there were population or ecological
concerns, they were downplayed.

This new baby boom beginning in the eighties didn't ring quite   34
so true. It was covered in the same glamorous but artificial veneer that
camouflaged a lot of unsavory things during the Reagan years: the
savings and loan business, the junk bond profiteers, the leveraged
buyouts. It smacked of privilege and acquisitiveness, of competition
and prestige, of Yuppism at its most grasping. It wasn't so much about
building families or loving children as it was about a generation of
self-centered boomers who were trying to "complete" themselves and
"have it all." They had given lip service to population and ecological
concerns in their 20s and early 30s; now they tossed aside principle
for procreation. They had put off having children as long as they
physiologically could while they indulged themselves in toys and drugs
and recreational sex; now that it was chic and trendy to be married,
have the condo, do the baby thing, they did so with a vengeance.

The euphemism "quality time," which really meant "I am having   35
a baby but someone else will have to raise it," was a phrase invented
during this time by the superwomen who played hardball in the board-
room and cooed to their infants in the bedroom. Their equally ambitious husbands found being a dad paid big dividends when it came to
promotions, too. The whole thing reeked of status-seeking at its shallow, materialistic worst.

But, I'm ashamed to say, I was buying it. Hey, I was first in line   36
at the checkout counter! I was totally sold on the notion that without
a child of my own, I was absolutely nothing. It didn't matter what
other things I had accomplished on this planet. The fact that I was
not a mother proved that I was a failure as a woman.

And, to tell the truth, there is something mesmerizing about the   37
concept of having a baby. The miracle of conception. The stages of
growth as the fetus moves and kicks. The thrill of knowing you are
creating a life within. Who could not be swayed by the romance of
such a biological miracle? Regardless of how logically you talk to
yourself, it is difficult as a woman to let go of the eternal seduction
of motherhood.

But what to do? I could not go through another miscarriage. I   38
would not even attempt to become pregnant again. I would, instead,
put all of my public relations and writing background to the ultimate
test: I would convince a complete stranger, a pregnant woman who
didn't want her baby, to give it to me! I would write heart-wrenching
copy and tempting "mommy resumes," complete with precious picture
books of me, my two dogs, my lovely home, my piano, my books, my
college degree . . . whatever it took, I would do it. I would overcome
any doubts in the mind of the prospective birth mother about my
single status. I could be mother and father. I could work all day and
diaper all night. I could offer love and affection, a spotless home,
music and sunlight. Eagerly, I printed up hundreds of flyers and began
my search.

Three years, eight thousand dollars, and two willing birth mothers   39
later, I had finally had enough. I walked away from the first birth
mother when she turned out to be flakier than a bowl of Raisin Bran.
I would not admit to myself that my own growing reluctance to enter
into single motherhood was also a key factor.

I began again and found another counselor, another attorney,   40
another birth mother. But two months before the delivery of the second
child, something odd happened. A friend told me we should begin
buying baby furniture, preparing the baby's room; she spoke of giving
me a baby shower. And I was extremely reluctant. I didn't want to
look at furniture. I most definitely didn't want a baby shower.

Later, after much agonizing thought, I realized that I didn't want   41
the baby, either. I called the birth mother and told her that I would
not be taking the baby. And with that, I closed the door on motherhood
for the last time.

The decision not to take the baby didn't come in a blazing burst   42
of insight.

What had happened in those three years to bring me out of my   43
motherhood craze?

For one thing, I had researched what would be the most important   44
decision I would ever make. I felt uncomfortable making an impulsive,
purely emotional decision about something so permanent, so life-
changing. (That's not like me at all, by the way. I tend to be impulsive
about everything.)

I must have spoken with hundreds upon hundreds of parents—   45
men, women, couples, friends, colleagues, complete strangers. I talked
at work. I talked on airplanes, in hotel lobbies, outside of meetings,
while waiting in lines, to my dentist, my doctor, my hairdresser, my
chiropractor, even to the information operator! I talked to anyone
who would listen.

Their responses to my announcement that I was going to adopt   46
a baby were less than encouraging. Over eighty percent of them advised
me to consider my decision carefully. Some went further.

"Why don't you get a dog instead?" "Don't do it." "Why would   47
you want to do that now, at this time in your life?" and "If I knew
what I was getting myself in for, I wouldn't have had kids at all."
Surprised? So was I. Then I realized: these parents were telling the
truth. They weren't at some party with friends or at a family reunion
bragging about their children. They didn't have to save face with me.
While they loved their children, for most of them parenthood had
been a very mixed bag of blessings.

Lying by the pool in Scottsdale, Arizona, on vacation one January,   48
I got into a conversation with a very attractive woman in her early
60s. She told me she had four grown children. I told her my usual
story about planning to adopt an infant.

"Why?" she asked, in a tone clearly indicating she thought me   49
insane. When I told her that I felt life would be meaningless without
children, that having a child was going to transform my life, she
confided that she was on the first vacation she had ever taken without
any of her four children knowing where she was.

"I love them, but I can't handle their problems anymore," she   50
said. Her youngest was 24, the oldest 32. Two were in the middle of
difficult divorces, her son had no money and had moved home for the
second time, one daughter had a baby but no husband and also was
moving home.

"You are never free from their problems," she said. "It doesn't   51
matter how old they get or how old—and tired—you get. I am truly
enjoying this time to myself. And I am planning to move away from

Vancouver, away from my grown children. It's time now for them to deal with their own problems."

She looked at me. "I wouldn't do it," she advised. "I just wouldn't   52
do it."

I talked to single mothers who had adopted. While they were   53
almost uniformly enthusiastic about their children and how much they loved them, I heard other things, too, things that disturbed me.

"I can't get out of the house on the weekends." "It's so hard when   54
Peter is sick. I have to miss work and I'm on commission." "I've just put a second mortgage on the house. Raising a child is so expensive." "I have no social life. I haven't dated in five years." "My daughter is at that age where she really wants a daddy. She cries a lot about it."

The realities of what single parenting would mean broke through   55
the pretty dream world I had concocted for myself and brought me back to earth with a thud. I wasn't willing to put the next twenty or thirty years—the best and perhaps only years I had left—into raising a child. I feared I had neither the patience, the energy, or the financial wherewithal to do a creditable job. I wasn't willing to give up the possibility of a loving relationship with a man (and most men would be uninterested in raising children at this age), opportunities to travel, and a comfortable, worry-free retirement for myself. I realized I cherished my quiet home and the time to read, rest, reflect, play the piano, and write. Perhaps it was selfish. I prefer to think of it as in my best self-interest, an enormously important factor to consider in the parenting decision. There would be no babies for me.

When I closed the door on parenthood for the final time, I expected   56
to suffer and mourn. But something funny happened instead. The relief of making a final decision was enormous. The fresh breeze of sanity and self-esteem blew once again into my life, cleaning out stale corners and depressing cobwebs. I let go of the notion that I had to have it all, that I was a failure without a child. I let go of the drive, the obsession, the grief. I stopped beating myself up. You've heard the old joke about hitting yourself on the head with a hammer because it feels so good when you stop? It does.

Something changed in my perception, as well. We are all victims   57
of tunnel vision in our lives. It just depends which tunnel you choose. I had seen only the children in the supermarket carts, never the distracted or tired expression on the mothers' faces as they dealt with the constant demands from small children. I had heard only the joyous sounds of childish laughter and singing. I had not been listening to the screams, the whines, the nonstop crying. I had a vision of carrying

my baby in her little pink booties proudly into the mall or to a friend's home. I had not thought about the 24-hour-a-day commitment, the 3 A.M. feedings or the $600 a month I would have to find in order to put her in daycare.

I had not considered the ear infections and the teething and the 58 frightened runs to the emergency room—nor the costs of additional health insurance. I had only seen (my tunnel vision again) the positives. I believe our society does us a disservice when it focuses only on the benefits of child-rearing. And I think parents who tell the truth are our greatest allies against ill-considered procreation and even child abuse by those who buy the myth and discover too late the difficult realities of parenting.

It's important that I make it clear that I am not bitter about being 59 childless, nor do I dislike children. I spent seventeen years teaching English in a high school classroom to 150 adolescents a day; I still enjoy teenagers. The decision not to have children was solely mine. What I speak out against is the pressure and the prejudice of a society that demands parenthood from us all and creates anxiety, despair, and frustration in those who do not want or cannot have children. Not everyone *should* have children. Not everyone wants them. Not everyone is capable of doing a good job of rearing them.

I now consider myself happily childless by choice. I could still, at 60 my age, opt to have my own children through adoption or the "miracles" of the fertility industry. But I choose to live my life from here on out without children of my own. There are those who say that childless adults don't know what they're missing.

I know. 61

I know what it is to desperately want a child. 62

I know what it is to lose a child. 63

I know what it is to obsessively grieve and despair because I did 64 not fit in to what society deemed the norm, what my peers and the media and even my government saw as acceptable and "fulfilled."

I know what it feels like to be alone, to be different, to be isolated, 65 to be ignored.

And while I realize I don't know all of what I've missed as a single 66 mother, I know enough. I've missed the chubby arms around the neck, the sticky kisses, the joys of teaching and giving, the goodnight prayers, the lullabies. I've missed the hallowed title of "Mom." I've missed the Halloween costumes and the piano recitals and the "growing" marks on the wall, baking cookies on rainy afternoons and making Christmas ornaments. I've missed the companionship and comfort of a grown son or daughter.

However, I've also missed total exhaustion, despair over finding   67
competent childcare, sleepless nights due to teething or frantic worrying about paying the bills, lack of time for my writing, my reading,
my animals, or my music, and perhaps pulling out my hair over drugs,
pregnancy, accidents. I've missed dealing with grown children who
never leave home, and I've missed weeping bitterly over inattentive or
selfish adult sons and daughters, as many of my mother's friends have
done.

We all make our choices. The challenge comes in living with them,   68
and living well with them and in peace. Taking personal responsibility
is part of the challenge of being comfortable with our choices; we
didn't let society, or our parents, or our friends make our decisions
for us.

I become more committed to and comfortable with living childfree   69
every day—less ambivalent, less defensive, more joyful, and best of
all, free to be myself. Helping you to be free to be you, to live your
life the way that suits you best, is what this book is all about.

THINKING ABOUT THE CONTENT

1. What were some of the reasons Lafayette wanted to have a child? Were
   these good reasons? Do you think many married people have children
   because subconsciously they think it is expected of them?
2. Lafayette feels that "this new baby boom beginning in the eighties didn't
   ring quite so true," at least compared with the baby boom after World
   War II (33). Are her comments true? Are we seeing any results of the
   1980s "baby boom" that bear her out?
3. If Lafayette had not had a miscarriage and brought her pregnancy to
   term, do you think she would be a happy mother at this point? What
   comments does she make that make you think as you do?
4. Do you think many people have preconceived, erroneous notions of what
   raising a family is like? Why do most couples want to have children and
   raise a family? Is there something wrong or odd about couples who don't
   want children? Is this a sign of selfishness?

LOOKING AT STRUCTURE AND STYLE

5. How well does Lafayette show the social influences placed on women to
   have children? Which paragraphs reflect or imply such influence?
6. Lafayette is quite open and frank in respect to her own life. Which
   paragraphs help establish this ingenuousness? Are such comments appropriate? Why or why not?

7. For what effect does Lafayette repeat the phrase "I know . . ." in paragraphs 61–65?
8. Is Lafayette's decision to remain childless well supported? Are you convinced she knows what she is doing? Why or why not?

EXPLORING DISCUSSION AND WRITING TOPICS

9. Lafayette says, "Taking personal responsibility is part of the challenge of being comfortable with our choices; we didn't let society, or our parents, or our friends make our decisions for us" (68). How easy is this to do? Is this the right approach to choosing a lifestyle?
10. Why do you want or not want to have children? Who should have children? Who should not?
11. Read more from Lafayette's book to learn about the ChildFree Network. What is its function? Is it necessary? Who benefits from it? What does its existence reflect about contemporary society and "traditional family values"?

Reprinted by permission. Courtesy of Carol Wilson Fine Arts, Inc.

DAVE BARRY

Dave Barry, a Pulitzer Prize winner based at the *Miami Herald,* writes a syndicated column that appears in several hundred newspapers. Author of more than seventeen books, including *Dave Barry's Greatest Hits, Dave Barry's Bad Habits, Dave Barry Does Japan, Dave Barry Is Not Making This Up, Dave Barry Slept Here: A Sort of History of the United States,* and *Babies and Other Hazards of Sex,* the *New York Times* has called him "the funniest man in America." But Barry responds by asking, "What do they know?"

The following selection is from *Dave Barry's Complete Guide to Guys.* If we are to believe the book jacket, "To research this guide—which is 100 percent mostly new material—Dave spent literally dozens of minutes sitting around at least looking thoughtful. He attempted to conduct intensive, soul-searching personal interviews with several guys he knows, although they ended up watching the playoffs instead." Here, Barry attempts to explain why women might have trouble understanding a "guy's lifestyle."

❦

Tips for Women: How To Have a Relationship with a Guy

Contrary to what many women believe, it's fairly easy to develop a long-term, stable, intimate, and mutually fulfilling relationship with a guy. Of course this guy has to be a Labrador retriever. With human guys, it's extremely difficult. This is because guys don't really grasp what women mean by the term *relationship.*

Let's say a guy named Roger is attracted to a woman named Elaine. He asks her out to a movie; she accepts; they have a pretty good time. A few nights later he asks her out to dinner, and again they enjoy themselves. They continue to see each other regularly, and after a while neither one of them is seeing anybody else.

And then, one evening when they're driving home, a thought occurs to Elaine, and, without really thinking, she says it aloud: "Do you realize that, as of tonight, we've been seeing each other for exactly six months?"

And then there is silence in the car. To Elaine, it seems like a very   4
loud silence. She thinks to herself: Geez, I wonder if it bothers him
that I said that. Maybe he's been feeling confined by our relationship;
maybe he thinks I'm trying to push him into some kind of obligation
that he doesn't want, or isn't sure of.

And Roger is thinking: Gosh. *Six months.*   5

And Elaine is thinking: But, hey, *I'm* not so sure I want this kind   6
of relationship, either. Sometimes I wish *I* had a little more space, so
I'd have time to think about whether I really want us to keep going
the way we are, moving steadily toward . . . I mean, where *are* we
going? Are we just going to keep seeing each other at this level of
intimacy? Are we heading toward *marriage?* Toward *children?* Toward
a *lifetime* together? Am I ready for that level of commitment? Do I
really even *know* this person?

And Roger is thinking: . . . so that means it was . . . let's see   7
. . . *February* when we started going out, which was right after I had
the car at the dealer's, which means . . . lemme check the odome-
ter. . . . *Whoa!* I am *way* overdue for an oil change here.

And Elaine is thinking: He's upset. I can see it on his face. Maybe   8
I'm reading this completely wrong. Maybe he wants *more* from our
relationship, *more* intimacy, *more* commitment; maybe he has sensed—
even before *I* sensed it—that I was feeling some reservations. Yes, I
bet that's it. That's why he's so reluctant to say anything about his
own feelings: He's afraid of being rejected.

And Roger is thinking: And I'm gonna have them look at the   9
transmission again. I don't care *what* those morons say, it's still not
shifting right. And they better not try to blame it on the cold weather
this time. *What* cold weather? It's eighty-seven degrees out, and this
thing is shifting like a goddamn *garbage truck,* and I paid those incom-
petent thieving cretin bastards *six hundred dollars.*

And Elaine is thinking: He's angry. And I don't blame him. I'd be   10
angry, too. God, I feel so *guilty,* putting him through this, but I can't
help the way I feel. I'm just not *sure.*

And Roger is thinking: They'll probably say it's only a ninety-day   11
warranty. That's exactly what they're gonna say, the scumballs.

And Elaine is thinking: Maybe I'm just too idealistic, waiting for   12
a knight to come riding up on his white horse, when I'm sitting right
next to a perfectly good person, a person I enjoy being with, a person
I truly do care about, a person who seems to truly care about me. A
person who is in pain because of my self-centered, schoolgirl romantic
fantasy.

And Roger is thinking: Warranty? They want a warranty? *I'll* give   13
them a goddamn warranty. I'll take their warranty and stick it right
up their. . . .

"Roger," Elaine says aloud.   14

"What?" says Roger, startled.   15

"Please don't torture yourself like this," she says, her eyes begin-   16
ning to brim with tears. "Maybe I should never have . . . Oh *God*, I
feel so. . . ." *(She breaks down, sobbing.)*

"What?" says Roger.   17

"I'm such a fool," Elaine sobs. "I mean, I know there's no knight.   18
I really know that. It's silly. There's no knight, and there's no horse."

"There's no horse?" says Roger.   19

"You think I'm a fool, don't you," Elaine says.   20

"No!" says Roger, glad to finally know the correct answer.   21

"It's just that. . . . It's that I . . . I need some time," Elaine says.   22

(There is a fifteen-second pause while Roger, thinking as fast as   23
he can, tries to come up with a safe response. Finally he comes up
with one that he thinks might work.)

"Yes," he says.   24

(Elaine, deeply moved, touches his hand.)   25

"Oh, Roger, do you really feel that why?" she says.   26

"What way?" says Roger.   27

"That way about time," says Elaine.   28

"Oh," says Roger, "Yes."   29

(Elaine turns to face him and gazes deeply into his eyes, causing   30
him to become very nervous about what she might say next, especially
if it involves a horse. At last she speaks.)

"Thank you, Roger," she says.   31

"Thank *you*," says Roger.   32

Then he takes her home, and she lies on her bed, a conflicted,   33
tortured soul, and weeps until dawn, whereas when Roger gets back to
his place, he opens a bag of Doritos, turns on the TV, and immediately
becomes deeply involved in a rerun of a tennis match between two
Czechoslovakians he has never heard of. A tiny voice in the far recesses
of his mind tells him that something major was going on back there
in the car, but he is pretty sure there is no way he would ever understand
what, and so he figures it's better if he doesn't think about it. (This is
also Roger's policy regarding world hunger.)

The next day Elaine will call her closest friend, or perhaps two   34
of them, and they will talk about this situation for six straight
hours. In painstaking detail, they will analyze everything she said

and everything he said, going over it time and time again, exploring every word, expression, and gesture for nuances of meaning, considering every possible ramification. They will continue to discuss this subject, off and on, for weeks, maybe months, never reaching any definite conclusions, but never getting bored with it, either.

Meanwhile, Roger, while playing racquetball one day with a mu-   35
tual friend of his and Elaine's, will pause just before serving, frown, and say: "Norm, did Elaine ever own a horse?"

We're not talking about different wavelengths here. We're talking   36
about different *planets,* in completely different *solar systems.* Elaine cannot communicate meaningfully with Roger about their relationship any more than she can meaningfully play chess with a duck. Because the sum total of Roger's thinking on this particular topic is as follows:

Huh?   37

Women have a lot of trouble accepting this. Despite millions of   38
years of overwhelming evidence to the contrary, women are convinced that guys must spend a certain amount of time thinking about the relationship. How could they not? How could a guy see another human being day after day, night after night, sharing countless hours with this person, becoming physically intimate—how can a guy be doing these things and *not* be thinking about their relationship? This is what women figure.

They are wrong. A guy in a relationship is like an ant standing   39
on top of a truck tire. The ant is aware, on a very basic level, that something large is there, but he cannot even dimly comprehend what this thing is, or the nature of his involvement with it. And if the truck starts moving, and the tire starts to roll, the ant will sense that something important is happening, but right up until he rolls around to the bottom and is squashed into a small black blot, the only distinct thought that will form in his tiny brain will be, and I quote,

Huh?   40

Which is exactly what Roger will think when Elaine explodes with   41
fury at him when he commits one of the endless series of petty offenses, such as asking her sister out, that guys are always committing in relationships because they have virtually no clue that they are in one.

"How *could* he?" Elaine will ask her best friends. "What was he   42
thinking?"

The answer is, He *wasn't* thinking, in the sense that women mean   43
the word. He can't: He doesn't have the appropriate type of brain. He

has a guy brain, which is basically an analytical, problem-solving type of organ. It likes things to be definite and measurable and specific. It's not comfortable with nebulous and imprecise relationship-type concepts such as *love* and *need* and *trust*. If the guy brain has to form an opinion about another person, it prefers to form that opinion based on something concrete about the person, such as his or her earned-run average.

So the guy brain is not well-suited to grasping relationships. But it's good at analyzing and solving mechanical problems. For example, if a couple owns a house, and they want to repaint it so they can sell it, it will probably be the guy who will take charge of this project. He will methodically take the necessary measurements, calculate the total surface area, and determine the per-gallon coverage capacity of the paint; then, using his natural analytical and mathematical skills, he will apply himself to the problem of figuring out a good excuse not to paint the house.   44

"It's too humid," he'll say. Or: "I've read that prospective buyers are actually attracted more to a house with a lot of exterior dirt." Guys simply have a natural flair for this kind of problem-solving. That's why we always have guys in charge of handling the federal budget deficit.   45

But the point I'm trying to make is that, if you're a woman, and you want to have a successful relationship with a guy, the Number One Tip to remember is: 46

1. Never assume that the guy understands that you and he have a relationship.   47

The guy will not realize this on his own. You have to plant the idea in his brain by constantly making subtle references to it in your everyday conversation, such as: 48

- "Roger, would you mind passing me a Sweet 'n' Low, inasmuch as we have a relationship?"   49

- "Wake up, Roger! There's a prowler in the den and we have a relationship! You and I do, I mean."   50

- "Good news, Roger! The gynecologist says we're going to have our fourth child, which will serve as yet another indication that we have a relationship!"   51

- "Roger, inasmuch as this plane is crashing and we probably have only about a minute to live, I want you to know that we've had   52 a wonderful fifty-three years of marriage together, which clearly constitutes a relationship."

Never let up, women. Pound away relentlessly at this concept,   53
and eventually it will start to penetrate the guy's brain. Some day he might even start thinking about it on his own. He'll be talking with some other guys about women, and, out of the blue, he'll say, "Elaine and I, we have, ummm. . . . We have, ahhh. . . . We . . . We have this *thing*."

And he will sincerely mean it.   54

The next relationship-enhancement tip is: 55

2. Do not expect the guy to make a hasty commitment.   56

By "hasty," I mean, "within your lifetime." Guys are *extremely*   57
reluctant to make commitments. This is because they never feel *ready*.

"I'm sorry," guys are always telling women, "but I'm just not   58
ready to make a commitment." Guys are in a permanent state of nonreadiness. If guys were turkey breasts, you could put them in a 350-degree oven on July Fourth, and they *still* wouldn't be done in time for Thanksgiving.

Women have a lot of trouble understanding this. Women ask   59
themselves: How can a guy say he's "not ready" to make a permanent commitment to a woman with whom he is obviously compatible; a woman whom he has been seeing for years; a woman who once drove *his* dog to the veterinarian in *her* new car when it (the dog) started making unusual stomach noises and then barfing prolifically after eating an entire birthday cake, including candles, that *she* made from scratch for *him* (the guy), the result being that her car will smell like a stadium rest room for the next five years, at the end of which this guy will probably still say he's "not ready"? And how come this same guy was somehow capable, at age seven, of committing himself to a lifelong, passionate, win-or-lose relationship with the Kansas City Royals, who have never so much as sent him a card?

A lot of women have concluded that the problem is that guys,   60
as a group, have the emotional maturity of hamsters. No, this is not the case. A hamster is much more capable of making a lasting commitment to a woman, especially if she gives it those little food pellets. Whereas a guy, in a relationship, will consume the pellets of companionship, and he will run on the exercise wheel of lust; but as soon as he senses that the door of commitment is about to close and trap him in the wire cage of true intimacy, he'll squirm

out, scamper across the kitchen floor of uncertainty and hide under the refrigerator of nonreadiness.[1]

This is natural behavior. Guys are born with a fundamental, geneti- 61
cally transmitted mental condition known to psychologists as: The Fear That If You Get Attached to a Woman, Some Unattached Guy, Somewhere, Will Be Having More Fun Than You. This is why all married guys assume that all unmarried guys lead lives of constant excitement involving hot tubs full of naked international fashion models; whereas in fact for most unmarried guys, the climax of the typical evening is watching an infomercial for Hair-in-a-Spray-Can while eating onion dip straight from the container. (This is also true of married guys, although statistically they are far more likely to be using a spoon.)

So guys are extremely reluctant to make commitments, or even 62
to take any steps that might *lead* to commitments. This is why, when a guy goes out on a date with a woman and finds himself really liking her, he often will demonstrate his affection by avoiding her for the rest of his life.

Women are puzzled by this. "I don't *understand*," they say. "We 63
had such a great time! Why doesn't he *call?*"

The reason is that the guy, using the linear guy thought process, 64
has realized that if he takes her out again, he'll probably like her even more, so he'll take her out *again,* and eventually they'll fall in love with each other, and they'll get married, and they'll have children, and then they'll have grandchildren, and eventually they'll retire and take a trip around the world, and they'll be walking hand-in-hand on some spectacular beach in the South Pacific, reminiscing about the lifetime of experiences they've shared together, and then several naked international fashion models will walk up and invite him to join them in a hot tub, and *he won't be able to do it.*

This is Basic Guy Logic. And it leads us to our final and most 65
important tip for women who wish to have a successful relationship with a guy:

3. Don't make the guy feel threatened. 66

Guys are easily threatened by the tiniest hint that they have become 67
somehow obligated, so you need to learn to give soothing, nonthreatening responses, especially in certain dangerous situations, as shown in the following table.

1. I am a professional writer. Do not try these metaphors at home.

Situation	Threatening Response	Nonthreatening Response
You meet a guy for the first time.	"Hello."	"I am a nun."
You're on your first date. The guy asks you what your hopes for the future are.	"Well, I'd like to pursue my career for a while, and then get married and maybe have children."	"A vodka Collins."
You have a great time on the date, and the guy asks you if you'd like to go out again.	"Yes."	"Okay, but bear in mind that I have only three months to live."
The clergyperson asks you if you take this man to be your lawful wedded husband, for richer and poorer, in sickness and in health, etc., 'til death do you part.	"I do."	"Well, sure, but not *literally.*"

THINKING ABOUT THE CONTENT

1. *Huh?*
2. What are the three tips Barry offers to women? What is "Basic Guy Logic"? Beneath the humor, are there any truths regarding the differences in male-female relationships? If so, what are they?
3. Ask your own question here.
4. If you have more to say, ask another question. (I'm not sure my editor is going to let me get away with this.)

LOOKING AT STRUCTURE AND STYLE

5. How does Barry use comparison-contrast as a humorous device? How far-fetched are his comparisons? Who seems more "real," Roger or Elaine? Who is mostly being made fun of?

EXPLORING DISCUSSION AND WRITING TOPICS

6. Write an essay called "Tips for Men: How to Have a Relationship with a Gal." Approach it humorously or seriously.
7. Discuss whether or not Elaine ever owned a horse.

Bruce Brawer's essays on cultural criticism have appeared in such journals as the *New Criterion* and the *American Spectator*. Probably best recognized as the author of *A Place at the Table: The Gay Individual in American Society*, Brawer takes his title from a speech by President Clinton in which he expresses hope for "an American home where everyone has a place at the table." Brawer contends that inviting homosexuals to the table need not disrupt our life together, but rather improve it. According to Brawer, the public debates about homosexuality have been conducted by "belligerent extremists" on both sides.

In *A Place at the Table*, Brawer deals only with male homosexuality, because lesbianism, he believes, is entangled with the issues of feminism, something other than his concerns in the book. Brawer wants his readers to "embrace my hope in the ultimate triumph of reason over irrationality, acceptance over estrangement, love over loathing," and to show that "there's no inherent conflict between homosexuality and decency."

In the following selection from Brawer's book, he discusses the prejudices and fears people have toward homosexuals, how they are perpetuated, and why a better understanding of gay lifestyles is important for both homosexuals and heterosexuals.

🌾

A Place at the Table

Of all prejudices, homophobia is the only one whose spread has been fostered by a widespread belief that good Christian values require it. At the same time, deep-seated though it may be, it is the prejudice that can be most dramatically challenged by a personal exposure to the object of prejudice. Since gays *do* come from everywhere, from every kind of family in every corner of the world, most heterosexuals have their first close encounter with homosexuality when they discover that a friend or relative or co-worker—someone whom they already know and trust and care about, whom they might never have suspected of being "different," and whom they would not in a million years think of as the Other—is in fact gay. A white racist can't suddenly discover that his teenage child is black, but countless homophobic parents have suddenly discovered their teenage children to be gay. In such situations, something's got to give. Either the loved one is rejected, turned out of the house, the very mention of his name prohibited, or—as occurs, fortunately, in most cases—the hated Other instantly ceases to be an Other and the misconceptions on which bigotry is founded begin to crumble. Every time I see a congregation full of fundamentalists on TV applauding an anti-gay sermon, I think that sooner or later some of these people will be told by their sons or daughters: "I'm gay." Of this there's no doubt; it will happen. And their assumptions will be jolted. Their sense of gays as something entirely Other will be shaken. In order to maintain this notion of gays as the Other, some of these people will reject their children, perhaps even tell them, "You're dead to me. I have no child." More, after a period of adjustment, will come to understand and accept.

The ultimate enemy of anti-gay prejudice, then, is the truth—the 2 truth that gays, who to many heterosexuals seem the most alien of Others, are in fact not by nature an Other at all. Rather, they are made into an Other by ill-informed prejudice—and are then despised for being that imagined Other. The reason for all these headlines about gays in the military, gays in the Boy Scouts, gays in the public-school curricula, and so forth is that, in the 1990s, gays are at last demanding in huge numbers that they be recognized as *not* being some exotic. Other, unsuited to participate in established institutions. They want to lead open, ordinary middle-class lives, not lives in the closet or on the bohemian fringe. Yet people who claim to stand for the values that underlie those ordinary lives continue to do everything they can to prevent gays from leading such lives.

If levels of homophobia remain high, it is largely because there 3 are still many heterosexuals who don't know (or who think they don't know) any gay people. To alter this state of affairs is by far the most important factor in eliminating anti-gay prejudice. And it has, fortunately, already begun to come to pass. As more gays have become more honest about their homosexuality, more heterosexual friends, relatives, and co-workers have rethought ill-informed prejudices. "Individual contact," Joseph Steffan writes, "is the most powerful weapon we have in the battle against homophobia, indeed, against all forms of prejudice. It is a battle that can only be won from the ground up. Simply knowing someone who is gay or lesbian . . . is the best way to overcome hatred." This is why both the gay subculture and the closet are, practically speaking, allies of homophobia. The subculture keeps gays largely segregated from the straight majority; the closet keeps their sexual orientation a secret. (Knowing someone who is gay or lesbian doesn't make a difference, after all, unless one knows that the person *is* gay or lesbian.)

Closeted homosexuals are right to criticize those subculture-oriented gays who through reckless political actions, fatuous public antics, or irresponsible stunts have helped to perpetuate offensive images of homosexuality. By the same token, though, if these closeted homosexuals make such criticisms, they have a responsibility to place themselves on the line, to help rectify those images, and to lend what they may see as their superior intelligence, self-control, and rationality to the cause. For such homosexuals simply to shrug nervously and say "It's best not to talk about these things" is scandalous; in these eight brief words is summed up the whole long, sad history of homosexuals' failure to win respect and vanquish stereotypes. 4

Most people who condemn homosexuals are not wicked. More often, they're uninformed. Not unintelligent—on the contrary, as I have said, they are often very intelligent—but uninformed. They may not be aware that they know any homosexuals, and consequently the word may conjure up for them a variety of strange, disturbing, but unrepresentative images. Or they may be insecure about their own sexual orientation, and thus may be rendered especially uncomfortable by any exposure to people who are openly gay. Or they may believe that to accord homosexuals full civil rights would be to attack the institution of marriage and invite social breakdown—an argument that is valid only if you assume that most husbands and fathers are suppressing powerful homosexual urges and that in a society where homosexuality did not pose so many difficulties they would be living with other men. 5

The opposition of many people to gay rights is built on a thorough misunderstanding of what homosexuality is and what gay rights would mean for society at large. During the 1992 election campaign, *USA Today* reported that Sandy Sumner, a young woman who campaigned door-to-door for Oregon's anti-gay measure, was convinced that "radical groups like Queer Nation represent most homosexuals, and that they want to take over schools and government." In the fall of 1992, the *New York Times* quoted a Brooklyn mother's complaint that New York City's proposed tolerance curriculum would teach her children that "if any man touches me and I'm a little boy, it's O.K., or if any woman touches me and I'm a little girl, it's O.K." 6

Where do people acquire such inaccurate ideas about what homosexuals want and about what the gay-rights movement seeks to accomplish? Often from propagandists like the Reverend Lou Sheldon, who 7 said in September 1992 that the newly enacted California law banning anti-gay job discrimination would "protect sex with animals and the rape of children as forms of political expression." Certainly from Rush Limbaugh, who has said, among many other things, that allowing gays into the armed forces would lead to the founding of Queer Nation chapters on military bases. And also from people like *Washington Times* columnist Samuel Francis, who described gay Eagle Scout James Dale's attempt to rejoin the Scouts as part of a "culture war" on the part of homosexuals. "For some reason," Francis wrote, homosexuals "would like to go camping out in the woods along with the packs of adolescent boys who compose the Scouts, and for some other reason the Scouts just don't want them. I think I know the reasons in both cases, but I'll leave them to your imagination." In another column, Francis wrote:

> A "society" that makes no distinction between sex within
> marriage and sex outside it, that does not distinguish
> morally and socially between continence and debauchery,
> normality and perversion, love and lust, is not really a society
> but merely the chaos of a perpetual orgy.
>   It is . . . to just such an orgy that the proponents of
> normalized and unrestricted homosexuality invite America.
> Maybe most Americans have reached the point at which
> they are ready to immerse themselves in the illusion that
> a perpetual orgy pretending to be a society really doesn't
> hurt anybody.

How many of Sheldon's followers, one wondered, would note his absurd equation of rape with consensual homosexual sex? How many of Limbaugh's viewers would understand that gays who go into the armed forces and gays who join Queer Nation are two very different kinds of people? And how many readers of Francis's remarks about the need to make distinctions would recognize that it was Francis who—by implicitly equating heterosexuality with love and continence and equating homosexuality with lust and orgies—was guilty of a refusal to make distinctions? For sexual orientation is one issue, sexual irresponsibility another; homosexuals are innately no less capable of falling in love and being faithful, and innately no more inclined to lewdness and promiscuity, than heterosexuals. Sheldon, Limbaugh, and Francis are not the only commentators who seek deliberately to equate homosexuality, in the public mind, with rape, radicalism, and raunchiness.

Many heterosexuals gripe that they're sick of hearing so much about   8
homosexuality. In a twist on the famous line in which Lord Alfred
Douglas described homosexuality as "the Love that dare not speak its
name," some have complained in recent years that homosexuality has
turned into "the love that won't shut up." During a recent talk-show
confrontation about the subject, for example, a heterosexual man
argued that for gays to talk about homosexuality constituted "straight-
bashing." "After all," he said, "*I* don't go around talking about being
straight!" Such a man simply doesn't realize how wrong he is, and
how unfair. As Joseph Steffan has noted, "the public expression of
heterosexuality is such an integral and basic part of our everyday
lives that it goes unrecognized." The proper response to the man who
complained of "straight-bashing" is that he "talks about" being straight
all the time without realizing it. He does so every time he mentions
his wife, every time he tells a joke about marriage, every time he
banters playfully with a waitress or female secretary. Indeed, from the
homosexual point of view, "the love that won't shut up" is heterosexuality; and the major reason why anti-gay prejudice endures, I think,
is that homosexuality, despite all the discussion of it that has taken
place on certain issues-oriented TV and radio shows, maintains an
extremely low profile in both popular culture and everyday life.

   Though the average American married couple may, in other words,   9
hear a good deal of talk about homosexuality in an abstract and general
sense, openly homosexual individuals are not an everyday part of their
life. They are not accustomed to meeting gay couples at church or the
P.T.A. It is likely that at least one of the couple's not-too-distant relatives is gay, but that relative's homosexuality is likely to be as long
absent from the realm of family conversation as the relative himself
has been absent from family gatherings. Nor is the couple used to
seeing gays as characters on TV sitcoms or dramas (unless tolerance
of homosexuality is itself the theme of a specific episode). Indeed, gays
continue to be depicted so rarely in mainstream movies and TV series
that when one such character does appear on *Melrose Place* or *Roseanne,* gay periodicals treat it as a major event. While heterosexual
celebrities talk freely with Jay Leno or David Letterman about their
romances or marriages, moreover, the overwhelming majority of homosexuals in public life keep their sexual identity entirely under wraps.

   If you're straight and you can't quite understand what I'm talking   10
about, take a look sometime at a rerun of the old *Andy Griffith* show.
If you're white, try to imagine what it's like being a black person
watching the same show. Think of it: a North Carolina town with no
blacks whatsoever. None. Where are they? White viewers (especially

non-Southerners) might not even notice the omission. But to a black person, at first sight, it must be stunning. What, many a black viewer must have wondered when he or she first saw the series, is this program saying about me? Well, that's what it's like being a gay man and watching virtually every TV drama and comedy. The assumption is always that every man is attracted only to women, that every teenage boy lusts after teenage girls.

Homosexuality is, of course, a staple of shows like *Donahue* and   11
Oprah—and gays owe much to the vigorous and articulate support of Phil Donahue, in particular, for gay rights. Yet while the conspicu-ousness of gays on programs like *Donahue* has in one respect been a very good thing, it has in another respect not been a blessing for homosexuals (or anyone), since a disproportionate number of the gays who appear on such programs tend to be highly politicized or to be people who (like many of these programs' heterosexual guests) want the world to know that they are sexually obsessed or promiscuous or kinky. Too often, the image of homosexuality communicated to the general public by such talk-show guests is sensational, counterproduc-tive, and extremely misleading. For too many viewers of these shows, homosexuality comes off not as an integral part of everyday reality but as the stuff of scandal, an excuse for freak shows, arguments, pietistic moralizing, and titillating revelations. (To quote a recent promotional announcement: "Is your husband secretly gay? Next *Oprah*.") Such shows reinforce the idea of homosexuality as something to argue about and worry about, as opposed to something to think about and learn about: it becomes a hot political issue, something with two inflexible opposing sides, rather than a matter on which people might reach a common understanding if only long-standing misconcep-tions and baseless mistrust were eliminated.

Indeed, it often seems as if the producers of these shows have   12
deliberately booked the most extreme people they could find on both sides of the issue—however small their constituencies and however discredited their arguments—and have thus, incidentally, helped to build lucrative public careers for irresponsible people. (One show, for example, featured a spokesman for the "Exodus Ex-Gay Ministries," which claimed to be able to turn homosexuals into heterosexuals—something that simply cannot be done.) The revealing fact is that when *Donahue* and *Oprah* cover themes other than homosexuality—for example, infidelity or family conflicts or health issues—openly gay individuals are rarely, and gay couples virtually never, included. The shows don't reflect the reality of homosexuals as people who have interests and problems like everyone else and whose lives are not

entirely about being gay. Ultimately, in short, these series reinforce the notion that homosexuality is not a part of the social fabric but an isolating, alienating trait.

There are, to be sure, scattered exceptions to the rule of gay   13
invisibility on TV and in the movies. There was, of course, *Longtime Companion*. The year 1993, moreover, saw the production of at least three potentially important projects: *Philadelphia,* which was touted as "the first big-budget Hollywood movie on homophobia"; *And the Band Played On,* an HBO miniseries adaptation of Randy Shilts's book about the AIDS crisis; and *Tales of the City,* the first TV miniseries to focus largely on gay life. (Like David Leavitt's gay novel *The Lost Language of Cranes,* which became a 1991 TV movie, *Tales of the City* scared off American producers with its gay content and is being adapted for British television.) Yet it remained to be seen what form these dramas would take and what sort of impact they would have.

Surely most of the exceptions to the rule of gay invisibility on TV   14
and in the movies give gays little to cheer about. The occasional gay-themed PBS program routinely looks at homosexuality through the single window of the subculture, and thereby serves only to reinforce mainstream stereotypes and prejudices. On local news programs where the homosexuality of hero cops or firemen or celebrity interviewees is routinely avoided, the subject of homosexuality tends to come up only in stories about AIDS and gay-rights issues or when someone—a priest, day-care worker, or scoutmaster—is accused of sexually abusing boys. (This practice of breaking the silence on homosexuality only to cover sex crimes tends, of course, to obscure the fact that homosexuals are no more likely than heterosexuals to sexually abuse children.)

As I've mentioned, prime-time shows like *Roseanne* and *Melrose*   15
Place have included gay characters—but these aren't *major* characters, portrayed fully enough so that viewers can feel involved in their lives; rather, they are invariably peripheral, placed in the background in self-conscious gestures of tolerance and diversity on the part of the producers. Yes, *One Life to Live* offered that admirable story line about a gay teenager's coming out—but it didn't dare to give the clean-cut, wholesome-looking young man an actual boyfriend. For a while it seemed that every other episode of *The Golden Girls* was about some friend or relative of one of the girls who turned out to be gay—an obvious attempt on the part of the show's producers to teach their audience a lesson in acceptance. But the episodes in question invariably treated homosexuality as an issue, and reinforced the idea that gay people never do anything except have sex and talk about being gay. Watching such programs, one could understand why some people say

they get sick of hearing about homosexuality. And one could not help reflecting that the first sign of real change will be when TV series have regular homosexual characters (not marginal ones) who have actual romantic relationships, who talk about something other than homosexuality, and whose family and work lives are treated in the same way as those of straight characters.

The most striking fact about anti-gay prejudice in America is not that   16
it has endured for so long; it is that Americans who disapprove of homosexuality have refused to face the deep contradictions inherent in their attitudes. But of course doing so would involve *thinking* about those attitudes, and homosexuality is something that many people simply don't want to think about.

For many, these attitudes seem to come terribly easily. Most people   17
who engage in anti-gay rhetoric, while claiming to speak from profound religious or moral conviction, haven't put much serious thought into their censures. The widely held view of homosexuality as "wrong" is not unlike antebellum Southern whites' notion that slavery was morally defensible: both attitudes are long-established, socially entrenched, taken for granted. One would think that any Christian halfway sincere in his religious beliefs—which demand of him that, above all else, he love and not hate—would be anguished at the thought of having to condemn millions of people for their sexual orientation. One would think that such a person might examine the relevant scripture in order to see if there was some basis for acceptance instead of condemnation; one would think he might read a book like John Boswell's *Christianity, Social Tolerance, and Homosexuality* in order to understand how it is that many good, intelligent people, straight and gay alike, sincerely see no contradiction between homosexual life and Christian belief. But such serious reflection and soul searching on the topic of homosexuality appear to take place far less often than they should. On the contrary, when it comes to discussions of the moral dimension of homosexuality, illogic, closed-mindedness, and the reiteration of age-old formulas are the order of the day.

What underlies most of this prejudice? Opponents of homosexual-   18
ity use different words. They contend variously that they find it "evil," "wrong," "sick." "Evil" is a religious person's verdict; "wrong" is a secular person's verdict; "sick" is the verdict of a person with pretensions to psychological expertise. Each verdict is the result of someone reaching for the nearest available term to label, and to damn, something that confuses him or makes him uncomfortable.

What can someone mean when he says that "homosexuality is   19
wrong"? That to be born homosexual makes one automatically a male-
factor? Or could it be that the crime lies in accepting one's sexuality
and in trying to lead a loving and committed life with another human
being? Or does the crime not begin until your hands touch? Your lips?
Your genitalia? Moreover, if homosexuality is wrong, who is wronged
by it—the homosexual person? Society in general? Young people who
are in danger of being "recruited"? Do these questions sound frivolous?
They're not. What's frivolous is to state unequivocally that homosexuality is "wrong" without asking oneself such questions and figuring
out exactly what one means.

And what of the argument that homosexuality is not wrong but   20
"sick"—a psychological disorder? This popular view is expressed by
one D. L. Forston, M.D., of Gary, Indiana, who in a letter to *The
New Republic* argues that "the depression, mental illness and substance
abuse associated with the lifestyle cannot be fully accounted for by
reaction to societal isolation and hostility. In short, homosexuality is
a personality disorder at best and a mental illness at worst." "Cannot
be fully accounted for"? How can Dr. Forston possibly know this? He
obviously has no idea what most homosexuals have to go through
day by day in the way of inadvertent reminders that they are considered
evil, depraved, emotionally disturbed, or just plain anomalous. Dr.
Forston's views notwithstanding, it has for many years seemed remarkable to me that, given these daily assaults, there aren't *more* gay alcoholics and depressives and so on.

Of course, if one considers homosexuality a personality disorder   21
or mental illness, then every homosexual is by definition an emotional
cripple, however sane and stable he may be in comparison to the
average heterosexual. But to make such a blanket diagnosis is prepos-
terous. Medical science has always classified psychological phenomena
as disorders, rather than as mere variations, on the basis of their
consequences in the real world. In other words, a given psychological
phenomenon cannot be objectively classified as a disorder unless it
gives rise, of itself, to some sort of maladjustment. A generation and
more ago, in a time when one could not even go to a gay bar without
fear of arrest, homosexuals suffered severe neuroses—or even psycho-
ses—at a rate higher than they do now and manifested higher rates of
alcoholism, drug addiction, and suicide. They suffered these problems
not because they were gay but because they had been raised to think
that homosexuality was an abomination, because they had to live with
the knowledge that virtually everyone around them considered them
morally corrupt, and because the fear of ostracism, denunciation, and

imprisonment forced them to keep their sexual orientation a secret. Only the most uncommon individuals could live with perfect sanity and serenity under such circumstances; most could not. So it was that psychiatrists designated homosexuality as a psychological disorder.

The almost universal opprobrium with which homosexuals once   22 lived has not entirely dissipated. Yet homosexuals are now permitted to live more openly and with less fear of persecution, and are accordingly more productive and more emotionally balanced than ever before. It is clear that self-respecting homosexuals who live openly among accepting people have no more problems or different problems than anyone else; in an accepting society, they can lead lives that are, in every respect but sexual orientation, indistinguishable from the lives of heterosexuals. This is not true of schizophrenics, psychotics, and other people classified as suffering from psychological disorders. Such people suffer real problems of adjustment that are caused entirely by their psychological disorders and that could not be avoided by any modifications in social attitudes or behavior. Given this simple practical fact, to label homosexuality a "sickness" or a "psychological disorder" is simply name calling—an attempt to pigeonhole and patronize something that the pigeonholer may well find threatening for reasons having to do with his own psychological problems. Certainly if homosexuality were a psychological disorder, it would have to be considered a unique one: for the "sufferers" who experience the greatest emotional health are those who confidently reject the idea that it is a psychological disorder, while the greatest psychological damage is suffered by those homosexuals who have allowed themselves to be persuaded that they're suffering from a sickness.

Some people compare homosexuality to various addictions. Comment-   23 ing on the gay-tolerance lessons in New York City's proposed Rainbow Curriculum, a local school board member told a TV news reporter: "We have a number of children in the school system whose parents are crack addicts. Are we supposed to tell them that that's OK? It might make them feel better but I don't think it's prudent." Similarly, in response to a *New York Times* editorial favoring tolerance of homosexuality, David Blankenhorn, the president of the Institute for American Values, wrote:

> You remind us that tolerance is an important social value. Yes, but you also imply that tolerance is a synonym for approval. As a nonsmoker, I tolerate smoking. But I do not approve of it. Even less do I believe that the public

school system should teach my child that smoking and non-smoking are equally praiseworthy.

Tolerance is not the only important value in life. Other values, such as the value of a child receiving the love of both a mother and a father, are also important. You reduce the issue to a false polarization: accept all possible family forms as morally equivalent or incur the accusation of intolerance.

Is tolerance always our society's highest-order value? Is there any circumstance in which society might have a legitimate stake in promoting certain behaviors while discouraging other behaviors? Your reflections on tolerance come across as simplistic moralizing.

The addiction most often compared to homosexuality is alcoholism. In a letter to *Newsweek*, Peter B. Langmuir of New Haven, Connecticut, wrote that "describing homosexuality as an acceptable alternative life-style is like encouraging the alcoholic to return to the bottle." The same comparison appears in an article by George W. Barger, a canon at Trinity Cathedral in Omaha, who considers himself to be motivated by compassion and generosity toward gays. "Despite our best efforts," writes Canon Barger, whose essay represents a typical ecclesiastical approach to the subject, "we don't know much about the developmental sequence of either [alcoholism or homosexuality]. . . . The socio-biological roots of homosexuality are obscure. Shall we label it a simple moral perversity? Is it best understood as an alternative lifestyle for a rather small percentage of persons?" As with alcoholism, Canon Barger suggests that further study is in order and points to alcohol rehabilitation programs as a model for dealing with homosexuals. "Why wouldn't something similar be a step forward in the homosexuality debate? The non-judgmental framework, the willingness to accept the personhood of the other despite personal moral misgivings, surely commend themselves. On the other hand, it would be equally legitimate to raise questions about ordination of practicing homosexuals, or the blessing of same-sex relationships."

Though his intentions may be virtuous, Canon Barger's essay is essentially a political document; he is interested less in promoting understanding between human beings than in achieving compromise between factions. What moral difference, after all, do the "developmental sequence" and "socio-biological roots" of homosexuality make? Is Canon Barger suggesting that homosexuality is or may be morally offensive in some way, and that a fuller scientific accounting of its origin might either mitigate its immorality or help us to decide whether it is indeed immoral? This proposition itself seems highly dubious in moral terms. Would any neurological discovery make Saddam Hussein less evil?

And what is one to make of Canon Barger's mention of alcohol   26
rehabilitation? To rehabilitate has two possible meanings in this context. It can mean "to restore to a former capacity"; but the word could not apply in this sense to homosexuals, for no true homosexual was ever anything other than homosexual. Or it can mean "to restore to a condition of health or useful and constructive activity"; but experience has shown that the most healthful, useful, and constructive thing for homosexuals to do, as far as their sexual orientation is concerned, is to be honest about it with themselves and others. As for the blessing of same-sex relationships, priests routinely bless all sorts of things other than heterosexual marriages—including houses, cars, pets, Saint Patrick's Day parades, and the work of clubs and committees. Why, then, should it be considered outrageous to bless a loving relationship between two Christians?

These four men—Langmuir, Blankenhorn, Barger, and the New   27
York school board member—all have something in common. When they think of homosexual people, they think immediately of sexual behavior. That's what homosexuality is to them: a kind of behavior that is deviant, disturbing, undesirable. But homosexuality is not something you do; it's something you *are*. To compare it to substance abuse or addiction is to suggest that, just as alcoholics are better off without alcohol and smokers better off without cigarettes, homosexuals are better off without homosexual behavior. To imply such a thing is to denigrate the importance in life of devoted, loving relationships. This implication is especially astonishing coming from a clergyman like Canon Barger or from a man who claims, as David Blankenhorn does, to care intensely about children's psychological development. Can such people not understand how callous it is to equate a committed human relationship to something like crack addiction, chain smoking, or alcoholism?

THINKING ABOUT THE CONTENT

1. Brawer says that the "ultimate enemy of anti-gay prejudice" is the truth (2). What truth? Whose truth?
2. Brawer discusses conceptions many people have of homosexuals that he says are not true: "it's wrong," "perverse," "it's sick," "it's an addiction," and so on. How well does he dispel them?

3. On the whole, Brawer seems to feel that television shows and movies, although they may frequently deal with homosexuality, do more of a disservice than a service to homosexual understanding. What is his reasoning? Have you seen any movies or programs such as those he mentions? Is he correct? Should the media deal differently or more frequently with homosexual issues? Why or why not?

4. Brawer feels that most people "who engage in anti-gay rhetoric, while claiming to speak from profound religious or moral conviction, haven't put much serious thought into their censures" (17). Do you agree? Why or why not?

5. Do you hold any of the antigay prejudices Brawer mentions? Where did you get your views? Does he present any arguments that cause you to think your views may be wrong? Why or why not?

LOOKING AT STRUCTURE AND STYLE

6. Discuss the effectiveness of the opening paragraph in stating topic, thesis, and attitude. Does it draw your interest? Why or why not?

7. Find some examples, such as the first sentence in paragraph 5, where Brawer seems careful not to antagonize his reader with views opposite from his. Is this a good technique in this case? Would Brawer be more effective in his argument if he were more antagonistic? Why or why not?

8. Discuss Brawer's tone. What particular passages develop tone?

9. To whom is Brawer writing? Does he anticipate his audience? How can you tell?

EXPLORING DISCUSSION AND WRITING TOPICS

10. Discuss your views on homosexuality. Should homosexuals have "a place at the table"? Why or why not?

11. Brawer admits that some subculture homosexuals themselves perpetuate offensive images of homosexuality that are then used to condemn homosexuality itself. What are some other subculture groups that perpetuate offensive images of themselves that create prejudices toward themselves?

When most people refer to welfare, they usually mean Aid to Families with Dependent Children (AFDC). AFDC actually started in 1935 as Aid to Dependent Children (ADC). The intent was to help poor widows stay at home and raise their children. Today the program is intended to help families meet their immediate financial needs and to help them become financially independent by requiring recipients to seek out job training and work experience. AFDC is the country's largest cash-assistance program for poor families.

Confusion abounds regarding AFDC. To some, as Rosemary Bray suggests in the next essay, federal welfare relief is a chance for many to get out of the poverty pocket and into the mainstream. Others see welfare as a waste of tax dollars. Congress and political pundits, looking to balance the federal budget, frequently target programs like AFDC as a "free lunch" and an incentive to not work. Indeed, one of the ten points of the Christian Coalition's *Contract with the American Family* calls for the abolishment of all federal welfare programs and suggests the money be given to the states in the form of block grants. That portion of the Coalition's *Contract* follows Bray's essay.

Rosemary Bray is the author of *Martin Luther King*, a children's biography, and her political memoir, *Unafraid of the Dark*. In the following essay, which originally appeared in *The New York Times Magazine*, she speaks as one whose lifestyle was aided by AFDC, but fears the welfare question is becoming a race question in the hands of those who would destroy it.

🌿

So How Did I Get Here?

Growing up on welfare was a story I had planned to tell a long   1
time from now, when I had children of my own. My childhood on Aid to Families with Dependent Children (AFDC) was going to be one of those stories I would tell my kids about the bad old days, an urban legend equivalent to Abe Lincoln studying by firelight. But I know now I cannot wait, because in spite of a wealth of evidence

about the true nature of welfare and poverty in America, the debate has turned ugly, vicious, and racist. The "welfare question" has become the race question and the woman question in disguise, and so far the answers bode well for no one.

In both blunt and coded terms, comfortable Americans more and   2
more often bemoan the waste of their tax money on lazy black women with a love of copulation, a horror of birth control, and a lack of interest in marriage. Were it not for the experiences of half my life, were I not black and female and of a certain age, perhaps I would be like so many people who blindly accept the lies and distortions, half-truths, and wrongheaded notions about welfare. But for better or for worse, I do know better. I know more than I want to know about being poor. I know that the welfare system is designed to be inadequate, to leave its constituents on the edge of survival. I know because I've been there.

And finally, I know that perhaps even more dependent on welfare   3
than its recipients are the large number of Americans who would rather accept this patchwork of economic horrors than fully address the real needs of real people.

My mother came to Chicago in 1947 with a fourth-grade educa-   4
tion, cut short by working in the Mississippi fields. She pressed shirts in a laundry for a while and later waited tables in a restaurant, where she met my father. Mercurial and independent, with a sixth-grade education, my Arkansas-born father worked at whatever came to hand. He owned a lunch wagon for a time and prepared food for hours in our kitchen on the nights before he took the wagon out. Sometimes he hauled junk and sold it in the open-air markets of Maxwell Street on Sunday mornings. Eight years after they met—seven years after they married—I was born. My father made her quit her job; her work, he told her, was taking care of me. By the time I was four, I had a sister, a brother, and another brother on the way. My parents, like most other American couples of the 1950s, had their own American dream—a husband who worked, a wife who stayed home, a family of smiling children. But as was true for so many African-American couples, their American dream was an illusion.

The house on the corner of Berkeley Avenue and 45th Street is   5
long gone. The other houses still stand, but today the neighborhood is an emptier, bleaker place. When we moved there, it was a street of old limestones with beveled-glass windows, all falling into vague disrepair. Home was a four-room apartment on the first floor, in

what must have been the public rooms of a formerly grand house. The rent was $110 a month. All of us kids slept in the big front room. Because I was the oldest, I had a bed of my own, near a big plate-glass window.

My mother and father had been married for several years before   6
she realized he was a gambler who would never stay away from the track. By the time we moved to Berkeley Avenue, Daddy was spending more time gambling, and bringing home less and less money and more and more anger. Mama's simplest requests were met with rage. They fought once for hours when she asked for money to buy a tube of lipstick. It didn't help that I always seemed to need a doctor. I had allergies and bronchitis so severe that I nearly died one Sunday after church when I was about three.

It was around this time that my mother decided to sign up for   7
AFDC. She explained to the caseworker that Daddy wasn't home much, and when he was he didn't have any money. Daddy was furious; Mama was adamant. "There were times when we hardly had a loaf of bread in here," she told me years later. "It was close. I wasn't going to let you all go hungry."

Going on welfare closed a door between my parents that never   8
reopened. She joined the ranks of unskilled women who were forced to turn to the state for the security their men could not provide. In the sterile relationship between herself and the State of Illinois, Mama found an autonomy denied her by my father. It was she who could decide, at last, some part of her own fate and ours. AFDC relegated marginally productive men like my father to the ranks of failed patriarchs who no longer controlled the destiny of their families. Like so many of his peers, he could no longer afford the luxury of a woman who did as she was told because her economic life depended on it. Daddy became one of the shadow men who walked out back doors as caseworkers came in through the front. Why did he acquiesce? For all his anger, for all his frightening brutality, he loved us, so much that he swallowed his pride and periodically ceased to exist so that we might survive.

In 1960, the year my mother went on public aid, the poverty   9
threshold for a family of five in the United States was $3,560, and the monthly payment to a family of five from the State of Illinois was $182.56, a total of $2,190.72 a year. Once the $110 rent was paid, Mama was left with $72.56 a month to take care of all the other expenses. By any standard, we were poor. All our lives were proscribed by the narrow line between not quite and just enough.

What did it take to live?   10

It took the kindness of friends as well as strangers, the charity of   11
churches, low expectations, deprivation, and patience. I can't begin to
count the hours spent in long lines, long waits, long walks in pursuit
of basic things. A visit to a local clinic (one housing doctors, a dentist,
and a pharmacy in an incredibly crowded series of rooms) invariably
took the better part of a day; I never saw the same doctor twice.

It took, as well, a turning of our collective backs on the letter of   12
a law that required reporting even a small and important miracle like
a present of five dollars. All families have their secrets, but I remember
the weight of an extra burden. In a world where caseworkers were
empowered to probe into every nook and cranny of our lives, silence
became defense. Even now, there are things I will not publicly discuss
because I cannot shake the fear that we might be hounded by the state,
eager to prosecute us for the crime of survival.

ALL MY MEMORIES of our years on AFDC are seasoned with unease.   13
It's painful to remember how much every penny counted, how even a
gap of 25 cents could make a difference in any given week. Few people
understand how precarious life is from welfare check to welfare check,
how the word "extra" has no meaning. Late mail, a bureaucratic mix-
up . . . and a carefully planned method of survival lies in tatters.

What made our lives work as well as they did was my mother's   14
genius at making do—worn into her by a childhood of rural poverty—
along with her vivid imagination. She worked at home endlessly,
shopped ruthlessly, bargained, cajoled, charmed. Her food store of
choice was the one that stocked pork and beans, creamed corn, sar-
dines, Vienna sausages, and potted meat all at 10 cents a can. Clothing
was the stuff of rummage sales, trips to Goodwill, and bargain base-
ments, where thin cotton and polyester reigned supreme. Our shoes
came from a discount store that sold two pairs for five dollars.

It was an uphill climb, but there was no time for reflection; we   15
were too busy with our everyday lives. Yet, I remember how much it
pained me to know that Mama, who recruited a neighbor to help her
teach me how to read when I was three, found herself left behind by
her eldest daughter, then by each of us in turn. Her biggest worry was
that we would grow up uneducated, so Mama enrolled us in parochial
school.

When one caseworker angrily questioned how she could afford   16
to send four children to St. Ambrose School, my mother, who emphatically declared, "My kids need an education," told her it was none of
her business. (In fact, the school had a volume discount of sorts; the

price of tuition dropped with each child you sent. I still don't quite know how she managed it.) She organized our lives around church and school, including Mass every morning at 7:45. My brother was an altar boy, I laid out the vestments each afternoon for the next day's Mass. She volunteered as a chaperon for every class trip, sat with us as we did homework she did not understand herself. She and my father reminded us again and again and again that every book, every test, every page of homework was in fact a ticket out and away from the life we lived.

MY LIFE ON WELFARE ended on June 4, 1976—a month after my 21st   17 birthday, two weeks after I graduated from Yale. My father, eaten up with cancer and rage, lived just long enough to know the oldest two of us had graduated from college and were on our own. Before the decade ended, all of us had left the welfare rolls. The eldest of my brothers worked at the post office, assumed support of my mother (who also went to work, as a companion to an elderly woman), and earned his master's degree at night. My sister married and got a job at a bank. My baby brother parked cars and found a wife. Mama's biggest job was done at last; the investment made in our lives by the State of Illinois had come to fruition. Five people on welfare for 18 years had become five working, taxpaying adults. Three of us went to college, two of us finished; one of us has an advanced degree; all of us can take care of ourselves.

Ours was a best-case phenomenon, based on the synergy of church   18 and state, the government and the private sector, and the thousand points of light that we called friends and neighbors. But there was something more: What fueled our dreams and fired our belief that our lives could change for the better was the promise of the civil rights movement and the war on poverty—for millions of African-Americans the defining events of the 1960s. Caught up in the heady atmosphere of imminent change, our world was filled not only with issues and ideas but with amazing images of black people engaged in the struggle for long-denied rights and freedoms. We knew other people lived differently than we did, we knew we didn't have much, but we didn't mind, because we knew it wouldn't be long. My mother borrowed a phrase I had read to her once from Dick Gregory's autobiography: "Not poor, just broke." She would repeat it often, as often as she sang hymns in the kitchen. She loved to sing a spiritual Mahalia Jackson had made famous: "Move On Up a Little Higher." Like so many others, Mama was singing about earth as well as heaven.

These are the things I remember every time I read another article   19
outlining America's welfare crisis. The rage I feel about the welfare
debate comes from listening to a host of lies, distortions, and exaggera-
tions—and taking them personally.

I am no fool. I know of few women—on welfare or off—with   20
my mother's grace and courage and stamina. I know not all women
on welfare are cut from the same cloth. Some are lazy, some are ground
down. Some are too young; many are without husbands. A few have
made welfare fraud a lucrative career; a great many more have pushed
the rules on outside income to their very limits.

I also know that none of these things justify our making welfare   21
a test of character and worthiness, rather than an acknowledgment of
need. Near-sainthood should not be a requirement for financial and
medical assistance.

But all manner of sociologists and policy gurus continue to equate   22
issues that simply aren't equivalent—welfare, race, rates of poverty,
crime, marriage, and childbirth—and to reach conclusions that serve
to demonize the poor. More than one social arbiter would have us
believe that we have all been mistaken for the last 30 years—that the
efforts to relieve the most severe effects of poverty have not only failed
but have served instead to increase and expand the ranks of the poor.
In keeping women, children, and men from starvation, we are told,
we have also kept them from self-sufficiency. In our zeal to do good,
we have undermined the work ethic, the family, and, thus, by association, the country itself.

So how did I get here?   23

DESPITE ATTEMPTS to misconstrue and discredit the social programs   24
and policies that changed—even saved—my life, certain facts remain.
Poverty was reduced by 39 percent between 1960 and 1990, according
to the Census Bureau, from 22.2 percent to 13.5 percent of the nation's
population. That is far too many poor people, but the rate is considerably lower than it might have been if we had thrown up our hands
and reminded ourselves that the poor will always be with us. Of black
women considered "highly dependent," that is, on welfare for more
than seven years, 81 percent of their daughters grow up to live productive lives off the welfare rolls, a 1992 Congressional report stated;
the 19 percent who become second-generation welfare recipients can
hardly be said to constitute an epidemic of welfare dependency. The
vast majority of African-Americans are now working or middle class,
an achievement that occurred in the past 30 years, most specifically
between 1960 and 1973, the years of expansion in the very same social

programs that it is so popular now to savage. Those were the same years in which I changed from girl to woman; learned to read and think; graduated from high school and college; came to be a working woman, a taxpayer, a citizen.

In spite of all the successes we know of, in spite of the reality that   25
the typical welfare recipient is a white woman with young children, ideologues have continued to fashion from whole cloth the specter of the mythical black welfare mother, complete with a prodigious reproductive capacity and a galling laziness, accompanied by the uncaring and equally lazy black man in her life who will not work, will not marry her, and will not support his family.

Why has this myth been promoted by some of the best (and the   26
worst) people in government, academia, journalism, and industry? One explanation may be that the constant presence of poverty frustrates even the best-intentioned among us. It may also be because the myth allows for denial about who the poor in America really are and for denial about the depth and intransigence of racism regardless of economic status. And because getting tough on welfare is for some a first-class career move; what better way to win a position in the next administration than to trash those people least able to respond? And, finally, because it serves to assure white Americans that lazy black people aren't getting away with anything.

Many of these prescriptions for saving America from the welfare   27
plague not only reflect an insistent, if sometimes unconscious, racism but rest on the bedrock of patriarchy. They are rooted in the fantasy of a male presence as a path to social and economic salvation and in its corollary—the image of woman as passive chattel, constitutionally so afflicted by her condition that the only recourse is to transfer her care from the hands of the state to the hands of a man with a job. The largely ineffectual plans to create jobs for men in communities ravaged by disinvestment, the state-sponsored dragnets for men who cannot or will not support their children, the exhortations for women on welfare to find themselves a man and get married, all are the institutional expressions of the same worn cultural illusion—that women and children without a man are fundamentally damaged goods. Men are such a boon, the reasoning goes, because they make more money than women do.

Were we truly serious about an end to poverty among women   28
and children, we would take the logical next step. We would figure out how to make sure women who did a dollar's worth of work got a dollar's worth of pay. We would make sure that women could go to work with their minds at ease, knowing their children were well

cared for. What women on welfare need, in large measure, are the things key to the life of every adult woman: economic security and autonomy. Women need the skills and the legitimate opportunity to earn a living for ourselves as well as for people who may rely on us; we need the freedom to make choices to improve our own lives and the lives of those dear to us.

"The real problem is not welfare," says Kathryn Edin, a professor   29
of sociology at Rutgers University and a scholar in residence at the Russell Sage Foundation. "The real problem is the nature of low-wage work and lack of support for these workers—most of whom happen to be women raising their children alone."

Completing a five-year study of single mothers—some low-wage   30
workers, some welfare recipients—Edin is quantifying what common sense and bitter experience have told millions of women who rotate off and on the welfare rolls: Women, particularly unskilled women with children, get the worst jobs available, with the least amount of health care, and are the most frequently laid off. "The work place is not oriented toward people who have family responsibilities," she says. "Most jobs are set up assuming that someone is minding the kids and doesn't need assistance."

But the writers and scholars and politicians who wax most rhap-   31
sodic about the need to replace welfare with work make their harsh judgments from the comfortable and supportive environs of offices and libraries and think tanks. If they need to go to the bathroom midsentence, there is no one timing their absence. If they take longer than a half hour for lunch, there is no one waiting to dock their pay. If their baby-sitter gets sick, there is no risk of someone having taken their place at work by the next morning. Yet these are conditions that the low-wage women routinely face, which inevitably leads to the cyclical nature of their welfare histories. These are the realities that many of the most vocal and widely quoted critics of welfare routinely ignore. In his book, *The End of Equality,* for example, Mickey Kaus discusses social and economic inequity, referring to David Ellwood's study on long-term welfare dependency without ever mentioning that it counts anyone who uses the services for at least one month as having been on welfare for the entire year.

In the heated atmosphere of the welfare debate, the larger society   32
is encouraged to believe that women on welfare have so violated the social contract that they have forfeited all rights common to those of us lucky enough not to be poor. In no area is this attitude more clearly demonstrated than in issues of sexuality and childbearing. Consider the following: A *Philadelphia Inquirer* editorial of December 12, 1990,

urges the use of Norplant contraceptive inserts for welfare recipients—in spite of repeated warnings from women's health groups of its dangerous side effects—in the belief that the drug "could be invaluable in breaking the cycle of inner-city poverty." (The newspaper apologized for the editorial after it met widespread criticism, both within and outside the paper.) A California judge orders a woman on welfare, convicted of abusing two of her four children, to use Norplant; the judge's decision was appealed. The Washington state legislature considers approving cash payments of up to $10,000 for women on welfare who agree to be sterilized. These and other proposals, all centering on women's reproductive capacities, were advanced in spite of evidence that welfare recipients have fewer children than those not on welfare.

The punitive energy behind these and so many other Draconian   33
actions and proposals goes beyond the desire to decrease welfare costs; it cuts to the heart of the nation's racial and sexual hysteria. Generated neither by law nor by fully informed public debate, these actions amount to social control over "those people on welfare"—a control many Americans feel they have bought and paid for every April 15. The question is obvious: If citizens were really aware of who receives welfare in America, however inadequate it is, if they acknowledged that white women and children were welfare's primary beneficiaries, would most of these things be happening?

WELFARE HAS BECOME a code word now. One that enables white Ameri-   34
cans to mask their sometimes malignant, sometimes benign racism behind false concerns about the suffering ghetto poor and their negative impact on the rest of us. It has become the vehicle many so-called tough thinkers use to undermine compassionate policy and engineer the reduction of social programs.

So how *did* I get here?   35

I kept my drawers up and my dress down, to quote my mother.   36
I didn't end up pregnant because I had better things to do. I knew I did because my uneducated, Southern-born parents told me so. Their faith, their focus on our futures are a far cry from the thesis of Nicholas Lemann, whose widely acclaimed book *The Promised Land* perpetuates the myth of black Southern sharecropping society as a primary source of black urban malaise. Most important, my family and I had every reason to believe that I had better things to do and that when I got older I would be able to do them. I had a mission, a calling, work to do that only I could do. And that is knowledge transmitted not just by parents, or school, or churches. It is a palpable thing,

available by osmosis from the culture of the neighborhood and the world at large.

Add to this formula a whopping dose of dumb luck. It was my sixth-grade teacher, Sister Maria Sarto, who identified in me the first signs of a stifling boredom and told my mother that I needed a tougher, more challenging curriculum than her school could provide. It was she who then tracked down the private Francis W. Parker School, which agreed to give me a scholarship if I passed the admissions test. 37

Had I been born a few years earlier, or a decade later, I might now be living on welfare in the Robert Taylor Homes or working as a hospital nurse's aide for $6.67 an hour. People who think such things could never have happened to me haven't met enough poor people to know better. The avenue of escape can be very narrow indeed. The hope and energy of the 1960s—fueled not only by a growing economy but by all the passions of a great national quest—is long gone. The sense of possibility I knew has been replaced with the popular cultural currency that money and those who have it are everything and those without are nothing. 38

Much has been made of the culture of the underclass, the culture of poverty, as though they were the free-floating illnesses of the African-American poor, rendering them immune to other influences: the widespread American culture of greed, for example, or cynicism. It is a thinly veiled continuation of the endless projection of "disease" onto black life, a convenient way to sidestep a more painful debate about the loss of meaning in American life that has made our entire nation depressed and dispirited. The malaise that has overtaken our country is hardly confined to African-Americans or the poor, and if both groups should disappear tomorrow, our nation would still find itself in crisis. To talk of the black "underclass threat" to the public sphere, as Mickey Kaus does, to demonize the poor among us and thus by association all of us—ultimately this does more damage to the body politic than do a dozen welfare queens. 39

When I walk down the streets of my Harlem neighborhood, I see women like my mother hustling, struggling, walking their children to school, and walking them back home. And I also see women who have lost both energy and faith, talking loud, hanging out. I see the shadow of men of a new generation, floating by with a few dollars and a toy, then drifting away to the shelters they call home. And I see, a dozen times a day, the little girls my sister and I used to be, the little boys my brothers once were. 40

Even the grudging, inadequate public help I once had is fading   41
fast for them. The time and patience they will need to re-create
themselves is vanishing under pressure for the big, quick mix and
the crushing load of blame being heaped upon them. In the big
cities and the small towns of America, we have let theory, ideology,
and mythology about welfare and poverty overtake these children
and their parents.

THINKING ABOUT THE CONTENT

1. How does Bray's description of her life on welfare differ from the image
   critics of the welfare program hold toward welfare families?
2. What advantages did AFDC afford Bray's family that otherwise might
   not have been possible? To what besides AFDC aid does Bray credit for
   her family's success?
3. Bray believes that some want to make welfare a racial issue. What does
   Bray believe is behind such attempts to end or curtail welfare? What
   myths does she claim are perpetrated to confuse people's views on welfare?
   Have you heard any of these myths? Are you knowledgeable regarding
   welfare statistics?
4. How, according to Bray, does the workplace itself create a need for welfare? What would need to be changed?
5. What might Bray's life be like now if AFDC had not been available to
   her family?

A McDonald's Right Next to You

(To the tune of "Daisy, Daisy," or "A Bicycle Built for Two.")
Lazy, lazy you in the welfare state
You're half crazy—what's gonna be your fate?
Babies outside of marriage
Don't deserve a carriage
But you'll enjoy
Being employed
At a McDonald's right next to you.

(From Cathy Crimmins and Tom Naeder's *Newt Gingrich's Bedtime Stories
for Orphans*. Dove, 1995, 31. Copyright © 1995. Reprinted by permission.)

LOOKING AT STRUCTURE AND STYLE

6. Describe Bray's attitude and tone. What particular passages contribute to both?
7. Bray uses both personal experience and facts to support her thesis. How well does she balance these two? Are both needed to make her argument more convincing?
8. How well does Bray counter the arguments against her views? What are some examples of those counterarguments?
9. How strong is Bray's conclusion? Is she convincing? Why or why not?

EXPLORING DISCUSSION AND WRITING TOPICS

10. If you have no particular idea for an essay in mind after reading Bray's essay, wait until you have read the following selection and consider some of the ideas presented later.

CHRISTIAN COALITION

In May 1995, the Christian Coalition announced its *Contract with the American Family*, a ten-point plan calling upon the government to be accountable for the cultural crisis that the members of the Coalition feel has afflicted America over the past three decades. One of the points calls for the "enactment of legislation to enhance contributions to private charities as a first step toward transforming the bureaucratic welfare state into a system of private and faith-based compassion." In effect, the Coalition calls for the abolishment of federal welfare programs and the enactment of legislation that would encourage private charities to take on the role.

The following selection from the *Contract* explains the proposal.

᭙

America's Welfare System Is a Tragic Failure *

Enactment of legislation to enhance contributions to private charities as a first step toward transforming the bureaucratic welfare state into a system of private and faith-based compassion.

A 1994 REPORT by the National Center for Policy Analysis details the growing evidence that private sector charities do a better job than government of "getting prompt aid to those who need it most, encouraging self-sufficiency and self-reliance, preserving the family unit and using resources [more] efficiently."   1

At the same time, it is clear that America's welfare system is a tragic failure. Despite record expenditures, poverty is getting worse, not better. Indeed, the current welfare system is actually contributing to poverty in America.   2

Federal, state, and local governments spend about $350 billion per year on seventy-nine means-tested programs aimed at assisting the poor; this is about 20 percent more than we spend on national defense.   3

*Editor's title

107

Yet today's poverty rate of 15.1 percent is higher than the 14.7 percent rate in 1966 when the War on Poverty began.

Even worse, the welfare system has caused the work ethic of the   4
lowest income groups to collapse and family breakup and illegitimacy to soar. In 1960, nearly two-thirds of households in the lowest one-fifth of the income distribution were headed by persons who worked. By 1991, this had declined to around one-third, with only 11 percent of the heads of households working full-time, year-round. And then there are the statistics on illegitimacy. The rate for African-Americans has risen from 28 percent in 1965 to 68 percent in 1991. The rate for whites was 4 percent in 1965, and among white high school dropouts it is now 48 percent. In ten major U.S. cities in 1991, more than half of all births occur out of wedlock.

The collapse of work and family has bred urban decay, crime, drug   5
addiction, and numerous other social afflictions. This social tragedy is the direct result of our current welfare system which rewards people for not working by giving them numerous benefits and penalizes those who return to work by taking away the benefits. The system rewards illegitimacy and family breakup by paying women generous rewards for having children while they are single and penalizes marriage by taking away the benefits from women who marry working men.

Simply stated, the current welfare system is a disaster for the poor,   6
the taxpayers, the economy, and the nation. Even more importantly, our current welfare system stands in direct contradiction to one of history's lessons about helping the poor: Private charity works better than government handouts. Christian Coalition believes that the time has come to remember our history lessons and begin to move back to a system of private charity.

A New Approach to Welfare

One way to accomplish this would be to abolish all major federal   7
welfare programs and give the money to the states in the form of block grants. States could then use those dollars to involve private and religious charitable organizations.

Another possibility is to give taxpayers the ability to "target"   8
their welfare tax dollars to private charitable organizations *or* the government. Both ideas are worth pursuing.

Federal funding for as many current federal welfare programs as   9
possible should be sent to the states with only one proviso: that the funds be used to help the poor. Each state would then be able to use

the funds, along with current state welfare funds, to design its own welfare programs. These grants would replace AFDC, food stamps, and public housing, among other so-called entitlement programs. Medicaid funds could be segregated in a separate grant with the requirement that they be spent on health care for the poor.

This would free each state to experiment with entirely new ap-   10
proaches to welfare. States might offer work instead of welfare. They might grant funds to well-run private charities. They might come up with entirely new approaches that no one has thought of yet.

The federal government should not impede innovation and experi-   11
mentation at the state level. Clearly the federal government does not know what the right approach to welfare is, and the right approach may vary from state to state. Moreover, any attempt to impose federal restrictions on the design of state welfare programs will tend to give Washington-based interest groups greater opportunity to influence policy and short circuit fundamental reforms. With open experimentation, by contrast, some states will be able to discover what works, and others can adopt and adapt the best approaches.

Increasing Credit for Charitable Contributions

The second possibility for reform would be a dollar-for-dollar tax   12
credit for contributions to private charities. Taxpayers could donate a percentage of their personal income tax payments, perhaps the share of total individual income taxes that currently goes to federal means-tested welfare programs. To the extent that a state's taxpayers utilized such credits, the state's welfare block grants would be reduced by an equal amount. Thus the revenue loss from the tax credits would be offset completely by reduced federal welfare grants to the states, leaving no effect on the deficit. Block grants plus tax credits would give taxpayers the ultimate control over welfare. If a state mis-spent its block grant funds, its taxpayers could shift the funds to the private alternatives that work better. Healthy market competition between the state programs and private charities would give state welfare bureaucracies a real incentive to perform well in reducing poverty.

A mountain of evidence and experience indicates that private   13
charities are far more effective than public welfare bureaucracies. Studies show, for example, that "as many as 80 percent of low-income people turn to the private sector first when facing a crisis." Private agencies engaged in job training for teenagers and for the mentally and physically handicapped have shown they can outperform government

agencies. Instead of encouraging counterproductive behavior, the best private charities use their aid to encourage self-improvement, self-sufficiency, and ultimate independence. The assistance of private charities may be contingent on ending drug use and alcoholism, completing necessary education, taking available work, avoiding out-of-wedlock births, maintaining families, and other positive behaviors. Private charities are also much better at getting aid promptly to those who need it most and at getting the most benefit out of every dollar.

With the tax credit, private organizations would be able to compete on a level playing field for welfare tax dollars. To the extent they convinced the taxpayers that they were doing a better job than state bureaucracies, private charities, rather than government, would be permitted to manage America's war on poverty.   14

Private Charities Are Efficient

Although volumes have been written about the failures of government welfare programs, the academic and scholarly community has paid surprisingly little attention to private sector charity. Yet the private sector is playing an extremely important role: In 1992, total charitable contributions reached $124 billion, with contributions by individuals accounting for 82 percent ($101.83 billion) of that total.   15

More than 85 percent of adult Americans make some charitable contribution each year. About half the adult population did volunteer work in 1991, contributing more than twenty billion hours of labor. The dollar value of these contributions of time is at least $176 billion. If the value of volunteer labor is included, private sector contributions to charitable causes are approximately the same as the poverty budgets of federal, state, and local governments combined.   16

Many citizens are not as generous in their contributions to private charitable organizations these days because they already are overtaxed. However, if given the choice between having their tax dollars subsidize government welfare programs or subsidize private charitable programs, many would prefer to designate the money to a private charity of their choice.   17

The reasons for this are several. Entitlement programs for welfare are so structured, for example, that benefits are granted solely on the basis of personal circumstances. Applicants do not have to give the reasons for their circumstances or explain how they plan to change them in the future. They do not even have to show a willingness to change. In the AFDC program, the requirements for eligibility essentially amount to: (1) low income, (2) very few assets, (3) dependent   18 children, and (4) no man in the household. Anyone satisfying these requirements is entitled to benefits. And the word *entitlement* means *right*—benefits cannot be withdrawn simply because recipients refuse to modify their behavior.

The philosophy of the private sector is quite different. The best   19 private charities do not view the giving of assistance as a "duty" or the receipt of assistance as a "right." Instead, they view charitable assistance as a tool recipients can use intelligently, not only to gain relief but also to change behavior. At many private charities the level of assistance varies considerably from individual to individual. Private agencies usually reserve the right to reduce assistance or withdraw it altogether if recipients do not make behavioral changes.

Many private charities require that a caseworker and an aid recipi-   20 ent develop a plan to move the recipient into self-sufficiency. For example:

- At Jessie's House, a transitional home for the homeless in Hampton, Massachusetts, shelter beyond one week is contingent upon evidence of individual improvement.

- At the Dallas Salvation Army, aid varies according to the caseworker's evaluation of the recipient's condition and record of behavioral improvement.

In contrast, entitlement programs grant recipients and potential   21 recipients of aid broad freedoms to exercise their preferences. In many cases, they choose poverty and, in effect, present the rest of us with a welfare bill. The preferences of public welfare recipients thereby determine the behavior of those who pay the bills.

The philosophy of the private sector is quite different. In general,   22 private agencies allow those who pay the bills to set the standards. Recipients of private sector welfare must adjust their behavior to the preferences of the rest of society, not the other way around.

If we accept the view that individuals should take responsibility   23 for supporting themselves and their families and that welfare assistance should be administered in a way that encourages this behavior, it follows that the approach of our best private charities is far superior to that of entitlement programs. Because individuals and individual circumstances differ, it is only through hands-on management that we can give relief without encouraging antisocial behavior.

Hands-on management includes the tailoring of aid to individual   24 needs and individual circumstances. Such support, counseling, and follow-up is virtually unheard of in federal welfare programs. Indeed, when public welfare recipients request counseling, they frequently are referred to private sector agencies.

A basic premise of the American system is that government is the last resort. In other words, the role of government is to do those socially desirable things that the private sector either will not or cannot do.   25

Ironically, in the field of social welfare this premise has been turned on its head. In the early years of the War on Poverty, federal welfare programs were a social safety net to provide services that the private sector, for one reason or another, did not. Now it is obvious that just the opposite is true—increasingly, the private sector reaches people government does not reach and offers essential services that government welfare programs do not provide.   26

Failing Those with the Greatest Need

If a humane welfare system means anything at all, it means getting aid first to people who need it most. One of the most astonishing and least-known facts about the welfare state is how miserably it fails to achieve this goal. Consider that only 41 percent of all poverty families receive food stamps; yet 28 percent of food stamp families have incomes above the poverty level. Only 23 percent of all poverty families live in public housing or receive housing subsidies; yet almost half of the families receiving housing benefits are not poor. Only 40 percent of all poverty families are covered by Medicaid; yet 40 percent of all Medicaid beneficiaries are not poor. Amazingly, 41 percent of all poverty families receive no means-tested benefit of any kind from government; yet more than half of all families who do receive at least one means-tested benefit are not poor.   27

Where do people in need turn for help when they are not getting government assistance? They turn to private charities. Ninety-four percent of all shelters for the homeless in the U.S. are operated by churches, synagogues, secular groups, and other voluntary organizations.   28

Our best private charities see independence and self-sufficiency as a primary goal for their "clients." Often this goal is accomplished by either encouraging or requiring aid recipients to contribute their labor to the agency itself.   29

But a major issue in the welfare–poverty industry is whether the recipient of aid should have to "do anything" in order to continue receiving welfare benefits. Nowhere is the controversy more evident than with respect to workfare.   30

Throughout the 1970s, a continuous political battle at the national   31
level raged over the question of whether welfare should be tied to
work. It appeared the welfare bureaucracy lost the battle when Congress passed the Work Incentive (WIN) program and the Community
Work Experience Program (CWEP). However, because it administers
these two programs, the bureaucracy that lost the battle won the war
by finding few AFDC recipients suitable for workfare and channeling
those who were suitable into training or school rather than jobs. The
1988 *Federal Family Support Act* mandated that all states create work-
for-welfare programs. But as happened with WIN and CWEP, this
program did not reduce the welfare rolls significantly.

Encouraging Compassion and Responsibility

A prevalent philosophy in the private sector is that most people are   32
fully capable of taking responsibility for their lives in the long term,
but that emergencies and crises occur for which help is both necessary
and desirable. As a consequence, private sector agencies make it surprisingly easy for recipients to obtain emergency relief. It really is true
that, in America, almost anybody can get a free lunch.

The near-universal characteristic of private sector charity is that   33
it's easy to get, but hard to keep. Most government programs, by
contrast, have the opposite characteristic: it's hard to get on welfare,
but easy to stay there. In the public sector, there are often long waiting
times between applying for assistance and receiving aid. In Texas, for
example, the waiting period is typically two to three weeks for food
stamps. For AFDC, the waiting period is typically a month after an
applicant completes the complicated and cumbersome application
forms.

Once accepted into the public welfare system, however, people   34
find it relatively easy to stay there for a long time: Of all women who
receive welfare in any given year, about 60 percent receive welfare the
next year. Among women receiving welfare for two consecutive years,
about 70 percent receive it a third year. Among women receiving
welfare for four consecutive years, about 80 percent receive it a fifth
year.

There is considerable evidence that private sector charity makes   35
far more efficient use of resources than do public welfare programs.
Although temporary relief in the form of food or shelter is fairly easy
to obtain from private agencies, long-term assistance or assistance in
the form of cash is far more difficult. For example, before the Dallas
Salvation Army will provide cash to help people defray the cost of

rent, recipients must present a court ordered eviction notice showing failure to pay rent.

Similarly, before that charity will give financial aid to defray the   36
costs of utilities, the recipient must present a notice of termination of service for failure to pay utility bills. Even when there is evidence of need, good private charities often seek to determine whether the potential recipient has access to other, untapped sources of assistance. For example, before the Dallas Salvation Army will provide continuing assistance to an individual, a caseworker informs the family including in-laws and requests assistance from them first. The caseworker also makes sure the individual applies for all other public and private aid for which he or she is eligible.

Private sector agencies appear to be much more adept at avoiding   37
unnecessary spending that does not benefit the truly needy. They know how to keep program costs down by utilizing volunteer labor and donated goods. Public housing placed in the hands of tenants costs less and is of higher quality than that owned and maintained by government. Private sector crime prevention programs, alcohol and drug abuse programs, and neighborhood preservation programs also have proved to be superior to public sector programs.

All of this supports one very important reality. In the words of   38
Acton Institute head Father Robert A. Sirico, "[G]overnment has no monopoly on compassion. Indeed, government is compassion's least able practitioner." Christian Coalition supports finding ways to ensure that the private sector is able to reassert itself as the rightful practitioner of charity to America's most needy.

THINKING ABOUT THE CONTENT

1. The proposal states that "it is clear that America's welfare system is a tragic failure" (2). Is this statement well supported? What proof is offered? How might Rosemary Bray ("So How Did I Get Here?") respond to that statement?
2. According to the proposal, "Federal, state, and local governments spend about $350 billion a year on . . . programs aimed at assisting the poor; this is about 20 percent more than we spend on national defense" (3). Should state and local government expenditures be included in a comparison of "national defense"? Is it wrong to spend more money on assisting the poor than on national defense? Why or why not?
3. What evidence is provided to support the contention that "private charity works better than government handouts"? (6) Is the evidence convincing? Why or why not? Do you think that private charities would be able to

receive enough contributions to carry on the work of helping the needy? Why or why not?

4. The proposal cites several statistics regarding amounts and numbers of people involved in receiving welfare aid. What is the source of these statistics?

5. In paragraph 4, how might the difference in wording used to cite the statistics on illegitimacy of African Americans and whites be considered racist? What seems to be the point?

6. Why do you agree or disagree with the proposal?

LOOKING AT STRUCTURE AND STYLE

7. What is the tone and attitude of the proposal? What passages help develop both?

8. To whom is the proposal addressed? Why do you think so?

9. Is enough support provided to convince the reader of the Coalition's position? Which arguments are the most convincing, and which are not?

EXPLORING DISCUSSION AND WRITING TOPICS

10. Research balanced information on welfare programs and recipients. What reports seem to substantiate Bray's claims (see previous essay) that the welfare question has become a race question? What reports refute such claims?

11. Write an essay that refutes some of the myths about welfare by reporting facts found in reliable publications. You might begin with *America's New War on Poverty: A Reader for Action* (Robert Lavelle, ed., Blackside, 1995)

12. What is your position on welfare? Should federal, state, or local governments be responsible for helping the poor or should it be the responsibility of charities and churches? Who should receive welfare and in what form?

13. Write your own essay entitled "How Did I Get Here? Where Am I Going?" What circumstances and advantages helped you get where you are now? What help, and from whom, will you need to get where you want to go? Can you do it on your own?

MICHAEL LERNER

Michael Lerner is the editor of TIKKUN, a bimonthly Jewish critique of politics, culture, and society. He has written several books, including *Jewish Renewal: A Path to Healing and Transformation* and *Jews and Blacks: Let the Healing Begin,* coauthored with Cornel West. In addition, Lerner keeps a busy speaking schedule and leads workshops on ethics and meaning. Much of his writing and speaking is concerned with mending the breaks in our social fabric through the betterment of community and family relationships.

After reading the Christian Coalition's *Contract with the American Family* (see the excerpt, page 112), Lerner decided the Religious Right "doesn't give two hoots about families, it only uses that issue to impose its reactionary agenda." In the following editorial from TIKKUN, Lerner shows why the Christian Coalition isn't pro-family enough and offers his own "A Meaning-Oriented Contract with American Families" in order to improve the lifestyle of all Americans.

ℵ

A Meaning-Oriented Contract with American Families

In May [1995] Ralph Reed, the executive director of Pat Robertson's Christian Coalition, unveiled its Contract with the American Family, a surprisingly visionless document that failed to articulate any coherent theory of why American families are in trouble. The family crisis is too serious to be used merely as a Trojan horse to push through Congress a potpourri of unrelated conservative political programs, yet that seems to be the immoral game now being played by the Religious Right.

Let's start by acknowledging what liberals and progressives often miss: There really is a problem with family life in America. Many people are fearful that the family—the only societal institution that explicitly has the task of caring for people regardless of how successful they have been in the competitive market—is now in crisis.

In a society in which people have learned to see each other as objects, rather than as embodiments of the spirit of God, people increasingly come to feel that everyone is applying market criteria to

1

2

3

116

personal life, always looking for "the best deal," always ready to abandon any given relationship if a better deal (someone more responsive, attractive, interesting, powerful, empathic, younger) suddenly becomes available. The more unsure people are about their "exchange value" on the market, the more they worry about the possibility that their own relationship will fall apart and they will be in a far more difficult position. Unlike the elegant lifestyle liberals who seem to have endless opportunities for new relationships and hence have seemingly little fear of divorce, many Americans feel that their lives would be much worse off if their marriage were to collapse. The freedom of endless opportunities for new relationships that liberals seem to celebrate actually feels to many of the "less elegant" set as endless opportunities for rejection, loneliness, and pain. No wonder they resonate to hate radio and its demeaning of these liberal lifestylers.

When the Christian Coalition speaks about families in crisis, 4 Americans hear that someone is addressing their needs. They may not ever focus on the details of the Contract with the American Family, but they get the message that the Right cares about what is happening to them in their personal lives while the Left only cares about some constitutional principles protecting the rights of individuals to make choices that seem unavailable or remote from the actual lives of the American majority.

The Right points out that the family crisis in America is based on 5 an excess of selfishness, and the Left's excessive focus on individual rights only plays into and strengthens people's desire to put their own individual needs above the needs of any community or any family to which they belong. This inability to commit to a "we," argue some right-wing theorists, forms the rotten core of liberal culture, contributing to the weakening of relationships in general, and to families in particular.

On this last point, the Right is at least partially correct. American 6 society does suffer from an excessive individualism, a narcissistic focus on one's own needs and desires without regard to the needs and desires of others.

But the Right now makes a destructive and hateful move by sug- 7 gesting that that ethos of selfishness has been caused by special interest groups (African Americans, feminists, gays and lesbians, Jews, immigrants, labor, etc.) using liberal big-government programs to pursue their own selfish needs. And so the Right proposes to dismantle government and put power back into the hands of the states and local governments (often implicitly reminding people of the good old days before the labor movement, the civil-rights movement, and the women's movement were able to use federal power to win rights and protections that they were powerless to win on the local level).

What the Right conveniently fails to notice is the powerful impact   8
of the economic marketplace in fostering a materialistic and cynical worldview, rewarding as wise men those who have been most effective in making a buck, while insisting that sophistication is measured by the amount one can manipulate others for the sake of maximizing one's own wealth and power. It is a worldview that marginalizes love and ridicules spiritual and ethical concerns.

Yet family life is strongest when it is embedded in a community   9
of meaning (e.g., a religious, national, or political community) that reflects some higher ethical and spiritual purpose. Within such communities, relationships are often focused on how the family might contribute its energies to some higher good, and that higher good, while often connected to the economic survival of the community, usually involves some shared ethical or spiritual values.

When communities of meaning break down, or when they become   10
little more than reflections of the materialistic and individualistic ethos of the market, individual relationships increasingly carry the burden of providing essential meaning. For many, the couple's happiness becomes the meaning of life.

Few individual relationships can fulfill that purpose, and this often   11
leaves people feeling deeply dissatisfied with their families or other loving relationships. They imagine that others are getting their meaning needs met in such relationships and that it is only their own individual failures that have kept them from finding similar satisfaction in their own families.

The Religious Right has exploited this pervasive anxiety, correctly   12
telling Americans that it is not their fault that their family life feels jeopardized, that the blame belongs instead to liberals and the allegedly selfish special interests (who are actually the groups who have been most trampled by the selfishness of a racist, sexist, and materialistic competitive market). Many Americans respond with gratitude toward the Right and anger toward these demonized groups.

The Left is unable to respond effectively to all this because the   13
Left doesn't understand that the hunger for love and for meaning and purpose stems from legitimate needs that are being daily frustrated in American society. That's precisely why we need a politics of meaning that can speak to these same needs yet provide a progressive alternative to the Right's analysis.

From the standpoint of a politics of meaning, a society that rewards   14
people for their selfishness should not be surprised that it faces a crisis
in families.

A society that rewards people in the world of work for their ability   15
to manipulate and control others should not be surprised that it has
fostered a narcissistic personality incapable of sustaining long-term
committed, loving relationships. A society that makes work unfulfilling
and alienating, and promotes a meritocratic ideology that encourages
people to blame themselves for having this kind of work, will produce
people who feel too burned out, depressed, or angry to have a lot of
energy for their families.

Any pro-families program that doesn't challenge the many ways   16
that the world of work and the psychic impact of the competitive
market have on undermining families is going to be more rhetoric than
reality. To be seriously pro-families we must challenge the "bottom
line" consciousness fostered by the market, with its privileging of
money and power and its implicit message that "looking out for number one" is the goal of life and that caring about others is a concern
only for the naive person.

The democratic Left has pointed out that families suffer when   17
they don't have enough economic support, child-care, and health-care
benefits. Yet we all know that the crisis in families is as likely to afflict
people in affluent suburbs as people in the poverty-stricken inner cities.
To the extent that they are unwilling to question how liberal culture
might participate in the same excessive individualism and narcissism
and materialism that is fostered by the market, liberals will never be
in a position to seriously address the breakdown of loving relationships
and families.

Moreover, liberals tend to think of "private life" as the sphere in   18
which people ought to seek meaning. Their task is finished, they seem
to believe, once they have guaranteed to each individual the opportunity to pursue his or her own path freed from any external imposition.
But this picture neglects our deep need for others, and our need to be
embedded in a larger framework of meaning and purpose.

The Right seems to be wiser when it notices that our individual   19
lives cannot be complete when we live in a public world that is devoid
of larger purpose and meaning. The technocratic and value-free version
of public space that was created by the liberal state, complete with
impersonal bureaucracies and an injunction to hide one's own real
identity in public lest it offend those who are different, is correctly
protested by the Right. Yet the Christian Coalition's solution would

in effect reimpose Christianity on the public sphere—and that is no solution. Those of us who grew up in a world before Supreme Court decisions protected us from forced recitals of "The Lord's Prayer" and forced participation in Christmas pageants and schools dominated by Christian symbolism have no desire to return to that kind of a world, in which our identities had to be denied in order to be part of public space.

What we need, instead, is something new and complex: a public   20 sphere that is meaning-friendly, but one that does not impose a particular system of meaning. How to build that is precisely one of the tasks we've set for ourselves in the creation of the Foundation for Ethics and Meaning. But we need a way to transform the values of the market, and to create a new bottom line in America, one that rewards institutions and individuals for ethical, spiritual, and ecological sensitivity, one that refuses to grant the title "efficient" or "productive" to institutions that tend to create narcissistic individuals incapable of sustaining loving relationships.

Because the Christian Coalition's Contract with American Families   21 has almost nothing to do with challenging the ethos of selfishness and materialism, it would do little to alleviate the real crisis in family life. Some conservative theorists have interesting things to say about the breakdown of the family, but this document is lifeless, formalistic, narrow in conception, missing the energy that an underlying vision could bring. Here is a classic instance in which the Right merely uses the issue of family rather than seriously addressing it. It recycles some of the traditional conservative agenda and cynically claims that this will strengthen family.

The Right's Contract

If you look at the details of the Christian Coalition's Contract, its   22 failure to live up to the Right's own best ideals becomes clear.

1. **A constitutional amendment to allow people to celebrate their**   23 **religion in public spaces.** It is irrelevant to challenging the ethos of selfishness and materialism and will do little to strengthen families. Moreover, the kind of religion that would likely result from moves such as a moment of silence in schools, the reintroduction of Christmas, and other religious behavior into public space— like the kind of religiosity that flourished there before Supreme Court decisions barred it—would be a curiously lifeless form of

public religion whose consequences would be to further the secularization process within religious forms. The fiery intensity of religious experience and the compassionate connection between human beings that is one of the best aspects of many religious communities would almost certainly be lost in most of these public-square religious observances. Far from making the society more religious, these observances are a disservice to God and undermine authentic spiritual life, replacing it with cheapened public showmanship.

2. **Transfer of funding of the federal Department of Education to families and local school boards.** The Christian Coalition endorses a U.S. Department of Education report that parental involvement in children's education results in higher student performance. But it then blames the lack of involvement on bureaucracies and administrative costs and federal restrictions. The claim is ludicrous on its face. Underlying the Right's concern is that federal standards have encouraged the development of curriculum that includes the experience of women, Blacks, and other minorities, as well as the placing of the U.S. experience in the context of world history. Yet understanding that America has been racist or sexist does little to undermine families. What liberals have failed to do is to help people understand that they need not feel personally critiqued when we acknowledge the reality of societal racism or sexism. A critique of sexism and racism need not imply a critique of the value of the lives of the majority of Americans— most of whom already feel critiqued enough simply by their failure to have "made it" in the economy, to have work that feels meaningful, or to have families in which they feel fully respected, recognized, and secure.

3. **Legislation to enhance parents' choice of schools.** There is much to be said for some form of school choice, if and only if it were class-weighted in ways that gave working people and the poor the same economic power to get high-quality schools that is now available to upper-middle-income people. If, for example, there was a sliding scale based on disposable income after the basic food, shelter, and clothing needs had been met, so that poor people might be given vouchers ten or fifteen times that of upper-middle-income people, we might have a fair system. But none of this would help alleviate the ethos of selfishness. The introduction of a marketplace in educational opportunities, while desirable for

other reasons, would probably further erode the kinds of social solidarity that contribute to family support.

4. **Enactment of a Parental Rights Act and defeat of the U.N. Convention on the Rights of the Child.** This is the Right's attempt to protect the sanctity of individual family life from those who would scrutinize it with "external" standards, like concern about physical or sexual abuse. Our society has only recently begun to consider how widespread that abuse is. Rather than challenge the distortions in daily life that create a society with so many physical or sexual abusers, the Right effectively protects the abusers behind the screen of family privacy. From our standpoint, the Christian Coalition proposal represents the real threat to the needs of families and allies it with the sickest and morally most obnoxious realities of American society.   26

5. **Family-Friendly Tax Relief.** Under this rubric, the Christian Coalition calls for a series of measures that pro-family progressives also support: tax relief for families with children, eliminating the marriage penalty, and allowing homemakers to contribute up to $2,000 annually toward an IRA, thereby providing equitable treatment of spouses who work at home.   27

6. **Freeing states to limit funds for abortions.** While we at TIKKUN support abortion rights, we also understand some of the legitimate concerns raised by the Catholic Church and other anti-abortion activists (though we are also aware of the hypocrisy of many who care about life only until the fetus is born, then manage to lose concern when the child moves into poverty induced by current class-oriented economic and social arrangements). The Right makes an important point when it questions the way liberals have defended abortion by placing the decision entirely in the realm of "individual choice," as though individual choices had no consequences for the rest of the society and as though we were accountable to no one but ourselves and our own desires. While we oppose the Right's attempt to legislate these issues, we do believe that liberals have too quickly reverted to a highly individualistic framework in defending abortion rights. Seeing ourselves as isolated monads possessing rights and entering into relationships with others through voluntary contracts—the exact model suggested by the theorists of capitalism—has contributed to the breakdown of loving relationships. So while we oppose the Right's paradoxical attempt to bring the state into personal life, and believe that choice needs to be protected (particularly from those who would coerce   28

or bomb abortion clinics out of existence or penalize doctors who perform them), we also think that the liberal world should be crusading for voluntary restraints on abortion, creating an ethos which goes beyond the "it's nobody's business but the woman involved" and which sees abortion as a kind of tragedy which may be appropriate in some circumstances but which should be dealt with as a tragedy rather than as "business as usual." While rejecting the Right's attempt to impose state control, we also ought to seek to create an ethos in the society that mourns the too-frequent need for abortion, and see that as a reason to speed societal changes that would make those abortions less necessary. Most women are already deeply conflicted and in much psychic pain when they undergo abortions. The appropriate attitude is not to make them feel guiltier. But it would be appropriate for the rest of us to mourn each time such an abortion is performed, and to see it as a further impetus to work for change of a society that made this choice seem the most plausible one to the woman involved. This attitude of collective penance is very different from the judgmental and recriminatory attitude of the Religious Right but also from the laissez-faire attitude of many liberals.

7. **Enactment of legislation to enhance contributions to private chari-** 29
ties as a first step toward transforming the bureaucratic welfare
state into a system of private and faith-based compassion.   This
is a valuable direction. Every citizen should be allowed to donate
$200 of his or her federal tax obligation to any nonprofit with a
total income of less than $20 million (this prevents these choices
from being totally manipulated by the wealthiest institutions, who
can buy television time to convince people to donate to them while
making smaller community-based institutions invisible). But while
it's a good idea, it will do little to undermine the larger ethos of
selfishness or to support family life.

8. **Restricting pornography. A good idea, though it should not be** 30
accomplished by big government legislation, but rather by market
pressures.   But even if we had no pornography, family life would
still be in deep trouble.

9. **Privatizing the arts, the National Endowment for the Humanities,** 31
the Corporation for Public Broadcasting, and Legal Services Cor-
poration.   This has absolutely nothing to do with families, and
is opportunistically tacked on to the Contract.

10. **Crime Victim Restitution.**   Funds given to states to build prisons 32
should encourage work, study, and drug-testing requirements for

prisoners in state correctional facilities, as well as requiring restitution to victims subsequent to release. Again, this has nothing to do with the problems facing families, though we support some of these notions.

A Meaning-Oriented Contract with American Families

We do not want government to be the vehicle for the pro-families   33
agenda we propose, and when we talk about families we mean to
include single-parent and homosexual families as well. Read our Meaning-Oriented Contract with American Families as a guide to what
we need to accomplish in civil society, developed through grass-roots
activities, not by the imposition of big government.

1. We promise the American people a campaign to reduce the total   34
   selfishness and materialism in society by popularizing a new "bottom line" in America that evaluates productivity of institutions
   by the degree to which they tend to produce human beings capable
   of sustaining loving and caring relationships and capable of ethical,
   spiritual, and ecological awareness and action. We demand of
   every corporation, governmental agency, and other major societal
   institutions that they produce a yearly "ethical impact report" that
   assesses the degree to which their activities, products, and mode
   of operation tend toward the creation of loving and caring relationships (and we insist that employees of these institutions, together
   with the public that receives the relevant goods or services, be
   participants in shaping this report without fear of management
   reprisals). We seek to publicly honor those who have contributed
   to the ethical and spiritual life of the community, and those who
   have dedicated their lives to caring for others.
2. Harnessing the technological advances of the computer-age, we   35
   advocate reducing the number of working hours for each individual to a thirty-hour work week, redistributing work so that everyone is employed, and thus allowing working people to have more
   time and energy for family life. More time and energy for family life
   may not be sufficient, but it is absolutely necessary to strengthen
   families.
3. We support voluntary measures increasing employee participation   36
   in fundamental decisions in shaping the world of work, thus decreasing the stress that results from powerlessness at work. As
   workers have less stress to bring home, some of the stresses in
   family life will be reduced.

4. We support the creation of family-support networks in every com-   37
   munity to provide voluntary frameworks of assistance for families
dealing with the inevitable tensions in family life. We will create
a family-support corps of volunteers in each neighborhood who
are available to provide in-home supplemental care for children
or the elderly. We will create Councils of Elders in each community
and we will struggle to get every societal institution to learn from
the accumulated wisdom of our communities' elders. To show
that the society values caring activities, we will struggle for higher
wages for child-care and health-care personnel, as well as for
teachers, family therapists and educators, and others engaged in
providing the infrastructure for a much wider framework of voluntary family supports.

5. We support the creation of television programs and networks   38
aimed at providing children's entertainment that avoids excessive
violence, rejects the manipulative use of sexuality common on
television, challenges the ethos of selfishness and materialism, and
focuses on developing ethical, ecological, and spiritual sensitivity.

6. While opposing the creation of any single framework of meaning   39
or purpose, either by the government or in civil society, we encourage a diversity of communities of meaning, and encourage people
to understand that their families are strengthened when they are
part of these larger communities. Similarly, while people should
be free to choose whatever form of family life they wish, we
encourage the development of small and medium-sized ethically,
spiritually, and/or ecologically oriented communities in which people are validated simply because they are created in the image of
God, and without regard to their accomplishments in the marketplace. Such communities will be an important adjunct to family
life.

7. We advocate one year of paid "family leave" to ensure that parents   40
are given enough time to be with their children in the first year
of life. We also support flexible work schedules so that parents
can be home when their children return from school.

8. We advocate changes in school curricula so that every educational   41
system teaches empathy, caring, individual responsibility, discipline, and respect for the experience of others. When parents visit
schools to select where they will use the vouchers discussed above,
schools must present them with full disclosure not only about the
level of academic achievement of previous graduates, but also
about the degree to which graduates have shown themselves to
embody these values in subsequent years.

9. We seek a society that provides full employment, housing, health   42
care, and child care, but that does so in ways that empower the
individual family without the imposition of bureaucratic constraints or a particular lifestyle. So when we have government
implementing programs, we want to see more done on the model
of the Canadian single-payer plan, less on the model of the bureaucratic monstrosity that was proposed as the Clinton health-care
plan.

10. We support the creation of public events at which families meet   43
to celebrate and honor as a community the hard work and energy
that so many people put into building families, while simultaneously providing a public space (through workshops, small group
discussions, educational forums, etc.) to explore the many remaining problems in family life. We will build ongoing public
campaigns to improve the quality of family life by improving the
total amount of loving and caring energy in the society, by hon-
oring and rewarding those who are best at expressing love and
caring in an ethical and spiritually centered way, and by challenging all those societal practices that undermine our ability to see
and treat each other as fundamentally deserving of love and caring.
And we will encourage people to spend less time in the pursuit
of power and wealth, more time in responding to the grandeur
of creation with awe, wonder, and radical amazement.

In the coming years, TIKKUN and the Foundation for Ethics and   44
Meaning will be trying to create a progressive pro-families coalition
to take this kind of pro-families agenda into the public arena. As a
first step, we will feature these ideas at our national Summit on Ethics
and Meaning in the spring of 1996, and we encourage you to create
regional and local summits at which these ideas can be discussed. And
we encourage you to challenge right-wing spokespeople who present
themselves as "the pro-family force," and left-wing people who attack
the Christian Coalition's Contract with the American Family while
ignoring the underlying hunger for loving relationships that drives so
many people into the arms of the Right's pro-family agenda.

Michael Lerner is the author of *The Politics of Meaning: Restoring Hope and Possibility in an Age of Cynicism and Despair*. Reprinted from *TIKKUN Magazine, a Bi-monthly Jewish Critique of Politics, Culture, and Society*. Subscriptions are $31.00 per year from *TIKKUN*, 251 West 100th Street, 5th floor, New York, NY 10025.

THINKING ABOUT THE CONTENT

1. What is it that Lerner believes liberals and progressives "often miss" regarding family life? What does Lerner believe is behind this crisis? How and what have liberals contributed to the crisis?
2. What does Lerner find wrong with the Right's *Contract with the American Family?* Why does he say the Right has "exploited" people's anxiety over community and family breakdowns? What reasons does he give? Do you agree or disagree?
3. Lerner takes each of the ten points of the Right's *Contract* and examines them. Why does he feel the *Contract* "recycles some of the traditional conservative agenda and cynically claims that this will strengthen family" (21)?
4. How does Lerner's *Meaning-Oriented Contract* differ from the Right's? Are each of his ten points directly related to helping families? Are they practical suggestions? Do you think they will work? Why or why not?
5. Lerner believes the Right is trying to enforce its agenda on government. Is Lerner, in his last paragraph, doing what he accuses the Right of doing? Why or why not?

LOOKING AT STRUCTURE AND STYLE

6. Lerner's opening paragraph establishes topic, thesis, attitude, and tone. How does he do that? Does he draw in your interest? Why?
7. Lerner not only criticizes the Right, but also the Left. To whom is he writing? What makes you think so? How different might his essay be if he had not included his criticism of liberals?
8. Was it necessary for Lerner to include all ten points of the Right's *Contract with the American Family?* Why or why not?
9. Are Lerner's arguments balanced? Is he convincing? Why or why not?

EXPLORING DISCUSSION AND WRITING TOPICS

10. Write an essay that evaluates Lerner's *Meaning-Oriented Contract.* Would it truly help families? Which points do you think should be brought to fruition? Are any of the points disguised political agendas?
11. Read the entire Christian Coalition's *Contract with the American Family.* Does Lerner evaluate it fairly? Would such a contract help families? Is it basically a political agenda?
12. Write your own contract with the American family. What do you think needs to be done to strengthen families? Indeed, is there really a problem with family life in America?
13. Pick either the Right's or Lerner's contract and discuss how implementation of either would change the average person's lifestyle.

SOME RESEARCH SOURCES ON LIFESTYLE ISSUES

The following sources may be useful if you choose to do more reading
or pursue a research project dealing with issues prompted by the
reading selections in this unit.

Anderson, Elijah. *Streetwise: Race, Class, and Change in an Urban Community.* New York: HarperCollins, 1990

Brawer, Bruce. *A Place at the Table.* New York: Poseidon, 1993.

Derber, Charles. *Money, Murder, and the American Dream.* London: Faber, 1993.

Fremon, Celeste. *Father Greg and the Homeboys: The Extraordinary Journey of Father Greg Boyle and His Work with the Latino Gangs of East L.A.* New York: Hyperion, 1995.

Gabler, Neal. *Winchell: Gossip, Power and the Culture Celebrity.* New York: Knopf, 1995.

Kowinski, William S. *The Malling of America.* New York: Morrow, 1985.

Lafayette, Leslie. *Why Don't You Have Kids: Living in Full Without Parenthood.* New York: Kensington, 1995.

Leach, William. *Land of Desire: Merchants, Power, and the Rise of a New American Culture.* New York: Pantheon, 1993.

Maracle, Lee. *Bobbi Lee: Indian Rebel.* San Francisco: Woman's Press, 1990.

Marcus, Eric. *Making History: The Struggle for Gay and Lesbian Equal Rights.* New York: HarperCollins, 1940–1990.

Marriott, Michel. "Living in 'Lockdown,' " *Newsweek* (January 23, 1995): 56–57.

Orenstein, Peggy. *School Girls.* New York: Doubleday, 1994.

Pipher, Mary. *Reviving Ophelia: Saving the Selves of Adolescent Girls.* New York: Putnam, 1994.

Riley, Patricia, ed. *Growing Up Native American.* New York: Morrow, 1993.

Rodriguez, Luis J. *Always Running: la vida loca, Gang Days in L.A.* Los Angeles: Curbstone Press, 1993.

Stan, Adele M., ed. *Debating Sexual Correctness.* New York: Delta, 1995.

Stolberg, Sheryl, "A World Without Welfare?" *Los Angeles Times Magazine,* (July 9, 1995): 6ff.

Wolf, Anthony E. *Get Out of My Life, But First Could You Drive Me and Cheryl to the Mall?* New York: HarperCollins, 1995.

Pride and Prejudice

A great many people think they are thinking when they are merely rearranging their prejudices.

—WILLIAM JAMES

When dealing with people, remember you are not dealing with creatures of logic, but with creatures of emotion, creatures bristling with prejudice, and motivated by pride and vanity.

—DALE CARNEGIE

He that is possessed with a prejudice is possessed with a devil, and one of the worst kinds of devils, for it shuts out the truth, and often leads to ruinous error.

—TRYON EDWARDS

We are a nation of many nationalities, many races, many religions—bound together by a single unity, the unity of freedom and equality. Whoever seeks to set one nationality against another, seeks to degrade all nationalities.

—FRANKLIN DELANO ROOSEVELT

Prejudice, which sees what it pleases, cannot see what is plain.

—AUBREY T. DE VERE

Prejudice is being down on something you're not up on.

—ANONYMOUS

The American ideal is not that we will all agree with each other; or even like each other every minute of the day. It is rather that we will respect each other's rights; especially the right to be different, and that, at the end of the day, we will understand that we are one people, one country, and one community, and that our well-being is inextricably bound up with the well-being of each and every one of our fellow citizens.

—ARTHUR J. KROPP

PRIDE AND PREJUDICE ARE SOMETIMES two sides of the same coin. Too much pride can lead to prejudice; prejudice can lead to too much pride.

What is pride? Dictionary definitions tell us it is a sense of one's dignity, value, or self-respect; a pleasure or satisfaction in an achievement, a possession, or an association. Nothing wrong with that. But the definitions continue, describing pride as arrogant or disdainful conduct; haughtiness; an excessively high opinion of oneself; conceit. Pride can start out as a harmless character trait, but when it is taken to extremes it can become dangerous and lead to problems. The Greeks called it *hubris,* a tragic character flaw of pride and arrogance that leads good men to their downfall. Too much pride can make us blind to the truth, resulting in racial, cultural, and religious chauvinism and discrimination.

Prejudice is prejudging others. Prejudice refers to negative reactions to other people that are based on a lack of experience, firsthand knowledge, or chauvinism. Prejudiced people tend to ignore evidence that does not fit their biased viewpoint. All of us have some degree of prejudice in the way in which we perceive and interact with others who are unlike us. Ill-conceived prejudice combined with hubris can become hateful and volatile.

Richard Brislin, in his book *Cross-Cultural Encounters: Face-to-Face Interaction,* describes so-called benefits or functions of prejudice. One "benefit" is what he calls the utilitarian or adjustment function. He suggests that showing certain kinds of prejudice provides rewards and avoids punishments. If, for instance, we want to be liked by a certain group of people, we tend to accept that group's prejudices. It's easier to accept their prejudices than for us to risk being disliked or to make the effort to analyze the bases of their prejudices.

Secondly, Brislin believes that prejudice serves as an ego-defensive function, a protection of our self-esteem. For example, we may be unsuccessful in certain courses in school so we create a prejudicial attitude toward those who are successful in order to protect our self-image. It's easier to call an A student a *nerd* than to admit we don't want to put in the effort to make better grades.

A third "benefit" of prejudice is what Brislin calls a value-expressive function. If we believe that our religion or political beliefs are valuable, the most correct, or even special and better than others, we may, as a way of expressing our values, hold prejudicial attitudes toward others who do not believe as we do. During most major wars, all sides have believed that God is on their side, and that their reasons for fighting are the "right" ones.

The last "benefit" of prejudice Brislin calls the knowledge function, which are prejudicial attitudes we hold because of our need to neatly organize our world by placing everything in its properly labeled box. When these "benefits" are taken to extremes, we get what Brislin calls redneck racism, which is characterized by a judgment that members of another group are inferior or deficient in some way and should be discriminated against.

The reasons for prejudice are many and complex. But for whatever reasons, at one time or another, groups of people in nearly every part of the world have developed prejudice against other groups that are different from them in some way. These prejudices have been based on nearly every factor imaginable—race, language, religion, social position, occupation, physical appearance, and so on. The United States is no different.

Discrimination against minority groups is unfortunately part of U.S. history. Native Americans, African Americans, Asian immigrants, Catholics, Jews, gays, and women, among others, have all been subjected to intolerance in one form or another. Since the civil rights movement began in the 1960s, much attention continues to be given to the need for more tolerance and understanding. Minority groups now seek to establish pride in members of their culture as a way to combat prejudice. But it has not been enough. As Elaine Pascoe suggests in *Racial Prejudice,* "Everyone in society is interconnected; whether we like it or not, we all pull together to move society in whatever direction it is taking. When someone is deprived [through prejudice] of the opportunity to contribute his or her potential, we are all losers."

The essays in this unit deal with the issues of pride, prejudice, and discrimination. Use them to risk contact with your own pride and prejudices.

VINCENT RYAN RUGGIERO

Both our pride and our prejudices develop from the way we see ourselves and others. Sometimes our sight is prone to error and needs corrective thinking. The philosopher John Locke believed that some people are more prone to errors than others:

> Those who seldom reason at all, but think and act as those around them do—parents, neighbors, the clergy, or anyone else they admire and respect. Such people want to avoid the difficulty that accompanies thinking for themselves.
>
> Those who are determined to let passion rather than reason govern their lives. Those people are influenced only by reasoning that supports their prejudices.
>
> Those who sincerely follow reason, but lack sound, overall good sense, and so do not look at all sides of an issue. They tend to talk with one type of person, read one type of book, and so are exposed to only one viewpoint. (*The Conduct of the Understanding*, Part 3)

To this list, Vincent Ryan Ruggiero adds one more type of person prone to errors in thinking: "people who never bother to reexamine an opinion once it has been formed."

Ruggiero, professor emeritus of humanities at the State University of New York at Delhi, is well known for his many books on critical thinking. The following selection is from his book, *Beyond Feelings: A Guide to Critical Thinking* (4th ed.), Mayfield Publishing Company, 1995.

◆

The Basic Problem: "Mine Is Better"

It's natural enough to like our own possessions better than other people's possessions.* Our possessions are extensions of ourselves. When first graders turn to their classmates and say, "My dad is bigger

---

* One exception to the rule occurs when we are *envying* others. But that is a special situation that doesn't contradict the point here.

than yours" or "My shoes are newer" or "My crayons color better," they are not just speaking about their fathers or their shoes or crayons. They are saying something about themselves: "Hey, look at me. I'm something special."

Several years later those children will be saying, "My car is faster 2 than yours," "My football team will go all the way this year," "My marks are higher than Olivia's." (That's one of the great blessings of students—though they may have to stoop to compare, they can always find someone with lower grades than theirs.)

Even later, when they've learned that it sounds boastful to *say* 3 their possessions are better, they'll continue to *think* they are: "My house is more expensive, my club more exclusive, my spouse more attractive, my children better behaved, my accomplishments more numerous."

All of this, as we have noted, is natural, although not especially 4 noble or virtuous or, in many cases, even factual. Just natural. The tendency is probably as old as humanity. History records countless examples of it. Most wars, for example, can be traced to some form of "mine is better" thinking. Satirists have pointed their pens at it. Ambrose Bierce, for instance, in his *Devil's Dictionary*, includes the word *infidel*. Technically, the word means "one who is an unbeliever in some religion." But Bierce's definition points up the underlying attitude in those who use the word. He defines *infidel* this way: "In New York, one who does not believe in the Christian religion; in Constantinople, one who does."

For many people, most of the time, the "mine is better" tendency is 5 balanced by the awareness that other people feel the same way about their things, that it's an unavoidable part of being a person to do so. In other words, many people realize that we all see ourselves in a special way, different from everything that is not ourselves, and that whatever we associate with ourselves becomes part of us in our minds. People who have this understanding and are reasonably secure and self-confident can control the tendency. The problem is that some people do not understand that each person has a special viewpoint. For them, "mine is better" is not an attitude that everyone has about his or her things. Rather, it is a special, higher truth about their particular situation. Psychologists classify such people as either egocentric or ethnocentric.

Egocentric People

Egocentric means centered or focused on one's own self and interested 6 only in one's own interests, needs, and views. Egocentric people tend to practice "egospeak." The term was coined by Edmond Addeo and Robert Burger in their book of the same name. Egospeak, they explain, is "the art of boosting our own egos by speaking only about what we want to talk about, and not giving a hoot in hell about what the other person wants to talk about." More important for our discussion is what precedes the outward expression of self-centeredness and energizes it: egocentric people's habit of mind. Following Addeo and Burger, we might characterize that habit as egoTHINK.

Because the perspective of egothink is very limited, egocentric people have difficulty seeing issues from a variety of viewpoints. The world exists for them and is defined by their beliefs and values: What disturbs them should disturb everyone; what is of no consequence to them is unimportant. This attitude makes it difficult for egocentric people to observe, listen, and understand. Why should a person bother paying attention to others, including teachers and textbook authors, if they have nothing valuable to offer? What incentive is there to learn when one already knows everything worth knowing? For that matter, why bother with the laborious task of investigating controversial issues, poring over expert testimony, and evaluating evidence when one's own opinion is the final, infallible arbiter? It is difficult, indeed, for an egocentric to become proficient in critical thinking.

Ethnocentric People

Ethnocentric means centered or focused on one's group. Unlike egocentric people, ethnocentrics are not absorbed in themselves but rather in their race, religion, ethnic group, or culture, which they believe is superior to all others. This belief they consider above the normal processes of examination and questioning. Faced with a challenge to it or even a situation in which they are called on to explain it, they will resist. In their minds there is no point in examining or questioning it. The matter is settled.

Ethnocentric people, of course, are not born but made. Their early training in the home creates the habits of mind that characterize them. As children, they tend to expect and need strong leadership and strict discipline from their parents and teachers. Also, they are rigid and inflexible in their views, unable to face problems for which the outcomes or answers are not clear. They have no patience with complex situations and meet their daily affairs with oversimplifications.

As adults, ethnocentric individuals tend toward inflexible categorizing. They recognize no middle ground to issues. Things are either all one way or all the other. If such people are not completely *for* something, they are completely *against* it. The political party or candidate of their choice, for example, is the savior of the country; the opposition can only lead the country to destruction.

For ethnocentrics, the measure of any person or idea, of course,   11
is the person's or idea's similarity to their race, their religion, their culture, their value system. Whatever blends with their outlook is worthy. Whatever differs from it is suspect, threatening, dangerous. This is a sad and undesirable attitude to take. But ethnocentric people find it quite satisfying. Psychologist Gordon Allport offers this explanation:

> By taking a negative view of great groups of mankind, we
> somehow make life simpler. For example, if I reject all
> foreigners as a category, I don't have to bother with them—
> except to keep them out of my country. If I can ticket,
> then, all Negroes as comprising an inferior and objectionable
> race, I conveniently dispose of a tenth of my fellow citizens.
> If I can put the Catholics into another category and reject
> them, my life is still further simplified. I then pare again and
> slice off the Jews . . . and so it goes.

Ethnocentric people's prejudice has an additional function. It fills   12
their need for an out-group to blame for real and imagined problems in society. Take any problem—crime in the streets, the drug trade, corruption in government, the assassination of a leader, a strike in a major industry, pornography, a rise in food prices—and there is a ready-made villain to blame it on: The "kikes" are responsible—or the "wops," "niggers," "spics," or "polacks." Ethnocentrics achieve instant diagnosis—it's as easy as matching column A to column B. And they get a large target at which they can point their anger and fear and inadequacy and frustration.

Controlling "Mine Is Better" Thinking

It's clear what the extreme "mine is better" attitude of egocentric and   13
ethnocentric people does to their judgment. It twists and warps it, often beyond correction. The effect of the "mine is better" tendencies of the rest of us is less dramatic, but no less real.

Our preference for our own thinking can prevent us from identi-   14
fying flaws in our own ideas, as well as from seeing and building upon other people's insights. Similarly, our pride in our own religion can lead us to dismiss too quickly the beliefs and practices of other religions and ignore mistakes in our religious history. Our preference for our

own political party can make us support inferior candidates and programs. Our allegiance to our own opinions can shut us off from other perspectives, blind us to unfamiliar truths, and enslave us to yesterday's conclusions.

Furthermore, our readiness to accept uncritically those who appeal to our preconceived notions leaves us vulnerable to those who would manipulate us for their own purposes. Historians tell us that is precisely why Hitler succeeded in winning control of Germany and very nearly conquering the world.   15

"Mine is better" thinking is the most basic problem for critical thinkers because, left unchecked, it can distort perception and corrupt judgment. The more mired we are in subjectivity, the less effective will be our critical thinking. Though perfect objectivity may be unattainable, by controlling our "mine is better" tendencies, we can achieve a significant degree of objectivity. One way to gain that control is to keep in mind that, like other people, we too are prone to "mine is better" thinking and that its influence will be strongest when the subject is one we really care about. As G. K. Chesterton observed,   16

> We are all exact and scientific on the subjects we do not
> care about. We all immediately detect exaggeration in an expo-
> sition of Mormonism or a patriotic speech from Paraguay.
> We all require sobriety on the subject of the sea serpent.
> But the moment we begin to believe in a thing ourselves,
> that moment we begin easily to overstate it; and the mo-
> ment our souls become serious, our words become a little
> wild.

The second way to control "mine is better" thinking is to be alert for signals of its presence. Those signals can be found both in our feelings and in our thoughts: 17

> *In feelings:* Very pleasant, favorable sensations, the de-
> sire to embrace a statement or argument immediately,
> without appraising it further. Or very unpleasant, negative
> sensations, the desire to attack and denounce a statement or
> argument without delay.
> *In thoughts:* Ideas such as "I'm glad that experts are
> taking such a position—I've thought it all along" and "No
> use wasting time analyzing this evidence—it must be conclu-
> sive." Or ideas such as "This view is outrageous because
> it challenges what I have always thought—I refuse to con-
> sider it."

Whenever you find yourself reacting this way, you can be reason-   18
ably sure you are being victimized by "mine is better" thinking. The
appropriate response is to resist the reaction and force yourself to
consider the matter fair-mindedly.

THINKING ABOUT THE CONTENT

1. Ruggiero says, "Our possessions are extensions of ourselves" (1). What
   does he mean? How can our possessions lead us toward pride or prejudice?
   What possessions do you see as extensions of yourself?
2. Explain the terms *egocentric* and *ethnocentric*. How can these characteristics lead to prejudice? Explain with some examples.
3. According to Ruggiero, "Ethnocentric people's prejudice has an additional
   function. It fills their need for an out-group to blame for real and imagined
   problems in society" (12). Cite some actual examples of this "need" at
   work today.
4. What cautions does Ruggiero say we need to take with "mine is better"
   thinking? Do you agree with him? Explain.

LOOKING AT STRUCTURE AND STYLE

5. How does Ruggiero use the first three paragraphs to show how the "mine
   is better" thinking develops? How do paragraphs 4 and 5 depend on the
   content of paragraphs 1–3?
6. How many outside sources does Ruggiero use? How do they help him
   support his views and explanations?
7. Describe Ruggiero's style, tone, and attitude.

Calvin and Hobbes   **by Bill Watterson**

EXPLORING DISCUSSION AND WRITING TOPICS

8. Discuss an example of your own "mine is better" thinking. When did you first become aware of it? What caused such pride? Have you changed or do you want to change your attitude?

9. In paragraph 4, Ruggiero says that history records countless examples of the tendency toward "mine is better" thinking. Pick two or three examples from history and discuss the causes and effects.

10. Explain to someone who is either egocentric or ethnocentric why it is necessary to investigate controversial issues from various viewpoints.

11. Trace any one "mine is better" thinking from childhood to adulthood and show how it can lead to prejudice.

GORDON ALLPORT

Gordon Allport, quoted in the preceding essay, "The Basic Problem: 'Mine Is Better' " by Vincent Ryan Ruggiero, was a professor of psychology at Harvard University until his retirement in 1962. During his career, he wrote numerous articles and books on personality and was considered a leading authority in his field. His most famous work, *The Nature of Prejudice,* was first published in 1954, when the country was still racially segregated and Senator Joseph McCarthy held public hearings in which he discredited many innocent people in the armed forces, members of the media, and public figures who held ideas differently from himself by calling them communists. McCarthy was finally censured by the U.S. Senate, but only after many people's reputations had been ruined. *McCarthyism,* the practice of publicizing accusations of political disloyalty or subversion with insufficient regard to evidence, serves as a strong reminder of how the manipulation of pride and prejudice can be used destructively.

Allport's *The Nature of Prejudice* is still as widely read and as timely today as it was the year of its publication. In the following passage from his book, Allport discusses the way language can reveal and express prejudice. "Most people," says Allport, "are unaware of this basic law of language—that every label applied to a given person refers properly only to one aspect of his nature."

᭠

The Nature of Prejudice

Without words we should scarcely be able to form categories at all. A dog perhaps forms rudimentary generalizations, such as small-boys-are-to-be-avoided—but this concept runs its course on the conditioned reflex level, and does not become the object of thought as such. In order to hold a generalization in mind for reflection and recall, for identification and for action, we need to fix it in words. Without words our world would be, as William James said, an "empirical sand-heap."   1

Nouns That Cut Slices

In the empirical world of human beings there are some [four] billion grains of sand corresponding to our category "the human race." We   2 cannot possibly deal with so many separate entities in our thought, nor can we individualize even among the hundreds whom we encounter in our daily round. We must group them, form clusters. We welcome, therefore, the names that help us to perform the clustering.

The most important property of a noun is that it brings many grains of sand into a single pail, disregarding that fact that the same grains might have fitted just as appropriately into another pail. To state the matter technically, a noun *abstracts* from a concrete reality some one feature and assembles different concrete realities only with respect to this one feature. The very act of classifying forces us to overlook all other features, many of which might offer a sounder basis than the rubric we select. Irving Lee gives the following example:

> I knew a man who lost the use of both eyes. He was called a "blind man." He could also be called an expert typist, a conscientious worker, a good student, a careful listener, a man who wanted a job. But he couldn't get a job in the department store order room where employees sat and typed orders which came over the telephone. The personnel man was impatient to get the interview over. "But you're a blind man," he kept saying, and one could almost feel his silent assumption that somehow the incapacity in one aspect made the man incapable in every other. So blinded by the label was the interviewer that he could not be persuaded to look beyond it.

Some labels, such as "blind man," are exceedingly salient and powerful. They tend to prevent alternative classification, or even cross-classification. Ethnic labels are often of this type, particularly if they refer to some highly visible feature, e.g., Negro, Oriental. They resemble the labels that point to some outstanding incapacity—*feeble-minded, cripple, blind man*. Let us call such symbols "labels of primary potency." These symbols act like shrieking sirens, deafening us to all finer discriminations that we might otherwise perceive. Even though the blindness of one man and the darkness of pigmentation of another may be defining attributes for some purposes they are irrelevant and "noisy" for others.

Most people are unaware of this basic law of language—that every label applied to a given person refers properly only to one aspect of his nature. You may correctly say that a certain man is *human, a philanthropist, a Chinese, a physician, an athlete*. A given person may be all of these; but the chances are that *Chinese* stands out in your mind as the symbol of primary potency. Yet neither this nor any other classificatory label can refer to the whole of a man's nature. (Only his proper name can do so.)

Thus each label we use, especially those of primary potency, distracts our attention from concrete reality. The living, breathing, complex individual—the ultimate unit of human nature—is lost to sight. The label magnifies one attribute out of all proportion to its true significance, and masks other important attributes of the individual. . . .

A category, once formed with the aid of a symbol of primary potency, tends to attract more attributes than it should. The category labeled *Chinese* comes to signify not only ethnic membership but also reticence, impassivity, poverty, treachery. To be sure . . . there may be genuine ethnic-linked traits, making for a certain *probability* that the member of an ethnic stock may have these attributes. But our cognitive process is not cautious. The labeled category, as we have seen, includes indiscriminately the defining attribute, probable attributes, and wholly fanciful, nonexistent attributes.

Even proper names—which ought to invite us to look at the individual person—may act like symbols of primary potency, especially if they arouse ethnic associations. Mr. Greenberg is a person, but since his name is Jewish, it activates in the hearer his entire category of Jews-as-a-whole. An ingenious experiment performed by Razran shows this point clearly, and at the same time demonstrates how a proper name, acting like an ethnic symbol, may bring with it an avalanche of stereotypes.

> Thirty photographs of college girls were shown on a screen to 150 students. The subjects rated the girls on a scale from one to five for *beauty, intelligence, character, ambition, general likability*. Two months later the same subjects were asked to rate the same photographs (and fifteen additional ones introduced to complicate the memory factor). This time five of the original photographs were given Jewish surnames (Cohen, Kantor, etc.), five Italian (Valenti, etc.), five Irish (O'Brien, etc.); and the remaining girls were given names chosen from the signers of the Declaration of Independence and from the Social Register (Davis, Adams, Clark, etc.).
>
> When Jewish names were attached to photographs there occurred the following changes in ratings:
>
> decrease in liking
>
> decrease in character

decrease in beauty

increase in intelligence

increase in ambition

For those photographs given Italian names there occurred:

decrease in liking

decrease in character

decrease in beauty

decrease in intelligence

Thus a mere proper name leads to prejudgments of personal attributes. The individual is fitted to the prejudice ethnic category, and not judged in his own right.

While the Irish names also brought about depreciated judgment, the depreciation was not as great as in the case of the Jews and Italians. The falling of likability of the "Jewish girls" was twice as great as for "Italians" and five times as great as for "Irish." We note, however, that the "Jewish" photographs caused higher ratings in *intelligence* and in *ambition*. Not all stereotypes of out-groups are unfavorable.

The anthropologist, Margaret Mead, has suggested that labels of 9
primary potency lose some of their force when they are changed from nouns into adjectives. To speak of a Negro soldier, a Catholic teacher, or a Jewish artist calls attention to the fact that some other group classifications are just as legitimate as the racial or religious. If George Johnson is spoken of not only as a Negro but also as a *soldier*, we have at least two attributes to know him by, and two are more accurate than one. To depict him truly as an individual, of course, we should have to name many more attributes. It is a useful suggestion that we designate ethnic and religious membership where possible with *adjectives* rather than with *nouns*.

Emotionally Toned Labels

Many categories have two kinds of labels—one less emotional and 10
one more emotional. Ask yourself how you feel, and what thoughts you have, when you read the words *school teacher*, and then *school marm*. Certainly the second phrase calls up something more strict, more ridiculous, more disagreeable than the former. Here are four

innocent letters: m-a-r-m. But they make us shudder a bit, laugh a bit, and scorn a bit. They call up an image of a spare, humorless, irritable old maid. They do not tell us that she is an individual human being with sorrows and troubles of her own. They force her instantly into a rejective category.

In the ethnic sphere even plain labels such as Negro, Italian, Jew, 11 Catholic, Irish-American, French-Canadian may have emotional tone for a reason that we shall soon explain. But they all have their higher key equivalents: nigger, wop, kike, papist, harp, canuck. When these labels are employed we can be almost certain that the speaker *intends* not only to characterize the person's membership, but also to disparage and reject him.

Quite apart from the insulting intent that lies behind the use of 12 certain labels, there is also an inherent ("physiognomic") handicap in many terms designating ethnic membership. For example, the proper names characteristic of certain ethic memberships strike us as absurd. (We compare them, of course, with what is familiar and therefore "right.") Chinese names are short and silly; Polish names intrinsically difficult and outlandish. Unfamiliar dialects strike us as ludicrous. Foreign dress (which, of course, is a visual ethnic symbol) seems unnecessarily queer.

But of all these "physiognomic" handicaps the reference to 13 color, clearly implied in certain symbols, is the greatest. The word Negro comes from the Latin *niger* meaning black. In point of fact, no Negro has a black complexion, but by comparison with other blonder stocks, he has come to be known as a "black man." Unfortunately *black* in the English language is a word having a preponderance of sinister connotations: the outlook is black, blackball, blackguard, blackhearted, black death, blacklist, blackmail, Black Hand. In his novel *Moby Dick,* Herman Melville considers at length the remarkably morbid connotations of black and the remarkably virtuous connotations of white.

Nor is the ominous flavor of black confined to the English 14 language. A cross-cultural study reveals that the semantic significance of black is more or less universally the same. Among certain Siberian tribes, members of a privileged clan call themselves "white bones," and refer to all others as "black bones." Even among Uganda Negroes there is some evidence for a white god at the apex of the theocratic hierarchy; certain it is that a white cloth, signifying purity, is used to ward off evil spirit and disease.

There is thus an implied value-judgment in the very concept 15 of *white race* and *black race.* One might also study the numerous unpleasant connotations of *yellow,* and their possible bearing on our conception of the people of the Orient.

Such reasoning should not be carried too far, since there are undoubtedly, in various contexts, pleasant associations with both black and yellow. Black velvet is agreeable; so too are chocolate and coffee. Yellow tulips are well liked; the sun and moon are radiantly yellow. Yet it is true that "color" words are used with chauvinistic overtones more than most people realize. There is certainly condescension indicated in many familiar phrases: dark as a nigger's pocket, darktown strutters, white hope (a term originated when a white contender was sought against the Negro heavyweight champion, Jack Johnson), the white man's burden, the yellow peril, black boy. Scores of everyday phrases are stamped with the flavor of prejudice, whether the user knows it or not.

We spoke of the fact that even the most proper and sedate labels for minority groups sometimes seem to exude a negative flavor. In many contexts and situations the very terms *French-Canadian, Mexican,* or *Jew,* correct and nonmalicious though they are, sound a bit opprobrious. The reason is that they are labels of social deviants. Especially in a culture where uniformity is prized, the name of *any* deviant carries with it *ipso facto* a negative value-judgment. Words like *insane, alcoholic, pervert* are presumably neutral designations of a human condition, but they are more: they are finger-pointings at deviance. Minority groups are deviants, and for this reason, from the very outset, the most innocent labels in many situations imply a shading of disrepute. When we wish to highlight the deviance and denigrate it still further we use words of a higher emotional key: crackpot, soak, pansy, greaser, Okie, nigger, harp, kike.

Members of minority groups are often understandably sensitive to names given them. Not only do they object to deliberately insulting epithets, but sometimes see evil intent where none exists. Often the word Negro is spelled with a small *n,* occasionally as a studied insult, more often from ignorance. (The term is not cognate with white, which is not capitalized, but rather with Caucasian, which is.) Terms like *mulatto* or *octoroon* cause hard feeling because of the condescension with which they have often been used in the past. Sex differentiations are objectionable, since they seem doubly to emphasize ethnic difference: why speak of Jewess and not of Protestantess, or of Negress and not of whitess? Similar overemphasis is implied in the terms like Chinaman or Scotchman; why not American man? Grounds for misunderstanding lie in the fact that

minority group members are sensitive to such shadings, while majority members may employ them unthinkingly.

The Communist Label

Until we label an out-group it does not clearly exist in our minds.   19
Take the curiously vague situation that we often meet when a person
wishes to locate responsibility on the shoulders of some out-group
whose nature he cannot specify. In such a case he usually employs
the pronoun "they" without an antecedent. "Why don't they make
these sidewalks wider?" "I hear they are going to build a factory
in this town and hire a lot of foreigners." "I won't pay this tax
bill; they can just whistle for their money." If asked "who?" the
speaker is likely to grow confused and embarrassed. The common
use of the orphaned pronoun *they* teaches us that people often
want and need to designate out-groups (usually for the purpose of
venting hostility) even when they have no clear conception of the
out-group in question. And so long as the target of wrath remains
vague and ill-defined specific prejudice cannot crystallize around it.
To have enemies we need labels.

Until relatively recently—strange as it may seem—there was no   20
agreed-upon symbol for *communist*. The word, of course, existed but
it had no special emotional connotation, and did not designate a public
enemy. Even when, after World War I, there was a growing feeling of
economic and social menace in this country, there was no agreement
as to the actual source of the menace.

A content analysis of the *Boston Herald* for the year 1920 turned   21
up the following list of labels. Each was used in a context implying
some threat. Hysteria had overspread the country, as it did after World
War II. Someone must be responsible for the postwar malaise, rising
prices, uncertainty. There must be a villain. But in 1920 the villain
was impartially designated by reporters and editorial writers with the
following symbols:

> alien, agitator, anarchist, apostle of bomb and torch,
> Bolshevik, communist, communist laborite, conspirator,
> emissary of false promise, extremist, foreigner, hyphenated-
> American, incendiary, IWW, parlor anarchist, parlor pink,
> parlor socialist, plotter, radical, red, revolutionary, Russian
> agitator, socialist, Soviet, syndicalist, traitor, undesirable.[1]

1. The IWW, or Industrial Workers of the World, was a radical labor organization
   that advocated violence. Syndicalism advocated that labor unions take over the
   government and industry.

From this excited array we note that the *need* for an enemy (some-   22
one to serve as a focus for discontent and jitters) was considerably
more apparent than the precise *identity* of the enemy. At any rate,
there was no clearly agreed-upon label. Perhaps partly for this reason the hysteria abated. Since no clear category of "communism"
existed there was no true focus for the hostility.

But following World War II this collection of vaguely interchange-   23
able labels became fewer in number and more commonly agreed upon.
The out-group menace came to be designated almost always as *communist* or *red*. In 1920 the threat, lacking a clear label, was vague; after
1945 both symbol and thing became more definite. Not that people
knew precisely what they meant when they said "communist," but
with the aid of the term they were at least able to point consistently
to *something* that inspired fear. The term developed the power of
signifying menace and led to various repressive measures against anyone to whom the label was rightly or wrongly attached.

Logically, the label should apply to specifiable defining attributes,   24
such as members of the Communist Party, or people whose allegiance
is with the Russian system, or followers, historically, or Karl Marx.
But the label came in for more extensive use.

What seems to have happened is approximately as follows. Having   25
suffered through a period of war and being acutely aware of devastating
revolutions abroad, it is natural that most people should be upset,
dreading to lose their possessions, annoyed by high taxes, seeing customary moral and religious values threatened, and dreading worse
disasters to come. Seeking an explanation for this unrest, a single
identifiable enemy is wanted. It is not enough to designate "Russia"
or some other distant land. Nor is it satisfactory to fix blame on
"changing social conditions." What is needed is a human agent near
at hand: someone in Washington, someone in our schools, in our
factories, in our neighborhood. If we *feel* an immediate threat, we
reason, there must be a near-lying danger. It is, we conclude, communism, not only in Russia but also in America, at our doorstep, in our
government, in our churches, in our colleges, in our neighborhood.

Are we saying that hostility toward communism is prejudice? Not   26
necessarily. There are certainly phases of the dispute wherein realistic
social conflict is involved. American values (e.g., respect for the person)
and totalitarian values as represented in Soviet practice are intrinsically
at odds. A realistic opposition in some form will occur. Prejudice enters
only when the defining attributes of "communist" grow imprecise,
when anyone who favors any form of social change is called a communist. People who fear social change are the ones most likely to affix
the label to any persons or practices that seem to them threatening.

For them the category is undifferentiated. It includes books, mov-   27
ies, preachers, teachers who utter what for them are uncongenial
thoughts. If evil befalls—perhaps forest fires or a factory explosion—it
is due to communist saboteurs. The category becomes monopolistic,
covering almost anything that is uncongenial. On the floor of the
House of Representatives in 1946, Representative Rankin called James
Roosevelt a communist. Congressman Outland replied with psychological acumen, "Apparently everyone who disagrees with Mr. Rankin is
a communist."

When differentiated thinking is at a low ebb—as it is in times of   28
social crises—there is a magnification of two-valued logic. Things are
perceived as either inside or outside a moral order. What is outside is
likely to be called "communist." Correspondingly—and here is where
damage is done—whatever is called communist (however erroneously)
is immediately cast outside the moral order.

This associative mechanism places enormous power in the hands   29
of a demagogue. For several years Senator McCarthy managed to
discredit many citizens who thought differently from himself by the
simple device of calling them a communist. Few people were able to
see through this trick and many reputations were ruined. But the
famous senator has no monopoly on the device. As reported in the
Boston Herald on November 1, 1946, Representative Joseph Martin,
Republican leader in the House, ended his election campaign against
his Democratic opponent by saying, "The people will vote tomorrow
between chaos, confusion, bankruptcy, state socialism or communism,
and the preservation of our American life, with all its freedom and its
opportunities." Such an array of emotional labels placed his opponent
outside the accepted moral order. Martin was re-elected. . . .

Not everyone, or course, is taken in. Demagogy, when it goes too   30
far, meets with ridicule. Elizabeth Dilling's book, *The Red Network*,
was so exaggerated in its two-valued logic that it was shrugged off by
many people with a smile. One reader remarked, "Apparently if you
step off the sidewalk with your left foot you're a communist." But it
is not easy in times of social strain and hysteria to keep one's balance,
and to resist the tendency of a verbal symbol to manufacture large
and fanciful categories of prejudiced thinking.

Verbal Realism and Symbol Phobia

Most individuals rebel at being labeled, especially if the label is uncom-   31
plimentary. Very few are willing to be called *fascistic, socialistic,* or
anti-Semitic. Unsavory labels may apply to others, but not to us.

An illustration of the craving that people have to attach favorable   32
symbols to themselves is seen in the community where white people
banded together to force out a Negro family that had moved in. They
called themselves "Neighborly Endeavor" and chose as their motto
the Golden Rule.[2] One of the first acts of this symbol-sanctified band
was to sue the man who sold property to Negroes. They then flooded
the house which another Negro couple planned to occupy. Such were
the acts performed under the banner of the Golden Rule.

Studies made by Stagner and Hartmann show that a person's   33
political attitudes may in fact entitle him to be called a fascist or a
socialist, and yet he will emphatically repudiate the unsavory label,
and fail to endorse any movement or candidate that overtly accepts
them. In short, there is a *symbol phobia* that corresponds to *verbal
realism*. We are more inclined to the former when we ourselves are
concerned, though we are much less critical when epithets of "fascist,"
"communist," "blind man," "school marm" are applied to others.

When symbols provoke strong emotions they are sometimes re-   34
garded no longer as symbols, but as actual things. The expressions
"son of a bitch" and "liar" are in our culture frequently regarded as
"fighting words." Softer and more subtle expressions of contempt may
be accepted. But in these particular cases, the epithet itself must be
"taken back." We certainly do not change our opponent's attitude by
making him take back a word, but it seems somehow important that
the word itself be eradicated.

Such verbal realism may reach extreme length.   35

> The City Council of Cambridge, Massachusetts, unani-
> mously passed a resolution (December, 1939) making it illegal
> "to possess, harbor, sequester, introduce or transport, within
> the city limits, any book, map, magazine, newspaper, pam-
> phlet, handbill or circular containing the words Lenin or
> Leningrad."

Such naiveté in confusing language with reality is hard to comprehend
unless we recall that word-magic plays an appreciable part in human
thinking. The following examples, like the one preceding are taken
from Hayakawa.[3]

> The Malagasy soldier must eschew kidneys, because in the
> Malagasy language the word for kidney is the same as

2. "Do unto others are you would have others do unto you."

3. S. I. Hayakawa, author of *Language in Thought and Action.*

that for "shot"; so shot he would certainly be if he ate a
kidney.

In May, 1937, a state senator of New York bitterly opposed
a bill for the control of syphilis because "the innocence
of children might be corrupted by a widespread use of the
term. . . . This particular word creates a shudder in every
decent woman and decent man."

This tendency to reify words underscores the close cohesion that   36
exists between category and symbol. Just the mention of "communist"
"Negro," "Jew," "England," "Democrats," will send some people into
a panic of fear or a frenzy of anger. Who can say whether it is the
word or the thing that annoys them? The label is an intrinsic part of
any monopolistic category. Hence to liberate a person from ethnic or
political prejudice it is necessary at the same time to liberate him from
word fetishism. This fact is well known to students of general semantics
who tell us that prejudice is due in large part to verbal realism and to
symbol phobia. Therefore any program for the reduction of prejudice
must include a large measure of semantic therapy.

THINKING ABOUT THE CONTENT

1. What does Allport mean by "labels of primary potency" (4)? What are
   some examples other than the ones Allport gives? Why should we be
   aware of the power of these labels? What part of speech are they? What
   happens when adjectives are applied to labels of primary potency?
2. Explain what Allport means by "emotionally toned labels." What are
   some examples? Do you ever use any of these labels? When? Why?
3. Recount how the word *communist* took on a negative connotation. What
   words or labels have similarly taken on "the identity of the enemy" today?
   Are there any people in the news who, like Senator Joseph McCarthy,
   use labels to denigrate their adversaries?
4. In paragraph 33, Allport uses the phrases *symbol phobia* and *verbal
   realism.* Give some of your own examples of each.
5. Have Allport's comments made you more aware of the connection between
   language and prejudice? Why? Do you tend to use labels of primary
   potency or verbal realism? Why?

LOOKING AT STRUCTURE AND STYLE

6. Is Allport's thesis or main point stated or implied? If stated, where?
7. What primary method does Allport use to support his thesis?

8. Describe Allport's attitude toward his subject.

EXPLORING DISCUSSION AND WRITING TOPICS

9. Write an essay that examines some of the language you use or have used that reflects a prejudice toward someone or some group. Where did you learn the language? Why have you developed the prejudice you hold?
10. Write an essay that discusses what Allport calls "nouns that cut slices." How do these words reflect and sustain prejudice?
11. Discuss a current news event that seems to have prejudice at its roots. How might language have contributed to the problem?
12. How might others categorize you? What labels might they apply to you or your culture? Which of these are acceptable? Which ones not?

SUSAN S. LANG

Susan S. Lang is a freelance writer who has held positions as a library media specialist and newspaper reporter. She has published more than one hundred articles. Her foremost concern is the growth of extremist groups in America. She worries that intolerance will become tolerated and that prejudices will become politically and socially acceptable unless we speak out against racism, hatred, and bigotry.

The following reading selection is taken from Lang's book *Extremists Groups in America,* in which she examines many of the radical religious, paramilitary, and racist groups in the United States. She discusses their hatred of Jews and blacks, how they recruit new members, and how such thoughts may be opposed. In the following portion from her book, she asks and looks for answers to the following questions: "Why do some people hate other people because of the color of their skin or the way they worship God?" "Why do some people taunt and brutalize total strangers who merely belong to a minority group and who have done nothing to hurt them?" "What causes such violent racism?"

❧

With Extreme Prejudice

Racism Throughout History

Hatred and cruelty based on differences—different skin colors, different religions, or different political beliefs—are nothing new. The Bible is full of conflicts arising between different groups: hostility toward Jews is described as early as 586 B.C.;[1] and in Ancient Rome, despised Christians were fed to lions for spectator sport. By the fourth century, Jews were blamed for Christ's death as well as for any other crimes that could be pinned on them.

Even the history of this nation, the freest and longest-living democracy in the world, is riddled with blind hate and violence against minorities. People of various religions and cultures have frequently been exploited, dominated, hunted, enslaved, or butchered. Many of

1. Allport, Gordon W. *The Nature of Prejudice* (Boston: Beacon Press, 1954), p. 247.

our earliest settlers fled from Europe because they were persecuted for their religious or political beliefs. Once they got here, however, they themselves became intolerant of outsiders.

The Puritans, for example, arrived in 1620 to escape religious corruption in England. Once here, their theocracy—government based on religion—refused to tolerate anyone who argued against their views. In 1635, Roger Williams was called a radical because he objected to laws telling him how to observe God. When the Puritans banished him from the Massachusetts Bay Colony, Williams founded Rhode Island, where he established a freer government based on tolerance for all—except for Roman Catholics. Catholics had to flee to Maryland, where they were welcome, but then *they* excluded other faiths.

Early on, Catholics were victims of loathing and disdain in a mostly Protestant America. When thousands of Catholics immigrated to the United States in the 1830s, they were resented because they competed for the same jobs as those already here. Catholic immigrants were attacked on the street, and their homes were stoned. Later, Catholic churches and homes were stormed and burned by rioting mobs, and dozens of people were killed.

In the 1840s, an anti-alien and anti-Catholic secret society was formed. The so-called Know Nothings provoked riots, terror, and national suspicion against Catholic Irish-Americans for almost twenty years.

By the time of the Civil War, many whites had already joined secret terrorist groups to hurt or even lynch Southern whites who were thought to oppose slavery or secession from the Union. When the war shattered the South's economy and ravaged its land, the Southern states were forced to accept Congress-imposed rule by Northern generals. Hard times hit almost every Southerner, no matter how wealthy or powerful the person had been before the war. Although the causes of the embittered South's anguish and frustration were complex, Southerners blamed the now-freed blacks for their misery.

In 1866, just after the war, a secret club named themselves the Ku Klux Klan and vowed to assert what they claimed was the superiority of the Southern white man. Its brand of fanatical racism quickly inspired intimidating night rides and cross-burnings throughout the South. Author Jules Archer, in *The Extremists: Gadflies of American Society,* says:

> Klansmen spread terror among Negroes to keep them from claiming their new rights. Wearing long white robes, masks

and pointed hoods, they flogged, beat and murdered Negroes. . . . Depicting themselves as gallant "knights" defending the purity of white womanhood, they sought to reestablish white supremacy.[2]

Ever since, the Ku Klux Klan has been stalking, intimidating, hanging,
and hurting blacks and other minorities. Many of today's extremists
stem from these "knights" of white terror.

Blacks and Catholics, however, haven't been the only victims of   8
American racism. As the West was "civilized," Native Americans were
scorned and slaughtered; their honor, life-style, land, and food were
plundered. And the Chinese, who had come to the United States with
high hopes for bright economic opportunities, were quickly disillu-
sioned. Instead of opportunities, they faced the hostility and disgust
of American whites and were paid poor wages to build the railroads
that so vastly improved the life-styles of those American whites.

By the early 1900s, it was the Jews' turn to be victimized. Automo-   9
bile baron Henry Ford helped fuel an already festering anti-Semitism
by publishing lies that the Jewish people were part of a conspiracy to
control the world and that they were to blame for World War I. Then
it was the American-Japanese's turn. Historian Richard Curry tells
what happened during World War II, just after Pearl Harbor:

> The government committed the worst single mass violation
> of civil liberties in American history. Yielding to racist
> pressures and war hysteria, the authorities forcibly removed
> all persons of Japanese ancestry from their homes . . .
> and "relocated" them. . . . They were herded together in
> barbed wire stockades and subjected to indignities of the
> worst sort. Ultimately, they were removed to concentration
> camps.[3]

In 1988, more than forty years later, the U.S. government finally approved reparations to the families of the interned American-Japanese
(although as of 1989 they still had not been paid).

Vile and vicious acts against people who are different have been   10
committed for thousands of years and, unfortunately, Americans have
proved no different than anyone else.

2. Archer, Jules. *The Extremists: Gadflies of American Society* (New York: Hawthorne
   Books, 1969), p. 99.

3. Curry, Richard O., John G. Sproat, and Kenyon C. Cramer. *The Shaping of America*
   (New York: Holt, Rinehart & Winston, 1972), p. 648.

What Are Racism, Prejudice, Stereotyping, and Discrimination?

Racism is the belief that one or more races are superior to others. 11
Prejudice is prejudging others. Gordon Allport, a professor emeritus
of psychology at Harvard University and an expert in prejudice, defines
prejudice as . . .

> [a] hostile attitude toward a person who belongs to a group,
> simply because he belongs to that group, and is therefore
> presumed to have the objectionable qualities ascribed to the
> group.[4]

The most common way that prejudice works is by stereotyping people,
that is, putting everyone from the same ethnic group together and
assuming they all have the same negative characteristics or behave in
the same objectionable way.

Stereotypes and prejudice apply not only to race or color but also 12
to any minority. People typically stereotype others because of their
differing religions, political beliefs, or cultures. But discrimination
doesn't end there. Prejudice can also be based on sex, age, education,
or socioeconomic status. And it can get even more petty. It can lie
with a group's accent, food habits, names, dress, even mannerisms.
All these cases have one thing in common: the belief that there's a
superior "in-group" that excludes an inferior "out-group." Prejudiced
individuals, for example, may not give a particular person a job simply
because they make negative associations with that person's sex, nationality, religion, age, accent, and so on.

How does such discrimination lead to blind violence against mi- 13
norities? When some people feel threatened and unhappy, it seems
easiest to blame someone else for their misery and anxiety. Immigrants
and minorities have always been easy targets or scapegoats. Through
the years and even today, many Americans believe that minorities
threaten their jobs, their homes, their racial purity.

Ironically, all Americans, with the exception of Native Americans, 14
are descendants of immigrants. America has always held its doors open
to refugees from all over the world. As President John F. Kennedy said,
"America is a nation of immigrants." Even our Founding Fathers were
immigrants. Nevertheless, established Americans often don't want the
recent immigrants to get a good job, a cozy home. They fear that
there's not enough of all that to go around, and if the Jews or the

4. Allport, *The Nature of Prejudice*, p. 7

Vietnamese refugees or others get that good job at the bank, that's one less job for them and their kind. In *American Racism: Exploration of the Nature of Prejudice,* authors Roger Daniels and Harry Kitano write:

> The built-up feeling of what is considered one's own territory, of what are considered one's rights and prerogatives as white men—can lead to a defensive position that results in extreme solutions. And the reasons for both defensive reactions and extreme solutions are symbolized by remarks such as, "They're taking my job," "They're moving next door to me," . . .[5]

Such people believe that their lives would be better if minorities were put in their place. They resent ethnic groups, such as Jews or Asians, for buying a nicer home, getting a better job, earning a higher salary. They believe that their own life-styles are threatened, that they have a lot to lose if they "let these people come in and take over."

Prejudice against others is caused by fear and ignorance. People understand their own families and neighbors and know how they do things if they are all from the same culture. However, some people recoil from people who are different. Such ethnocentrism—the belief that one's own group is the best, the only "right" or "normal" one—can cause fear. Such fear can generate hate, which, in turn, can trigger violence. [15]

Some individuals take it upon themselves to protect their own people, their own culture, their own religion. Although such nationalism or patriotism can be a good thing and is the driving force behind any army at war, it can become distorted and twisted to wreak hatred and prejudice against innocent victims. [16]

How the Desire for Change Can Cause Extremism

Whether it's family, community, society, or government, some people like things to stay just the way they are. These people are called "moderates," and they are content with the status quo, the way things are. Many people, though, want some change. Those people, who have new ideas for change, are called "liberals," and on the Line of Change that follows, they fall to the left of the center. Traditionalists who want [17]

5. Daniels, Roger, and Harry H. L. Kitano. *American Racism: Exploration of the Nature of Prejudice* (Englewood Cliffs, N.J.: Prentice Hall, 1970), p. 9.

to preserve the best of the past or to change things back to the way they used to be are called "conservatives"; they fall to the right of the center. Often, liberals are called "left wing" and conservatives "right wing."

Far-Left Extremists	Liberals	Moderates	Conservatives	Far-Right Extremists
	Leftists		Rightists	

Some people, though, want change, and they want that change *now.* They are not willing to work gradually, by bargaining, negotiating, or reconciling with others to convince other people of their ideas and to make up a majority that can eventually change the system. Instead, they want a lot of change, they want it now, and they are personally willing to risk a great deal to achieve that change. Because they carry things to the extreme, they are called "extremists."

"The extremist does not recognize or accept the legitimacy of 18 dissent and is unwilling to compromise. . . ."[6] says political scientist William Moore. Rather than accepting a pluralistic society—one that consists of different social groups that have a balance of power— extremists are antipluralist. They violate the rules of how change is achieved in a democratic, pluralistic society.

Extremists who want a totally new system are called "radical 19 leftists," "revolutionaries," or "left-wing extremists." Typically, the radical left wants a dramatically altered government structure, more government control over the economy (as in Socialism and Communism), more social welfare programs, antitrust laws, and strong labor unions. If these extremists are violent, they will typically attack officials, police, industrialists, and the military. Sometimes, left-wing extremists or radicals are revolutionaries, members of minority groups such as blacks or Native Americans who not only want more power and equality but also advocate breaking away from the government to form their own. Such groups are called "separatists"—they want a separate state.

Right-wing extremists, on the other hand, don't want a *new* state; 20 they want things the way they *used* to be, before the Jews or blacks or others, for example, came into political power. They usually attack social groups based on racial, ethnic, or religious differences. They typically want as little government regulation as possible. They also

6. Moore, Willian V. *Extremism in the United States: A Teaching Resource Focusing on Neo-Nazism* (National Education Association, 1983), p. 15.

want as few social welfare programs as possible, and fewer and less powerful labor unions. Right-wing extremists tend to believe in "rugged individualism"; they'd rather arm themselves, take the law into their own hands as much as possible (this is known as *vigilantism*), and take care of their own problems rather than have a strong government do it for them. Often, right-wing extremists are from a majority group, such as some whites who don't want immigrants and minorities coming in and changing the country. They are also sometimes members of (or are protected by) the police or the power structure. "Their vigilante activities may thus become a sort of part-time job, lasting a good deal longer than most terrorist careers of the Left."[7] They'd rather that America stay "pure," the way they think it used to be.

Thus, extremists are antipluralistic—they refuse to accept that all   21 social groups have a right to coexist in American society; they tend to use illegitimate methods, such as violence, to achieve their goals; and they do not represent the views of the majority.

Extremism in American History

Extremism is not in itself wrong. In fact, extremism is the driving   22 force behind innovation and creative change. Even democracy and Christianity were once extremist minority views, considered subversive and ludicrous by the majority. Many significant events in American history were caused by those considered extremists at the time. The revolutionaries of 1776, for example, were a small minority fed up with what they believed was oppressive rule by the British crown. These so-called Founding Fathers—primarily wealthy, highly educated colonial aristocrats with too much to lose if the British continued to control and tax them—felt forced to use left-wing tactics to achieve political separatism. They took up arms to overthrow the status quo. The Tories, on the other hand, were the right-wing reactionaries of the times. These colonists, one-third of the total, wanted the Crown of England to maintain its control as it had for 150 years.

Over fifty years later, the abolitionists became the extremists of   23 the day. For more than two centuries, slaves had been the foundation upon which the economic and social structure of the South had rested. When the voice of abolition permeated the South, it was considered radical and dangerous.

7. Rubenstein, Richard. *Alchemists of Revolution: Terrorism in the Modern World* (New York: Basic Books, 1987), p. 128.

To management and government, the labor union movement in   24
the early 1900s was extremist. At that time, there were no laws protecting the wages, workday, or safety of workers. The radical voice of
workers demanding better wages and improved working conditions
was such a threat to the control, power, and wealth of management
that goons were hired to break strikes, to intimidate union members,
and even to murder leaders. It is only due to the persistence and
perseverance of extremist laborers that today we have minimum wages,
laws limiting long working hours, and safety regulations in the workplace.

In the 1960s, the violence and rioting of Southerners resisting   25
racial desegregation and civil rights for blacks were extreme. Peaceful
black marchers were stormed; a black church was bombed, killing
four children. In reaction, the extreme left black nationalist movement
was born: Black Muslims advocated that white men were evil and
that blacks should break all contact with them. Another part of the
movement, led by Malcolm X, urged blacks to arm themselves in self-
defense against racist attacks.

The Bill of Rights protects the rights of any group to express their   26
ideas:

AMENDMENT I:
FREEDOM OF RELIGION, SPEECH, PRESS,
ASSEMBLY, AND PETITION

Congress shall make no law respecting an establishment of
religion or prohibiting the free exercise thereof; or abridg-
ing the freedom of speech, or of the press; or the right of
the people peaceably to assemble, and to petition the Government for a redress of grievances.

In other words, all Americans have the right to express their ideas, no
matter how extreme or hateful. Extremist ideas are to be tolerated in
a democratic country; but when those ideas cause a split from the
democratic process and turn to violence against others, that extremism
has become dangerous.

How Prejudice Leads to Extremism

Although the United States of America is probably the most demo-   27
cratic, the wealthiest, and the freest nation in the world, many Americans are not content with their lives and the way things are. As our

country has become increasingly technological, complicated, and centralized, the "haves" and "have nots" have become more pronounced. Both the "never-hads" and the "once-hads"[8] feel increasingly ignored and shut out, powerless, and deprived of a piece of the pie that they believe is rightfully theirs. They believe that the political, military, and economic powers that control their lives are way beyond their influence and are, to some extent, the source of their problems. Some citizens view the government as too powerful, yet too ineffectual. They feel alienated from the government and are distrustful of it.

Sociologist David Bouchier, in his book *Radical Citizenship: The New American,* writes: 28

> There is a pervasive sense of powerlessness in everyday life and work, and as a consequence of all th[is], there is an anxious search for safe, personal, and individualistic satisfactions that will insulate one against the chaos of public life and the emptiness of private life.[9]

In addition to powerlessness and alienation, some Americans believe that the criminal justice system is totally inadequate to protect them:

> The triple-bolted doors, electronic security systems, the places and times which must be avoided, the awareness of empty streets and lobbies, dark corners, loitering youths, the legal or illegal carrying of guns, Mace canisters, or electronic zappers might seem to the outsider more like postholocaust conditions of anarchy than the ordinary routines of a civilized community. Compared with the other Western democracies, the level of crime in the United States is fearful.[10]

As a result, more and more Americans are arming themselves. Vigilantism (where people take the law into their own hands) is on the rise. Powerless people can then become dangerous people. Bouchier also writes:

> Powerless people tend to be fascinated by power and to identify with it. The fantasies of power, heroism, revenge,

---

8. Lipset, Seymour Martin, and Earl Raab. *The Politics of Unreason: Right-Wing Extremism in America, 1790–1970* (New York: Harper & Row, 1970).

9. Bouchier, David. *Radical Citizenship: The New American Activism* (New York: Schocken Books, 1987), p. 10.

10. Ibid.

violence, and redemption that have increasingly taken over television and movie screens must be filling some gap in people's lives.[11]

The price we pay to live in a free society is to abide by the rules of that society. If we are frustrated and discontent with those rules, it is our responsibility to work toward changing them. But once people take the law into their own hands, democracy and a free society are threatened.

How Frustration Leads to Hatred

The more frustrated people are with their lives, the more aggressive they become. Even an infant will kick and scream when she doesn't get what she wants. The baby's frustration will be vented through aggression. If the baby feels that her mother is thwarting her from her desire, she will vent that frustration on her parent: the mother is the source of the frustration.

Likewise, when people become frustrated because they don't have what they think is a good enough job or an adequate income to satisfy their needs and desires, they tend to find some person or some group to blame for their frustration. The resultant anger may turn to aggression toward the person or group perceived to be the source of the frustration. Sometimes, their perception of who is frustrating them is accurate—their boss, their mayor, their parent. Sometimes, though, these angry feelings are displaced, and the anger and the blame are put on "other objects, specifically upon available out-groups."[12] In other words, it's dumped on scapegoats. When raging frustration is combined with racism and prejudice, the frustrated person or group will blame an entire race or nation.

Frustration against an individual will cause anger, but since anger, writes psychologist Allport, is a temporary emotional state, it will pass, perhaps after an argument or even after a fistfight. But when frustration is pitted against an entire group, it causes hatred. Such hatred may be understandable: as, for example, when the Nazis during World War II exterminated more than nine million people, including six million Jews (75 percent of the European Jewish population), thus justifiably arousing hatred from around the world. Often, though, frustrated people end up feeling ready to hate. According to Allport:

29

30

31

11. Ibid., p 18

12. Allport, *The Nature of Prejudice*, p. 349.

> The sentiment has little relation to reality, although it may
> be the product of a long series of bitter disappointments
> in life. These frustrations become fused into a kind of "free-
> floating hatred." . . . He must hate something. The real
> roots of the hatred may baffle him, but he thinks up some
> convenient victim and some good reason.[13]

Prejudiced people who become haters are always on the lookout for danger; they sense that something or some group is about to threaten their well-being, writes Allport. This constant fear and this anxiety cause feelings of inadequacy and a loss of control. These emotions erode one's self-esteem. Jealousy that others are getting better jobs and guilt that they are not getting the better job may be part of their psychology. Such people have a strong need to blame and feel superior to others. They come to believe that the hated group or person is wholly to blame. It not only gives them an avenue along which to vent their frustration, but it also helps them to rid themselves of any guilt that may linger because of their prejudiced feelings.

Demagogues

These dynamics of powerlessness, alienation, frustration, and anger are at the root of hate and bigotry and may help to explain why some people blindly hate, assault, and murder strangers. These bigots are often goaded into violence by leaders, or demagogues, who appeal to their vulnerable and fragile states of mind. Throughout history, demagogues have gained power and popularity by appealing to the emotions, passions, and prejudices of others, and they commonly use the same messages of protest and hate. According to the authors of *Prophets of Deceit,* who studied the speeches of many demagogues, the messages are remarkably similar. They are:

You've been cheated.
There is a widespread conspiracy against us.
The conspirators are sexually corrupt, too.
Our present government is corrupt.
Doom is just around the corner.
Capitalism and Communism both threaten us.
We can't trust the foreigners.

13. Ibid., p. 364.

Our enemies are low animals.
There is no middle ground.
There must be no polluting of blood (we must remain racially pure).
But with disaster around the corner, what can you do?
The situation is too urgent to permit the luxury of thought.
Everybody is against me (they're trying to shut me up).[14]

Then demagogues describe how wonderful it would be if . . . and prescribe their own course of action, often a violent one. The listeners are assured that they're not to blame, that they are the true patriots, the true nationalists, and that they are superior to others. People who have a great deal to lose are vulnerable to the rhetoric of demagogues, but so are people who have very little to lose. They might already be unemployed, poor, or imprisoned. Poor teenagers living in an inner city, for example, may believe that they have few bright prospects for the future and that they have nothing to lose by trying to create change. Such people are willing to risk a lot because they have so little to lose.

THINKING ABOUT THE CONTENT

1. In paragraph 2, Lang says, "Even the history of this nation, the freest and longest-living democracy in the world, is riddled with blind hate and violence against minorities." What examples does Lang provide to support her statement?

2. Besides the examples Lang provides of religious and racial groups who have been victimized or ill-treated by those who felt they were superior, are there any mistreated groups of which you are aware that she fails to mention?

3. Lang claims that many Americans hold prejudices because they fear that minorities threaten their jobs, their homes, and/or their racial purity. Are these valid fears? Explain.

4. In paragraph 17, Lang defines *moderates, liberals, traditionalists, conservatives,* and *extremists.* Do you fit any of these definitions? Explain.

5. Explain Lang's views on *extremists* and *extremism.*

6. Do you believe that "all Americans have the right to express their ideas, no matter how extreme or hateful" (26)?

7. How do demagogues use prejudice, fear, and hatred to gain power and get people to act violently? Have you been, or do you think you ever could be, caught up in a wave of hatred or violence? Explain.

14. L. Lowenthal, and N. Guterman. *Prophets of Deceit: A Study of the Techniques of the American Agitator* (New York: Harper, 1949), in Allport, pp 414–15.

Looking at Structure and Style

8. How clearly does Lang's thesis come through? What do you think it is? Is it implied or stated directly?
9. In paragraphs 7, 9, 11, 14, 18, 26, 28, 31, and 32, the author quotes other sources. Are these quotes useful in supporting the points she is making? Do they give more credence to what she claims? Are they necessary, especially if some readers disagree with her views?
10. How would you describe Lang's tone and attitude?
11. Find some examples of paragraphs that use the following writing patterns: example, cause-effect, comparison-contrast, definition.

Exploring Discussion and Writing Topics

12. Pick one of the examples from U.S. history that Lang uses to show prejudicial treatment of a particular religious or minority group and research it further. Then write a summary of what you learn.
13. In paragraph 11, Lang quotes from Gordon Allport's book, *The Nature of Prejudice,* a portion of which precedes this selection. Read all or selected portions of the book and write your evaluation of what you read.
14. Discuss a prejudice you hold toward someone or some group. Why do you feel the way you do? What caused you to feel as you do? Is your prejudice based on a stereotype? What might you do about it? What harm might come from your prejudice?
15. Write an essay arguing against a particular extremist viewpoint, such as white supremacy, mandatory school prayer, or banning gays in the military.
16. Research more recent violent acts of extremist groups or individuals, such as the 1995 bombing of the federal building in Oklahoma. Was pride, prejudice, or both a contributing motivator behind such acts? What do extremists hope will be gained by such acts?

JONATHAN RAUCH

Jonathan Rauch is a writer for the *Economist* magazine and author of *Kindly Inquisitors: The New Attacks on Free Thought,* published by the University of Chicago Press. In both his book and the following essay from *Harper's,* Rauch expresses concern over the trend in universities, workplaces, news media, and government agencies to declare that "there is no place for racism, sexism, homophobia, Christian-bashing, and other forms of prejudice in public debate or even private thought." To rid society of prejudice is not only a "sweet" dream, Rauch feels, but "the very last thing society should do is seek to utterly eradicate racism and other forms of prejudice."

According to Rauch, we should not try to do away with prejudices and dogmas, but channel them, "making them socially productive by pitting prejudice against prejudice and dogma against dogma, exposing all to withering public criticism." What survives, he argues, is our base of knowledge.

※

In Defense of Prejudice

The war on prejudice is now, in all likelihood, the most uncontroversial social movement in America. Opposition to "hate speech," formerly identified with the liberal left, has become a bipartisan piety. In the past year, groups and factions that agree on nothing else have agreed that the public expression of any and all prejudices must be forbidden. On the left, protesters and editorialists have insisted that Francis L. Lawrence resign as president of Rutgers University for describing blacks as "a disadvantaged population that doesn't have that genetic, hereditary background to have a higher average." On the other side of the ideological divide, Ralph Reed, the executive director of the Christian Coalition, responded to criticism of the religious right by calling a press conference to denounce a supposed outbreak of "name-calling, scapegoating, and religious bigotry." Craig Rogers, an evangelical Christian student at California State University, recently filed a $2.5 million sexual-harassment suit against a lesbian professor of psychology, claiming that anti-male bias in one of her lectures violated campus rules and left him feeling "raped and trapped."

In universities and on Capitol Hill, in workplaces and newsrooms,   2
authorities are declaring that there is no place for racism, sexism, homophobia, Christian-bashing, and other forms of prejudice in public debate or even in private thought. "Only when racism and other forms of prejudice are expunged," say the crusaders for sweetness and light, "can minorities be safe and society be fair." So sweet, this dream of a world without prejudice. But the very last thing society should do is seek to utterly eradicate racism and other forms of prejudice.

I suppose I should say, in the customary I-hope-I-don't-sound-too-   3
defensive tone, that I am not a racist and that this is not an article favoring racism or any other particular prejudice. It is an article favoring intellectual pluralism, which permits the expression of various forms of bigotry and always will. Although we like to hope that a time will come when no one will believe that people come in types and that each type belongs with its own kind, I doubt such a day will ever arrive. By all indications, *Homo sapiens* is a tribal species for whom "us versus them" comes naturally and must be continually pushed back. Where there is genuine freedom of expression, there will be racist expression. There will also be people who believe that homosexuals are sick or threaten children or—especially among teen-agers—are rightful targets of manly savagery. Homosexuality will always be incomprehensible to most people, and what is incomprehen-sible is feared. As for anti-Semitism, it appears to be a hardier virus than influenza. If you want pluralism, then you get racism and sexism and homophobia, and communism and fascism and xenophobia and tribalism, and that is just for a start. If you want to believe in intellectual freedom and the progress of knowledge and the advancement of science and all those other good things, then you must swallow hard and accept this: for as thickheaded and wayward an animal as us, the realistic question is how to make the best of prejudice, not how to eradicate it.

Indeed, "eradicating prejudice" is so vague a proposition as to be   4
meaningless. Distinguishing prejudice reliably and nonpolitically from non-prejudice, or even defining it crisply, is quite hopeless. We all feel we know prejudice when we see it. But do we? At the University of Michigan, a student said in a classroom discussion that he considered homosexuality a disease treatable with therapy. He was summoned to a formal disciplinary hearing for violating the school's policy against speech that "victimizes" people based on "sexual orientation." Now, the evidence is abundant that this particular hypothesis is wrong, and

any American homosexual can attest to the harm that the student's hypothesis has inflicted on many real people. But was it a statement of prejudice or of misguided belief? Hate speech or hypothesis? Many Americans who do not regard themselves as bigots or haters believe that homosexuality is a treatable disease. They may be wrong, but are they all bigots? I am unwilling to say so, and if you are willing, beware. The line between a prejudiced belief and a merely controversial one is elusive, and the harder you look the more elusive it becomes. "God hates homosexuals" is a statement of fact, not of bias, to those who believe it; "American criminals are disproportionately black" is a statement of bias, not of fact, to those who disbelieve it.

Who is right? You may decide, and so may others, and there is 5 no need to agree. That is the great innovation of intellectual pluralism (which is to say, of post-Enlightenment science, broadly defined). We cannot know in advance or for sure which belief is prejudice and which is truth, but to advance knowledge we don't need to know. The genius of intellectual pluralism lies not in doing away with prejudices and dogmas but in channeling them—making them socially productive by pitting prejudice against prejudice and dogma against dogma, exposing all to withering public criticism. What survives at the end of the day is our base of knowledge.

What they told us in high school about this process is very largely 6 a lie. The Enlightenment tradition taught us that science is orderly, antiseptic, rational, the province of detached experimenters and high-minded logicians. In the popular view, science stands for reason against prejudice, open-mindedness against dogma, calm consideration against passionate attachment—all personified by pop-science icons like the magisterially deductive Sherlock Holmes, the coolly analytic Mr. Spock, the genially authoritative Mr. Science (from our junior-high science films). Yet one of science's dirty secrets is that although science as a whole is as unbiased as anything human can be, scientists are just as biased as anyone else, sometimes more so. "One of the strengths of science," writes the philosopher of science David L. Hull, "is that it does not require that scientists be unbiased, only that different scientists have different biases." Another dirty secret is that, no less than the rest of us, scientists can be dogmatic and pigheaded. "Although this pigheadedness often damages the careers of individual scientists," says Hull, "it is beneficial for the manifest goal of science," which relies on people to invest years in their ideas and defend them passionately. And the dirtiest secret of all, if you believe in the antiseptic popular view of science, is that this most ostensibly rational of enterprises depends on the most irrational of motives—ambition, narcissism, animus, even revenge. "Scientists acknowledge that among their motivations are natural curiosity, the love of truth, and the desire to help humanity, but other inducements exist as well, and one of them is to 'get that son of a bitch,' " says Hull. "Time and again, scientists whom I interviewed described the powerful spur that 'showing that son of a bitch' supplied to their own research."

Many people, I think, are bewildered by this unvarnished and all too human view of science. They believe that for a system to be unprejudiced, the people in it must also be unprejudiced. In fact, the opposite is true. Far from eradicating ugly or stupid ideas and coarse or unpleasant motives, intellectual pluralism relies upon them to excite intellectual passion and redouble scientific effort. I know of no modern idea more ugly and stupid than that the Holocaust never happened, nor any idea more viciously motivated. Yet the deniers' claims that the Auschwitz gas chambers could not have worked led to closer study and, in 1993, research showing, at last, how they actually did work. Thanks to prejudice and stupidity, another opening for doubt has been shut.

An enlightened and efficient intellectual regime lets a million prejudices bloom, including many that you or I may regard as hateful or grotesque. It avoids any attempt to stamp out prejudice, because stamping out prejudice really means forcing everyone to share the same prejudice, namely that of whoever is in authority. The great American philosopher Charles Sanders Peirce wrote in 1877: "When complete agreement could not otherwise be reached, a general massacre of all who have not thought in a certain way has proved a very effective means of settling opinion in a country." In speaking of "settling opinion," Peirce was writing about one of the two or three most fundamental problems that any human society must confront and solve. For most societies down through the centuries, this problem was dealt with in the manner he described: errors were identified by the authorities—priests, politburos, dictators—or by mass opinion, and then the error-makers were eliminated along with their putative mistakes. "Let all men who reject the established belief be terrified into silence," wrote Peirce, describing this system. "This method has, from the earliest times, been one of the chief means of upholding correct theological and political doctrines."

Intellectual pluralism substitutes a radically different doctrine: we kill our mistakes rather than each other. Here I draw on another great philosopher, the late Karl Popper, who pointed out that the critical method of science "consists in letting our hypotheses die in our stead." Those who are in error are not (or are not supposed to be) banished or excommunicated or forced to sign a renunciation or required to submit to "rehabilitation" or sent for psychological counseling. It is the error we punish, not the errant. By letting people make errors—even mischievous, spiteful errors (as, for instance, Galileo's insistence on Copernicanism was taken to be in 1633)—pluralism creates room to challenge orthodoxy, think imaginatively, experiment boldly. Brilliance and bigotry are empowered in the same stroke.

Pluralism is the principle that protects and makes a place in human   10 company for that loneliest and most vulnerable of all minorities, the minority who is hounded and despised among blacks and whites, gays and straights, who is suspect or criminal among every tribe and in every nation of the world, and yet on whom progress depends: the dissident. I am not saying that dissent is always or even usually enlightened. Most of the time it is foolish and self-serving. No dissident has the right to be taken seriously, and the fact that Aryan Nation racists or Nation of Islam anti-Semites are unorthodox does not entitle them to respect. But what goes around comes around. As a supporter of gay marriage, for example, I reject the majority's view of family, and as a Jew I reject its view of God. I try to be civil, but the fact is that most Americans regard my views on marriage as a reckless assault on the most fundamental of all institutions, and many people are more than a little discomfited by the statement "Jesus Christ was no more divine than anybody else" (which is why so few people ever say it). Trap the racists and anti-Semites, and you lay a trap for me too. Hunt for them with eradication in your mind, and you have brought dissent itself within your sights.

The new crusade against prejudice waves aside such warnings.   11 Like earlier crusades against antisocial ideas, the mission is fueled by good (if cocksure) intentions and a genuine sense of urgency. Some kinds of error are held to be intolerable, like pollutants that even in small traces poison the water for a whole town. Some errors are so pernicious as to damage real people's lives, so wrongheaded that no person of right mind or goodwill could support them. Like their forebears of other stripe—the Church in its campaigns against heretics, the McCarthyites in their campaigns against Communists—the modern anti-racist and anti-sexist and anti-homophobic campaigners are totalists, demanding not that misguided ideas and ugly expressions be corrected or criticized but that they be eradicated. They make war not on errors but on error, and like other totalists they act in the name of public safety—the safety, especially, of minorities.

The sweeping implications of this challenge to pluralism are not, I   12
think, well enough understood by the public at large. Indeed, the new
brand of totalism has yet even to be properly named "Multiculturalism," for instance, is much too broad. "Political correctness" comes
closer but is too trendy and snide. For lack of anything else, I will call
the new anti-pluralism "purism," since its major tenet is that society
cannot be just until the last traces of invidious prejudice have been
scrubbed away. Whatever you call it, the purists' way of seeing things
has spread through American intellectual life with remarkable speed,
so much so that many people will blink at you uncomprehendingly or
even call you a racist (or sexist or homophobe, etc.) if you suggest
that expressions of racism should be tolerated or that prejudice has
its part to play.

The new purism sets out, to begin with, on a campaign against   13
words, for words are the currency of prejudice, and if prejudice is
hurtful then so must be prejudiced words. "We are not safe when these
violent words are among us," wrote Mari Matsuda, then a UCLA law
professor. Here one imagines gangs of racist words swinging chains
and smashing heads in back alleys. To suppress bigoted language seems,
at first blush, reasonable, but it quickly leads to a curious result.
A peculiar kind of verbal shamanism takes root, as though certain
expressions, like curses or magical incantations, carry in themselves
the power to hurt or heal—as though words were bigoted rather than
people. "Context is everything," people have always said. The use of
the word "nigger" in *Huckleberry Finn* does not make the book an
"act" of hate speech—or does it? In the new view, this is no longer
so clear. The very utterance of the word "nigger" (at least by a non-
black) is a racist act. When a *Sacramento Bee* cartoonist put the word
"nigger" mockingly in the mouth of a white supremacist, there were
howls of protest and 1,400 canceled subscriptions and an editorial
apology, even though the word was plainly being invoked against
racists, not against blacks.

Faced with escalating demands of verbal absolutism, newspapers   14
issue lists of forbidden words. The expressions "gyp" (derived from
"Gypsy") and "Dutch treat" were among the dozens of terms stricken
as "offensive" in a much-ridiculed (and later withdrawn) *Los Angeles
Times* speech code. The University of Missouri journalism school issued
a *Dictionary of Cautionary Words and Phrases,* which included
"*Buxom:* Offensive reference to a woman's chest. Do not use. See
'Woman.' *Codger:* Offensive reference to a senior citizen."

As was bound to happen, purists soon discovered that chasing   15
around after words like "gyp" or "buxom" hardly goes to the roots
of the problem. As long as they remain bigoted, bigots will simply

find other words. If they can't call you a kike then they will say Jewboy, Judas, or Hebe, and when all those are banned they will press words like "oven" and "lampshade" into their service. The vocabulary of hate is potentially as rich as your dictionary, and all you do by banning language used by cretins is to let them decide what the rest of us may say. The problem, some purists have concluded, must therefore go much deeper than laws: it must go to the deeper level of ideas. Racism, sexism, homophobia, and the rest must be built into the very structure of American society and American patterns of thought, so pervasive yet so insidious that, like water to a fish, they are both omnipresent and unseen. The mere existence of prejudice constructs a society whose very nature is prejudiced.

This line of thinking was pioneered by feminists, who argued that 16 pornography, more than just being expressive, is an act by which men construct an oppressive society. Racial activists quickly picked up the argument. Racist expressions are themselves acts of oppression, they said. "All racist speech constructs the social reality that constrains the liberty of nonwhites because of their race," wrote Charles R. Lawrence III, then a law professor at Stanford. From the purist point of view, a society with even one racist is a racist society, because the idea itself threatens and demeans its targets. They cannot feel wholly safe or wholly welcome as long as racism is present. Pluralism says: There will always be some racists. Marginalize them, ignore them, exploit them, ridicule them, take pains to make their policies illegal, but otherwise leave them alone. Purists say: That's not enough. Society cannot be just until these pervasive and oppressive ideas are searched out and eradicated.

And so what is now under way is a growing drive to eliminate 17 prejudice from every corner of society. I doubt that many people have noticed how far-reaching this anti-pluralist movement is becoming.

In universities: Dozens of universities have adopted codes proscrib- 18 ing speech or other expression that (this is from Stanford's policy, which is more or less representative) "is intended to insult or stigmatize an individual or a small number of individuals on the basis of their sex, race, color, handicap, religion, sexual orientation or national and ethnic origin." Some codes punish only persistent harassment of a targeted individual, but many, following the purist doctrine that even one racist is too many, go much further. At Penn, an administrator declared: "We at the University of Pennsylvania have guaranteed students and the community that they can live in a community free of sexism, racism, and homophobia." Here is the purism that gives "political correctness" its distinctive combination of puffy high-mindedness and authoritarian zeal.

In school curricula: "More fundamental than eliminating racial   19
segregation has to be the removal of racist thinking, assumptions,
symbols, and materials in the curriculum," writes theorist Molefi Kete
Asante. In practice, the effort to "remove racist thinking" goes well
beyond striking egregious references from textbooks. In many cases it
becomes a kind of mental engineering in which students are encouraged
to see prejudice everywhere; it includes teaching identity politics as an
antidote to internalized racism; it rejects mainstream science as "white
male" thinking; and it tampers with history, installing such dubious
notions as that the ancient Greeks stole their culture from Africa or
that an ancient carving of a bird is an example of "African experimental
aeronautics."

In criminal law: Consider two crimes. In each, I am beaten brutally;   20
in each, my jaw is smashed and my skull is split in just the same way.
However, in the first crime my assailant calls me an "asshole"; in the
second he calls me a "queer." In most states, in many localities, and,
as of September 1994, in federal cases, these two crimes are treated
differently: the crime motivated by bias—or deemed to be so motivated
by prosecutors and juries—gets a stiffer punishment. "Longer prison
terms for bigots," shrilled Brooklyn Democratic Congressman Charles
Schumer, who introduced the federal hate-crimes legislation, and those
are what the law now provides. Evidence that the assailant holds
prejudiced beliefs, even if he doesn't actually express them while committing an offense, can serve to elevate the crime. Defendants in hate-
crimes cases may be grilled on how many black friends they have and
whether they have told racist jokes. To increase a prison sentence only
because of the defendant's "prejudice" (as gauged by prosecutor and
jury) is, of course, to try minds and punish beliefs. Purists say, Well,
they are dangerous minds and poisonous beliefs.

In the workplace: Though government cannot constitutionally   21
suppress bigotry directly, it is now busy doing so indirectly by requiring
employers to eliminate prejudice. Since the early 1980s, courts and
the Equal Employment Opportunity Commission have moved to bar
workplace speech deemed to create a hostile or abusive working environment for minorities. The law, held a federal court in 1988, "does
require that an employer take prompt action to prevent . . . bigots
from expressing their opinions in a way that abuses or offends their
co-workers," so as to achieve "the goal of eliminating prejudices and
biases from our society." So it was, as UCLA law professor Eugene
Volokh notes, that the EEOC charged that a manufacturer's ads using
admittedly accurate depictions of samurai, kabuki, and sumo were
"racist" and "offensive to people of Japanese origin"; that a Pennsylvania court found that an employer's printing Bible verses on paychecks

was religious harassment of Jewish employees; that an employer had to desist using gender-based job titles like "foreman" and "draftsman" after a female employee sued.

On and on the campaign goes, darting from one outbreak of prejudice to another like a cat chasing flies. In the American Bar Association, activists demand that lawyers who express "bias or prejudice" be penalized. In the Education Department, the civil-rights office presses for a ban on computer bulletin board comments that "show hostility toward a person or group based on sex, race or color, including slurs, negative stereotypes, jokes or pranks." In its security checks for government jobs, the FBI takes to asking whether applicants are "free of biases against any class of citizens," whether, for instance, they have told racist jokes or indicated other "prejudices." Joke police! George Orwell, grasping the close relationship of jokes to dissent, said that every joke is a tiny revolution. The purists will have no such rebellions. 22

The purist campaign reaches, in the end, into the mind itself. In a lecture at the University of New Hampshire, a professor compared writing to sex ("You and the subject become one"); he was suspended and required to apologize, but what was most insidious was the order to undergo university-approved counseling to have his mind straightened out. At the University of Pennsylvania, a law lecturer said, "We have ex-slaves here who should know about the Thirteenth Amendment"; he was banished from campus for a year and required to make a public apology, and he, too, was compelled to attend a "sensitivity and racial awareness" session. Mandatory re-education of alleged bigots is the natural consequence of intellectual purism. Prejudice must be eliminated! 23

Ah, but the task of scouring minds clean is Augean. "Nobody escapes," said a Rutgers University report on campus prejudice. Bias and prejudice, it found, cross every conceivable line, from sex to race to politics: "No matter who you are, no matter what the color of your skin, no matter what your gender or sexual orientation, no matter what you believe, no matter how you behave, there is somebody out there who doesn't like people of your kind." Charles Lawrence writes: "Racism is ubiquitous. We are all racists." If he means that most of us think racist thoughts of some sort at one time or another, he is right. If we are going to "eliminate prejudices and biases from our society," then the work of the prejudice police is unending. They are doomed to hunt and hunt and hunt, scour and scour and scour. 24

What is especially dismaying is that the purists pursue prejudice in the name of protecting minorities. In order to protect people like me (homosexual), they must pursue people like me (dissident). In order 25 to bolster minority self-esteem, they suppress minority opinion. There are, of course, all kinds of practical and legal problems with the purists' campaign: the incursions against the First Amendment; the inevitable abuses by prosecutors and activists who define as "hateful" or "violent" whatever speech they dislike or can score points off of; the lack of any evidence that repressing prejudice eliminates rather than inflames it. But minorities, of all people, ought to remember that by definition we cannot prevail by numbers, and we generally cannot prevail by force. Against the power of ignorant mass opinion and group prejudice and superstition, we have only our voices. If you doubt that minorities' voices are powerful weapons, think of the lengths to which Southern officials went to silence the Reverend Martin Luther King Jr. (recall that the city commissioner of Montgomery, Alabama, won a $500,000 libel suit, later overturned in *New York Times* v. *Sullivan* [1964], regarding an advertisement in the *Times* placed by civil-rights leaders who denounced the Montgomery police). Think of how much gay people have improved their lot over twenty-five years simply by refusing to remain silent. Recall the Michigan student who was prosecuted for saying that homosexuality is a treatable disease, and notice that he was black. Under that Michigan speech code, more than twenty blacks were charged with racist speech, while no instance of racist speech by whites was punished. In Florida, the hate-speech law was invoked against a black man who called a policeman a "white cracker"; not so surprisingly, in the first hate-crimes case to reach the Supreme Court, the victim was white and the defendant black.

In the escalating war against "prejudice," the right is already learn-   26
ing to play by the rules that were pioneered by the purist activists of the left. Last year leading Democrats, including the President, criticized the Republican Party for being increasingly in the thrall of the Christian right. Some of the rhetoric was harsh ("fire-breathing Christian radical right"), but it wasn't vicious or even clearly wrong. Never mind: when Democratic Representative Vic Fazio said Republicans were "being forced to the fringes by the aggressive political tactics of the religious right," the chairman of the Republican National Committee, Haley Barbour, said, "Christian-bashing" was "the left's preferred form of religious bigotry." Bigotry! Prejudice! "Christians active in politics are now on the receiving end of an extraordinary campaign of bias and prejudice," said the conservative leader William J. Bennett. One discerns, here, where the new purism leads. Eventually, any criticism of any group will be "prejudice."

Here is the ultimate irony of the new purism: words, which plural-   27
ists hope can be substituted for violence, are redefined by purists *as*

violence. "The experience of being called 'nigger,' 'spic,' 'Jap,' or 'kike' is like receiving a slap in the face," Charles Lawrence wrote in 1990. "Psychic injury is no less an injury than being struck in the face, and it often is far more severe." This kind of talk is commonplace today. Epithets, insults, often even polite expressions of what's taken to be prejudice are called by purists "assaultive speech," "words that wound," "verbal violence." "To me, racial epithets are not speech," one University of Michigan law professor said. "They are bullets." In her speech accepting the 1993 Nobel Prize for Literature in Stockholm, Sweden, the author Toni Morrison said this: "Oppressive language does more than represent violence; it is violence."

It is not violence. I am thinking back to a moment on the subway   28
in Washington, a little thing. I was riding home late one night and a squad of noisy kids, maybe seventeen or eighteen years old, noisily piled into the car. They yelled across the car and a girl said, "Where do we get off?"

A boy said, "Farragut North."   29
The girl: "*Faggot* North!"   30
The boy: "Yeah! Faggot North!"   31
General hilarity.   32

First, before the intellect resumes control, there is a moment of   33
fear, an animal moment. Who are they? How many of them? How dangerous? Where is the way out? All of these things are noted preverbally and assessed by the gut. Then the brain begins an assessment: they are sober, this is probably too public a place for them to do it, there are more girls than boys, they were just talking, it is probably nothing.

They didn't notice me and there was no incident. The teenage   34
babble flowed on, leaving me to think. I became interested in my own reaction: the jump of fear out of nowhere like an alert animal, the sense for a brief time that one is naked and alone and should hide or run away. For a time, one ceases to be a human being and becomes instead a faggot.

The fear engendered by these words is real. The remedy is as clear   35
and as imperfect as ever: protect citizens against violence. This, I grant, is something that American society has never done very well and now does quite poorly. It is no solution to define words as violence or prejudice as oppression, and then by cracking down on words or thoughts pretend that we are doing something about violence and oppression. No doubt it is easier to pass a speech code or hate-crimes law and proclaim the streets safer than actually to make the streets

safer, but the one must never be confused with the other. Every cop or prosecutor chasing words is one fewer chasing criminals. In a world rife with real violence and oppression, full of Rwandas and Bosnias and eleven-year-olds spraying bullets at children in Chicago and in turn being executed by gang lords, it is odious of Toni Morrison to say that words are violence.

Indeed, equating "verbal violence" with physical violence is a treacherous, mischievous business. Not long ago a writer was charged with viciously and gratuitously wounding the feelings and dignity of millions of people. He was charged, in effect, with exhibiting flagrant prejudice against Muslims and outrageously slandering their beliefs. "What is freedom of expression?" mused Salman Rushdie a year after the ayatollahs sentenced him to death and put a price on his head. "Without the freedom to offend, it ceases to exist." I can think of nothing sadder than that minority activists, in their haste to make the world better, should be the ones to forget the lesson of Rushdie's plight: for minorities, pluralism, not purism, is the answer. The campaigns to eradicate prejudice—all of them, the speech codes and workplace restrictions and mandatory therapy for accused bigots and all the rest—should stop, now. The whole objective of eradicating prejudice, as opposed to correcting and criticizing it, should be repudiated as a fool's errand. Salman Rushdie is right, Toni Morrison wrong, and minorities belong at his side, not hers.

36

THINKING ABOUT THE CONTENT

1. Rauch believes that there will never be a time "when no one will believe that people come in types and that each type belongs with its own." Do you agree? Why or why not?

2. "The realistic question," argues Rauch, "is how to make the best of prejudice, not how to eradicate it" (3). Does the author support his argument with sound reasoning? Explain why you do or do not agree with him.

3. What is Rauch's definition of *intellectual pluralism*? What does he mean when he says with pluralism "we kill our mistakes rather than each other"(9)? What are the challenges to pluralism, according to Rauch. Do you think intellectual pluralism exists or can exist? Explain.

4. What does Rauch mean by *purism* (12)? What examples does he provide to support his contention that the "new purism" is on a campaign against words? How does purism differ from pluralism?

5. According to Rauch, how far reaching is the antipluralist movement becoming?

6. Did Rauch's implication that he was a homosexual (25) cause you to react differently to his thesis? Explain.

LOOKING AT STRUCTURE AND STYLE

7. In what paragraph is the thesis best stated? How well does the author prepare us for his thesis?
8. What is the function of paragraphs 4 and 5?
9. For what purpose does Rauch discuss scientists and people's perception of scientists? What does it have to do with his thesis?
10. What is the function of paragraphs 18–23?
11. What purpose is served by the author's personal anecdote in paragraphs 28–34?

EXPLORING DISCUSSION AND WRITING TOPICS

12. Rauch disagrees with Toni Morrison and those of like mind who feel that "Oppressive language does more than represent violence; it is violence" (27). He agrees with Salman Rushdie that "without the freedom to offend, it [freedom] ceases to exist" (36). Take a stand and argue for or against Morrison's or Rushdie's statement.
13. Write about a time when you were hurt by words. What prompted the incident? What feelings did you have then? What feelings do you have now?
14. Do some research into one of the areas where Rauch says the antipluralist movement is reaching (universities, school curricula, criminal law, the workplace) and discuss just how far-reaching it is. Is he right? What examples support or refute Rauch?

Upon its fiftieth anniversary in 1995, the United Nations proclaimed it the Year of Tolerance. Ironically, that same year the United States was to experience the bombing of the federal building in Oklahoma; the growing popularity of bigoted hosts on radio talk shows such as Gordon Liddy, convicted conspirator in the Watergate scandals, who advocated the killing of government agents; increased enrollment in armed militia groups intolerant of the federal and state governments; a rise in anti-Semitic demonstrations; and political candidates fanning intolerance toward immigrants, with some even claiming the United States should withdraw its membership from the United Nations.

In the previous essay, "In Defense of Prejudice," Jonathan Rauch argues that the expression of various forms of bigotry and hatred cannot be outlawed or done away with and should even be protected. The following essay by Flora Lewis, a syndicated newspaper columnist, also has something to say about prejudice and abusive language.

ᴪ

Tolerance Can Be Learned

1 "You have to be taught / Before it's too late, / Before you are six, or seven or eight, / To hate all the people your relatives hate. / You have to be carefully taught."

2 The satirical song from the musical "South Pacific," mocking the prejudices of American servicemen encountering islanders during World War II, was based on a common utopian thesis—that hatred is unnatural.

3 Jean-Jacques Rousseau, a beam of the Enlightenment (in his writings but not in his personal life), promoted the idea that untutored man is a "noble savage," and that evil thoughts and deeds are the result of pollution by civilization.

4 At the end of the 20th century, we know better, or we ought to. It is tolerance that has to be taught, as the headlines remind us every day—from Bosnia, from Chechnya, from Rwanda, from Oklahoma City, from Tokyo's subway, from the series of 50th anniversary commemorations of the end of organized Nazi atrocities.

As William Golding expostulated in "Lord of the Flies," "inno-   5
cent" children can be outrageously cruel, without any lessons or real
provocation.

Bigotry can come easily to people uncertain of their own identity,   6
to be defined by rejecting "the other." It offers a sense of belonging
in the dominant, or would-be dominant, group, by sharing a hatred
of outsiders. It offers protection, by automatically marking friend and
foe beforehand, in the many parts of the world accustomed over long
centuries to anticipate war, not peace.

The recognition that tolerance cannot be taken for granted and   7
that prejudice, persecution and hatred cannot be considered just peculiar aberrations from human nature underlies the United Nations decision to proclaim this year, its 50th anniversary, the Year of Tolerance.
Unesco is seeking to promote the teaching of tolerance.

Looking behind the headlines, it is evident that there is something   8
in the idea that wanton violence expressing intolerance isn't all that
spontaneous. History does offer a nourishing soil, and there is scarcely
a human group, whether national, ethnic, religious or whatever, which
cannot find grounds for grievance somewhere in the past.

But that is always selective history, selected to be lethal by ignoring   9
all the parts of reasonable coexistence, of mutual support. It is, in
almost all the flagrant contemporary examples of malevolence, deliberately exploited by the few as a means of achieving and consolidating
power. It isn't irresistible, but it takes deliberate, conscious will to
resist.

Joining the angry American debate after the Oklahoma City bomb-   10
ing over whether the spread of rabid, hate-filled talk radio inspired
violence, Senator Max Baucus of Montana pointed out that free speech
is not only a guarantee, it is a duty. He recounted an incident in the
town of Billings, where there is a concentration of extreme right-
wingers, after attacks on two Jewish homes. The people of the town
rallied in demonstrative support of their Jewish and black fellow citizens.

"And the skinheads fled," Mr. Baucus wrote. "We must all make   11
hate mongers unwelcome in our towns and communities."

He is right. Hate cannot be outlawed when it stops at speech, but   12
it can and must be shamed and shouted down.

There are natural instincts available to help teach tolerance, partic-   13
ularly to children. They are curiosity, the appeal of variety, the adventure of learning. Nobody likes to feel that he or she is being used for
someone else's selfish purpose, so exposing the power mechanics behind the appeals for intolerance can be an antidote.

What do we mean by tolerance? Basically, it is hating, if there is   14
to be hate, not for who you are but for what you do. It does not mean
that anything goes, but rather that sacred is as sacred does.

"Multiculturalism," in the American campus jargon for rejecting   15
established values, can be intolerant, too, with its claim for a monopoly
of virtue, aggressively asserted. Dead white males, whose place in the
cultural hagiography it denounces, do have value. So do live ones, for
that matter. They are not to be denied their right to dignity, in a claimed
right to hate.

In the last five years there have been 90 armed conflicts in the   16
world (not counting terrorist attacks) and they have produced 20
million refugees. Only four were wars between states; the rest were
internal, people exploding with hate for each other in the same country.

Countries that consider themselves civilized are not immune. Tol-   17
erance may not come naturally, but it can be learned.

THINKING ABOUT THE CONTENT

1. Do you agree or disagree with the song lyrics quoted in the first paragraph?
   Why or why not?
2. Lewis disagrees with Rousseau's belief that "evil thoughts and deeds are
   the result of pollution by civilization" (3). Do you agree with Lewis or
   Rousseau? Why?
3. Do you think Lewis and Rauch are in agreement regarding the need to
   protect prejudiced language? Is the incident that occurred in Billings,
   Montana (10–11), an example that also supports Rauch's thesis? On what
   points regarding prejudice might Lewis and Rauch agree or disagree?
4. What is the point Lewis makes in paragraphs 9 and 10? How does it
   help support her thesis?
5. What is Lewis's definition of *tolerance?* Do you believe in tolerance? Have
   you learned tolerance? Explain.
6. What are Lewis's opinions regarding multicultural studies on U.S. college
   campuses (15)?

LOOKING AT STRUCTURE AND STYLE

6. How does Lewis use the first three paragraphs to establish her thesis?
   What is their function?
7. How does Lewis use paragraphs 4 and 5 to establish and support her
   thesis?
8. What is the point of paragraph 16? What does it have to do with the
   author's thesis?

9. To what audience does the author aim her essay? What in the essay leads you to think so?

EXPLORING DISCUSSION AND WRITING TOPICS

10. Write an essay arguing why hateful radio talk shows should or should not be allowed on the air.
11. Discuss why schools or colleges should or should not have rules pertaining to the use of hateful or bigoted speech toward any group or person on campus.
12. How far should the term *free speech* be taken? Is there a limit?

JI-YEON MARY YUHFILL

Ji-Yeon Mary Yuhfill, a South Korean, moved to the United States with her family in 1970. She holds a master's degree in cognitive science from Stanford University and a doctorate in history from the University of Pennsylvania. Yuhfill has worked as a reporter for the *Omaha World-Herald* and *New York Newsday*.

The following essay, which originally appeared in the *Philadelphia Inquirer* (1991), opposes those who believe that a multicultural curriculum would fragment the United States into ethnic groups. Yuhfill believes students should be provided with any information that can help them "access critically the reasons for the inconsistencies between the ideals of the U.S. and social realities." Such a curriculum, she argues, could sustain pride in one's culture without the prejudice that can sometimes accompany false pride.

ﯗ

Let's Tell the Story of All America's Cultures

1   I grew up hearing, seeing and almost believing that America was white—albeit with a little black tinged here and there—and that white was best.

2   The white people were everywhere in my 1970s Chicago childhood: Founding Fathers, Lewis and Clark, Lincoln, Daniel Boone, Carnegie, presidents, explorers and industrialists galore. The only black people were slaves. The only Indians were scalpers.

3   I never heard one word about how Benjamin Franklin was so impressed by the Iroquois federation of nations that he adapted that model into our system of state and federal government. Or that the Indian tribes were systematically betrayed and massacred by a greedy young nation that stole their land and called it the United States.

4   I never heard one word about how Asian immigrants were among the first to turn California's desert into fields of plenty. Or about Chinese immigrant Ah Bing, who bred the cherry now on sale in groceries across the nation. Or that plantation owners in Hawaii imported labor from China, Japan, Korea and the Philippines to work

the sugar cane fields. I never learned that Asian immigrants were the only immigrants denied U.S. citizenship, even though they served honorably in World War I. All the immigrants in my textbook were white.

I never learned about Frederick Douglass, the runaway slave who   5
became a leading abolitionist and statesman, or about black scholar W. E. B. Du Bois. I never learned that black people rose up in arms against slavery. Nat Turner wasn't one of the heroes in my childhood history class.

I never learned that the American Southwest and California were   6
already settled by Mexicans when they were annexed after the Mexican-American War. I never learned that Mexico once had a problem keeping land-hungry white men on the U.S. side of the border.

So when other children called me a slant-eyed chink and told me   7
to go back where I came from, I was ready to believe that I wasn't really an American because I wasn't white.

America's bittersweet legacy of struggling and failing and getting   8
another step closer to democratic ideals of liberty and equality and justice for all wasn't for the likes of me, an immigrant child from Korea. The history books said so.

Well, the history books were wrong.   9

Educators around the country are finally realizing what I realized   10
as a teenager in the library, looking up the history I wasn't getting in school. America is a multicultural nation, composed of many people with varying histories and varying traditions who have little in common except their humanity, a belief in democracy and a desire for freedom.

America changed them, but they changed America too.   11

A committee of scholars and teachers gathered by the New York   12
State Department of Education recognizes this in their recent report, "One Nation, Many Peoples: A Declaration of Cultural Interdependence."

They recommend that public schools provide a "multicultural   13
education, anchored to the shared principles of a liberal democracy."

What that means, according to the report, is recognizing that   14
America was shaped and continues to be shaped by people of diverse backgrounds. It calls for students to be taught that history is an ongoing process of discovery and interpretation of the past, and that there is more than one way of viewing the world.

Thus, the westward migration of white Americans is not just a   15
heroic settling of an untamed wild, but also the conquest of indigenous peoples. Immigrants were not just white, but Asian as well. Blacks

were not merely passive slaves freed by northern whites, but active fighters for their own liberation.

In particular, according to the report, the curriculum should help   16
children "to access critically the reasons for the inconsistencies between
the ideals of the U.S. and social realities. It should provide information
and intellectual tools that can permit them to contribute to bringing
reality closer to the ideals."

In other words, show children the good with the bad, and give   17
them the skills to help improve their country. What could be more
patriotic?

Several dissenting members of the New York committee publicly   18
worry that America will splinter into ethnic fragments if this multicultural curriculum is adopted. They argue that the committee's report
puts the focus on ethnicity at the expense of national unity.

But downplaying ethnicity will not bolster national unity. The   19
history of America is the story of how and why people from all over
the world came to the United States, and how in struggling to make
a better life for themselves, they changed each other, they changed the
country, and they all came to call themselves Americans.

E pluribus unum. Out of many, one.   20

This is why I, with my Korean background, and my childhood   21
tormentors, with their lost-in-the-mist-of-time European backgrounds,
are all Americans.

It is the unique beauty of this country. It is high time we let all   22
our children gaze upon it.

THINKING ABOUT THE CONTENT

1. Yuhfill states she grew up in the 1970s "seeing and believing that America
   was white—albeit with a little black tinged here and there—and that
   white was best" (1). To what does she blame this upbringing? Would she
   find such a presence today? Explain.
2. What sort of prejudice did Yuhfill experience as a child? Why does she
   believe she was treated this way? What effect did it have on her?
3. Yuhfill recounts historical events about nonwhites that she never learned
   in her textbooks. Did your history textbooks detail most of these events
   or were you unaware of many of them? Were you taught that the expansion
   and development of the United States was mostly a "white man's history"
   or taught that "white was best"?
4. Yuhfill argues that "downplaying ethnicity will not bolster national unity"
   (19). Do you agree? Explain.

LOOKING AT STRUCTURE AND STYLE

5. What might you infer prompted Yuhfill to write this essay? To whom is she writing?
6. Is Yuhfill's thesis stated or implied? If stated, where?
7. Paragraphs 3 through 6 all begin with "I never heard" or "I never learned." Explain the effect of this repetition.
8. How well does Yuhfill support her conclusion? Do you agree with her? Why or why not?

EXPLORING DISCUSSION AND WRITING TOPICS

9. Write an argument for or against a multicultural public school curriculum. What should be taught? What effect might such a curriculum have on pride and prejudice?
10. Research some current history textbooks by looking in the index or table of contents for some of the names of people and historical events Yuhfill mentions. Are most of them covered in contemporary textbooks? Do contemporary history books appear balanced in coverage?
11. Reflect on your own elementary and high school education. Was it similar to Yuhfill's or did you receive a more multicultural approach to U.S. history? Did learning of any of these events affect your feelings of pride or prejudice? Explain.

The following selection first appeared in Marilyn P. Davis's *Mexican Voices/American Dreams: An Oral History of Mexican Immigration to the United States*. Davis taped interviews with several people of Mexican heritage, then transcribed and edited them for her book, thus the readings are informal and conversational.

"It's My Country Too" is the written interview with Juan Cadena, outreach coordinator for the Muscatine (Iowa) School District and former director of the Muscatine Migrant Committee. Notice both the pride and the prejudice that comes through in the interview.

♦

It's My Country Too

I work for the Muscatine Migrant Committee. We're a government- 1 funded organization that's been in existence for over twenty years. We provide medical help for migrants and seasonal farm workers. I've been the director of the program since 1971.

"Migrant" and "immigrant" are not synonymous. Our definition 2 of a migrant is someone who has earned half of their income within a twelve-consecutive-month period in the past twenty-four months. And the fact that they're from Mexico or any other country or are white or speak Spanish or don't speak Spanish is really not relevant. On the other hand, 99 percent of the migrants are Mexican-Americans and *mexicanos*. With seasonal farm workers it's just the opposite, 90 percent are white, European-Americans from Iowa. I don't know what percentage of the migrants are Mexican citizens. Fifteen years ago, a great percentage of our migrants were from Texas and were American citizens by birth. In the last three or four years we have had a higher proportion of Mexican citizens than before.

I grew up in the Midwest. I was born in Texas, but we moved 3 to Saginaw, Michigan, when I was ten years old. When we first moved to Carleton, just across the Saginaw River, there was a little—what we call *colonia*. It didn't amount to much, there were only eight migrant houses, and we lived right down the tracks in another little house near the sugar beet company. We made friends

with everybody in the *colonia*. We all went to the same school.
Well, a couple of years later my father bought a house about three
or four miles from there, in the Buena Vista neighborhood. We
were only half a block from Saginaw, but I kept in contact with
the people from the *colonia*.

We used to have Mexican dances. First in a real small hall,   4
then we graduated to the auditorium, then to the armory. By the
1960s, "Los Relámpagos del Norte" came and there were two
thousand people at the dance. It just grew and grew. After I left
Saginaw in the seventies, Vincente Fernández came to the Civic
Center and they had a real turnout.

So there is a substantial number of Hispanics in Saginaw. The   5
community college, when we left, had over 200 Mexicans enrolled.
A few years ago, I went back and they had 400 in the community
college.

When I was a community organizer we had clubs in each of   6
the high schools for Mexican kids, to encourage them to go to
college. One school had over 250 kids. The Graduation Club was
started back in the forties for all the Mexicans who are going to
graduate from high school. They have their own prom and bring
speakers such as Senator Chavez and Senator Montoya, to give a
special commencement. The kids still go to graduation with their
respective schools, but they also have a separate one just for
Mexicans.

I don't know if they still do, but in Saginaw they used to   7
celebrate the *diez de septiembre* and *cinco de mayo*. I don't think
half of them know what the heck's being celebrated. That's the
truth. I was in San Antonio and these Mexicans, my wife, Martha's
cousins, live in an affluent, nice neighborhood on the north side.
They were all excited because they were going to this Festival San
Jacinto and Martha says, "Well what is the celebration about?"
And they didn't know. *¿Verdad, Martha?* They didn't know. I knew,
but I didn't say nothing. They said, "*No sabemos lo que es,* but
we have a lot of fun." But this whole holiday is about when the
mexicanos got whipped by the whites here in San Jacinto and they
don't even know. They're going out there to celebrate. So you know
they don't even care. Even the whites don't know what the San
Jacinto's about anymore, and nobody gives a hoot.

In Saginaw I had no real close friends that were not Mexicans.   8
I wasn't unfriendly with anyone, but I really never got associated
with whites very much until I went in the army. Actually in those
years I never paid any attention to who was from Mexico and who

was from Texas, who was from Saginaw, who was from out of
town, no attention whatsoever. I never even thought about it until
I came here.

And here, when we first came to Muscatine it was like I was   9
wearing a sign on my forehead, "I'm Mexican." It wasn't just my
perception, because when my relations would come down from Saginaw to visit, they would say, "What's wrong with the people in Muscatine? They stare at you." Well, that's not true anymore, but that was
the situation when we first came here in '71. It was like a little cultural
shock for me too, because I was confronted with this, "You're a Mexican." I knew I was a Mexican, but I didn't want people to be looking
at me like, "Hey, Mexican!" They didn't say it, but that's the feeling
you got. In Saginaw it wasn't that way at all—the relationship between
whites and Mexicans is real good. There's really not that obvious
discrimination. There was a little bit in the forties but not after that.
Now there's even a lot of intermarriage.

See here, it was pretty bad. I was standing in line at the bank one   10
day—this is one example—and this guy says, "This is the way Mexicans line up for food stamps," and everybody was ha-ha-ha. Well I
didn't laugh. I felt like grabbing the guy and throwing him through
the window. But I was going to a church council meeting, I was
president. Now how would I be getting into a fight? I was getting a
little more religious, so I started thinking and acting different. A few
years before I probably would have tried to throw him through the
window.

Another time I called this number for a house to rent. I guess he   11
was busy and didn't notice that I had an accent. So when we got there
he said, "Stop right there, I'm not renting to no Mexicans!" You know
it was kind of comical.

I said, "Did I hear what you said?"   12

He said, "That's right, I don't rent to Mexicans."   13

I said, "Oh Christ!" So I called the civil rights commission, I was   14
going to do something, but I never followed up on it.

A couple, Anglo friends, did a consumers' report here. We would   15
send a Mexican couple, or pretend-to-be couple, to rent an apartment,
and the landlord would say there wasn't any place to rent. Then our
Anglo friends would come right behind them an hour later and, like
magic, they would have a vacancy. After about twenty cases, they
wrote a report. Those landlords were mad! But see we started exposing
all that foolishness. Then in the schools there was also a lot of discrimination. I'm sure there still is, to some extent, but it has changed a lot.
¿Verdad, Martha? There's a lot of good Anglos in this community.

I was considered real militant in Saginaw, and when I came here 16
I was in the mood that I could do anything. That's the way I was. I
sort of enjoyed it, you know. I was thirty-four, so I was no young kid.
But nothing scared me, nothing.

I don't know. We had this old Mexican guy that was being ripped 17
off in West Liberty. This was a long time ago, but this justice of the
peace had rented a place to the Mexican. In the first place it was small,
a real shack. But beyond that there's no way that any thinking person
could have expected the old guy to pay this kind of rent for the amount
of money he was earning. So a friend and I, he was a law student, we
went over there. Out comes this justice of the peace, and this guy
looks like he's from *Petticoat Junction,* had his striped coveralls with
this little hat and the whole bit. He said, "We don't want all those
Mexicans coming into town. They park their cars and half of the time
they're leaking oil and they leave all those oil spots all over and all
that." My friend was saying, "Write that down, Juan." And I was
writing notes, writing notes.

The justice of the peace would tell his lawyer, "They're gonna get 18
me. They're gonna get us, Ernie."

"Ah, don't worry about it." But you could see he was all worried. 19
So finally the lawyer said, "Juan, I'll talk to you, I don't want to talk
to your friend. I'll talk to you, just you and I."

See, we were playing the good cop, bad cop. I went in but told 20
my friend, "You stay out of here." Then I told the justice's lawyer,
"Well, I'll keep this lawyer away from here if you cut the rent in half
and. . . ." And this is exactly what the man had wanted. He agreed
to everything.

"You're not going to take it any further than this?" 21

I said, "No, we'll forget the whole thing." 22

So we went back for the old goat to sign the papers and he said, 23
"Well, I'm sorry what I said about Mexicans, it's not only Mexicans
that do that, niggers and Puerto Ricans do the same."

Can you believe that? He was serious. God, I'll never forget that. 24
How can you get angry with somebody like that? You can't, these
people are crazy. He was apologizing and insulting us at the same
time. I've noticed that people are like that. If you really look at them,
they're hilarious. The only time I'm really worried about a racist person
is if they're in a position to determine someone's economic or social
future.

Before I came here I was a coordinator for the grape boycott, for 25
Cesar Chavez in the Saginaw area. We confronted a lot of people,
people who would spit on us and say, "Go back to Mexico, you

wetbacks!" And we were all from the United States. A lot of Anglos were helping us out, but in a way I was a racist. I wanted Mexicans to be doing something for Mexicans, but we were all American citizens. When I joined the grape boycott movement it was being led by some seventeen-year-old Anglo girl, and 99 percent of the people doing the marching were Anglos, nuns, and priests. I took it over and chased them all out. I didn't tell them directly to leave, but in a month or so they were all gone except the real hard-nosed. I would have 100 or 150 and they were all Mexicans. *¿Verdad, Martha?* The Anglos didn't want me because I was coming across too hard. They wanted to make waves but not BIG waves, and I was making REAL BIG waves.

But here in Muscatine it was a different ballgame than Saginaw.   26
If you're really trying to do something useful and to really help or change conditions, you have to adapt to the conditions that you're dealing with. You can't just sing the same songs.

In Saginaw there really wasn't that many poor people. Now I'm   27
used to it, but when we came here, we went riding around to the southside. We saw Anglos, blue-eyed, blond kids with stringy hair and dirty faces, scroungy looking, and I said, "Well wait a minute, I thought I would have to go to the Ozarks to see this. Not Iowa, the breadbasket of America." I thought everybody would be like you know, *Ozzie and Harriet.* But you see a lot of poor people, and really I don't know how you would say it, riff-raff maybe.

We don't have that in Saginaw. There's a large middle class, and   28
everybody works in the plants, and they all make a lot of money. There I could say, "Look at the way the poor Mexicans live here." Because there were a few poor Mexicans. But here, I can't say that because we have as many poor whites.

Another difference, in Saginaw everybody works side by side there   29
at the plants, and it doesn't matter whether you're white, yellow, or blue. You earn the same kind of money, the same kind of education and everything else.

People wanted me to get involved with the union here too, like   30
the grape boycott. But I said, "It isn't going to work. In Saginaw we used to go to a supermarket. I would take six people and we would turn away 50 percent of the people. Here you can take 200 people and you aren't going to turn 5 percent of the people away. They don't identify with the union. In Saginaw everybody was union." I don't care if they were Polish or Mexican or black, they were all union people. So it was real easy to close down a store. Here it wouldn't work. People are not union oriented. Cesar Chavez came and people

said, "Let's get him down to organize." It isn't going to work. The whole thing was a different world, and I found that out real quick.

I've read a lot of books. The bible has influenced me. I've read Espinoza, Jung, Marx, Ché Guevara, Fidel Castro, Mao Tse-tung, Gandhi, and Franz Fanon. Spicer, an anthropologist, influenced me too.   31

In school when I was growing up in Texas, the history books were always lying. My dad would correct the history like Pancho Villa and the Alamo, and say, "This is a bunch of lies. These *gringos* are telling you a bunch of lies." So I started thinking for myself. I remember once the nuns wanted us to sign some papers they were going to drop over China and I didn't sign them. My sister Lupe didn't sign it either. She was the only one in her class and I was the only one in mine. I said, "How do I know communism is wrong? How do I know that they're not right and I'm wrong?" White people have been lying to us all these years, and they have discriminated against us in Texas, so how come they're supposed to be so good? They broke all those treaties with the Indians and treated them like dogs, and now they're going to tell me that they're good and the Chinese are bad. I said, "No. I hope the Chinese come and take this country over." That's what I told them.   32

And the nuns would say, "We're going to have Father come and talk to you because you're a communist." I said, "How can I be a communist? You don't even know what a communist is." I didn't completely buy that little trick of the land of the free and the home of the brave. The United States, I do agree, is probably the best country in the world. And I'm glad I'm an American citizen and was born in this country. But the point is, you can't just swallow everything that they try to tell us, especially when it comes to minorities. I always saw the United States as an extension of Europe, and if you were not of European ancestry somehow you weren't American. What the heck, I was born here, but if I said anything against the United States they would say, "Why don't you go back to Mexico." Well, why don't you go back to Europe. Why should you be trying to send me to Mexico. What's the difference?   33

Like one guy—we were at a school board hearing where I was pushing for bilingual education—he told the superintendent of schools, "You mean to tell me this man"—talking about me, I was sitting right in front of him—"expects us to teach his kids Spanish in school?"   34

And then I told the superintendent, "You mean to tell me that this man here expects me to teach his kid English in school?"   35

He said, "What do you mean, you speak Spanish at home, don't you?"   36

I said, "Well what do you speak at home, Chinese? If you expect   37
me to teach my kid Spanish at home, then you teach your kid English
at home."

He said, "Well I don't mind, maybe you people already living here   38
have the right to speak Spanish, but I'm talking about the other people
coming in."

"Fine, I'm okay if you speak English, but all new people coming   39
in should speak Spanish. What makes you right and me wrong?"

He said, "Well because we're the majority."   40

I said, "No, no, no, what about Zimbabwe? You white Europeans   41
want to push your culture and your language everywhere. In Zimbabwe
you're the minority." I wanted to make the same argument. If he would
say my argument wasn't right, it would be because he thought I was
a second-class citizen, but why should he be more of a citizen than
me? I'm a taxpayer. It's my money too. It's my country too. It's my
school system too. It's a matter of perceiving what we're all about
here in the United States.

THINKING ABOUT THE CONTENT

1. What sort of things or accomplishments does Cadena speak of with pride?
   Are they worthy of pride? Why or why not?
2. What kind of prejudice does Cadena describe? Does he reveal any prejudice himself? If so, what is it?
3. Are Cadena's arguments for bilingual education programs valid? Why or
   why not? Does the fact that whites are a minority in Zimbabwe a good
   argument in paragraph 41? Why or why not?
4. Is Cadena's view that America is "an extension of Europe" correct (33)?
   Why or why not?

LOOKING AT STRUCTURE AND STYLE

5. Since this is an edited version of an oral interview, it is difficult to discuss
   style and structure; however, does the editor capture Cadena's personality
   and attitude? Explain.

EXPLORING DISCUSSION AND WRITING TOPICS

6. Reread paragraph 31. If you have (or want to) read any of the works by
   the authors mentioned, explain why and in what way they might influence
   someone's way of thinking, especially someone or some group that might
   be subjected to prejudice frequently.

7. Write about a time you felt "culture shock" by entering a situation or place where you felt you were not welcomed or were made to feel different.

8. Discuss your own pride. What things about yourself, your family, heritage, friends, or country are you most proud? Do you have too much pride? not enough?

VIVIAN GORNICK

A journalist, Vivian Gornick's work has appeared in numerous publications, including the *Atlantic*, the *Los Angeles Times*, the *Nation*, *Tikkun*, and the *Washington Post*. In addition, Gornick has written five books, including *Essays in Feminism*, *In Search of Ali Mahmoud*, and *Fierce Attachments: A Memoir*.

In the following selection, which appeared in the March/April 1989 issue of *Tikkun*, Gornick uses examples from her own life to reflect the pride and the prejudice she felt as she discovered not only her awareness of herself as Jewish but also a woman.

𝒲

Twice an Outsider: On Being Jewish and a Woman

When I was growing up, the whole world was Jewish. The heroes were Jewish and the villains were Jewish. The landlord, the doctor, the grocer, your best friend, the village idiot, the neighborhood bully: all Jewish. We were working-class and immigrant as well, but that just came with the territory. Essentially, we were Jews on the streets of New York. We learned to be kind, cruel, smart, and feeling in a mixture of language and gesture that was part street slang, part grade-school English, part kitchen Yiddish. We learned about politics and society in much the same way: down the block were a few Orthodox Jews, up the block a few Zionists, in between a sprinkling of socialists. For the most part, people had no politics at all, only a cautious appetite for the goods of life. It was a small, tight, hyphenated world that we occupied, but I didn't know that; I thought it *was* the world.

One Sunday evening when I was eight years old my parents and I were riding in the back seat of my rich uncle's Buick. We had been out for a drive and now we were back in the Bronx, headed for home. Suddenly, another car sideswiped us. My mother and my aunt shrieked. My uncle swore softly. My father, in whose lap I was sitting, said out the window at the speeding car, "That's all right. Nothing but a bunch of kikes in here." In an instant I knew everything. I knew there was a world beyond our streets, and in that world my father was a humiliated man, without power or standing. By extension, we were all vulnerable out there; but *we* didn't matter so much. It was my father, my handsome, gentle father, who mattered. My heart burned for him. I burrowed closer in his lap, pressed myself against his chest. I wanted to warm the place in him that I was sure had grown cold when he called himself a kike.

That was in the middle of the Second World War—*the* watershed   3
event for the men and women of my generation. No matter what your social condition, if you were a child growing up in the early 1940s you entered the decade destined for one kind of life and came out of it headed for another. For those of us who had gone into the war the children of intimidated inner-city Jews, 1945 signified an astonishing change in the atmosphere. The end of the war brought frozen food and nuclear fission, laundromats and anti-communists, Levittown and the breakup of the college quota system. The trolley tracks were torn up, and the streets paved over. Buses took you not only to other parts of the Bronx but into Manhattan as well. When my brother graduated from the Bronx High School of Science in 1947 my father said, "Now you can become a salesman." But my cousin Joey had been a bombardier in the Pacific and was now one of the elite: a returned GI at City College. My brother sat down with my father and explained that even though he was not a genius he had to go to college. It was his right and his obligation. My father stared at his son. Now we were in the new world.

When I was sixteen a girl in the next building had her nose straight-   4
ened; we all trooped in to see Selma Shapiro lying in state, swathed in bandages from which would emerge a person fit for life beyond the block. Three buildings away a boy went downtown for a job, and on his application he wrote "Arnold Brown" instead of "Arnold Braunowitz." The news swept through the neighborhood like wildfire. A nose job? A name change? What was happening here? It was awful; it was wonderful. It was frightening; it was delicious. Whatever it was, it wasn't stasis. Things felt lively and active. Chutzpah was on the rise, passivity on the wane. We were going to run the gauntlet. That's what it meant to be in the new world. For the first time we could *imagine* ourselves out there.

But who exactly do I mean when I say we? I mean Arnie, not Selma.   5
I mean my brother, not me. I mean the boys, not the girls. My mother stood behind me, pushing me forward. "The girl goes to college, too," she said. And I did. But my going to college would not mean the same

thing as my brother's going to college, and we all knew it. For my brother, college meant getting from the Bronx to Manhattan. But for me? From the time I was fourteen I yearned to get out of the Bronx, but get out into *what?* I did not actually imagine myself a working person alone in Manhattan and nobody else did either. What I did imagine was that I would marry, and that the man I married would get me downtown. He would brave the perils of class and race, and somehow I'd be there alongside him.

The greater chain of social being obtained. Selma straightened her 6
nose so that she could marry upward into the Jewish middle class. Arnie changed his name so that he could wedge himself into the Christian world. It was the boys who would be out there facing down the terrors of the word "kike," not the girls. The boys would run the gauntlet, for themselves and for us. We would be standing not beside them but behind them, egging them on. And because we knew we'd be behind them, we—the girls—never experienced ourselves directly as Jews. I never shivered inside with the fear of being called a kike. I remember that. Somehow I knew that if I were insulted in that way I might feel stunned, but the fear and shame would be once removed. I knew I'd run home to Arnie, and I'd say, "Arnie, they called me a kike," and he'd look miserable, and I'd say, "Do something!" and the whole matter would be out of my hands the minute I said, "Do something." It was Arnie who'd have to stand up to the world, search his soul, test his feelings, discover his capacity for courage or action. Not me. And that is why Arnie grew up to become William Paley, and the other boys on the block—the ones who sneered and raged and trembled, who knew they'd have to run that gauntlet, get into that new world like it or not, and were smart and sensitive, and hated and feared and longed for it all—they grew up to become Philip Roth and Woody Allen. Me and Selma? We grew up to become women.

The confusion is historic; the distinction is crucial.   7

Woody Allen is exactly my age. I remember as though it were   8
yesterday listening to Allen's first standup comic monologues in the late fifties at the Bitter End Café. We were all in our twenties, my friends and I and Allen. It was as though someone on the block had suddenly found it in himself to say to a world beyond the street, "Listen. You wanna know how it is? This is how it is," and with more courage than anxiety he had shaped our experience. This wasn't Milton Berle or Henny Youngman up there, a Borscht Belt comic speaking half Yiddish, half English, all outsiderness. No, this was one of us, describing how it felt to be our age and in our place: on the street, at

a party, in the subway, at home in the Bronx or Brooklyn, and then out there, downtown, in the city. Half in, half out.

Philip Roth, of course, cut closer to the bone. His sentence struc- 9 ture deepened the experience, drove home better than Allen could the pain and the excitement, the intelligence and the anguish, the hilarity and the madness of getting so close you could touch it and *still* you weren't inside.

Behind Allen and Roth stood Saul Bellow, who made the words 10 "manic" and "Jewish" synonymous, whose work glittered with a wild flood of feeling that poured from a river of language, all pent-up brilliance, the intelligence driven to an edge of hysteria that resembled Mel Brooks as much as it did Philip Roth. Although Bellow had been writing since the forties, it was only now in the fifties and sixties that his work and its meaning traveled down from a small community of intellectual readers to the reading populace at large. Here was a street-smart writing Jew who was actually extending the American language, using us—our lives, our idiom—to say something about American life that had not been said before. In the process, he gave us—me and my contemporaries—the equipment to define ourselves, and therefore become ourselves.

These men are on a continuum. From Milton Berle and Mel Brooks 11 to Saul Bellow, Philip Roth, and Woody Allen—the subtle alterations of tone and voice among them constitute a piece of social history, chart a progress of the way Jews felt about themselves in America, embody a fine calibration of rage, resentment, and hunger.

My mother hated Milton Berle, and I understood why—he was 12 hard to take. But I laughed against my will, and I knew he was the real thing. To see the idiom of your life coming back at you, shaped and enlarged by a line of humorous intelligence as compelling as a poem in the sustained nature of its thesis and context, was to experience one of life's deepest satisfactions. When that famous chord of recognition strikes, it is healing—illuminating and healing.

Milton Berle was my first experience of an artist's work applied 13 to the grosser materials of my own environment. Berle, operating at a lower level of genius, was just as sinister as the Marx brothers. It was the wildness of his humor and the no-holds-barred atmosphere that it generated. Berle was coarse and vulgar, fast and furious, frightening in the speed of his cunning and his rage. My mother was repelled. She knew this was Jewish self-hatred at its most vicious.

Mel Brooks was more of the same, only ten years younger, and 14 the ten years made a difference. A few years ago Brooks reminisced about how, when he began writing for Sid Caesar, his mother asked him how much money he was making, and he told her sixty dollars a week. He knew if he told her what he was really making she'd have a heart attack. "The heart," he said. "It would attack her." That story was for us: Woody Allen built on it. Brooks—also marked by a Borscht Belt coarseness that spoke to an uneducated sense of America, a lack of conversance with the larger culture—was still the shrewd, wild Jew talking, but his tone was a bit sadder, a bit quieter than Milton Berle's, less defended against the fears that dominated our lives. The lessened defense was the sign of change.

With Woody Allen, we passed through into a crucial stage of development. Allen built a persona, an identity, a body of work out of the idea of the mousy Jew who makes a fool of the gentile rather than of another Jew. This had not happened before. Its meaning was unmistakable.   15

The Woody Allen character is obsessed with getting laid. Everyone else does it; he alone can't do it. Everywhere he goes—in the street, on the subway, at a party—he gazes mournfully at the golden shiksas all around him, always beyond reach. It's not a Jewish girl he's trying to get into bed; it's Diane Keaton. The Jewish girl is Brooklyn; Annie Hall is Manhattan.   16

And what does sexual success mean? It means everything. It means the defeat of all that life bitterly withholds, already characterized by the fact that one has been born a Jew instead of Humphrey Bogart. If Allen can just get that blue-eyed beauty into bed. He wants it so bad he's going to die of it. He's going to expire from this hunger right there before your eyes.   17

The humor turns on Allen's extraordinary ability to mock himself. He's as brilliant as Charlie Chaplin at making wonderful his own smallness. And he's as successful as Chaplin at making a hero of the little man, and a fool of the withholding world in the person of the pretty girl. When Diane Keaton wrings her hands and moans, "I can't," and Allen blinks like a rabbit and says, "Why? Because I'm Jewish?"—he accomplishes a minor miracle on the screen. The beautiful woman is made ridiculous. The golden shiksa has become absurd, inept, incapable: the insincere and the foolish cut down to size so that Allen can come up to size.   18

When was the first time I saw it? Which movie was it? I can't remember. I remember only that at one of them, in the early seventies, I suddenly found myself listening to the audience laugh hysterically while Allen made a dreadful fool of the girl on the screen, and I realized that he had to make a fool of her, that he would always have to make   19 a fool of her, because she was the foil, the instrument of his unholy deprivation, the exasperating source of life's mean indifference. I said to myself, "This is dis-*gust*-ing," and as I said it I knew I'd been feeling this way all my life: from Milton Berle to Saul Bellow to Woody Allen. I had always laughed, but deep inside I'd frozen up, and now I saw why. Milton Berle with his mother-in-law jokes, Saul Bellow with the mistresses who hold out and the wives who do him in, Mel Brooks and Woody Allen with the girl always and only the carrot at the end of the stick. Every last one of them was trashing women. Using women to savage the withholding world. Using us. Their mothers, their sisters, their wives. To them, we weren't friends or comrades. We weren't even Jews or gentiles. We were just girls.

At that moment I knew that I would never again feel myself more   20 of a Jew than a woman. I had never suffered as men did for being a Jew in a Christian world because, as a Jew, I had not known that I wanted the world. Now, as a woman, I knew I wanted the world and I suffered.

Hannah Arendt, watching the Nazis rise to power in Germany,   21 had denied the meaning of her own Jewishness for a long time. When she acknowledged it, she did so by saying, "When one is attacked as a Jew, one must defend oneself *as a Jew*. Not as a German, not as a world-citizen, not as an upholder of the Rights of Man [emphasis in original]." I read that and I was ready to change the sentences to read, "When one is attacked as a woman, one must defend oneself *as a woman*. Not as a Jew, not as a member of the working class, not as a child of immigrants."

My father had to be Jewish; he had no choice. When he went downtown   22 he heard "kike." I live downtown, and I do not hear "kike." Maybe it's there to be heard and I'm not tuned in, but it can't be there all that much if I don't hear it. I'm out in the world, and this is what I *do* hear:

I walk down the street. A working-class man puts his lips together   23 and makes a sucking noise at me.

I enter a hardware store to purchase a lock. I choose one, and the   24 man behind the counter shakes his head at me. "Women don't know how to use that lock," he says.

I go to a party in a university town. A man asks me what I do. I   25 tell him I'm a journalist. He asks if I run a cooking page. Two minutes later someone asks me not if I have a husband but what my husband does.

I go to another party, a dinner party on New York's Upper West   26
Side. I'm the only woman at the table who is not there as a wife. I speak
a few sentences on the subject under discussion. I am not responded to.
A minute later my thought is rephrased by one of the men. Two other
men immediately address it.

Outsiderness is the daily infliction of social invisibility. From low-   27
grade humiliation to life-threatening aggression, its power lies in the
way one is seen, and how that in turn affects the way one sees oneself.
When my father heard the word "kike" the life force within him
shriveled. When a man on the street makes animallike noises at me,
or when a man at a dinner table does not hear what I say, the same
thing happens to me. This is what makes the heart pound and the
head fill with blood. This is how the separation between world and
self occurs. This is outsiderness alive in the daily way. It is here, on
the issue of being a woman, not a Jew, that I must make my stand
and hold my ground.

A few years ago I taught at a state university in a small Western   28
town. One night at a faculty party a member of the department I was
working in, a man of modest intelligence, said of another teacher
who had aroused strong feeling in the department, "He's a smart Jew
crashing about in all directions." I stared at this man, thinking, "How
interesting. You *look* civilized." Then I said, quite calmly, "What a
quaint phrase. In New York we don't hear ourselves described as smart
Jews any more. Is that still current out here?" The man turned dull
red, and the exchange was at an end.

A few weeks later at another party I saw this same man engaged   29
in conversation with another member of the department, a woman. I
knew this woman, and in my view her gifts of mind and spirit were
comparable to the man's. She was not a scholar and he was not a
scholar. She was not intellectual and neither was he. They were both
hard-working university teachers. I watched the two standing together,
talking. The woman gestured widely as she spoke, smiled inordinately,
fingered her hair. Her eyes were bright; her tone was eager. She ex-
claimed; she enthused; she performed. The man stood there, pulling
at a pipe, silent, motionless, his body slack, his face immobile, his
entire being unreadable except for his eyes and his mouth: in them an
expression of mockery and patronage as the woman grew ever more
frantic in her need to gain a response. It was clear that the harder she
tried, the more secure he felt. At a certain point it became obvious
that he was deliberately withholding what he knew she needed. I was
watching a ritual exchange of petition and denial predicated on a

power structure that in this instance turned wholly on his maleness and her femaleness.

I watched these two for a long time, and as I watched I felt my   30
throat tighten, my arms and legs begin to tingle, a kind of sick feeling spread through my chest and belly. I wanted to put her up against the wall, but I wanted to put him through the wall. I realized I'd been absorbing this kind of thing twenty times a day in this department, in this university, in this town; and it was making me ill.

This daily feeling, this awareness of the subtle ways in institutional   31
life that the most ordinary men accord each other the simplest of recognitions and withhold these recognitions from the equally ordinary women with whom they work, is palpable, and it burns inside every woman who experiences it—whether she is aware of what is happening or has numbed herself to what is happening.

When I hear an anti-Semitic remark I am hurt, I am angered, but I   32
am not frightened. I do not fear for my life or my livelihood or my right to pursue the open expression of my convictions. When I hear a sexist remark I feel all of the above. I feel that stomach-churning rage and pain that tells me that I am in trouble, that I am up against threat and wipeout. I am in the presence of something virulent in the social scheme directed against me not because of what I actually am but because of an immutable condition of birth. Something I might once have experienced as a Jew but today can feel only as a woman.

Bellow, Roth, Allen: these are writers who have had only the taste   33
of their own lives as the stimulus for creative work—and a rich, lively taste it has been: tart and smart, full of bite and wisdom. But these writers were allowed to become so fabulously successful precisely because the stigma of Jewishness was lading even as they were re-cording it. When Bellow wrote *Herzog,* being Jewish was no longer the open wound it had been when he wrote *The Victim;* and by the time Allen and Roth were coming into their own they were far more integrated into the larger world than their work suggested. Therefore, for Allen or Roth to go on making the golden shiksa the foil, or for Bellow to keep portraying the Jewish intellectual who can't arrive as his foil, is tiresome and unpersuasive. It does not speak to the lives that any of us are now living. Such work strikes no chord of recognition; it strikes only chords of memory and sentiment. The thing about outsiderness is that one feels it in the flesh every day; one feels oneself invisible in the ordinary social way. These are requirements of the condition.

This invisibility once made Jews manic and blacks murderous. It 34
works on women in a variety of ways:

I leaned across the counter in the hardware store and said to the 35
man who had told me women didn't know how to use the lock I'd
chosen, "Would you say that to me if I were black?" He stared lightly
at me for a long moment. Then he nodded, "Gotcha," he said.

To the man at the university party I explained my work in great 36
and careful detail. The man, a sixty-year-old Ivy Leaguer, was frankly
puzzled at why I spoke of something fairly simple at such excessive
length. I knew this was the first time he had heard what I was *really*
saying, and I didn't expect it to sink in. What I did expect was that
the next time he heard a woman speak these words, they would begin
to take hold.

At the dinner party in New York I made a scene. I brought harmless 37
sociability to an end. I insisted that everyone see that the little social
murders committed between men and women were the real subtext
of the evening, and that civilized converse was no longer possible
unless this underlying truth was addressed. I did this because these
were liberal intellectuals. They had heard it all before, many times,
and *still* they did not get it. It was as terrible for me to go home that
evening with the taste of ashes in my mouth as it was for everyone
else—we had all come expecting the warm pleasures of good food and
good conversation—but I couldn't have lived with myself that night
if I hadn't spoken up. Just as I would have had to speak up if the
conversation had suddenly turned politely anti-Semitic. Which it would
not have in this company.

The Jewishness inside me is an education. I see more clearly, can 38
think more inventively, because I can think analogously about "them"
and "us." That particular knowledge of being one among the many is
mine twice over. I have watched masters respond to "them" and "us,"
and I have learned. I wouldn't have missed being Jewish for the world.
It lives in me as a vital subculture, enriching my life as a writer, as an
American, and certainly as a woman.

Reprinted from *TIKKUN Magazine, a Bi-monthly Jewish Critique of Politics, Culture, and Society.*
Subscriptions are $31.00 per year from TIKKUN, 251 West 100th Street, 5th floor, New York, NY
10025.

THINKING ABOUT THE CONTENT

1. Gornick's essay reflects both a pride and prejudice of sorts. In what does she show pride? in what prejudice?
2. What does Gornick mean when she says she is twice an outsider? What does she mean when she states, "Outsiderness is the daily infliction of social invisibility"(27)? Have you ever experienced being an outsider? Explain.
3. How does Gornick make use of the work of such well-known Jewish talents as Milton Berle, Mel Brooks, Woody Allen, Saul Bellow, and Philip Roth to establish her thesis? What does she admire and what does she dislike about their work? Do you agree with her interpretation of their work? Explain.
4. Gornick says that she will "never again feel myself more of a Jew than a woman" (20). What does she mean? Why does she feel that way?
5. In paragraphs 35–37, Gornick recounts how she countered what she considered antifeminists remarks and situations. Do you think she reacted appropriately in each case? Explain.
6. Gornick says her "Jewishness inside me is an education" (38). What does she mean? What kind of education was it? What does she feel it prepared her for?

LOOKING AT STRUCTURE AND STYLE

7. Gornick divides her essay into four parts with breaks at the end of paragraphs 4, 21, and 31. What is the function of each of the four sections?
8. Gornick uses a variety of examples to develop her argument. From where do her examples come? How well do they work?
9. To whom do you think Gornick is writing? Explain your reasoning.

EXPLORING DISCUSSION AND WRITING TOPICS

10. Gornick describes the difference in the way girls and boys were raised in her Jewish community. Do these distinctions still exist today? Should distinctions be drawn? Are boys raised with different expectations than girls in some communities?
11. Gornick says she is threatened more by a sexist remark than she is by an anti-Semitic remark. Do you feel the same way? What kinds of prejudicial remarks personally offend you?
12. Begin an essay with the phrase "When I was growing up, the whole world was _____." Then recount a time or incident that changed your view of the world and your place in it.

THOMAS KENEALLY

While Steven Spielberg's film *Schindler's List* was widely acclaimed by the film world and most moviegoers when it appeared in 1994, it also created a negative stir among others. Spielberg was blamed for reminding people of an ugly period in history, of taking advantage of the Holocaust in order to make money from the film. Others blamed Jews for "always raising the issue of their persecution." Forget the Holocaust and put it behind us, some said. It's an old story. After all it's a Jewish problem, isn't it?

Thomas Keneally, author of the book from which the movie was made and a Distinguished Professor in University of California at Irvine's English and comparative literature department, disagrees. In the following essay, Keneally argues that the Holocaust should never be forgotten, that the prejudice that brought about the Holocaust is not a Jewish problem, but a European one, the apex of centuries of cross-cultural hatreds. To remember the Holocaust, he says, is to "receive the warnings inherent in it."

❦

The Holocaust: Never to Be Forgotten

The great irony is that people discover race hate the way lovers 1
discover love. It always seems utterly new and fresh to the hater, who like the lover feels that he has invented the emotion. And like love, race hate always expresses itself in the same clichés uttered as if the hater had discovered the principles of the universe. "They take our jobs." "They're everywhere." "They lust after our women." "They're just too damn different."

Racism is as human as love. In defining ourselves, the tribe we 2
belong to, its mores, we are tempted to believe in the inferiority of the culture and mores of other groups. Prejudice is the hairy backside of what we all need: a sense of identity. Sometimes, the more grand the cultural identity, the greater is the temptation to racism. The officers of the *Einsatzgruppen,* the SS killing squads, all loved their Mozart and their Goethe.

Often, particularly in America, race hate or group hate seems 3
rootless, as in the now famous case of the two young men who attacked

204

a Vietnamese stroller in Laguna Beach because they thought he was gay. It did not seem that the young men had any measurable reason, any damage they could point to or quantify, to explain why they wanted to beat the hell out of either Asians or gays. Did America's war experiences provide them with a primitive spur? The AIDS epidemic? A long bow to draw to believe that their own immune systems would somehow be strengthened by assaulting a perhaps-gay Vietnamese beach-walker.

We often righteously sneer at the racial and religious violence in   4
Northern Ireland and in the Balkans, but hate in both these cases is based on versions of history and measurable blood spilled in the past. There is more than legend to what the Serbs and Croatians did to each other since the Middle Ages, and to what Bosnian Muslims may once have done under Turkish rule. Catholics and Protestants in Northern Ireland can similarly point to historic massacres, even though they may be written too simple-mindedly into their respective maps of the world and their folk songs. In all cases, the hate is merely augmented rather than caused by religious difference. But at least the Northern Irish Catholics can point to very real injustices and miseries they have suffered. Protestants can point to their own heap of bodies, the real fear of IRA gunmen and of being absorbed into a Republic of Eire in which their civil rights may be curtailed for the sake of Catholic doctrine.

Race hate in America is not often based on any real disadvantage   5
suffered by the hater. It is based on stereotypes or rumor. But that's all the serpent in the gut needs to start secreting its poison.

Over every question of race or group hate lies the shadow of the   6
Holocaust, and for the moment the Holocaust questions are associated with Steven Spielberg's film of my book. As a Gentile, an Australian of Irish Catholic background, I have no hesitation in saying that the Holocaust should be talked about again and again and should not be forgotten. The reason is that the Holocaust is the most extreme version of rootless race hate in European history. Classic European anti-Semitism was based more on the idea that the Jews had killed Christ and were engaged in an anti-European philosophic and financial conspiracy than on any measurable harm done to Europe. No one could point to Jewish massacres of Christians, though in Poland and Germany vague but intense hate was able to be engineered into blaming Jews for the economic problems of both countries. But who could say, my mother was raped by a Jew, my father hanged by one?

The SS mastered the ultimate challenge of genocide: If you get the   7
hated group where you want them—behind wire—how do you ensure

that your now-perfected kingdom isn't sullied by too many corpses lying around and giving mute evidence of what happened to them? It's a question of processing the hated group. The Nazis devised the most bureaucratic, most extreme, most technological means of doing that. No question that the Cambodian tyrant Pol Pot would have loved to have been able to organize such methods to punish those of his own people who lacked "political correctness." No question that the tyrant Mengistu of Ethiopia would have loved to have been able to apply a final solution to the Eritreans of the Horn of Africa. But the Nazis really did it, and they were Europeans.

As a European who grew up very far from the scene, I don't feel   8 uselessly guilty about that, but I feel amazed and appalled. On a recent Sunday in Chicago, I met an elderly couple, the Schlesingers. A tall, sober-looking man and a small-boned, extremely handsome woman, they had been prisoners in Oskar Schindler's work camps. It struck me again, the ridiculous idea to which all the resources of the Reich were devoted—the idea that European civilization and the Schlesingers could not be allowed to coexist. The Schlesingers, urbane and pleasant as they are, could not be permitted to go on breathing. Only Schindler's intervention and their own intelligence ensured that they did continue to breathe.

Maybe one shouldn't be surprised, since the racist always talks   9 in terms of mass extermination. The last station on the hate line in his head is always something like Auschwitz, which stands as the most graphic instance of the kind of place to which hatred takes people.

And now the further great irony is that Jews like Steven Spielberg   10 are actually blamed for remembering, for reviving the memory that is not only Jewish but human. The Jews, we are told by the haters, remember their disasters in a particularly and hatefully Jewish way. And what about the fact that the Israeli right wing uses the Holocaust as a sanction for the persecution of Palestinians? Instead of addressing that real political problem, let's work on forgetting the Holocaust as fast as we can. Christians are allowed to remember the crucifixion of their Messiah, which occurred some time in the first century A.D.; Jews should be disqualified from remembering their dead of 1939–1945 because they are too good at it, too damn . . . Jewish!

But the Holocaust remains for me not a Jewish problem but a   11 European one. The Germans themselves are grappling with a conflict about this among their historians—how to fit this unique event into German history, into the German and European imagination. And that is not the Jews' fault. It is the fault of Europe, which has pursued anti-Semitism consistently since the Middle Ages and has still not yet repented of it. It is the grand Europe that all us people from the new world love to visit and rightly admire that brought race hate to its ultimate conclusion. That is why it is important for Gentiles to retain the memory of the Holocaust, and to receive the warnings inherent in it.

THINKING ABOUT THE CONTENT

1. How much do you know about the Holocaust? Is it enough to be able to agree or disagree with Keneally's viewpoint?
2. Keneally says the Holocaust should be talked about again and again. Do you agree? Why? What can we learn from remembering it?
3. Do you agree or disagree with what Keneally says in paragraph 5? Why? Can you provide examples to support or refute the point being made?
4. Keneally makes the case that the Holocaust is not a Jewish problem but a European one, in fact "the fault of Europe" (11). What do you think? Is he historically correct?
5. In the last paragraph Keneally says, "It is important for Gentiles to retain the memory of the Holocaust, and to receive the warnings inherent in it." What are the warnings?

LOOKING AT STRUCTURE AND STYLE

6. Is Keneally's thesis stated or implied? If stated, where?
7. What is the function of paragraph 4? How does it tie in with Keneally's thesis, if it does?
8. How smoothly does Keneally move from one point to the next? Is the transition easy to follow? Give some examples.
9. Where in the essay can you find some touches of a sarcastic tone?
10. Explain some of the following phrases Keneally uses:
    a. "Prejudice is the hairy backside of what we all need: a sense of identity" (2).
    b. "But that's all the serpent in the gut needs to start secreting its poison" (5).
    c. "The last station on the hate line in his [the racist's] head is always something like Auschwitz, which stands as the most graphic instance of the kind of place to which hatred takes people." (9).

EXPLORING DISCUSSION AND WRITING TOPICS

11. In paragraph 3, Keneally discusses an example of what he calls *rootless racism*. Write an essay that defines the term. Is it a good term for the kind of violence shown against the Vietnamese stroller mentioned in paragraph 3?

12. Write a critique of the movie or the book *Schindler's List.*
13. Research the Holocaust, and write an argument for or against the idea that the Holocaust must never be forgotten.
14. Pick an ethnic group and discuss the stereotypes associated with that group. How and why do those stereotypes sometimes lead to hate by some nonmembers of that group? How do these stereotypes lead to hatred and prejudice?
15. Some people believe that the Holocaust never happened, that it is all propaganda. Do you think it possible to create such a hoax? Why might some people wish to deny the existence of historical records?
16. Write about a current event of which you have some knowledge (see paragraph 4 for examples or use your own experience) and discuss the role of hate and prejudice as it pertains to the current event.

An Interview between Louis Farrakhan and Sylvester Monroe

In the 1930s, a black Islamic sect was founded by a Southern farm laborer named Elijah Muhammad who wanted to form a black nation and keep the races segregated. Malcolm X became a charismatic spokesman for the organization, and a young Louis Farrakhan became one of his followers. Malcolm X was later to break away from Muhammad goals and shed the idea of a separate black union. Because of his split, Malcolm X was assassinated by three of Muhammad's followers.

In 1981, Louis Farrakhan, still an outspoken advocate of antiwhite policies, announced the rebirth of the Nation of Islam and declared himself its "minister" and leader. Since then he has become what some consider the most controversial African-American leader for his "dual message of self-help and hate." While Farrakhan's message to blacks is independence and self-reliance, fairly or unfairly, most of his media attention has been from his racial slurs against Jews. He has been quoted, some say out of context, as calling Judaism a "dirty and gutter religion," and Hitler "a very great man" ("wickedly great," he later explained). Farrakhan, whose speaking fee ranges between $15,000 to $20,000, has powerful allure, as witnessed by his speech outdrawing a World Series game on the same night, filling the 16,500-seat Los Angeles Sports Arena, and his ability to draw 25,000 to the New York Convention Center. In October 1995, Farrakhan sponsored what was called the Million Man March on Washington, D.C., where hundreds of thousands of black men peacefully congregated to hear black leaders call for self-reliance and spiritual renewal in the African-American communities.

In late 1993, when Farrakhan's aid Khallid Abdul Muhammad spoke to students at Kean College in New Jersey, he blamed the Holocaust on its victims and attacked Jews for "sucking our blood in the black community." The speech set off sparks between Jewish and African-American leaders. While Farrakhan rebuked his aide and demoted him, he did not apologize for his anti-Jewish stance. *Time* magazine's February 18, 1994, issue made Farrakhan its cover story. The following is an excerpt from that issue, an interview with *Time* correspondent Sylvester Monroe.

"They Suck the Life from You"

TIME: *What is the message that the Nation of Islam is imparting to* 1
African Americans?

FARRAKHAN: That God is interested in us, that God has heard our
moaning and our groaning under the whip and the lash of our
oppressors and has now come to see about us. That's the appeal.

TIME: *How does the Nation of Islam take a person who has hit* 2
bottom with drugs or alcohol or crime and remake that person?

FARRAKHAN: Well, we can't do it without the help of God, and we
can't do it until we can reconnect that person to the source of truth
and goodness that is Allah.

So once we can reconnect him to God and show him his relationship to God, then you give him the knowledge of himself, his history.
So by teaching us our history beyond the cotton fields, beyond our
slave history in America, and teaching us our connection to the great
rulers of ancient civilizations, the great builders of the pyramids and
the great architects of civilization and teaching us our relationship
to the father of medicine, the father of law, the father of mathematics
and science and religion, this makes us desire now to come up out
of our ignorance and achieve the best that we possibly can achieve.
And this is what begins to transform the person's life.

TIME: *It has sometimes appeared that you were building this sense* 3
of self-esteem by putting down another people.

FARRAKHAN: Now the truth of the matter is that white supremacists
built a world on that ideology. If that system of white supremacy is
based on falsehood, then the truth will attack that system at its
foundation and it will begin to tumble down.

Now the truth of the matter is, whites are superior. They are
not superior because they are born superior. They are superior because they have been the ruling power that God has permitted them
to rule. They have had the wisdom and the guidance to rule while
most of the dark world or the darker people of the world have been,
as they have called it, asleep.

Now it's the awakening of all the darker people of the world,
and we are awakening at the level that the white world is now
beginning to decline. And this is what Brother Khallid was talking
about in his speech; I could not say he's a liar, [that] he's wrong.
But this should never be taught out of the spirit of mockery.

And so to tear down another people to lift yourself up is not proper. But to tell the truth, to tear down the mind built on a false premise of white supremacy, that is nothing but proper because that will allow whites to relate to themselves as well as to other human beings as human beings.

TIME: *So what Khallid did, was that wrong?*   4

FARRAKHAN: To me, it is highly improper in that you make a mockery over people. So why should we mock them? Why should we goad them into a behavior that is so easy for them to do harm to black people? And that's why I rebuked him.

TIME: *Have Khallid's remarks damaged your relationship with the*   5
mainstream black civil rights leadership?

FARRAKHAN: I don't feel that we can go down the road to liberation without a John Jacob, without a Jesse Jackson, without a Dorothy Height, without a Coretta Scott King or a Congressional Black Caucus or an N.A.A.C.P.

I mean, I have grown to the point by God's grace, that I see the value of each and every one of these persons to the overall struggle of our people.

I feel that not only do they have something to offer me, but I have something to offer them. I'm not trying to be mainstream. I don't even know what that is. I don't know whether any black has ever achieved mainstream. But I do know this. I want the unity of black organizations and black leaders that we might form a united front and seriously discuss what we can do to better the condition of our people.

TIME: *Has there been any discussion about just that?*   6

FARRAKHAN: We have never got to the point where we would sit down to open up these kinds of discussions. Unfortunately, there are those who saw in me a poison that would infect that group. And so they used their influence to push that group away from me. Even if they liked me, they could not associate with me for fear of what it would do to them professionally and economically.

So now we have to get to this talk of anti-Semitism. Am I really, anti-Semitic? Do I really want extermination of Jewish people? Of course, the answer is no. Now here's where the problem is. When I am accused of being a Hitler, a black Hitler, because of my oratorical ability and my ability to move people, there is fear that I'm not under control. By the grace of God, I shall never be under the control of those who do not want the liberation of our people. I cannot do that.

The idea is to isolate me, and hopefully, through the media and everybody calling me a hater, a racist, an anti-Semite, that I would just dry up and go away.

Now they have done this for 10 years, and I have not gone away. Now fortunately or unfortunately, they have forced other black leaders into silence on the basic issues of race and color and economics, and Farrakhan now has emerged as the voice that speaks to the hurt of our people.

Now I'm going to come to something that may get me in a lot of trouble. But I've got to speak the truth. What is a bloodsucker? When they land on your skin, they suck the life from you to sustain their life.

In the '20s and '30s and '40s, up into the '50s, the Jews were the primary merchants in the black community. Wherever we were, they were. What was their role? We bought food from them; we bought clothing from them; we bought furniture from them; we rented from them. So if they made profit from us, then from our life they drew life and came to strength. They turned it over to the Arabs, the Koreans and others, who are there now doing what? Sucking the lifeblood of our own community.

Every black artist, or most of them who came to prominence, who are their managers, who are their agents? Does the agent have the talent or the artist? But who reaps the benefits? Come on. We die penniless and broke, but somebody else is sucking from us. Who surrounds Michael Jackson? Is it us?

See, Brother, we've got to look at what truth is. You throw it out there as if to say this is some of the same old garbage that was said in Europe. I don't know about no garbage said in Europe.

But I know what I'm seeing in America. And because I see that black people, Sylvester, in the intellectual fields and professional fields are not going to be free until there is a new relationship with the Jewish community, then I feel that what I'm saying has to ultimately break that relationship.

Just like they felt it necessary to break my relationship with the Black Caucus, I feel it absolutely necessary to break the old relationship of the black intellectual and professional with the Jewish community and restructure it along lines of reciprocity, along lines of fairness and equity.

TIME: *How much does this black/Jewish controversy actually wind 7 up hurting black people?*

FARRAKHAN: I did not recognize the degree to which Jews held control over black professionals, black intellectuals, black entertainers, black sports figures; Khallid did not lie when he said that.

My ultimate aim is the liberation of our people. So if we are to be liberated, it's good to see the hands that are holding us. And we need to sever those hands from holding us that we may be a free people, that we may enter into a better relationship with them than we presently have.

So yes, in one sense it's a loss, but in the ultimate sense it's a gain. Because when I saw that, I recognized that the black man will never be free until we address the problem of the relationship between blacks and Jews.

TIME: *If you could tell the readers of TIME magazine anything you want to tell them about Farrakhan or the Nation of Islam, what would you say to them, or do you even care?* 8

FARRAKHAN: Of course I care.

I would hope that the American people and black people would give us a chance to speak to them not on a 30-second sound bite or not even through TIME magazine or any other white-managed magazine or newspaper but allow us to come to the American people to state our case.

I would hope that before the House of Representatives or the Senate will follow the advice of others to do things to hurt the Nation of Islam and our efforts in America at reforming our people, that you would invite us before the Senate or before members of the House of Representatives to question me and us on anything that I have ever said in the past.

And if they can show me that I'm a racist or an anti-Semite, with all of the legal brilliance that's in the government, and I, from that lofty place will apologize to the world for misrepresenting what I believed to be the truth.

THINKING ABOUT THE CONTENT

1. What, based on the interview, seems to be the message that the Nation of Islam is imparting? What is your opinion of the message?
2. How well do you think Farrakhan answered the third question? Is Farrakhan "putting down another people" (the Jews)? whites?
3. Farrakhan says in answer to *Time*'s sixth question, "Am I really anti-Semitic? . . . Of course, the answer is no." Yet, later in his answer he seems to call Jews "bloodsuckers," and says, "black people . . . in the intellectual fields and professional fields are not going to be free until

there is a new relationship with the Jewish community. . . ." Can what
he says be called anti-Semitic? Explain.

4. Is Farrakhan correct to blame the Jewish merchants from the 1920s to
the 1950s for "sucking the lifeblood" of the black community? If true,
how did they do this? What did Farrakhan expect them to do?

5. What proof does Farrakhan offer that Jews hold "control over black
professionals, black intellectuals, black entertainers, black sports figures"
(7)?

6. Farrakhan has been accused of being "a black Hitler," stirring up hatred
against the Jews as Hitler did in the 1930s. Does Farrakhan defend himself
against this accusation? What do you think? Is he a demagogue?

LOOKING AT STRUCTURE AND STYLE

7. How well do you think Farrakhan answered the questions put to him?
Was he direct or evasive in some cases? Discuss your opinion.

8. Select and react to some of the language Farrakhan uses. How would
you describe his rhetoric? Would you be interested in hearing him speak?
Explain.

EXPLORING DISCUSSION AND WRITING TOPICS

9. Research the Nation of Islam and write about one aspect of it: its founders,
its tenets, its history, its appeal, its contribution to the African-American
community, and so on.

10. Support or refute the Nation of Islam's idea of black segregation.

11. Write about what you would need to know to understand better what
Farrakhan means by "the liberation of our people" (7). Or, write what
you think he means.

12. In historical fact, Jews played a major role in supporting the black civil
rights movement and are among the first to be heard from in demanding
special preference for blacks. Do some research and write an essay that
counters Farrakhan's statement that Jewish people have oppressed African
Americans.

Cornel West, professor of African American studies and philosophy of religion at Harvard University, is considered by many to be one of the most eloquent, logical, and significant black voices in America today. His book *Race Matters* is widely read and held in high regard. He, along with liberal Jewish intellectual Michael Lerner (See the unit on Lifestyles) have coauthored *Jews and Blacks: Let the Healing Begin,* in which both men trade experiences and ideas that challenge our thinking about race.

The following essay was one of several by Jewish and African-American scholars who were asked to express their views as part of *Time* magazine's cover story on Louis Farrakhan from which the previous reading selection was taken. West believes that we have "failed miserably" to talk about the underlying issue regarding the furor over the Nation of Islam and Louis Farrakhan, which is "how to talk about and fight all forms of xenophobia in American life."

How Do We Fight Xenophobia?

The fundamental issue regarding the unadulterated bigotry of Khallid Abdul Muhammad, the anti-Semitic claims of Minister Louis Farrakhan and the vicious demonization of both black Islamic fellow citizens by the mainstream media is—how do we talk about and fight all forms of xenophobia in American life? So far, we have failed miserably. Instead we have become even more polarized, owing to our distrust of one another and our flagrant disregard for the transformative possibilities of high-quality public conversation. 1

Let us go back to the beginning of this sad episode, namely, Minister Louis Farrakhan's remarks about Hitler, Judaism and the link of Jewish power to black social misery. Most Americans believe Minister Farrakhan praised Adolf Hitler and, by implication, condoned the evils done to the Jewish people. Yet this is simply wrong. As Minister Farrakhan has noted on many occasions, his statement that Hitler was "wickedly great"—like Alexander, Caesar, Napoleon and Stalin— meant that Hitler was famous for his pernicious ability to conquer, destroy and dominate others. Furthermore, Hitler hated black people 2 with great passion. And given Minister Farrakhan's devotion to the cause of black freedom, he would not claim that Hitler was *morally* great. Nevertheless, the main stream press portrayed Minister Farrakhan as a Nazi—that is, a devil in our midst. Surely, if we believe Minister Farrakhan was *morally* wrong to have once held that whites were devils, it is wrong of us to believe he is a devil.

His obsession with connecting black social misery to Jewish power,   3
including his ugly characterization of Judaism as a "gutter religion" used to legitimate the state of Israel at the expense of Palestinians, is vintage anti-Semitic ideology. Judaism—like any religion—can be used for good or bad. His claim that Jews owned 75% of enslaved Africans in this country at a time when there were about 4 million black slaves and 5,000 Jewish slaveholders reveals this obsession. In fact, in 1861, Jews constituted roughly 0.2% of Southerners (20,000 out of 9 million) and 0.3% of slaveholders (5,000 out of 1,937,625).

Minister Farrakhan may be rightly upset that antislavery activism   4
was not predominant among the 150,000 Jews then in America, or that there is no record of any Southern rabbi who publicly criticized slavery—but there were militant Jewish abolitionists (including Northern rabbis) such as Isidor Busch, Michael Helprin, Rabbi David Einhorn and August Bondi (who fought with John Brown). The expulsion of Jews from Tennessee by Ulysses S. Grant's Order No. 11 in 1862 and new waves of poor East European Jews would yield a more antiracist activism among American Jewry. But even though Minister Farrakhan's anti-Semitic claims are false and hurtful, this does not mean that he is a Nazi or that he has a monopoly on anti-Semitism in American.

If we are to engage in a serious dialogue about blacks and Jews,   5
and how best to fight xenophobia, we must not cast all anti-Semitic statements as pro-Nazi ones, vilify black anti-Semites and soft-pedal white anti-Semites (or Jewish antiblack or anti-Arab racists) or overlook the role of some Jewish conservatives as defenders of policies that contribute to black social misery. We cannot proceed if we assume the worst of each other—that the majority of black people are unreconstructed anti-Semites or that the majority of Jews are plotting conspiracies to destroy black people. I have great faith and confidence in the moral wisdom of most blacks and Jews in regard to vulgar racist bigotry—yet our communities are shot through with more subtle forms. This is why it is incumbent upon blacks and Jews to fight *all* forms of xenophobia even as we try to alleviate the poverty and paranoia that feed so much despair and distrust in our time.

As for my brothers, Khallid Abdul Muhammad and Minister Louis   6
Farrakhan, I beseech you in the precious name of the black freedom

struggle and in the compassionate spirit of Islam to channel your efforts of black self-help in ways that do not mirror the worst of what American civilization has done to black people.

We rightly will not permit a double-standard treatment that casts 7 you less than human, but we also must not allow your—or anyone else's—utterance to tar the black freedom struggle with the brush of immorality. For the sake of Fannie Lou Hamer, Abraham Joshua Heschel and El-Hajj Malik el-Shabazz—and those many thousands gone—we can do no other.

THINKING ABOUT THE CONTENT

1. What is *xenophobia*? How does it relate to racial and religious prejudice? to Louis Farrakhan's remarks about Jews?
2. In many places, the media reported that Louis Farrakhan praised Hitler as "a great man." How does West attempt to explain Farrakhan's remarks? Is he convincing? Why?
3. What is West's reaction to the mainstream press portraying Farrakhan as "a Nazi—that is, a devil in our midst" (2)? Is his reasoning balanced?
4. West says that any religion "can be used for good or bad" (3). What does he mean? Can you think of some examples to support this claim?
5. What does West suggest we must do "if we are to engage in serious dialogue about blacks and Jews, and how best to fight xenophobia" (5). What do you think of his suggestions?

LOOKING AT STRUCTURE AND STYLE

6. What audience does West seem to be addressing? How does he switch audiences in the last two paragraphs?
7. How would you describe the tone of the essay? What are some words or phrases West uses to establish his tone?
8. What is the primary function of paragraphs 3–4?
9. What attitude toward Louis Farrakhan's anti-Semitism does West hold? What words help reveal his attitude?
10. How well does West argue his claim that Farrakhan should not be labeled a "devil" (2) or a "Nazi" (4)?

EXPLORING DISCUSSION AND WRITING TOPICS

11. Write an essay defining xenophobia and its effects.
12. Read all or parts of Cornel West's *Race Matters* and write your evaluation or reactions to some of his views.
13. Write an essay on how any religion "can be used for good or bad (3)."

14. Write an essay showing why society cannot proceed if races assume the worst of each other.

SOME RESEARCH SOURCES DEALING WITH PREJUDICE

The following sources may be useful if you choose to do more reading or pursue a research project dealing with issues prompted by the reading selections in this unit.

Allport, Gordon. *The Nature of Prejudice.* New York: Addison-Wesley, 1979.

Cole, Jim. *Filtering People: Understanding and Confronting Our Prejudices.* Philadelphia: New Society, 1990.

Davis, Angela. *Women, Culture, and Politics.* New York: Random House, 1989.

DeMott, Benjamin. *The Trouble with Friendship: Why Americans Can't Think Straight About Race.* New York: Grove/Atlantic, 1996.

Hackett, David A. *The Buchenwald Report.* Boulder: Westview Press, 1995.

Hockenos, Paul. *Free to Hate.* New York: Routledge, 1994.

Lang, Susan. *Extremist Groups in America.* New York: Franklin Watts, 1990.

Lerner, Michael, and Cornel West. *Jews and Blacks: Let the Healing Begin.* New York: TIKKUN, 1995.

Marin, Peter. *Freedom and its Discontents.* South Royalton, VT: Steerforth, 1995.

Moe, Barbara. *Coping with Bias Incidents.* Rosen Publishing Group, 1993.

Osborn, Kevin. *Tolerance.* New York: Rosen Publishing Group, 1990.

Paris, Erna. *The End of Days: The Story of Tolerance, Tyranny and the Expulsion of the Jews from Spain.* New York: Prometheus, 1995.

Pascoe, Elaine. *Racial Prejudice.* New York: Rosen Publishing Group, 1985.

Ridgeway, James. *Blood in the Face: The KKK, Aryan Nations, Nazi Skinheads, and the Rise of the New White Culture.* New York: Thunder Mouth, 1995.

Ruggiero, Vincent Ryan. *Beyond Feelings: A Guide to Critical Thinking.* Mountain View, CA: Mayfield, 1995.

Sandel, Michael J. "America's Search for a New Public Philosophy," *Atlantic Monthly* (March 1996): 57ff.

Race and Rights

At the heart of racism is the religious assertion that God made a creative mistake when He brought some people into being.

—FRIEDRICH OTTO HERTZ

The existence of any pure race with special endowments is a myth, as is the belief that there are races all of whose members are foredoomed to eternal inferiority.

—FRANZ BOAS

Mere connection with what is known as a superior race will not permanently carry an individual forward unless the individual has worth.

—BOOKER T. WASHINGTON

In the gain or loss of one race all the rest have equal claim.

—JAMES RUSSELL LOWELL

No matter how much respect, no matter how much recognition whites show towards me, as far as I'm concerned, as long as it is not shown to every one of our people in this country, it doesn't exist for me.

—MALCOLM X

The difference of race is one of the reasons why I fear war may always exist; because race implies difference, difference implies superiority, and superiority leads to predominance.

—BENJAMIN DISRAELI

The ultimate end of all revolutionary social change is to establish the sanctity of human life, the dignity of man, the right of every human being to liberty and well-being.

—EMMA GOLDMAN

I have a dream that one day this nation will rise up and live out the true meaning of its creed: "We hold these truths to be self-evident that all men are created equal." . . . I have a dream that my four little children will one day live in a nation where they will not be judged by the color of their skin but by the content of their character. I have a dream today.

—MARTIN LUTHER KING, JR.

WHILE THE CIVIL RIGHTS MOVEMENT provoked the end of official racial segregation, racism remains a serious divisive social issue in the United States. Some argue that discriminatory practices and segregationist laws have been abolished and wonder why there is a problem, but others argue that racism still has not diminished in any significant way. The media frequently describes the United States as a racist society, and that view seems to have created a mood of cultural despair about the possibility of racial progress. Questions being raised are: Is racial prejudice innate, or is it culturally acquired? Does the United States owe blacks compensation for the legacy of slavery as some blacks demand? Did the civil rights movement succeed or fail in diminishing racism? Are those involved in the civil rights establishment perpetuating racism in order to keep their jobs? Are there "race activists" deliberately poisoning the minds of the younger generation? Can persons of color be racists?

Yehudi Webster, an African-American sociologist at California State University, writes in *The Racialization of America*, "It is not 'race' but a *practice* of racial classification that bedevils the society." He argues that racial statistics create a reality of racial division, which then requires solutions such as school busing, affirmative action, and multicultural education. Such programs, Webster believes, heighten racial awareness, which then creates more problems and animosity. "By creating social welfare programs based on race rather than on need, the government sets citizens against one another because of perceived racial differences." Along these lines, writers Shelby Steele, Stephen Carter, and Stanley Crouch speak for black individualism and a "common humanity" based on national identity rather than racial identity.

On the other hand, Jon Michael Spencer, a professor of African-American studies at the University of North Carolina, feels that "to relinquish the notion of race—even though it's a cruel hoax—at this particular time is to relinquish our fortress against the powers and the principalities that still try to undermine us." For Spencer, "Race is not an essence but rather a metaphor pointing to cultural and historical differences." These differences he attributes to "whites and African peoples having existed for centuries at the opposite ends in the master-slave dialectic." In agreement is Molefi Kete Asante, chairman of Temple University's department of African-American studies, who is often called the "father of Afrocentricity." Asante espouses black consciousness, black pride, and believes in a cultural and psychological affinity with Africa.

Then there are those who agree with Dinesh D'Souza, who argues in his highly controversial book *The End of Racism,* that "the generation that marched with Martin Luther King, Jr. may be too committed to the paradigm of racial struggle to see the possibility of progress." D'Souza believes it is time to stop advocating that race matters as the basis for identity and public policy, suggesting that blacks themselves are part of the race problem and experience "a kind of schizophrenia between their racial and American identities."

Writing about race in the *New Yorker,* Lawrence Wright says, "Whatever the word *race* may mean elsewhere in the world, or to the world of science, it is clear that in America the categories are arbitrary, confused, and hopelessly intermingled. In many cases, Americans don't know who they are, racially speaking." Wright cites a National Center for Health Statistics study that found 5.8 percent of the people who called themselves black were seen as white by a census interviewer, nearly one-third of the people identifying themselves as Asian were classified as white or black by observers, and 70 percent of the people who claimed to be Native Americans were identified as white or black. As Wright points out, such discrepancies "cast doubt on the dependability of race as a criterion for any statistical survey." Yet, racial statistics are used in such practices as monitoring and enforcing civil rights laws, in hiring and jury selection, in discriminatory housing practices, and in apportionment of political power.

While the issue of black and white race relationships has perhaps dominated the history of this country, our population encompasses many other racial and cultural identities as well. The reading selections in this unit deal with some of that diversity and its problems.

ANDREW HACKER

Andrew Hacker, professor of political science at Queens College, has authored several books, including *The End of the American Era, The United States: A Statistical Portrait of the American People,* and *Two Nations: Black and White, Separate, Hostile, Unequal* from which the following selection is taken. In *Two Nations,* Hacker offers a disturbing analysis of the conditions that he believes keep blacks and whites "dangerously far apart in their ability to participate fully in the American Dream." He asks, "Are we 'one nation under God' or two nations manacled by race?"

In this section from *Two Nations,* Hacker says, "Of course, no one who is white can understand what it is like to be black in America. Still, were they to spend time in a black body, here are some of the things they would learn."

❦

Being Black in America

Most white Americans will say that, all things considered, things   1
aren't so bad for black people in the United States. Of course,
they will grant that many problems remain. Still, whites feel there has
been steady improvement, bringing blacks closer to parity, especially
when compared with conditions in the past. Some have even been
heard to muse that it's better to be black, since affirmative action
policies make it a disadvantage to be white.

What white people seldom stop to ask is how they may benefit from   2
belonging to their race. Nor is this surprising. People who can see do not
regard their vision as a gift for which they should offer thanks. It may
also be replied that having a white skin does not immunize a person from
misfortune or failure. Yet even for those who fall to the bottom, being
white has a worth. What could that value be?

Let us try to find out by means of a parable: suspend disbelief for   3
a moment, and assume that what follows might actually happen:

The Visit

You will be visited tonight by an official you have never
met. He begins by telling you that he is extremely embarrassed.

The organization he represents has made a mistake, something that hardly ever happens.

According to their records, he goes on, you were to have been born black: to another set of parents, far from where you were raised.

However, the rules being what they are, this error must be rectified, and as soon as possible. So at midnight tonight, you will become black. And this will mean not simply a darker skin, but the bodily and facial features associated with African ancestry. However, inside you will be the person you always were. Your knowledge and ideas will remain intact. But outwardly you will not be recognizable to anyone you now know.

Your visitor emphasizes that being born to the wrong parents was in no way your fault. Consequently, his organization is prepared to offer you some reasonable recompense. Would you, he asks, care to name a sum of money you might consider appropriate? He adds that his group is by no means poor. It can be quite generous when the circumstances warrant, as they seem to in your case. He finishes by saying that their records show you are scheduled to live another fifty years—as a black man or woman in America.

How much financial recompense would you request?

When this parable has been put to white students, most seemed 4
to feel that it would not be out of place to ask for $50 million, or $1 million for each coming black year. And this calculation conveys, as well as anything, the value that white people place on their own skins. Indeed, to be white is to possess a gift whose value can be appreciated only after it has been taken away. And why ask so large a sum? Surely this needs no detailing. The money would be used, as best it could, to buy protections from the discriminations and dangers white people know they would face once they were perceived to be black.

Of course, no one who is white can understand what it is like to 5
be black in America. Still, were they to spend time in a black body, here are some of the things they would learn.

In the eyes of white Americans, being black encapsulates your identity. 6
No other racial or national origin is seen as having so pervasive a personality or character. Even if you write a book on Euclidean algorithms or Renaissance sculpture, you will still be described as a "black

author." Although you are a native American, with a longer lineage than most, you will never be accorded full membership in the nation or society. More than that, you early learn that this nation feels no need or desire for your physical presence. (Indeed, your people are no longer in demand as cheap labor.) You sense that most white citizens would heave a sigh of relief were you simply to disappear. While few openly propose that you return to Africa, they would be greatly pleased were you to make that decision for yourself.

Your people originated in Africa, and you want to feel pride in 7 your homeland. After all, it was where humanity began. Hence your desire to know more of its peoples and their history, their culture and achievements, and how they endure within yourself. W. E. B. Du Bois said it best: "two thoughts, two unrecognizable stirrings, two warring ideals in one black body."

Yet there is also your awareness that not only America, but also 8 much of the rest of the world, regards Africa as the primal continent: the most backward, the least developed, by almost every modern measure. Equally unsettling, Africa is regarded as barely worth the world's attention, a region no longer expected to improve in condition or status. During its periodic misfortunes—usually famine or slaughter—Africa may evoke compassion and pity. Yet the message persists that it must receive outside help, since there is little likelihood that it will set things right by itself.

Then there are the personal choices you must make about your 9 identity. Unless you want to stress a Caribbean connection, you are an American and it is the only citizenship you have. At the same time, you realize that this is a white country, which expects its inhabitants to think and act in white ways. How far do you wish to adapt, adjust, assimilate, to a civilization so at variance with your people's past? For example, there is the not-so-simple matter of deciding on your diction. You know how white people talk and what they like to hear. Should you conform to those expectations, even if it demands denying or concealing much of your self? After all, white America gives out most of the rewards and prizes associated with success. Your decisions are rendered all the more painful by the hypocrisy of it all, since you are aware that even if you make every effort to conform, whites will still not accept you as one of their own.

So to a far greater degree than for immigrants from other lands, 10 it rests on you to create your own identity. But it is still not easy to follow the counsel of Zora Neale Hurston: "Be as black as you want to be." For one thing, that choice is not always left to you. By citizenship and birth, you may count as an American, yet you find yourself agreeing with August Wilson when he says "We're a different people." Why else can you refer to your people as "folks" and "family," to one another as "sisters" and "brothers," in ways whites never can?

There are moments when you understand Toni Morrison's riposte, 11 "At no moment in my life have I ever felt as though I were an American." This in turn gives rise to feelings of sympathy with figures like Cassius Clay, H. Rap Brown, Lew Alcindor, and Stokely Carmichael, who decided to repatriate themselves as Muhammad Ali, Jamil Abdullah al-Amin, Kareem Abdul-Jabbar, and Kwame Touré.

Those choices are not just for yourself. There will be the per- 12 plexing—and equally painful—task of having to explain to your children why they will not be treated as other Americans: that they will never be altogether accepted, that they will always be regarded warily, if not with suspicion or hostility. When they ask whether this happens because of anything they have done, you must find ways of conveying that, no, it is not because of any fault of their own. Further, for reasons you can barely explain yourself, you must tell them that much of the world has decided that you are not and cannot be their equals; that this world wishes to keep you apart, a caste it will neither absorb nor assimilate.

You will tell your children this world is wrong. But, because that 13 world is there, they will have to struggle to survive, with scales weighted against them. They will have to work harder and do better, yet the result may be less recognition and reward. We all know life can be unfair. For black people, this knowledge is not an academic theory but a fact of daily life.

You find yourself granting that there are more black faces in places 14 where they were never seen before. Within living memory, your people were barred from major league teams; now they command the highest salaries in most professional sports. In the movies, your people had to settle for roles as servants or buffoons. Now at least some of them are cast as physicians, business executives, and police officials. But are things truly different? When everything is added up, white America still prefers its black people to be performers who divert them as athletes and musicians and comedians.

Yet where you yourself are concerned, you sense that in mainstream occupations, your prospects are quite limited. In most areas of employment, even after playing by the rules, you find yourself hitting a not-so-invisible ceiling. You wonder if you are simply corporate wallpaper, a protective coloration they find it prudent to display. You begin to suspect that a "qualification" you will always lack is white pigmentation.

In theory, all Americans with financial means and a respectable   15
demeanor can choose where they want to live. For over a generation, courts across the country have decreed that a person's race cannot be a reason for refusing to rent or sell a residence. However, the law seems to have had little impact on practice, since almost all residential areas are entirely black or white. Most whites prefer it that way. Some will say they would like a black family nearby, if only to be able to report that their area is integrated. But not many do. Most white Americans do not move in circles where racial integration wins social or moral credit.

This does not mean it is absolutely impossible for a black family   16
to find a home in a white area. Some have, and others undoubtedly will. Even so, black Americans have no illusions about the hurdles they will face. If you look outside your designated areas, you can expect chilly receptions, evasive responses, and outright lies: a humiliating experience, rendered all the more enraging because it is so repeated and prolonged. After a while, it becomes too draining to continue the search. Still, if you have the income, you will find an area to your liking; but it will probably be all black. In various suburbs and at the outer edges of cities, one can see well-kept homes, outwardly like other such settings. But a closer view shows all the householders to be black.

This is the place to consider residential apartheid—and that is   17
what it is—in its full perspective. Black segregation differs markedly from that imposed on any other group. Even newly arrived immigrants are more readily accepted in white neighborhoods.

Nor should it be assumed that most black householders prefer   18
the racial ratios in areas where they currently reside. Successive surveys have shown that, on average, only about one in eight say they prefer a neighborhood that is all or mostly black, which is the condition most presently confront. The vast majority—some 85 percent—state they would like an equal mixture of black and white neighbors. Unfortunately, this degree of racial balance has virtually no chance of being realized. The reason, very simply, is that hardly any whites will live in a neighborhood or community where half the residents are black. So directly or indirectly, white Americans have the power to decide the racial composition of communities and neighborhoods. Most egregious have been instances where acts of arson or vandalism force black families to leave. But such methods are exceptional. There are other, less blatant, ways to prevent residential integration from passing a certain "tipping" point.

Here we have no shortage of studies. By and large, this research   19
agrees that white residents will stay—and some new ones may move
in—if black arrivals do not exceed 8 percent. But once the black
proportion passes that point, whites begin to leave the neighborhood
and no new ones will move in. The vacated houses or apartments will
be bought or rented by blacks, and the area will be on its way to
becoming all black.

What makes integration difficult if not impossible is that so few   20
whites will accept even a racial composition reflecting the overall
national proportion of 12 or 13 percent. In this regard, one or two
attempts have been made to impose ceilings on the number of black
residents in housing projects and developments, so as not to frighten
away whites. Starrett City in New York has used this strategy, as has
Atrium Village in Chicago. According to some legal readings these
procedures are unconstitutional, since they treat racial groups differently. Those administering such "benign quotas" have found they must
maintain two sets of waiting lists. This has been necessary to ensure
that the next families chosen for vacant apartments will preserve the
prevailing racial ratio. Given the preference of most blacks for integrated housing, quite a few tend to apply, and they invariably outnumber the whites on the list. The result is that black applicants have to wait
longer, and are less likely to get their first choice of accommodation.

Whites and blacks who want to achieve and maintain interracial   21
housing—itself a rarity—find they are forced to defend "benign quotas" that are biased against some blacks, since there are fewer "black"
places. Racial quotas also tend to put blacks on the spot. On the one
hand, few are willing to publicly support a ceiling for people of their
race. Even so, most of the black householders already in residence
would prefer that the racial ratio remain stabilized. After all, they
themselves underwent a wait because they wanted to live in a racially
integrated setting. Yet preserving the equation pits them against other
blacks impatient to get in.

If many whites say they support racial integration in principle,   22
even if this only means a token black neighbor, at least as many do
not want any blacks living near them at all. One question, certainly,
is how far this resistance is based solely on race, or whether the reasons
have more to do with culture or class. White people themselves vary
in income and other signals of status, and every section of the nation
has hierarchies among white neighborhoods. Even in an area where
everyone earns essentially the same income, many residents would not
want a homosexual couple on their block, or a neighbor who parked
a business van ("PARAGON PEST CONTROL") in his driveway every

night. Simply being a fellow white is not enough to make a person a desired neighbor.

This granted, we can try to isolate the element of race by positing   23
some "ideal" black neighbors: persons with professional credentials or those who hold administrative positions in respected organizations. Give them sophisticated tastes; make them congenial in demeanor; and have them willing to care about their property and the area as a whole. And allow, further, that a fair number of whites might not object to having one or two such households nearby. Why, then, would such open-minded neighbors start worrying if the number of black families—granting that all of them are impeccably middle class—seems to be approaching a racial "tipping" point?

The first reason is that there is no assurance that the black propor-   24
tion will stay below the "tipping" figure. Word gets around among black families when a "white" neighborhood appears willing to accept a measure of integration. Rental and real estate agents are also quick to note this fact and begin recommending the area to black customers. As a result, whenever homes and apartments become vacant, a visible number of those coming to look at them appear to be black. Nor should this be surprising. Some black Americans want more interracial exposure for themselves and their children. Others may not share this wish, but they know that better schools and safer streets are more apt to be where whites are.

Longitudinal studies, based on tracing census tracts, show that   25
whites begin to move out once the black proportion reaches somewhere between 10 and 20 percent. Moreover, this happens even when the blacks who move in have the same economic and social standing as the white residents. What is it, then, that makes white Americans unwilling to risk having black neighbors? Some of the reasons are familiar and openly stated. Others involve fears less easily articulated or admitted.

To the minds of most Americans, the mere presence of black people   26
is associated with a high incidence of crime, residential deterioration, and lower educational attainment. Of course, most whites are willing to acknowledge that these strictures do not apply to all blacks. At the same time, they do not want to have to worry about trying to distinguish blacks who would make good neighbors from those who would not. To which is added the suspicion that if more black families arrive, it would take only one or two undesirables to undermine any interracial amity.

Even if all one's black neighbors were vouchsafed to be middle class   27
or better, there may still be misgivings about their teenaged children. To

start, there is the well-known wariness of white parents that their children—especially their daughters—could begin to make black friends. Plus the fear that even less intimate contacts will influence the vocabulary and diction, even the academic commitments, of their own offspring. And if white parents are already uneasy over the kinds of music their children enjoy, imagine their anxieties at hearing an even greater black resonance. Along with the worry that some of the black youths on the block might display a hostile demeanor, clouding the congenial ambience most Americans seek.

Americans have extraordinarily sensitive antennae for the color- 28 ations of neighborhoods. In virtually every metropolitan area, white householders can rank each enclave by the racial makeup of the residents. Given this knowledge, where a family lives becomes an index of its social standing. While this is largely an economic matter, proximity to blacks compounds this assessment. For a white family to be seen as living in a mixed—or changing—neighborhood can be construed as a symptom of surrender, indeed as evidence that they are on a downward spiral.

If you are black, these white reactions brand you as a carrier of 29 contaminations. No matter what your talents or attainments, you are seen as infecting a neighborhood simply because of your race. This is the ultimate insult of segregation. It opens wounds that never really heal and leaves scars to remind you how far you stand from full citizenship.

Except when you are in your own neighborhood, you feel always on 30 display. On many occasions, you find you are the only person of your race present. You may be the only black student in a college classroom, the only black on a jury, the sole black at a corporate meeting, the only one at a social gathering. With luck, there may be one or two others. You feel every eye is on you, and you are not clear what posture to present. You realize that your presence makes whites uncomfortable; most of them probably wish you were not there at all. But since you are, they want to see you smile, so they can believe that you are being treated well. Not only is an upbeat air expected, but you must never show exasperation or anger, let alone anything that could look like a chip on your shoulder. Not everyone can keep such tight control. You don't find it surprising that so many black athletes and entertainers seek relief from those tensions.

Even when not in white company, you know that you are forever 31 in their conversations. Ralph Ellison once said that to whites, you are an "invisible man." You know what he meant. Yet for all that, you and your people have been studied and scrutinized and dissected, caricatured, and pitied or deplored, as no other group ever has. You see yourself reduced to data in research, statistics in reports. Each year, the nation asks how many of your teenagers have become pregnant, how many of your young men are in prison. Not only are you continually on view; you are always on trial.

What we have come to call the media looms large in the lives of   32
almost all Americans. Television and films, newspapers and magazines, books and advertising, all serve as windows on a wider world, providing real and fantasized images of the human experience. The media also help us to fill out our own identities, telling us about ourselves, or the selves we might like to be.

If you are black, most of what is available for you to read and   33
watch and hear depicts the activities of white people, with only rare and incidental allusions to persons like yourself. Black topics and authors and performers appear even less than your share of the population, not least because the rest of America doesn't care to know about you. Whites will be quick to point out that there have been successful "black" programs on radio and television, as well as popular black entertainers and best-selling authors. Yet in these and other instances, it is whites who decide which people and productions will be underwritten, which almost always usually means that "black" projects will have to appeal to whites as well. You sometimes sense that much that is "black" is missing in artists like Jessye Norman and Toni Morrison, Paul Robeson, and Bill Cosby, who you sense must tailor their talents to white audiences. You often find yourself wishing they could just be themselves, among their own people.

At the same time, you feel frustration and disgust when white   34
America appropriates your music, your styles, indeed your speech and sexuality. At times, white audiences will laud the originality of black artists and performers and athletes. But in the end, they feel more comfortable when white musicians and designers and writers—and athletic coaches—adapt black talents to white sensibilities.

Add to this your bemusement when movies and television series   35
cast more blacks as physicians and attorneys and executives than one will ever find in actual hospitals or law firms or corporations. True, these depictions can serve as role models for your children, encouraging their aspirations. At the same time, you do not want white audiences to conclude that since so many of your people seem to be doing well, little more needs to be done.

Then there are those advertisements showing groups of people.   36
Yes, one of them may be black, although not too black, and always

looking happy to be in white company. Still, these blacks are seldom in the front row, or close to the center. Even worse, you think you have detected a recent trend: in advertisements that include a person of color, you see Asians being used instead of blacks.

To be sure, textbooks and lesson plans now include allusions to "contri-   37
butions" made by Americans of many ancestries. Children are taught how the Chinese built the railroads, and that Hispanics have a vibrant and varied culture. Even acknowledging these nods, the curriculums of the nation's schools and colleges focus mainly on the achievements of white people. The emphasis is on English origins, and that those settlers brought their institutions and ideas from the British Isles. Most Americans with European ancestors can identify with this "Anglo-Saxon" past. Descendants of slaves do not find it as easy. Whether black children are alienated by the content of the curriculum is a matter of controversy, which will be considered later on. At this point, it can be said that few teachers attempt to explain how the human beings consigned to slavery shaped the structure and sensibilities of the new nation. Apart from brief allusions to a Sojourner Truth or a Benjamin Banneker, your people appear as passive victims and faceless individuals.

In much the same vein, white children can be led to see how the   38
travails of Shakespeare's heroes shed light on the human condition. Or that Jane Austen's heroines have messages for Americans of today. Nor is this impossible for black Americans. Ralph Ellison, raised in rural Alabama, recalled that reading Ezra Pound and Sigmund Freud give him a broader sense of life. Jamaica Kincaid has cited Charlotte Brontë as her first literary influence. Yet no matter how diligently you think about these authors and their ideas, you find that much of your life is not reflected in European learning. You often feel that there is a part of yourself, your soul, that Europe cannot reach. As in Countée Cullen's lines:

> What is Africa to me:
> Copper sun or scarlet sea,
> Jungle star or jungle track,
> Strong bronzed men, or regal black,
> Women from whose loins I sprang
> When the birds of Eden sang?

Whether you would like to know more white people is not an   39
easy question to answer. So many of the contacts you have with them are stiff and uneasy, hardly worth the effort. If you are a woman, you

may have developed some cordial acquaintances among white women at your place of work, since women tend to be more relaxed when among themselves. Still, very few black men and women can say that they have white "friends," if by that is meant people they confide in or entertain in their homes.

Of course, friendships often grow out of shared experiences. People with similar backgrounds can take certain things for granted when with one another. In this respect, you and white people may not have very much in common. At the same time, by no means all your outlooks and interests relate to your race. There probably are at least a few white people you would like to know better. It just might be that some of them would like to know you. But as matters now stand, the chances that these barriers will be broken do not appear to be very great. [40]

Societies create vocabularies, devising new terms when they are needed, and retaining old ones when they serve a purpose. Dictionaries list words as obsolete or archaic, denoting that they are no longer used or heard. But one epithet survives, because people want it to. Your vulnerability to humiliation can be summed up in a single word. That word, of course, is "nigger." [41]

When a white person voices it, it becomes a knife with a whetted edge. No black person can hear it with equanimity or ignore it as "simply a word." This word has the force to pierce, to wound, to penetrate, as no other has. There have, of course, been terms like "kike" and "spic" and "chink." But these are less frequently heard today, and they lack the same emotional impact. Some nonethnic terms come closer, such as "slut" and "fag" and "cripple." Yet, "nigger" stands alone with its power to tear at one's insides. It is revealing that whites have never created so wrenching an epithet for even the most benighted members of their own race. [42]

Black people may use "nigger" among themselves, but with a tone and intention that is known and understood. Even so, if you are black, you know white society devised this word and keeps it available for use. (Not officially, of course, or even in print; but you know it continues to be uttered behind closed doors.) Its persistence reminds you that you are still perceived as a degraded species of humanity, a level to which whites can never descend. [43]

You and your people have problems, far more than your share. And it is not as if you are ignorant of them, or wish to sweep them under a rug. But how to frame your opinions is not an easy matter. For example, what should you say about black crime or addiction or out-of-wedlock pregnancies? Of course, you have much to say on these and other topics, and you certainly express your ideas when you are [44] among your own people. And you can be critical—very critical—of a lot of behavior you agree has become common among blacks.

However, the white world also asks that black people conduct 45 these discussions in public. In particular, they want to hear you condemn black figures they regard as outrageous or irresponsible. This cannot help but annoy you. For one thing, you have never asked for white advice. Yet whites seem to feel that you stand in need of their tutelage, as if you lack the insight to understand your own interests. Moreover, it makes sense for members of a minority to stand together, especially since so many whites delight in magnifying differences among blacks. Your people have had a long history of being divided and conquered. At the same time, you have no desire to be held responsible for what every person of your color thinks or does. You cannot count how many times you have been asked to atone for some utterances of Louis Farrakhan, or simply to assert that he does not speak for you. You want to retort that you will choose your own causes and laments. Like other Americans, you have no obligation to follow agendas set by others.

As it happens, black Americans can and do disagree on racial 46 matters, not to mention a host of other issues. Thus a survey conducted in 1990 found that 78 percent of those polled said they preferred to think of themselves as "black," and another 20 percent chose "African-American," while the remaining 2 percent stayed with "Negro." Another study by a team of black social scientists found that less than a quarter of the blacks they polled felt that black parents should give their children African names. Indeed, on a wide range of matters, there is no fixed, let alone official, black position. Yet it is amazing how often white people ask you to tell them how "black people" think about some individual or issue.

Then there are the accusations of inconsistency. As when you seem 47 to favor taking race into consideration in some areas, but not in others. Or that you support a double standard, which allows separate criteria to be used for blacks in employment or education. Well, as it happens, you do believe:

- That discrimination against blacks remains real and calls for radical remedies; yet you cannot take seriously the argument that these compensatory actions will cause whites to suffer from "reverse" discrimination.

- That blacks have every right to attend dominantly white schools; yet once they are there, they should not be taken to task for spending much of their time with classmates of their own race.

- That it is important to preserve historically black colleges; yet you would feel entitled to object if some other schools were to designate themselves as "historically white."

- That racism is often the key reason why white voters rally behind white candidates; yet when blacks support a candidate of their own race, you do not see this as expressing racism.

- That while you reject censorship, you would prefer that a book like *Huckleberry Finn* not be assigned in high school classes, since its ubiquitous use of "nigger" sustains a view of blacks that can only hurt your people. Nor are you persuaded that the typical teacher can make clear Mark Twain's intentions, or put them in perspective, for white teenagers.

It will often seem to you as if black people's opinions are constantly under scrutiny by the white world. Every time you express an opinion, whites seem to slap it on their dissecting table, showing that blacks want the best of both ways. In fact, you have answers on these issues, but whites take so much delight in citing alleged "inconsistencies" that they hardly hear what you have to say. 48

You may, by a combination of brains and luck and perseverance, make it into the middle class. And like all middle-class Americans, you will want to enjoy the comforts and pleasures that come with that status. One downside is that you will find many white people asking why you aren't doing more to help members of your race whom you have supposedly left behind. There is even the suggestion that, by moving to a safer or more spacious area, you have callously deserted your own people. 49

Yet hardly ever do middle-class whites reflect on the fact that they, too, have moved to better neighborhoods, usually far from poorer and less equable persons of their own race or ethnic origins. There is little evidence that middle-class whites are prepared to give much of themselves in aid of fellow whites who have fallen on misfortune. Indeed, the majority of white Americans have chosen to live in sequestered suburbs, where they are insulated from the nation's losers and failures. 50

Compounding these expectations, you find yourself continually subjected to comparisons with other minorities or even members of your own race. For example, you are informed that blacks who have emigrated from the Caribbean earn higher incomes than those born in the United States. Here the message seems to be that color by itself is not an insurmountable barrier. Most stinging of all are contrasts with recent immigrants. You hear people just off the boat (or, nowadays, a 51 plane) extolled for building businesses and becoming productive citizens. Which is another way of asking why you haven't matched their achievements, considering how long your people have been here.

Moreover, immigrants are praised for being willing to start at the   52
bottom. The fact that so many of them manage to find jobs is taken as evidence that the economy still has ample opportunities for employment. You want to reply that you are not an immigrant, but as much a citizen as any white person born here. Perhaps you can't match the mathematical skills of a teenager from Korea, but then neither can most white kids at suburban high schools. You feel much like a child being chided because she has not done as well as a precocious sister. However, you are an adult, and do not find such scolding helpful or welcome.

No law of humanity or nature posits a precise format for the family.   53
Throughout history and even in our day, households have had many shapes and structures. The same strictures apply to marriage and parental relationships. All this requires some emphasis, given concerns expressed about "the black family" and its presumed disintegration. In fact, the last several decades have seen a weakening of domestic ties in all classes and races.

Black Americans are fully aware of what is happening in this   54
sphere. They know that most black children are being born out of wedlock and that these youngsters will spend most of their growing years with a single parent. They understand that a majority of their marriages will dissolve in separation or divorce, and that many black men and women will never marry at all. Black Americans also realize that tensions between men and women sometimes bear a violence and bitterness that can take an awful toll.

If you are black, you soon learn it is safest to make peace with   55
reality: to acknowledge that the conditions of your time can undercut dreams of enduring romance and "happily ever after." This is especially true if you are a black woman, since you may find yourself spending many of your years without a man in your life. Of course, you will survive and adapt, as your people always have. Central in this effort will be joining and sustaining a community of women—another form of a family—on whom you can rely for love and strength and support.

If you are a black woman, you can expect to live five fewer years   56
than your white counterpart. Among men, the gap is seven years. Indeed, a man living in New York's Harlem is less likely to reach sixty-five than is a resident of Bangladesh. Black men have a three times greater chance of dying of AIDS, and outnumber whites as murder

victims by a factor of seven. According to studies, you get less sleep, are more likely to be overweight, and to develop hypertension. This is not simply due to poverty. Your shorter and more painful life results, in considerable measure, from the anxieties that come with being black in America.

If you are a black young man, life can be an interlude with an 57
early demise. Black youths do what they must to survive in a hostile world, with the prospect of violence and death on its battlefields. Attitudes can turn fatalistic, even suicidal: gladiators without even the cheers of an audience.

When white people hear the cry, "the police are coming!" for them 58
it almost always means, "help is on the way." Black citizens cannot make the same assumption. If you have been the victim of a crime, you cannot presume that the police will actually show up; or, if they do, that they will take much note of your losses or suffering. You sense police officials feel that blacks should accept being robbed or raped as one of life's everyday risks. It seems to you obvious that more detectives are assigned to a case when a white person is murdered.

If you are black and young and a man, the arrival of the police 59
does not usually signify help, but something very different. If you are a teenager simply socializing with some friends, the police may order you to disperse and get off the streets. They may turn on a search-light, order you against a wall. Then comes the command to spread your legs and empty out your pockets, and stand splayed there while they call in your identity over their radio. You may be a college student and sing in a church choir, but that will not overcome the police presumption that you have probably done something they can arrest you for.

If you find yourself caught up in the system, it will seem like alien 60
terrain. Usually your judge and prosecutor will be white, as will most members of the jury, as well as your attorney. In short, your fate will be decided by a white world.

This may help to explain why you have so many harsh words for 61
the police, even though you want and need their protection more than white people do. After all, there tends to be more crime in areas where you live, not to mention drug dealing and all that comes in its wake. Black citizens are at least twice as likely as whites to become victims of violent crimes. Moreover, in almost all of these cases, the person who attacks you will be black. Since this is so, whites want to know, why don't black people speak out against the members of their race who are causing so much grief? The reason is partly that you do not want to attack other blacks while whites are listening. At least

equally important is that while you obviously have no taste for violence, you are also wary of measures that might come with a campaign to stamp out "black crime." These reasons will receive fuller consideration in a later chapter. At this point you might simply say that you are not sure you want a more vigorous police presence, if those enforcers are unable to distinguish between law-abiding citizens and local predators. Of course, you want to be protected. But not if it means that you and your friends and relatives end up included among those the police harass or arrest.

The national anthem sings of America as "the land of the free." The Pledge of Allegiance promises "liberty and justice for all." The Declaration of Independence proclaims that all human creatures are "created equal."

If you are black, you cannot easily join in the anthem's refrain, reciting the pledge, or affirming that your country is committed to equality. While you grant that the United States is "your" country, you may define your citizenship as partial and qualified. It is not that you are "disloyal," if that means having your first allegiance elsewhere. Rather, you feel no compelling commitment to a republic that has always rebuffed you and your people.

We know from surveys that during the Cold War era, black Americans felt less antipathy toward nations then designated as our enemies, since they saw themselves less threatened by the Soviet Union or Cuba or China than did most white Americans. Nor were they so sure why they or their children were asked to risk their lives fighting people of color in places like Vietnam and Panama and the Middle East. And if the United States finds itself increasingly at odds with Islamic countries or other movements in the Third World, even more black Americans may find themselves wondering where their own allegiances lie.

As you look back on the way this nation has treated your people, you wonder how so many have managed to persevere amid so much adversity. About slavery, of course, too much cannot be said. Yet even within living memory, there were beaches and parks—in the North as well as in the South—where black Americans simply could not set foot. Segregation meant separation without even a pretense of equal facilities. In Southern communities that had only a single public library or swimming pool, black residents and taxpayers could never borrow a book or go for a swim. Indeed, black youths were even forbidden to stroll past the pool, lest they catch a glimpse of white girls in their bathing costumes.

62

63

64

65

How did they endure the endless insults and humiliations?   66
Grown people being called by their first names, having to avert
their eyes when addressed by white people, even being expected to
step off a sidewalk when whites walked by. Overarching it all was
the terror, with white police and prosecutors and judges possessing
all but total power over black lives. Not to mention the lynchings
by white mobs, with victims even chosen at random, to remind all
blacks of what could happen to them if they did not remain
compliant and submissive.

You wonder how much that has changed. Suppose, for example,   67
you find yourself having to drive across the country, stopping at gaso-
line stations and restaurants and motels. As you travel across the heart
of white America, you can never be sure of how you will be received.
While the odds are that you will reach your destination alive, you
cannot be so sure that you will not be stopped by the police or spend
a night in a cell. So you would be well advised to keep to the speed
limit, and not exceed it by a single mile. Of course, white people are
pulled over by state troopers; but how often are their cars searched?
Or if a motel clerk cannot "find" your reservation, is it because she
has now seen you in person? And are all the toilet facilities at this
service station really out of order?

The day-to-day aggravations and humiliations add up bit by bitter   68
bit. To take a depressingly familiar example, you stroll into a shop to
look at the merchandise, and it soon becomes clear that the clerks are
keeping a watchful eye on you. Too quickly, one of them comes over
to inquire what it is you might want, and then remains conspicuously
close as you continue your search. It also seems that they take an
unusually long time verifying your credit card. And then you and a
black friend enter a restaurant, and find yourselves greeted warily,
with what is obviously a more anxious reception than that given to
white guests. Yes, you will be served, and your table will not necessarily
be next to the kitchen. Still, you sense that they would rather you had
chosen some other eating place. Or has this sort of thing happened so
often that you are growing paranoid?

So there is the sheer strain of living in a white world, the rage   69
that you must suppress almost every day. No wonder black Americans,
especially black men, suffer so much from hypertension. (If ever an
illness had social causes, this is certainly one.) To be black in America
means reining in your opinions and emotions as no whites ever have
to do. Not to mention the forced and false smiles you are expected to
contrive, to assure white Americans that you harbor no grievances
against them.

Along with the tension and the strain and the rage, there come   70
those moments of despair. At times, the conclusion seems all but self-
evident that white America has no desire for your presence or any
need for your people. Can this nation have an unstated strategy for
annihilating your people? How else, you ask yourself, can one explain
the incidence of death and debilitation from drugs and disease; the
incarceration of a whole generation of your men; the consignment of
millions of women and children to half-lives of poverty and dependency?* Each of these debilities has its causes; indeed, analyzing them
has become a minor industry. Yet with so much about these conditions
that is so closely related to race, they say something about the larger
society that has allowed them to happen.

This is not to say that white officials sit in secret rooms, plotting   71
the genocide of black America. You understand as well as anyone that
politics and history seldom operate that way. Nor do you think of
yourself as unduly suspicious. Still, you cannot rid yourself of some
lingering mistrust. Just as your people were once made to serve silently
as slaves, could it be that if white America begins to conclude that
you are becoming too much trouble, it will find itself contemplating
more lasting solutions?

THINKING ABOUT THE CONTENT

1. Why does Hacker believe it is not easy to follow Zora Neale Hurston's
   counsel, "Be as black as you want to be" (10)? Why might you feel as
   Toni Morrison that, "At no moment in my life have I ever felt as though
   I were an American" (10)? How would you respond to such a statement?
2. Hacker says that despite the theory that all Americans with financial
   means and a respectable demeanor can choose where they want to live,
   it is, in fact, almost impossible for blacks. What proof does he offer?
3. What does Hacker call the "ultimate insult of segregation" (29)? What
   long-lasting problems does this create? Is the United States still segregated
   in some ways? Explain.
4. Why does Hacker state that even though there are successful "black"
   programs on radio and television, as well as black entertainers and best-
   selling authors, that much that is "black" is missing? Do his examples
   support his contention?

---

* In 1990, when a sample of black Americans were asked if they thought that the
government was deliberately encouraging drug use among black people, 64 percent
felt that this might be true. When asked if they suspected that AIDS had been purposely
created by scientists to infect black people, 32 percent believed there might be some
truth in this view.

5. What are some of the hypocrisies compounded by the way the white system views black Americans? Does Hacker exaggerate?

6. How did reading this selection affect your own views of black and white relations?

LOOKING AT STRUCTURE AND STYLE

7. Hacker, who is white, assumes the persona of a black American. How well do you think he does this?

8. Describe the attitude and tone of the selection. How are both achieved?

9. How well does Hacker support his arguments? In what points is he the strongest? the weakest?

EXPLORING DISCUSSION AND WRITING TOPICS

10. Write an essay to an African American asking him or her to spend some time in a white body. What are some of the things he or she would learn?

11. Reread Hacker's opening paragraph. Write an essay in response to the statements in it.

12. Write an essay about your mistrust of a race different from yours. What is it you mistrust? Is it real or imaginary? What is the source of the mistrust? What can you do about it?

13. Write an essay arguing for or against affirmative action.

GERALD EARLY

In addition to being a contributing editor to *Civilization*, Gerald Early won the 1994 National Book Critics Circle Award for his book of criticism, *The Culture of Bruising: Essays on Prizefighting, Literature, and Modern American Culture*. He is also the author of *Daughters: On Family and Fatherhood*, *Tuxedo Junction: Essays on American Culture*, and *How the War in the Streets Is Won*, a book of poetry. In 1994 Early gave the opening address at a Library of Congress conference on black diaspora.

As director of the African and Afro-American studies program at Washington University in St. Louis, Early deals constantly with questions about Afrocentrism. Early says, "Since writing about Malcolm X for *Harper's* a few years ago, I have tried, perhaps foolishly, to depolemicize a very polemical issue. I have been dissatisfied with most of what I have read on the subject." The following essay from *Civilization* magazine is part of his "continuing effort to get it right."

〰

Understanding Afrocentrism

The White man will never admit his real references. He will steal everything you have and still call you those names.
—*ISHMAEL REED*
Mumbo Jumbo (1972)

Furthermore, no one can be thoroughly educated until he learns as much about the Negro as he knows about other people.
— *CARTER G. WOODSON*
The Mis-Education of the Negro (1933)

[Alexander] Crummell's black nationalism was marked by certain inconsistencies, but they derived from the inconsistencies and hypocrisy of American racism, rather than from any intellectual shortcomings on his part. It was impossible to create an ideology that responded rationally to an irrational system.
—*WILSON JEREMIAH MOSES*
Alexander Crummell: A Study of Civilization and Discontent (1989)

243

In a span of three weeks during the early spring semester of 1995,   1
Angela Davis and bell hooks, two notable black leftist, feminist
thinkers, visited the campus of Washington University in St. Louis,
invited by different student groups. They were generally well received,
indeed, enthusiastically so. But there was, for each of them during
these visits, something of a jarring note, both involving black students.

Professor Davis, entertaining questions during a panel session after   2
having spoken earlier on the subject of prison reform, was asked by
a black woman student what she had to offer black people as a solution
to their problems. The student went on to explain that she did not
consider herself an African-American. She was simply an African,
wishing to have nothing to do with being an American or with America
itself. She wanted black people to separate themselves entirely from
"Europeans," as she called white Americans, and wanted to know
what Davis could suggest to further that aim.

Davis answered that she was not inclined to such stringent race   3
separation. She was proud of being of African descent but wished to
be around a variety of people, not just people like herself. Davis felt
further that blacks should not isolate themselves but accept in partnership anyone who was sincerely interested in the cause of overthrowing
capitalism, a standard and reasonable Marxist response to the "essen-
tializing" of race in a way that would divert true political engagement
"against the system." The student was visibly annoyed with the answer,
which presumably smacked of "white" intellectualism.

Professor bell hooks, after her address on ending racism and sexism   4
in America—love, I think, was the answer—was asked by a black
woman student how feminism was relevant to black women. Hooks
explained that feminism was not only for white women, that black
women needed to read more feminist texts, even if some of them were
racist. After all, Karl Marx was racist but he did give the world a
brilliant analysis of capitalism. She had said in her speech how disappointed she was that her black women students at City College of New
York were not inclined to embrace feminism, rejecting it as something
white. She felt that these black women were unduly influenced by
black male rappers who bashed feminism. The answer did not persuade
or please the student.

Later that day, I heard many black undergraduates dismiss hooks's   5
talk as not addressing the needs of black people, as being too geared
to the white feminists in the audience. Some were disturbed that hooks
would feel that they formed their opinions on the basis of listening to
rap records. None of this was said, necessarily, with hostility, but

rather with regret and a shade of condescension that only the young can so keenly and innocently express when speaking about the foolishness of their elders.

I recall a fairly recent incident where a black student, a very bright   6
young woman, asked if, when doing research, one had to acknowledge racist books. I told her that a certain amount of objectivity was part of the discipline of being a scholar. Anger at unjust or inaccurate statements and assessments was understandable, but personalizing everything often caused a kind of tunnel vision where crude self-affirmation seemed to be the only fit end of scholarship. She responded that she would refuse to acknowledge racist sources, that if the book was racist, then everything it said was tainted and should be disregarded.

The attitudes of these students have been shaped by Afrocentrism,   7
an insistence by a growing number of black Americans to see the world from an "African-centered" perspective in response to the dominant "European-centered" perspective to which they feel they have been subjected throughout their lives. Afrocentrism is many things and has many degrees of advocacy. It can range from the commercialism and pretense of the shallow holiday called Kwanza (no shallower, it should be said, than the commercialized celebration of Christmas) to the kente-cloth ads and nationalist talk that one finds in most black publications these days; from talk about racist European scholarship to a view that world culture is essentially African in origin and that Europeans are usurpers, thieves, and generally inferior. On the one hand, we have the recent cover story "Is Jesus Black?" in *Emerge,* an Afrocentric-tinged news magazine for the black middle class. The answer in this instance, of course, is clearly yes. (Obviously, this is grounds for competing claims between blacks and Jews; whatever can be said about Jesus' skin color or the religious movement that bears his name, there is no question that he was a Jew.) On the other hand, we have the first explicitly Afrocentric Hollywood Western in Mario Van Peebles's 1993 film *Posse,* a jumbled multicultural critique of white *fin de siècle* imperialism and the myth of how the West was won.

No doubt, Afrocentrists specifically and black folk generally found   8
it to be a signal victory that in the recent television dramatization of the love affair between Solomon and Sheba, Sheba was played by a black actress and Solomon by a swarthy Hispanic. In the 1959 Hollywood film version of *Solomon and Sheba,* directed by King Vidor—who, incidentally, made the first all-black Hollywood film—Solomon was played by Yul Brynner and Sheba by Gina Lollobrigida. It is safe to say that the real Solomon and the real Sheba, if they ever existed,

did not look remotely like any of the actors who ever played them. But whom we want them to look like is very important. The Afrocentrists will feel their triumph to be complete when black actors portray Beethoven, Joseph Haydn, Warren G. Harding, Alexander Hamilton, Hannibal, Abraham Lincoln, Dwight Eisenhower, Cleopatra, Moses, Jesus Christ and Saint Augustine. Many African-Americans are inclined to believe that any noted white with ambiguous ancestry must be black. They are also inclined to believe that any white with dark skin tones, one who hangs around blacks or who "acts black" in some way is truly black. At various times in my life, I have heard blacks argue vehemently that Madonna, Phoebe Snow, Keith Jarrett, Mae West, Ava Gardner and Dorothy Parker were black, even though they did not have a shred of evidence to support the claims. Blacks have always been fascinated by "passing," by the possibility that some whites are really black—"fooling old massa," so to speak.

Afrocentrism is an intellectual movement, a political view, a historically   9 traceable evolution, a religious orthodoxy. It derives, in part, from Negritude and Pan-Africanism, which stressed the culture and achievements of Africans. Both movements were started by Africans, West Indians and African-Americans in response to European colonialism and the worldwide oppression of African-descended people. But Afrocentrism is also a direct offshoot of earlier forms of black nationalism, in which blacks around the world believed they had a special destiny to fulfill and a special consciousness to redeem. More important, Afrocentrism is a mood that has largely erupted in the last 10 to 15 years in response to integration or, perhaps more precisely, to the failure of integration. Many blacks who have succeeded in the white world tend to feel most Afrocentric, although I think it would be a mistake to see Afrocentrism purely as middle-class, since significant numbers of working-class blacks are attracted to some elements of it. The bourgeois, "midcult" element of Afrocentrism, nonetheless, is very strong. "Integrated" middle-class blacks see it as a demonstration of their race loyalty and solidarity with their brothers and sisters throughout the world, whether in American cities or on African farms. (It is worth noting the economic clout of the black middle class, which can be seen in the growing number of black Hollywood films and filmmakers, in new black magazines ranging from *Body and Soul* to *The Source* to *Upscale,* and in the larger audience for black books. It is the market power of this class that has given Afrocentrism its force as a consumer ideology.)

So the middle-class black, having had more contact with whites   10
and their institutions, is expected to speak for and to other blacks.
Afrocentrism, like Negritude and Pan-Africanism, is meant to be an
ideological glue to bring black people together, not just on the basis
of color but as the expression of a cultural and spiritual will that
crosses class and geographical lines. As W. E. B. Du Bois wrote in
1940:

> Since the fifteenth century these ancestors of mine and their
> other descendants have had a common history; have suffered
> a common disaster and have one long memory. . . . The
> real essence of this kinship is its social heritage of slavery; the
> discrimination and insults; and this heritage binds together
> not simply the children of Africa, but extends through
> yellow Asia and into the South Seas. It is this unity that
> draws me to Africa.

Louis H. Farrakhan, the head of the Nation of Islam, is probably   11
the most familiar figure associated with Afrocentrism. (Muhammad
Ali introduced Islamic conversion to an even bigger public, suffering
greatly for his religious and political beliefs and becoming the most
noted and charismatic dissident of his era. Ali's prodigious athletic
abilities and his genial temperament succeeded in endearing him to
the American public despite his religion. He never became a member
of Farrakhan's sect.) Farrakhan is a fiery preacher, prone to making
extreme statements, with a militant flair and a racist edge, that have
the conviction of truth among some blacks. He especially exploits the
idea that he is a heroic black man at grave risk for daring to tell the
truth about the white man. (Malcolm X used this device effectively,
too.) He is also a master demagogue who exploits the paranoia of his
audience. But then, as a friend once said to me, "What black person
isn't justified in being at least half-paranoid?"

Farrakhan has found three effective lines of entry among blacks,   12
particularly young blacks, that draw on the Afrocentric impulse: First,
that Islam is the true religion of black people. (This has led to a move
among black Christian leaders to point out with great vehemence the
African origins of Christianity, to make it, in effect, a black religion.)
Second, that black people need business enterprise in their community
in order to liberate themselves (an old belief among blacks, going back
to at least the early part of the 19th century). And third, that Jews of
European descent (what he calls "false Jews") are not to be trusted, a
charge that exploits the current tension between blacks and Jews—and

that Farrakhan has used to move into the black civil-rights establishment. All three positions enjoy remarkable support within the black
middle class, a situation that has helped Farrakhan tap people's insecu-
rities for his own purposes. The Nation of Islam may be famous for
converting addicts and criminals, but above all, it wants, as all religions
do, to win over the middle class, with its money, its respectability and
its organizational know-how.

Whatever might be said of Farrakhan's importance as a political   13
figure in the black community or in the United States, he is a minor
figure in the development of Afrocentrism. His position in the history
of Afrocentrism is similar to that of, say, Rush Limbaugh in the development of American conservatism. He is, like Limbaugh, a figure the
media can use to give a sellable face and voice to a unique temper
among a group of people. For both Limbaugh and Farrakhan represent
an intense sentimentality in American life, a yearning for a fantasized,
idealized past of racial grandeur and simplicity. This sentimentality
appeals powerfully to the black middle class, which yearns for a usable,
untainted past. This partly explains why Farrakhan and the Muslims
can often be found speaking to black college students.

In thinking about the connection between class and nationalistic   14
feelings, it should be recalled that in Harriet Beecher Stowe's 1852
novel, *Uncle Tom's Cabin*, the most light-complexioned blacks, the
ones with the greatest skills, George, Eliza and Cassy, return to Africa
at the novel's end to retrieve their degraded patrimony. It might be
said that this is purely Stowe's own perverse vision, since some of the
fiercest advocates for returning to Africa have been Martin Delany,
Alexander Crummell and Marcus Garvey, all very dark men. Yet there
is more than a little truth to the idea that class, caste and race consciousness are closely interwoven. Nationalism of whatever sort has almost
always been an affair of a disaffected middle class. And until the 1920s,
the black middle class in America was disproportionately made up of
light-skinned people.

The paradox of the bourgeois aspect of Afrocentrism is that it   15
rejects cosmopolitanism as being "white" or "Eurocentric." Yet Afrocentrism has no other way of seeing cosmopolitanism except on the
"Eurocentric" model, so it tries to make Africa for black Americans
the equivalent of what Europe is for white Americans: the source of
civilization. Indeed, by trying to argue that Africa is the source of
Western civilization, the Afrocentric sees the African, symbolically, as
the mother of white Europe (just as the black mother, the mammy, is
the mythic progenitor of the white South, or so Langston Hughes
seemed to believe in his famous short story "Father and Son," which

became his even more famous play, *Mulatto*). The African becomes, in this view, the most deeply cultured person on the planet, which matches his status as the oldest person on the planet, with the longest and deepest genetic history. In short, Afrocentrism becomes another form of the American apologizing for being American to people he imagines are his cultural superiors. Afrocentrism tries to mask a quest for American filiopiety behind a facade of African ancestor and culture worship.

It would be easy, on one level, to dismiss Afrocentrism as an expression, 16 in white workplaces and white colleges, of intimidated black folk who are desperately trying to find a space for themselves in what they feel to be alien, unsympathetic environments. Seen this way, Afrocentrism becomes an expression of the low self-esteem and inferiority that blacks feel most intensely when they are around whites; their response is to become more "black," estranged from the environment that they find so unaccepting of them. The greatest psychic burden of the African-American is that he must not only think constantly about being different but about what his difference means. And it might be suggested that Afrocentrism does not solve this problem but merely reflects it in a different mirror. There is a certain amount of truth to this, especially at a time when affirmative action, which promotes group identification and group difference, tends to intensify black self-consciousness. And black people, through no fault of their own, are afflicted with a debilitating sense of self-consciousness when around whites. When whites are in the rare situation of being a minority in a sea of blacks, they often exhibit an abject self-consciousness as well, but the source of that self-consciousness is quite different. The white is used to traveling anywhere in the world and having his cultural inclinations accommodated. The black is neither used to this nor does he realistically expect it. The European exults in his culture while the African is utterly degraded by his. That blacks should want to free themselves from the white gaze seems not merely normal but essential to the project of reconstructing themselves as a people on their own terms. And the history of blacks in the United States has been an ongoing project—tragic, pathetic, noble, heroic, misguided, sublime—of self-reconstruction.

Afrocentrism, like a good many nationalistic ideologies, might be 17 called the orthodoxy of the book, or more precisely, the orthodoxy of the books. Afrocentrism is an attempt to wed knowledge and ideology. Movements like Afrocentrism, which feels both its mission and its authority hinge on the revelation of a denied and buried truth, promote a fervent scholasticism, a hermeneutical ardor among true believers for compilations of historical minutiae on the one hand, and for grand philosophical tracts on the other. The former might be best represented by George G. M. James's *Stolen Legacy,* published in 1954, the latter by Mustafa El-Amin's *Al-Islam, Christianity, and Freemasonry* and *Freemasonry, Ancient Egypt, and the Islamic Destiny.* These books were not written by professional historians or by college professors. The fact that several classic Afrocentric texts have been written by amateurs gives Afrocentrism its powerful populist appeal, its legitimacy as an expression of "truth" that white institutional forces hide or obscure. At the same time, this leaves it vulnerable to charges of being homemade, unprofessional, theoretically immature and the like. It is one of the striking aspects of Afrocentrism that within the last 20 years it has developed a cadre of academics to speak for it, to professionalize it, to make it a considerable insurgency movement on the college campus.

There are several texts that might be considered the literary and intellectual cornerstones of the Afrocentrism movement. Molefi K. Asante, professor and chair of African-American studies at Temple University in Philadelphia, is credited with inventing the name "Afrocentrism" or "Afrocentricity" (although currently the term "Africentrism" is on the rise in certain quarters, probably because there is a group of black folk who, for some reason, despise the prefix "Afro," as if the word "Africa" itself were created by the people of the continent rather than by Europeans). Asante's very short books, including *The Afrocentric Idea,* published in 1987, and *Afrocentricity: The Theory of Social Change,* published in 1980, are frequently the starting points for people seeking a basic explanation of this ideology. As defined by Asante, Afrocentrism seems to take the terms and values of Eurocentrism—intense individualism, crass greed, lack of spirituality, warlike inclinations, dominance and racism, dishonesty and hypocrisy—and color their opposites black, giving us a view of black people not terribly different from the romantic racism of Harriet Beecher Stowe and other whites like her in the 19th and 20th centuries. I cannot recount the number of "race sensitivity" meetings I have attended where blacks begin to describe themselves (or those they perceive to be Africans) as more spiritual, more family-oriented, more community-oriented, more rhythmic, more natural and less combative than whites. All of which is, of course, a crock of nonsense, largely the expression of wishes for qualities that blacks see as absent from their community life now. But, thanks to Asante, this has become the profile of the African in the Afrocentric vision.

18

Martin Bernal's massively researched two-volume *Black Athena*   19
(published in 1987 and 1991) is a popular title in Afrocentric circles,
in large measure because Bernal, a professor at Cornell, is one of the
few white scholars to take Afrocentrism seriously—William Piersen,
Robert Farris Thompson and Andrew Hacker, in decidedly different
ways, are others—and one of the few to write an academic treatise in
its defense that forces whites to take it seriously too. (The irony that
blacks still need whites, in some measure, to sell their ideas and themselves to other whites is not entirely lost on those who have thought
about this.)

    Black Athena supports three major contentions of the Afrocen-   20
trists: 1) ancient Egypt was a black civilization; 2) the Greeks derived
a good deal, if not all, of their philosophy and religion from the
Egyptians; 3) European historiography has tried strenuously and with
clear political objectives to deny both. Bernal's book provoked a scath-
ing attack by Mary R. Lefkowitz, a professor at Wellesley, who charac-
terizes Afrocentrism as a perversion of the historiography of antiquity
and a degradation of academic standards for political ends. Lefkowitz
has also battled with Tony Martin, a cultural historian, barrister and
Marcus Garvey specialist, who began using and endorsing the Nation
of Islam's anti-Semitic *The Secret Relationship Between Blacks and
Jews* (Vol. 1) in his classes on slavery at Wellesley. Martin responded
in 1993 with his own account of the dispute, *The Jewish Onslaught:
Despatches from the Wellesley Battlefront,* which elaborates his claims
of Jewish racism and the hypocrisy of academic freedom.

    Maulana Karenga, professor and chair of black studies at Califor-   21
nia State University at Long Beach, created the black philosophical
code called the Kawaida, which was the inspiration for Kwanza and
the seven principles (Nguzo Saba) that the holiday celebrates. The code
contains a bit of Marxism to create a "theoretical" ambiance. Karenga
is also author of the popular *Introduction to Black Studies,* used by
many colleges in their introductory courses, despite its rather tenden-
tious manner, which he tries to pass off as sharp-minded Marxism,
and the fact that the book is weak on a good many aspects of African-
American life and culture.

    Perhaps the most popular Afrocentric text is Chancellor Williams's   22
*The Destruction of Black Civilization: Great Issues of a Race From
4500 B.C. to 2000 A.D.* (published in 1987), an account of his exhaustive
research trips to Africa. Although not directly trained in the study of
African history, Williams studied under William Leo Hansberry, a
history professor at Howard University and probably the leading black
American authority on Africa during the 1930s, 1940s and 1950s.

Hansberry did path-breaking work in an utterly neglected field, eventually becoming known as "the father of African studies" in the United States. (Scholars, until recently, did not think Africa had a "history." The continent, especially its sub-Saharan regions, had an "anthropology" and an "archaeology," folkways to be discovered and remains to be unearthed, but never a record of institutions, traditions, political ideologies and complex societies.) Williams also did research on African history at Oxford and at the University of London, where, because of colonialism, interest in the nature of African societies was far keener than in the United States. His book *The Re-Birth of African Civilization,* an account of his 1953–1957 research project investigating the nature of education in Europe and Africa, calls for Pan-African education of blacks in Africa and around the world. Williams concluded that "European" and "Eurocentric" education was antithetical, both politically and intellectually, to African interests, a common refrain in Afrocentrist thought.

Most Afrocentric scholars at universities today genuflect at the [23] intellectual altar of Cheikh Anta Diop, a Senegalese humanist and scientist who began his research into African history in 1946, as the battle against European colonialism in Africa was beginning. Diop saw his mission as undermining European colonialism by destroying the European's claim to a superior history. He was tenacious in demonstrating that Africa had a "real" history that showed that Africans were the product of civilizations and not of the jungle. This claim to history was a sign to the African that he was an equal player in the family of man, and was essential to any demand for independence.

For Diop, it was not enough to reconstruct African history; it was [24] also necessary to depict a unified Africa, an idea that, whether myth or fact, was considered ideologically crucial by the Pan-African movement to overthrow European imperialism. Like every other oppressed people, the African could face the future only if he could hark back to some version of his past, preferably a past touched with greatness. This could be done only by running African history and civilization through Egypt, the only African civilization that impressed European intellectuals. As jazz and cultural critic Stanley Crouch suggested, Egypt is the only African civilization that has monuments, a physical legacy that indicates history as understood in European terms. Thus, for black people in Africa to be unified, for black people around the world to feel unified, ancient Egypt had to be a "black" civilization and serve as the origin of all blackness and, even more important, all whiteness. We know from scientific evidence that Africa is the place of origin for human life. If it is also true that Egypt is the oldest civilization from which Europeans borrowed freely (Bernal makes a persuasive argument for the influence of Egypt on European intellectuals through the 19th century), then Africans helped shape Western culture and were major actors in history, not bit players in the unfolding drama of European dominance.

Diop's doctoral dissertation, based on the idea that Egypt was 25 African and that European civilization was largely built on Egyptian ideas, was rejected at the University of Paris in 1951. The story goes that he was able to defend his dissertation successfully only in 1960 when he was accompanied into the examination room by an army of historians, sociologists and anthropologists who supported his views, or at least his right as a responsible scholar to express them. By then, with African independence in full swing, his ideas had a political currency in Africa as an expression of Pan-Africanism. And no one supported the idea of a unified Africa more than Egypt's then-president, Gamal Abdel Nasser, probably the most powerful independent leader on the continent. Like Gandhi, Nasser called himself a black man, and he envisioned an Africa united in opposition to Israel and South Africa. It was a good moment for Diop to be saying what he was saying. At the 1956 Conference of Negro-African Writers and Artists in Paris, Diop was one of the most popular speakers, although black American James Baldwin was not much impressed with his thesis. (Admittedly, for Baldwin this was pretty new stuff.) For his part, Diop, a Marxist, thought the American delegation was blindly anticommunist and naively committed to the integrationist policies of the civil-rights movement.

Diop produced a number of volumes translated into English, some 26 based on his dissertation. They include *The African Origin of Civilization: Myth or Reality, Civilization or Barbarism: An Authentic Anthropology* and *The Cultural Unity of Negro Africa*. For Diop, everything turned on establishing that ancient Egypt was a black civilization: "The history of Black Africa will remain suspended in air and cannot be written correctly until African historians dare to connect it with the history of Egypt." Moreover, Diop felt that the African could not remove the chains of colonialism from his psyche until he had a fully reconstructed history—in other words, until he had a usable past. Diop was brilliant and clearly obsessed. His importance in the formation of African-American intellectual history does not depend on whether his historical theories are correct. (Although there is considerable debate about ancient Egypt—not surprising, since there is no documentation of the claim in the language of the people who lived there at the time—it is now conceded by virtually everyone that the Egyptians were a mixed-race people.) Diop's work transcends questions of historical accuracy and enters the realm of "belief." Much of what Diop wrote may be true (he had vast amounts of evidence to support his claims) but, as a Marxist, he was not motivated simply by the quest for positivistic, objective "truth." He wanted to use the supposed objectivity of scientific research for political ends.

Diop brought together three important elements in understanding the origins of Afrocentrism: first, the tradition of professional, politically motivated historical research that buttresses the claims of untrained, amateur historians; second, the explicit connection between knowledge of one's "proper" history and one's psychological and spiritual well-being; third, the connection between "proper" knowledge of one's history and the realization of a political mission and purpose. If European history functioned as an ideological and political justification for Europe's place in the world and its hope for its future, why shouldn't African history function in the same manner? This is the reasoning of the Pan-Africanists and Afrocentrists who see "proper" history as the version that is most ideologically and politically useful to their group. Diop's research supports the idea of a conspiracy among white historians to discredit or ignore black civilization. Without a "proper" knowledge of African history, Diop argues, blacks will remain politically impotent and psychologically crippled. These ideas have become the uncritical dogma of Afrocentrism. By the time Diop died in 1986, he had been virtually canonized by an important set of black American scholars who identified themselves as Afrocentric.

Diop is useful for Afrocentrism today not only because of his monumental research but because he was an African, thus linking Afrocentrism to Africa itself and permitting the black American to kneel before the perfect intellect of the "purer" African. But Diop's ideas about ancient black civilization in Egypt and the importance of fuller knowledge of its history had been advanced earlier by several African-American intellectuals, including W. E. B. Du Bois in his momentous book *Black Folk, Then and Now: An Essay in the History and Sociology of the Negro Race,* which appeared in 1939. Du Bois said he was inspired to write about the glories of the Negro past after hearing a lecture in 1906 at Atlanta University by the preeminent white anthropologist Franz Boas, debunker of racism and mentor of Zora Neale Hurston. Du Bois's work remains, despite the more richly researched efforts of Diop, Bernal and St. Clair Drake in *Black Folk Here and There* (published in two volumes in 1987 and 1990), the best and most readable examination of the subject. Indeed, his work must be seen in a larger historical context, dating back to the founding of the American Negro Academy in 1897, when he and other black intellectuals tried to organize themselves for the purpose of producing scholarship that defended the race and promoted race consciousness. Yet Du Bois's book is not the central work of the Afrocentric movement by a black American writer.

That book would be Carter G. Woodson's *The Mis-Education of* 29 *the Negro,* originally published in 1933. Woodson, a Harvard Ph.D. in history who launched both the Association for the Study of Negro Life and History (1915) and Negro History Week (1926), was as obsessed with the reconstruction of the Negro past as Diop or Du Bois. He churned out dozens of books on virtually every aspect of African and African-American history. Some were wooden, opaque or just plain sloppy, and several are unreadable (even in the opinion of his assistant, the late, brilliant black historian Lorenzo Greene), indicating the haste with which they were composed. Even so, Woodson was a serious and demanding scholar. Greene thought of him, at times, as having the pious devotion of a Franciscan friar and the crotchety temper of an eccentric intellectual consumed by his work.

The Mis-Education of the Negro, although written by a man 30 who endorsed Booker T. Washington and the Tuskegee method, was generally critical of black education. Black people, Woodson argued, were not being educated in a way that would encourage them to press their own political and economic interests or make them a viable social group in the United States. They were, in fact, being educated against their own interests, largely because their education was controlled by whites who saw advantage in giving blacks an inferior education. Moreover, Woodson made the explicit connection between "improper" education, including a lack of knowledge about the black past, and the psychological degradation of the Negro, his internalized sense of inferiority. In short, a white-controlled education led to Uncle Tomism and black sellouts, to a defective Negro who suffered from false consciousness, or, more precisely, "white" consciousness. Some of this argument was restated in black sociologist E. Franklin Frazier's seminal 1957 work, *Black Bourgeoisie.* The black middle class was almost exclusively the target of this indictment—a fact that prompted that class to romanticize certain aspects of black lower-class life, particularly its antisocial and criminal elements, in an effort to demonstrate its solidarity with "authentic" black experience. This was true with the Black Panthers in the late 1960s and it continues with rap music

today. Another consequence is that the black middle class insists on
a degree of race loyalty that sometimes thwarts any critical inquiry
that does not promote race unity.

Much of Woodson's argument resonates with blacks today because   31
it seems to endorse the idea of Afrocentric schools and especially
the idea that knowledge of a glorious African past would give black
youngsters self-esteem, reduce violence and criminality in black neighborhoods, and lead to the spiritual and political uplift of black people.
This is why history is actually a less important discipline to the rise
of Afrocentrism than psychology. After all, the reconstruction of black
history was always connected with the reconstruction of the black
mind, a mind that existed before the coming of the white man—or at
least a mind that could be free of the white man and his image of
what black people were.

In some ways, the rise of Afrocentrism is related to the rise of   32
"black psychology" as a discipline. The Association of Black Psychologists was organized in 1968, a time when a number of black professional offshoots were formed in political and ideological protest against
the mainstream, white-dominated versions of their organizations.
Somewhat later came the *Journal of Black Psychology*, given impetus
by the initial assaults against black intelligence or pointed suggestions
of black genetic inferiority by Richard Herrnstein, Arthur Jensen and
others in the early 1970s; this was also the time of the first wave
of court challenges against affirmative action. The black psychology
movement argued for new modes of treatment for black mental illness,
the medical efficacy of using black history to repair a collectively
damaged black psyche, and the destruction of "Eurocentrism and the
values it spawned—from the idealization of white standards of beauty
to the scientific measurement of intelligence—as totally inimical to the
political and psychological interests of black people. Rationality, order,
individualism, dominance, sexual repression as well as sexual license,
aggression, warmaking, moneymaking, capitalism itself—all soon became "white values."

That all of this happened during the era of Vietnam War protests,   33
when white Western civilization was coming under withering intellectual attack from the radical left, is not without significance. Radical
white intellectuals, who otherwise had no more use for a black epic
history than a white one, found the black version useful as a weapon
against "Eurocentrism," which, as a result of the Vietnam War, they
held in utter contempt. In short, Jean-Paul Sartre and Susan Sontag
were as instrumental, albeit indirectly, in the formation of Afrocentrism
as, say, the Black Power movement of the late 1960s or the writings

of African psychiatrist Franz Fanon, whose *The Wretched of the Earth* became the revolutionary psychological profile of the oppressed black diaspora. Also occurring at this time was the movement on white college campuses to establish black studies programs, which provided a black intellectual wedge into the white academy. These programs, largely multidisciplinary, required an ideological purpose and mission to bind together the various disciplines, which is why many began to articulate some kind of Afrocentrism or, as it was called in the 1970s, "black aesthetic"—in other words, an ideological framework to give black studies a reason for being. When used to challenge the dominance of Western thought, Afrocentrism becomes part of a multicultural wave of complaint and resentment against the white man by a number of groups that feel they have been oppressed.

In an age of dysfunction and psychotherapy, no one can have   34
greater claim to having been made dysfunctional by political oppression than the African-American, who was literally a slave; and no one can have a greater need for recourse to psychotherapy in the form of Afrocentrism. But what made the black psychology movement possible was the rise of the Nation of Islam, particularly the rise of Malcolm X.

The charismatic Muslim minister did two things. First, he forced   35
the white mainstream press to take notice of black nationalism, Pan-Africanism and the concept of African unity. Previously these ideas had been marginalized as ridiculous or even comic expressions of black nationalism, to be read by blacks in black barbershops and beauty salons as they thumbed through the Ripley's-Believe-It-or-Not-type work of the self-taught black historian J. A. Rogers (*One Hundred Amazing Facts About the Negro, Five Negro Presidents* and the like). Malcolm X revitalized the ideas of Marcus Garvey, the great black nationalist leader of the 1910s and 1920s, whose Universal Negro Improvement Association became, for a time, one of the most popular black political groups in America. Malcolm, like Garvey, felt that the Negro still needed to be "improved" but, unlike Garveyites, the Muslims did not offer costumes and parades but sober suits, puritanical religion, dietary discipline and no-nonsense business practices. Malcolm himself was also, by his physical appearance alone, a figure who would not be dismissed as a buffoon, as Garvey often was by both blacks and whites. According to Malcolm's *Autobiography*, his father had been a Garveyite as well as a wife beater who favored his lighter-skinned children. Malcolm's Islamic-based black nationalism, his sexual abstinence, which lasted from his religious conversion until his marriage a decade later, and his triumph over his own preference

for lighter-skinned blacks and whites were all meant to demonstrate, vividly, how he superseded his father as a nationalist and how the Nation of Islam had superseded Garveyism.

Malcolm enlisted a body of enforcers, the feared Fruit of Islam,   36 grim-faced men who, one imagines, were supposed to personify the essence of an unbowed yet disciplined black manhood. In this way, he dramatically associated black nationalism with a new type of regenerated black male. It was said in the black community, and may still be, that no one bothers a Muslim for fear of retribution from the Fruit of Islam. Certainly, there was a point in the development of the Fruit of Islam and the Nation itself in the 1960s and early 1970s (Malcolm was assassinated in 1965) when both were closely associated with racketeering and gangster activity. During this period, many East Coast mosques were among the most terrifying organizations in the black community.

Second, Malcolm, in his *Autobiography,* also managed to link the   37 psychological redemption of the Negro with his reacquaintance with his history. The prison chapters of the *Autobiography* have become nearly mythic as a paradigm of black reawakening. Malcolm's religious conversion became, in a sense, the redemption of the black male and the rehabilitation of black masculinity itself. Lately, we have seen two major black male public figures who were incarcerated for serious crimes, Marion Barry and Mike Tyson, use the Malcolm paradigm to resuscitate their standing with the black public. The martyrdom of Malcolm gave this paradigm a blood-endorsed political heroism that has virtually foreclosed any serious criticism of either its origins or its meaning.

It is extraordinary to contemplate how highly regarded Malcolm   38 X is in the black community today, especially in comparison with Martin Luther King. (When I wrote an article for *Harper's* that was critical of Malcolm X, I received three death threats.) Despite the fact that King's achievements were enormous—and that Malcolm left really nothing behind other than a book—King's association with integration, with nonviolence, even with Christianity has reduced him in the eyes of many blacks. When blacks in major cities, inspired by figures like Malcolm X and the romanticization of Africa that Malcolm's nationalism wrought, began to organize African-oriented celebrations, such as my aunts did in Philadelphia with the creation of the Yoruba-inspired Odunde festival in 1975, then Afrocentrism has succeeded not only in intellectual spheres but on the grass-roots level as well. Its triumph as the legitimation of the black mind and the black aesthetic vision was complete.

Afrocentrism may eventually wane in the black community but   39
probably not very soon. Moreover, a certain type of nationalistic mood,
a kind of racial preoccupation, will always exist among blacks. It
always has, in varying degrees. Homesickness is strong among black
Americans, although it is difficult to point to a homeland. What Afrocentrism reflects is the inability of a large number of black people to
deal with the reality of being American and with the meaning of their
American experience.

Stanley Crouch is right in pointing out that the Afrocentrist is   40
similar to the white Southerner after the Civil War. To black nationalists, the lost war was the "war of liberation" led by black "revolutionaries" in the late 1960s, which in their imagination was modeled on the
struggles against colonialism then taking place around the world. (The
enslavement of the Africans, of course, was an earlier lost war, and it
also weighs heavily on the Afrocentrist. He, like the white Southerner,
hates the idea of belonging to a defeated people.) This imaginative
vision of a restored and indomitable ethnicity is not to be taken lightly.
In a culture as driven by the idea of redemption and as corrupted by
racism as this one, race war is our Armageddon. It can be seen in
works as various as Thomas Jefferson's *Notes on the State of Virginia,*
David Walker's *Appeal to the Colored Citizens of the World,* Joseph
Smith's *Book of Mormon,* D. W. Griffith's *Birth of a Nation* and Mario
Van Peebles's *Posse.*

Today, Afrocentrism is not a mature political movement but rather a   41
cultural style and a moral stance. There is a deep, almost lyrical poi-
gnancy in the fantasy of the Afrocentrist, as there is in the white
Southerner's. What would I have been had I not lost the war? The
Afrocentrist is devoted to his ancestry and his blood, fixated on the
set of traditions that define his nobility, preoccupied with an imagined
lost way of life. What drives the Afrocentrist and the white Southerner
is not the expression of a group self-interest but concern with pride
and honor. One group's myth is built on the surfeit of honor and pride,
the other on the total absence of them.

Like the white Southerner, the Afrocentrist is in revolt against   42
liberalism itself, against the idea of individual liberty. In a way, the
Afrocentrist is right to rage against it, because liberalism set free the
individual but did not encourage the development of a community
within which the individual could flower. This is what the Afrocentrist
wishes to retrieve, a place for himself in his own community. Wilson
Jeremiah Moses, a black historian, is right: Afrocentrism is a historiography of decline, like the mythic epic of the South. The tragedy is that

black people fail to see their "Americanization" as one of the great human triumphs of the past 500 years. The United States is virtually the only country where the ex-masters and the ex-slaves try to live together as equals, not only by consent of the ex-masters but by the demand of the ex-slaves. Ironically, what the Afrocentrist can best hope for is precisely what multiculturalism offers: the idea that American culture is a blend of many white and nonwhite cultures. In the end, although many Afrocentrists claim they want this blending, multiculturalism will not satisfy. For if the Euro-American is reminded through this that he is not European or wholly white, the African-American will surely be reminded that he is not African or wholly black. The Afrocentrist does not wish to be a mongrel. He wants, like the Southerner, to be pure.

Afrocentrism is intense now because blacks are in a special period   43
of social development in a nation going through a period of fearsome transition. Social development, by its nature, is ambivalent, characterized by a sense of exchange, of gaining and losing. Afrocentrism, in its conservatism, is opposed to this ambivalence and to this sense of exchange. What blacks desire during these turbulent times is exactly what whites want: the security of a golden past that never existed. A significant number of both blacks and whites want, strangely, to go back to an era of segregation, a fantasy time between 1920 and 1955, when whites felt secure in a stable culture and when blacks felt unified and strong because black people were forced to live together. Afrocentrism wants social change without having to pay the psychic price for it. Perhaps many black folk feel that they have paid too much already, and who is to say they are not right.

The issue raised by Afrocentrism is the meaning and formation   44
of identity, which is the major fixation of the American, especially the black American. In a country that relentlessly promotes the myth of self-reliance because it is unable to provide any sense of security in a cauldron of capitalistic change, identity struggle is so acute because so much is at stake. Afrocentrism may be wrong in many respects, and it certainly can be stifling and restrictive, but some of its impulses are right. In a culture where information and resources of knowledge are the main levers for social and economic advancement, psychological well-being has become increasingly important as, in the words of one scholar, "a social resource," just as "social networks of care and community support [have become] central features of a dynamic economy." Black folk know, and rightly so, that their individual identities are tied to the strength of their community. The struggle over black identity in the United States has been the struggle over the creation of a

true black community here. What integration has done to the individual black mind in the United States is directly related to what it has done to the black community. This is the first lesson we must learn. The second is that perhaps many black folk cling to Afrocentrism because the black *American* experience still costs more, requires more courage, than white Americans—and black Americans—are willing to admit.

THINKING ABOUT THE CONTENT

1. Early says, "Afrocentrism is many things and has many degrees of advocacy" (7). What are some of the examples of Afrocentrism that Early uses to help define it? Why is Afrocentrism difficult to define specifically? What is its appeal for a growing number of blacks?

2. Early compares Louis Farrakhan, head of the Nation of Islam, with the conservative talk-show host Rush Limbaugh. In what ways does he find them similar? What are their salable techniques?

3. What does Early mean when he says, "The paradox of the bourgeois aspect of Afrocentrism is that it rejects cosmopolitanism as being 'white' or 'Eurocentric' " (15)? Does this mean Early is denouncing Afrocentrism? Why or why not?

4. What fault does Early seem to find with Molefi K. Asante's definition of Afrocentrism? Why does he call Asante's views of African Americans "a crock of nonsense" (18)? What do you think?

5. What is the importance of Cheikh Anta Diop's research to the Afrocentric movement? Why does Early believe W. E. B. Du Bois deserves more credit than Diop's? Why is Malcolm X held in higher regard by many in the black community today than Martin Luther King, Jr.? Of what importance is the work of these three men to Afrocentrism?

6. Early believes that "Afrocentrism may be wrong in many respects . . . but some of its impulses are right" (44). What does he find wrong and right about Afrocentrism? What are your opinions regarding the Afrocentric movement?

LOOKING AT STRUCTURE AND STYLE

7. What is the function of the first six paragraphs? How does Early use them to establish his subject and thesis? How well does paragraph 7 make the transition into the subject?

8. How well does Early define Afrocentrism? Where in his essay does he make distinctions of the various components of Afrocentrism? How thoroughly does he explain each portion of the definition?

9. To whom is Early writing? What passages either directly or indirectly reveal Early's opinions of Afrocentrism? How knowledgeable does Early seem on the subject?

EXPLORING DISCUSSION AND WRITING TOPICS

10. Develop Early's comment, "What blacks desire during these turbulent times is exactly what whites want: the security of a golden past that never existed" (43). Is he right? What is "turbulent" about the times? What is the appeal of "a fantasy time between 1920 and 1955" for both blacks and whites (43)?

11. Respond to Early's comment in the last sentence that "the black *American* experience still costs more, requires more courage, than white Americans—and black Americans—are willing to admit" (44).

12. Do you think that Afrocentrism can eventually bring harmony to an integrated society, or will it further segregate and develop tension between races?

bell hooks (Gloria Watkins) has taught at Oberlin College and is Distinguished Professor of English at City College in New York. A teacher, poet, and activist, hooks focuses her writing mainly on the politics of gender, race, and class, as can be seen in her column, "Sisters of the Yam" in *Z* magazine, and her books *Ain't I a Woman: Black Women and Feminism; Talking Back: Thinking Feminist, Thinking Black; Feminist Theory: From Margin to Center; Black Looks: Race and Representation; Yearning: Race, Gender, and Cultural Politics; Teaching to Transgress: Education as the Practice of Freedom;* and *Killing Rage: Ending Racism.*

In the following essay from *Killing Rage* (1995), hooks voices concern over the mistaken notion that the work of African-American intellectuals is seen by many blacks as a "sell-out" to white supremacy further estranging themselves from the plight of the black community; over the lack of voice and encouragement in academia given to black intellectuals, especially black women intellectuals; and over the lack of unity between black academics and intellectuals. Professor hooks challenges the black academic and intellectual communities to work more closely in finding ways to reach the black community and bringing about black self-determination.

ℳ

Black Intellectuals: Choosing Sides

Throughout much of our history in the United States, African Americans have been taught to value education—to believe that it is necessary for racial uplift, one of the means by which we can redress wrongs engendered by institutionalized racism. The belief that education was a way to intervene in white supremacist assumptions that black folks were intellectually inferior, more body than mind, was challenged when unprecedented numbers of black students entered colleges and universities, graduated with degrees, yet found that racist assumptions remained intact. It was challenged by the reality of racial assimilation—the creation of a cultural context wherein those educated black folks who had "made it" often internalized white supremacist thinking about blackness. Rather than intervening in the status quo, assimilated educated black folks often became the gatekeepers, mediating between the racist white power structure and that larger mass of black folks who were continually assaulted, exploited, and/or oppressed. Nowhere was this trend more evident than in colleges and universities. Even historically black colleges upheld white supremacist biases in the shaping of curricula, programs of study, and social life.

When militant black resistance to white supremacy erupted in   2
the sixties with the call for black power, the value of education was questioned. The ways in which many educated black folks acted in complicity with the existing racist structure were called out. Even though some black academics and/or intellectuals responded to the demand for progressive education that would not reflect white supremacist biases, the vast majority continued to promote conservative and liberal notions of assimilation. Against a backdrop wherein black academics and/or intellectuals were viewed as "suspect," as potential traitors to the cause of black self-determination, young black critical thinkers who saw ourselves as revolutionaries entered colleges and universities in the seventies prepared to do battle. We were there to acquire an education but we were not there to passively consume the education offered by the colonizer. We were often lone individuals profoundly isolated, not only from the white world but from the world of assimilated conservative blackness that was more the norm.

Unlike insurgent black critical thinker/philosopher Cornel West,   3
who cites his experience as an undergraduate at Harvard as the time when he underwent an "intellectual conversion" because studying there opened "a whole new world of ideas," I made my commitment to intellectual life in the segregated black world of my childhood. While I agree with West that it is useful "to be connected to a person or subculture that has devoted himself, herself or itself to the life of the mind," I do not see this as the only cultural context where intellectual quest can be nurtured and sustained. Indeed, rampant anti-intellectualism at Stanford University threatened to thwart my longing to devote myself to the life of the mind. This environment was an extremely hostile place for any black student militantly resisting white supremacy—engaging in a process of decolonization. The black scholars there who were committed to intellectual life were often uninterested in those of us who came from underprivileged-class backgrounds, who were not the offspring of the black elite, and in most cases were not male. This seemed especially true of the small number of radical and politicized black male professors. Ironically, my desire to do intellectual work had been much more affirmed in the segregated community I grew up in than at Stanford University, where I encountered not only

racist assumptions about the intelligence of black folks, sexist ideas about female intellectuality, and class elitism but also prejudicial attitudes towards southerners. Intellectual work differs from academic work precisely because one does not need to undertake a formal course of study or strive for degrees to live the life of the mind. Despite class, gender, or race, individuals can choose intellectual work even if that choice is never affirmed by teachers or academic institutions. Formal education can and often does enrich an organic intellectual process but it is not essential to the making of an intellectual. I did not attend college to become an intellectual, nor did I attain a doctorate for that reason. These paths led me into the academic profession, which is not necessarily a location where intellectual work is affirmed.

Too often we confuse academic and intellectual work. Certainly, 4 I entered college naively assuming it would be a place where a life of the mind would be affirmed only to discover the difference between working to be an academic and doing intellectual work. The heart of intellectual work is critical engagement with ideas. While one reads, studies, and at times writes, a significant part of that work is time spent in contemplation and reflection. Even though an exchange of ideas can and does take place in a communal context, there is necessarily a private solitary dimension to intellectual work. It is that need for time that has often precluded African Americans, particularly those among us who grow up without class privilege, from becoming intellectuals. Those of us who choose intellectual life usually pursue academic careers so that we will have time to do our work. My earliest models for black intellectual life were not academics; they were writers, specifically Lorraine Hansberry and James Baldwin. Unlike most black academics I encountered as a student, these writers were readers, thinkers, political activists, committed to education for critical consciousness; they were individuals exuding radical openness. They were not narrow-minded. Their openness to ideas, to engaging in critical dialogues with diverse audiences, set a powerful example.

The intellectual work of writers like Baldwin and Hansberry tends 5 to be obscured when discussions of black intellectual traditions focus on academics or writers who teach in university settings. Most black academics (like their white and non-white counterparts) are not intellectuals. No unitary black intellectual tradition can be developed if black academics stubbornly resist acknowledging the work of writers who are also major critical thinkers or if attention is only given those thinkers who manage to acquire recognition in the white mainstream. There are not many African Americans who choose to devote themselves to an intellectual life, and those who do who are not connected to the academy, who may not publish widely or at all, have no visibility. Concurrently, many young black intellectuals abandon their zeal for a life of the mind in the process of becoming and/or working as academics or seeking more financially rewarding occupations.

Since so few black folks choose to devote themselves to intellectual   6
life, there is no strong intellectual community. Black academics and/or intellectuals have the greatest opportunity to form bonds with one another. Yet those bonds often are established not on the basis of respect for work but rather via a process of networking wherein exchanges of favors or personal likes and dislikes overdetermine allegiances. The competitive hierarchical structure of academe militates against the formation of intellectual community based on open-minded sharing of ideas. Among marginalized groups, like African Americans, the most open-minded individuals are more likely to be isolated. That isolation is likely to be intensified if their intellectual work is linked to progressive politics.

When I began teaching in the same institution as Cornel West, I   7
was able to bond with him and experience the joy of intellectual community. Sharing with him both progressive politics and a vision of intellectual life was the connection that enabled us to write *Breaking Bread: Insurgent Black Intellectual Life*. When I approached him with this project, we were both uncertain about whether or not there would really be an audience for such a discussion. Our primary intent was to affirm the primacy of intellectual work in contemporary African-American life. We wanted to repudiate the notion that to become a black intellectual and/or academic means that one assimilates and surrenders passionate concern with ending white supremacy, with uplifting black people. Through this act of intervention we hoped to encourage more black folks to choose intellectual work.

When I wrote my essay for the book, I was particularly interested   8
in exploring the conditions that must exist for black females to choose intellectual life. Many black women academics often dismiss and devalue intellectual work, particularly the work of peers. Even though there are so few of us, competition for mainstream attention, jockeying for male approval, or narrow judgmental attitudes tend to pit us against one another. In my own life, commitment to feminist politics has been the force that challenges me to seek a solidarity and sisterhood with black women that transcends the will to compete or engage in petty trashing. When patriarchal support of competition between women is coupled with competitive academic longing for status and influence, black women are not empowered to bond on the basis of shared commitment to intellectual life or open-minded exchange of ideas.

Empowered to be hostile towards and policing of one another, black female academics and/or intellectuals often work to censor and silence one another. This is especially the case when dissenting perspectives emerge. Since many women in the academy are conservative or liberal in their politics, tensions arise between those groups and individuals, like myself, who advocate revolutionary politics.

I was reminded of these splits recently when the conference "Black Women in the Academy: Defending Our Name, 1894–1994" was convened. The brochure for the conference introduced it with a statement that read:

> Black women have come in for a large share of negative criticism in the form of both open and coded discourse generated by the Anita Hill–Clarence Thomas hearings last year, and political discourse generated by electoral campaigns over the course of the last year largely centered on the issue of welfare reform and "family values." These events have generated the most intense public consideration of the character and morality of Black women this country has witnessed since the 1890's.

I found this statement discouraging. Implicitly it suggests that black women come to voice, are recognized as meaningful presences, only when we are granted visibility by white-dominated mass media, that it is this public's recognition that is worthy of debate and response. Such a statement deflects attention away from the work black women continually do to bring our concerns to public attention. That black women academics would gather under a rubric that suggests we come to "defend our name" rather than to proclaim and celebrate our academic and/or intellectual work was troubling. Politically, I rejected the public premise of this conference. It embraced a rhetoric and positionality of victimhood without problematizing this stance. It tacitly assumed that black women would all identify our circumstances with those individuals who were being highlighted by mainstream political culture. Although I longed to be among a gathering of black women from various disciplines, I knew that my presence would not have been welcomed by those participants who wanted more than anything to have the conference superficially project a unitary vision of black women in the academy. There was nothing in the prefatory statement that acknowledged diversity of opinion or political affiliations. The demand for a unitary vision leads to the exclusion of voices, the silencing of dissent. Exclusion is one way to punish those whose views are not deemed correct or acceptable. Fear of isolation serves to check individual black women's critical thought and curtails their interest in progressive politics. Black women in the academy, who are busy defending their name, may not be at all interested in engaging in rigorous intellectual discussion and debate. To a grave extent black female intellectuals with progressive politics are assailed from all sides. We confront white supremacy, as well as the sexism of black people (especially black men), which continues to overvalue black male intellectuals and undervalue the work of black females, even as we then find ourselves rejected by individual black women with more conservative politics who either feel threatened or assume a policing role in order to silence diverse perspectives.

Lack of solidarity and intellectual community among black women leaves us particularly vulnerable in relation to highly competitive sexist black male thinkers who see themselves as the movers and shakers defining black intellectual tradition. Much of their scholarship is written as though they read none of the work of black women critical thinkers. Seeing themselves as shaping the tradition, these black males often assign black female thinkers supportive roles. Subordinating our work to that of powerful males, they attempt to keep in place racialized sexist hierarchies that deem their work more valuable. This thinking persists even though the work of an individual black woman thinker may be much more well read, reaching a much more diverse audience than comparable work by male counterparts. Black male thinkers act in complicity with a white power structure wherein sexist thinking supports devaluing black women as critical thinkers even as that same structure acknowledges the power and excellence of black women's fiction writing. When it comes to nonfiction writing, white-dominated mass media often make no distinction between individual black women based on our work. We are often lumped together so that if a representative is desired any one will do. Major magazines and newspapers that seek out the opinions of black male thinkers who are deemed important because of their work act as though any black female voice will do, the assumption being that none of our voices is particularly distinct or deserving of attention based on the specific nature of our work. Unfortunately, collectively black women intellectuals (as distinct from black women academics) do not produce a substantial body of work that would serve as an intervention challenging the assumption that we are merely following behind male thinkers. Often black males define the nature of public discourse about the role of the black intellectual in ways that deflect attention away from individual black female thinkers whose work may be more exemplary in its connection of theory and practice, in its engagement with progressive politics.

When I have participated in discussions about the role of black   11
intellectuals convened by male thinkers, there has been a refusal to
acknowledge those of us who do not passively embrace the assumption
that our work fails to reach a diverse audience of black folks, that
there is necessarily a gap between intellectual work and progressive
political activism. Intellectual work can itself be a gesture of political
activism if it challenges us to know in ways that counter and oppose
existing epistemologies (ways of knowing) that keep us colonized,
subjugated, etc. Intellectual work has that potential only if the individual is committed to a progressive political vision of social change. All
too often we invest in a unitary model of "the" black intellectual. Yet
the nature of our intellectual work and its meaning is overdetermined
by our politics.

As an African-American intellectual who has never felt that intel-   12
lectual work separated me either from my segregated poor and working-class community and family of origin or from masses of ordinary
black people, I understand that a false dichotomy has been constructed
in our culture that socializes us to believe that the work of black
intellectuals will necessarily estrange us from blackness. Many of us
are socialized to embrace this dichotomy, to see it as "natural" and
embrace it without interrogation. Black intellectuals who choose to
do work that addresses the needs and concerns of black liberation
struggle, of black folks seeking to decolonize their minds and imagina-
tions, will find no separation has to exist between themselves and
other black people from various class backgrounds. This does not
mean that our work will be embraced without critique, or that we
will not be seen as suspect, only that we can counter the negative
representations of black intellectuals as uppity assimilated traitors by
the work we do. Black intellectuals who are not concerned with the
issue of changing this society so that the conditions exist for black
self-determination will most likely do their work in such a way that
it will not appeal to black folks across class. Black intellectuals who
are committed to ending domination, exploitation, and oppression in
all its myriad manifestations, racism, sexism, class elitism, etc., will
be politically challenged to interrogate the way we work, what we do,
how we speak and write, to see whether or not we are working in a
manner that crosses boundaries. I have made specific decisions about
the nature of my work in the interest of making it accessible to a
broader audience. Those decisions involve doing writing that may not
impress my academic peers. When I decided to write a self-help book
on black women and self-recovery, I expressed in the introduction to
this work my fear that such an act would actually further de-legitimize

me in the eyes of academic colleagues of all races. To take that risk seems minor given the possible good that can come when the effort is made to share knowledge informed by progressive politics in diverse ways.

The desire to share knowledge with diverse audiences while cen- 13 tralizing black folks and our struggle for self-determination, without excluding non-black audiences, requires different strategies from those intellectuals normally deploy to disseminate work. Black intellectuals committed to sharing knowledge across class see public speaking in a different way from most of our peers. Recognizing that masses of folks lack basic reading skills, we know that we must use lectures, radio, television, and conversation in diverse settings to share information. Given the cultural context of white supremacist patriarchy, it is unlikely that any black intellectual who is continually working to cross boundaries will receive the same levels of attention given those folks who assimilate and who are primarily concerned with speaking to a white audience. The degree to which black intellectuals will work in a manner that challenges existing structures of domination will be determined by the nature of their political commitment. Importantly, that commitment need not be static. It changes. There may be work that a progressive intellectual wants to do that aims to address a diverse audience, even as that same individual may choose to do work that speaks specifically to select audiences, work that may use difficult language or jargon that is not accessible to everyone. Strategically, progressive black intellectuals must work from multiple locations. To do such work one necessarily takes risks that require sacrifice—that may include forfeiting opportunities for status and privilege that might undermine one's capacity to engage in dialogue across boundaries. Whether or not an individual thinker chooses to make such sacrifices is not a static process. We make multiple choices depending on our circumstances. Ultimately, depth of political commitment to progressive social change informs our will to sacrifice.

Political activism may be expressed by the type of work progres- 14 sive black intellectuals choose to do. To politically counter anti-intellectual and/or academic thought in black life that persists in portraying educated black folks as traitors (a representation that has concrete foundation), insurgent black critical thinkers must be accountable. That means the work we individually do, and the work of our peers, must be continually interrogated. Unfortunately, when the issue of accountability is superficially raised, the work of powerful black males who are seen as possible traitors is often spotlighted. Often the work of black intellectuals who continually endeavor to frame our discourses in ways that are inclusive of our commitment to black self-determination is discounted. Competitive and sexist battles between black males over issues of leadership often deflect attention away from the work of black women intellectuals which may be far more exemplary in relation to issues of crossing borders, educating for critical consciousness outside the academy. As long as sexist thinking informs public discourse around the role of black intellectuals, as long as black men dominate the discussion, the voices of black female intellectuals will not be heard. Our works are rarely quoted or critically engaged by our male peers. Even when the rare black male thinker incorporates an understanding of gender and/or feminism that stems from his engagement with the work of black women, he may not cite that work. If the work of black women is not valued, then we are not seen as embodying standards of intellectual rigor and excellence coupled with progressive political actions that create a context for change in diverse black communities in ways that could be mirrored by black male peers and students. Until more black women, and our allies in struggle, publicly challenge these biases and omissions within all arenas of public discourse, discussions of the role black intellectuals can assume in black liberation struggle will always be overdetermined by the actions of men.

In the past year I have been on two panels discussing the role of black intellectuals where the intent was more to delineate the shortcomings of famous, individual black males and to castigate them for failing to address the needs of ordinary folks than real engagement of the issues. Black intellectuals must choose to act in the service of black liberation. That choice emerges from our politics. Black intellectuals, like everyone, should be accountable for the political choices we make and for the ways those choices shape our lives, our visions, and our work. Clearly, many black intellectuals and/or academics are not choosing to espouse radical or revolutionary progressive politics. A useful discussion of the role of black intellectuals would not only critically examine why this is so, it would also articulate strategies of constructive intervention and contestation. There is no one function, no one location intellectuals who choose progressive politics must inhabit in society. This is especially true for black intellectuals. Ideally, we should be present everywhere, represented in all walks of life, just as our work should be multilayered, ever-changing, and diverse. And these same criteria should apply to those who engage our work. Most importantly there should be more of us.

Insurgent black intellectuals can increase our numbers by contin-   16
ually reminding everyone that intellectual work need not be done
solely in academic settings. Nor is it healthy for most progressive
black intellectual thought to emerge solely in the service of educational institutions. These locations limit and overdetermine discourse.
Concurrently, without in any way diminishing the importance of
academic work, we need to vigilantly clarify ways in which academic
work does differ from intellectual work. The labor we do as
academics is valuable but it is not inherently intellectual. Making
a distinction between the two types of work, even though they
sometimes overlap and converge, allows everyone to appreciate the
different nature of commitment that is required when one is primarily
concerned with advancing an academic career, in contrast to con-
structing a life where one can be devoted fully and deeply to
intellectual work. Having chosen to balance an academic career
with a primary commitment to intellectual work, I see firsthand
the tensions between the two choices. My primary engagement is
with ideas, not personalities or networks. Racial openness is essential
for intellectual work, independent thinking. Allegiances to institutions
or powerful factions within those locations often constrain and
inhibit independent thought. It is this concrete reality that has led
so many intellectuals to eschew involvement in spheres of power
that can impinge on our commitment to radical openness, to unfet-
tered thought. Fear of surrendering this state of open-mindedness
has often led intellectuals to deny the political implications of their
work, to act as though they do not embrace political positions
because they think it might mean losing "objectivity." There is no
politically neutral intellectual work. Knowing this should empower
intellectuals to make political choices that we can claim while still
holding on to an ethical commitment of open engagement with
ideas. Intellectuals can offer any radical movement for social change
transformative visions and insights. Black intellectuals who are
committed to an inclusive struggle to end systems of domination
(imperialism, racism, sexism, class elitism) can bring to black liberation struggle a radically new vision of social change. Challenging
black intellectuals, Cornel West encourages us to create "a public
dialogue with the black community and within the American community in which certain kinds of alternative ways of looking at the
world and changing the world are made available to people." If
black intellectuals begin our work with this intent, then we show
by our example that we act in solidarity with every black person
who is committed to black self-determination.

THINKING ABOUT THE CONTENT

1. What is hooks's definition of an intellectual? How does she define the difference between academic and intellectual work? Do you agree? Explain.
2. Why does hooks believe that bonds between the black academic and intellectual communities are not being formed? According to hooks, what part do the "progressive politics" of some black intellectuals have in the lack of such a formation?
3. Professor hooks says that a "false dichotomy has been constructed in our culture that socializes us to believe that the work of black intellectuals will necessarily estrange us from blackness" (12). What does she mean? How, according to hooks, can black intellectuals eradicate such beliefs?
4. In paragraph 15, hooks states, "Black intellectuals must choose to act in the service of black liberation." What does hooks feel is the responsibility of black intellectuals? Is she correct? Explain.

LOOKING AT STRUCTURE AND STYLE

5. hooks claims that "rampant anti-intellectualism" existed at Stanford University during her attendance there. What examples does she supply? Are these examples of "anti-intellectualism"?
6. Describe hooks's style. Provide some examples from the essay that exemplify her style.
8. Several of hooks's paragraphs are lengthy, for example 3, 9, 10, and 16. Discuss their structure and function. Do they work well despite the length? As an editor, would you change them? If so, how?

EXPLORING DISCUSSION AND WRITING TOPICS

9. Professor hooks considers herself an intellectual. Read some other works by or about her and write an essay that discusses whether she is fulfilling the role she establishes for black intellectuals to follow.
10. Professor hooks contends that academia, even in black colleges, has and often continues to uphold white supremacist biases. Are you finding that to be true in your current education? Explain.
11. Write an essay that reflects your definitions of an academic and an intellectual. You may or may not want to discuss how they are similar or different from those of hooks's.

DINESH D'SOUZA

Dinesh D'Souza is a first-generation immigrant from India and became a citizen of the United States in 1991. In the Preface to his book *The End of Racism*, D'Souza states:

> My inclinations are strongly antiracist and sympathetic to minorities. My family endured European colonialism in India for many generations. . . . In the United States I am no stranger to xenophobia, prejudice, and discrimination. I also feel a particular debt to the civil rights movement, whose campaign on behalf of black equality helped to expand rights and opportunities for all citizens. Yet, I am not an uncritical cheerleader for every parade that carries the minority banner.

In *The End of Racism*, D'Souza is certainly no cheerleader for those involved in today's civil rights movement. He argues that if blacks want an end to racism they must have a "cultural renaissance" and rebuild the African-American community so as to become "unhyphenated Americans."

As did an earlier work of his, *Illiberal Education*, D'Souza created quite a storm. Two cofellows at the American Enterprise Institute where D'Souza is a research fellow, resigned in protest of the book's publication, claiming that D'Souza inflames rather than enlightens public discussions of race. The following selection is taken from the last pages of *The End of Racism*.

᎒

The End of Racism

Once we have set aside the false remedies premised on relativism—proportional representation and multiculturalism—it is possible to directly address America's real problem, which is partly a race problem and partly a black problem. The solution to the race problem is a public policy that is strictly indifferent to race. The black problem can be solved only through a program of cultural reconstruction in which society plays a supporting role but which is carried out primarily by African Americans themselves. Both projects need to be pursued simultaneously; neither can work by itself. If society is race neutral but blacks remain uncompetitive, then equality of rights for individuals will lead to dramatic inequality of result for groups, liberal embarrassment will set in, and we are back on the path to racial preferences. On the other hand, if blacks are going to reform their community, they have a right to expect that they will be treated equally under the law. Although America has a long way to go, many mistakes have been made, and current antagonisms are high, still there are hopeful signs that the nation can move toward a society in which race ceases to matter, a destination that we can term "the end of racism."

While politicians and pundits continue to debate who should bene-   2
fit from race-based programs, the country is entering a new era in which old racial categories are rapidly becoming obsolete. The main reason for this is intermarriage. Exogamy rates have been extremely high for white ethnic groups for almost a generation. Intermarriage rates for Asians and Hispanics are also substantial and rising. Some 25 percent of Hispanics now marry outside their group. About one-third of Asians living in the United States are married to non-Asians. Although many states as late as 1967 outlawed such unions, today about 5 percent of blacks marry whites. Ten percent of African American men between the ages of fifteen and thirty-four are married to white women. Each year approximately fifty thousand births are recorded to black and white couples.[1]

The rapid increase in mixed-race children means that, in the not-   3
too-distant future, it will be virtually impossible to sort Americans into precise categories for the purposes of maintaining government statistics and enforcing racial preferences. Already the Census Bureau has been compelled by demographic necessity to consider abandoning its archaic system of classification which forces all citizens into a Procrustean bed of six basic groups: white, black, Hispanic, Asian/Pacific Islander, American Indian, and other. For some civil rights activists, such change is an alarming prospect. Consequently, many vehemently oppose a proposal being entertained by the government to introduce a new "multiracial" category, because it might diminish the size of the black population and reduce its affirmative action claims in voting and the work force. "To relinquish the notion of race," black studies professor Jon Michael Spencer says, "is to relinquish our fortress against the powers and principalities that still try to undermine us."[2]

1. Richard Alba, "Assimilation's Quiet Tide," *The Public Interest* (spring 1995), 17; "Mixed Babies," *American Demographics* (June 1994), 39.

2. Cited by Lawrence Wright, "One Drop of Blood," *New Yorker* (July 25, 1994).

Yet by ending racial classification, and limiting government use   4
of ethnic data for scholarly research, Americans across the ideological
spectrum can take an important step toward transcending the historic
barriers of race. Far from treating mixed-race children as an embarrassment to the existing regime of racial head-counting, liberals should
welcome the emerging *café au lait* society. It is also time to reject the
advice of an older generation of scholars who continue to fight the
old battles of the civil rights movement, and to place confidence in
the new generation of young people, who are a hopeful sign for the
twenty-first century.

All the evidence shows that young people today are strongly com-   5
mitted to the principle of equality of rights. They are not disfigured
by the racism that afflicted earlier generations of Americans. For most
young whites born after the civil rights movement, it is absurd and
unthinkable to place people of a different race in the back of the bus,
or to require them to drink out of a separate water fountain. Yet these
young people who go to the same schools as blacks, dress in similar
ways, and listen to the same music, find it just as ridiculous to arbi-
trarily single out African Americans or other groups for special preferences based on color. A recent survey by Peter Hart's polling firm
showed vast majorities of whites and blacks united in their agreement
that success should be the result of education, hard work, and equal
treatment under the law.[3]

Older whites mistake young people's sense of fair play, which   6
produces a resistance to racial nepotism, for a resurgence of racism.
Here is an amazing spectacle: a new generation, which has no record
of legal discrimination and which is by all evidence not racist, is accused
of racism by an earlier generation which has demonstrated its racist
ideology and participated in the enforcement of legal discrimination
against blacks. Against their better instincts, young people are being
corrupted into thinking of themselves in racial terms and into developing identities and hostilities that will only prove a barrier to further
reducing the vestiges of racism in America. An incredible fund of
goodwill is being squandered.

Liberals should stop listening to the fashionable prophets of de-   7
spair who once led the nation nobly and admirably, but who have

3. People for the American Way, *Democracy's Next Generation: A Study of American
   Youth on Race,* survey by Peter Hart Research Associates, Washington, D.C., 1992,
   pp. 12–19, 95–100; see also Charlotte Steeh and Howard Schuman, "Young White
   Adults: Did Racial Attitudes Change in the 1980s?" *American Journal of Sociology*
   98 (September 1989), 340–67.

now become reactionary fogies. So committed are they to the paradigm of racial struggle that they are unable to see and seize new opportunities. Civil rights mythographers are fond of painting Martin Luther King as the Moses of the movement, who, in his own prophetic words, would never reach the Promised Land. What has not been noted is the obvious corollary to this elegant myth: like the Hebrews whom Moses shepherded through the desert for 40 years, today's civil rights leaders are too steeped in the mentality of Egypt to be admitted into Canaan; they may have to die out altogether before a new generation can arise to claim the fruits of their long and largely successful struggle against racial discrimination in this country. These bitter and bewildered old idolators should invest their earnings from racial soothsaying and take a well-earned retirement from the civil rights debate. A new liberal vision, which can strengthen and inspire the burgeoning idealism of the younger generation, would reject biology as the basis for group claims of superiority, acknowledge dysfunctionalities in black culture, insist upon strict government race neutrality, and support policies that encourage productive habits of behavior among African Americans and indeed all citizens.

Blacks as a group stand at a historic junction. Very few people in the civil rights leadership recognize this: convinced that racism of a hundred varieties stands between African Americans and success, most of the activists are ready to do battle once again with this seemingly elusive and invincible foe. Yet the agenda of securing legal rights for blacks has now been accomplished, and there is no point for blacks to increase the temperature of accusations of racism. Historically whites have used racism to serve powerful entrenched interests, but what interests does racism serve now? Most whites have no economic stake in the ghetto. They have absolutely nothing to gain from oppressing poor blacks. Indeed the only concern that whites seem to have about the underclass is its potential for crime and its reliance on the public purse. [8]

By contrast, it is the civil rights industry which now has a vested interest in the persistence of the ghetto, because the miseries of poor blacks are the best advertisement for continuing programs of racial preferences and set-asides. No one is more committed to the one-drop rule, and more likely to resist its demise, than these professional blacks whose livelihoods depend on maintaining a large and resentful African American coalition. Publicly inconsolable about the fact that racism continues, these activists seem privately terrified that it has abated. Formerly a beacon of moral argument and social responsibility, the civil rights leadership has lost much of its moral credibility, and has [9] a fair representation of charlatans who exploit the sufferings of the underclass to collect research grants, minority scholarships, racial preferences, and other subsidies for themselves. Progressive blacks who wish to keep the spirit of the civil rights movement alive might consider a sit-in at the offices of the NAACP at which they demand that the organization commit itself to measures to address the plight of the poorest blacks.

The real issue in America today is not whether Cornel West can get a taxi. If he dresses well he is less likely to be mistaken for a criminal, and if one cab passes him by, another will come along to take him to the dining room at the Harvard faculty club. The supreme challenge faced by African Americans is the one that Booker T. Washington outlined almost a century ago: the mission of building the civilizational resources of a people whose culture is frequently unsuited to the requirements of the modern world. Writes African American pastor Eugene Rivers: 10

> Unlike many of our ancestors, who came out of slavery and entered this century with strong backs, discipline, a thirst for literacy, deep religious faith, and hope in the face of adversity, we have produced . . . a new jack generation ill-equipped to secure gainful employment even as productive slaves.[4]

Sadly, the habits that were needed to resist racist oppression or secure legal rights are not the ones needed to exercise personal freedom or achieve success today. As urged by black reformers, both conservative and liberal, the task ahead is one of rebuilding broken families, developing educational and job skills, fostering black entrepreneurship, and curbing the epidemic of violence in the inner cities. Since the government is not in a good position to improve socialization practices among African Americans, the primary responsibility for cultural restoration undoubtedly lies with the black community itself. "When we finally achieve the right of full participation in American life," Ralph Ellison wrote, "what we make of it will depend upon our sense of cultural values, and our creative use of freedom, not upon our racial identification."[5] 11

Reformers like Glenn Loury, William Raspberry, and John Sibley Butler have offered specific recommendations for black self-improvement. Raspberry has proposed that middle-class African Americans voluntarily establish Big Brother programs in which they "adopt" poor 12

---

4. Eugene Rivers, "On the Responsibility of Intellectuals in the Age of Crack," *Boston Review* (September–October 1992).

5. Ralph Ellison, *Shadow and Act* (New York: Random House, 1964), p. 271.

black children and expose them to more productive habits of behavior. The National Urban League has a pilot program to convince successful blacks who have benefited from affirmative action to invest in the economic revitalization of inner cities. Another proposal is for black groups to conduct summer camps in which students are taught entrepreneurial skills. John Sibley Butler argues that blacks should emulate Koreans and set up rotating credit associations which establish pools of capital for members to set up new businesses. Reformers such as Robert Woodson, Charles Ballard, Kimi Gray, Jesse Peterson, Johnny Ray Youngblood, and Reginald Dickson are going beyond advocacy, setting up teen-pregnancy programs, family support initiatives, community job training, instruction in language and social demeanor, resident supervision of housing projects, and privately run neighborhood schools. Even some of the old civil rights veterans are starting to realize that old panaceas won't work. As Harlem's Reverend Calvin Butts puts it, "Our community has now become the dumping ground for every social service in the world. Harlem's salvation is not more AIDS hostels, drug rehab centers, homeless shelters, or low-income housing, but more businesses and middle-class people who buy condos or coops."[6]

We can sympathize with the magnitude of the project facing African Americans. In order to succeed, they must rid themselves of aspects of their past that are, even now, aspects of themselves.[7] The most telling refutation of racism, as Frederick Douglass once said about slavery, "is the presence of an industrious, enterprising, thrifty and intelligent free black population."[8] For many black scholars and activists, such proposals are anathema because they seem to involve ideological sellout to the white man and thus are viewed as not authentically black. Frantz Fanon, a leading black anticolonialist writer, did not agree. What is needed after the revolution, Fanon wrote, is "the

13

6. Cited by Paul Klebnikov, "Showing Big Daddy the Door," *Forbes* (November 9, 1992), 154.

7. As Orlando Patterson writes: "Blacks now face a historic choice. To survive, they must abandon their search for a past, must indeed recognize that they lack all claim to a distinctive cultural heritage, and that the path ahead lies not in myth-making and historical reconstruction, which are always doomed to failure, but in accepting the epic challenge of their reality. Black Americans can be the first group in the history of mankind who transcend the confines and grip of a cultural heritage, and in so doing, they can become the most truly modern of all peoples—a people . . . whose style of life will be a rational and continually changing adaptation to the exigencies of survival at the highest possible level of existence." See Orlando Patterson, "Toward a Future That Has No Past," *The Public Interest* (Spring 1972), 60–61.

8. Frederick Douglass *Life and Times of Frederick Douglass* (New York: Collier Books, 1962), p. 289.

liberation of the man of color from himself. However painful it may be for me to accept this conclusion, I am obliged to state it: for the black man, there is only one destiny, and it is white."[9] In this Fanon is right: for generations, blacks have attempted to straighten their hair, lighten their skin, and pass for white.[10] But what blacks need to do is to "act white," which is to say, to abandon idiotic Back-to-Africa schemes and embrace mainstream cultural norms, so that they can effectively compete with other groups.

There is no self-esteem to be found in Africa or even in dubious   14
ideologies of blackness. "Let the sun be proud of its achievement," Frederick Douglass said.[11] Instead, African Americans should take genuine pride in their collective moral achievement in this country's history. Blacks as a group have made a vital contribution to the expansion of the franchise of liberty and opportunity in America. Through their struggle over two centuries, blacks have helped to make the principles of the American founding a legal reality not just for themselves but also for other groups. As W. E. B. Du Bois put it, "There are no truer exponents of the pure human spirit of the Declaration of Independence than the American Negroes."[12]

Yet rejection in this country produced what Du Bois termed a   15
"double consciousness," so that blacks experience a kind of schizophrenia between their racial and American identities. Only now, for the first time in history, it is possible for African Americans to transcend this inner polarization and become the first truly modern people, unhyphenated Americans. Black success and social acceptance now are both tied to rebuilding the African American community. If blacks can achieve such a cultural renaissance, they will teach other Americans a valuable lesson in civilizational restoration. Thus they could vindicate both Booker T. Washington's project of cultural empowerment and Du Bois's hope for a unique African American "message" to the world.

---

9. Frantz Fanon, *Black Skin, White Masks* (New York: Grove Weidenfeld, 1967), pp. 8, 10.

10. The first black millionaire, Madame C. J. Walker, made her fortune selling skin dye and hair-straightening cosmetics to blacks. "We wanted to be light-skinned so bad," one activist recalls, "we would walk in the shade." See Audrey Edwards and Craig Polite, *Children of the Dream* (New York: Doubleday, 1992), p. 17.

11. Frederick Douglass, "The Nation's Problem," in Howard Brotz, ed., *Negro Social and Political Thought, 1850–1920* (New York: Basic Books, 1966), pp. 316–17.

12. W. E. B. Du Bois, *The Souls of Black Folk*, Penguin Books, New York, 1982, p. 11; see also W. E. B. Du Bois, *The Gift of Black Folk* (Millwood, N.Y.: Kraus-Thomson, 1975), p. 139.

Even more, it will be blacks themselves who will finally discredit racism, solve the American dilemma, and become the truest and noblest exemplars of Western civilization.

THINKING ABOUT THE CONTENT

1. D'Souza dismisses what he calls "false remedies . . . proportional representation and multiculturalism" and believes there can be an end of racism with a public policy that is indifferent to race and a "program of cultural reconstruction in which society plays a supporting role but which is to be carried out primarily by African Americans themselves." Are "proportional representation" and "multiculturalism" false remedies? What is your reaction to his proposal?

2. What does D'Souza mean by "a cultural reconstruction" of the black community? What specific areas does he call upon black reformers to address? Is it the black community's responsibility to address these issues?

3. What does D'Souza have against today's civil rights leaders? What effect does he feel they are having on the younger generation? What do you think of his argument?

4. What are D'Souza's arguments against Afrocentrism (explained in Gerald Early's "Understanding Afrocentrism")? Why does he feel African-Americans need to drop the hyphen? What do you think?

LOOKING AT STRUCTURE AND STYLE

5. What words or phrases develop D'Souza's attitude and tone? To whom is he writing? Why do you think so?

6. What is the point of paragraph 2? What relation does it have with D'Souza's argument? Is this an effective argument?

EXPLORING DISCUSSION AND WRITING TOPICS

7. Discuss whether or not you think ending racial classification and the limiting of government usage of ethnic data for scholarly research will help end racism. What is the purpose and value of racial classification at present?

8. React to D'Souza's last paragraph; or, read other portions of *The End of Racism* and discuss your reaction.

ISHMAEL REED

Ishmael Reed grew up in working-class neighborhoods in Buffalo, New York, attended Buffalo public schools and the University of Buffalo. He has taught at Harvard, Yale, and Dartmouth, and for twenty years has been on the faculty at the University of California at Berkeley. He a Harvard Signet Fellow, a Yale Calhoun Fellow, and the author of more than twenty books, including novels, essays, plays, and poetry. Some of his works include *Japanese by Spring, Writin' Is Fightin', Mumbo Jumbo, A Secretary of the Spirits,* and *Mother Hubbard.* He has been a finalist for the Pulitzer Prize and was twice nominated for the National Book Award. Reed is also the founder of the Before Columbus Foundation. He is one of two Americans to receive the 1993 Suzukinu Hanayagi Award from the Osaka Community Foundation.

The following selection appears in Reed's *Airing Dirty Laundry,* a collection of essays on a wide range of subjects from indictments of the media establishment for "selling out black America" to the revival of bebop music. Here, Reed recounts how he discovered who his ancestors were and argues that, "The Afrocentric exploration of the black past only scratches the surface."

เจ

Distant Cousins

I *am* a native of the South, and it was not until last April that I began 1
to understand how native I am. It's quite possible that I am a twenty-plus generation southerner.

Among my ancestors are those who roamed the mountains of 2
Tennessee for thousands of years, Irish people who left the Irish frontier in the late 1700s, and at least one Danish woman from Stonewall, Tennessee, who for now remains a mystery. (When I discovered that, I began to realize why I had such an affinity for Kierkegaard in my late teenage years.) And that's what searching for the details of one's background is similar to: a whodunit. But every time I've found a new fact, a new lead, I've discovered that my fiction has been ahead of me.

The made-up moments in my creative work arising from another 3
murky part of consciousness seem to have had a better take on my

origin than I. For example, in the early 1970s I read of a state called
Franklin that was almost admitted to the Union. All I knew about it
was that its population was black, Indian, and white and that it was
led by an idealistic governor named Sevier. I wrote a poem called "The
Lost State of Franklin." This work was the basis for a performance
created by Carla Blank and her Japanese collaborator, Susuhi Hanayagi.

When I visited my father's sisters and brother for the first time,   4
last year, I discovered that their homestead was located not too far
from the site of Governor Sevier's home and that the street before the
one they lived on was named Franklin.

I found that others knew details about me that were lost to me.   5
Native Americans in the Southwest, Pacific Northwest, and Alaska
knew about my ancestry before I was able to locate it. Leslie Silko,
after hearing me read from my work, told me that I was an Indian.
A group of Native Americans with whom we were joshing around in
Ellensburg, Washington, removed a headdress from a white man who
claims Native American ancestry and placed it on my head. That's
more like it, they said.

After learning of my Cherokee great-grandmother, I phoned my   6
friend Andy Hope and asked, in jest, why, given the fact that I had a
Native American heritage, I wasn't invited to Returning-of-the-Gift
Festival held in Oklahoma City. Andy said he hoped I wouldn't be
bitten by a mosquito so that my Native American blood would be
drained. Some of the comments of these Indian writers came back to
me in April as, en route to Alcoa from Knoxville, we passed through
a section of land called the Old Cherokee Trail, and while discussing
my ancestry, the lost part, with aunts I'd never seen, I was told that
my grandfather's mother was a Cherokee who was spared the trip
west, the Trail of Tears, during which thousands of Cherokee Indians
were uprooted from their traditional homelands in Tennessee. I was
informed that my grandfather attended Cherokee school.

The Afrocentric exploration of the black past only scratches the   7
surface. A full examination of the ancestry of those who are referred
to in the newspapers as blacks and African Americans must include
Europe and Native America. The pursuit of this journey requires the
sort of intellectual courage that's missing in contemporary, politically
correct America, where certain words cannot be spoken and certain
secrets cannot be unearthed and certain investigations are frowned
upon.

Black Americans who desire to uncover their past face problems.   8
They must encounter not only the intellectual timidity of some black

Americans, but red racism (Native American novelist and critic Gerald
Vizenor surprised me with his comments about the racist views some
Native Americans hold toward blacks). Yet probably the thorniest
impediment to the discovery of the black past is southern denial. The
inability of some southerners, not only laymen but academicians, to
face the fact of miscegenation is such an explosive issue that this word,
which simply means "mix," has taken on a sinister meaning. The denial
that generations of southern white men have lived in polygamous
arrangements is a hypocrisy that exists to this day. As someone whose
fiction plays with the hypocrisy, I was delighted to point out in my
latest novel, *Japanese by Spring,* that among the recent candidates for
president who were running or about to run on the "immorality in
the inner city" ticket, two were fathers of out-of-wedlock children,
two were accused by a blond lobbyist of having engaged in assignations
with her, and one was accused by a beauty queen of receiving more
than a massage from her when he visited her in a New York hotel. In
fact, a Civil War writer named Martha Higgens wrote that plantation
owners still thought of themselves as good husbands and fathers.
Maybe this is why an exploration of the African American past can
become so dangerous: an exploration that would reduce the newspaper,
bureaucrat, and think-tank idea of a Black America, a place inhabited
with people of an uninterrupted African genealogy, to speciousness.

Black people growing up in the 1940s and 1950s were told by   9
their education that if they behaved like Anglos and assumed an Anglo
identity, opportunities would appear. In order to become this other
identity, one had to reject one's past. I think this is why there appears,
frequently, a scene in the novel of assimilation, by those not only of
black but of white ethnic background, in which the narrator invites
college friends home and is ashamed of his or her parents speaking
English with a German, Italian, Irish, or Yoruba syntax. Our parents
were viewed by our education as dumb and backward, and the sooner
we abandoned their attitudes and style, it was proposed, the better
our chances for success. It took me many years to understand that my
parents' style was in some ways hipper and more sophisticated than
mine. In the 1950s, they were listening to the blues, Charles Brown,
and others, while I was listening to West Coast jazz.

An exploration of those ancestors who lay behind their generation   10
was considered unthinkable. You'd find yourself in some cotton field,
and if you went back further than that, you might find yourself in a
jungle surrounded by these teeth-gnashing natives. My education told
me that I was an uncivilized infidel and that I could be redeemed only
by cutting all ties to my background.

Travel, world events, and my contact with black intellectuals   11
would change my outlook. At the age of fifteen, I traveled to Paris as
part of a YMCA delegation and, while there, met with Africans for
whom my education had not prepared me: students who were studying
at the Sorbonne, articulate and intellectual.

The type of colonialism that today's students could only imagine   12
began to fade in the 1960s. New and dynamic leaders arose in Africa—
Patrice Lumumba and Kwame Nkrumah. I remember watching a
shaken Adlai Stevenson being interrupted by black demonstrators as he
sought to defend some backward American African policy. I excitedly
turned to my mother and shouted at her that some black people were
interrupting Stevenson's speech. Adlai Stevenson had been my hero.

In high school, when the teacher asked students to select countries   13
to represent during United Nations Day assembly, we black students
were too embarrassed to choose Africa. We preferred to represent
someplace like Norway.

At the beginning of the 1960s, African Americans were claiming   14
Africa. I met Malcolm X, who put it plain. In what was to be the
beginning of a number of exchanges I had with him in both Buffalo
and New York City, he said that black history was cotton-patch history
as it was being taught. He was right. In the textbooks we read, the
blacks seemed to be having a great time. Real party animals. So what
was the fuss? We hadn't read W. E. B. Du Bois's *Black Reconstruction,*
and so the Reconstruction period became another source of embarrassment, since our view of the Reconstruction period was framed by
D. W. Griffith.

During the early 1960s, African Americans changed their style.   15
Many stopped straightening their hair in favor of an Afro fashion. I
went to New York and joined a black writers' workshop called Umbra,
and we wrote poetry about the greatness of African civilization. I
began to name my style after that of nonacademic folklore based upon
the secret allusions to the Hoodoo culture I'd heard the old black
people whisper about. If folklore was a despised culture, then I would
embrace it. I would base my literary style upon a culture that embarrassed middle-class blacks and of which the white literary culture knew
little, at least the northern white literary culture. I would wave this
lost aesthetic in their faces. My use of what I called Neo-Hoodooism
was an act of literary defiance. Little did I know that I was embarking
on an aesthetic journey that would ultimately take me to the Yoruba
people of West Africa.

Black Pride did wonders for the emotions. It was a great intellec-   16
tual high. It made you feel good. It's significant, I think, that after the

collapse of the Black Power movement, some of its leaders turned to physical drugs. But however exhilarating Black Power was, it could not put out of one's mind those rumors: family stories of ancestors who "could have been white," or who were white.

I was in my late thirties when one day, sitting at a table with my eighty-year-old grandmother, I asked her the identity of her father. (To this day, I wonder why it took me so long.) 17

She said he was an Irishman who had to leave Chattanooga for his role in organizing the pipe workers. It all came back to me—the early years, 1940, 1942, when I lived with my grandmother's brother on 1019 Elm Street in Chattanooga, before my mother returned to take me to Buffalo, New York. There was a pipe manufacturing plant located at the bottom of a hill from the house. Across the street from my uncle's house sat a huge mansion that dominated the neighborhood. It must have been about twenty acres. Built in the Spanish hacienda style, it was owned by the eccentric owner of the pipeworks. His name was pronounced Montegue, and my grandmother's brother remembered him as a man who, despite his wealth, walked down the hill toward his factory wearing overalls and a dirty rag around his neck. I remember staring for hours at the mansion, wondering what lay behind those walls. There were rumors that the mansion was haunted, but not, I was beginning to discover, as haunted as my genealogy. Nobody had ever told me that there was a connection between this man and an ancestor of mine. 18

When I hired a professional genealogist to trace my ancestry on my mother's side, I discovered that the name of the man whom my grandmother identified as an Irishman was Marion Shaw Coleman, who was born in December of 1869 in either Alabama or Georgia. The surprises wouldn't end with this discovery of an Irish American on my grandmother's side. In an interview I conducted with my mother and her cousin, I uncovered another ancestor of Irish American background, on my grandfather's side. My mother's cousin, whom we call "Sister," said that her grandfather, my mother's father's father, was a mean Irishman. My genealogical chart identified this man as Ezekiel Hopson or Hopkins, born in Alabama between 1854 and 1859. His father, Pleasant Hopson, was born in about 1830. 19

These European ghosts in the African American past have been shoveled under by the passionate claims made by the "pure race" theorists, black and white, who hold so much sway over our political and cultural life. These relatives would prove that racial supremacy is, as you say down here in Little Rock, a dog that won't hunt. 20

The late humanitarian John Maher introduced me at a meeting   21
of the Celtic Foundation as an Irish American poet. His reasoning was
that if a drop of black blood made me black, why didn't a drop of
Irish blood make me Irish? The people at my table—Irish American
celebrities—seemed stunned. Pete Hamill, however, shook my hand.
Feminist Dierdre English stunned both me and the audience by an-
nouncing that I was an Irish American, all right, because I was a "liar
and a thief." I then understood why her last name was English. Ms.
English is ignorant of the fact that blacks and whites have been sneaking
back and forth across the racial fences since they came in contact with
each other in the early seventeenth century. Later I wasn't surprised
to read her comments—printed in the *New York Times*—about the
African slave trade, comments that must be the most ignorant on
record.

I asked the late Sarah Fabio, a poet who was called the mother   22
of black studies and whose features betrayed a European heritage,
how one would reconcile the obvious European strain in the blood of
an African American with the African American's identification with
Africa, and she said that she was black because it was the black people
who nurtured her. She had a point. Marion Shaw Coleman left his
African American wife, whose maiden name was Mary E. Hardy,
with a number of children whom she had to support by operating a
restaurant in Chattanooga for more than twenty years. White American males may be the original runaway fathers of the African American
experience.

In the census report of about 1870, Ezekiel Hopson's/Hopkins's   23
children's names are listed. Under "Racial Classification," some children are listed "Black." Other children are listed "White." On the
document, *White* has been crossed out and the letter *M* for *mulatto* is
substituted. According to family oral history, the children who looked
white or near white were beneficiaries of the family's assets and eventually abandoned their darker relatives. Don't look for a story in the
Atlantic Monthly, Harper's, or the *New York Times Magazine* about
how darker relatives were cheated out of millions of dollars in assets
by white and near-white relatives. There are millions missing from the
American black family. These millions have long since passed over
into whiteness.

In 1983, I came in contact with family members whom I'd never   24
seen. Children of a father I'd never met. And this is how I found that
there were Europeans and Native Americans on this side of the family
tree.

The complex racial background of those who are referred to as   25
black Americans has seldom been submitted to serious scrutiny. One
could understand why the Identity Crisis nonfiction is a popular genre
among assimilated intellectuals, but the fact that I could obtain as
much information as I did for only $100 indicates that Identity Crisis
intellectuals aren't seriously interested in discovering their roots, or
are afraid of what they might find. Besides, millions of dollars are
involved in continuing the black-white polarization. Think of all of
the journalists and op-ed writers, along with a profit-feeding media,
that would be out of business were there a fresh and revised look at
race in America. If one allows the Native American ancestry of blacks,
then W. E. B. Du Bois's theory of double consciousness, which has
thrilled black intellectuals for decades, would fold.

I still haven't pieced together all the strains of my identity, but   26
I'm much closer than I was before that day when I decided to ask my
grandmother about her father, and his father. I know now why it took
me so long to ask her the question. I also know that there's no such
thing as Black America or White America, two nations, with two
separate bloodlines. America is a land of distant cousins.

THINKING ABOUT THE CONTENT

1. Based on his own ancestry, why does Reed feel that a full examination
   of African-American ancestry must include Europe and Native America?
   How does his own ancestry argue against Afrocentrism?
2. Why does Reed believe "the thorniest impediment to the discovery of the
   black past is southern denial" (8)? Denial of what?
3. According to Reed, how does "the newspaper, bureaucrat, and think-
   tank idea of a Black America" differ from what he feels can be found by
   an exploration of ancestry (8)? What image of himself as an African
   American was Reed taught? How does that teaching and thought differ
   from today's? What brought about the change?
4. What does Reed say or imply about Afrocentrism? Is he convincing?

LOOKING AT STRUCTURE AND STYLE

5. Is Reed's conclusion stated or implied? If stated, where?
6. What passages help develop Reed's attitude and tone?
7. To whom is Reed writing? What makes you think so? How successful is
   he in presenting his views on Afrocentrism?

EXPLORING DISCUSSION AND WRITING TOPICS

8. Research as much or your family tree as you can. Discuss your own family ancestry. Who are your "distant cousins"? What does it tell you about who you are?
9. Discuss why it is or is not important to know one's ancestry.
10. Reed says "there's no such thing as Black America or White America" (26). Discuss why you agree or disagree.

SUSAN GARVER AND PAULA McGUIRE

Susan Garver, a freelance editor, and Paula McGuire, an editor for an educational publishing company, are contributors to the Coming of America Series, six books centering on different ethnic groups. Each book, using diaries, letters, photographs, and interviews, focuses on the American immigrant experience.

In the following selection from one of the books in the series, *Coming to North American from Mexico, Cuba, and Puerto Rico* (1991), Garver and McGuire reveal what it was like for Mexican immigrants during the Great Depression when the typical attitude in the United States toward immigration was "America for the Americans."

᭙

America for the Americans

When the Americans from the North moved into Mexican territory   1
in the early 1800s, they looked down on the Mexican people. As the years went by, this contempt showed itself in the way United States employers treated Mexican laborers. When the United States needed workers, they encouraged emigration from Mexico but gave the Mexicans the worst jobs at the lowest pay. Mexican farm workers were laid off as soon as a job was done and were constantly on the move. The majority of Mexican immigrants ended up living in make-shift shanty-towns and *barrio* slums.

There were some North Americans who believed that the Mexi-   2
cans preferred this way of life, as one reporter described:

> . . . they are unsettled as a class, move readily from place
> to place, and do not acquire or lease land to any extent.
> But their most unfavorable characteristic is their inclination
> to form colonies and live in a clannish manner. Wherever
> a considerable group of Mexicans are employed, they live
> together, if possible, and associate very little with members
> of other races. . . . In the cities their colonization has be-
> come a menace.[1]

---

1. Samuel Bryan, "Mexican Immigrants in the United States," *The Survey,* 28 (September 7, 1912), 729.

Even those Mexicans who managed to save enough money to   3
move to a good part of town suffered from discrimination. In an
interview a Mexican woman spoke about a neighbor's experience:

> They bought a new stucco house, but there is a very bad
> American who lives next door. The American says bad things
> to her, and calls her a "dirty Mexican," and she is just as
> clean as clean can be. My friend only lived three months there.
> She was so happy with her new house, she fixed it up so
> cute, and it was a nice house. They planted garden, flow-
> ers, and lawn. She worked all day to make it nice, but . . .
> she wants to move now.[2]

As long as there was a need for cheap labor, the Mexican presence   4
was tolerated. That need evaporated in the early 1930s. When the
United States found itself in the middle of the Depression, the Mexican
immigrant was no longer needed or wanted. Millions of citizens had
been thrown out of work—why should Mexicans be given jobs when
there weren't enough for Americans? Measures were taken to prevent
Mexicans from getting the few available jobs. California, for example,
passed a law in 1931 barring aliens from employment on public works
projects. Signs that read "No Niggers, Mexicans, or Dogs Allowed"
and "Only White Labor Employed" were posted.

The suggestion was that the Mexican go home to Mexico. Many   5
Mexicans did return to Mexico voluntarily, in fact. In the early 1930s
more returned to Mexico than immigrated to the United States. The
United States government helped by tightening immigration restrictions, increasing border patrol activities, and making strong efforts to
find and deport illegal aliens.

But many of the Mexicans in the United States were citizens.   6
Although wholesale deportation was illegal, some officials suggested
it. Then, some city governments who could not afford to keep so many
people on welfare during the Depression days offered Mexicans their
fare to the border if they would leave. Implicit was the threat that
their welfare payments would be discontinued. One researcher figured
out that the cost of welfare for some nine thousand Mexicans in Los
Angeles for one year was $800,000. It would cost the city less than
$150,000 to ship the same number to Mexico City. An arrangement
was made with officials of the Southern Pacific Railroad, which agreed
to transport Mexicans from Los Angeles to Mexico City for $14.70

2. Emory S. Bogardus, *The Mexican in the United States,* p. 28.

per person. The first trainload departed in February 1931, and the trips continued for several years.

Jorge Acevedo, a victim of repatriation, described the early-morning arrival of vans in Maravilla, a Mexican-American area in Los Angeles: 7

> Families were not asked what they would like to take along, or told what they needed . . . or even where they were going. "Get in the truck." . . . . Families were separated. . . .
> They pushed most of my family in one van, and somehow in all the shouting and pushing I was separated and got stuck in another van. It was a very big one with boards across it for us to sit on. Nobody knew what was happening or where we were going. Someone said, to a health station.
> We drove all day. The driver wouldn't stop for bathroom nor food nor water. The driver was drinking and became happier as he went along. . . . It was dark when he finally ran the truck off the road. Everyone knew by now that we had been deported. Nobody knew why, but there was a lot of hatred and anger.[3]

During the period 1900–1930, one million Mexicans immigrated   8
to the United States. In the early 1930s, some 300,000 Mexicans and Mexican-Americans were sent back over the border. At least half of them were American-born, and therefore American citizens. Repatriation was especially hard on Mexican-Americans who were United States citizens—either naturalized or native-born Acevedo, who was a native-born North American, was determined to return to Los Angeles, his home.

> One of the reasons I made it back was because I was alone. The others who were dumped into Mexico tried to travel back across the border in families and groups. They were easily spotted and turned back. I was young and strong, and I kept walking. I traveled at night, crawling into some hole or under some brush during the day. I kept off the roads when I had to and went around the larger villages. In this way, then, I walked through the northern part of Mexico, and made my way back to El Paso, Texas.[4]

3. Charles J. and Patricia L. Bustamante, *The Mexican-American and the United States* (Mountain View, Cal.: Patty-Lar Publications, 1969), p. 34.

4. Ibid.

After a few months and a twenty-five-hundred-mile trip, Acevedo   9
arrived in Los Angeles. Later he became a prominent community leader
and in 1967 was appointed director of the War on Poverty in Santa
Clara Country, California.

The repatriation program created problems in Mexico. It took   10
time to resettle the thousands of people who were pouring into the
country every week. Reported one journalist:

> . . . in early January more than ten thousand *repatriados*
> camped and starved, huddled together, waiting for a kind
> government to provide them with transportation so that
> they could move on. . . . Then, later in the month, the
> [Mexican] government sent a train of thirty-three box cars
> . . . and then a second train . . . to take them south and
> scattered them over the country. . . .[5]

For those Mexicans who could stay on in the United States, condi-   11
tions were usually appalling—inadequate relief money, poor housing,
racial prejudice, and segregated schooling. Often a needy Mexican
family received less assistance than a needy American one: the Mexicans "needed less."

Hostility toward Mexicans and Mexican-Americans during the   12
Depression spilled over into the school system. Many schools were
segregated because of their location "near the camp" or on "the other
side of the tracks." Other schools were deliberately segregated. It was
said that Mexican children would be more comfortable and more
confident when competing and learning only with other Mexican children. But segregation made an already tense situation worse. A Mexican who attended a segregated school said:

> In the first place it gave me the feeling of inferiority which
> I found hard to overcome. In the second place, it forms
> dislike, distrust, and even hatred of the American children.
> In the third place the Mexican children do not get to
> associate with the American children and pick up their cus-
> toms, habits and vice versa. . . .[6]

Segregation caused serious problems for some second-generation   13
Mexican-Americans. They had been denied the chance to become

5. Robert McLean, "Goodbye, Vicente," *The Survey,* 66 (May 1931), 182.

6. Ruth L. Martinez, *The Unusual Mexican: A Study in Acculturation* (San Francisco:
R and E Research Associates, 1973).

"Americanized." At the same time, they did not feel that they were Mexicans, for many of them had never been to Mexico. As one writer put it, the Mexican-American is a "hybrid":

> He is unable to reconcile the ideas of the old with those of the new. He accepts some of each and discards some of each. Sometimes he is wise in his choice, sometimes he is exceedingly foolish. . . . His parents are Mexicans. His children may be American. He, himself, is neither; he is both—a hybrid.[7]

Some Mexican children did attend integrated schools, where they [14] were forbidden to speak Spanish even when they were playing in the schoolyard. Cesar Chavez, the well-known Mexican-American labor leader, spoke of the frustration that this caused him.

> In class one of my biggest problems was the language. Of course, we bitterly resented not being able to speak Spanish, but they insisted that we had to learn English. They said that if we were American, then we should speak the language, and if we wanted to speak Spanish, we should go back to Mexico.[8]

Punishment was immediate if the teacher heard the students speak- [15] ing their native language. But Chavez had no wish to give up the language and customs of his people and could not understand why he was being told to do so.

> It's a terrible thing when you have your own language and customs, and those are shattered. I remember trying to find out who I was and not being able to understand. Once, for instance, I recall saying I was a Mexican. The teacher was quick to correct me. "Oh, no, don't say that!" she said. But what else could I say? In a nice way she said, "You are an American. All of us are Americans," and she gave me a long explanation I couldn't understand. I went home and told my mother, "Mama, they tell me I'm an American!" To me an American was a white man. My mother couldn't really give me a satisfactory answer either. She said I was a citizen,

7. May Lanagan, *Second Generation Mexicans in Belvedere* (master's thesis, University of Southern California, 1932), p. 17.

8. Jacques E. Levy, *Cesar Chavez: Autobiography of La Causa* (New York: W. W. Norton, 1975), p. 24.

but I didn't know what a citizen meant. It was too complicated.[9]

The poor treatment of Mexicans in the United States during the   16
1930s finally led to action. Mexicans began to form labor unions and
to demand decent wages and fair treatment. Angry employers reacted
by branding union organizers as Communists and demanding that
they be deported. One Mexican who suffered this fate was Jesus Pal-
lares, who helped to organize unions at several mining camps in New
Mexico. A government relief office worker described what happened
next.

> Attempts were made by my office to intimidate Pallares by
> withholding relief and by inventing reasons by which he could
> be removed from relief jobs. . . . Threats were made to
> starve his family in order to involve him in an argument which
> the relief agency hoped would give rise to violence on his
> part. . . . Such violence never took place, even though
> situations were carefully prepared in advance such as the
> placing of a hammer on the supervisor's desk within his easy
> reach. . . . A complaint was made to Washington on the
> vague and flimsy basis that Pallares was a "trouble-
> maker."[10]

During the same period in California, Mexican fruit pickers were   17
organizing, calling for wage increases and transportation assistance.
The growers' own great cooperative organization has been created as
a result of the oppression and exploitation by brokers and shippers in
the past. Still, they refused to accept the organization of their workers.
The growers' opposition to the Mexican citrus-fruit pickers in Orange
County was particularly ruthless. When the union struck, retaliation
came in the form of vigilantes, strikebreakers, slanted newspaper stories, and a state motor patrol in the area to "direct law-and-order
activities." The sheriff stated: "It is a fight between the entire population
of Orange County and a bunch of Communists." However, dozens
and dozens of non-Communist Mexican fruit pickers were jailed, including 116 who were arrested while traveling on the highway. They
were charged with riot and placed under a bail of five hundred dollars
each. They were held for two weeks before a judge finally released
them and criticized the authorities for their actions.

9. Ibid.

10. Philip Stevenson, "Deporting Jesus," *The Nation* (July 18, 1936), 69.

During the strike, the newspapers upheld "law-abiding citizens" 18
and carried headlines such as "Vigilantes Battle Citrus Workers in War
on Reds." Only one newspaper defended the fruit pickers. The Los
Angeles *Evening News* reported:

> Be it known that the "heroic band of vigilantes," twenty-
> eight in number, who last Friday with clubs and tear-gas
> bombs stole up on a peaceful meeting of 150 Mexican fruit
> pickers in Placentia, fell upon the dumbfounded workers
> without warning, smashed jaws and cracked heads, dis-
> persed the group save one striker smashed into uncon-
> sciousness and left lying on the ground, were exactly this:
>   Twenty-eight Los Angeles bums, recruited from
> streets and beer-halls through a detective agency and paid
> eight dollars a day by the citrus growers to foment violence
> and terrorize the striking Mexican pickers.[11]

This was just one of the strikes against the California growers in 19
the 1930s. Mostly unsuccessful and always blamed on the influence
of the Communists [or "Reds"], these strikes nevertheless were laying
the groundwork for successful labor organization in the future.

The years of the Depression had a strong effect on the typical 20
North American's attitude toward immigration. Earlier slogans such
as "Land of Opportunity" and "Refuge of the Oppressed" were replaced by "America for the Americans." It was not until economic
conditions improved after World War II that Mexican-Americans,
along with other minority groups, could begin again to claim their
civil rights as United States citizens.

THINKING ABOUT THE CONTENT

1. Why did conditions worsen for the Mexican immigrant during the Great
   Depression? How is the Mexican immigrant being treated today?
2. What is meant by a Mexican-American "hybrid"? Can this term be applied
   to other racial or ethnic groups? Explain.
3. What problems were created by the repatriation program of the 1930s?
   What kind of action did the program eventually lead to?
4. What tactics were used by those who treated the Mexicans unfairly? Why
   do you suppose such racial prejudice exists?

11. Quoted in Frank Stokes, "Let the Mexicans Organize," *The Nation* (December 19,
    1936), p. 731.

LOOKING AT STRUCTURE AND STYLE

5. To whom do you think the authors are writing? Support your contention.
6. How well do the authors support their historical overview? Is the support reliable?
7. Describe the authors' tone. How is this tone created?

EXPLORING DISCUSSION AND WRITING TOPICS

8. Compare and contrast the situation of the Mexican American today with that of the 1930s.
9. Read from Carver and McGuire's book and compare and contrast the treatment of Mexican immigrants with those from Cuba or Puerto Rico. Or, read from one of the other books in the Coming to America series that deals with the treatment of immigrants from Asia, the British Isles, or Europe.
10. Is immigration a problem in America today? Should immigration be stopped, slowed, opened? Who should be allowed in? What are government policies on immigration?

LINDA CHAVEZ

Linda Chavez has been a senior fellow of the Manhattan Institute and a former director of the U.S. Commission on Civil Rights. She is a frequent contributor to publications such as *Fortune,* the *Wall Street Journal,* and *USA Today.*

The publication of her book *Out of the Barrio: Toward a New Politics of Hispanic Assimilation* (1991) created quite a stir, especially among Hispanics leaders. Some were angered at her stance on bilingual education, immigration policies, and affirmative action because it went against the grain with Hispanic policymakers. Her position that young Hispanics are no longer victims of social prejudice or governmental policies seems to be supported by a 1992 survey of racial attitudes among young people conducted by Peter Hart Research Associates for People for the American Way. The study found that only 9 percent of young Hispanics surveyed believed that Hispanics' socioeconomic status was hindered by prejudice or discrimination. Instead, the report showed that those surveyed felt lower education and difficulty with English explained why some "Hispanics tend to be worse off in terms of jobs, income, and housing."

Chavez, in her introduction to the 1992 paperback edition of *Out of the Barrio,* states that she hopes the book "will provoke real and sustained debate on how best to achieve the economic, social, and political integration of the Hispanic community."

What follows is excerpted from her book.

᙮

Out of the Barrio

A ssimilation has become a dirty word in American politics. It in-   1
vokes images of people, cultures, and traditions forged into a colorless alloy in an indifferent melting pot. But, in fact, assimilation, as it has taken place in the United States, is a far more gentle process, by which people from outside the community gradually became part of the community itself. Descendants of the German, Irish, Italian, Polish, Greek, and other immigrants who came to the United States bear little resemblance to the descendants of the countrymen their forebears left behind. America changed its immigrant groups—and

was changed by them. Some groups were accepted more reluctantly than others—the Chinese, for example—and some with great struggle. Blacks, whose ancestors were forced to come here, have only lately won their legal right to full participation in this society; and even then civil rights gains have not been sufficiently translated into economic gains. Until quite recently, however, there was no question but that each group desired admittance to the mainstream. No more. Now ethnic leaders demand that their groups remain separate, that their native culture and language be preserved intact, and that whatever accommodation takes place be on the part of the receiving society.

Hispanic leaders have been among the most demanding, insisting   2
that Hispanic children be taught in Spanish; that Hispanic adults be allowed to cast ballots in their native language and that they have the right to vote in districts in which Hispanics make up the majority of voters; that their ethnicity entitle them to a certain percentage of jobs and college admissions; that immigrants from Latin America be granted many of these same benefits, even if they are in the country illegally. But while Hispanic leaders have been pressing these claims, the rank and file have been moving quietly and steadily into the American mainstream. Like the children and grandchildren of millions of ethnic immigrants before them, virtually all native-born Hispanics speak English—many speak only English. The great majority finish high school, and growing numbers attend college. Their earnings and occupational status have been rising along with their education. But evidence of the success of native-born Hispanics is drowned in the flood of new Latin immigrants—more than five million—who have come in the last two decades, hoping to climb the ladder as well. For all of these people, assimilation represents the opportunity to succeed in America. Whatever the sacrifices it entails—and there are some—most believe that the payoff is worth it. Yet the elites who create and influence public policy seem convinced that the process must be stopped or, where this has already occurred, reversed.

From 1820 to 1924 the United States successfully incorporated a   3
population more ethnically diverse and varied than any other in the world. We could not have done so if today's politics of ethnicity had been the prevailing ethos. Once again, we are experiencing record immigration, principally from Latin America and Asia. The millions of Latin immigrants who are joining the already large native-born Hispanic population will severely strain our capacity to absorb them, unless we can revive a consensus for assimilation. But the new politics of Hispanic assimilation need not include the worst features of the Americanization era. Children should not be forced to sink or swim in classes in which they don't understand the language of instruction.

The model of Anglo conformity would seem ridiculous today in a country in which 150 million persons are descended from people who did not come here from the British Isles. We should not be tempted to shut our doors because we fear the newcomers are too different from us ever to become truly "American." Nonetheless, Hispanics will be obliged to make some adjustments if they are to accomplish what other ethnic groups have.

Language and Culture

Most Hispanics accept the fact that the United States is an English-speaking country; they even embrace the idea. A *Houston Chronicle* poll in 1990 found that 87 percent of all Hispanics believed that it was their "duty to learn English" and that a majority believed English should be adopted as an official language.[1] Similar results have been obtained in polls taken in California, Colorado, and elsewhere. But Hispanics, especially more recent arrivals, also feel it is important to preserve their own language. Nearly half the Hispanics in the *Houston Chronicle* poll thought that people coming from other countries should preserve their language and teach it to their children. There is nothing inconsistent in these findings, nor are the sentiments expressed unique to Hispanics. Every immigrant group has struggled to retain its language, customs, traditions. Some groups have been more successful than others. A majority of Greek Americans, for example, still speak Greek in their homes at least occasionally.[2] The debate is not about whether Hispanics, or any other group, have the right to retain their native language but about whose responsibility it is to ensure that they do so.

The government should not be obliged to preserve any group's distinctive language or culture. Public schools should make sure that all children can speak, read, and write English well. When teaching children from non–English-speaking backgrounds, they should use methods that will achieve English proficiency quickly and should not allow political pressure to interfere with meeting the academic needs of students. No children in an American school are helped by being held back in their native language when they could be learning the

---

1. Jo Ann Zuniga, "87% in Poll See Duty to Learn English," *Houston Chronicle* (July 12, 1990).

2. Commission on Civil Rights, *The Economic Status of Americans of Southern and Eastern European Ancestry* (Washington, D.C.: Government Printing Office, 1986), p. 45.

language that will enable them to get a decent job or pursue higher education. More than twenty years of experience with native-language instruction fails to show that children in these programs learn English more quickly or perform better academically than children in programs that emphasize English acquisition.

If Hispanic parents want their children to be able to speak Spanish   6
and know about their distinctive culture, they must take the responsibility to teach their children these things. Government simply cannot— and should not—be charged with this responsibility. Government bureaucracies given the authority to create bicultural teaching materials homogenize the myths, customs, and history of the Hispanic peoples of this hemisphere, who, after all, are not a single group but many groups. It is only in the United States that "Hispanics" exist; a Cakchiquel Indian in Guatemala would find it remarkable that anyone could consider his culture to be the same as a Spanish Argentinean's. The best way for Hispanics to learn about their native culture is in their own communities. Chinese, Jewish, Greek, and other ethnic communities have long established after-school and weekend programs to teach language and culture to children from these groups. Nothing stops Hispanic organizations from doing the same things. And, indeed, many Hispanic community groups around the country promote cultural programs. In Washington, D.C., groups from El Salvador, Guatemala, Colombia, and elsewhere sponsor soccer teams, fiestas, parades throughout the year, and a two-day celebration in a Latin neighborhood that draws crowds in the hundreds of thousands.[3] The Washington Spanish Festival is a lively, vibrant affair that makes the federal government's effort to enforce Hispanic Heritage Month in all of its

3. In May 1991, a riot broke out in a Latino neighborhood in Washington, D.C., where many new immigrants live (many of them illegal aliens). Both the local and national media described the two nights of arson and looting in political terms, as an expression of the alienation of the Hispanic community. In fact, fewer than half of the people arrested during the incident were Hispanic; most were young black males from a nearby neighborhood. There were few injuries and no deaths, and much criticism was directed at the police by local residents for standing by while young men looted stores, many of which were owned by Latinos. The Washington, D.C., metropolitan area is home to nearly a quarter of a million Hispanics, more than 80 percent of whom live in the suburbs of the city, far from the neighborhood where this incident occurred. Nonetheless, national Hispanic leaders, including members of the Hispanic Congressional delegation, flocked to the scene of the violence to portray as typical of the area's Latino population the problems which occurred in the few blocks of this urban settlement of recent immigrants.

agencies and departments each September seem pathetic by comparison. The sight and sound of mariachis strolling through the cavernous
halls of the Department of Labor as indifferent federal workers try to
work above the din is not only ridiculous; it will not do anything to
preserve Mexican culture in the United States.

Hispanics should be interested not just in maintaining their own,   7
distinctive culture but in helping Latin immigrants adjust to their
American environment and culture as well. Too few Hispanic organizations promote English or civics classes, although the number has increased dramatically since the federal government began dispensing
funds for such programs under the provisions of the Immigration
Reform and Control Act, which gives amnesty to illegal aliens on the
condition that they take English and civics classes.[4] But why shouldn't
the Hispanic community itself take some responsibility to help new
immigrants learn the language and history of their new country, even
without government assistance? The settlement houses of the early
century thrived without government funds. The project by the National
Association of Latino Elected and Appointed Officials (NALEO) to
encourage Latin immigrants to become U.S. citizens is the exception
among Hispanic organizations; it should become the rule.

Political Participation

The real barriers to Hispanic political power are apathy and alienage.   8
Too few native-born Hispanics register and vote; too few Hispanic immigrants become citizens. The way to increase real political power is not
to gerrymander districts to create safe seats for Hispanic elected officials
or treat illegal aliens and other immigrants as if their status were unimportant to their political representation; yet those are precisely the tactics
Hispanic organizations have urged lately. Ethnic politics is an old and
honored tradition in the United States. No one should be surprised that
Hispanics are playing the game now, but the rules have been changed
significantly since the early century. One analyst has noted, "In the past,
ethnic leaders were obliged to translate raw numbers into organizational
muscle in the factories or at the polls. . . . In the affirmative-action
state, Hispanic leaders do not require voters, or even protestors—only
bodies."[5] This is not healthy, for Hispanics or the country.

4. For fiscal year 1989 the federal government distributed nearly $200 million in grants
   to state and local governments to assist in providing English and civics classes for
   adults and other services for those eligible for amnesty.
5. Peter Skerry, "Keeping Immigrants in the Political Sweatshops," *Wall Street Journal*
   (Nov. 6, 1989).

Politics has traditionally been a great equalizer. One person's vote 9
was as good as another's, regardless of whether the one was rich and
the other poor. But politics requires that people participate. The great
civil rights struggles of the 1960s were fought in large part to guarantee
the right to vote. Hispanic leaders demand representation but do not
insist that individual Hispanics participate in the process. The emphasis
is always on rights, never on obligations. Hispanic voter organizations
devote most of their efforts toward making the process easier—election
law reform, postcard registration, election materials in Spanish—to
little avail; voter turnout is still lower among Hispanics than among
blacks or whites. Spanish posters urge Hispanics to vote because it
will mean more and better jobs and social programs, but I've never
seen one that mentions good citizenship. Hispanics (and others) need to
be reminded that if they want the freedom and opportunity democracy
offers, the least they can do is take the time to register and vote. These
are the lessons with which earlier immigrants were imbued, and they
bear reviving.

Ethnic politics was for many groups a stepping-stone into the 10
mainstream. Irish, Italian, and Jewish politicians established political
machines that drew their support from ethnic neighborhoods; and
the machines, in turn, provided jobs and other forms of political patronage to those who helped elect them. But eventually, candidates
from these ethnic groups went beyond ethnic politics. Governor Mario
Cuomo (D) and Senator Alfonse D' Amato (R) are both Italian American politicians from New York, but they represent quite different
political constituencies, neither of which is primarily ethnically based.
Candidates for statewide office—at least successful ones—cannot afford to be seen merely as ethnic representatives. Ethnic politics may
be useful at the local level, but if Hispanic candidates wish to gain
major political offices, they will have to appeal beyond their ethnic
base. Those Hispanics who have already been elected as governors
and U.S. senators (eight, so far) have managed to do so.

Education

Education has been chiefly responsible for the remarkable advance- 11
ments most immigrant groups have made in this society. European
immigrants from the early century came at a time when the education
levels of the entire population were rising rapidly, and they benefited
even more than the population of native stock, because they started
from a much lower base. More than one-quarter of the immigrants
who came during the years from 1899 to 1910 could neither read nor

write.[6] Yet the grandchildren of those immigrants today are indistinguishable from other Americans in educational attainment; about one-quarter have obtained college degrees. Second- and third-generation Hispanics, especially those who entered high school after 1960, have begun to close the education gap as well. But the proportion of those who go on to college is smaller among native-born Hispanics than among other Americans, and this percentage has remained relatively constant across generations, at about 10–13 percent for Mexican Americans. If Hispanics hope to repeat the successful experience of generations of previous immigrant groups, they must continue to increase their educational attainment, and they are not doing so fast enough. Italians, Jews, Greeks, and others took dramatic strides in this realm, with the biggest gains in college enrollment made after World War II.[7] Despite more than two decades of affirmative action programs and federal student aid, college graduation rates among native-born Hispanics, not to mention immigrants, remain significantly below those among non-Hispanics.

The government can do only so much in promoting higher education for Hispanics or any group. It is substantially easier today for a Hispanic student to go to college than it was even twenty or thirty years ago, yet the proportion of Mexican Americans who are graduating from college today is unchanged from what it was forty years ago. When the former secretary of education Lauro Cavazos, the first Hispanic ever to serve in the Cabinet, criticized Hispanic parents for the low educational attainment of their children, he was roundly attacked for blaming the victim. But Cavazos's point was that Hispanic parents must encourage their children's educational aspirations and that, too often, they don't. Those groups that have made the most spectacular socioeconomic gains—Jews and Chinese, for example—have done so because their families placed great emphasis on education. 12

Hispanics cannot have it both ways. If they want to earn as much as non-Hispanic whites, they have to invest the same number of years in schooling as these do. The earnings gap will not close until the 13

6. Richard A. Easterlin, "Immigration: Economic and Social Characteristics," in Stephan Thernstrom, ed., *Harvard Encyclopedia of American Ethnic Groups* (Cambridge, Mass.: Harvard University Press, 1981), p. 478.

7. See Richard Alba, *Ethnic Identity: The Transformation of White America* (New Haven: Yale University Press, 1990), p. 7. Both men and women born after 1930 showed large gains, although the gains were higher for men, probably reflecting the increase in college attendance by veterans under the G. I. Bill.

education gap does. Native-born Hispanics are already enjoying earnings comparable to those of non-Hispanic whites, once educational differences are factored in. If they want to earn more, they must become better educated. But education requires sacrifices, especially for persons from lower-income families. Poverty, which was both more pervasive and severe earlier in this century, did not prevent Jews or Chinese from helping their children get a better education. These families were willing to forgo immediate pleasures, even necessities, in order to send their children to school. Hispanics must be willing to do the same—or else be satisfied with lower socioeconomic status. The status of second- and third-generation Hispanics will probably continue to rise even without big gains in college graduation; but the rise will be slow. Only a substantial commitment to the education of their children on the part of this generation of Hispanic parents will increase the speed with which Hispanics improve their social and economic status.

Entitlements

The idea of personal sacrifice is an anomaly in this age of entitlements. 14 The rhetoric is all about rights. And the rights being demanded go far beyond the right to equality under the law. Hispanics have been trained in the politics of affirmative action, believing that jobs, advancement, and even political power should be apportioned on the basis of ethnicity. But the rationale for treating all Hispanics like a permanently disadvantaged group is fast disappearing. What's more, there is no ground for giving preference in jobs or promotions to persons who have endured no history of discrimination in this country—namely, recent immigrants. Even within Hispanic groups, there are great differences between the historical discrimination faced by Mexican Americans and Puerto Ricans and that faced by, say, Cubans. Most Hispanic leaders, though, are willing to have everyone included in order to increase the population eligible for the programs and, therefore, the proportion of jobs and academic placements that can be claimed. But these alliances are beginning to fray at the edges. Recently, a group of Mexican American firemen in San Francisco challenged the right of two Spanish Americans to participate in a department affirmative action program, claiming that the latter's European roots made them unlikely to have suffered discrimination comparable to that of other Hispanics. The group recommended establishing a panel of twelve

Hispanics to certify who is and who is not Hispanic.[8] But that is hardly the answer.

Affirmative action politics treats race and ethnicity as if they were   15
synonymous with disadvantage. The son of a Mexican American doctor or lawyer is treated as if he suffered the same disadvantage as the child of a Mexican farm worker; and both are given preference over poor, non-Hispanic whites in admission to most colleges or affirmative action employment programs. Most people think this is unfair, especially white ethnics whose own parents and grandparents also faced discrimination in this society but never became eligible for the entitlements of the civil rights era. It is inherently patronizing to assume that all Hispanics are deprived and grossly unjust to give those who aren't preference on the basis of disadvantages they don't experience. Whether stated or not, the essence of affirmative action is the belief that Hispanics—or any of the other eligible groups—are not capable of measuring up to the standards applied to whites. This is a pernicious idea.

Ultimately, entitlements based on their status as "victims" rob   16
Hispanics of real power. The history of American ethnic groups is one of overcoming disadvantage, of competing with those who were already here and proving themselves as competent as any who came before. Their fight was always to be treated the same as other Americans, never to be treated as special, certainly not to turn the temporary disadvantages they suffered into the basis for permanent entitlement. Anyone who thinks this fight was easier in the early part of this century when it was waged by other ethnic groups does not know history. Hispanics have not always had an easy time of it in the United States. Even though discrimination against Mexican Americans and Puerto Ricans was not as severe as it was against blacks, acceptance has come only with struggle, and some prejudices still exist. Discrimination against Hispanics, or any other group, should be fought, and there are laws and a massive administrative apparatus to do so. But the way to eliminate such discrimination is not to classify all Hispanics as victims and treat them as if they could not succeed by their own efforts. Hispanics can and will prosper in the United States by following the example of the millions before them.

8. "Spanish Progeny Are Not Hispanic, S. F. Group Insists," *San Diego Union* (Nov. 24, 1990). Ironically, both Spanish American firemen would have been promoted in the department even without benefit of affirmative action; they received the third- and sixth-highest scores on exams administered to sixty-eight persons for twenty promotion slots.

THINKING ABOUT THE CONTENT

1. What are some of the policies Hispanic leaders demand as a means for Hispanic assimilation into the American mainstream? Why does Chavez believe these policies do not reflect the needs of Hispanics? Do you agree with her? Explain.
2. What support does Chavez offer for her viewpoint? How do they seem contrary to the arguments of Hispanic leaders who disagree with her?
3. Chavez says that "the government should not be obliged to preserve any group's distinctive language or culture" (5). Why do you agree or disagree with her?
4. What does Chavez mean by "ethnic politics" (10)? What does she claim are the real barriers to Hispanic political power?
5. Chavez says that, "Education has been chiefly responsible for the remarkable advancements most immigrant groups have made in this society" (11). What examples does she provide to support this statement?
6. What are your views regarding affirmative action? What has led you to this viewpoint?

LOOKING AT STRUCTURE AND STYLE

7. How well does Chavez argue her stance against affirmative action policies and entitlement programs as they now stand? Is she convincing? Is her support valid?
8. Describe Chavez's tone. Who is her audience? Do you think she offends those who do not agree with her? Why or why not?

EXPLORING DISCUSSION AND WRITING TOPICS

9. Discuss your views of affirmative action or entitlement programs for minorities. Support your position with as many facts as possible.
10. In a country with such a diverse ethnic population, should any special groups be granted government help? Who are they and why?
11. Are the problems Hispanics may face in assimilating into the mainstream of American life different from those that other groups, such as African Americans, Asians, and Native Americans, faced? Discuss.
12. To what extent is it the government's obligation or duty to help ethnic or minority groups better themselves or assimilate into society?

CLARA E. RODRIGUEZ

Clara E. Rodriguez, a Puerto Rican born in New York, holds a bachelor's degree from City College of New York and a doctorate from Washington University in St. Louis. She is a professor of sociology at Fordham University and author of several books and articles, among them *Puerto Ricans* and *Born in the U.S.A.*, as well as *The Puerto Rican Struggle*, which she coedited.

The following essay, which appeared in the *Boston Globe*, discusses the difference between the definition of race in the United States and that of Latinos. Because of the rapid growth of the Latino population in the United States, which in some areas is faster than whites, Rodriguez believes this population change may change the way race has historically been defined and used.

ᵂ

Salsa in the Melting Pot

Predictions proliferate about the impact that the fast-growing Latino   1
population will have on the United States. Latinos, those citizens who trace their roots to Puerto Rico, Mexico and other Spanish-speaking Caribbean and South and Central American countries, will constitute the largest single "minority" group by the turn of the century. (Indeed, some argue this is already the case but that Latinos who are here illegally have not been counted by the census.) As a result, U.S. food, music, language, literature, visual arts, family values and personal warmth will all be invigorated by Latino influences. The old U.S. melting pot—what some Latinos call the *sancocho,* after the lusty Caribbean stew—will be flavored with a big splash of salsa.

That is good news, but it is old news. There is another area, critical   2
and unrecognized, where Latinos may have their greatest impact, and this is the way race is viewed and understood. Although there is general acceptance of the fact that there is only one human race with infinite variation and some population clusters, "race," as people experience it, is a cultural construct. How "races" or racial paradigms are determined varies from culture to culture, as does the meaning of the term "race." Each system of racial classification is seen to be—by those who utilize it—the only correct way of viewing individuals.

Latinos perceive race and react to it in ways that are fundamentally   3
different from those of Euro-Americans. To Latinos, race is more
cultural than physical. And while physical or "racial" characteristics
may distinguish people from one another, they are not, in themselves,
the basis for sub-group segregation. This is not to say that race is
unimportant in Latin America or among Latinos; rather, it is different.
The enslavement of both Africans and indigenous peoples was widespread, and it was often accompanied by cruel and harsh treatment.
The emphasis on the racial superiority of white Europeans is an inherent part of the colonial legacy in Latin America. This legacy is often
subtly manifested, e.g., in common parlance, kinky hair is referred to
as *pelo malo* (bad hair), and standards of beauty seldom deviate from
the European model.

The Traditional U.S. View of Race

In the United States, race has historically been seen as a black–white   4
dichotomy. There were essentially two races: white and not white,
which most often meant black. The white race was defined by the
absence of any nonwhite blood, and the black race was defined by the
presence of any black blood. Thus, the offspring of Native American
Indians, Asians or whites who intermarried with blacks became black.
Race was genetically or biologically defined, and it could not change
over a person's lifetime, or as a person moved from one part of the
United States to another.

The 1896 decision of the U.S. Supreme Court in the *Plessy* vs.   5
Ferguson case legitimated this dualistic view of race. In this case, the
petitioner averred that since he was ". . . seven eighths Caucasian
and one eighth African blood; and that the mixture of colored blood
was not discernible in him . . ." that he was entitled to the rights and
privileges of citizens of the white race. The Supreme Court decided
against the plaintiff, thus further legitimizing the genetic or blood-
quantum definition of race and sanctioning Jim Crow legislation.

This U.S. view of race, as an either/or condition where the basis   6
for racial distinctions is biological, is in contrast to the Latin-American
view, where race is conceived of as a continuum, with one's place along
the continuum determined partly by social factors. In Latin America,
race refers to a group of people who are felt to be somehow similar
in their essential nature. That essential nature depends on biology
but also on physical appearance, class, education, manners and other
"social" variables. Thus, while in the United States race has been
an ascribed characteristic that does not change after birth, or from

country to country, in Latin America race can change over time or from place to place. Consequently, a man can go from being white in Puerto Rico to mulatto in Mexico to black in the United States.

This more "ambiguous" concept of race has been a strong theme   7
in Latin-American literature and political thought. It had its antecedents in Spain and Portugal and was redefined in the New World, the Amerindian colonies. In Brazil, for example, up to 40 racial categories have been enumerated, while in the Spanish Caribbean, race ranges along a continuum of racial categories. Latinos have a number of intermediate categories, e.g., *mestizo, triguano, indio, moreno,* etc., not known in the United States. But most important, for many Latinos, cultural identity often supersedes racial identity; while for other Latinos, racial identity is often fused with their cultural identity. By contrast, in the United States, non-Hispanic whites, when identifying themselves or others racially, tend to use the "traditional" racial categories, i.e., white, black, Asian and Native American Indian. These categories are used regardless of the ethnic or cultural identity of the individuals being racially classified.

The Census and U.S. Latinos

The fact that Latinos and Euro-Americans have different ways of   8
racial identification has become more critical with the rapid growth of Hispanics in the United States. In the 1980 census, 40 percent of all the Latinos in the United States responded they were "other—Spanish" to the race question, while less than 2 percent of the non-Hispanic population in any state responded they were "other." The 1990 census showed a dramatic surge in the "other" category—10 million people listed their race as "other." This category increased by 45.1 percent since 1980, making it the second fastest-growing of all the racial categories, right behind Asian.

While some observers see this as indicating confusion, I see it as   9
a clear rejection of the U.S. biracial categorization, in favor of a category that indicates one is not culturally, socially or politically white or black, that one is something else, perhaps another "social race." Thus, for example, one may appear to be physically white or black but identify in terms of one's national origin or as a multiracial person. For many of these "others," there may be a physical component to race, but racial identity is ultimately a subjective sense of what one is (culturally), not what one looks like to others.

Physical and Cultural Identities

Because of its emphasis on biological descent, the U.S. race perspective 10
tends to utilize physical characteristics to determine cultural identities.
Thus, Asian-appearing people are considered Asian even though they
may never have been to Asia, i.e., they may be from the Andes, the
Philippines or from Mexico. Within this U.S. racial perspective, cultural
distinctions, such as the fact that while growing up some may speak
(or spoke) Korean, while others spoke Tibetan, are irrelevant. Ironically, what are perhaps prime identifiers, i.e., national origin, culture
or language, are ignored. Similarly, Panamanians who are Spanish-
speaking but appear to be African-Americans are also asked to shed
their unique culture and language and become "black and not Hispanic." Lastly, Latin Americans of Scandinavian appearance are seen
to be non-Hispanic and sometimes placed into the position of having
to prove their Hispanicity.

This tendency to classify individuals according to their race and 11
not their culture continues the assimilationist thrust of the melting-
pot theorists, while it preserves the inequities attendant on the dualistic
race order in the United States. The long experience of African-Americans and Native American Indians from different tribes—which are
really different nations, with unique cultures—exemplifies this dual
process of homogenization and minoritization.

The Latino view of race—as a social, not biological, phenome- 12
non—turns all this on its head. For Latinos, culture is the more important aspect of who someone is.

The Challenge to U.S. Society

This Latino view of race, as cultural first and physical second, poses 13
a fundamental challenge to the historic place of race in U.S. society.
Moreover, the influx of increasing numbers of other racially and ethnically diverse peoples to these shores is bound to force a reexamination
of the U.S. view of race. As minorities become the "emerging majority,"
and as whites become a "minority" in some urban areas, the dichoto-
mous view of race in the United States, wherein one is white or non-
white, will become less and less useful as a means of distinguishing
groups and individuals.

We can only hope that this process of growing racial and cultural 14
diversity in America will be seen and appreciated as a positive, enriching force. Then, and only then, when the American dream is framed

as a cultural rainbow, can America fulfill its pluralistic heritage and promise.

THINKING ABOUT THE CONTENT

1. Rodriguez argues that Latinos perceive or define race differently than the more traditional way it has been defined in the United States. What is the difference between the two definitions? What difference does it make?
2. Why are social and cultural factors more important to Latinos than biological factors? Do you agree? Explain.
3. Would it be better to classify people by culture rather than race? Why?
4. What changes might occur in our society if race were to be viewed as Rodriguez claims Latinos do?

LOOKING AT STRUCTURE AND STYLE

5. How does Rodriguez lead into her thesis? Is the thesis implied or stated? If stated, where?
6. What support does Rodriguez give for her definition of the traditional U.S. view of race and that of the Latino? Is the support convincing? Explain.

EXPLORING DISCUSSION AND WRITING TOPICS

7. React to Rodriguez's last sentence.
8. Explain why it is or is not important to classify people either by race or culture. Is any classification necessary? Why?
9. Recount how being classified as a member of a particular race has helped or harmed you at some point in your life.

In April 1992 one of the worst racially inspired riots of the century broke out in South-Central Los Angeles, California. Frustration and anger over what many saw as injustice in the first jury verdict of the police beating of Rodney King, an African American, erupted into violence, unleashing burning, looting, shootings, and mass destruction of property. Entire neighborhoods were engulfed in flames.

Among those areas threatened and targeted was Koreatown. Korean store owners suddenly found themselves targets in the riots. Answering calls for help from a Korean-language radio station, volunteers armed themselves and turned their stores and mini-malls into small fortresses. For hours, they fought a back-and-forth battle with several hundred looters until the police arrived. Eight out of ten Korean stores were burned or looted. Whatever fragile relationships Koreans had developed with their black and Latino customers was severely damaged along with their stores, homes, and dreams.

The following essay by Arthur Hu appeared in *The New Republic* in June 1992, two months after the Los Angeles riot. Hu, a writer for *Asian Week,* points out here how black violence and racial remarks against Asians were given little or no attention by the mainstream media, and "virtually no Asian Americans [were] called on to explain the situation from their point of view."

ﷺ

Us and Them

Spike Lee's vision of violence has truly become the Real Thing. Throughout the time of the conflagration in Los Angeles, I saw virtually no Asian Americans called on to explain the situation from their point of view. Yet Asians were not just victims of collateral damage; they were often a strategic target. Although much of what went on was black violence directed at Asians, the only racism that was lamented in the mainstream media was white violence against blacks.   1

The unfortunate timing of the mild sentence given to Soon Ja Du for shooting Latasha Harlins about a year ago in Los Angeles was a   2 key factor in the degree of black outrage that resulted in the rioting of April 29 and 30. Activists of ill will had already spread the word that a black girl had been shot in the back by a Korean merchant over a carton of juice. They didn't mention that the woman running the store had been assaulted by the girl before she fired, or that the context for this action was widespread violence against Korean shopkeepers. Korean entrepreneurs in South-Central Los Angeles ran a 1 in 250 chance of being killed while pursuing their business last year, about the same odds as a tour of duty in Vietnam. Stretch that to a career of thirty years, and the chances go up to 1 in 16, not a much better chance of survival than their young black male customers. Around eight out of ten Korean stores were burned or looted in the riots. One hundred in Koreatown alone. Three of the fifty-one killed were Asian—a high proportion when you consider that Asians constitute less than 0.5 percent of the population in South-Central Los Angeles.

Racist remarks were parlayed without comment by the various local and national news media and talk shows, as if one kind of racism were morally appropriate and another weren't: "Those Koreans don't respect us. . . . Those whites are subhuman, they don't even belong here. . . . The Koreans were part of the system, and so are you! . . . Burn the Chinese stores! Fuck the Koreans, we're glad they're gone. . . . Well, burning an apartment is a tragedy, but the liquor stores had to go. . . . We're sick of 400 years of oppression by Koreans!"

It is not as if Korean-Americans are far more economically powerful than black Americans. Even though household incomes were close to the national average, extended and intact families meant that Koreans in 1980 (the latest Census figures available) had a per capita income of only $5,544, which was closer to the $4,545 for blacks than the $7,808 for whites. The average small store brings in no more money than a good union manufacturing job. The difference is that Koreans have the highest number of self-employed of any ethnic group, and their willingness to work very hard for very little money gives them a competitive advantage in inner-city neighborhoods where supermarkets fear to tread. Blacks have also generally ceded the worst entry-level jobs such as janitors and maids to immigrants. Thus Latinos and Asians toil at subminimum wages, living in tiny cubicles and shacks in order to send money to their families in the old country, while many black teens turn their noses at jobs at McDonald's or Safeway at double the minimum wage.

One-hundred-and-twelve-hour work weeks, plus unpaid family labor, is common among Koreans. Many have college degrees that won't get them decent jobs because of discrimination or language problems. Asian students who live in housing projects and go to inner-city schools rack up grades, test scores, and graduation rates that are the envy of white suburban students. Koreans don't get special loans; they just work three jobs, save, sacrifice, and borrow from loan pools built by family and friends. It seems that Koreans are despised solely because they are the smallest local representative of the "capitalist system," or are of a different race and culture.

Many Asian Americans feel frustrated by the double standards 6 involved in the reporting of criminal cases. In the King case, the race of the policemen, Rodney King, and his jurors was considered relevant. But consider the case of Gregory Calvin Smith, a black man who raped twenty women in San Jose, California. Half his victims were Asian. He got a death sentence for raping and shooting a Japanese exchange student. Yet Smith's picture was never shown; mention of his race was omitted in every article and local TV story. If the King case had been covered without reference to race, the L.A. riot may never have erupted. It's good the Asians don't have an Al Sharpton who can exploit such situations, but Asian resentment and confusion is inevitable when even Asian American leaders minimize the existence of anti-Asian prejudice when it is perpetrated by black Americans.

Many residents of South-Central already realize how, as one told 7 the *Los Angeles Times*, "those damn fools destroyed our neighborhood for nothing." It's not the Koreans who now have no place to cash their checks and no place to buy their groceries. When the supermarket chains leave for good, many will wish for the Koreans to return.

My son is eight months old today. I'm going to teach him not to 8 hate, not to kill, not to lie, and not to steal. I will show him how to fend for himself and his family by using his own resources and industry. I pray that one day everybody else can do the same. I know it's harder when you are poor, but there is no other way. Because only when that day comes will riots like those we've just witnessed in L.A. be a distant memory.

THINKING ABOUT THE CONTENT

1. Who are the "Us and Them" referred to in the title? What does the title imply?
2. Why does Hu feel Asian stores were targeted during the riots?
3. React to the last sentence in paragraph 4. Do you believe this is true? Explain.
4. What does Hu mean by "the double standards involved in the reporting

of criminal cases" (6)? Do you think the Los Angeles riots might have
been avoided if the King case had been covered without reference to race?

5. Hu refers to Al Sharpton in paragraph 6. What inferences can we draw
   from his comments regarding Sharpton and Asian Americans?

6. What is Hu's solution to ending racism? Do you think his way is possible?
   Explain.

LOOKING AT STRUCTURE AND STYLE

7. Is Hu's thesis clear? Is it stated or implied? If stated, where?

8. Describe Hu's tone. What words or phrases help establish his tone?

9. What is the point of paragraph 3? What paragraph pattern is used?

10. Why does Hu use all the quotations in paragraph 3? What is similar in
    their message?

11. How well does Hu support his views? Is his reasoning mostly logical or
    emotional? Explain with examples from the essay.

EXPLORING DISCUSSION AND WRITING TOPICS

12. Respond to Hu's remark that blacks have "generally ceded the worst
    entry-level jobs such as janitors and maids to immigrants" (4).

13. Explain why you would or would not teach a child of yours what Hu
    intends to teach his son.

14. Discuss whether Hu's remarks can help establish better race relations
    between blacks and the Asian community.

15. Research the 1992 Los Angeles riot. Write on some aspect of it that
    interests you.

AMY WANG

Amy Wang was born in Pittsburgh two years after her parents came to the United States from Taiwan. Graduating from Cornell University in 1990, Wang received her master's degree in journalism from Columbia University in 1993. That same year, Wang worked as a copy editor at the *Philadephia Inquirer* and published the following essay in the *Inquirer*'s Sunday magazine.

Wang discusses her own experience with being treated as racially different and how it affects the way she responds to others.

❧

The Same Difference

It was on my way home that the moment of truth swept by—again.   1

There we were, a friend and I, heading north on the Pennsylvania   2
Turnpike to central New York to visit my parents. Somehow our conversation had parted the curtains before my childhood memories, and before I knew it, I was telling him about an incident I have never quite forgotten.

As I spoke, it was almost as if my adult self were back in Pittsburgh,   3
watching; strange how in my memory the sun is always glinting through a bright haze on that day. The trees are bare, or nearly so, with dark branches that reach out to splinter the sun's rays. I am walking alone, down a white concrete sidewalk littered with leaves, twigs, buckeyes. School is out for the day, and everyone is going home.

From behind come shouts, and I turn to see a group of children   4
from school. A moment passes, and I realize they are shouting at me. I listen for several seconds before the words whip into clarity:

Chink! Hey, chink! Chinky chinky chink!   5

They are running. I am frozen, my heart the only part of me   6
moving, and it is pounding. Then one of them stoops, picks up a twig and hurls it at me. It lands short, a foot away on the sidewalk. Then I turn, still blocks from home, and run. The twigs keep coming, clattering close behind as the others shout and follow. As I run, I think of the steep steps to the front door and despair.

But when I reach the steps and turn around, only silence follows.   7
And when my mother answers the doorbell's ring, she sees only her

daughter, cheeks a little flushed, waiting to be let in. Almost instinc-
tively, I know I must not tell her. It would only hurt her, and there is
nothing she can do. Besides, it is nothing I want to discuss.

"Wow," he said. "And you were in sixth grade when this happened?"   8
    "Six," I said. "I was 6 when this happened. I was in first grade."   9
    He was clearly appalled, his eyes in far focus as he tried to under-   10
stand how such a thing could happen to a small child. I was concentrating on the road, but even a sidelong glance showed he did not, could
not, quite understand. And it was then that I felt the familiar stab of
disappointment: the realization that no matter how long we traveled
together, we would always be on parallel roads, moving on either side
of a great divide. I would never know his assurance as he made his
way through a world where his skin color was an assumption, and he
would never know my anxiety as I made my way through a world
where my skin color was an anguish.

    We were silent, and after a while he fell asleep. "Wake me up   11
when we get to Allentown," he had said as he drifted off, and we both
smiled, remembering a classmate who had once padded an expense
account for profit by driving from New York to Allentown and back
twice in two days.

    The thought of the old mill town triggered memories of another   12
old mill town, where I had gotten my first job out of college. It was
at the local newspaper, working nights on the copy desk. Our shifts
ended at 1 A.M., and I often drove home through deserted streets, the
hush broken only by the whir of an occasional street-cleaning machine
or the clanking of a distant garbage truck. The other drivers on the
streets at that hour seemed just as weary, just as intent on getting
to bed.

    In such an atmosphere I often dream, and so to this day a shadowy,   13
slowed-down quality suffuses the memory of turning my head and
looking out the side window one night just in time to see an old red
Dodge draw up in the next lane at a traffic light. Inside, four young
white crewcut men dressed in denim and flannel strain toward me,
their faces distorted with hate, their mouths twisted with invective.
Our windows are closed, so I am spared their actual words, but their
frenzied pantomime leaves little to be imagined.

    When the light turns green I pull away hastily, but they cruise   14
alongside for the next few blocks. By the time they tire of me and
swing into a left turn, I am seething with fear and rage. I wait until
they are committed to the turn, then raise my middle finger. One of
them looks back for a final insult, sees my gesture, and gapes—but

only for a moment. He turns, and I know he is screaming at the driver to turn back. I gun it.

They never come after me, and I make it home alive. Numb, I   15
crawl into bed. It is only after I lie down that I realize how they might have hurt me, the four of them with their huge Dodge against my tiny Nissan, and I begin to shake. As my mind tumbles, the phone rings. For a moment I think it is them, and then logic returns. I answer, and it is my boyfriend, calling from Boston. I tell him what happened, melting into tears. He is sympathetic, but then he asks: "How do you know they weren't yelling at you because you were a woman?"

I don't, of course, but that is not the point. His whiteness rushes   16
through the line with the very question. "It doesn't matter," I tell him, and suddenly I can't stand to hear his voice. I tell him I don't want to discuss it anymore, and hang up.

Somewhere along Route 79 in New York he said, "This is beautiful."   17
I smiled, remembering the years I spent in Finger Lakes country: middle school, high school, college. Here were trees I had climbed, hills I had sledded down, malls I knew by heart; here were roads that led to memories and people who knew my history.

And it was because I had to come back here that another He was   18
able to betray me. It was during the first summer I spent away from home, working at a magazine in New York. Picture now a pavilion on the grounds of a quiet country club where the staff is enjoying the annual company picnic, and there I am by the jukebox, hovering over the glassed-in 45s as a light mist dampens the grass. As the Contours wail "Do You Love Me," I sway to the beat, attracting a stranger's eyes. In a moment he is introducing himself; in an hour he is sitting by me in the bus taking us back to the city; in a week he is asking me out to dinner.

I am no longer thinking clearly. On my last day at the magazine,   19
he watches as I clean out my desk, then asks me, in a low but urgent tone, not to forget him. He tells me he wants my address, and a sudden foreboding chill nearly stuns me with its iciness, sending shivers through my hand as I write out the address and phone number. Then I ask for his address and phone number. I do not think to ask him not to forget me.

Weeks go by without a word, and then one night, I know. The   20
chill comes back: For days I hate white men, all of them, they all bear the blame for his misdeed. But I have known too many good ones for my fury to last, and finally I am forced to admit that I have been a fool, and that this time, at least, it had nothing to do with race.

"It could have happened to anyone," a (white male) friend tells   21
me. "It happens to everyone."

I am not immediately consoled. But time goes on, and finally, so   22
do I.

By the time we pulled into my parents' driveway, it was nearly din-   23
nertime. I sprang out, glad to stretch, and bounded into the house,
but he was slow to follow, and I had discarded my shoulder bag and
greeted everyone by the time he finally appeared in the doorway. I
went to introduce him, wondering why he was hanging back. Then
he raised his eyes to mine as he came up the stairs, and I realized he
was nervous: He was in my world now, and he was finally getting an
inkling of what I went through every day.

Payback time. At last.   24

Then my mother was there, smiling and shaking his hand, and   25
my father was right behind her, also smiling.

"Welcome," he said.   26

For a moment, I could see the horizon, where parallel lines some-   27
times seem to meet.

Thinking about the Content

1. Wang states "the moment of truth swept by—again" (1). What does she
   mean? Why does she say "again"?
2. Why does Wang feel that telling her mother about being called a "chink"
   and chased would only hurt her mother and "is nothing I want to discuss"
   (7)? Should she have discussed this episode with her mother? Explain.
3. Do you think the boys in the red Dodge were making racial slurs at
   Wang or merely provoking her because she was a woman alone? What
   differences does it make, if any? Explain.
4. What does she mean by, "Payback time. At last" (24)?
5. Wang says that she and her male friend will always travel "parallel roads"
   (10) and ends by saying "parallel lines *sometimes* [my emphasis] seem to
   meet" (27). What does she mean? Do you think she will always hold this
   attitude? Will the lines ever meet for her?

Looking at Structure and Style

6. Is Wang's thesis implied or stated? If stated, where? What is her thesis?
7. Wang uses several one-sentence paragraphs throughout, for example,
   paragraphs 1, 5, 22, 24, and 27. How effective are these? As an editor,
   would you make any suggestions for revision? Explain.
8. How well does Wang support her reason for enjoying "payback time"?

Does she provide enough reasons or support for readers to be sympathetic to her feelings?

9. Describe her tone. What words or phrases help establish that tone?

EXPLORING DISCUSSION AND WRITING TOPICS

10. Discuss a time when you became aware that your parents held a bias toward some ethnic or racial group. What words were used? How did you react? Have you absorbed the same feelings?

11. Discuss a time when you either felt the sting of prejudice for the first time or caused someone else hurt or pain because of your own bias.

12. Write an essay that explores the use of offensive words that apply to different racial or ethnic groups. What power do these words have?

An active member of the American Indian Anti-Defamation League, Ward Churchill is a writer and former professor of American Indian studies at the University of Colorado. Some of his works include *Indians Are Us: Culture and Genocide in Native North America* and *Fantasies of the Master Race: Literature, Cinema, and the Colonization of American Indians.*

In the following essay taken from a longer piece in *Z* magazine, "Crimes Against Humanity," Churchill discusses the racism some Native Americans find in the use of their native names, images, and symbols by professional sports teams and shows what things might be like if the use of ethnic names were spread beyond Native American names.

〜

The Indian Chant and
the Tomahawk Chop

During the past couple of seasons, there has been an increasing wave of controversy regarding the names of professional sports teams like the Atlanta "Braves," Cleveland "Indians," Washington "Redskins," and Kansas City "Chiefs." The issue extends to the names of college teams like Florida State University "Seminoles," University of Illinois "Fighting Illini," and so on, right on down to high school outfits like the Lamar (Colorado) "Savages." Also involved have been team adoption of "mascots," replete with feathers, buckskins, beads, spears and "warpaint" (some fans have opted to adorn themselves in the same fashion), and nifty little "pep" gestures like the "Indian Chant" and "Tomahawk Chop."

A substantial number of American Indians have protested that use of native names, images and symbols as sports team mascots and the like is, by definition, a virulently racist practice. Given the historical relationship between Indians and non-Indians during what has been called the "Conquest of America," American Indian Movement leader (and American Indian Anti-Defamation Council founder) Russell Means has compared the practice to contemporary Germans naming their soccer teams the "Jews," "Hebrews," and "Yids," while adorning their uniforms with grotesque caricatures of Jewish faces taken from the Nazis' anti-Semitic propaganda of the 1930s. Numerous demonstrations have occurred in conjunction with games—most notably during the November 15, 1992 match-up between the Chiefs and Redskins in Kansas City—by angry Indians and their supporters.

In response, a number of players—especially African Americans and other minority athletes—have been trotted out by professional team owners like Ted Turner, as well as university and public school officials, to announce that they mean not to insult but to honor native people. They have been joined by the television networks and most major newspapers, all of which have editorialized that Indian discomfort with the situation is "no big deal," insisting that the whole thing is just "good, clean fun." The country needs more such fun, they've argued, and "a few disgruntled Native Americans" have no right to undermine the nation's enjoyment of its leisure time by complaining. This is especially the case, some have argued, "in hard times like these." It has even been contended that Indian outrage at being systematically degraded—rather than the degradation itself—creates "a serious barrier to the sort of intergroup communication so necessary in a multicultural society such as ours."

Okay, let's communicate. We are frankly dubious that those advancing such positions really believe their own rhetoric, but, just for the sake of argument, let's accept the premise that they are sincere. If what they say is true, then isn't it time we spread such "inoffensiveness" and "good cheer" around among *all* groups so that *everybody* can participate *equally* in fostering the round of national laughs they call for? Sure it is—the country can't have too much fun or "intergroup involvement"—so the more, the merrier. Simple consistency demands that anyone who thinks the Tomahawk Chop is a swell pastime must be just as hearty in their endorsement of the following ideas—by the logic used to defend the defamation of American Indians—should help us all really start yukking it up.

First, as a counterpart to the Redskins, we need an NFL team called "Niggers" to honor Afro-Americans. Half-time festivities for fans might include a simulated stewing of the opposing coach in a large pot while players and cheerleaders dance around it, garbed in leopard skins and wearing fake bones in their noses. This concept obviously goes along with the kind of gaiety attending the Chop, but also with the actions of the Kansas City Chiefs, whose team members—prominently including black team members—lately appeared on a poster looking "fierce" and "savage" by way of wearing Indian regalia.

Just a bit of harmless "morale boosting," says the Chiefs' front office. You bet.

So that the newly-formed Niggers sports club won't end up too   6 out of sync while expressing the "spirit" and "identity" of Afro-Americans in the above fashion, a baseball franchise—let's call this one the "Sambos"—should be formed. How about a basketball team called the "Spearchuckers"? A hockey team called the "Jungle Bunnies"? Maybe the "essence" of these teams could be depicted by images of tiny black faces adorned with huge pairs of lips. The players could appear on TV every week or so gnawing on chicken legs and spitting watermelon seeds at one another. Catchy, eh? Well, there's "nothing to be upset about," according to those who love wearing "war bonnets" to the Super Bowl or having "Chief Illiniwik" dance around the sports arenas of Urbana, Illinois.

And why stop there? There are plenty of other groups to include.   7 "Hispanics"? They can be "represented" by the Galveston "Greasers" and San Diego "Spics," at least until the Wisconsin "Wetbacks" and Baltimore "Beaners" get off the ground. Asian Americans? How about the "Slopes," "Dinks," "Gooks," and "Zipperheads"? Owners of the latter teams might get their logo ideas from editorial page cartoons printed in the nation's newspapers during World War II: slant-eyes, buck teeth, big glasses, but nothing racially insulting or derogatory, according to the editors and artists involved at the time. Indeed, this Second World War–vintage stuff can be seen as just another barrel of laughs, at least by what current editors say are their "local standards" concerning American Indians.

Let's see. Who's been left out? Teams like the Kansas City "Kikes,"   8 Hanover "Honkies," San Leandro "Shylocks," Daytona "Dagos," and Pittsburgh "Polacks" will fill a certain social void among white folk. Have a religious belief? Let's all go for the gusto and gear up the Milwaukee "Mackerel Snappers" and Hollywood "Holy Rollers." The Fighting Irish of Notre Dame can be rechristened the "Drunken Irish" or "Papist Pigs." Issues of gender and sexual preference can be addressed through creation of teams like the St. Louis "Sluts," Boston "Bimbos," Detroit "Dykes," and the Fresno "Fags." How about the Gainesville "Gimps" and Richmond "Retards," so the physically and mentally impaired won't be excluded from our fun and games?

Now, don't go getting "overly sensitive" out there. None of this   9 is demeaning or insulting, at least not when it's being done to Indians. Just ask the folks who are doing it, or their apologists like Andy Rooney in the national media. They'll tell you—as in fact they *have* been telling you—that there's been no harm done, regardless of what their victims think, feel, or say. The situation is exactly the same as when those with precisely the same mentality used to insist that Step 'n' Fetchit was okay, or Rochester on the Jack Benny Show, or Amos and Andy, Charlie Chan, the Frito Bandito, or any of the other cutsey symbols making up the lexicon of American racism. Have we communicated yet?

Let's get just a little bit real here. The notion of "fun" embodied 10 in rituals like the Tomahawk Chop must be understood for what it is. There's not a single non-Indian example used above which can be considered socially acceptable in even the most marginal sense. The reasons are obvious enough. So why is it different where American Indians are concerned? One can only conclude that, in contrast to the other groups at issue, Indians are (falsely) perceived as being too few, and therefore too weak, to defend themselves effectively against racist and otherwise offensive behavior.

Fortunately, there are some glimmers of hope. A few teams and 11 their fans have gotten the message and have responded appropriately. Stanford University, which opted to drop the name "Indians" from Stanford, has experienced no resulting drop-off in attendance. Meanwhile, the local newspaper in Portland, Oregon, recently decided its long-standing editorial policy prohibiting use of racial epithets should include derogatory team names. The Redskins, for instance, are now referred to as "the Washington team," and will continue to be described in this way until the franchise adopts an inoffensive moniker (newspaper sales in Portland have suffered no decline as a result).

Such examples are to be applauded and encouraged. They stand 12 as figurative beacons in the night, proving beyond all doubt that it is quite possible to indulge in the pleasure of athletics without accepting blatant racism into the bargain.

THINKING ABOUT THE CONTENT

1. Why is using the names "Chiefs," "Redskins," and "Braves" considered insulting and racist by Native Americans? Do you agree with Churchill that the way the names, as well as the use of "war bonnets," and gestures such as "the tomahawk chop," are offensive and racist? Do you think Churchill is being overly sensitive? Why or why not?
2. Some of the arguments for continuing to use Native American names, symbols, and images are that it is "no big deal," it is "good, clean fun," and "no offensiveness is involved, and "a few disgruntled Native Americans" have no right to complain and disrupt the fun intended (3). What do you think of these excuses? Are they valid? Can other arguments not

ROB ROGERS, Reprinted by permission of United Feature Syndicate, Inc.

mentioned put forth as a reason for continuing to use the adopted names and gestures used?

3. Are Churchill's analogies between stereotypes of Native Americans and those of other ethnic groups effective? Do you find any analogies more offensive than others? Why or why not?

4. To what extent do you agree or disagree with Churchill?

LOOKING AT STRUCTURE AND STYLE

5. What words or phrases help establish Churchill's attitude and tone? Why is the tone appropriate?

6. To whom is Churchill writing? What makes you think so?

7. Examine Churchill's transitional elements. How does he move from one stereotype to the next? Is it effective?

EXPLORING DISCUSSION AND WRITING TOPICS

8. Research a sports team that uses a Native American name and symbols. Why was that name selected? Who was involved in the selection? Have there been protests against the name?

9. Write an essay on the power of maintaining racism by stereotyping eth-

nic groups. How has this force been used to create and promote racial tension?

10. Write an essay explaining why sports teams such as the Atlanta Braves or Cleveland Indians should or should not change their names.

SOME RESEARCH SOURCES ON RACIAL ISSUES

The following sources may be useful if you choose to do more reading or pursue a research project dealing with issues prompted by the reading selections this unit.

Asante, Molefi K. *The Afrocentric Idea.* Philadelphia: Temple University Press, 1987.

Bell, Derrick. *Faces at the Bottom of the Well: The Permanence of Racism.* New York: Basic Books, 1992.

Chavez, Linda. *Out of the Barrio.* New York: Basic Books, 1992.

De Alva, Jorge Klor, Earl Shorris, and Cornel West. "Our Next Race Question: The Uneasiness Between Blacks and Latinos," *Harper's* (April 1996), 55–63.

Du Bois, W. E. B. *The Souls of Black Folk.* New York: Penguin, 1982.

D'Souza, Dinesh. *The End of Racism.* New York: Free Press, 1995.

Ezekiel, Ralphael S. *The Racist Mind.* New York: Viking, 1995.

Gates Jr., Henry Louis. *Loose Canons: Notes on the Culture Wars.* New York: Oxford, 1992.

Hacker, Andrew. *Two Nations: Black and White, Separate, Hostile, Unequal.* New York: Scribner's, 1992.

Herrnstein, Richard J., and Charles Murray. *The Bell Curve: Intelligence and Class Structure in American Life.* New York: Free Press, 1994.

hooks, bell. *Killing Rage: Ending Racism.* New York: Henry Holt, 1995.

Ice T. *The Ice Opinion: Who Gives a Fuck?* New York: St. Martin's, 1994.

Jacoby, Russell, and Naomi Glauberman, *The Bell Curve Debate.* New York: Times Books, 1995.

Jaynes, Gerald D., and Robin M. Williams. *A Common Destiny: Blacks and American Society.* New York: National Academy Press, 1989.

Keyes, Alan. *Masters of the Dream: The Strength and Betrayal of Black America.* New York: Morrow, 1995.

King Jr., Martin Luther. *Where Do We Go From Here: Chaos or Community.* Boston: Beacon Press, 1968.

Loury, Glenn C. *One by One from the Inside Out: Race and Responsibility in America.* New York: Free Press, 1995.

Massey, Douglas, and Nancy Denton. *American Apartheid: Segregation and the Making of the Underclass.* Cambridge, MA: Harvard University Press, 1993.

Morrison, Toni. *Race-ing Justice, En-gendering Power.* Pantheon, 1992.

Reed, Ismael. *Airing Dirty Laundry.* New York: Free Press, 1993.

Ridgeway, James. *Blood in the Face: The KKK, Aryan Nations, Nazi Skinheads, and the Rise of the New White Culture.* New York: Thunder Mouth, 1995.

Steele, Shelby. *The Content of Our Character: A New Vision of Race in America.* New York: St. Martin's, 1990.

West, Cornel. *Race Matters.* Boston: Beacon Press, 1993.

Religion and Faith

Many have quarreled about religion that never practiced it.

—BENJAMIN FRANKLIN

Every man, either to his terror or consolation, has some sense of religion.

—JAMES HARRINGTON

To swallow and follow, whether old doctrine or new propaganda, is a weakness still dominating the human mind.

—CHARLOTTE P. GILLMAN

It is the test of a good religion whether you can joke about it.

—GILBERT K. CHESTERTON

Our hope of immortality does not come from any religions, but nearly all religions come from that hope.

—ROBERT GREEN INGERSOLL

Measure not men by Sundays, without regarding what they do all the week after.

—THOMAS FULLER

Religion has not civilized man, man has civilized religion.

—ROBERT GREEN INGERSOLL

Religion is a candle inside a multicolored lantern. Everyone looks through a particular color, but the candle is always there.

—MOHAMMED NEGUIB

You can change your faith without changing gods, and vice versa.

—STANISLAW J. LEC

All religions must be tolerated, for every man must get to heaven in his own way.

—FREDERICK THE GREAT

Science without religion is lame; religion without science is blind.

—ALBERT EINSTEIN

THE UNITED STATES IS THE most religiously diverse nation in the world. According to J. Gordon Melton, compiler of the *Encyclopedia of American Religions,* in addition to the mainstream Judeo-Christian faiths that populated the original colonies, America now has between 700 and 800 "nonconventional" denominations. Half are "imported variants of standard world religions, mostly Asian." The other half is a potpourri of everything from Branch Davidians to New Agers.

According to the Pluralism Project run by Harvard University's Diana Eck, there are seven Buddhist temples in Salt Lake City, two Sikh gurdwaras in Phoenix, a Taoist temple in Denver, a Jain Center in Blairstown, New Jersey, and five mosques in Oklahoma City. It is estimated that as of 1994 the United States has 1,139 houses of worship for Muslims, 1,515 for Buddhists, and 412 for Hindus.

In contrast with religious violence in places such as Belfast, Bosnia, Beirut, and Bombay, conflicts in doctrine in the United States seem to manage tolerance on the whole, taking religious conflicts to the courts and to print. As you will see in the following essays, disagreement occurs not only *between* different religious doctrines, but *within* a singular faith's doctrine. For instance, a person who claims to be a Christian may disagree with another Christian on ways to interpret the Bible. From the Scopes trial in 1926 to the battle over creationism in the 1990s, from the civil rights movement to the feminist and the gay and lesbian movements, the Bible as literal truth has been strongly debated. Interpretations of the Bible continue to be used to deny human rights on issues from homosexuality to war, always with God on "our" side.

During the mid-1990s, religious scholars and theologians were publishing research that questioned some fundamental beliefs of Christianity. Spurred by new findings contained in two ancient libraries, the Dead Sea Scrolls and the Nag Hammai manuscripts, along with the publication of books such as Robert W. Funk's *The Five Gospels,* which boldly asserts that Jesus only said 18 percent of the things attributed to him, Christian believers were given a jolt.

Along these lines, Burton Mack's *The Lost Gospel* contends that the Bible's New Testament contains only four of five gospels, the fifth having been lost and recently discovered. Referred to as the "Book of

Q" (Q for Quelle, or "source" in German) Mack and others contend that Q was made up of quotes from Jesus that the New Testament gospel writers, Matthew, Mark, Luke, and John, inserted selectively in their own books. The result, says Mach, is a mythical figure of Jesus, because the writers of Q "were not Christians and did not think Jesus a messiah or the Christ. They did not regard his death as divine . . . and did not imagine that he had been raised from the dead." Instead, says Mack, "they thought of him as a teacher whose teaching made it possible to live with verve in troubled times."

In *Jesus and the Riddle of the Dead Sea Scrolls,* Barbara Thiering presents Jesus as a man who was married twice, had three children, and came from Qumran, home of the Dead Sea Scrolls. She contends that Jesus did not die on the cross but was drugged and later revived.

John P. Meier's *A Marginal Jew: Rethinking the Historical Jesus,* distinguishes Jesus the man from what later teachings made him out to be. Meier believes Jesus was one of seven children who probably married, but remained celibate for religious reasons.

To add more fuel to the often fiery biblical debate, current research findings and translations indicate that the Bible as it exists today excludes many other competing texts because of fierce political and religious rivalry between Jewish, Christian, and Gnostic sects, revealing the Bible to be a selectively censored and distorted version of ancient religious literature.

While Christianity is still the predominant religion of the United States, referring to the nation as "Christian" is misplaced. The nation's traditional consensus faith is biblical monotheism, which also includes Judaism. However, Islam, the world's third great monotheistic faith is growing through immigration and conversion and may soon overtake Judaism as America's second largest belief system.

What are we to make of all this? In his book *Zen Keys,* Thich Nhat Hanh calls upon us to honor the best aspects of *all* religious traditions. He points out that religious institutions worldwide are becoming more political than spiritual, motivated by material and political interests and worldly conflicts with the result that their spiritual tasks are being neglected. Perhaps Hanh is correct when he says:

> Technological civilization continually creates new needs of consumption, most of which are not important. This civiliza-tion has also created suffering and tragedies. Religions must be conscious of our need to awaken to our true humanity. Churches must work to rebuild communities in which a

sane and healthy life can be lived, realizing that true happiness does not rest in the consumption of goods paid for by
suffering, famine, and death, but in a life enlightened by
the insight into interbeing and the recognition of our deep
responsibility to be true to ourselves and to help our neighbors.

This unit contains some interesting viewpoints on religion and
religious figures, some of which may even irritate or challenge your
beliefs. Risk the contact with an open mind.

MARGARET ISHERWOOD

Margaret Isherwood received a degree in moral science from Cambridge. She was a lecturer at the Froebel Educational Institute, served as the dean of women at Olivet College, Michigan, and was a psychologist at the Oak Lane Country Day School near Philadelphia. She later worked with Dr. Fritz Kunkel and a group of religious-oriented counselors in Los Angeles.

Although written in 1970, the following selection from Isherwood's book *Searching for Meaning: A Religion of Inner Growth for Agnostics and Believers* stays timely today. Isherwood believes that life's meaning for us can only unfold as we grow in mind and spirit. For her, "religion is not primarily a matter of believing but of growing and becoming whatever we have it in us to become." For Isherwood, the evolutionary process has given humans the power of conscious choice, so it is our responsibility to use our wisdom and insight to save man from extinction.

The following selection from her book explains what led her to "abandon the attempt to prove the existence of a mysterious and incomprehensible 'person' [God] existing somewhere in outer space and build up faith in life on what can be known in experience."

%

Searching for Meaning

There must be a large number of people who went through a similar 1 experience to that which befell me in my late teens, though it may be doubted whether loss of faith is such a traumatic experience today as it was fifty years ago. Asking questions is now more generally encouraged from childhood onward, and many more interests compete with religion for our attention. At the same time, thoughtful people of all ages find themselves wondering about life.

There is a deep longing to know whether there is a God or at 2 least a "something" that gives significance to the whole process, especially when faced with suffering: one's own, and the weight of suffering everywhere. There is also a deep need to feel that it matters, *sub specie aeternitatis*, how one lives, that it is really important to try to discipline the tiger and the ape within us and to contribute to life whatever lies in our power.

It is psychologically and spiritually dangerous to meet these needs ₃ or answer these questions in terms of a rigid and debatable theology. To do so is one of the most effective ways of emptying out new life with the "bathwater" of outworn dogmas. "Believe nothing because you have been told it." The advice of the Buddha to his disciples, was extreme but wiser than the opposite methods of early indoctrination advocated by Ignatius Loyola: "Give me a child till he is seven years old, and I will give him to you for the rest of his life."

Faith Lost and Found

In my late teens the system of beliefs forming the mold that contained ₄ my faith in life crumbled overnight. In actual fact the disaster could not have been as sudden as it appeared. Behind the scenes the acids of modernity had been at work for some little time but I had unconsciously erected a barrier against them. When the barrier broke the result was devastating, for the narrow biblical theology in which I had been nurtured was said to contain the fixed and unalterable truth for all time, and I did not know where else to turn for illumination or guidance. If this story of evolution was true, then the Bible was not. The ground gave way under my feet. I was in what is now called an "existential vacuum," a vacuum caused by the loss of any meaning for existence.

Cambridge did nothing to resolve my dilemma. My emotional ₅ foundations had been overthrown, and part of me continued trying to reestablish the Father-God who had been such a support and comfort during the long and dreary years at an unmirthful boarding school for the daughters of poor clergy. I was told by a fellow college student that I should never be a good philosopher if I did not abandon such wishful thinking: and from all my professors and their teaching I imbibed the impression that reason alone could be relied on as the way to truth. They may not have intended this, but I did not intend to be "duped" a second time, and reason seemed to give the only security against this. I did, however, sometimes consult with ministers. All were alike in making religion primarily a matter of belief, and as I could not coerce myself into believing something that was not proved, even though I felt guilty for not believing, I seemed to get nowhere.

Yet of course I was getting somewhere without realizing it. There ₆ was Pascal's strange paradox: "Thou wouldst not seek me if thou hadst not already found me," which must mean something and which suggested one was on the right track so long as one was seeking. But it was many years before I ceased worshipping the goddess reason as the *only* avenue to truth, and before I came to realize that there were other orders of knowledge as well as factual, and other modes of knowing than by the intellect. It took many years to abandon the futile attempt to find God at the end of a syllogism and to understand that feeling-experience could bring a kind of knowledge just as valid as knowledge of scientific or mathematical facts and no more to be doubted than these.

One of the most important of my "facts of experience" occurred   7
very early in life, but its memory had been wiped out for some time, and later with loss of faith I became too involved with God the Father to pay much attention to a "mere" experience. In my old age that experience has fitted into place and become more important than anything I learned from books and university lectures.

It came about as follows: As a young child I was extremely fortu-   8
nate in having free contact with the beauty of the earth, with woods and meadows, hills, lanes and a stream on whose banks grew forget-me-nots, willow-herb and lacy meadow sweet. It was my delight to wander in these meadows. On one quiet Sunday afternoon at the age of nine I carried a baby sister down the sandy lane at the end of the garden.

Crossing the stream by the stepping stones, I laid her down under   9
some sweet-smelling lime trees that were in bloom. Everything was very quiet save for the burbling water and the lazy munching of the melancholy cows. I was not thinking of anything in particular, but I must have absorbed the total ambience very deeply, for after nearly seventy years it is all still quite clear and still "holy ground."

The "Thing" happened suddenly but quietly, as if I had awakened   10
from a dream. It is well known that we have no language in which to describe the experience of the noumenal.

> To those who know Thee not, no words can paint
> And those who know Thee know all words are faint.

So, like the prophet Ezekiel, I must fall back on symbolic terms and say, "The Heavens were opened," or, "It was as if a veil had been drawn and I saw the far country," which was not "far" but all around, filling me with wonder and gladness.

I remember saying, "Now I know what Heaven is like." Then I   11
found myself repeating the twenty-third Psalm: "He maketh me to lie down in green pastures; he leadeth me beside the still waters." I had a vague feeling this must somehow be connected with what they were talking about in church—little as I ever understood of that save for a few Scripture passages of outstanding beauty.

When the moment had passed I seem to have thought no more   12
about it. I had often had somewhat similar moments, as with the
discoveries of the first snow-drop, the apple blossom in spring and
the translucent yellow maple trees in autumn. The aesthetic and the
mystic are very close, and the one can obviously prepare the way to the
other without necessarily taking one "through" into the transcendent.
Both, for those who want to express it that way, can be called experiences of "God."

But I did not know that. "God" for me was the name of a person   13
who was my loving Father in Heaven. Later, when I was uprooted
from that paradisiacal environment and shades of the prison house
began to close, I needed this loving Father badly and derived great
comfort from his existence and the assurance that he had everything
under control and would eventually exchange this vale of tears for
eternal bliss if one obeyed the command to "Endure hardness as a
good soldier of Jesus Christ."

It was a grim philosophy but perhaps a less unwise extreme than   14
indulgent permissiveness. In a way I believe that it served me well until
I left school and made the shattering discovery that there were people
who did not believe in any of it.

The discovery was altogether too sudden. A more intelligent reli-   15
gious education, even in adolescence, would have prepared me for
new ways of looking at things and would have explained that one
must, all through life, grow and outgrow earlier ways of thinking and
feeling; that as we grow toward greater maturity, deeper and fuller
meaning will continuously unfold. It was a sorry thing that I should
have spent so many years hunting for childhood's personal God when
all the time I had known that experience of *Le Milieu Divin* in the
meadows. It was strange that I should "know" the truth that *this life
is not all,* and not know that I knew it, still less be able to relate it to
the theology of the churches.

This is why I suggest that today, instead of endlessly debating the   16
existence of God the Father, the Supreme Being, we make clear that,
since nobody can know whether such a "person" exists, we use the
term "God," if and when we use it, as a symbol for the highest we
know and that we should explicitly say that we are so using it; that
we should, like the Buddha, leave aside all argument about God's
existence and concentrate rather on those things with which God, if
he exists, must be primarily and profoundly concerned, with self-
transforming and the increase of wisdom and understanding, with
significant living and dying, with truth and goodness, beauty and
love. Such concentration would undoubtedly please him more than

disputation concerning his existence, singing his praises, or begging
his forgiveness.

A Hindu sage once said: "When a Westerner is faced with a theo-   17
logical problem he says, "I will consider this intellectually." The Hindu
says, "I will try to raise my level of consciousness." The Hindu way
is the more sensible, because when the level of consciousness is raised
we can see further and see things differently. As Paul truly said, as we
are at present we can only see "as through a glass darkly" and can
only know "in part."

This is one of the most difficult steps in growing toward maturity,   18
the relinquishing of our treasured "certainties" and accepting the fact
that much of our knowledge can be only partial. Of Blake's poem
"The Tiger" a child remarked, "It's nearly all questions." That is also
true of life; there are more questions than answers, and when the
answers do come through, they often arrive in unexpected ways from
unexpected sources, so that we do not always recognize them.

Paul also said that when he became a man he put away childish   19
things. Many of us fail to do this or to help children to do it, especially
with regard to our thinking about God. We cling to the childhood's
image even when we regard ourselves as "grown up." Intelligent children are, by the age of seven, quite capable of beginning to understand
the meaning of abstract thinking. Christian children hear in church
that God is a spirit and that the Holy Spirit is the third "Person"
of the Trinity. This is meaningless, and unless they are helped to put
some content into the word "spirit" and to seek out its presence operating both in the external world and in themselves, it may remain
meaningless through life. The first step is to distinguish between concrete and abstract, between visible and invisible realities. That things
like love and wavelengths are real although they cannot be seen is an
important discovery for a child trying to get a more intelligible concept
of God than "the Man up there." It means that spirit too can be real,
but, like love, can be known only in its operations and its effects.

When tragedy descends, the usual response of people with a per-   20
sonal and perhaps an anthropomorphic concept of God is to ask "Why?
Why did this have to happen to me? Why did God allow it? He is
omnipotent and so could have stopped it. 'Not a sparrow falls without
his knowing,' So, Why?" Since there is no answer to such questions, the
necessity of outgrowing the personal and understanding the spiritual
concept of God is obvious. Otherwise the preacher is inevitably manufacturing atheists.

How do we find God as spirit? A man struck suddenly blind   21
admitted the temptation to give in to self-pity, but added "I find there

is another force in me on which I can draw and which enables me to say, 'I can manage; I am equal to this.' " Quite young children can, without being priggish about it, understand that story and relate it to themselves.

Such understanding will reveal that what is called "God the Holy   22
Spirit" is the force in us that makes for courage, humility and love. It is what St Paul meant when he referred to "the power that worketh in us" (*Ephesians III, 20*).

When religion is thus built up through discussion and on an experi-   23
mental basis, it will not break down. In my case it had been based on authoritarian statements that must not be questioned because they had been "once and for all delivered." At the end of that long searching I decided that the teaching of Jesus remained valid but that the teaching of the church *about* Jesus was debatable, that this should therefore be taken symbolically and the deeper esoteric meaning of such things as the Christmas and Easter festivals be made clear. Some things are truer than the literal truth, and the significance of the symbol as a carrier of meaning was one of the things that helped to awaken me to the realization that religion is an inward thing and that the true significance of the mythos lies in its inner and hidden meanings, not in the recorded outer events. For example, the statement that Christ rose from the dead, understood symbolically, is capable of various interpretations that are meaningful for us quite independently of whether we happen to believe it literally or not. That is not the important thing. Taken literally it seems to collide with modern knowledge, and so the literalist discards the doctrine without concerning himself with hidden mean-ings—without ever realizing that life and death are both parts of a complementary process.

Carl Jung writes: "The danger that a mythology understood too   24
literally, and as taught by the church, will suddenly be repudiated lock stock and barrel is today greater than ever. Is it not time that the Christian mythology, instead of being wiped out, was understood sym-bolically for once?" Incidentally he adds that "there is no need of the Easter event as a guarantee of immortality, because long before the coming of Christianity mankind believed in a life after death" (*The Undiscovered Self.*)

Another brick for the new structure I was slowly building for faith   25
in life was the study of evolution. Let those who wished insist that it was a purposeless and purely mechanical process brought about by natural selection and the survival of the fittest—with chance variations; the fact remained that from the dust this process had produced a

Socrates, a Jesus and a Shakespeare. This was something to fill one with a great wonder. It indicated that "something" was at work.

Yet another kind of country that began to develop my interest in "other dimensions" was the realm of the paranormal. As described earlier I had already, as a child, had a simple mystic experience of a "beyond." Now that parapsychology has at last been freed from the taint of "unscientific," one can begin to see the connection between mystic or cosmic consciousness and paraconsciousness, and the support given by the one to the other.

Lastly, the loosening of my tenacious hold on reason as the only avenue to truth was further aided by acquaintance with Eastern religions, especially Buddhism, which is generally regarded by the West as atheistic and therefore "not a real religion at all." And certainly, if religion means primarily belief in God, is not an atheistic religion a contradiction in terms?

Again the answer came slowly over the years: start at a new place. Abandon the attempt to prove the existence of a mysterious and incomprehensible "person" existing somewhere in outer space and build up faith in life on what can be known in experience. I saw that the language and imagery in which truth is expressed must vary with the stage of development; that there are "grades of significance," and that as we let go of Childhood's God, we can become more aware of those things in life that may justly be called divine, which induce in us what Rudolf Otto called "a sense of the holy" and Schweitzer called "reverence for life." In short, that there is a larger reality which transcends the phenomenal world, which can become known to us only as our personalities become capable of apprehending it.

In one of his letters to Minanlabain, A. E. (Lord Russell) wrote, "I believe the only news of any interest does not come from the great cities or from the councils of state, but from some lonely watcher on the hills who has a momentary glimpse of infinitude and feels the universe rushing at him."

THINKING ABOUT THE CONTENT

1. Isherwood believes "It is psychologically and spiritually dangerous" to answer the question of God's existence "in terms of rigid and debatable theology" (3). What does she mean? Do you agree? Explain.

2. What does Isherwood mean by "facts of experience" described in paragraphs 7–11? What do such experiences have to do with our thinking about God? Have you had such experiences?

3. What would Isherwood consider an "intelligent religious education" (15)? Do you agree? Explain.

4. "Instead of endlessly debating the existence of God the Father," what does Isherwood suggest we do (16)? How would this approach alter certain people's views of God? Do you agree with her? Why or why not?

5. How does Isherwood define "God the Holy Spirit" (22)? Why does she feel it is important to "outgrow" the personal and understand "the spiritual concept of God" (20)? Do you agree? Explain.

6. Isherwood says, "Another brick for the new structure I was slowly building for faith in life was the study of evolution" (25). Does she accept the study of evolution as valid? Do you agree with her? Explain.

7. Why does Isherwood feel we need to loosen the "hold on reason as the only avenue to truth" (27)? What other avenues besides reason does she feel can lead us to "let go of Childhood's God" (28)?

LOOKING AT STRUCTURE AND STYLE

8. To whom is Isherwood writing? Why do you think so?

9. How well versed in her subject is Isherwood? From what sources does she draw much of her support?

10. Isherwood uses her personal growth experiences in coming to an understanding of her dilemma over God. Is this a useful technique for the development of her thesis? Why or why not?

EXPLORING DISCUSSION AND WRITING TOPICS

11. Write an essay that argues for the benefit of one statement over the other:

    Believe nothing because you have been told it.

    —*BUDDHA*

    Give me a child till he is seven years old, and I will give him to you for the rest of his life.

    —*LOYOLA*

12. Discuss your religious upbringing. Was it rigid? Was it understandable as a child? Do you still believe what you were taught as a child?

13. Is the teaching of evolution contrary to the belief in a God the Father?

14. Summarize Isherwood's belief system.

NORMAN CORWIN

Norman Corwin is the author of more than a dozen books, among them: *The Plot to Overthrow Christmas, Seems Radio Is Here to Stay, Thirteen by Corwin, More by Corwin, We Hold These Truths, The World of Carl Sandburg, Prayer for the '70s, Holes in the Stained Glass Window,* and *Trivializing America: The Triumph of Mediocrity.* In the latter book, from which this selection is taken, Corwin discloses examples of what he sees as the general erosion of values in our national ethos. For Corwin, America's "demise is far less likely to be from a nuclear blow (not without destroying whoever deals the blow) than from the wasting effects of trivialization" in most everything from entertainment to religion. His call is a summons to war against the bad taste and sleazy standards that he feels have contaminated life in the United States.

In the following selection, Corwin deals with what he sees as the trivialization of religion in the United States.

ᴪ

Trivializing Religion

Of all systems of abstract thought, religion has the widest spread. It overlooks life, death, morality, ethics, justice, divinity, speaks for creation, superintends the cosmos, deals in myths and mysteries, mediates the soul, accommodates hope, fear, power, charity, devotion, mercy. Yet for all of that, much of it is steeped in trivia.

The same writ that alludes to Arcturus and his sons, and to loosing the bands of Orion, dwells on the number of brass sockets, staves of shittim wood and twined linen hangings in the construction of an altar; it inveighs against anklets, wimples and crisping pins in the dress of women; fusses over dietary and architectural details, rites of purification, stipulates physical defects which exclude a priest from office, sets the exact number of oil lamps and cakes of shrewbread to be placed in the holy of holies.

Goodness and mercy, green pastures, still waters, restoration of the soul, transit of the valley of the shadow of death, eternal life in the house of the Lord, are gathered into six sentences of a single psalm, yet there are tedious rounds of hair-splitting, and mysterious configurations such as the numbers 666 and 144,000 which occur in consecutive verses of The Revelation. "Here is wisdom," is written by way of introduction to the first figure; concerning the 144,000 we learn only that "they"—not otherwise identified—were not defiled with women, they were virgins; that they followed the Lamb wherever he went, and that they, and they alone, were able to learn a new song sung by the "voice of harpers harping with their harps" (Rev. 14: 1–4). Biblical commentators, after many calisthenics, still cannot satisfactorily explain these numbers.

Veneration and trivialization constantly cross in religion. The 4 1,807-page compendium, *Exhaustive Concordance of The Bible*, by James Strong, S.R.D., LL.D., actually lists every last *a, an, as, are, be, but, by, for, from, he, hers, his, I, in, it, me, not, of, on, she, that, the, thee, unto, upon, was* and *were*. The placement of each of these words by chapter and verse is meticulously arranged in an appendix of 18 parallel columns per page of fine print, page after page after page—an Amazon of trivia, useful to nobody, but laid out in full because each article, pronoun and preposition is, after all, in the *Bible*, and the Bible, like Everest, is *there*.

Still, this is an inoffensive and pure-minded form of trivia. Sacredness, like taste, is beyond dispute. A hair of the prophet, a shroud, an ark, a wall, the black stone of Mecca, a capitalized pronoun—so long as the sanctity in which believers envelop such articles and particles is not imposed on non-believers by fire, sword or mandate, no harm is done. Gourmands of the spirit, no less than of food and drink, are entitled to their indulgences. The trivialities of pilpulism, the waste of time and breath in wrangling over how many angels can dance on the head of a pin, are too trifling to frazzle the fabric of a whole society. It is when the *concept* of a divinity, of a godhead, of God, is itself petty, when the ineffable is rendered not only effable but picayune, that trivialization causes damage by lowering sights and values. And while whittling God down to anthropomorphic size and character is practiced universally, there are certain uniquely American ways of doing it which employ showmanship, salesmanship, mass media, gimmickry, and entreprenurial messiahship.

There is an ancient Hindu merchant's prayer which asks for advantageous trading, high interest and great wealth, and it is so unblushingly cheeky that we smile when we read it:

Indra, may I gather wealth from my purchases! . . . With my prayers, I sing this divine song, that I may gain hundredfold! . . . May what I get in barter render me a gainer!

May the accruing of gain be auspicious . . . (may I) gain
wealth through wealth . . . may Indra place luster into it
for me.[1]

The exclamation marks are in the original prayer, and at this distance
we may be charmed or amused by the earnest insistence of the votary.
He is merely asking for fat profits. He does not claim that he knows
the Vedic gods personally, that he has met Indra face to face, been
anointed by heaven, or armed with divine authority.

    In contrast to this candid Hindu, Americans who pray to gain   7
wealth through wealth, tend to brag about God's personal confidence
in them. Nelson Bunker Hunt, Texas billionaire, a Croesus on the
world level of Paul Getty, the Greek shipping magnates and the Saudi
oilmen, is foursquare for religiousness. "The important thing to have,"
he said at an investment seminar for millionaires, "is a spiritual environment in this country that will mean we can keep the money we make."
Not long before, he had tried to corner the world supply of silver, and
had lost so heavily that he had to be bailed out by a government-
approved loan of $1.1 billion. It took a consortium of banks to do it.
Earlier, Hunt had also been deep in oil and soybeans. In his many
investments he had no doubt hoped for God's blessing. In turn he gave
his own blessing to William R. Bright, founder of the Campus Crusade
for Christ and director of a $49 million evangelical complex that
included a "Christian Embassy" and a travel agency. Hunt's benedic-
tion took two forms—money, and a declaration that Bright was "the
closest thing to Jesus on earth." The object of this praise was in no
position to dispute it, since he himself announced that he was "commis-
sioned by God to save the world."

    One of Mr. Bright's strategies for saving the world was the forma-   8
tion of a constellation called, with stunning fatuity, "History's Handful." Its goal was 1,000 donors willing to donate or raise $1 million
each. Bright harvested $170 million from History's Handful by the
middle of 1980. Nelson Bunker Hunt alone gave $10 million, but on
Bright's scale this was modest. According to *Newsweek*,[2] at a "Christian briefing" in Houston

> - Bright explained how [donors] could be enshrined in his
> "Golden Globe Hall of Honor." For $100 million, a donor
> can become a "world sponsor"; for half that, a "hemisphere

---

1. Alfonso M. Dinola, *The Prayers of Man* (London: Heinemann, 1962), 191.

2. *Newsweek* (June 18, 198): 55.

sponsor," and for $25 million, a "continental sponsor."
A mere $25,000 buys only the sponsorship of a single earthly
mission.

The director of financial planning for Bright's Great Commission 9
Foundation, William C. Wagner, explained the compatibility of Holy
Script with holy scrip:

> The Bible is the inerrant word of God—the undisputed book
> on financial success. There are some 500 verses in the Bible
> on prayer, but there are over 2,000 on money and posses-
> sions.

At the same investment seminar, John W. O'Donnell of Newport Beach,
Ca., one of the foremost tax-shelter advisers in the country, had a
supply-side view of the Creator: "The Lord is the all-time capitalist,
not a socialist."

A clear line of descent, or ascent, from the Hindu merchant who 10
prayed to gain a hundredfold, to the modern investor, was indicated
by David Jackson of Denver in the course of a lecture on barter-trading
as a way to avoid taxes:

> The Good Lord has entrusted assets to you and made you
> an agent. The master has a duty to cooperate with you.
> He will indemnify and compensate you. Real estate agents
> get 7 to 10%; attorneys, maybe 33 to 40%. God has said
> you can have a 90% agency. With generosity like that, don't
> you feel bad about limiting it to 10%?

Oftener than not, American evangelists profess to know God very 11
well and to have inside tracks to Jesus, but the one who knows God
best would appear to be Morris Cerullo, self-proclaimed "Prophet of
God," whose Third World Crusade appearances have attracted more
than 100,000 congregants to a single service. He claims in his autobiography, *From Judaism to Christianity*, that he met God face to face in
Paterson, N.J., and was lifted into heaven, where he encountered "The
Presence of God" in the form of a six-foot-high flaming ball.

> My eyes were drawn to the place where the glory of God
> was standing in the heavens, and right where He had been
> standing, there was a hole in the sky in the form of two
> footprints. It was as if someone had taken a knife and cut
> a hole in a great big cake of cheese and one could see right
> through it. . . . I knew what I had to do. I put my feet

> in the indentations that had been made by the Presence of
> God, and to my utter amazement, my feet fit perfectly
> into those footprints. They were the exact size.

This trumps the story of Cinderella's shoe, and for the first time reveals
that God has the foot size of a short, stocky man.

Cerullo shares with the religious millionaires of the investment   12
seminar an appreciation of God's power to indemnify and compensate.
His World Evangelism organization bought the El Cortez Hotel in San
Diego for $7.5 million and sold it two years later for $12 million.
Early in 1982 a corporation financed by Cerullo announced plans to
build a $50 million hotel-condominium resort on the Smoky Moun-
tains of Tennessee. But spreading the word of God and making big
deals in real estate are only two of Cerullo's interests. Others include
a lively antagonism toward women's rights, homosexual rights, and
the rights of the elderly because they "all fit in with the sinister evil
forces designed to tear down the structure of our society as Satan
makes his last great spectacular onslaught."

Whatever one may think of Satan, who is unpopular in all but a   13
few exotic cults, he is a large abstraction, adversary to God himself,
physical opponent of the Archangel Michael, prominent in the Books
of Isaiah, Job and the non-canonical Enoch, and a luminous figure in
pages of Aeschylus, Sophocles, Seneca, Dante, Milton and Goethe. But
Satan, too, has been trivialized to accommodate American prophets
and statesmen. One might expect Morris Cerullo to believe Satan is
busy making tracks in a spectacular onslaught, but what of a U.S.
Army general, later to become Secretary of State, who speculated that
the erasure of 18 minutes of Richard M. Nixon's voice from a Watergate tape might have been the doing of a demonic force?

Satan and his associates, like God and Jesus, have been scaled   14
down to petty activities. Larry Gohorn, former president of General
Automation and a participant in the great investment seminar, declared
that in 1978 God commanded him to "get the banking system operational," and told a reporter in 1981 that he had been "personally
attacked by demons."

Alexander Haig was not the only one to think that demons had   15
been nasty to President Nixon. Billy Graham, evangelist closest to the
White House in the era of conservative presidents, was shocked by
Watergate—not because of the criminal conspiracy which it exposed,
but because Nixon, whom Graham had thought to be "every inch a
Christian gentleman," had used so many expletives. Graham blamed

it on sleeping pills and demons. "Even the Greek word for them both is the same. My conclusion is that it was just all those sleeping pills, they just let a demon-power come in and play over him."

Small wonder that fundamentalist Christians in some of the west- 16
ern states early in 1982 circulated rumors that Procter & Gamble's corporate symbol of a crescent moon with a bearded face, in profile, looking at a group of 13 stars, was connected with satanism and devil worship. The company was hard put to find where the rumors originated. A woman in Phoenix said she heard about the supposed link between P & G and Satan at a fundamentalist Christian seminar. Other sources cited the Trinity Broadcasting Network of Tustin, Ca., producer of Christian TV programs delivered to 1.3 million viewers by cable, as the responsible party. Trinity denied it. Finally P & G gave up its moon, stars, and suspect eidolon.

Religious broadcasting is highly profitable, and resoundingly suc- 17
cessful both in terms of affluence and influence. The Christian Broad-casting Network (CBN), which has a $20 million production facility in Virginia Beach, Va., draws more mail than all three commercial networks combined, and receives income estimated to exceed $1 mil-lion per week.[3] Jerry Falwell's Moral Majority sermons are carried by 395 TV stations and 500 radio outlets. The Southern Baptist Radio and Television Commission, seeking to take advantage of "new oppor-tunity," drew up plans for a 105-station denominational network. National Catholic Telecommunications announced it was "adding an-other dimension to the church's work, to reach out more effectively." The United Methodist Church publicly instituted a $25 million cam-paign for what it called "TV Presence and Ministry."

These major Christian denominations went about the broadcast- 18
ing business with relative sedateness, compared to the gimmickry of the evangelists. Among the latter group, Oral Roberts, founder of Oral Roberts University, offered his broadcast audiences a "blessing-pact plan" through which he would "earnestly pray" that any gift given to his ministry will be returned "in its entirety from a totally unexpected source," and promised that if, after a year, this did not happen, the donation would be immediately refunded with no questions asked. In 1983 Roberts moved to higher ground following a seven-hour conver-sation with Jesus in which Jesus gave him "marching orders" and chided him and his supporters for dragging their feet with donations for a three-building medical complex Roberts was installing in Oklahoma.

3. *Watch* (August 1980).

"When," Jesus asked with apparent impatience, "when are you and your partners going to obey me? When?"

The partners alluded to were "prayer partners," whom Jesus in-   19
structed Roberts to ask for $240 each. In return they would receive 48 tapes containing Roberts' commentaries on books of the New Testament, plus 14 special blessings that included money and success. Though Roberts did not quote Jesus on the cause of cancer, he advised his prayer partners in a 12-page fund-raising letter that "I have become keenly aware of how Satan is trying to take control of the cells and cause them to multiply out of their divinely placed order." As to the size of the suggested donation, Jesus was quoted verbatim: "Tell them this is not Oral Roberts asking [for the $240], but their Lord."

Roberts is but one of many preachers who exchange goods or   20
tokens for tithes. Among others were revivalist A.A. Allen, who sold pieces of his original revival tent as "Prosperity Blessing Cloths," and guaranteed possession of these swatches to reward the buyer with good health and economic security. Dr. Frederick J. ("Reverend Ike") Eikerenkoetter II, likewise offered a "prayer cloth" for healing pur-poses.[4] "Money," he said, "is God in action."

The money is very good. Jesus might be appalled, but then there   21
were no investment seminars or transmitters in Jerusalem. His ministry did not divide its time between sports and the word of God, as does Gannett-owned radio station KPRZ in Los Angeles, which features local and nationally syndicated ministers and gospel music six days a week, but on Saturday carries Stanford and Notre Dame football games, and, in season, the entire Los Angeles Kings hockey league schedule. The station's general manager explained, "By carrying Kings hockey, we have preempted some of our Christian advertisers because, frankly, the revenues are greater. We're still committed to the Christian format, but we're also committed to making money."

It follows that if God is trivialized, Jesus is next in line. Bruce   22
Barton, advertising nabob (Batten, Barton, Durstine & Osborne), as-sured America in his best-selling book, *The Man Nobody Knows,* that Jesus

> . . . was a salesman at heart . . . he would be a national
> advertiser today, as he was the great advertiser of his own
> day. . . . Take any one of the parables no matter which—
> you will find that it exemplifies all the principles on which
> advertising textbooks are written . . . his language was

4. John Wilson, *Religion in American Society* (New York: Prentice-Hall, 1978).

marvelously simple . . . all the greatest things in life are
one-syllable things—love, joy, home, hope, child, wife, trust,
faith, God. . . .

What Barton neglected to mention was that all the meanest things in
life are one-syllable things too: hate, sin, greed, lust, pain, whore, slave,
pimp, bawd, crook, rape, rage, gloom, doubt, war, fiend, ghoul, brat,
pox, plague, throe, curse, woe, groan, moan, stroke, death. And some
of the greatest things in life are polysyllabic . . . happiness, beauty,
brotherhood, kindness, amity, benevolence, charity, consideration, patience, plenitude, wholesomeness, prosperity . . . they make a long
list, longer than the monosyllables so close to Barton's Jesus.

Jesus might not be pleased to learn that he would be big on   23
Madison Avenue; that Billy Graham compared his Sermon on the
Mount to President Eisenhower's first foreign policy address; that Jerry
Falwell advertises over TV the *Jesus First LP Album;* that Ken Foure,
featured speaker of "Spiritual Emphasis Week" at Grace College, an
evangelical Christian school in Indiana, was a used car salesman who,
in his own words, "switched the pitch to Christ."

Of course, not only Christian evangelists have found fat pickings   24
in America. Imported faiths, some of them as exotic as an albino
dzeggetai, have reaped riches from this fertile land. To name only one,
there is Mahataj Ji, a teenage guru whose shepherding in America
earned him a fleet of sports cars, a Rolls-Royce or two, and a $22,000
British Jensen touring car used especially for festivals.

And why not? If so many other things in America society are   25
marked down like goods in a bargain basement, in order to keep
merchandise moving and cash flowing in, why not God? Exaltation
and edification are all very well, but there is a time and place for
everything, and it is only sound to keep prayer cloths and blessing-
pact packages circulating where they can do the most good. To trivializers God is a resource and religion is a technique, and the combo is
unbeatable.

THINKING ABOUT THE CONTENT

1. In what ways does Corwin think much of religion is "steeped in trivia"
   (1)? Who are the "trivializers"? Is he correct? Why or why not?
2. What does he mean by the statement, "Veneration and trivialization constantly cross in religion" (4)? What are some of his examples of veneration
   and trivialization? Do you agree with his examples? Why or why not?
3. What is the contrast drawn in the difference between the Hindu merchant's

prayer and the American's who pray to gain wealth? Why is or is not the significance different?

4. Corwin published *Trivializing America* in 1986. Is religion still being trivialized? What contemporary events or examples of religious trivialization continue to support or refute Corwin's thesis?

LOOKING AT STRUCTURE AND STYLE

5. Describe Corwin's attitude and tone. What particular passages contribute to both?

6. To whom is Corwin writing? Why do you think so? Who might be offended by some of his comments?

7. What is the function of paragraphs 2–4? Why does he seem to excuse the examples in those paragraphs as "inoffensive and pure-minded form of trivia" (5)?

8. How well does Corwin support his thesis? Are his use of statistics verifiable?

EXPLORING DISCUSSION AND WRITING TOPICS

9. Watch one of the religious broadcasting channels, such as the Christian Broadcasting Network, the Trinity Broadcasting Network, or The Faith and Values Channel. Do some of the evangelists "trivialize" religion? Does Corwin exaggerate? Are religious messages mixed with politics or business? To which audience are the networks aimed?

10. Research balanced views on one of the people Corwin calls religious trivialists in his comments, such as Oral Roberts, Nelson B. Hunt, William R. Bright, Jerry Falwell, or Morris Cerullo. Is he being unfair? Are these people using religion to gain power and money? Do they trivialize in the name of religion? If, so how do they get away with it?

John Shelby Spong

The Episcopal bishop of Newark, John Shelby Spong is the author of numerous books, including *Honest Prayer, This Hebrew Lord, Christpower, Into the Whirlwind: The Future of the Church, Beyond Moralism, Living in Sin? A Bishop Rethinks Sexuality,* and *Rescuing the Bible from Fundamentalism.* The outspoken Bishop Spong is often controversial because of his strong views against fundamentalism and his attempts to bring racial minorities, women, and homosexuals into what he calls "the full life of his church." Spong wants "to bring the Bible into the twentieth century by focusing on its eternal truths" rather than the historical, philosophical, and scientific deviations that have caused some people to discount the Bible all together.

In his book *Rescuing the Bible from Fundamentalism,* Spong reveals how literal interpretations of the Bible have been used to justify slavery, ban books, deny the rights of gays and lesbians, subordinate women, and justify war. Combining current biblical scholarship and modern science, Spong wants to "lift the Scriptures out of the prejudices and cultural biases of today and liberate the Bible's message of hope for all people." The first chapter of the book is reprinted here.

❦

Sex Drove Me to the Bible

Sex drove me to the Bible!   1
This statement is literally true, but not in the sense that most would   2
interpret it. In 1988 my book entitled *Living in Sin? A Bishop Rethinks Human Sexuality* was published by Harper and Row. In that book I was led to question traditional religious attitudes and traditional religious definitions on a wide variety of sexual issues, from homosexuality to premarital living arrangements. There was an immediate outcry from conservative religious circles in defense of something they called biblical morality.

Proof Texting and Prejudice

This appeal to the Bible to justify and to sustain an attitude that was   3
clearly passing away had a very familiar ring to me. I grew up in

America's segregated South with its rich evangelical biblical heritage. Time after time I heard the Bible quoted to justify segregation. I was told that Ham, Noah's son, had looked on Noah in his nakedness, and for this sin he had been cursed to servitude and slavery along with all his progeny (Gen. 9:25–27). It did not occur to those quoting this Scripture to raise questions about what kind of God was assumed in this verse, or whether or not they could worship such a God. Since they could not identify themselves with those who were the victims of this cruelty, the God to whom they ascribed this victimizing power did not appear to them to be seriously compromised.

It also did not seem to matter that this corporate condemnation   4
of millions of people to servitude because of their ancestor's indiscretion might also contradict other parts of the sacred text. The prophet Ezekiel, for example writes:

> What do you mean by repeating this proverb concerning
> the land of Israel, 'The fathers have eaten sour grapes, and
> the children's teeth are set on edge'? As I live, says the Lord
> God, this proverb shall no more be used by you in Israel.
> Behold, all souls are mine; the soul of the father as well as
> the soul of the son is mine: the soul that sins shall die. (Ezek.
> 18:2–4)

The only concern of the one who quoted the texts in my early life was to maintain that person's prejudice, to enable that person to avoid having to change destructive attitudes.

I lived in Lynchburg, Virginia, in the late 1960s, when independent   5
Baptist preacher Jerry Falwell was just beginning his rise to national prominence. Intense racism was certainly in the air at that time, and Jerry Falwell played to these feelings as his popularity grew. To start a "Christian school" in that period of history was a popular response to the Supreme Court order to dismantle the segregated school system endemic to the South since the Civil War. Teachers in Falwell's school had to take an oath of conformity to biblical inerrancy, and by that same view of Scripture, Jerry Falwell could justify his emotional commitment to segregation, although, in fairness to Mr. Falwell, it needs to be said that he has moved away from these negative attitudes as the years have gone by.

It was in this period of history that the segregationist governor   6
of Georgia, Lester Maddox, became a candidate for president of the United States and was supported by many southern fundamentalists. Maddox was a Georgia restaurateur who battled for his "constitutional right" to serve only a segregated public. He gave out ax

handles at his restaurant as a hint of the way he thought those who wanted to desegregate public businesses might be discouraged from doing so.

With ease, many texts out of the Hebrew Scriptures could be   7 quoted to justify the need for God's chosen people to keep themselves separate and apart from those judged to be unchosen, heathen, or evil. That was, and is, a major theme in the books of both Ezra and Nehemiah, for example (Ezra 10:12, 15; Neh. 13:1–3). Of course those texts could be countered by other texts to produce ambivalence or relativity in biblical truth, but fundamentalists could not tolerate this. Those whose religious security is rooted in a literal Bible do not want that security disturbed. They are not happy when facts challenge their biblical understanding or when nuances in the text are introduced or when they are forced to deal with either contradictions or changing insights. The Bible, as they understand it, shares in the permanence and certainty of God, convinces them that they are right, and justifies the enormous fear and even negativity that lie so close to the surface in fundamentalistic religion. For biblical literalists, there is always an enemy to be defeated in mortal combat.

Sometimes that enemy is Satan—the devil literalized and made   8 very real and serving the primary purpose of removing responsibility from the one who has fallen into sin. Onetime-popular American evangelist Jimmy Swaggart, when caught in a New Orleans motel with a prostitute, explained his behavior by just such an appeal to Satan. His evangelistic enterprises were so successful, he stated, that the devil was being hurled back into darkness by this white knight of a preacher. So the devil launched a counterattack and lured evangelist Swaggart into a trap and dealt a mortal blow to his soul-winning ministry. If the devil can ensnare a heroic figure like Swaggart, so the argument went, think what he (the devil is always male, witches are always female) can do to the lesser persons who are mere church members.

In evangelical circles, child discipline tends to be quite physical,   9 both because children are thought to be "born in sin" and therefore evil and because the Book of Proverbs teaches parents that "he who spares the rod hates his son, but he who loves him is diligent to discipline him" (Prov. 13:24). One disobedient lad, facing corporal punishment in "the woodshed," is said to have argued for a suspended sentence by saying, "It wasn't my fault, father. The devil made me do it." To which the father replied, "Well son, I guess it is my duty to beat the devil out of you!" Blaming the devil is a popular but not always successful maneuver. It did not work for Mr. Swaggart.

If the devil is not the enemy, then, according to the fundamentalists, 10
a rival church frequently is the focus of the negative energy that roots
in fear. The story is told of a little town in east Tennessee, hardly big
enough to support one church, where on opposite sides of the main
street stood the First Baptist Church and the Second Baptist Church.
When a visitor inquired as to why there were two Baptist churches in
this single tiny town, the visitor was told, "This Baptist church says,
'there ain't no hell,' and this other Baptist church says, 'the hell there
ain't.' "

If not a rival church, then religious liberals, secular modernists, 11
God-denying communists, or some other incarnation of evil becomes
the enemy. Irrational religious anger demands a target. Television evangelists use physical and verbal means to act out their negativity and
thereby to relieve some of this energy in the lives of their congregations.
It is an interesting exercise, when viewing television evangelists, to
turn off the sound and watch the facial contortions and violent gestures.
Seldom do they communicate the love of God.

When a fundamentalist Christian sees the Antichrist in someone 12
who is disturbing his or her religious security, it becomes not merely
justifiable but downright righteous to utter words of condemnation
and prayers for the early demise of that enemy. Indeed, you can even
believe that you are God's anointed one to rid the world of this demonic
figure.

One irate reader of a newspaper article wrote that he was praying 13
that the next plane I took would crash, carrying me to my grave. The
next time I boarded a flight I felt I should stop at the front of the
plane and say, "Folks, there is something you need to know before
this plane takes off." If I did so, it might result in a wider seat selection.
I wonder, however, at the incongruity of that letter writer who sincerely
believes himself to be a Christian and yet somehow does not calculate
the fact that his prayers for the early demise of someone he abhors
might also require the sacrificial deaths of a planeload of supposedly
innocent people. Yet that is the nature of religious anger. Once again,
the words spoken and the deeds proposed are simply not in touch
with the gospel of the God who so loved the world and who, in the
person of Jesus, invited all to "come unto him."

A major function of fundamentalist religion is to bolster deeply 14
insecure and fearful people. This is done by justifying a way of life
with all of its defining prejudices. It thereby provides an appropriate
and legitimate outlet for one's anger. The authority of an inerrant Bible
that can be readily quoted to buttress this point of view becomes an

essential ingredient to such a life. When that Bible is challenged, or relativized, the resulting anger proves the point categorically.

The same mentality exists in the more sophisticated mainline   15
churches on more rational levels and with more complex and emotional issues. These churches would be embarrassed if they had to defend the patterns of segregation among southern fundamentalists, but many of them are quite convinced that their prejudice toward women, for example, is a justified part of God's plan in creation. It is for them God-given and biblically based. It is no surprise, then, that the twentieth-century battle for the rights of women in the church and for the casting off of the male-imposed definition of women has produced heated and emotional ecclesiastical conflict.

From the Pope, John Paul II, to the former Presiding Bishop of the   16
Episcopal Church, John Maury Allin, to the Archbishop of Canterbury, Robert Runcie, to the outspoken Anglican Bishop of London, Graham Leonard, the most remarkable words have been spoken to prove that the "unbroken tradition of two thousand years of an all-male priesthood" is not a manifestation of the prejudice and sin of a patriarchal, sexist society, but is rather a manifestation of the unchanging will of God supported by "the word of God" in the Bible. Each spoke for that point of view that was distinctly uncomfortable as the sexual stereotypes of the past began to be discarded.

In separate ways, but with a patriarchal consistency, the various   17
Christian leaders accepted a definition of women that precluded the possibility that a woman could represent God at the altar. Without daring to say so outright, they were nevertheless suggesting that women are not created in the image of God. Only men share that honor. Paul had made that argument in the First Epistle to the Corinthians—"For a man ought not to cover his head, since he is the image and glory of God; but woman is the glory of man. (For man was not made from woman, but woman from man. Neither was man created for woman but woman for man." [1 Cor. 11:7–9].) Paul drew in that same epistle the conclusion that, therefore, "the women should keep silent in the churches. For they are not permitted to speak, but should be subordinate, as even the law says. If there is anything they [women] desire to know, let them ask their husbands at home. For it is shameful for a woman to speak in church" (1 Cor. 14:34, 35).

If this passage is taken literally, if the Bible is regarded as the   18
"inerrant word of God," then no woman can sing in a choir, participate in a liturgy, teach Sunday school, or be ordained as a pastor or a priest. Churches with women participating in any of these areas, and that includes every church in Christendom on some level, have thus ignored,

reinterpreted, dismissed, or relativized these biblical passages. The new sexual consciousness, and most especially the feminist aspect of that consciousness, is clearly on a collision course with "sacred tradition" as both church and Scripture have defined it. At every point thus far, "sacred tradition" has been bent to accommodate the emerging insights. This will not change. It is only a matter of time before all vestiges of the ecclesiastical oppression of women will come to an end. A woman bishop of Rome, sitting on the throne of Saint Peter as pope, is inevitable. The Bible quoted to oppose this rising tide of consciousness will itself be a casualty unless it is freed from the straitjacket of literal fundamentalism.

The issue of homosexuality is another reality in sexual thinking and practice that places pressure on Holy Scripture. Once again, this prejudice is so deep, so widely assumed to be self-evident, that all major churches have in the past simply quoted the Bible to justify their continued oppression and rejection of gay and lesbian persons. The Sodom and Gomorrah story is cited uncritically to be a biblical account, and therefore a justification, of God's condemnation of this behavior. Yet a closer reading of this narrative reveals it to be a strange story involving hospitality laws in a nomadic society that our world of superhighways, bright lights, and chain motels cannot even imagine. It is a story about gang rape, which cannot ever be anything but evil. It is a narrative that expresses violent malevolence toward women that few people today, even among the fundamentalists, would be eager to condone. [19]

In the biblical world of male values, the humiliation of a male was best achieved by making the males act like women in the sex act. To act like a woman, to be the passive participant in coitus, was thought to be insulting to the dignity of the male. This, far more than homosexuality, was the underlying theme of the Sodom story. The hero of this tale was Lot, a citizen of Sodom, who offered the sanctuary of his home to the angelic messengers and who protected them from the sexual abuse of the men of Sodom. Few preachers go on to tell you that Lot protected these messengers by offering to the mob for their sexual sport his two virgin daughters. You may "do to them as you please" (Gen. 19:8), Lot asserted. [20]

The story goes on to say that Lot, despite this violent betrayal of his daughters, was accounted righteous by God. As the tiny righteous remnant of Sodom, Lot and his family were spared by God from the destruction that befell that infamous city. The story continues to tell us of Lot's subsequent drunkenness and his seduction into incest by his scheming daughters (Gen. 19:30–36). Once again, the purpose of [21] a claim of biblical literalism is revealed to be not to call people to the values of justice, but to justify existing prejudice by keeping oneself secure inside a way of life that cannot be challenged by any new insight. Among fundamentalists, the selective use of a text, ignoring vast areas of reality, is commonplace.

There are certainly other places in Scripture where homosexuality 22 is condemned. Both the Torah and Saint Paul can be cited. However, the question of biblical authority arises anew when scientific data, which the fifth- and sixth-century B.C.E. authors of the Torah and Saint Paul could not have imagined, throws new light on the origin and cause of homosexuality. Such data available today suggest that homosexual orientation is not a matter of choice but a matter of ontology; that is, it is of the being of the individual, not the doing.

It also suggests that this phenomenon has been present in human 23 life since the dawn of human history, that it is present in higher mammals that presumably fall below the level of volition, and that there has been no appreciable success despite all the efforts of modern science, including psychiatry, in changing the givenness of this reality for the vast majority of persons. Then perhaps it begins to dawn on us that life has within it wide varieties. We have male vocal ranges from countertenor to bass and female vocal ranges from lyric soprano to a contralto that could be and sometimes is a baritone. We have male physical ranges from the muscular athlete to the soft, delicate man and female physical ranges from the well-conditioned athlete who can compete on an equal basis with the vast majority of males to the frail woman who lives out the male stereotype of helplessness.

So also we have ranges in male sexual orientation from those who 24 constitute the majority and who relate to women sexually, though, it might be added, with a wide variety of sexual appetites; to those who, because of the way their brains were sexed in utero, as many scientists would now suggest, find desire only in their response to those of their own gender. (Lest some reader make too quick and simplistic a correlation of these categories, let me quickly say that I know countertenors who are heterosexual and basses who are homosexual. I know male athletes who are gay and I know heterosexual males who in physical appearance would be called effeminate. The stereotypes of the ages do not hold when scrutinized.)

The authors of the Bible did not have the knowledge on this 25 subject that is available to us today. The sexual attitudes in Scripture used to justify the prejudiced sexual stereotypes of the past simply are not holding in this generation. They are not in touch with emerging contemporary knowledge.

So it was that sex drove me to the Bible. The new emerging sexual   26
consciousness and the passing of ancient stereotypes challenged the
authority of Scripture, raised profound questions about the authenticity of biblical insights, and created for me and for many others a crisis
of faith.

The Rescue Effort

It is not a new crisis. Tension has existed between the church and the   27
scientific community for hundreds of years. Galileo was excommunicated for his suggestion that the earth was not the center of the created
order. Isaac Newton and his clockwork universe were at odds with
those who pray to an intervening deity. People like Bishop Samuel
Wilberforce and his modern-day descendants, called creationists, were
sent into orbit as they tried to neutralize the impact of Charles Darwin.
This tension has increasingly resulted in an anti-intellectual approach
to Christianity on the part of literal-minded, conservative Christians
and a departure from the organized Christian church into the secular
city by scores of modern men and women for whom the mythologi-
cal framework of the Christian story no longer has any translatable
meaning.

Above all, it has placed the Bible in jeopardy. If the only people   28
who talk about the Bible are fundamentalists and their more sophisticated city cousins, who wince defensively when the "traditions of the
church" are challenged by new insights, then fewer and fewer people
are going to take seriously a book or a church that appears to them
to be so antiquated.

When attention is turned to the mainline churches, where a well-   29
educated ministry has always been required, it becomes obvious that
they have, by and large, simply ignored the Bible. The average pew
sitter in the average mainline church, both Catholic and Protestant,
is, to say it bluntly, biblically illiterate. The offering to the world by
the mainline churches of a viable option and alternative to biblical
fundamentalism is, therefore, not forthcoming. The options, our people
are made to feel, are either to live in continued ignorance or to abandon
the church altogether for life apart from any religious convictions. The
biblical scholarship of the past two hundred years has simply not been
made available to the man or the woman in the pew. So mainline
Christians allow the television preachers to manipulate their audiences,
most times to their own financial gain, by making the most absurd
biblical claims without their being called to accountability in the name
of truth.

It is for these reasons that I have found it imperative to put another   30
voice into the public arena. My purpose in this volume is first to rescue
the Bible from the exclusive hands of those who demand that it be
literal truth and second to open that sacred story to levels of insight
and beauty that, in my experience, literalism has never produced. I
hope to call people into an appreciation of the living "Word of God"
that lurks so often hidden and undiscovered beneath the literal words
of the text.

For biblical scholars, this volume will be very elementary. For   31
those who have only vague recollections of biblical stories, it will be
both insightful and expanding. Depending on how much the Bible has
been made into an idol for my readers, my book will be regarded as
either enlightening or disturbing. My hope is that it will help members
of the Christian churches to allow their soon-to-be-twenty-first-century
minds to become aware of and to embrace a biblical truth that, while
not literal, is certainly timeless.

I write as a Christian who loves the church. I am not a hostile   32
critic who stands outside religion desiring to make fun of it. I am not
a Marxist who believes that religion is the opiate of the people. I am
not a Madalyn Murray O'Hair who believes that God should be
expunged from public life. I am a bishop in the Anglican (Episcopal)
church who was raised as a biblical fundamentalist and who, when I
left that fundamentalism, did not leave my love of the Bible or my
desire to serve God through the church.

There will be some who, upon reading this volume, will be dis-   33
turbed and even angry. I regret that. I have no desire to make uncomfortable anyone's fragile life. In a strange way, discomfort and even
anger bear witness to the dawning of new possibilities; so while it
saddens me to cause distress, it also awakens in me a sense of gratitude.
At the same time, I suspect that voices will be raised among the liberal
Christians proclaiming that there is nothing new here and, therefore,
no reason to take this book seriously. Or they will fasten on a date
or a fact that they can challenge, even successfully, to discredit the
whole work. There is not much new here, and some of my dates
and "facts" are still debated in theological circles. Nonetheless, I will
continue to argue that these insights, drawn largely from that deep
and impressive literature of biblical scholarship over the past one
hundred years, have not yet become operative in the church primarily
because they have not yet become operative in those very clergy who
will dismiss this as "old hat."

It is my deepest hope that there will be others who will discover   34
in the pages of this book a means through which they can return to
church in honesty or be enabled to worship God with a renewed

integrity in the church that they have never left. I believe that their name is legion. They are members of my family and among my closest friends. I write for them because the goal of my professional life has been to combine scholarship with faith, to bring honesty and the authenticity of citizenship in the modern world to the activity of worship while continuing to walk in the faith tradition established by Jesus of Nazareth whom I call Lord and Christ. Time will tell whether or not so lofty a goal has been achieved.

Thinking about the Content

1. Why does Spong feel that biblical literalists need to be challenged? What social problems that he feels are caused by biblical literalists does he discuss? How does the Bible itself lie at the cause of some of the text's interpretation problems?
2. Spong feels that, "A major function of fundamentalist religion is to bolster deeply insecure and fearful people" (14). Why does he feel this way? Do you agree? Why or why not?
3. If the Bible were to be taken literally and the advice in every passage followed, what might a Christian lifestyle be like? For instance, what position would women have in the home and church? What other differences would take place?
4. Why does Spong feel that the average mainline churches, both Catholic and Protestant, will not be forthcoming with an alternative to fundamentalism? Do you think he is right when he calls the average churchgoer "biblically illiterate" (29)? Are you?

Looking at Structure and Style

5. How effective is the opening paragraph? How well does it grab your attention?
6. What is the point of paragraph 32? Why does Spong feel it important to say what he is not as well as what he is? Does this help give more credence to his thesis?
7. Spong implies that the ministry of biblical fundamentalism is not as well educated as the ministry of mainline churches. How does he do this?
8. What is Spong's attitude and tone? Provide some examples of passages that supply both.

Exploring Discussion and Writing Topics

9. Find some passages in the Bible that if taken literally would be destructive to one or more elements of society. If possible, explain why such passages may be in the Bible and how else they might be interpreted.

10. Research a specific incident in U.S. history where the literal interpretation of the Bible was used to deny some aspect of human rights.

11. Spong believes that if the Bible is continued to be read literally and mainstream church members continue to remain ignorant of the Bible that the Bible may be cast aside as both dated and irrelevant. Do you think that might happen? What would be the result?

12. Is an understanding of the Bible important? Why? To whom? In what ways? How much of it have you read? Do you know its history as well as its contents?

JOSEPH CAMPBELL

Joseph Campbell, an author and editor, was for many years a member of the literature faculty at Sarah Lawrence College. He is the author of the four-volume study of world mythologies collectively entitled *The Masks of God*. He also authored *The Hero with a Thousand Faces*, *The Flight of the Wild Gander*, *The Inner Reaches of Outer Space*, and *Myths to Live By*. Campbell was also featured and interviewed in the popular PBS series conducted by Bill Moyers, *The Power of Myths*.

While scientists treat the evolution of humans by concentrating on the physical traits that bind us, such as posture, brain, number and arrangement of teeth, the thumb, and so on, Campbell believes that we should also concentrate on the psychological character of man. Campbell asserts that the most evident distinguishing psychological sign that binds is man's organization of his life according primarily to mythic aims and laws. In many of his works, Campbell revealed the commonality of myths in diverse cultural groups. While many of the myths bear a similarity, they are often given contrasting interpretations over time.

In the following selection from *Myths to Live By*, Campbell discusses interpretations of a Judeo-Christian myth and a Buddhist myth.

🌿

The Emergence of Mankind

In relation to the first books and chapters of the Bible, it used to be the custom of both Jews and Christians to take the narratives literally, as though they were dependable accounts of the origin of the universe and of actual prehistoric events. It was supposed and taught that there had been, quite concretely, a creation of the world in seven days by a god known only to the Jews; that somewhere on this broad new earth there had been a Garden of Eden containing a serpent that could talk; that the first woman, Eve, was formed from the first man's rib, and that the wicked serpent told her of the marvelous properties of the fruits of a certain tree of which God had forbidden the couple to eat; and that, as a consequence of their having eaten of that fruit, there followed a "Fall" of all mankind, death came into the world, and the couple was driven forth from the garden. For there was in the center of that garden a second tree, the fruit of which would have given them eternal life; and their creator, fearing lest they should now take and eat of that too, and so become as knowing and immortal as himself, cursed them, and having driven them out, placed at his garden gate "cherubim and a flaming sword which turned every way to guard the way to the tree of life."

It seems impossible today, but people actually believed all that   2 until as recently as half a century of so ago: clergymen, philosophers, government officers, and all. Today we know—and know right well—that there was never anything of the kind: no Garden of Eden anywhere on this earth, no time when the serpent could talk, no prehistoric "Fall," no exclusion from the garden, no universal Flood, no Noah's Ark. The entire history on which our leading Occidental religions have been founded is an anthology of fictions. But these are fictions of a type that have had—curiously enough—a universal vogue as the founding legends of other religions, too. Their counterparts have turned up everywhere—and yet, there was never such a garden, serpent, tree, or deluge.

How account for such anomalies? Who invents these impossible   3 tales? Where do their images come from? And why—though obviously absurd—are they everywhere so reverently believed?

What I would suggest is that by comparing a number from different   4 parts of the world and differing traditions, one might arrive at an understanding of their force, their source and possible sense. For they are not historical. That much is clear. They speak, therefore, not of outside events but of themes of the imagination. And since they exhibit features that are actually universal, they must in some way represent features of our general racial imagination, permanent features of the human spirit—or, as we say today, of the psyche. They are telling us, therefore, of matters fundamental to ourselves, enduring essential principles about which it would be good for us to know; about which, in fact, it will be necessary for us to know if our conscious minds are to be kept in touch with our own most secret, motivating depths. In short, these holy tales and their images are messages to the conscious mind from quarters of the spirit unknown to normal daylight consciousness, and if read as referring to events in the field of space and time—whether of the future, present, or past—they will have been misread and their force deflected, some secondary thing outside then taking to itself the reference of the symbol, some sanctified stick, stone, or animal, person, event, city, of social group.

Let us regard a little more closely the Biblical image of the garden.   5

Its name, Eden, signifies in Hebrew "delight, a place of delight,"   6 and our own English word, Paradise, which is from the Persian, *pairi-*, "around," *daeza,* "a wall," means properly "a walled enclosure." Apparently, then, Eden is a walled garden of delight, and in its center stands the great tree; or rather, in its center stand two trees, the one of the knowledge of good and evil, the other of immortal life. Four rivers flow, furthermore, from within it as from an inexhaustible source, to refresh the world in the four directions. And when our first parents, having eaten the fruit, were driven forth, two cherubim were stationed (as we have heard) at its eastern gate, to guard the way of return.

Taken as referring not to any geographical scene, but to a landscape of the soul, that Garden of Eden would have to be within us. Yet our conscious minds are unable to enter it and enjoy there the taste of eternal life, since we have already tasted of the knowledge of good and evil. That, in fact, must then be the knowledge that has thrown us out of the garden, pitched us away from our own center, so that we now judge things in those terms and experience only good and evil instead of eternal life—which, since the enclosed garden is within us, must already be ours, even though unknown to our conscious personalities. That would seem to be the meaning of the myth when read, not as prehistory, but as referring to man's inward spiritual state.

Let us turn now from this Bible legend, by which the West has been enchanted, to the Indian, of the Buddha, which has enspelled the entire East; for there too is the mythic image of a tree of immortal life defended by two terrifying guards. That tree is the one beneath which Siddhartha was sitting, facing east, when he wakened to the light of his own immortality in truth and was known thereafter as the Buddha, the Wakened One. There is a serpent in that legend also, but instead of being known as evil, it is thought of as symbolic of the immortal inhabiting energy of all life on earth. For the serpent shedding its skin, to be, as it were, born again, is likened in the Orient to the reincarnating spirit that assumes and throws off bodies as a man puts on and puts off clothes. There is in Indian mythology a great cobra imagined as balancing the tablelike earth on its head: its head being, of course, at the pivotal point, exactly beneath the world tree. And according to the Buddha legend, when the Blessed One, having attained omniscience, continued to sit absorbed for a number of days in absolute meditation, he became endangered by a great storm that arose in the world around him, and this prodigious serpent, coming up from below, wrapped itself protectively around the Buddha, covering his head with its cobra hood.

Thus, whereas in one of these two legends of the tree the service of the serpent is rejected and the animal itself cursed, in the other it is accepted. In both, the serpent is in some way associated with the

tree and has apparently enjoyed its fruits, since it can slough its skin
and live again; but in the Bible legend our first parents are expelled
from the garden of that tree, whereas in the Buddhist tradition we are
all invited in. The tree beneath which the Buddha sat corresponds,
thus, to the second of the Garden of Eden, which, as already said, is
to be thought of not as geographically situated but as a garden of the
soul. And so, what then keeps us from returning to it and sitting like
the Buddha beneath it? Who or what are those two cherubim? Do the
Buddhists know of any such pair?

One of the most important Buddhist centers in the world today   10
is the holy city of Nara, Japan, where there is a great temple sheltering
a prodigious bronze image, 53 ½ feet high, of the Buddha seated cross-
legged on a great lotus, holding his right hand lifted in the "fear not"
posture; and as one approaches the precincts of this temple, one passes
through a gate that is guarded, left and right, by two gigantic, marvelously threatening military figures flourishing swords. These are the
Buddhist counterparts of the cherubim stationed by Yahweh at the
garden gate. However, here we are not to be intimidated and held off.
The fear of death and desire for life that these threatening guardsmen
arouse in us are to be left behind as we pass between.

In the Buddhist view, that is to say, what is keeping us out of the   11
garden is not the jealousy or wrath of any god, but our own instinctive
attachment to what we take to be our lives. Our senses, outward-
directed to the world of space and time, have attached us to that world
and to our mortal bodies within it. We are loath to give up what we take
to be the goods and pleasures of this physical life, and this attachment is
the great fact, the great circumstance or barrier, that is keeping us out
of the garden. This, and this alone, is preventing us from recognizing
within ourselves that immortal and universal consciousness of which
our physical senses, outward-turned, are but the agents.

According to this teaching, no actual cherub with a flaming sword   12
is required to keep us out of our inward garden, since we are keeping
ourselves out, through our avid interest in the outward, mortal aspects
both of ourselves and of our world. What is symbolized in our passage
of the guarded gate is our abandonment of both the world so known
and ourselves so known within it: the phenomenal, mere appearance
of things seen as born and dying, experienced either as good or as
evil, and regarded, consequently, with desire and fear. Of the two big
Buddhist cherubim, one has the mouth open, the other, the mouth
closed—in token (I have been told) of the way we experience things
in this temporal world, in terms always of pairs-of-opposites. Passing
between, we are to leave such thinking behind.

But is that not the lesson, finally, of the Bible story as well? Eve   13
and then Adam ate the fruit of the knowledge of good and evil, which
is to say, of the pairs-of-opposites, and immediately experienced themselves as different from each other and felt shame. God, therefore, no
more than confirmed what already had been accomplished when he
drove them from the garden to experience the pains of death and
birth and of toil for the goods of this world. Furthermore, they were
experiencing God himself now as totally "other," wrathful and dangerous to their purposes, and the cherubim at the garden gate were representations of this way—now theirs—of experiencing both God and
themselves. But as we are told also in the Bible legend, it would actually
have been possible for Adam to "put forth his hand and take also of
the tree of life, and eat, and live forever." And in the Christian image
of the crucified redeemer that is exactly what we are being asked to
do. The teaching here is that Christ restored to man immortality.
His cross, throughout the Middle Ages, was equated with the tree of
immortal life; and the fruit of that tree was the crucified Savior himself,
who there offered up his flesh and his blood to be our "meat indeed"
and our "drink indeed." He himself had boldly walked, so to say, right
on through the guarded gate without fear of the cherubim and that
flaming turning sword. And just as the Buddha, five hundred years
before, had left behind all ego-oriented desires and fears to come to
know himself as the pure, immortal Void, so the Western Savior left
his body nailed to the tree and passed in spirit to atonement—at-one-
ment—with the Father: to be followed now by ourselves.

The symbolic images of the two traditions are thus formally equiv-   14
alent, even though the points of view of the two may be difficult to
reconcile. In that of the Old and New Testaments, God and man are
not one, but opposites, and the reason man was expelled from the
garden was that he had disobeyed his creator. The sacrifice on the
cross, accordingly, was in the nature not so much of a realization of
at-one-ment as of penitential *atonement*. On the Buddhist side, on the
other hand, man's separation from the source of his being is to be
read in psychological terms, as an effect of misdirected consciousness,
ignorant of its seat and source, which attributes final reality to merely
phenomenal apparitions. Whereas the level of instruction represented
in the Bible story is that, pretty much, of a nursery tale of disobedience
and its punishment, inculcating an attitude of dependency, fear, and
respectful devotion, such as might be thought appropriate for a child
in relation to a parent, the Buddhist teaching, in contrast, is for self-
responsible adults. And yet the imagery shared by the two is finally
older by far than either, older than the Old Testament, much older

than Buddhism, older even than India. For we find the symbolism of the serpent, tree, and garden of immortality already in the earliest cuneiform texts, depicted on Old Sumerian cylinder seals, and represented even in the arts and rites of primitive village folk throughout the world.

Nor does it matter from the standpoint of a comparative study of symbolic forms whether Christ or the Buddha ever actually lived and performed the miracles associated with their teachings. The religious literatures of the world abound in counterparts of those two great lives. And what one may learn from them all, finally, is that the savior, the hero, the redeemed one, is the one who has learned to penetrate the protective wall of those fears within, which exclude the rest of us, generally, in our daylight and even our dreamnight thoughts, from all experience of our own and the world's divine ground. The mythologized biographies of such saviors communicate the messages of their world-transcending wisdom in world-transcending symbols—which, ironically, are then generally translated back into such verbalized thoughts as built the interior walls in the first place. I have heard good Christian clergymen admonish young couples at their marriage ceremonies so to live together in this life that in the world to come they may have life everlasting; and I have thought, Alas! The more appropriate mythic admonishment would be, so to live their marriages that in *this* world they may experience life everlasting. For there is indeed a life everlasting, a dimension of enduring human values that inheres in the very act of living itself, and in the simultaneous experience and expression of which men through all time have lived and died. We all embody these unknowingly, the great being simply those who have wakened to their knowledge—as suggested in a saying attributed to Christ in the Gnostic *Gospel According to Thomas:* "The Kingdom of the Father is spread upon the earth and men do not see it."

Mythologies might be defined in this light as poetic expressions of just such transcendental seeing; and if we may take as evidence the antiquity of certain basic mythic forms—the serpent god, for example, and the sacred tree—the beginnings of what we take today to be mystical revelation must have been known to at least a few, even of the primitive teachers of our race, from the very start.

THINKING ABOUT THE CONTENT

1. Do you agree with Campbell's interpretation of the Adam and Eve story and the meaning of the Buddha story? Why or why not?
2. What commonalities does Campbell find between the Garden of Eden

story and that of Buddha's enlightenment? To what does he attribute the similarities to these and other common myths?

3. What does Campbell mean by "messages to the conscious mind" (4)? Do you agree? Why or why not? What other reasons might explain similarities in ancient myths from diverse geographical and cultural backgrounds?

4. Does Campbell's interpretation of the two myths contradict the principal beliefs of the Judeo-Christian and Buddhist traditions?

5. Campbell says it doesn't matter if Christ or Buddha ever actually lived and performed the miracles associated with their teachings. Why does he say that? Do you agree or disagree? Why?

LOOKING AT STRUCTURE AND STYLE

6. What is the function of paragraph 1? How is the first sentence of paragraph 2 used as a transition? Is it effective?

7. What is the function of paragraph 3? Are the questions answered?

8. What rhetorical patterns does Campbell use to develop his thesis? Is his thesis implied or stated? If stated, where?

EXPLORING DISCUSSION AND WRITING TOPICS

9. Read the Gnostic *Gospel According to Thomas*. Since it contains sayings attributed to Christ, why do you think the framers of the present-day Bible did not include this text?

10. Trace the use of serpents in ancient myths. What do they symbolize? What similarities and differences are there in their use?

TONY HENDRA and SEAN KELLY

It is the test of a good religion whether you can joke about it.
—GILBERT K. CHESTERTON

Based on the above quote, the following selection from Tony Hendra's and Sean Kelly's book *Not the Bible* is reprinted here. Compare this interpretation of the creation story with those of Stone, Spong, and Campbell in previous reading selections.

❦

The Book of Creation

Chapter 1

In the beginning God created Dates. 1

And the date *was* Monday, July 4, 4004 B.C. 2

And God said, Let there be light; and there was light. And *when* 3 there was Light, God saw the Date, *that* it was Monday, and he *got* down to work; for verily, he had a Big Job *to do.*

And God made pottery shards and Silurian mollusks and pre- 4 Cambrian limestone strata; and flints and Jurassic Mastodon tusks and Picanthropus erectus skulls and Cretaceous placentals made he; and those cave paintings at Lasceaux. And that was *that,* for the first Work Day.

And God saw that he had made many wondrous things, *but* that 5 he had not wherein to put *it* all. And God said, Let the heavens be divided from the earth; and *let* us bury all of these Things which we have made in the earth; *but* not too deep.

And God buried all the Things which he had made, and that was 6 *that.*

And the morning and the evening *and* the overtime were Tuesday. 7

And God said, Let there be water; and let the dry *land* appear; 8 and that was *that.*

And God called the dry *land* Real Estate; and the water called he 9 *the* Sea. And in the land and beneath *it* put he crude *oil,* grades one through six; and *natural* gas put he thereunder, and prehistoric carboniferous forests yielding anthracite and other ligneous matter; and all these called he Resources; and *he* made them Abundant.

And likewise all that was *in* the Sea, even unto two hundred 10
miles from the dry *land,* called he resources; all that was therein, *like* manganese nodules, for instance.

And the morning unto the evening *had been* an long day; *which* 11
he called Wednesday.

And God said, Let the earth bring forth abundantly every moving 12
creature I *can* think of, with or without backbones, with or without wings or feet, or fins or claws, vestigial limbs and all, right *now;* and let each *one* be of a separate species. For lo, I can make *whatsoever* I like, *whensoever* I like.

And the earth brought forth abundantly *all* creatures, great and 13
small, with and without backbones, with and without wings and feet and fins and claws, vestigial limbs and all, *from* bugs *to* brontosauruses.

But God blessed them all, saying, Be fruitful and multiply and 14
Evolve Not.

And God looked upon the species he had made, and saw that the 15
earth was exceedingly crowded, and he said *unto* them, Let each species compete for what it needeth; for Healthy Competition is My Law. And the species competeth amongst themselves, the cattle and the creeping things, the dogs and the dinosaurs; and some madeth it and some didn't; and the dogs ate the dinosaurs and God was pleased.

And God took the bones from the dinosaurs, and caused them to 16
appear *mighty* old; and cast he them about the land and the sea. And he took every tiny *creature* that had not madeth it, and caused *them* to become fossils; and cast he them about *likewise.*

And just to put matters beyond the valley of the shadow of a 17
doubt God created carbon dating. And *this* is the origin of species.

And in the Evening of the day which *was* Thursday, God saw that 18
he had put in *another* good day's work

And God said, Let us make man in our image, after our likeness, 19
which is tall and well-formed and pale of hue: and let us *also* make monkeys, which resembleth us not in any wise, *but* are short and ill-formed and hairy. And God added, Let man *have* dominion over the monkeys and the fowl of the air and every species, endangered or otherwise.

So God created Man in His *own* image; tall and well-formed and 20
pale of hue created He him, and nothing at all like the monkeys.

And God said, Behold I have given you every herb-bearing seed, 21
which is upon the face of the earth. But ye shalt not smoketh it, *lest* it giveth *you* ideas

And to every beast of the earth and every fowl of the air I have   22
given also every green herb, and to them it shall be for *meat*. But they
shall be *for you*. And the Lord God your Host suggesteth that the
flesh of cattle goeth well with that of the fin and the claw; thus shall
Surf be wedded unto Turf.

And God saw everything he had made, and he saw that it was   23
very good; and God said, It *just* goes to show Me what the private
sector can accomplish. With a lot of fool regulations this could have
taken *billions of years*

And on the evening of the fifth day, *which had been* the roughest   24
day yet, God said, Thank me it's Friday. And God made the weekend.

Chapter 2

Thus the heavens and the earth were finished, and *all* in five days, and   25
all less than six thousand years *ago;* and if thou believest it not, in a
sling *shalt* thou find thy hindermost quarters.

Likewise God took the dust of the ground, and the slime of the   26
Sea and the scum of the earth and formed Man therefrom; and *breathed*
the breath of life right in his face. And he *became* Free to Choose.

And God made an Marketplace eastward of Eden, in which the   27
man was free *to* play. And this *was* the Free Play of the Marketplace.

And out of the ground made the LORD God *to grow* four trees: 28
the Tree of Life, and the Liberty Tree, and the Pursuit of Happiness
Tree, and the Tree of the Knowledge of Sex.

And the LORD God commanded the man, saying, This is my Law,   29
which is called the Law of Supply and Demand. Investeth thou in the
trees of Life, Liberty, and the Pursuit of Happiness, and thou shalt
make for thyself an *fortune*. For *what* fruit thou eatest not, that thou
mayest sell, and with the seeds thereof expand *thy* operations.

But of the fruit of the tree of the Knowledge of Sex, thou mayest   30
not eat; nor mayest thou invest therein, nor profit thereby nor expand
its operations; for that is a mighty waste of seed.

And the man was exceeding glad. But he asked the lord God: 31
Who then *shall* labor in this Marketplace? For am I not management,
being tall and well-formed and pale of hue?

And the LORD God said unto himself, Verily, this kid hath the   32
potential which is Executive.

And out of the ground the LORD God formed every beast of the   33
field and every fowl of the air, and brought them unto Adam to labor
for him. And they labored for peanuts.

Then Adam was again exceeding glad. But he spake once more 34
unto the LORD God, saying, Lo, I am free to play in the Marketplace
of the LORD, and have cheap labor in plenty; but to whom shall I sell
my surplus fruit and realize a fortune thereby?

And the LORD God said unto himself, Verily, this is an Live One. 35

And he caused a deep sleep to fall upon Adam and he took from 36
him one of his ribs, which was an spare rib.

And the spare rib which the LORD God had taken from the man, 37
made he woman. And he brought her unto the man, saying:

This is Woman and she shall purchase your fruit, to eat it; and 38
ye shall realize a fortune thereby. For Man produceth and Woman
consumeth, wherefore she shall be called the Consumer.

And they were both decently clad, the Man and the Woman, from 39
the neck even unto the ankles, so they were not ashamed.

Chapter 3

Now the snake in the grass was *more* permissive than any beast of 40
the field which the LORD God *had* made. And he said *unto* the woman,
Why hast thou accepted this lowly and submissive *role?* For art thou
not human, *even* as the man is human?

And the woman said unto the snake in the grass, the LORD God 41
hath ordained that I am placed under the man, and must do whatsoever
he telleth me to do; for is *he* not the Man?

But the snake in the grass laughed a cunning laugh, and said 42
unto the woman, Is it not right and just that thou shouldst fulfill thy
potential? For art thou not comely in thy flesh, even as the man is
comely in his flesh?

And the woman said, Nay, I know not, for hath not the LORD 43
God clad us decently, from the neck even unto the ankles; and forbidden
that we eat of the Tree of the Knowledge of Sex?

But the snake in the grass said unto the woman, whispering even 44
into her very ear, saying, Whatsoever feeleth good, do thou *it;* and
believeth thou me, it feeleth *good.*

And when the woman saw the fruit of the Tree of the Knowledge 45
of Sex, that it was firm and plump and juicy, she plucked thereof, and
sank her teeth *therein,* and gave also to her husband, *and* he likewise
sank his teeth *therein.*

And the eyes of *both* of them were opened, and they saw that 46
they were not naked.

And the woman loosened *then* Adam's uppermost garment, and 47
he likewise loosened hers; and she loosened his nethermost garment,

and the man *then* loosened her nethermost garment; until they were
out of their garments both, and *likewise* of their minds.

And, lo!, they did dance *upon* the grass of the ground, and they   48
did rock backward, and roll forward continually.

And as they did rock and roll, the serpent that *was* cunning did   49
play upon a stringéd *instrument* of music, and did smite his tail upon
the ground in an hypnotic rhythm; and he did sing *in a voice* that was
like unto four voices: She loveth you, yea, yea, yea.

THINKING ABOUT THE CONTENT

1. What is your reaction to this parody of the first book of the Bible, Genesis?
   Do you find it funny or offensive? Why?
2. What are some of the contemporary events, beliefs, or establishments
   being parodied? How well did the authors need to know the Bible in
   order to write their version?
3. Writing comedy is not easy. How well do the authors succeed in taking
   a serious subject and making it funny?

LOOKING AT STRUCTURE AND STYLE

4. Compare the structure of this selection with the structure of Genesis.
   What are some of the techniques used to give this parody a look of biblical
   authenticity?
5. Why do the authors italicize so many words? Is there a reason for it or
   is it random?
6. How does the language used help create a biblical tone? What are some
   examples?
7. To whom are the authors writing? What makes you think so?

EXPLORING DISCUSSION AND WRITING TOPICS

8. Is the test of a good religion whether you can joke about it? Respond to
   Chesterton's quote.
9. If the reading selection offends you, explain why.

A Vietnamese poet and Buddhist monk, Zen master Thich Nhat Hanh has been called a rare combination of mystic, scholar, and activist. During the Vietnam War, he was the chairman of the Vietnamese Buddhist Peace Delegation and nominated by Dr. Martin Luther King, Jr., for the Nobel Peace Prize. He is the author of more than twenty-five books, including *Being Peace, The Diamond that Cuts Through Illusions, Love in Action, The Miracle of Mindfulness, The Moon Bamboo, Peace in Every Step, Zen Keys,* and *Living Buddha, Living Christ.*

In the following selection from his book *Living Buddha, Living Christ,* Hanh challenges comments made by Pope John Paul II in *Crossing the Threshold of Hope* in which the Pope insists that Jesus is the only Son of God. Hanh argues that teaching the belief that Christianity offers the only way to salvation, negating all other religions, fosters intolerance and discrimination.

☙

Living Buddha, Living Christ

Who Is Not Unique?

John Paul II, in *Crossing the Threshold of Hope,* insists that Jesus is the only Son of God: "Christ is absolutely original and absolutely unique. If He were only a wise man like Socrates, if He were a 'prophet' like Muhammed, if He were 'enlightened' like Buddha, without any doubt He would not be what He is. He is the one mediator between God and humanity." This statement does not seem to reflect the deep mystery of the oneness of the Trinity. It also does not reflect the fact that Christ is also the Son of Man. All Christians, while praying to God, address Him as Father. Of course Christ is unique. But who is not unique? Socrates, Muhammed, the Buddha, you, and I are all unique. The idea behind the statement, however, is the notion that Christianity provides the only way of salvation and all other religious traditions are of no use. This attitude excludes dialogue and fosters religious intolerance and discrimination. It does not help.

The Difference Is in Emphasis

It is a natural tendency of man to personify qualities like love, freedom,   2
understanding, and also the ultimate. In Buddhism, the Perfection of
Wisdom (*Prajñaparamita*) is described as the Mother of all Buddhas,
and Indian Buddhists did represent it in the form of a female person.
The teaching of the Buddha, the Dharma, is also represented as a body,
the Dharmakaya. Buddhists make offerings to the historical Buddha
as well as to the Dharmakaya. But they know that Dharmakaya is not
a person in the sense of the five aggregates: form, feelings, perceptions,
mental states, and consciousness. It is like Freedom being personified
as a Goddess. Freedom is not a body made of the five aggregates. The
ultimate can be represented as a person, but the ultimate cannot be
just an assembly of the five aggregates. The true body of Jesus is His
teaching. The only way to touch Him is to practice His teaching. The
teaching of Jesus is His living body, and this living body of Christ
manifests itself whenever and wherever His teaching is practiced.

Buddhists and Christians alike, in dialogue, want to recognize   3
similarities as well as differences in their traditions. It is good that an
orange is an orange and a mango is a mango. The colors, the smells,
and the tastes are different, but looking deeply, we see that they are
both authentic fruits. Looking more deeply, we can see the sunshine,
the rain, the minerals, and the earth in both of them. Only their
manifestations are different. Authentic experience makes a religion a
true tradition. Religious experience is, above all, human experience.
If religions are authentic, they contain the same elements of stability,
joy, peace, understanding, and love. The similarities as well as the
differences are there. They differ only in terms of emphasis. Glucose
and acid are in all fruits, but their degrees differ. We cannot say that
one is a real fruit and the other is not.

Real Dialogue Brings Tolerance

The absence of true experience brings forth intolerance and a lack of   4
understanding. Organized religions, therefore, must create conditions
that are favorable for true practice and true experience to flower.
Authentic ecumenical practices help different schools within a tradition
learn from one another and restore the best aspects of the tradition
that may have been eroded. This is true within both Buddhism and
Christianity. Today in the West, all schools of Buddhism are present,
and through their interactions with one another, mutual learning is
taking place, and the elements that have been lost in one tradition

can be revived by another. The Roman Catholic church, the Eastern Orthodox church, and the Protestant churches could do the same. And it is possible to go even further. Different religious traditions can engage in dialogue with one another in a true spirit of ecumenism. Dialogue can be fruitful and enriching if both sides are truly open. If they really believe that there are valuable elements in each other's tradition and that they can learn from one another, they will also rediscover many valuable aspects of their own tradition through such an encounter. Peace will be a beautiful flower blooming on this field of practice.

Real dialogue makes us more open-minded, tolerant, and under-   5
standing. Buddhists and Christians both like to share their wisdom and experience. Sharing in this way is important and should be encouraged. But sharing does not mean wanting others to abandon their own spiritual roots and embrace your faith. That would be cruel. People are stable and happy only when they are firmly rooted in their own tradition and culture. To uproot them would make them suffer. There are already enough people uprooted from their tradition today, and they suffer greatly, wandering around like hungry ghosts, looking for something to fill their spiritual needs. We must help them return to their tradition. Each tradition must establish dialogue with its own people first, especially with those young people who are lost and alienated. During the last fifteen years while sharing the Buddha's Dharma in the West, I always urged my Western friends to go back to their own traditions and rediscover the values that are there, those values they have not been able to touch before. The practice of Buddhist meditation can help them do so, and many have succeeded. Buddhism is made of non-Buddhist elements. Buddhism has no separate self. When you are a truly happy Christian, you are also a Buddhist. And vice versa.

We Vietnamese have learned these lessons from our own suffering.   6
When Christian missionaries came to Vietnam several hundred years ago, they urged us to abandon the cult of ancestral worship and to abandon our Buddhist tradition. Later, when they offered to help us in refugee camps in Thailand and Hong Kong, they also urged us to give up our roots. The good will to help and to save us was there, but the correct understanding was not. People cannot be happy if they are rootless. We can enrich one another's spiritual lives, but there is no need to alienate people from their ancestors and their values. This situation calls for more understanding. Church authorities must strive to understand the suffering of their own people. The lack of understanding brings about the lack of tolerance and true love, which results in the alienation of people from the church. True understanding comes

from true practice. Understanding and love are values that transcend all dogma.

Thinking about the Content

1. What does Hanh find wrong with the Pope's statement, "He [Jesus] is the one mediator between God and humanity" (1)? How does Hanh view Christ? What does Hanh mean by the statement, "The true body of Jesus is His teaching"(2)?
2. What does Hanh suggest the Catholic church, the Eastern Orthodox church, and the Protestant churches should do? What does he mean by a "true spirit of ecumenism" (4)?
3. Explain what Hanh means by the statement, "When you are a truly happy Christian, you are also a Buddhist. And vice versa" (5).
4. Do you feel you need to know more about Buddhism to truly understand what Hanh is saying here? What seems to be his message?

Looking at Structure and Style

5. Hahn begins by quoting a passage from Pope John Paul II's *Crossing the Threshold of Hope* and negating the statement. How well does he support his position? Who might he not convince?
6. What words develop Hanh's attitude and tone? To whom does he seem to be writing?

Exploring Discussion and Writing Topics

7. Explore in an essay what Hanh means by, "Religious experience is, above all, human experience" (3). How does this tie in with his statement, "The true body of Jesus is His teaching" (2)?
8. How does Buddhist Hanh's appreciation of Jesus' teachings differ or compare with a more traditional Christian view of Jesus? Of what importance are Jesus' teaching to a non-Christian?
9. With whom do you agree regarding Jesus' uniqueness, the Pope or Hanh? What is more important, to believe that Jesus is the Son of God or in his teachings as a man on earth? Why?
10. Read more of Hanh's *Living Buddha, Living Christ* (or one of his other works) and evaluate his conclusions.
11. Discuss why you think so many religions exist in the world. Why do so many claim to be "the" religion of God? What is the importance of religion in one's life? What are the dangers of religious beliefs?

Islam, one of the world's largest religions, continues to have a dramatic effect on the world today. In America, because of political events, the effect is often negative or prejudiced in the way it is presented. In her book *Muhammad: A Biography of the Prophet*, Karen Armstrong recounts where "inaccurate images of Islam became one of the accepted ideas of Europe and continues to affect our perceptions of the Muslim world." Through her studies of the Crusades, the Qu'ran (Koran), the conflict in the Middle East, and the life of Mohammed, Armstrong is no longer a "believing or practicing Christian," nor does she belong to any other official religion. But her studies have caused her to evaluate Islam carefully.

Armstrong has written seven books, among them *The First Christian: St. Paul's Impact On Christianity, Tongues of Fire, The Gospel According to Woman, Holy War: The Crusades and Their Impact on Today's World*, and *Muhammad*, the Introduction of which follows.

๛

Introduction to Muhammad: A Biography of the Prophet

A s we approach the end of the twentieth century, religion has once again become a force to be reckoned with. We are witnessing a widespread revival which would have seemed inconceivable to many people during the 1950s and 1960s when secularists tended to assume that religion was a primitive superstition outgrown by civilised, rational man. Some confidently predicted its imminent demise. At best religion was a marginal and private activity, which could no longer influence world events. Now we realise that this was a false prophecy. In the Soviet Union, after decades of official atheism, men and women are demanding the right to practise their faith. In the West, people who have little interest in conventional doctrine and institutional churches have shown a new awareness of spirituality and the inner life. Most dramatically, perhaps, a radical religiosity, which we usually call "fundamentalism", has erupted in most of the major religions. It is an intensely political form of faith and some see it as a grave danger to world and civic peace. Governments ignore it at their peril. Yet

again, as so often in the past, an age of scepticism has been followed by
a period of intense religious fervour: religion seems to be an important
human need which cannot easily be discarded or pushed to the side-
lines, no matter how rational or sophisticated our society. Some will
welcome this new age of faith, others will deplore it, but none of us
can dismiss religion as irrelevant to the chief concerns of our century.
The religious instinct is extremely powerful and can be used for good
and ill. We must, therefore, understand it and examine its manifestations carefully, not only in our own society but also in other cultures.

Our dramatically shrunken world has revealed our inescapable   2
connection with one another. We can no longer think of ourselves as
separate from people in distant parts of the globe and leave them to
their own fate. We have a responsibility to each other and face common
dangers. It is also possible for us to acquire an appreciation of other
civilizations that was unimaginable before our own day. For the first
time, people all over the world are beginning to find inspiration in
more than one religion and many have adopted the faith of another
culture. Thus Buddhism is enjoying a great flowering in the West,
where Christianity had once reigned supreme. But even when people
have remained true to the faith of their fathers, they have sometimes
been influenced by other traditions. Sir Sarvepalli Rudhakrishnan
(1888–1975), the great Hindu philosopher and statesman, for example,
was educated at the Christian College of Madras and strongly affected
the religious thought of people of both East and West. The Jewish
philosopher Martin Buber (1878–1965), who wrote his doctoral thesis
on the two medieval Christian mystics Nicholas of Cusa and Meister
Eckhart, has been read enthusiastically by Christians and has had a
profound influence on their ideas and spirituality. Jews tend to be less
interested in Buber than are Christians, but they do read the Protestant
theologian Paul Tillich (1886–1965) and the modernist thinker Harvey
Cox. The barriers of geographical distance, hostility and fear, which
once kept the religions in separate watertight compartments, are beginning to fall.

Although much of the old prejudice remains, this is a hopeful   3
development. It is particularly heartening, after centuries of virulent
Christian anti-Semitism, to see Jewish and Christian scholars attempting to reach a new understanding. There is an incipient perception
of the deep unity of mankind's religious experience and a realisation
that traditions which "we" once despised can speak to our own condition and revitalise our spirituality. The implication of this could be
profound: we will never be able to see either our own or other peoples'
religions and cultures in quite the same way again. The possible result

of this has been compared to the revolution that science has effected in the outlook of men and women throughout the world. Many people will find this development extremely threatening and they will erect new barricades against the "Other," but some are already beginning to glimpse broader horizons and find that they are moved by religious ideals that their ancestors would have dismissed with contempt.

But one major religion seems to be outside this circle of goodwill 4 and, in the West at least, to have retained its negative image. People who are beginning to find inspiration in Zen or Taoism are usually not nearly so eager to look kindly upon Islam, even though it is the third religion of Abraham and more in tune with our own Judaeo-Christian tradition. In the West we have a long history of hostility towards Islam that seems as entrenched as our anti-Semitism, which in recent years has seen a disturbing revival in Europe. At least, however, many people have developed a healthy fear of this ancient prejudice since the Nazi Holocaust. But the old hatred of Islam continues to flourish on both sides of the Atlantic and people have few scruples about attacking this religion, even if they know little about it.

The hostility is understandable, because until the rise of the Soviet 5 Union in our own century, no polity or ideology posed such a continuous challenge to the West as Islam. When the Muslim empire was established in the seventh century CE, Europe was a backward region. Islam had quickly overrun much of the Christian world of the Middle East as well as the great Church of North Africa, which had been of crucial importance to the Church of Rome. This brilliant success was threatening: had God deserted the Christians and bestowed his favour on the infidel? Even when Europe recovered from the Dark Ages and established its own great civilisation, the old fear of the ever-expanding Muslim empire remained. Europe could make no impression on this powerful and dynamic culture: the Crusading project of the twelfth and thirteenth centuries eventually failed and, later, the Ottoman Turks brought Islam to the very doorstep of Europe. This fear made it impossible for Western Christians to be rational or objective about the Muslim faith. At the same time as they were weaving fearful fantasies about Jews, they were also evolving a distorted image of Islam, which reflected their own buried anxieties. Western scholars denounced Islam as a blasphemous faith and its Prophet Muhammad as the Great Pretender, who had founded a violent religion of the sword in order to conquer the world. "Mahomet" became a bogy to the people of Europe, used by mothers to frighten disobedient children. In Mummers' plays he was presented as the enemy of Western civilisation, who fought our own brave St George.

This inaccurate image of Islam became one of the received ideas   6
of Europe and it continues to affect our perceptions of the Muslim
world. The problem has been compounded by the fact that, for the
first time in Islamic history, Muslims have begun to cultivate a passionate hatred of the West. In part this is due to European and American
behaviour in the Islamic world. It is a mistake to imagine that Islam
is an inherently violent or fanatical faith, as is sometimes suggested.
Islam is a universal religion and there is nothing aggressively Oriental
or anti-Western about it. Indeed, when Muslims first encountered the
colonial West during the eighteenth century many were impressed by
its modern civilisation and tried to emulate it. But in recent years this
initial enthusiasm has given way to bitter resentment. We should also
remember that "fundamentalism" has surfaced in most religions and
seems to be a world-wide response to the peculiar strain of late-twenti-
eth-century life. Radical Hindus have taken to the streets to defend
the caste system and to oppose the Muslims of India; Jewish fundamentalists have made illegal settlements on the West Bank and the Gaza
Strip and have vowed to drive all Arabs from their Holy Land; Jerry
Falwell's Moral Majority and the new Christian Right, which saw the
Soviet Union as the evil empire, achieved astonishing power in the
United States during the 1980s. It is wrong, therefore, to assume that
Muslim extremists are typical of their faith. It would be just as mistaken
to see the late Ayatollah Khomeini as the incarnation of Islam as to
dismiss the rich and complex tradition of Judaism because of the
immoral policies of the late Rabbi Meir Kahane. If "fundamentalism"
seems particularly rife in the Muslim world, this is because of the
population explosion. To give just one telling example: there were only
9 million Iranians before the Second World War; today there are 57
million and their average age is seventeen. Radical Islam, with its
extreme and black-and-white solutions, is a young person's faith.

Most Westerners do not know enough about traditional Islam to   7
assess this new strain and put it in a proper perspective. When Shiites
in the Lebanon take hostages in the name of "Islam" people in Europe
and America naturally feel repelled by the religion itself, without realis-
ing that this behaviour contravenes important legislation in the Qu'ran
about the taking and treatment of captives. Regrettably, the media and
the popular press do not always give us the help we need. Far more
coverage, for example, was given to the Muslims who vociferously
supported Ayatollah Khomeini's *fatwa* against the British author Salman Rushdie than to the majority who opposed it. The religious authorities of Saudi Arabia and the sheikhs of the prestigious mosque

of al-Azhar in Cairo both condemned the *fatwa* as illegal and un-Islamic: Muslim law does not permit a man to be sentenced to death without trial and has no jurisdiction outside the Islamic world. At the Islamic Conference of March 1989, forty-four out of the forty-five member states unanimously rejected the Ayatollah's ruling. But this received only cursory attention in the British press and left many people with the misleading impression that the entire Muslim world was clamouring for Rushdie's blood. Sometimes the media seems to stir up our traditional prejudices, as was particularly apparent during the OPEC oil crisis of 1973. The imagery used in cartoons, advertisements and popular articles was rooted in old Western fears of a Muslim conspiracy to take over the world.

Many people feel that Muslim society justifies our stereotypical [8] view of it: life seems cheap; governments are sometimes corrupt or tyrannical; women are oppressed. It is not uncommon for people to blame this state of affairs on "Islam." But scholars warn us not to over-emphasise the role of any religion on a given society and Marshall G. S. Hodgson, the distinguished historian of Islam, points out that the aspects of the Muslim world condemned in the West are characteristic of most pre-modern societies: life would not have been very different here three hundred years ago. But sometimes there seems to be a definite desire to blame the faith itself for every disorder in the Muslim world. Thus feminists frequently condemn "Islam" for the custom of female circumcision. This despite the fact that it is really an African practice, is never mentioned in the Qu'ran, is *not* prescribed by three of the four main schools of Islamic jurisprudence, and was absorbed into the fourth school in North Africa where it was a fact of life. It is as impossible to generalise about Islam as about Christianity; there is a wide range of ideas and ideals in both.

A clear example of stereotyping is the common assumption that [9] the Islam practised in Saudi Arabia is the most authentic form of the faith. Seemingly more archaic, it is supposed to resemble that practised by the first community of Muslims. Because the West has long considered the regime in Saudi Arabia obnoxious, it tends to write off "Islam" too. But Wahhabism is only an Islamic sect. It developed in the eighteenth century and was similar to the Christian Puritan sect that flourished during the seventeenth century in England, the Netherlands and Massachusetts. The Puritans and the Wahhabis both claimed to be returning to the original faith, but both were really an entirely new development and a response to the unique conditions of the time. Both Wahhabism and Puritanism exerted an important influence in the Muslim and Christian worlds respectively, but it is a mistake to view either sect as normative in their religion. Reform movements in any faith attempt to return to the original spirit of the founder, but it is never possible to reproduce former conditions entirely.

I am not claiming that Islam is entirely faultless. All religions are [10] human institutions and frequently make serious mistakes. All have sometimes expressed their faith in inadequate and even in abhorrent ways. But they have also been creative, enabling millions of men and women to find faith in the ultimate meaning and value of life, despite the suffering that flesh is heir to. To put "Islam" into an unholy category of its own or to assume that its influence has been wholly or even predominantly negative is both inaccurate and unjust. It is a betrayal of the tolerance and compassion that are supposed to characterise Western society. In fact Islam shares many of the ideals and visions that have inspired both Judaism and Christianity Consequently it has helped people to cultivate values that it shares with our own culture. The Judaeo-Christian tradition does not have the monopoly on either monotheism or concern for justice, decency, compassion and respect for humanity.

Indeed, the Muslim interpretation of the monotheistic faith has [11] its own special genius and has important things to teach us. Ever since Islam came to my attention, I have been increasingly aware of this. Until a few years ago, I was almost entirely ignorant about the religion. The first inkling I had that it was a tradition that could speak to me came during a holiday in Samarkand. There I found the Islamic architecture to express a spirituality that resonated with my own Catholic past. In 1984 I had to make a television programme about Sufism, the mysticism of Islam, and was particularly impressed by the Sufi appreciation of other religions—a quality that I had certainly not encountered in Christianity! This challenged everything that I had taken for granted about "Islam" and I wanted to learn more. Finally, during a study of the Crusades and the current conflict in the Middle East, I was led to the life of Muhammad and to the Qu'ran, the scripture that he brought to the Arabs. I am no longer a believing or practising Christian nor do I belong to any other official religion. But at the same time as I have been revising my ideas about Islam, I have also been reconsidering the religious experience itself. In all the great religions, seers and prophets have conceived strikingly similar visions of a transcendent and ultimate reality. However we choose to interpret it, this human experience has been a fact of life. Indeed, Buddhists deny that there is anything supernatural about it: it is a state of mind that is natural to humanity. The monotheistic faiths, however, call this transcendence "God." I believe that Muhammad had such an experience and made a distinctive and valuable contribution to the spiritual experience of humanity. If we are to do justice to our Muslim neighbours, we must appreciate this essential fact. . . .

The Gulf War of 1991 showed that, whether we like it or not, 12 we are deeply connected with the Muslim world. Despite temporary alliances, it is clear that the West has largely lost the confidence of people in the Islamic world. A breakdown in communications is never the fault of one party and if the West is to regain the sympathy and respect that it once enjoyed in the Muslim world it must examine its own role in the Middle East and consider its own difficulties vis-à-vis Islam. That is why the first chapter of this book traces the history of Western hatred for the Prophet of Islam. But the picture is not entirely black. From the earliest days, some Europeans were able to achieve a more balanced view. They were always in a minority and they had their failings but this handful of people tried to correct the errors of their contemporaries and rise above received opinion. It is surely this more tolerant, compassionate and courageous tradition that we should seek to encourage now.

THINKING ABOUT THE CONTENT

1. Is Armstrong correct regarding the view most Americans have of Islam? Does the media tend to stereotype or support negative and prejudicial views? What are your views of Islam? Where did you get them?
2. Why have Muslims begun to cultivate a passionate hatred of the West? Are the reasons justified?
3. How did the Crusades contribute to present-day prejudice toward Muslims? How do fundamentalist Muslims help perpetrate prejudicial images toward Muslims?
4. Armstrong seems to imply that Islam is no better or no worse than Christianity. Why does she think this? What do you think?
5. Why is it important or not important to study and know about more than one religion? What effect might such study have on any religion in which one was raised? Why might some people be afraid of other religions?

LOOKING AT STRUCTURE AND STYLE

6. Armstrong begins by citing "a widespread revival" of religion at the end of the twentieth century (1). How does she build on that to lead into her discussion of Islam?
7. What is the function of paragraph 6? How effective is Armstrong in showing fundamentalism exists outside Islam? Are her examples true?

8. How useful is paragraph 11? Does Armstrong's inclusion of personal experiences with religion help or hinder her argument? Why?
9. To what audience is Armstrong writing? Does she keep that audience interested? Why or why not?

Exploring Discussion and Writing Topics

10. Research recent newspaper and magazine articles dealing with Islamic countries. How are the Muslims portrayed? Is there a distinction drawn between radical groups and Muslims as a whole?
11. Discuss why understanding and tolerating other religious beliefs is important.

The following perspective on Islam was written by a man who was a hostage in Iran for 444 days between 1979 and 1981. Moorhead Kennedy is president of Moorhead Kennedy Associates, an organization that trains executives to deal with unfamiliar cultures. Kennedy feels that Muslims, disappointed with secular nationalism, seek self-determination through social and religious unity. Because Islam will soon become the second-largest U.S. religious group after Christianity and ahead of Judaism, Kennedy suggests four steps for coming to terms and better understanding Islam. The following selection, "Why Fear Fundamentalism?", appeared in the Commentary section of the *Los Angeles Times* on March 15, 1993.

۱۶

Why Fear Fundamentalism?

"The West does not want independence based on Islamic thoughts 1 for Islamic countries," Iranian President Hashemi Rafsanjani said recently. "They are confronting an important movement, and they do not like it." Indeed, finding a kind word about Islamic fundamentalism is not easy. An Op-Ed piece in the *New York Times* characterized this important movement as "rage, religious fury, holy war, and political hypocrisy"—and that was before the explosion at the World Trade Center, attributed to Muslim fundamentalists.

Quite apart from the profound injustice done to millions of law- 2 abiding Muslims, equating Islamic fundamentalism with terrorism closes minds at a time when the American public badly needs to understand this important world movement.

To whatever extent it may ultimately prevail in the vast area 3 stretching from Morocco to Mindanao in the Philippines and in several former Soviet republics, Islamic fundamentalism is a vital and growing force. It has great appeal for young people, notably Palestinian and Jordanian university students. A version of it is increasingly visible and influential in our own African-American community. In its various manifestations, Islam will become, before long, the second-largest American religious grouping, after Christianity and ahead of Judaism.

Americans will have to come to terms with Islamic fundamental- 4 ism. Where should we start?

First, we need to understand that Islam is not only a faith, like   5
Christianity. It is also a political system, a legal system and a way of
life. Even the Israelis, normally astute about developments in the Arab
world, missed this reality. Even as they closed universities in the occupied territories, they encouraged seminary study, hoping to turn the
minds of their subject people away from Arab nationalism toward the
peaceful ways of religion.

Instead they got Hamas, championing the liberation of Palestine   6
not for reasons of Arab nationalism, but for Islam. The expulsion of
432 Hamas followers to no-man's-land on the Lebanese border became
Israel's most acute diplomatic embarrassment of recent years.

In Hamas, Israel is faced with an uncompromising maximalist   7
approach, that of total liberation of the sacred land of Palestine as
demanded by God, who will repay martyrs for this cause with everlasting life. In contrast to a Western-style movement like the Palestine
Liberation Organization, which is willing to compromise, Islamic fundamentalism is a formidable opponent. The difference between the
PLO's approach and that of the fundamentalists has to do with how
each views the West.

Starting from a position, real and perceived, of inferiority, the   8
Middle East has been trying to come to terms with the West. Its
coping device was imitation, perhaps most evident in Western-style
nationalism and the evolution of national states, complete with ideologies, parliaments, anthems and flags. Imitative Arab nationalism found
its culmination in Gamal Abdel Nasser, its low point in Nasser's humiliating defeat by Israel in 1967.

A great many Arabs concluded that they had been following the   9
wrong model. They could never be successful trying to be what they
were not. Similarly, in 1979, in Iran, the westernizing Shah was overthrown. "We no longer have to be imitation Americans," the Islamic
revolutionaries cried. "We can be ourselves." The basic question, "Who
am I?" is answered by many in Muslim countries through a return to
their Islamic roots.

Why the deep anger, the rage, directed against the United States?   10
Because our culture, pervasive and appealing, is what the fundamentalists are trying to expel from deep within themselves and their societies.
Yet, as they reject our culture, they are forced to recognize its superiority in many important respects. Their continuing dependence on it
deepens their anger. They rail against our culture's recreational sex,
widespread alcoholism and drug abuse as "Western decadence"; by
contrast, they hold themselves to be freshly inspired to decency.

Islamic fundamentalism has its own very positive side. Its medical   11
clinics in the poorest parts of Cairo, for example, evidencing in a
practical way the duty of Muslims to care for the poor, are a source
of popularity and respect.

Islamic law, the Sharia, or "path to salvation," is the sum of duties   12
required by God of human beings, with respect not only to God, but
also to one's fellows. It is the infusion of divine purpose into human
relationships that distinguishes Islamic law from the secular jurisprudence of Western countries. The restoration of the Sharia as the
operating national legal code is a cardinal feature of Islamic fundamentalism.

At Harvard Law School, I analyzed the differences between the   13
Islamic law of inheritance and that of Massachusetts. Islamic law
struck me as far more humane, for example in its recognition of family
relationships and its provisions for aging parents.

With its main tenets fixed in the 10th century, the Sharia is inade-   14
quate for many of the needs of modern society. As a social statement
of ethical principle, however, the Sharia is hard to surpass.

How, then, can the United States come to terms with this vital   15
and important movement? Let me suggest four initial steps:

- *Work hard on the flash points.* For example, the longer the Arab-
  Israeli peace process is delayed, the stronger will be the influence
  of the extremists. Future flash points should be identified and
  worked on; don't overlook the largely Muslim former Soviet republics.

- *Understand motives.* The key to the battle against terrorism is
  understanding. Unless we understand the reasons for anger against
  the United States on the part of an extremist fringe, we cannot
  effectively anticipate and counter the actions they are likely to
  take. Failure in this battle extends beyond the loss of life and
  property; it also poisons the domestic atmosphere with heightened
  discrimination and threats against the rights of a significant minority.

- *Set a better example.* The more uncaring and corrupt our own
  society, including the political process, appears to be, the more
  we strengthen that side of Islamic fundamentalism that most re-
  sents us. Domestic reforms make effective propaganda abroad.

- *Take it seriously.* Evidence greater understanding and sympathy
  for fundamentalism's more praiseworthy goals. Identify what
  unites our better sides.

Upon my return from hostage captivity in Iran, a senior State   16
Department official remarked, "Who would ever have thought that
all this could have happened, because of religion?" The same disdainful
attitude continues to prevail in Washington. Has anyone there thought
to publish a comparison between the better goals of the Islamic fundamentalists and those expressed in President Clinton's inaugural speech?

Rafsanjani is calling upon the West to grow up, to stop being   17
afraid of what we are unwilling to understand, to accord to others
rights that we claim for ourselves and our allies and to have the
courage to make common cause even with those whose means appear
unfamiliar, bizarre or even (possibly) dangerous.

THINKING ABOUT THE CONTENTS

1. How does Islam differ from Christianity? Why does it make dealing with Islamic countries more difficult?
2. What does Kennedy feel was the Israelis' mistake in their handling of the Palestinian situation? Would an Israeli understanding of the Islamic faith have made a difference?
3. What effect on U.S. society do you think the growing number of Muslims in the United States will have? Do you feel the need to learn more about Islam? Why or why not?
4. What does Kennedy assert is the difference between the Palestine Libera- tion Organization and the Hamas? Why is it important to understand the difference?
5. What is your opinion of Kennedy's four suggestions? After 444 days of captivity by Islamic fundamentalists, do you think you would have the same attitude Kennedy seems to have regarding Muslims? Why or why not?

LOOKING AT STRUCTURE AND STYLE

6. Who is Kennedy's audience? What examples from the essay support your view?
7. Why do you think Kennedy waits until paragraph 16 to mention his captivity in Iran?
8. Describe the tone of the essay and give some examples that lend that tone.

EXPLORING DISCUSSION AND WRITING TOPICS

9. Do what Kennedy suggests in paragraph 16. Draw a comparison between the better goals of the Islamic fundamentalists and President Clinton's inaugural speech.

10. Research some aspect of Islam and discuss why you could or could not accept that aspect of Islamic faith. Then show why a Muslim who held that aspect of faith could not accept your viewpoint.

In the following essay, Akbar S. Ahmed, a Pakistani scholar, offers a close look at the negative relations between Westerners and Muslims. Why, the author asks, is Islam—a religion advocating goodness, cleanliness, tolerance, learning, and piety—so misunderstood and reviled? Part of the problem, he argues, is a difference in moral philosophies. Pious Muslims believe Western culture lacks a moral philosophy and is too interested in individualism, in a desire to dominate, and in acquiring material items through a philosophy of consumerism. He argues that the true spirit of Islam is medicine for the rootlessness and heartlessness that Western culture has spread around the world. While chastising the West, Ahmed also sees fault in the way Muslims are responding to the West and calls for more faith, virtue, and tolerance among Muslims as well.

Ahmed's essay, printed here as it appeared excerpted in *Utne Reader,* was originally published in *New Perspectives Quarterly.*

🌿

Terror and Tolerance

A political cartographer with a bold eye for simplification would   1
divide the world map in the 1990s into two major categories: the civilizations that are *exploding*—reaching out, expanding, bubbling with scientific ideas, economic plans, political ambitions, cultural expression—and those that are *imploding,* collapsing in on themselves with economic, political, and social crises that prevent any serious attempt at major initiatives. The former are exploding with optimism, with sights firmly fixed on the future; the latter are weighed down by their history, traditions, "certainties," their ethnic and religious hatreds.

Western, or globalizing, civilization—in essence the G-7 industrial-   2
ized nations—is exploding. Much of the rest of the world is imploding.

Pious Muslims know that the problem with the G-7 globalizing   3
civilization is the hole where the heart should be—the vacuum inside, the absence of a moral philosophy. What gives the West its dynamic energy is individualism, the desire to dominate, the sheer drive to acquire material items through a philosophy of consumerism at all costs, to hoard. Such frenetic energy keeps society moving.

Patience, pace, and equilibrium, by contrast, are emphasized in   4
Islam. Haste is the devil's work, the Prophet warned. But the postmodern age is based on speed. In particular, the media thrive on and are
intoxicated by speed, change, news. The unceasing noise, dazzling
color, and restlessly shifting images of the MTV culture beckon and
harass. Silence, withdrawal, and meditation—advocated by all the
great religions—are simply not encouraged by the media.

The American mass media have achieved what American political   5
might could not: world domination. Hollywood has succeeded where
the Pentagon failed. The link between the two is established in the
fact that films and defense equipment are the two largest export earners
in the U.S. economy. J. R. Ewing has triumphed in a way that John
Foster Dulles could not even have dreamed of The world watches
American reruns with hypnotic fascination: Across the world people
ask "Who shot J. R.?" and "Who killed Laura Palmer?" The American
dream is seen as irresistible.

Muslim parents blanch at the modern Western media because of   6
the universality, power, and pervasiveness of these subversive images;
because of their malignity and hostility toward Islam.

The nonstop television images are of couples performing sex, men   7
inflicting terrible pain. The videocassettes that accompany pop songs
produce ever more bizarre images, from Madonna masturbating to
Michael Jackson's transmogrification into a panther. These intrusions
corrode the innermost structure of balance and authority in that cruci-
ble of all civilization, the family, adding to the crumbling authority
structures of the West that have been under attack now for the last
two generations.

Many of the moral stands on which Islam never conceded, such   8
as its steadfast opposition to the abuse of alcohol and drugs, are
now widely accepted in the West. Many in the West are also now
reevaluating divorce, the challenge to parental authority, the marginali-
zation of old people, the regular relocation of the home because of
work. All devastate the family.

The legitimate question being raised by Muslims is the following: 9
Why should they be dragged along the path of the West's social experimentation, which they know diverges from their own vision of society?
Why should they disrupt their domestic situation for temporary values,
however overpowering in their immediate and glamorous appeal?

Why is Islam—a religion advocating goodness, cleanliness, toler-   10
ance, learning, and piety—so misunderstood and reviled? *Jihad* has
become a dirty word in the media, representing the physical threat of
a barbaric civilization. Yet the concept is noble and powerful. It is the

desire to improve oneself, to attempt betterment and to struggle for the good cause. It is Tennysonian in its scope: to strive, to seek and not to yield.

This misunderstanding between Islam and the West feeds the Mus- 11 lim incapacity to respond coolly and meaningfully. Muslims being killed on the West Bank or in Kashmir, their mosques being threatened with demolition in Jerusalem or in Ayodhya, India, are seen throughout the Muslim world on television and cause instant dismay and anger.

Muslims throughout the world cite examples of gross injustice, 12 particularly where they live as a minority in non-Muslim countries. (This group forms a large percentage of the total number of Muslims in the world today.)

Muslims themselves are not blameless. Muslim leaders of Muslim 13 nations are failing to feed and clothe the poor. The greatest emphasis in Islamic teachings is given to the less privileged. This, alas, remains a neglected area, as leaders prefer to fulminate against their opponents.

Muslim leaders are also failing in another crucial area. Muslims 14 who live in the West and complain about racism would do well to turn their gaze on their own societies. Pakistanis have been killing Pakistanis, on the basis of race, in the most brutal manner possible for years in Sind province; political messages are carved into the buttocks of ethnic opponents. Kurds have been gassed and bombed in Iraq, and attacked in Turkey, by fellow Muslims for decades.

Many Muslim leaders, heads of government, right across the Mus- 15 lim world, have met a violent end. They have been shot (Anwar Sadat), hanged (Zulfikar Ali Bhutto of Pakistan), and blown up in the air (Zia ul-Haq, also of Pakistan). What Muslims have done to their leaders is more than matched by what the leaders did to their Muslim followers. Nightmare images are seared in the mind. State power—the army and police—has been responsible for the massacre of innocent country folk and even entire towns in Syria, in East Pakistan (now Bangladesh), in Iraq, and in Iran.

Furthermore, much of the unprecedented wealth from oil revenues 16 has been squandered on an unprecedented scale, in an unprecedented style. Call girls in London and casinos in the south of France, ranches in the United States and chalets in Switzerland diverted money that could have gone into health care, education, and closing the vast gaps between rich and poor. These antics provided legitimate ammunition for Western satirists; they became the caricature of a civilization. Ordinary Muslims have good cause to complain.

Also in need of pursuit is the notion of a just and stable state. 17 Contemplating the prospects for the 21st century, some Middle East experts conclude that the lack of "a civil society" is the great bane of the Muslims. Repression and stagnation—in spite of a certain record of durability in some states—mark their societies. Lawyers and journalists are unable to work freely, and businessmen operate in economies that may be labeled socialist or capitalist but in either case are controlled by the state.

The main Muslim responses to the West appear to be chauvinism   18
and withdrawal. This is both dangerous and doomed. The self-imposed isolation, the deliberate retreat, is not Islamic in spirit or content. Muslims who are isolated and self-centered imagine that passionate faith is exclusive to them. Yet a similar religious wave exists in Christianity, Hinduism, and Buddhism. Preferring to ignore this, Muslims will point out that the Western world is intimidated by them and fears their zeal. That Salman Rushdie was driven underground is cited as one proof of this. It seems that Muslim spokesmen are in danger of being intoxicated by their own verbosity.

The increasing stridency in their tone is thus linked to the larger   19
Muslim sense of anger and powerlessness. They advocate confrontation and violence, an eye for an eye; this confirms Western stereotypes of Muslims. They argue that moderation has failed and that extremism will draw attention to their problems. Perhaps in the atmosphere of violence and blind hatred, of injustice and inequality, their position has a certain logic. They will force Muslim problems onto the agenda where more sober voices have failed, and because we live in an interconnected world, no country can isolate itself from—or immunize itself against—Muslim wrath. Nevertheless, violence and cruelty are not in the spirit of the Koran or the life of the Prophet.

The Muslim voices of learning and balance—in politics and among   20
academics—are being drowned by those advocating violence and hatred. Two vital questions with wide-ranging implications arise: In the short term, has one of the world's greatest civilizations lost its ability to deal with problems except through violent force? In the long term, would Muslims replace the central Koranic concepts of *adl* and *ahsan* (balance and compassion), *ilm* (knowledge), and *sabr* (patience) with the bullet and the bomb?

Islam is a religion of equilibrium and tolerance, suggesting an   21
encouraging breadth of vision, fulfillment of human destiny in the universe. Balance is essential to Islam, especially in society; and the crucial balance is between *din* (religion) and *dunya* (world); it is a balance of, not a separation between, the two. The Muslim lives in the now, in the real world, but within the frame of religion, with a mind to the afterlife. So, whether it is in business, the academy, or

politics, the moral laws of Islam must not be forgotten. In the postmodern world, *dunya* is upsetting the balance, invading and appropriating *din*.

Yet the non-Muslim media, by their hammer-headed onslaught, have succeeded in portraying a negative image and may even succeed in changing Muslim character. Muslims, because of their gut response to the attack—both vehement and vitriolic—are failing to maintain the essential features of Islam. Muslim leaders have dug themselves into a hole in viewing the present upsurge simplistically as a confrontation with the West.   22

But Allah is everywhere. The universal nature of humanity is the main assumption in the Koran. God's purview and compassion take in everyone, "all creatures." The world is not divided into an East and a West: "To Allah belong the East and West: Whithersoever Ye turn, there is Allah's countenance" (Surah 2:115). Again and again God points to the wonders of creation, the diversity of races and languages in the world. Such a God cannot be parochial or xenophobic. Neither can a religion that acknowledges the wisdom and piety of over 124,000 "prophets" in its folklore be isolationist or intolerant. With its references to the heavens above, the Koran encourages us to lift up our heads and look beyond our planet, to the stars.   23

The divine presence is all around; it can be glimpsed in the eyes of a mother beholding her infant, the rising of the sun, a bird in flight, the first flowers of spring. The wonders and mystery of creation cannot be the monopoly of any one people. The Sufi mystics of Islam, for example, see God everywhere, even among the godless, not only in the mosque. In their desire for knowledge, compassion, and cleanliness many non-Muslims possess ideal Muslim virtues. We note goodness and humanity in people like Mother Teresa, Nelson Mandela, and Václav Havel. Islam has always shown the capacity to emerge in unexpected places and in unexpected times. The true understanding of Islam will therefore be critical in the coming years—and not only for Muslims.   24

THINKING ABOUT THE CONTENT

1. What philosophical differences exist between what Ahmed calls "pious Muslims" and the industrialized nations? Do you think these differences can be resolved? Which of the two philosophies as the author describes them do you subscribe to? Why?

2. Ahmed indicts the American media for bringing about the corrosion of the American family, claiming that many of the "moral stands on which

Islam never conceded . . . are now widely accepted in the West" (8). What are some of his examples of these moral stands? Do you think Americans, on the whole, have accepted what Muslims have not? Would Christian groups agree or disagree with Ahmed regarding the corroding of the family?

3. What are your responses to the questions Ahmed raises in paragraph 9? How is the West involved in the formation of these questions? What does Ahmed mean by "the West's social experimentation" (9)?

4. Ahmed says that Muslims themselves are not blameless in causing Islam to be misunderstood. In what ways are they to blame? How are some angered Muslims going against their own religious teachings?

5. How have the violent incidents Ahmed cites, or others more recent, affected your views toward Muslims? Are you prejudiced in your views toward Islam? Why or why not?

LOOKING AT STRUCTURE AND STYLE

6. To what audience is Ahmed writing? What leads you to that conclusion?
7. Is Ahmed's accusations against the American media accurate and well balanced? What other examples could he have used?
8. What is the author's thesis? Is it implied or stated? If stated, where?
9. What is the tone of the essay? How is the tone established?

EXPLORING DISCUSSION AND WRITING TOPICS

10. Discuss how Moorhead Kenndey's four steps for coming to terms with Islamic fundamentalism in the preceding essay ("Why Fear Fundamentalism") might also be a useful starting point for angry Muslims.

11. Discuss the similarities and differences in the family values as held by Muslims, Jews, and Christians.

12. Interview someone holding a religious view different from yours. What are the basic similarities and differences? What do you admire and/or dislike about that person's faith?

13. Karl Marx is often quoted as having said that religion is "the opiate of the people." Do you see any truth in this? What might he have meant? Can you provide any examples that support the statement?

MERLIN STONE

Merlin Stone has taught art and art history at several universities, worked as a sculptor, and exhibited widely. Through her interest in art and particularly sculpture, she became fascinated in archeology and ancient religion.

In her book, *When God Was a Woman,* Merlin Stone archeologically documents the story of the religion of the Goddess who reigned supreme in the Near and Middle East. Known by many names—Astarte, Isis, Ishtar, Nammu, Aruru—among them, the Goddess was once revered as the wise creator and source of universal order. Under her rule, woman's roles were different: they bought and sold property, traded goods in the markets, and inherited titles to property that passed from mother to daughter.

Stone's book, the product of ten years of research, traces what she sees as an ancient patriarchal conspiracy, "the wholesale rewriting of myth and religious dogma," to make the Goddess out to be a wanton and depraved figure. In the following section from her book, which comes after her detailed examination of female deities over thousands of years, Stone explains how early Hebrew leaders turned the tables on female deities with the creation story of Adam and Eve, making women feel subservient to men and a male deity.

🌾

When God Was a Woman

Let us take a closer look at the tale of creation and the subsequent loss of Paradise as related by the Hebrew leaders and later adopted and cherished by the advocates of Christianity. As we compare the Levite creation story with accounts of the Goddess religion, we notice how at each turn, in each sentence of the biblical myth, the original tenets of the Goddess religion were attacked.

Stephen Langdon wrote, "Thus beyond all doubt the Nippurian school of Sumerian theology originally regarded man as having been created from clay by the great mother goddess." Professor Kramer tells us, "In a tablet which gives a list of Sumerian gods the goddess Nammu, written with the ideogram for 'sea' is described as 'the mother who gave birth to heaven and earth.'" One Sumerian prayer goes as follows: "Hear O ye regions, the praise of Queen Nana, Magnify the

Creatress, Exalt the dignified, Exalt the glorious One, draw nigh unto the Mighty Lady." The Egyptians wrote, "In the beginning there was Isis, Oldest of the Old. She was the Goddess from whom all becoming arose." Even in Babylonian periods there were prayers to Mami or Aruru as the creator of human life. Yet the worshipers of Yahweh, perhaps one thousand years later, asserted that it was a male who initially created the world. It was the first claim to male kinship— maleness was primal.

According to legends of Sumer and Babylon, women and men had   3
been created simultaneously, in pairs—by the Goddess. But in the male religion it was of ultimate importance that the male was made first, and in the image of his creator—the second and third claims to male kinship rights. We are next told that from a small rather insignificant part of man, his rib, woman was formed. Despite all that we know about the biological facts of birth, facts the Levites certainly knew as well, we are assured that the male does not come from the female, but the female from the male. We may be reminded of the Indo-European Greek story of Athena being born from the head of Zeus.

Any unpleasant remnant or reminder of being born of woman   4
had to be denied and changed. Just as in the myth of the creation through an act of masturbation by the Egyptian Ptah, the Divine Ancestress was written out of reality. We are then informed that the woman made in this manner was presented as a gift to the man, declaring and assuring her status—among those who accepted the myth—as the property of the male. It tells us that she was given to him to keep him from being lonely, as "a helper fit for him." Thus we are expected to understand that the sole and divine purpose of women's existence is to help or serve men in some way.

The couple so designed was placed in the Garden of Eden—   5
paradise—where the male deity warned them not to eat any of the fruit of the tree of knowledge of good and evil. To the ancient Hebrews this tree was probably understood to represent the sacred sycamore fig of the Goddess, the familiar *asherah* which stood beside the altars of the temples of the Goddess and Her Baal. The sacred branch being passed around in the temple, as described by Ezekiel, may have been the manner in which the fruit was taken as "communion." According to Egyptian texts, to eat of this fruit was to eat of the flesh and the fluid of the Goddess, the patroness of sexual pleasure and reproduction. According to the Bible story, the forbidden fruit caused the couple's conscious comprehension of sexuality. Upon eating the fruit, Adam and Eve became aware of the sexual nature of their own bodies, "And they knew that they were naked." So it was that when the male deity

found them, they had modestly covered their genitals with aprons of
fig leaves.

But it was vitally important to the construction of the Levite myth   6
that they did not both decide to eat the forbidden fruit together, which
would have been a more logical turn for the tale to take since the
fruit symbolized sexual consciousness. No, the priestly scribes make
it exceedingly clear that the woman Eve ate of the fruit first—upon
the advice and counsel of the serpent.

It can hardly have been chance or coincidence that it was a serpent   7
who offered Eve the advice. For people of that time knew that the
serpent was the symbol, perhaps even the instrument, of divine counsel
in the religion of the Goddess. It was surely intended in the Paradise
myth, as in the Indo-European serpent and dragon myths, that the
serpent, as the familiar counselor of women, be seen as a source of
evil and be placed in such a menacing and villainous role that to listen
to the prophetesses of the female deity would be to violate the religion
of the male deity in a most dangerous manner.

The relationship between the woman and the serpent is shown to   8
be an important factor, for the Old Testament related that the male
deity spoke directly to the serpent, saying, "I will put enmity between
you and the woman and between your seed and her seed." In this way
the oracular priestesses, the prophetesses whose advice and counsel
had been identified with the symbolism and use of the serpent for
several millenia, were now to be regarded as the downfall of the whole
human species. Woman, as sagacious advisor or wise counselor, human
interpreter of the divine will of the Goddess, was no longer to be
respected, but to be hated, feared or at best doubted or ignored. This
demand for silence on the part of women, especially in the churches,
is later reflected in the passages of Paul in the New Testament. According to the Judaic and Christian theology, woman's judgment had
led to disaster for the whole human species.

We are told that, by eating the fruit first, woman possessed sexual   9
consciousness before man and in turn tempted man to partake of the
forbidden fruit, that is, to join her sinfully in sexual pleasures. This
image of Eve as the sexually tempting but God-defying seductress was
surely intended as a warning to all Hebrew men to stay away from
the sacred women of the temples, for if they succumbed to the temptations of these women, they simultaneously accepted the female deity—
Her fruit, Her sexuality and, perhaps most important, the resulting
matrilineal identity for any children who might be conceived in this
manner. It must also, perhaps even more pointedly, have been directed
at Hebrew women, cautioning them not to take part in the ancient

religion and its sexual customs, as they appear to have continued to do, despite the warnings and punishments meted out by the Levite priests.

The Hebrew creation myth, which blamed the female of the species   10
for initial sexual consciousness in order to suppress the worship of the Queen of Heaven, Her sacred women and matrilineal customs, from that time on assigned to women the role of sexual temptress. It cast her as the cunning and contriving arouser of the physical desires of men, she who offers the appealing but dangerous fruit. In the male religions, sexual drive was not to be regarded as the natural biological desires of women and men that encouraged the species to reproduce itself but was to be viewed as woman's fault.

Not only was the blame for having eaten the fruit of sexuality,   11
and for tempting Adam to do the same, laid heavily upon women, but the proof or admission of her guilt was supposedly made evident in the pain of childbirth, which women were assured was their eternal chastisement for teaching men such bad habits. Eve was to be severely punished as the male deity decreed: "I will greatly multiply your pain in childbearing; in pain you shall bring forth children, yet your desire shall be for your husband and he shall rule over you."

Making use of the natural occurrence of the pains of the pressure   12
of a human child passing from the womb, through a narrow channel, into the outside world, the Levite writer pretended to prove the omnipotent power of his deity. Not only was woman to bear the guilt for sexual consciousness, but according to the male deity her pain in bearing a child was to be regarded as punishment, so that all women giving birth would thus be forced to identify with Eve.

But perhaps most significant was the fact that the story also stated   13
that it was the will of the male deity that Eve would henceforth desire *only* her husband, redundantly reminding us that this whole fable was designed and propagated to provide "divine" sanction for male supremacy and a male kinship system, possible only with a certain knowledge of paternity.

We are perhaps all too familiar with the last line of the decree,   14
which announced that from that time on, as a result of her sin and in eternal payment for the defiant crime which she had committed against the male deity, her husband was awarded the divine right to dominate her, to "rule over" her, to totally assert his authority. And in guilt for what she had supposedly done in the very beginning of time, as if in confession of her poor judgment, she was expected to submit obediently. We may consider here the more practical reality that, once the economic security of women had been undermined by the institution

of male kinship, women were forced into the position of accepting
this one stable male provider as the one who "ruled the roost."

Once these edicts had been issued, the couple was expelled from   15
the Garden of Eden, the original paradise where life had been so easy.
From that time on they were to labor for their livelihood, a most severe
warning to any woman who might still have been tempted to defy the
Levite Yahweh. For hadn't it been just such a woman, listening to the
advice of the serpent, eating the forbidden fruit, suggesting that men
try it too and join her in sexual consciousness, who had once caused
the downfall and misery of all humankind?

THINKING ABOUT THE CONTENT

1. According to Stone, how did the Levite creators of the Adam and Eve
   myth use the story to make women subservient to men and a male deity?
   Does her explanation seem plausible? How do you interpret the Adam
   and Eve story? Does it conflict with Stone's?
2. Why does Stone believe that a snake is interpreted as evil in the creation
   story? Why do you think the Hebrew elders decided to use a snake in
   the story?
3. Do you agree with Stone's thesis? Why do you think that those of the
   Jewish, Christian, and Islamic faiths generally think of God as male?
   What other reasons might there be besides Stone's interpretation for this
   belief?
4. What effect do you think the creation story involving Adam and Eve has
   had on our attitudes toward family and social values?

9 CHICKWEED LANE™   by Brooke

Reprinted by permission: Tribune Media Services.

Looking at Structure and Style

5. To what audience is Stone writing? What examples support your view?
6. What words or phrases establish Stone's attitude and tone?
7. Discuss Stone's organizational pattern. How does she move from her opening statement to her final conclusion? Is the presentation well organized and easy to follow? Why or why not?

Exploring Discussion and Writing Topics

8. Write your own interpretation of the creation story involving Adam and Eve.
9. Research one of the female deities mentioned in the reading selection and report on her.
10. Pick another story from the Bible that supports Stone's contention that Judeo-Christian Biblical stories stress women's subservience and interpret it.
11. Explain what effect worshipping a female deity would have upon the status of women and men in cultures where a Goddess rather than a God was extolled.
12. Read the following essay by Dennis Prager, "Why God Must Be Depicted as a Father and Not as a Mother." Pick a position similar to Stone's or Prager's and write a reasoned essay of your own regarding the gender of God.

DENNIS PRAGER

Dennis Prager is a talk-show host on KABC in Los Angeles and WABC in New York. He writes *Ultimate Issues,* a quarterly journal on Judaism and society. The following essay appeared in the *Los Angeles Times* in response to a 1994 Presbyterian conference on "re-imagining God as a female deity." He and Merlin Stone (see "When God Was a Woman") might make good debating adversaries. Unlike Stone, who believes that a once strong female deity gave way to patriarchy and sexism over the ages, Prager believes that a depiction of God as masculine is "essential to the fundamental purposes of the Bible and Judeo-Christian society." Prager believes that those who argue for a female deity or even a gender-neutral Bible should stop to consider the consequences, which he spells out in the following selection.

ಳ

Why God Must Be Depicted as a Father and Not as a Mother

1 Most people believe that the Bible, the book that introduced humanity to God, refers to God in the masculine because of the patriarchy and sexism of the ancient world.

2 It is true that the Bible was written within a patriarchal context, and it is true that there is sexism in Bible-based religion. But I do not believe that these facts explain why God is depicted as a "father" rather than as a "parent" or "mother" (a neutered "It" would be unacceptable because the biblical God is a personal God).

3 The depiction of God in masculine terms, I believe, is essential to the Bible's fundamental moral purposes. To understand why, one must posit two premises: that the Hebrew Bible's primary concern is promoting good behavior, and that the primary perpetrators of evil behavior, such as violence against innocents, are males, especially young males.

4 From these facts I derive three reasons that it is in men's *and women's* best interests to depict God in the masculine.

5 Before offering these reasons, a personal note is in order: I strongly support women's equality, and I strongly affirm that God is neither male nor female and that both men and women are created in God's

image (Genesis 1:27). In addition, my own religious life is quite egalitarian, and I regard the notion that either sex is superior as nonsense.

Boys Take Rules From Men

When males are young, they need to feel accountable to a male authority figure. Without a father or some other male rule giver; young men are likely to do great harm. Almost any mother will tell you that if there is no male authority figure to give a growing boy rules, it is very difficult for her to control his wilder impulses. For this reason, a God depicted in masculine terms, not a goddess, not a "Mother in heaven," must be the source of such commandments as "Thou shall not murder" and "Thou shall not steal." 6

Women who feel discriminated against because of the male depiction of God should reflect on the consequences of a goddess- or mother-based religious/ethical code. Any discomfort they feel because of a masculine depiction of God is not comparable to the pain they will endure if boys are not civilized into good men. 7

The need for male authority figures is illustrated by the current criminal population in the United States. The absence of a father or other male authority in the formative years of a boy's life is the most important contributing factor to his turning to criminal behavior: A widely accepted figure is that *70 percent* of the violent criminals in American prisons did not grow up with a father. 8

If the father figure/rule giver that boys need is not on earth, a loving and morally authoritative Father in heaven can often serve as an effective substitute. 9

But the last thing that a boy growing up without a father needs is a female figure to worship. He already has one—his mother—and to develop healthfully, he needs to separate from her, not bond with another mother figure. Otherwise, he will spend his life expressing his masculinity in ways that are destructive to women and men. 10

Males Need a Male Role Model

To transform a wild boy into a good man, a male model is as necessary as a male rule giver. 11

When the Bible depicts God as merciful, caring for the poor and the widow, and as a lover of justice, it is not so much interested in describing God, who is, after all, largely indescribable, but in providing a model for human emulation. Especially male emulation. 12

If God were depicted as female, young men would deem traits   13
such as compassion, mercy, and care for the downtrodden as feminine,
and, in their pursuit of their masculinity, reject them. But if God, i.e.,
our Father in heaven, who is, on occasion, even a warrior, cares for
the poor and loves justice, mercy, and kindness, then these traits are
also masculine, and to be emulated.

The argument that this is sexist, since girls need moral female   14
models, is both irrelevant and untrue. It is irrelevant because the problem of mayhem and violence is overwhelmingly a male one—and this
is the problem with which the Bible is most concerned. It is untrue
because girls are able to retain their femininity and their decency with
a male-depicted God. Girls, too, view their fathers as rule givers. Of
course, girls need female role models—but not to avoid violence.

The Male is More Rule-Oriented

A third reason for depicting God in masculine terms is the indispens-   15
ability of law to a just and humane society.

"Law and order" can be code words for repression, but they are   16
in fact the building blocks of a decent society. It is therefore natural
and desirable that God be identified with the gender that is more
naturally disposed to rules and justice—males. Females are more naturally inclined toward feelings and compassion, two essential qualities
for a decent *personal* life, but not for the governance of *society.* A
male depiction of God helps make a law-based society possible. And
the Hebrew Bible is nothing if not law-based.

It is ironic that some women, in the name of feminism, are at-   17
tempting to emasculate the God of Western religious morality. For if
their goal is achieved, it is women who will suffer most from lawless
males.

We have too many absent fathers on earth to begin to even enter-   18
tain the thought of having no Father in heaven.

Thinking about the Content

1. For what three reasons does Prager think the depiction of God in masculine
   terms is vital? Is his argument logical? Why do you agree or disagree with
   him?
2. How do you respond to Prager's statement that God is "on occasion a
   warrior" (13)? Is this a good image of God to pass on to young males?
   Why or why not?
3. Is it true, as Prager says, that young girls also "need female role models—

but not in order to avoid violence" (14)? Is this a good reason for claiming a male deity?

4. Prager claims he is not sexist. Is he convincing? Why or why not?

5. Prager says he acknowledges that "God is neither male nor female (15)." Is this statement contradictory to his thesis? Why or why not?

6. Why do you think males do or do not respond better to the idea of a Father in Heaven than to a Mother in Heaven? Would women respond better to a Mother in Heaven? Why or why not?

LOOKING AT STRUCTURE AND STYLE

7. How well does Prager state his thesis? Does he support his thesis with fact or opinion?

8. What is the author's tone? What passages give that tone?

9. What kind of support does Prager offer for each of his three reasons for depicting God as a father in the Bible? Is it convincing?

EXPLORING DISCUSSION AND WRITING TOPICS

10. Write an essay that discusses how different women might be if the Bible referred to a female deity, a Mother in Heaven. How might that change our current social structure? Would men be more violent as Prager asserts?

11. Counterargue each of Prager's three reasons for depicting God as a father.

12. Discuss whether it is important for God to be depicted as one gender or the other in order for society to understand and follow the moral principles of the Bible and Judeo-Christian faiths.

SOME RESEARCH SOURCES ON RELIGION AND FAITH

The following sources may be useful if you choose to do more reading or pursue a research project dealing with issues prompted by the reading selections in this unit.

Armstrong, Karen. *Muhammad: A Biography of the Prophet*. New York: HarperCollins, 1992.

Barnstone, Willis, ed. *The Other Bible*. New York: HarperCollins, 1984.

Beck, Norman. *Mature Christianity in the 21st Century*. New York: Crossroad, 1995.

Campbell, Joseph. *The Hero with a Thousand Faces*. Princeton: University of Princeton Press, 1968.

———, with Bill Moyers. *The Power of Myth*. New York: Doubleday, 1988.

Carmody, Denise L., and John Tully Carmody. *Mysticism: Holiness East and West*. New York: Oxford, 1996.

Cleary, Thomas. *The Essential Koran: The Heart of Islam*. New York: Harper-Collins, 1993.

Coote, Robert B., and Mary P. Power. *Politics, and the Making of the Bible*. New York: Fortress Press, 1990.

Delbanco, Andrea. *The Death of Satan*. New York: Farrar-Straus, 1994.

Fiorenza, Elisabeth Schussler. *Bread Not Stone: The Challenge of Feminist Biblical Interpretation*. Boston: Beacon, 1984.

Flew, Antony. *Atheistic Humanism*. New York: Prometheus, 1994.

Hanh, Thich Nhat. *Living Buddha, Living Christ*. New York: Putnam's, 1995.

Isherwood, Margaret. *Searching for Meaning*. Philadelphia: MacRae Smith, 1970.

Keller, Werner. *Diaspora: The Post-Biblical History of the Jews*. New York: Harcourt, 1989.

Kertzer, Rabbi Morris N. *What Is a Jew?* New York: Macmillan, 1988.

Mack, Burton, L. *The Lost Gospel: The Book of Q and Christian Origins*. New York: HarperCollins, 1993.

Merton, Thomas. *Seeds of Contemplation*. New York: Dell, 1988.

Miles, Jack. *God: A Biography*. New York: Vintage, 1995.

Murray, William J. *Let Us Pray*. New York: Morrow, 1995.

Neusner, Jacob. *From Politics to Piety: The Emergence of Pharisaic Judaism*. Englewood Cliffs N.J.: Prentice-Hall, 1973.

Pagals, Elaine. *The Origin of Satan*. New York: Random House, 1995.

Russell, Letty M. *Feminist Interpretation of the Bible*. Westminster Press, 1985.

Smith, Huston. *The World's Religions*. New York: HarperCollins, 1991.

Spong, John Shelby. *Rescuing the Bible from Fundamentalism*. New York: HarperCollins, 1991.

Steinberg, Milton. *Basic Judaism*. New York: Harcourt, 1975.

Stone, Merlin. *When God Was a Woman*. New York: Dorset, 1976.

Wilson, A. N. *Jesus*. New York: Norton, 1992.

Responsibility

Responsibility is the price of greatness.

—WINSTON CHURCHILL

Every human being has a work to carry on within, duties to perform abroad, influence to exert, which are peculiarly his, and which no conscience but his own can teach.

—WILLIAM ELLERY CHANNING

Responsibility educates.

—WENDELL PHILLIPS

You will find men who want to be carried on the shoulders of others, who think that the world owes them a living. They don't seem to see that we must all lift together and pull together.

—HENRY FORD II

The Buck Stops Here.

—HARRY S TRUMAN

Responsibility is the thing people dread most of all. Yet it is the one thing in the world that develops us, gives us manhood or womanhood fiber.

—FRANK CRANE

When pupils study subjects that are too remote from their experience, that arouse no native curiousity, and that are beyond their power of understanding, they begin to use a measure of value and of reality for school subjects different from the measure they employ for affairs of life that make a vital appeal. They tend to become intellectually irresponsible; they do not ask for the meaning *of what they learn, in the sense of what difference it makes to the rest of their beliefs and to their actions.*

—*JOHN DEWEY*

৬ ৬
৬

Responsibility: something for which one is responsible, such as a
duty, an obligation, or a burden; moral, legal, or mental
accountability.

IN THE 1830s, THE FRENCH philosopher Alexis de Tocqueville was
intrigued by the American character and society. Based on observation
and conversations with Americans, Tocqueville's book *Democracy in
America* focused on family life, religious traditions, and participation
in local politics in an attempt to show how they formed the American
character. He felt that the characteristic of "individualism" that he saw
helped to create the kind of person "who could sustain a connection
to a wider political community and thus ultimately support the mainte-
nance of free institutions." But he also warned that this same individualism might "eventually isolate Americans one from another and
thereby undermine the conditions of freedom." Tocqueville believed
that the survival of free institutions depends upon the relationship
between private and public life, the way citizens do or do not participate
in their society. What are the social forces, he asked, that could control
and limit the tendency toward a despotic government?

Tocqueville and others since feel that active citizenship requires
the existence of well-established groups and institutions, from families
to political parties, as well as new social movements and coalitions
responsive to social and political needs when they arise. The United
States has a history of social movements, particularly in times of difficulty. From abolition to prohibition, from organized labor to civil
rights, energetic social movements, led and followed by people feeling
their social responsibility as citizens, have sometimes changed the
course of government and national lifestyles. These reforming impulses
more often than not went beyond serving merely as a lobby for special
interest groups. These movements involved people at all levels into
the politics of community.

Over time, these social movements often have a pendulum effect.
For instance, welfare liberalism began during the 1930s when Franklin
D. Roosevelt's New Deal government spent massive resources as a
means to bring the United States out of the Great Depression. But by
the 1980s, the Reagan Administration called government "overgrown
and overweight." In a 1984 speech Reagan said, "It is time to reject
the notion that advocating government programs is a form of personal
charity. Generosity is a reflection of what one does with his or her
resources—and not what he or she advocates the government do with

everyone's money." Picking up this theme in the mid-1990s, the Republican administration pushed on by the efforts of Christian Coalition movement seeks to swing the pendulum as far away from New Deal liberalism as possible and do away with government welfare and rely on the public's charity to help the disadvantaged.

But as the authors of *Habits of the Heart* point out, what Tocqueville admired about American individualism may be disintegrating because we have put our own good, as individuals, as groups, as a nation, ahead of the common good:

> Our problems today are not just political. They are moral and have to do with the meaning of life. We have assumed that as long as economic growth continued, we could leave all else to the private sphere. Now that economic growth is faltering and the moral ecology on which we have tacitly depended is in disarray, we are beginning to understand that our common life requires more than an exclusive concern for material accumulation. . . .
>
> Perhaps enduring commitment to those we love and civic friendship toward our fellow citizens are preferable to restless competition and anxious self-defense. [Robert N. Bellah et al., *Habits of the Heart* (New York: HarperCollins, 1986), 295.]

At times we read of our faltering "moral ecology" as we allow legislative bodies to pass laws that benefit or favor a few at the expense of the less privileged, that provide tax breaks or boons for the favored campaign donors, that provide funds for less needy projects than others. We read of government officials taking bribes from influence peddlers, lying to their constituents, abusing their power. We read of police officers breaking the law they are supposed to uphold. We read of large corporations flaunting environmental laws by dumping toxic waste into our streams and lakes, releasing harmful pollutants in the air, abusing workers for the sake of company profits. We read of communities rioting in the streets, looting, burning, physically harming others because of differences in skin color or religious beliefs. And we even read of students on college campuses publicly voicing disapproval of those of another race or country.

What we don't always hear about are the many commendable socially responsible happenings. We hear little about the person volunteering time three nights a week at the library to teach an adult how to read. Or the inner-city volunteers at the drug and rehabilitation centers who want to help others help themselves to a better life. We don't hear much about the many nonprofit organizations that help the mentally, physically, or economically disabled. Many of the functions of those organizations depend on individual gifts of money and goods, but we don't hear much about these givers' generosity. Nor do we hear about the millions who donate money to the many charitable organizations and health research foundations founded to help every human misfortune and illness imaginable. And against the established wisdom of Wall Street, mutual funds have been formed that seek out investments in companies that practice corporate social responsibility, treat their employees well, are sensitive to the communities where they operate, and are environmentally sensitive.

But what exactly does it mean to be responsible and act responsibly? With news so heavily weighed toward the negative, one can easily become cynical and overlook the many daily, simple, and grand acts of social responsibility. We cannot always easily recognize what our responsibilities are, what our obligations are, what we should do, and what actions to take, if any.

Some of us react to social injustice or wrongdoing by joining the shouting crowd; some of us quietly sign petitions; some of us hope our vote will count. Others of us do nothing, disengage ourselves from the "affairs of others," and withdraw into indifference or the fear of risking contacts with people or ideas that may unsettle us.

John Dewey, in his famous book *How We Think,* does not view responsibility as a moral trait but as an attitude:

> Like sincerity or whole-heartedness, responsibility is usually
> conceived as a moral trait rather than as an intellectual
> resource. But it is an attitude that is necessary to win the
> adequate support of desire for new points of view and
> new ideas and of enthusiasm for and the capacity for absorp-
> tion in subject matter. . . . To be intellectually responsi-
> ble is to consider the consequences of a projected step; it
> means to be willing to adopt these consequences when they
> follow reasonably from any position already taken. Intellec-
> tual responsibility secures integrity; that is to say, consistency
> and harmony in belief. It is not uncommon to see persons
> continue to accept beliefs whose logical consequences they
> refuse to acknowledge. They profess certain beliefs but are
> unwilling to commit themselves to the consequences that flow
> from them. [John Dewey, *How We Think* (Lexington, Mass.:
> D. C. Heath, 1960); 32.]

The essays in this section deal with various opinions on responsibility as individuals and as a community. Some opinions you will agree with, some you will not; some may affect you, others may irritate you. In all cases, don't accept or dismiss any viewpoints until you have analyzed both the author's reasoning and your own.

© 1995 Washington Post Writers Group. Reprinted with permission.

Professor of humanities at the University of the Arts in Philadelphia, Camille Paglia is the author of *Sexual Personae: Art and Decadence from Nefertiti to Emily Dickinson,* and two collections of her essays and interviews, *Sex, Art, and American Culture,* and *Vamps and Tramps.* Not afraid to say what is on her mind, Paglia has written much on popular culture, which she defines as "an eruption of the never-defeated paganism of the West."

Ever since the publication of *Sexual Personae,* Paglia has, as someone said, "attracted controversy the way a magnet draws iron fillings." Called by some "an academic rottweiler," Paglia states in her introduction to *Sex, Art, and American Culture* that there is a "gap between academe and the mass media, which is our culture." According to Paglia, "Professors of humanities, with all their leftist fantasies, have little direct knowledge of American life and no impact whatever on public policy."

The following essay first appeared in *New York Newsday* on January 27, 1991, under the title "Rape: A Bigger Danger than Feminists Know." Paglia argues that the college date-rape debate is "smothering in propaganda churned out by the expensive northeastern colleges and universities, with their overconcentration of boring, uptight academic feminists and spoiled, affluent students," and that we should not look for sexual enlightenment from academe, "which spews out mountains of books but never looks at life directly."

ꙮ

The Date-Rape Debate[*]

R ape is an outrage that cannot be tolerated in civilized society. Yet   1
feminism, which has waged a crusade for rape to be taken more seriously, has put young women in danger by hiding the truth about sex from them.

In dramatizing the pervasiveness of rape, feminists have told young   2
women that before they have sex with a man, they must give consent

---

*Editor's title.

416

as explicit as a legal contract's. In this way, young women have been convinced that they have been the victims of rape. On elite campuses in the Northeast and on the West Coast, they have held consciousness-raising sessions, petitioned administrations, demanded inquests. At Brown University, outraged, panicky "victims" have scrawled the names of alleged attackers on the walls of women's rest rooms. What marital rape was to the Seventies, "date rape" is to the Nineties.

The incidence and seriousness of rape do not require this kind of   3
exaggeration. Real acquaintance rape is nothing new. It has been a horrible problem for women for all of recorded history. Once fathers and brothers protected women from rape. Once the penalty for rape was death. I come from a fierce Italian tradition where, not so long ago in the motherland, a rapist would end up knifed, castrated, and hung out to dry.

But the old clans and small rural communities have broken down.   4
In our cities, on our campuses far from home, young women are vulnerable and defenseless. Feminism has not prepared them for this. Feminism keeps saying the sexes are the same. It keeps telling women they can do anything, go anywhere, say anything, wear anything. No, they can't. Women will always be in sexual danger.

One of my male students recently slept overnight with a friend in   5
a passageway of the Great Pyramid in Egypt. He described the moon and sand, the ancient silence and eerie echoes. I will never experience that. I am a woman. I am not stupid enough to believe I could ever be safe there. There is a world of solitary adventure I will never have. Women have always known these somber truths. But feminism, with its pie-in-the-sky fantasies about the perfect world, keeps young women from seeing life as it is.

We must remedy social injustice whenever we can. But there are   6
some things we cannot change. There are sexual differences that are based in biology. Academic feminism is lost in a fog of social construc-tionism. It believes we are totally the product of our environment. This idea was invented by Rousseau. He was wrong. Emboldened by dumb French language theory, academic feminists repeat the same hollow slogans over and over to each other. Their view of sex is naïve and prudish. Leaving sex to the feminists is like letting your dog vacation at the taxidermist's.

The sexes are at war. Men must struggle for identity against the   7
overwhelming power of their mothers. Women have menstruation to tell them they are women. Men must do or risk something to be men. Men become masculine only when other men say they are. Having sex with a woman is one way a boy becomes a man.

College men are at their hormonal peak. They have just left their 8
mothers and are questing for their male identity. In groups, they are
dangerous. A woman going to a fraternity party is walking into Testos-
terone Flats, full of prickly cacti and blazing guns. If she goes, she
should be armed with resolute alertness. She should arrive with girlfriends and leave with them. A girl who lets herself get dead drunk at
a fraternity party is a fool. A girl who goes upstairs alone with a
brother at a fraternity party is an idiot. Feminists call this "blaming
the victim." I call it common sense.

For a decade, feminists have drilled their disciples to say, "Rape 9
is a crime of violence but not of sex." This sugar-coated Shirley Temple
nonsense has exposed young women to disaster. Misled by feminism,
they do not expect rape from the nice boys from good homes who sit
next to them in class.

Aggression and eroticism are deeply intertwined. Hunt, pursuit, 10
and capture are biologically programmed into male sexuality. Generation after generation, men must be educated, refined, and ethically
persuaded away from their tendency toward anarchy and brutishness.
Society is not the enemy, as feminism ignorantly claims. Society is
woman's protection against rape. Feminism, with its solemn Carry
Nation repressiveness, does not see what is for men the eroticism or
fun element in rape, especially the wild, infectious delirium of gang
rape. Women who do not understand rape cannot defend themselves
against it.

The date-rape controversy shows feminism hitting the wall of its 11
own broken promises. The women of my Sixties generation were the
first respectable girls in history to swear like sailors, get drunk, stay
out all night—in short, to act like men. We sought total sexual freedom
and equality. But as time passed, we woke up to cold reality. The old
double standard protected women. When anything goes, it's women
who lose.

Today's young women don't know what they want. They see that 12
feminism has not brought sexual happiness. The theatrics of public
rage over date rape are their way of restoring the old sexual rules that
were shattered by my generation. Because nothing about the sexes has
really changed. The comic film *Where the Boys Are* (1960), the ultimate
expression of Fifties man-chasing, still speaks directly to our time. It
shows smart, lively women skillfully anticipating and fending off the
dozens of strategies with which horny men try to get them into bed.
The agonizing date-rape subplot and climax are brilliantly done. The
victim, Yvette Mimieux, makes mistake after mistake, obvious to the
other girls. She allows herself to be lured away from her girlfriends and
into isolation with boys whose character and intentions she misreads.

Where the Boys Are tells the truth. It shows courtship as a dangerous game in which the signals are not verbal but subliminal.

Neither militant feminism, which is obsessed with politically correct language, nor academic feminism, which believes that knowledge and experience are "constituted by" language, can understand preverbal or nonverbal communication. Feminism, focusing on sexual politics, cannot see that sex exists in and through the body. Sexual desire and arousal cannot be fully translated into verbal terms. This is why men and women misunderstand each other.

Trying to remake the future, feminism cut itself off from sexual history. It discarded and suppressed the sexual myths of literature, art, and religion. Those myths show us the turbulence, the mysteries and passions of sex. In mythology we see men's sexual anxiety, their fear of woman's dominance. Much sexual violence is rooted in men's sense of psychological weakness toward women. It takes many men to deal with one woman. Woman's voracity is a persistent motif. Clara Bow, it was rumored, took on the USC football team on weekends. Marilyn Monroe, singing "Diamonds Are a Girl's Best Friend," rules a conga line of men in tuxes. Half-clad Cher, in the video for "If I Could Turn Back Time," deranges a battleship of screaming sailors and straddles a pink-lit cannon. Feminism, coveting social power, is blind to woman's cosmic sexual power.

To understand rape, you must study the past. There never was and never will be sexual harmony. Every woman must take personal responsibility for her sexuality, which is nature's red flame. She must be prudent and cautious about where she goes and with whom. When she makes a mistake, she must accept the consequences and, through self-criticism, resolve never to make that mistake again. Running to Mommy and Daddy on the campus grievance committee is unworthy of strong women. Posting lists of guilty men in the toilet is cowardly, infantile stuff.

The Italian philosophy of life espouses high-energy confrontation. A male student makes a vulgar remark about your breasts? Don't slink off to whimper and simper with the campus shrinking violets. Deal with it. On the spot. Say, "Shut up, you jerk! And crawl back to the barnyard where you belong!" In general, women who project this take-charge attitude toward life get harassed less often. I see too many dopey, immature, self-pitying women walking around like melting sticks of butter. It's the Yvette Mimieux syndrome: make me happy. And listen to me weep when I'm not.

The date-rape debate is already smothering in propaganda churned out by the expensive Northeastern colleges and universities, with their overconcentration of boring, uptight academic feminists and spoiled, affluent students. Beware of the deep manipulativeness of rich students who were neglected by their parents. They love to turn the campus into hysterical psychodramas of sexual transgression, followed by assertions of parental authority and concern. And don't look for sexual enlightenment from academe, which spews out mountains of books but never looks at life directly.

As a fan of football and rock music, I see in the simple, swaggering masculinity of the jock and in the noisy posturing of the heavy-metal guitarist certain fundamental, unchanging truths about sex. Masculinity is aggressive, unstable, combustible. It is also the most creative cultural force in history. Women must reorient themselves toward the elemental powers of sex, which can strengthen or destroy. 18

The only solution to date rape is female self-awareness and self-control. A woman's number one line of defense is herself. When a real rape occurs, she should report it to the police. Complaining to college committees because the courts "take too long" is ridiculous. College administrations are not a branch of the judiciary. They are not equipped or trained for legal inquiry. Colleges must alert incoming students to the problems and dangers of adulthood. Then colleges must stand back and get out of the sex game. 19

THINKING ABOUT THE CONTENT

1. Why does Paglia blame the feminists for putting young women in danger of date rape? Do you agree with her? Explain.
2. Paglia says, "Academic feminism is lost in a fog of constructionism" (6). What does she mean? Do you agree or not? Why?
3. Why does Paglia disagree with the statement, "Rape is a crime of violence but not of sex"? What are your views?
4. Does Paglia seem to blame date-rape incidents more on women than on men? Explain.
5. What advice does Paglia give young women regarding what she calls "woman's cosmic sexual power" (14) and on how to deal with a male student's vulgar remark? How does it contrast with what she calls feminist propaganda? What does she feel is a "woman's number one line of defense" (19)? Is she correct?
6. Why does Paglia feel that the consequences of date rape are not the domain or responsibility of college administrations? Do you agree? If not, what do you feel their responsibility is?

LOOKING AT STRUCTURE AND STYLE

7. Who is Paglia's audience? Who might agree and who might disagree with her views?

8. Paglia blames feminism for "hiding the truth about sex" from young women. How well does she argue her point? Are her arguments convincing? Did she change your views at all?
9. Describe Paglia's tone and style. Provide some examples that develop her tone.

EXPLORING DISCUSSION AND WRITING TOPICS

10. Does your campus have rules and regulations regarding date rape? If so, examine them for their value. Do they seem written more as a protection from the administration being held responsible in the event of a student rape charge, or are they written to alert incoming students to the problems and dangers of rape? If your campus does not have any rules or regulations, argue why it should or why it is suitable in not having any.
11. Pick a point in Paglia's essay and counterargue her viewpoint.
12. Discuss the "date-rape crisis" on your campus. Is it an acknowledged problem? How have date-rape incidents been handle?
13. Read parts or all of one of the following and compare the views with those of Paglia and/or yourself:

Aldrich, Nelson W. "How to Avoid Date Rape," *The Wilson Quarterly* (spring 1994).

Pollitt, Katha. "Not Just Bad Sex," in *Reasonable Creatures*. New York: Knopf, 1994.

Roiphe, Katie. *The Morning After: Sex, Fear, and Feminism on Campus*. Boston: Little, Brown, 1993.

Sweet, Ellen. "Date Rape: The Story of an Epidemic and Those Who Deny It," *Ms.* (October 1985).

Wolfe, Naomi. "Are You a Bad Girl?", *Glamour* (November 1991).

Deborah Fallows

Deborah Fallows received a B.A. from Radcliffe and a Ph.D. in linguistics from the University of Texas. She worked as a research linguist at the Center for Applied Linguistics in Washington, D.C., and as an assistant dean at the School of Languages and Linguistics at Georgetown University. After becoming pregnant with her second child, Fallows gave up her career to stay home with her children. Since then, she has become known as a spokesperson for full-time mothers, arguing that "it is not possible to be both a full-time career woman and a full-fledged mother." Her views have been expressed in articles in *Newsweek, Washington Monthly,* and her 1985 book, *A Mother's Work.*

The following essay, which appeared in *Washington Monthly,* explains why she gave up her career to be a full-time mother and the responsibilities she feels parenting, especially motherhood, entails.

❧

Why Mothers Should Stay Home

About 18 months ago, when our first son was three years old and our second was about to be born, I decided to stop working and stay at home with our children. At the time, I wrote an article about the myth of the superwoman, saying that contrary to the prevailing notion of the day, it was not possible to be both a full-time career woman and a full-fledged mother. I said that while everyone recognizes the costs a stay-at-home mother pays in terms of power, prestige, money, and advancement in traditional careers, we are not always aware of or do not so readily admit what a full-time working woman loses and gives up in terms of mothering.

I've been at home with our children for almost a year and a half now, and I've learned a number of things about my choice. My convictions about the importance of mothering, which were based more on intuition than experience at the time, run even deeper and stronger. Nothing means more to me now than the hours I spend with my children, but I find myself coping with a problem I hadn't really foreseen. It is the task of regearing my life, of learning to live as a full-time mother without a professional career but still with many of the interests and ambitions that I had before I had children. And this is the hard part. It means unraveling those long-held life plans for a certain kind of career and deciding which elements are possible to keep and which I must discard. Perhaps even more important, it means changing the way I've been taught to think about myself and value the progress of my life.

My mother became a mother in 1946; she had gone to college, studied music, and worked for a year at her father's office. Then she married and had my sister by the time she was 22. She wasn't expected to have a career outside the home, and she didn't. When I was growing up, the only mothers who worked were those who, as we whispered, "had to." Even the high school teachers, who we recognized probably weren't doing it just for the money, were slightly suspect.

But between my mother's time and our own, the climate of opportunity and expectations for women started to change. Betty Friedan and *The Feminine Mystique* came between all of those mothers and all of us daughters. The small town in northern Ohio where I grew up was not exactly a hotbed of feminist activity, but even there the signals for young women were changing in the mid-sixties. We were raised with a curious mixture of hope of becoming homecoming queen and pressure to run for student council president. When I was 11, the mothers in our neighborhood bundled off their awkward, preadolescent daughters to Saturday morning charm classes, where we learned how to walk on a straight line, one foot directly in front of the other, and the proper way to don a coat. We all felt a little funny and humiliated, but we didn't say anything. By the time we were 17, we were May Queens, princesses, head drum majorettes, and cheerleaders, but we were also class valedictorians, editors of the school paper and yearbook, student directors of the school band, and candidates for six-year medical programs, Seven Sisters colleges, and honors programs at the Big Ten universities. I admit with some embarrassment that my two most thrilling moments in high school were being chosen for the homecoming court and being named first-chair trumpet in the concert band.

This was the way we were supposed to achieve—to be both beautiful and brilliant, charming and accomplished. It was one step beyond what our mothers did: we were aiming to be class presidents, not class secretaries; for medical school, not nursing school; we were building careers, not just jobs to tide us over before we landed husbands and started raising babies.

When I made my decision to stop working and stay home with our children, it was with a mixture of feelings. Part was defiance of the background I've just described—how could feminism dare tell me that I couldn't choose, with *pride,* motherhood alone? Part was anxiety—how could I keep some grasp on my extramothering self, on the things I had really enjoyed doing before I had children? I didn't want to become what the world kept telling me housewives are—ladies whose interests are confined to soap operas and the laundry. Certainly I knew from my own mother and from other women who had spent their middle years as full-time mothers that it was possible to be a thoughtful and sensitive person and still be a mother. But I didn't know how, and I didn't know where to turn to ask. Even my mother didn't have the answers. She was surprised when I told her I wanted to stop working and stay home with my kids. "You young women seem to handle everything so easily, so smoothly," she told me. "I never knew you were so torn between being a mother and being a professional."

The arrival of children in a woman's late twenties or early thirties   7
can be handy, of course, because it means you can finish your education and start a career before taking "time out" to start your family. But it's also awkward.

At my tenth college reunion last June, I found that many of my   8
friends had just become partner or vice-president of one thing or another, doctor-in-charge of some ward, tenured professor, editor-in-chief, and so forth. In these moments, I feel as if everyone is growing up around me. My reactions, though human, are not altogether pretty. I feel sorry for myself—there but for two small children go I. I feel frustrated in being passed over for things I know I could handle as well as or better than the next person. I feel anxious, wondering if I am going to "lose my touch," get rusty, boring, old, trivial too quickly. And I am afraid that in putting aside my professional ambitions just now, I may be putting aside forever the chance to attain the levels I once set for myself.

All of us, I think, spend time once in a while pondering the "what   9
ifs" of our lives, and we all experience momentary pangs of self-pity over the course we've taken. I know I'm not an exception to this, but I also know that when I add up the pluses and minuses my choice was right for me, and it might be right for other women.

The Importance of "Quantity" Time

The first adjustment on that first morning that I dressed for mother-   10
hood rather than for success was to believe intellectually in what I felt emotionally: that it was as important, as worthy for me to spend my time with my small children as to study, do research, try cases, or invest a bank's money. Furthermore, I had to believe it was worth it

to the children to have me—not someone else—there most of the time. There are a thousand small instances I have witnessed over the past year and a half that illustrate this feeling. One that stays in my mind happened last summer.

I had just dropped off our older son at the morning play camp at   11
the neighborhood school. I was about to drive off when a little boy about eight years old burst out of the school and ran down the front steps in tears. His mother was on her way down the walk and of course she saw him. She led him over to the steps, took his hands in hers, looked him directly in the eyes, and talked with him softly but deliberately for a few minutes, calming him down so he could go back inside happily and she could go on her way. What I recognized in that instant was something I'd been trying to put my finger on for months. I'd witnessed dozens of similar events, when a child was simply over-whelmed by something, and I knew there was a difference—a distinct difference in the way parents respond at such moments from the way I had seen babysitters or maids act, however loving and competent they may have been. Parents seem to have some combination of self-assurance, completeness, deliberateness, and consistency. If that boy had been my son, I would have wanted to be with him, too.

Perhaps this one episode was no more important than the many   12
reprimands or comforts I give my children during the day. But the more I'm around my children, the more such instances I happen to see and deal with. Perhaps a thousand of these episodes add up to the values and security I want to give my children.

I spend a lot of time with my children at playgrounds. We often   13
go out on nice afternoons when our older son gets home from school, sampling new ones or returning to old favorites. I particularly like playgrounds because of the balance they afford: they encourage the kids to strike out on their own but let me be there as a fallback. I've watched my older son in his share of small fistfights and scuffles, and I have been able to let him fight without intervening. He knows I'm there and runs back as often for protection as for nice things like a "Mom, see what I can do." Or our younger son toddles toward the big slide and needs me to follow him up and hold him as we slide down together. After so many hours, we've developed a style of play. I think my children know what to expect of me and I have learned their limits. I've watched the styles of many mothers and children, and you often can see, after a time, a microcosm of their lives together. I've also seen plenty of children there with full-time maids. The maids have their own styles, which usually are different from the mothers'. I've never seen a maid slide down a slide with her small charge, but

I have seen plenty scold children for climbing too high on the jungle gym, and I've seen plenty step in to stop the sand fights before anyone gets dirty or hurt. There's a reason for this, of course: a maid has a lot to explain if a youngster arrives home with a bloody nose, but a mother doesn't. Sometimes, I think, the nose is worth the lesson learned from it, yet that is something only a parent—not a maid or babysitter—can take the responsibility to decide.

It has taken me a few years to realize I have very high standards   14
for my role as a mother. I don't have to be a supermom who makes my children's clothes (I really can't sew), who does all the volunteer work at school (I do my share), or who cooks gourmet meals (we eat a lot of hamburgers). But I have to be around my children—a lot. I have to know them as well as I possibly can and see them in as many different environments and moods as possible in order to know best how to help them grow up—by comforting them, letting them alone, disciplining and enjoying them, being dependable but not stifling. What I need with them is time—in quantity, not quality.

I'm not talking about being with my children every minute of the   15
day. From the time they were several months old, we sent them out for short periods to the favorite neighborhood babysitter's. By the time he was two and a half, our older son was in a co-op nursery school (my husband and I would take turns doing parent duty for the 17 kids); now he's in prekindergarten for a full school day. These periods away from me are clearly important for my sanity, as well as for my children's socialization, their development of trust in people, and their ability to experience other ways of living. But there is a big difference between using childcare from 8 to 6, Monday through Friday, and using a babysitter or a nursery school three mornings a week.

I realize that not everyone enjoys the luxury of choice. Some of   16
my female friends work because it's the only way to make ends meet. But I think a lot of people pretend they have less room for choice than they really do. For some women, the reason may be the feeling—which is widespread among men—that their dignity and success are related to how much money they earn. For others, there is a sense of independence that comes with earning money that is hard to give up. (I know that I felt freer to buy things, especially for myself, or spend money on babysitters when I was contributing to the family income.) And still others define "necessities" in an expensive way: I've heard more than one woman say she "has to work" to keep up payments on the second house. Such a woman is the parallel to the government appointee who "has to resign" from his post to return to his former profession because he "can no longer afford government service."

Even though some women do have a choice, I am not suggesting   17
that all the responsibility for home and children should lie with the
mother. While my husband and I are an example of a more traditional
family, with a breadwinning father, a full-time mother, and two
children, he shares with me many of the family responsibilities: night-
tending, diapering, bathing, cooking, and playtime. A woman's decision to stay home or work is, at worst, a decision made by herself
and, at best, a decision made with her spouse.

But with all these qualifications noted, I still know that my own   18
choice is to stay with my children. Why does this seem to be at odds
with the climate of the times, especially among certain feminists? I
think it is because of a confused sense of ambition—based, in turn,
on a mistaken understanding of what being a housewife or mother
actually means.

While the world's idea of the comparative importance of career   19
and motherhood may have changed a good deal since my mother's
time, the general understanding of what motherhood means for those
who choose it has not changed or advanced. And that may be the real
problem for many women of my generation: who can blame them for
shying away from a commitment to full-time motherhood if they're
told, despite raising children, that motherhood is a vapid life of chores,
routines, and TV? I couldn't stand motherhood myself if that were
true. One of my many discoveries as a mother is that motherhood
requires not the renunciation of my former ambitions but rather their
refinement.

Even for those who intend to rush straight back to work, mother-   20
hood involves some interruption in the normal career plan. Separating
people, even temporarily, from their professional identities, can help
them see the difference between the ambition to *be*—to have an impressive job title to drop at cocktail parties—and the ambition to *do* specific
things that seem satisfying and rewarding. The ambition to be is often
a casualty of motherhood; the ambition to do need not be.

I see many of my friends intensely driven to keep doing things,   21
to keep involved in their former interests, or to develop entirely new
ones that they can learn from and grow with. In the free time they
manage to set aside—thanks to babysitters, co-op babycare, naptimes,
grandmothers' help, and husbands like mine who spend a lot of time
with the children—they are thinking and doing.

Women I have talked to have described how, after some months   22
or years of settling into motherhood, their sense of what work is worth,
and what they're looking for in work, has greatly changed. They are
less tolerant, more selective, more demanding in what they do. One

woman said that before she had children she would focus on a "cause," and was willing to do just about anything as her job toward that cause. Now she's still interested in advancing the cause, but she had no patience for busywork. In the limited time she can spare from her family, she wants to do things that really count, work in areas where her efforts make a difference. I'm not suggesting narcissism here but a clearer focus on a search for some long-range goal, some tangible accomplishment, a feeling so necessary during the season of child-raising when survival from one end of the day to the other is often the only achievement.

Each one's search is different, depending on factors like her husband's job (if she has a husband) and the extent of his role as a caretaker, her children's needs, her family's financial situation, and her personal lifestyle.   23

One of my friends had taught English in public high schools for the last ten years. She was the kind of teacher you remember fondly from your own childhood and hope your kids are lucky enough to have because she's dedicated, demanding, and creative. She expanded her subject to include other humanities, keeping herself several steps ahead of her students by reading and studying on her own, traveling to see museums and exhibits firsthand, collecting slides and books as she goes. She has a new baby daughter now and has stopped working to stay home with her child. She's decided to go back to school next fall, taking one or two courses at a time, to pursue a master's in fine arts—a chance to study formally what she's mostly taught herself and to return to her job someday with an even better background and more ideas for her teaching.   24

Going to school can be perfect for new mothers, as many in my own mother's generation found. It requires very little time away from home, which means cutting down on time away from the children as well as on child-care costs. It can be cheap, as with my friend, who can attend a virtually tuition-free state university. You can pace your work to suit demands at home by carefully choosing the number of courses you take and the type of work required. And it's physically easy but intellectually challenging—the complement to the other demands of the early years of mothering.   25

Other mothers I know do different things with their time. One friend, formerly a practicing lawyer and now a full-time mother, volunteers some of her time to advising the League of Women Voters on legal matters. Another, formerly a producer at a big radio station, now produces her own shows, albeit at a slower pace. A third quit her job   26 to raise her daughter but spends a lot of time on artistic projects, which she sells.

But if there's no real blueprint for what a modern mother should 27 be, you wouldn't know it from what comes through in the media. On the *Today Show* last summer, for instance, Jane Pauley interviewed Felice Schwartz, the president of Catalyst, an organization that promotes career development for women. They were discussing women's changing life-styles. Ms. Schwartz said that now women are going back to work full-time four months after having children, while 15 years ago they were taking 20 years off to have them. "Isn't that fantastic progress?" she said. Fantastic it certainly is; progress it is not, except toward the narrowest and least generous notion of what achievement means for humanity. Progress such as this is a step not toward "liberation" but toward the enslavement to career that has been the least attractive aspect of masculine success.

What it is really like to be a mother today seems to be a secret 28 that's kept from even my contemporaries who may be considering motherhood themselves. At a dinner recently, I sat near a young woman about my age, a New York television producer and recently anointed White House fellow. She and my husband and I were having a conversation about bureaucracy and what she found new or interesting or surprising about it in her new position. After several minutes, she turned away from my husband to me directly and said, "And how old are your children, Debbie?" It wasn't the question—not at all—but the tone that was revealing, the unattractive, condescending tone I've heard many older people use with youngsters, or doctors with patients. If I'd had her pegged as a fast-track superachiever, she had me pegged as little mother and lady of the house.

Hurt and anger were the wrong feelings at a moment like that, 29 although I felt them. Instead, I should have felt sorry for her, not because of her own choice but because she had no sense that a choice exists—waiting to be made by women like her and like me. The choice is *not* to be either a career woman or a dumb housewife. The issue is one that she, a woman at the age when careers take off and childbearing ability nears its eleventh hour, should be sensitive to and think about.

THINKING ABOUT THE CONTENT

1. Fallows says it is "not possible to be both a full-time career woman and a full-fledged mother" (1). Are her arguments convincing? Do you agree with her? Explain.

2. What, according to Fallows, are the responsibilities of a full-fledged mother? Would some consider these responsibilities old-fashioned or dated today? Why?

3. Fallows has a husband who financially supports her family. When discussing the responsibilities of motherhood, does she take into account those single mothers who are sole bread winners or who must work for financial reasons? Does this affect her argument?

4. Fallows says, "What it is really like to be a mother today seems to be a secret that's kept from even my contemporaries who may be considering motherhood themselves" (28). What is the secret? Who is keeping it secret and why?

LOOKING AT STRUCTURE AND STYLE

5. How well does Fallows support her thesis? Are her examples of responsible motherhood enough to sustain her viewpoint? Why or why not?

6. To whom is Fallows writing? Who might agree with her? Who might disagree? What makes you think so?

7. Fallows doesn't mention it in her essay, but obviously she is working at home as a writer. Does this weaken or strengthen her argument? Explain.

EXPLORING DISCUSSION AND WRITING TOPICS

8. Write a rebuttal to Fallows, countering any fallacies or weaknesses you think her thesis may contain.

9. Discuss the responsibilities of fatherhood or motherhood today. Are they different from any other generation? If so, how and why?

10. Write a response to someone who is considering giving up a career for motherhood. What would you advise her?

Reprinted by permission. Courtesy of Don Wright.

CHARLES DERBER

In spring 1989 a teenage gang brutally attacked, beat, stabbed, raped, and left for dead a jogger in New York's Central Park for no other reason, they later admitted, than to have some fun. Receiving national news coverage, the incident was labeled *wilding,* a term the captured youths themselves used to describe their behavior. What received most news attention was the lack of remorse and the smug indifference shown by the youths for what they had done.

In his book *Money, Murder, and the American Dream,* Charles Derber builds on this brutal incident of antisocial mentality, broadening the term *wilding* to mean any ruthless pursuit of self-interest at the expense of others. He reveals links between criminal wilding on the street, emotional wilding in families, economic wilding on Wall Street, and political wilding in Washington. The following passage taken from his book discusses what he calls "the politics of civil society" and its responsibility.

Charles Derber is a professor of sociology at Boston College and has also authored *The Pursuit of Attention, Power in the Highest Degree,* and *The Nuclear Seduction.*

🌿

Civic Responsibility

A New Bill of Rights? The Politics of Civil Society

America's romance with individualism and the free market has its 1
virtues, but it has clouded Americans' understanding of what makes society tick. Civil society arises only when people develop strong obligations to the larger "us" that can override the perennial, very human preoccupation with "me, me, me." Such larger commitments bloom only under special conditions, when the community shows that it cares so deeply for each of its members that each, in turn, fully understands his debt to society and seeks to pay it back in full.

The Japanese and Europeans, in their very different ways, seem 2
to appreciate this "deal" or contract that preserves civil society. The Japanese corporation smothers the Japanese worker in a cocoon of secure employment, health benefits, housing, and other social necessities that make it almost impossible for workers to imagine life outside

of the group. Through their expansive welfare states, the Europeans deliver their own bushel of benefits and entitlements that the citizen recognizes as indispensable to personal survival and happiness. Both systems bring their own serious problems, but succeed in creating the allegiance to the larger community that breeds immunity to the wilding epidemic.

Each civil society has to find its own way of inspiring its members' 3 devotion, but all must deliver those rock bottom necessities essential to the pursuit of life, liberty, and happiness. These include a minimal level of personal safety, food, shelter, and a livelihood. "Social orphans" deprived of these essentials are unable to fulfill any larger obligation to society, for their existence is entirely consumed by the brutish struggle for personal survival.

This leads to the idea of "social citizenship," an extension of the 4 familiar but narrower concept of political citizenship. The rights to health care, housing, and a job can be seen as social rights, parallel to our political rights to vote and to free speech enshrined in our constitution. Political rights apply to all citizens automatically, because they are the precondition of democracy as a system. Analogously, social rights should be extended automatically to everyone, for they are the precondition of civil society's survival.

The Japanese deliver such social rights through a paternalistic 5 corporate extended family, largely private, while the Europeans do it through the welfare state. America will have to find its own way. Ideally, the emerging institutions of the social market would, in the long run, provide a local, democratic, and nonstatist solution. One possibility is an American version of the success achieved by Mondragon, a remarkable complex of over one hundred industrial cooperatives in the Basque region of Spain. Mondragon has succeeded during the past forty years in guaranteeing job security, housing, health care, and education to its members with scarcely any help from the state. Workers in the cooperatives have created cooperative schools, hospitals, insurance companies, and banks that offer robust social security from birth to death. The Mondragon complex, which is the largest manufacturer of durable goods in Spain and employs thousands of "worker-owners," has never permanently laid off a worker, reproducing the equivalent of the Japanese system of lifetime employment, while also entrepreneuring new cooperatives in one of the most impressive rates of job creation in the world.

Whether an American social market could evolve in such a direc- 6 tion is purely speculative, but clearly there are ways to provide social rights that are realistic, democratic, and do not require big government. America is the only major industrialized country not to offer health

care as a social right to all its citizens. The problem could be easily
rectified through a national health care system that is neither bureaucratic nor necessarily public. The 1990s has already seen the proliferation of a variety of proposals for privately financed national health
care, relying on the existing network of health deliverers and insurers
and largely financed by employers. More comprehensive publicly financed plans, including the Health USA Act of 1991 proposed by
Nebraska senator Bob Kerrey, could simultaneously solve problems
of cost and access without creating a huge government bureaucracy.
Similarly, proposals abound for providing affordable housing in ways
that integrate private and public financing mechanisms and do not
make Uncle Sam everybody's landlord.[1]

   While government is not the preferred agent, it is the guarantor   7
of last resort. When people are homeless, starving, or jobless, civil
society has failed, and a wilding virus is activated. It is not silly idealism
or bleeding heart liberalism, but a conservative and prudent defense
of the social order that requires public action.

   For this reason, legal scholars like Columbia University law profes-   8
sor Louis Henkin are pointing to "genetic defects" in our Bill of Rights
that constitutionally guarantee political but not social citizenship
rights. Chief Justice William Rehnquist, in a 1989 court opinion, argued that the Constitution confers "no affirmative right to governmental aid, even when such aid may be necessary to secure life." This leads
constitutional attorney Paul Savoy, former dean of John F. Kennedy
University School of Law, to point out that "Our civil rights and civil
liberties are rights in the negative sense" and "do not include affirmative
obligations on government. We do not have a constitutional right,"
Savoy observes, "to have the state provide us with health care, or give
us shelter if we are homeless, or prevent a child from being beaten or
from starving to death." A coalition of unions, environmentalists, and
community groups has responded by calling for a second Bill of Rights
that would entitle all citizens to the elementary social rights of shelter,
food, and health care.[2]

   Social rights are not a free ride for the population, for with them   9
come demanding social obligations. Citizenship is an intimate dance
of rights and obligations, and "social citizens" need to embrace enthusiastically the moral obligations that come with their new entitlements.
This means not only willingly paying the taxes required to keep civil

---

1. For a review of health care proposals, see *The American Prospect,* Summer, 1991.

2. Paul Savoy, "Time for a Second Bill of Rights," *The Nation,* June 17, 1991,
pp. 815–16.

society healthy, but also devoting time and effort, as we detail below, to "community-building" at work, in the neighborhood and in the country at large.

The problem with the Left is that it demands rights without spelling out the obligations that have to accompany them; the problem with the Right is that it expects obligations to be fulfilled without ceding social rights in return. Both positions are absurd, since rights and obligations are flip sides of civil society's coin of the realm. We need a new politics that marries the Left's moral passion for rights with the Right's sober recognition of duty.

Defending Our Lives: Getting from Here to There

But what do we do now? Americans are a pragmatic people and want down-to-earth answers. While there is no recipe or magic formula, we can act now to stop the wilding epidemic. If we want to survive with our humanity intact, we really have no alternative.

Since the wilding epidemic is a cancer that can destroy society, we are all patients fighting to stay alive. Obviously, if we each felt we had a desperate illness, we would mobilize ourselves to act immediately, to save ourselves. But since wilding is a societal disease and not a biological illness, individuals can feel a deceptive immunity. It is possible to feel healthy, have fun, and enjoy life as society begins to come undone.

But as the epidemic spreads, everyone will increasingly feel at risk. The personal meaning of the wilding epidemic is that we each have to spend more and more time simply defending our lives. Defending our property, defending our livelihood, defending our health, defending our physical safety, defending our ego. This imposes a terrible burden on the individual, and it can easily fuel the "me" mentality at the heart of the problem, but it also unlocks the riddle of what to do. Not only will the illusion of immunity diminish, but the wisdom of dealing with the underlying disease and not just the symptoms will become more apparent.

One can start defending one's life, as Albert Brook's film comedy of that title suggests, either wisely or foolishly. The shortsighted approach involves trying to save oneself by abandoning everyone else, exemplified by the suburbanites who cocoon within homes wired with the latest security technology and refuse to pay taxes to support the center city. Robert Reich suggests that such a "politics of secession" is sweeping upper middle-class America. If so, it is a blind and morally unsustainable choice, for it creates short-term symptomatic relief while worsening the disease.

Since the disease is social, so too must be the cure. As the social 15
infrastructure begins to ulcerate and bleed, the rational long-term way
to defend one's life is to help repair the damaged societal tissue, whether
it be potholes in the road, hungry people sleeping on grates, or socio-
pathic competitiveness in the office. "Doing the right thing," then, is
defending one's life by cooperating to build up community strength
and bolster personal and collective resistance. This requires no saintly
sacrifice for the common good, but tough-minded and clear-eyed assessment of where the threat lies. When facing a wilding threat, the
first question to ask is, "What in myself or my social environment is
creating this threat?" Once that question is answered, the next is,
"What can I do about it?" Some cases will require purely personal
change, falling back on all one's psychological and moral strength, as
well as love and support from family, friends or mentors, to counter
wilding impulses within oneself or susceptibility to wilding influence
in the environment. Most cases will also require acting for some form
of social change to extirpate the external poison, whether at work, in
the neighborhood, or in the White House, typically achievable only
with the help of others.

Fortunately, the wisdom of social action is obvious in a huge 16
variety of circumstances, and Americans are already responding, especially where their own health is involved. When kids in Woburn,
Massachussets, were getting sick because of toxic chemicals, parents
got together to clean up the toxic dump and hold the wilding factory
accountable. In the 1990s, Americans are recognizing that staying
healthy has become a political-action project requiring a massive environmental clean-up, and they are not waiting for lackadaisical governments to take the lead. "People are recognizing they can in fact control
their environment," Hal Hiemstra, a Washington environmental activist notes. "They're starting to say, 'we've had it.' " The *Boston Globe*
reports that "an environmental wake-up call" is "being sounded nationwide by communities alarmed by the federal government's inertia and
inspired by their own sense of power to reshape the landscape." The
activists are not only defending their life but, the *Globe* observes, are
"local heroes on planetary matters."[3]

Heroes of a different sort are the suburban communities around 17
Minneapolis, who swam against the tide and rejected the "politics of
secession," the suburban wilding that has helped push Bridgeport,
Connecticut, into Chapter Eleven bankruptcy and left New York City
and hundreds of other cities tottering on the brink. The Minnesota

3. Larry Tye, "Local Heroes on Planetary Matters," *Boston Globe,* June 22, 1991, p. 3.

suburbs joined with Minneapolis in the mid-1980s and formed a regional pact "whereby any community enjoying 40 percent more than the average growth of the region in any given year would have to share with the other signers of the pact." Such apparent sacrifice for the larger good is just plain common sense, since if the city center failed, it would bring the surrounding communities down with it. The great irony, as John Shannon of the Urban Institute notes, "is that Minneapolis is now enjoying boom times and must pay *out* to the suburbs." A modern Aesop's fable, it shows how cooperation for the common good is, indeed, a form of enlightened self-interest.[4]

We can begin to cure the wilding sickness by doing more of what   18
we have always done well and doing it better: taking responsibility for our lives through civic participation. Tocqueville was amazed at the richness of America's democracy; its dense web of voluntary associations and democratic town meetings made it unique. "The free institutions which the inhabitants of the United States possess, and the political rights of which they make so much use," Tocqueville explains, "remind every citizen, and in a thousand ways, that he lives in society." In other words, democracy, and more democracy, is the best antidote for wilding and the most nourishing food for the social infrastructure.

Americans have become apathetic and indifferent to national poli-   19
tics, but we still retain our propensity to join together in what Tocqueville called "an immense assemblage of associations." One researcher suggests that there are now over 500,000 self-help groups in the United States with over 15 million members; many, whether alcoholics, abused children, battered spouses, or "codependents," are casualties of the wilding epidemic who by joining with others are taking enlightened first steps toward not only recovering personally but rebuilding civil society. The same can be said of the millions of others involved in volunteer efforts or political activism at local or higher levels.

In a recent study, the Kettering Institute of Dayton, Ohio, con-   20
cluded that Americans' indifference to national politics reflected less pure selfishness or apathy than despair about leaders and the absence of real choices. America desperately needs a new generation of political leaders who will tell the truth about the wilding crisis and articulate a new moral vision. But since no such leaders are now in view, the burden falls on the rest of us, where it ultimately belongs. It remains to be seen whether Americans will find in themselves the emotional and moral strength to forge a new collective dream.

4. Renee Loth, "Small Cities, Big Problems," *Boston Globe,* June 23, 1991, pp. A25, A28.

THINKING ABOUT THE CONTENT

1. How does Derber define *civil society?* Do you feel you have a debt to society? Why or why not?
2. In what ways, according to the author, do the Japanese and Europeans represent an understanding of a civil society?
3. What does Derber mean by *social citizenship?* Is U.S. society an example of social citizenship? Explain.
4. Why are some people calling for a "second Bill of Rights" (8)? What would such an act provide that our current Constitution does not provide? Do you feel it is necessary? Explain.
5. In paragraph 15, Derber suggests what to do when facing a wilding threat. Does this seem to be a feasible approach? When might it work and when not?
6. Derber cites a Kettering Institute study that "concluded that Americans' indifference to national politics reflected less pure selfishness or apathy than despair about leaders and the absence of real choices" (20). Do you agree or disagree with the study based on your own personal feelings about "civil society" and your place in it? Why or why not?

LOOKING AT STRUCTURE AND STYLE

7. Do you think Derber's broadened definition of the term *wilding* is appropriate? Explain.
8. Derber claims the "epidemic" of wilding is spreading (13). What words or phrases does he use to continue this disease-like analogy?
9. To what audience do you think Derber is writing? Why do you think so?
10. Reread the concluding paragraph. How well does it bring together the point Derber wants to make?

EXPLORING DISCUSSION AND WRITING TOPICS

11. If you accept Derber's use of the term *wilding,* provide some examples from one of the following areas: criminal wilding on the street, emotional wilding in families, economic wilding on Wall Street, or political wilding in Washington. Try to examine the cause, the effect, and the possible cure.
12. Research one of the self-help groups Derber mentions in paragraph 19. Why was the group formed? How is the group or organization helping to rebuild a civil society?
13. Recount some examples of people who have felt a responsibility toward their society. What have they done that has bettered society? What did it cost them?
14. What are you doing to repay what Derber calls your "debt" to society? Do you feel you have a responsibility to making, maintaining, or establishing a civil society? What is it? Does society owe you? If so, what and why?

DAVID MOBERG

The following essay by David Moberg from the November 29, 1993, issue of *In These Times* deals with the need for more corporate responsibility, arguing that individual irresponsibility is encouraged by corporate irresponsibility. In the nineteenth century, corporations increased their influence over state legislation, resulting in increasing power and privileges to big business. Indeed, in 1886, the U.S. Supreme Court ruled that a private corporation should be considered and treated as a natural person and should have the same rights as an individual under the Bill of Rights. This power, according to Moberg and others he cites, has created many of the social problems we face today.

๕

Suite Crimes

Who could possibly oppose "responsibility" and favor "irresponsibility"? As Lee Iacocca might say, it's a "no-brainer." Politically, it's easy enough to oppose teenagers dropping out of school, getting pregnant at age 14, and shooting their neighbors randomly. 1

Yet most current advocates of responsibility who focus on urging the poor to be more upright and less of a problem to the rest of us offer an extremely truncated moral vision. We may reasonably ask people to be responsible—but we need also to explain to them what they should be responsible for, and to whom they should be responsible. 2

It is necessary but not sufficient for them to follow the laws and to do what they can to take care of themselves. Being responsible means caring about others around you—family, neighbors, fellow workers or anyone else that your actions may affect. It means being socially concerned and accountable, willing to own up to the consequences of one's actions. 3

If a young man fathers a child, then it is not unreasonable to expect him to support and nurture that child. There is little argument about that proposition. Yet if a corporate executive makes a decision to close an inner-city factory—a move that will make it more difficult for many young men to support their children—he is likely to be applauded as a wizard of corporate restructuring and rewarded with 4 bonuses of millions of dollars. If he can get the same work done in Mexico for one-tenth the labor cost, he's simply a shrewd businessman.

Who will denounce him as irresponsible? In the Candidean world of free-market economics, his pursuit of narrow self-interest ultimately produces public good. Why not see the runaway father's narrow self-interest in the same entrepreneurial light?

The rampant irresponsibility of many individual Americans is largely the product of a culture dominated by corporations that are themselves systematically irresponsible, except to their shareholders—and often not even to them. Capitalism of yore assumed that the owner of a business was in some sense responsible for that enterprise, even if his power was used ruthlessly and against the social good. Now most owners have a distant, contingent and often fleeting relationship to the corporation—as blocks of stocks, options on stocks, or even financial futures based on the stock market are rapidly, incessantly traded. These investors don't want to take responsibility for business even in the conventional capitalist sense.

America has always been an extremely individualistic society, but the individualism of the yeoman farmer or mechanic assumed a vision of a relatively egalitarian, democratic society resting on a base of hardworking, independent producers. In practice, there were also many forms of cooperation and mutual support. The contemporary consumerist culture—built up over the past century with credit, advertising, assiduous marketing and the creation of identities through purchases—breeds a much narrower, self-obsessed individualism. At most, the consumer's responsibility is to pay the minimum balance on the credit card bill.

The general culture reflects the irresponsibility at the top. In terms of values, it is not clear that much of the middle and upper-middle class is so much more morally responsible than the poor. Is profiting from the revolving door between business and government morally superior to resorting to welfare?

Members of the upper-middle class have more opportunities and more money, but that is not entirely a result of their being more responsible. Likewise, the limitations placed on the poor are not all a result of their being irresponsible. If there is proportionately more social irresponsibility among the poor—and given that charitable giving as a percentage of income tends to be greater among the poor, that's not immediately evident—we can find it simultaneously understandable, unfortunate, undesirable and inexcusable.

The gross irresponsibilities of some of the poor—especially street crimes—are more immediate and comprehensible menaces than the suite crimes of some corporate executives. In both cases, it is possible to explain the actions of individuals in large part by looking at the social and economic forces that shape their lives—and still expect them as citizens and moral agents to take responsibility for what they do with their lives. But, unlike the irresponsible poor, the executive or owner of a corporation often can escape legal responsibility for his actions, hiding behind the corporate shield.

If we really want to make people more responsible, we must start   11
with the most powerful influences on society. In recent years, we've witnessed auto companies calculate the cost of lost lives from their faulty cars and decide it's cheaper to kill innocent people than to redesign their vehicles. We've seen a pharmaceutical company market a drug for animals to humans and jack up the price a hundredfold. Corporations, often with taxpayer assistance, have closed plants and fled overseas to politically repressive regimes. Though workers have the legal right to organize and act collectively, corporations typically do everything they can—including breaking the law—to crush the faintest sign of workplace democracy.

Three-fourths of manufacturers in 1991 made no effort to prevent   12
pollution and reduce toxic chemical usage, according to a recent study of toxic waste releases by the Citizens Fund, the research arm of Citizen Action. "Companies talk a good game about preventing pollution," Citizen Action environmental director Ed Hopkins says, "but when it comes to actually doing something, pitifully few take any responsible action."

Corporate irresponsibility has its immediate harms—unsafe or   13
unaffordable products, dangerous or alienated work environments, unemployment and growing inequality, ravaged urban centers, widespread pollution. Yet it also sets the tenor for society: political democracy is deeply corrupted and the idea of a social compact becomes laughable. Why should workers be responsible when their bosses aren't? Why should the poor be responsible when their legislative representatives aren't?

When Bill Clinton began campaigning, he talked about the need   14
for a new social covenant, about responsibility from corporations as well as from workers and welfare recipients. But in office, the Clinton administration has shown little stomach for demanding corporate responsibility. True, taxes on the rich were raised. But the revenue from those tax hikes was committed to reducing the debt and making the bond traders happy, not to public investments that might lead to jobs.

Clinton did not lay the groundwork for a social covenant when   15
his administration negotiated a labor side agreement to NAFTA that did not protect the right to organize unions. Citizens were not encouraged to assume more responsibility when Clinton's Environmental

Protection Agency permitted the operation of a hazardous waste incinerator near a school and homes in East Liverpool, Ohio, even after it
had failed government tests.

Writers Richard L. Grossman and Frank T. Adams, advocates for   16
both the environment and workers, argue that Americans must resurrect an old political tradition to insure greater corporate responsibility.
In a recent pamphlet entitled "Taking Care of Business: Citizenship
and the Charter of Incorporation," Grossman and Adams observe that
corporations operate on the basis of charters that are granted by state
governments. In the early 19th century, citizens demanded strict definitions of charters. These terms included limits on the length of a charter
and clauses reserving the right to revoke it. There was widespread
distrust of corporations, which were seen as threats to democracy and
to working people.

During the late 19th century, as corporations increased their influ-   17
ence over state legislatures, the states "gave corporations limited liability, decreased citizen authority over corporate structure, governance,
production and labor, and ever longer terms for the charters themselves," Grossman and Adams observe.

Far worse, the courts began to expand corporate privileges: judges   18
gave some corporations the right to take private property with minimal
compensation. Courts also eliminated jury trials to determine harm
and damages from corporate actions. And through the doctrine of
"the right to contract," judges stripped legislatures of much of their
powers over corporations. Moreover, the courts reduced corporate
liability, and the liability of individual corporate officers, and gave
management the power to stop civil rights at the plant gate.

In 1886, the Supreme Court ruled that a private corporation was   19
a natural person with the same rights as an individual under the Bill
of Rights or the 14th Amendment, which guarantees due process under
law. Courts began to rule that many laws took corporate property
without due process, a line of argument recently expanded by the free
market "law and economics" ideologists. They argue that virtually any
federal social or regulatory legislation, including most of the New Deal
and its legacy, represents unlawful "takings" of private property.

Grossman and Adams argue for a new movement to challenge the   20
charters of corporations that have demonstrated social irresponsibility.
Community groups have in recent years used bank charter laws and,
in particular, the provisions of the Community Reinvestment Act, to
challenge the expansion plans of banks that have miserable lending
records to minorities and poor neighborhoods.

Despite some remaining state charter laws that open interesting   21
political opportunities, Grossman and Adams' idea would be best

pursued by demanding national chartering of corporations. More than a decade ago, Ralph Nader promoted a Corporate Democracy Act as part of such national chartering. Corporations, he argued, should be forced to abide by broad responsibilities to workers, communities, the environment and to the well-being of the national economy if they are to be entitled to any privileges—including the right to exist.

Greater corporate social responsibility is essential for any signifi-   22
cant increase of individual responsibility to society. Contrary to the holy text of irresponsible competition, both the experience of many successful national economies and recent theoretical work even in economics demonstrate that cooperation and social responsibility can improve national economic performance. If there is a growing clamor for more personal responsibility, then reasserting society's power to create and control corporations is the responsible move to make.

THINKING ABOUT THE CONTENT

1. How does Moberg define *responsibility?* Do you agree? Explain.
2. Moberg believes that, "The rampant irresponsibility of many individual Americans is largely the product of a culture dominated by corporations that are themselves systematically irresponsible, except to their shareholders—and often not even to them" (6). What evidence does he provide to support this statement? Is he convincing?
3. What are Moberg's suggestions for making people more responsible? Do you think people need to be more responsible than they are? Explain.
4. What are some examples of corporate irresponsibility? Do you believe corporate irresponsibility is widespread? On what do you base your answer?
5. Moberg touts the pamphlet "Taking Care of Business: Citizenship and the Charter of Incorporation" by Grossman and Adams, which argues for a "new movement to challenge the charters of corporations that have demonstrated social irresponsibility" (20). Does this seem like a good movement? Why or why not? Are you interested enough in reading the Grossman and Adams pamphlet that you would send away for it? Why or why not?
6. Once aware of corporate irresponsibility, do you feel any responsibility to pursue ways to make corporations more responsible? Why or why not?

LOOKING AT STRUCTURE AND STYLE

7. To what audience is Moberg writing? Who does he feel is responsible for instigating change in corporate irresponsibility?
8. How well does Moberg's analogy work regarding the responsibility of a father to his child and that of a corporate executive to his community in paragraph 4?

9. Moberg uses rhetorical questions in paragraph 13. Are they useful in leading the reader to accept his thesis? Explain.
10. What examples from the essay help establish Moberg's attitude and tone?

EXPLORING DISCUSSION AND WRITING TOPICS

11. Argue the idea that shareholders should be held responsible for any damage caused by the corporation's irresponsibility.
12. Explore in an essay Moberg's comment: "Members of the upper middle class have more opportunities and more money, but that is not entirely a result of their being more responsible" (9).
13. How responsible should society be toward its poor? Is there a line were the individual's responsibility ends and society's begins?
14. Discuss why there should or should not be state and federal agencies that serve as "watchdogs" to make certain corporations act responsibly.

At the time he wrote the following article, Doug Bandow was a senior fellow at the libertarian Cato Institute in Washington, D.C. The article, excerpted here, originally appeared in the spring 1992 issue of *Business and Society Review* and then reprinted as it appears here in the September/October 1993 issue of *Utne Reader*. As you read, examine the reasons Bandow provides for his argument that businesses do good by doing well.

❧

Social Responsibility: A Conservative View

Just what do companies owe? And to whom? The minimalist position   1
on the responsibility of business is expressed by Nobel laureate economist Milton Friedman and neoconservative commentator Irving Kristol, among others. In their view, a firm is solely responsible to its owners—the shareholders in the case of a corporation. Thus, for managers to engage in other endeavors, such as charitable giving, is to violate their fiduciary duty.

Although these views are dismissed as backward by today's apos-   2
tles of corporate social responsibility, Friedman and Kristol are correct as far as the large picture is concerned. Corporations are specialized institutions created for a specific purpose. They are only one form of enterprise in a very diverse society with lots of different organizations. Churches exist to help people fulfill their responsibilities toward God in community with one another. Governments are instituted most basically to prevent people from violating the rights of others. Philanthropic institutions are created to do good works. Community associations are to promote one or another shared goal. And businesses are established to make a profit by meeting people's needs and wants.

Shouldn't business nevertheless "serve" society? Yes, but the way   3
it best does so is by satisfying people's desires in an efficient manner. There are, in fact, few tasks more pressing than what Nobel laureate economist Friedrich A. von Hayek calls "maintaining a human popula-

tion of this world 400 or 500 times as large as that which man could achieve in the natural hunting and gathering stage."

In short, businesses should concentrate on being good businesses. They shouldn't be charged with saving souls. Nor should they be expected to house the homeless, preserve a sense of community, or do any of many other important tasks for which other institutions have been created.

Does this mean that firms have no responsibilities other than making money? Of course not, just as individuals have obligations other than making money. But while firms have a duty to respect the rights of others, they are under no obligation to promote the interests of others. The distinction is important. Companies have responsibilities not to spew harmful pollutants into people's lungs and break contracts with their workers. They do not, however, have any obligation to underwrite a local symphony or provide their workers with popular benefits, such as family leave.

This does not mean that firms should be prohibited from promoting other goals when they desire to do so. In this regard, at least, Friedman and Kristol are wrong in opposing the idea of corporate philanthropy. E. B. Knauft may be right when he argues that charitable giving promotes a firm's bottom line. This kind of "selfishness" is a perfectly honorable reason for giving—after all, everyone benefits. Similarly, offering family leave or improved health care benefits may be a savvy step to attract top-quality workers. Going beyond the norm in pollution control may help attract environmentally conscious consumers.

Even if the firm receives no direct financial benefit from such activities, they are legitimate as long as the stockholders are aware of management's activities. When the jeans company Levi Strauss went public, for instance, it informed prospective shareholders that it intended to continue its ambitious policy of charitable giving. If shareholders are willing to funnel some of their resources through a firm to promote philanthropy or generous employee benefits, or whatever, then so be it. But this is different from philanthropic organizations browbeating companies to donate money or government mandating that they do so.

Social responsibility has become a catchword on the left, an excuse for ever-expanding government control of business. It's time that business fought back and explained that it has no more special responsibilities than anyone else. In the end, society will benefit most if business concentrates on doing its job well, rather than trying to solve the rest of the world's problems.

THINKING ABOUT THE CONTENT

1. Do you agree with Milton Friedman and Irving Kristol that a business is responsible solely to its owners or shareholders? Why or why not?
2. In what ways does Bandow both agree and disagree with Friedman and Kristol? Do you agree with Bandow? Explain.
3. Bandow says, "Social responsibility has become a catchword on the left, an excuse for ever-expanding government control of business" (8). Does he support this contention? Is he correct?
4. Bandow calls for businesses to fight back and to explain "that it has no more special responsibilities than anyone else" (8). To whom does he want this explained? What is your reaction to his idea of social responsibility?

LOOKING AT STRUCTURE AND STYLE

5. How does Bandow use the two opening paragraphs to establish his topic and thesis?
6. Does the quote of Nobel laureate Friedrich A. von Hayek used in paragraph 3 help support Bandow's thesis? Explain.
7. What specific thesis support does the author use? Is it mostly fact or opinion?
8. To whom is the author writing? What examples support your answer?

EXPLORING DISCUSSION AND WRITING TOPICS

9. Write an essay explaining your views on why businesses should or should not concentrate only on being good, profitable businesses.
10. Pick a well-known corporation, such as Exxon, Ford, or Apple. Explain what social responsibilities that particular company has to society and why it should fulfill them.
11. Some large corporations underwrite or provide funds for such things as the local symphony, charity events, or programs on PBS. Are such actions done under government pressure, for tax breaks, from a feeling of social responsibility, or as a form of advertising? Do some research to see what companies fund what types of charities and why.
12. Define the term *social responsibility* as it applies to business.
13. Do large businesses and corporations have a social responsibility beyond the goal of making money for its investors? Why or why not?

The following essay first appeared in the March/April 1992 issue of *Business Ethics* and then reprinted as it appears here in the September/October 1992 issue of *Utne Reader*. Majorie Kelly, a businesswoman, raises some interesting questions regarding responsibility: Does the creation of wealth cause poverty? Does gaining wealth obligate us to help the less fortunate? Should we, individually or collectively as a nation, feel responsible for helping the poor, the sick, the aged?

☙

Are You too Rich if Others Are too Poor?

Can you never be too rich or too thin, as the saying goes? It seems to make sense from a personal point of view, doesn't it? You simply can't be too rich.

Wanting money above all else is an obsession unique to our times, says Jacob Needleman in *Money and the Meaning of Life* (Doubleday, 1991). It's not that the forces of nature have changed, for we live on the same human plane on which Moses lived. Rather, the forces that once took various channels today act uniformly through money. Needleman writes:

"In other times and places, not everyone has wanted *money* above all else; people have desired salvation, beauty, power, strength, pleasure, propriety, explanations, food, adventure, conquest, comfort. But now and here, money—not necessarily even the things money can buy, but *money*—is what everyone wants. The outward expenditure of mankind's energy now takes place in and through money."

One of the consequences of our single-mindedness is that we have come to lack a sense of financial obesity: a cultural consensus that enough is enough and too much is grotesque. As a society we do have such a feeling about food (you *can* eat too much), and many of us have it about fitness (weight lifters *can* be grossly muscle-bound). But we lack any such revulsion to vast sums of money.

That's beginning to change, and the issue that's driving the change is excessive CEO pay. But I note that people react less to the *absolute* level of executive pay than to pay in relation to performance, or in relation to workers' wages. Among the pieces of legislation on CEO

447

pay currently circulating, for example, the most prominent would tie executive pay to worker pay—eliminating the tax deductibility for any salary more than 25 times that of the lowest-paid worker. Surprisingly, a recent poll found that such a move had the support of three out of five voters. And it was favored more highly by Republicans than Democrats.

Here we approach the nub of what I hope is an emerging new 6 consensus on wealth: Can you be too rich when others are so poor? It's a question that prosperous Americans might be called upon to face in the years ahead, and it is a question that is distinctly uncomfortable.

The other morning, as I sat in the warmth of my apartment, hot 7 coffee in hand, reading my morning *New York Times*, I saw on page one a photo of a refugee mother stumbling ashore, with four small children in tow. Clearly she owned nothing but the clothes on her back—and there I was, preparing to go off and plot how to bring more money into my business, and not incidentally how to bring more money into my life. At such moments I ask myself: Has my money got anything to do with her poverty? Am I or my nation or my business colleagues somehow responsible for this woman's plight?

The question enters territory governed by one of our unconscious 8 but profound beliefs about money, that it is a zero-sum game, and that for one person to have more means another has less. In short, that wealth is made on the backs of the poor.

There's a kind of reflexive reaction in us that says this might be 9 true, and there are some very caring people who are quite convinced that it is true. Their redistribution argument: Wealth generates poverty, therefore you solve poverty by redistributing wealth. For those of us concerned with social justice, this scenario has a kind of siren-song appeal, based as it is on compassion—an irresistible motive—and offering as it does a manageable solution to an age-old problem.

But there's an assumption here that is only partly accurate, and 10 that is that money is a physical commodity that can be moved about, something like a pile of marbles. This assumption was central to the 70-year experiment in redistribution that we know as communism— the experiment that so tragically and so disappointingly failed. Yet it seemed to be based on such a good idea: If capitalists are hoarding all the wealth, take it from them and spread it around. Yet what happened is that instead of being redistributed, the wealth somehow dissipated, and whole nations sank into poverty.

I suspect the truth is that money has a dual nature. For if the zero- 11 sum theory holds part of the truth of money, the other part is this: that prosperity can beget prosperity.

There is no denying that at times wealth has been made on the   12
suffering of others—as in the slave trade, or sweatshops. But if we are
truly to understand the magic of money, we must equally acknowledge
the times it does not behave in a zero-sum fashion—as when a company
develops computer software that becomes popular, or starts a consulting service that takes off. Such products or services can enrich the
clients who use them, make the companies who developed them
wealthy, and allow both to pay excellent wages to their employees.
There are no losers here, and no plunder—and not much more environmental damage than we all do in the normal course of living. Such
creation of wealth does not cause anyone's poverty. For indeed,
such businesspeople create the successful society in which many may
flourish.

I do not mean here to justify the trickle-down theory, for I don't   13
support it. But I am groping for a genuinely difficult truth about money,
a truth that may come hard to those of us working for greater fairness
in the world—that perhaps we must allow individuals to pursue vast
wealth. Perhaps we never can have equality of wealth, any more than
we can have an end of suffering. It is a sobering thought, but it may
be a comforting one as well: that we must allow ourselves an ethically
earned prosperity, for denying it to ourselves will not enrich anyone
else.

But if our guilt may be at an end there, our obligation is not.   14
For even if wealth doesn't cause poverty, I believe it does have some
relationship to it, and that relationship takes the form of a duty to
care. Those with money have an obligation to care for those without,
just as the healthy have a responsibility to care for the sick, or the
young to care for the old. And if it's not as simple as sharing the
marbles, perhaps it's the role of the fortunate to find a way to share
the magic.

THINKING ABOUT THE CONTENT

1. Kelly quotes Jacob Needleman who says, "The outward expenditure of
   mankind's energy now takes place in and through money" (3). Does Kelly
   agree? Do you agree? Do you think people want money above everything
   else? Do you? Explain your answer.
2. Can you be too rich when others are so poor? When might being wealthy
   be the cause of others being poor?
3. In paragraph 7, Kelly asks if she, her country, or her business colleagues
   are somehow responsible for others being poor. How does she answer
   her own question? Do you agree with her? Explain your viewpoint.

4. What are Kelly's arguments against communism and for capitalism? Do they make sense? Are they too simplistic?
5. Kelly states that perhaps we can never have equality of wealth any more than we can have an end of suffering, and that denying propserity earned will not enrich anyone else. Explain why you agree or disagree.

LOOKING AT STRUCTURE AND STYLE

6. Kelly finally answers the question in her title in the last paragraph. Does this work well?
7. Who is her audience? Why do you think so?
8. Is her use of the quotation from Needleman's book appropriate? Why or why not?

EXPLORING DISCUSSION AND WRITING TOPICS

9. How do you think the woman in paragraph 7 would respond to Kelly's title? Be that woman and write an answer to Kelly's title question.
10. Currently many chief executive officers (CEOs) of large corporations draw huge salaries as their companies make profits for shareholders. But in many cases, employees are being laid off or losing benefits. Are CEOs acting irresponsibly in accepting such salaries and bonuses when their employees are losing their jobs? Are they too rich if their employees are poor? Argue your point.
11. Argue for or against Kelly's statement, "Those with money have an obligation to care for those without, just as the healthy have a responsibility to care for the sick, or the young to care for the old" (14).
12. Read all or part of Jacbo Needleman's *Money and the Meaning of Life* and write your reaction to his thesis.
13. Research a period in U.S. history when those with wealth did not show responsibilty toward the poor, the sick, or the elderly. What was the outcome?

The ideas in the following essay, written for the September/Ocotber 1993 issue of *Utne Reader*, are taken from Paul Hawken's books *The Ecology of Commerce* and *Our Future and the Making of Things*. While Hawken praises those companies with a social conscience and their attempts to integrate social, ethical, and environmental principles in their business, he warns that not enough is being done if we are to stop abusing our natural resources: "If every company on the planet were to adopt the environmental and social practices of the best companies—of, say, the Body Shop, Patagonia, Ben and Jerry's—the world would still be moving toward environmental degradation and collapse." Here, Hawken submits a twelve-point plan "to create a sustainable future that includes a set of design strategies for people to follow."

❦

A Declaration of Sustainability

I recently performed a social audit for Ben & Jerry's Homemade Inc., America's premier socially responsible company. After poking and prodding around, asking tough questions, trying to provoke debate, and generally making a nuisance of myself, I can attest that their status as the leading social pioneer in commerce is safe for at least another year. They are an outstanding company. Are there flaws? Of course. Welcome to planet Earth. But the people at Ben & Jerry's are relaxed and unflinching in their willingness to look at, discuss, and deal with problems.

In the meantime, the company continues to put ice cream shops in Harlem, pay outstanding benefits, keep a compensation ratio of seven to one from the top of the organization to the bottom, seek out vendors from disadvantaged groups, and donate generous scoops of their profits to others. And they are about to overtake their historic rival Häagen-Dazs, the ersatz Scandinavian originator of super-premium ice cream, as the market leader in their category. At present rates of growth, Ben & Jerry's will be a $1 billion company by the end of the century. They are publicly held, nationally recognized, and rapidly growing, in part because Ben wanted to show that a socially responsible company could make it in the normal world of business.

451

Ben & Jerry's is just one of a growing vanguard of companies 3 attempting to redefine their social and ethical responsibilities. These companies no longer accept the maxim that the business of business is business. Their premise is simple: Corporations, because they are the dominant institution on the planet, must squarely face the social and environmental problems that afflict humankind. Organizations such as Business for Social Responsibility and the Social Venture Network, corporate "ethics" consultants, magazines such as *In Business* and *Business Ethics,* non-profits including the Council on Economic Priorities, investment funds such as Calvert and Covenant, newsletters like *Greenmoney,* and thousands of unafflicted companies are drawing up new codes of conduct for corporate life that integrate social, ethical, and environmental principles.

Ben & Jerry's and the roughly 2,000 other committed companies 4 in the social responsibility movement here and abroad have combined annual sales of approximately $2 billion, or one-hundredth of 1 percent of the $20 trillion sales garnered by the estimated 80 million to 100 million enterprises worldwide. The problems they are trying to address are vast and unremittingly complex: 5.5 billion people are breeding exponentially, and fulfilling their wants and needs is stripping the earth of its biotic capacity to produce life; a climactic burst of consumption by a single species is overwhelming the skies, earth, waters, and fauna.

As the Worldwatch Institute's Lester Brown patiently explains in 5 his annual survey, *State of the World,* every living system on earth is in decline. Making matters worse, we are having a once-in-a-billion-year blowout sale of hydrocarbons, which are being combusted into the atmosphere, effectively double glazing the planet within the next 50 years with unknown climatic results. The cornucopia of resources that are being extracted, mined, and harvested is so poorly distributed that 20 percent of the earth's people are chronically hungry or starving, while the top 20 percent of the population, largely in the north, control and consume 80 percent of the world's wealth. Since business in its myriad forms is primarily responsible for this "taking," it is appropriate that a growing number of companies ask the question, How does one honorably conduct business in the latter days of industrialism and the beginning of an ecological age? The ethical dilemma that confronts business begins with the acknowledgment that a commercial system that functions well by its own definitions unavoidably defies the greater and more profound ethic of biology. Specifically, how does business face the prospect that creating a profitable, growing company requires an intolerable abuse of the natural world?

Despite their dedicated good work, if we examine all or any of   6
the businesses that deservedly earn high marks for social and environmental responsibility, we are faced with a sobering irony: If every
company on the planet were to adopt the environmental and social
practices of the best companies—of, say, the Body Shop, Patagonia, and
Ben & Jerry's—the world would still be moving toward environmental
degradation and collapse. In other words, if we analyze environmental
effects and create an input-output model of resources and energy, the
results do not even approximate a tolerable or sustainable future. If
a tiny fraction of the world's most intelligent companies cannot model
a sustainable world, then that tells us that being socially responsible
is only one part of an overall solution, and that what we have is not
a management problem but a design problem.

At present, there is a contradiction inherent in the premise of a   7
socially responsible corporation: to wit, that a company can make the
world better, can grow, and can increase profits by meeting social and
environmental needs. It is a have-your-cake-and-eat-it fantasy that
cannot come true if the primary cause of environmental degradation
is overconsumption. Although proponents of socially responsible business are making an outstanding effort at reforming the tired old ethics
of commerce, they are unintentionally creating a new rationale for
companies to produce, advertise, expand, grow, capitalize, and use up
resources: the rationale that they are doing good. A jet flying across
the country, a car rented at an airport, an air-conditioned hotel room,
a truck full of goods, a worker commuting to his or her job—all
cause the same amount of environmental degradation whether they're
associated with the Body Shop, the Environmental Defense Fund, or
R. J. Reynolds.

In order to approximate a sustainable society, we need to describe a   8
system of commerce and production in which each and every act is
inherently sustainable and restorative. Because of the way our system
of commerce is designed, businesses will not be able to fulfill their
social contract with the environment or society until the system in
which they operate undergoes a fundamental change, a change that
brings commerce and governance into alignment with the natural
world from which we receive our life. There must be an integration
of economic, biologic, and human systems in order to create a sustainable and interdependent method of commerce that supports and fur-
thers our existence. As hard as we may strive to create sustainability
on a company level, we cannot fully succeed until the institutions

surrounding commerce are redesigned. Just as every act of production and consumption in an industrial society leads to further environmental degradation, regardless of intention or ethos, we need to imagine—and then design—a system of commerce where the opposite is true, where doing good is like falling off a log, where the natural, everyday acts of work and life accumulate into a better world as a matter of course, not a matter of altruism. A system of sustainable commerce would involve these objectives:

1. It would reduce absolute consumption of energy and natural resources among developed nations by 80 percent within 40 to 60 years.

2. It would provide secure, stable, and meaningful employment for people everywhere.

3. It would be self-actuating as opposed to regulated, controlled, mandated, or moralistic.

4. It would honor human nature and market principles.

5. It would be perceived as more desirable than our present way of life.

6. It would exceed sustainability by restoring degraded habitats and ecosystems to their fullest biological capacity.

7. It would rely on current solar income.

8. It should be fun and engaging, and strive for an aesthetic outcome.

Strategies for Sustainability

At present, the environmental and social responsibility movements consist of many different initiatives, connected primarily by values and beliefs rather than by design. What is needed is a conscious plan to create a sustainable future, including a set of design strategies for people to follow. For the record, I will suggest 12.

1. Take back the charter.

Although corporate charters may seem to have little to do with sustainability, they are critical to any long-term movement toward restoration of the planet. Read *Taking Care of Business: Citizenship and the Charter of Incorporation*, a 1992 pamphlet by Richard Grossman and Frank T. Adams (Charter Ink, Box 806, Cambridge, MA 02140). In it you find a lost history of corporate power and citizen involvement that addresses a basic and crucial point: Corporations are chartered by, and exist at the behest of, citizens. Incorporation is not a right but a privilege granted by the state that includes certain considerations such as limited liability. Corporations are supposed to be under our ultimate authority, not the other way around. The charter of incorporation is a revocable dispensation that was supposed to ensure accountability of the corporation to society as a whole. When Rockwell criminally despoils a weapons facility at Rocky Flats, Colorado, with plutonium waste, or when any corporation continually harms, abuses, or violates the public trust, citizens should have the right to revoke its charter, causing the company to disband, sell off its enterprises to other companies, and effectively go out of business. The workers would have jobs with the new owners, but the executives, directors, and management would be out of jobs, with a permanent notice on their résumés that they mismanaged a corporation into a charter revocation. This is not merely a deterrent to corporate abuse but a critical element of an ecological society because it creates feedback loops that prompt accountability, citizen involvement, and learning. We should remember that the citizens of this country originally envisioned corporations to be part of a public-private partnership, which is why the relationship between the chartering authority of state legislatures and the corporation was kept alive and active. They had it right.

2. Adjust price to reflect cost.

The economy is environmentally and commercially dysfunctional be- 11
cause the market does not provide consumers with proper information. The "free market" economies that we love so much are excellent at setting prices but lousy when it comes to recognizing costs. In order for a sustainable society to exist, every purchase must reflect or at least approximate its actual cost, not only the direct cost of production but also the costs to the air, water, and soil; the cost to future generations; the cost to worker health; the cost of waste, pollution, and toxicity. Simply stated, the marketplace gives us the wrong information. It tells us that flying across the country on a discount airline ticket is cheap when it is not. It tells us that our food is inexpensive when its method of production destroys aquifers and soil, the viability of ecosystems, and workers' lives. Whenever an organism gets wrong information, it is a form of toxicity. In fact, that is how pesticides work. A herbicide kills because it is a hormone that tells the plant to grow faster than its capacity to absorb nutrients allows. It literally grows itself to death. Sound familiar? Our daily doses of toxicity are

the prices in the marketplace. They are telling us to do the wrong thing for our own survival. They are lulling us into cutting down old-growth forests on the Olympic Peninsula for apple crates, into patterns of production and consumption that are not just unsustainable but profoundly shortsighted and destructive. It is surprising that "conservative" economists do not support or understand this idea, because it is they who insist that we pay as we go, have no debts, and take care of business. Let's do it.

3. Throw out and replace the entire tax system.

The present tax system sends the wrong messages to virtually everyone, encourages waste, discourages conservation, and rewards consumption. It taxes what we want to encourage—jobs, creativity, payrolls, and real income—and ignores the things we want to discourage—degradation, pollution, and depletion. The present U.S. tax system costs citizens $500 billion a year in record-keeping, filing, administrative, legal, and governmental costs—more than the actual amount we pay in personal income taxes. The only incentive in the present system is to cheat or hire a lawyer to cheat for us. The entire tax system must be incrementally replaced over a 20-year period by "Green fees," taxes that are added onto existing products, energy, services, and materials so that prices in the marketplace more closely approximate true costs. These taxes are not a means to raise revenue or bring down deficits, but must be absolutely revenue neutral so that people in the lower and middle classes experience no real change of income, only a shift in expenditures. Eventually, the cost of non-renewable resources, extractive energy, and industrial modes of production will be more expensive than renewable resources, such as solar energy, sustainable forestry, and biological methods of agriculture. Why should the upper-middle class be able to afford to conserve while the lower income classes cannot? So far the environmental movement has only made the world better for upper-middle class white people. The only kind of environmental movement that can succeed has to start from the bottom up. Under a Green fee system the incentives to save on taxes will create positive, constructive acts that are affordable for everyone. As energy prices go up to three to four times their existing levels (with commensurate tax reductions to offset the increase), the natural inclination to save money will result in carpooling, bicycling, telecommuting, public transport, and more efficient houses. As taxes on artificial fertilizers, pesticides, and fuel go up, again with offsetting reductions in income and payroll taxes, organic farmers will find that

12

their produce and methods are the cheapest means of production (because they truly are), and customers will find that organically grown food is less expensive than its commercial cousin. Eventually, with the probable exception of taxes on the rich, we will find ourselves in a position where we pay no taxes, but spend our money with a practiced and constructive discernment. Under an enlightened and redesigned tax system, the cheapest product in the marketplace would be best for the customer, the worker, the environment, and the company. That is rarely the case today.

4. Allow resource companies to be utilities.

An energy utility is an interesting hybrid of public-private interests. A utility gains a market monopoly in exchange for public control of rates, open books, and a guaranteed rate of return. Because of this relationship and the pioneering work of Amory Lovins, we now have markets for "negawatts." It is the first time in the history of industrialism that a corporation has figured out how to make money by selling the absence of something. Negawatts are the opposite of energy: They represent the collaborative ability of a utility to harness efficiency instead of hydrocarbons. This conservation-based alternative saves ratepayers, shareholders, and the company money—savings that are passed along to everyone. All resource systems, including oil, gas, forests, and water, should be run by some form of utility. There should be markets in negabarrels, negatrees, and negacoal. Oil companies, for example, have no alternative at present other than to lobby for the absurd, like drilling in the Arctic National Wildlife Refuge. That project, a $40 billion to $60 billion investment for a hoped-for supply of oil that would meet U.S. consumption needs for only six months, is the only way an oil company can make money under our current system of commerce. But what if the oil companies formed an oil utility and cut a deal with citizens and taxpayers that allowed them to "invest" in insulation, super-glazed windows, conservation rebates on new automobiles, and the scrapping of old cars? Through Green fees, we would pay them back a return on their conservation investment equal to what utilities receive, a rate of return that would be in accord with how many barrels of oil they save, rather than how many barrels they produce. Why should they care? Why should we? A $60 billion investment in conservation will yield, conservatively, four to ten times as much energy as drilling for oil. Given Lovins' principle of efficiency extraction, try to imagine a forest utility, a salmon utility, a copper utility, a Mississippi River utility, a grasslands utility. Imagine a system

13

where the resource utility benefits from conservation, makes money from efficiency, thrives through restoration, and profits from sustainability. It is possible today.

5. Change linear systems to cyclical ones.

Our economy has many design flaws, but the most glaring one is that nature is cyclical and industrialism is linear. In nature, no linear systems exist, or they don't exist for long because they exhaust themselves into extinction. Linear industrial systems take resources, transform them into products or services, discard waste, and sell to consumers, who discard more waste when they have consumed the product. But of course we don't consume TVs, cars, or most of the other stuff we buy. Instead, Americans produce six times their body weight every week in hazardous and toxic waste water, incinerator fly ash, agricultural wastes, heavy metals, and waste chemicals, paper, wood, etc. This does not include CO_2, which if it were included would double the amount of waste. Cyclical means of production are designed to imitate natural systems in which waste equals food for other forms of life, nothing is thrown away, and symbiosis replaces competition. Bill McDonough, a New York architect who has pioneered environmental design principles, has designed a system to retrofit every window in a major American city. Although it still awaits final approval, the project is planned to go like this: The city and a major window manufacturer form a joint venture to produce energy-saving super-glazed windows in the town. This partnership company will come to your house or business, measure all windows and glass doors, and then replace them with windows with an R-8 to R-12 energy-efficiency rating within 72 hours. The windows will have the same casements, molding, and general appearance as the old ones. You will receive a $500 check upon installation, and you will pay for the new windows over a 10- to 15-year period in your utility or tax bill. The total bill is less than the cost of the energy the windows will save. In other words, the windows will cost the home or business owner nothing. The city will pay for them initially with industrial development bonds. The factory will train and employ 300 disadvantaged people. The old windows will be completely recycled and reused, the glass melted into glass, the wooden frames ground up and mixed with recycled resins that are extruded to make the casements. When the city is reglazed, the residents and businesses will pocket an extra $20 million to $30 million every year in money saved on utility bills. After the windows are paid for, the figure will go even higher. The factory, designed to be transportable, will move

14

to another city; the first city will retain an equity interest in the venture. McDonough has designed a win-win-win-win-win system that optimizes a number of agendas. The ratepayers, the homeowners, the renters, the city, the environment, and the employed all thrive because they are "making" money from efficiency rather than exploitation. It's a little like running the industrial economy backwards.

6. Transform the making of things.

We have to institute the Intelligent Product System created by Michael   15
Braungart of the EPEA (Environmental Protection Encouragement Agency) in Hamburg, Germany. The system recognizes three types of products. The first are *consumables,* products that are either eaten, or, when they're placed on the ground, turn into dirt without any bioaccumulative effects. In other words, they are products whose waste equals food for other living systems. At present, many of the products that should be "consumable," like clothing and shoes, are not. Cotton cloth contains hundreds of different chemicals, plasticizers, defoliants, pesticides, and dyes; shoes are tanned with chromium and their soles contain lead; neckties and silk blouses contain zinc, tin, and toxic dye. Much of what we recycle today turns into toxic by-products, consuming more energy in the recycling process than is saved by recycling. We should be designing more things so that they can be thrown away—into the compost heap. Toothpaste tubes and other non-degradable packaging can be made out of natural polymers so that they break down and become fertilizer for plants. A package that turns into dirt is infinitely more useful, biologically speaking, than a package that turns into a plastic park bench. Heretical as it sounds, designing for decomposition, not recycling, is the way of the world around us.

The second category is *durables,* but in this case, they would not be   16
sold, only licensed. Cars, TVs, VCRs, and refrigerators would always belong to the original manufacturer, so they would be made, used, and returned within a closed-loop system. This is already being instituted in Germany and to a lesser extent in Japan, where companies are beginning to design for disassembly. If a company knows that its products will come back someday, and that it cannot throw anything away when they do, it creates a very different approach to design and materials.

Last, there are *unsalables*—toxins, radiation, heavy metals, and   17
chemicals. There is no living system for which these are food and thus they can never be thrown away. In Braungart's Intelligent Product System, unsalables must always belong to the original maker, safeguarded by public utilities called "parking lots" that store the toxins

in glass-lined barrels indefinitely, charging the original manufacturers rent for the service. The rent ceases when an independent scientific panel can confirm that there is a safe method to detoxify the substances in question. All toxic chemicals would have molecular markers identifying them as belonging to their originator, so that if they are found in wells, rivers, soil, or fish, it is the responsibility of the company to retrieve them and clean up. This places the problem of toxicity with the makers, where it belongs, making them responsible for full-life cycle effects.

7. Vote, don't buy.

Democracy has been effectively eliminated in America by the influence   18
of money, lawyers, and a political system that is the outgrowth of the first two. While we can dream of restoring our democractic system, the fact remains that we live in a plutocracy—government by the wealthy. One way out is to vote with your dollars, to withhold purchases from companies that act or respond inappropriately Don't just avoid buying a Mitsubishi automobile because of the company's participation in the destruction of primary forests in Malaysia, Indonesia, Ecuador, Brazil, Bolivia, Canada, Chile, Siberia, and Papua New Guinea. Write and tell them why you won't. Engage in dialogue, send one postcard a week, talk, organize, meet, publish newsletters, boycott, patronize, and communicate with companies like General Electric. Educate non-profits, organizations, municipalities, and pension funds to act affirmatively, to support the ecological CERES (formerly *Valdez*) Principles for business, to invest intelligently, and to *think* with their money, not merely spend it. Demand the best from the companies you work for and buy from. You deserve it and your actions will help them change.

8. Restore the "guardian."

There can be no healthy business sector unless there is a healthy   19
governing sector. In her book *Systems of Survival*, author Jane Jacobs describes two overarching moral syndromes that permeate our society: the commercial syndrome, which arose from trading cultures, and the governing, or guardian, syndrome that arose from territorial cultures. The guardian system is hierarchical, adheres to tradition, values loyalty, and shuns trading and inventiveness. The commercial system, on the other hand, is based on trading, so it values trust of outsiders, innovation, and future thinking. Each has qualities the other lacks. Whenever

the guardian tries to be in business, as in Eastern Europe, business doesn't work. What is also true, but not so obvious to us, is that when business plays government, governance fails as well. Our guardian system has almost completely broken down because of the money, power, influence, and control exercised by business and, to a lesser degree, other institutions. Business and unions have to get out of government. We need more than campaign reform: We need a vision that allows us all to see that when Speaker of the House Tom Foley exempts the aluminum industry in his district from the proposed Btu tax, or when Philip Morris donates $200,000 to the Jesse Helms Citizenship Center, citizenship is mocked and democracy is left gagging and twitching on the Capitol steps. The irony is that business thinks that its involvement in governance is good corporate citizenship or at least is advancing its own interests. The reality is that business is preventing the economy from evolving. Business loses, workers lose, the environment loses.

9. Shift from electronic literacy to biologic literacy.

That an average adult can recognize one thousand brand names and logos but fewer than ten local plants is not a good sign. We are moving not to an information age but to a biologic age, and unfortunately our technological education is equipping us for corporate markets, not the future. Sitting at home with virtual reality gloves, 3D video games, and interactive cable TV shopping is a barren and impoverished vision of the future. The computer revolution is not the totem of our future, only a tool. Don't get me wrong. Computers are great. But they are not an uplifting or compelling vision for culture or society. They do not move us toward a sustainable future any more than our obsession with cars and televisions provided us with newer definitions or richer meaning. We are moving into the age of living machines, not, as Corbusier noted, "machines for living in." The Thomas Edison of the future is not Bill Gates of Microsoft, but John and Nancy Todd, founders of the New Alchemy Institute, a Massachusetts design lab and think tank for sustainability. If the Todds' work seems less commercial, less successful, and less glamorous, it is because they are working on the real problem—how to live—and it is infinitely more complex than a microprocessor. Understanding biological processes is how we are going to create a new symbiosis with living systems (or perish). What we can learn on-line is how to model complex systems. It is computers that have allowed us to realize how the synapses in the

20

common sea slug are more powerful than all of our parallel processors
put together.

10. Take inventory.

We do not know how many species live on the planet within a factor   21
of ten. We do not know how many are being extirpated. We do not
know what is contained in the biological library inherited from the
Cenozoic age. (Sociobiologist E. O. Wilson estimates that it would
take 25,000 person-years to catalog most of the species, putting aside
the fact that there are only 1,500 people with the taxonomic ability
to undertake the task.) We do not know how complex systems interact—how the transpiration of the giant lily, *Victoria amazonica,* of
Brazil's rainforests affects European rainfall and agriculture, for example. We do not know what happens to 20 percent of the CO_2 that is
off-gassed every year (it disappears without a trace). We do not know
how to calculate sustainable yields in fisheries and forest systems. We
do not know why certain species, such as frogs, are dying out even
in pristine habitats. We do not know how the long-term effects of
chlorinated hydrocarbons on human health, behavior, sexuality, and
fertility. We do not know what a sustainable life is for existing inhabitants of the planet, and certainly not for future populations. (A Dutch
study calculated that your fair share of air travel is one trip across the
Atlantic in a lifetime.) We do not know how many people we can feed
on a sustainable basis, or what our diet would look like. In short, we
need to find out what's here, who has it, and what we can or can't
do with it.

11. Take care of human health.

The environmental and socially responsible movements would gain   22
additional credibility if they recognized that the greatest amount of
human suffering and mortality is caused by environmental problems
that are not being addressed by environmental organizations or companies. Contaminated water is killing a hundred times more people than
all other forms of pollution combined. Millions of children are dying
from preventable diseases and malnutrition.

   The movement toward sustainability must address the clear and   23
present dangers that people face worldwide, dangers that ironically
increase population levels because of their perceived threat. People
produce more children when they're afraid they'll lose them. Not until
the majority of the people in the world, all of whom suffer in myriad

preventable yet intolerable ways, understand that environmentalism means improving their lives directly will the ecology movement walk its talk. Americans will spend more money in the next 12 months on the movie and tchotchkes of *Jurassic Park* than on foreign aid to prevent malnutrition or provide safe water.

12. *Respect the human spirit.*

If hope is to pass the sobriety test, then it has to walk a pretty straight   24
line to reality. Nothing written, suggested, or proposed here is possible unless business is willing to integrate itself into the natural world. It is time for business to take the initiative in a genuinely open process of dialogue, collaboration, reflection, and redesign. "It is not enough," writes Jeremy Seabrook of the British Green party, "to declare, as many do, that we are living in an unsustainable way, using up resources, squandering the substance of the next generation however true this may be. People must feel subjectively the injustice and unsustainability before they will make a more sober assessment as to whether it is worth maintaining what is, or whether there might not be more equitable and satisfying ways that will not be won at the expense either of the necessities of the poor or of the wasting fabric of the planet."

Poet and naturalist W. S. Merwin (citing Robert Graves) reminds   25
us that we have one story, and one story only, to tell in our lives. We are made to believe by our parents and businesses, by our culture and televisions, by our politicians and movie stars that it is the story of money, of finance, of wealth, of the stock portfolio, the partnership, the country house. These are small, impoverished tales and whispers that have made us restless and craven; they are not stories at all. As author and garlic grower Stanley Crawford puts it, "The financial statement must finally give way to the narrative, with all its exceptions, special cases, imponderables. It must finally give way to the story, which is perhaps the way we arm ourselves against the next and always unpredictable turn of the cycle in the quixotic dare that is life; across the rock and cold of lifelines, it is our seed, our clove, our filament cast toward the future." It is something deeper than anything commercial culture can plumb, and it is waiting for each of us.

Business must yield to the longings of the human spirit.The most   26
important contribution of the socially responsible business movement has little to do with recycling, nuts from the rainforest, or employing the homeless. Their gift to us is that they are leading by trying to do something, to risk, take a chance, make a change—any change. They are not waiting for "the solution," but are acting without guarantees

of success or proof of purchase. This is what all of us must do. Being visionary has always been given a bad rap by commerce. But without a positive vision for humankind we can have no meaning, no work, and no purpose.

THINKING ABOUT THE CONTENT

1. Hawken believes that "Corporations, because they are the dominant institution on the planet, must squarely face the social and environmental problems that afflict humankind" (3). Is he correct? How are some of the companies he praises, like Ben and Jerry's, showing social responsibility? Why isn't what such companies are doing enough? What must companies do, according to Hawken, if there is to be a sustainable future?
2. Which of the twelve steps Hawken offers seems most operational? Which seem least likely to happen? What do you think of his plan? Is it too "visionary"? Do you think it could ever be put into effect? Why or why not?
3. What information regarding consumer consumption or industrial waste most surprised you? Will the information change your purchasing habits? Why or why not?
4. Are you concerned about the sustainability of the future? Is it important to worry about our environment? Would you work for a company that you knew was polluting or contributing to the waste of natural resources if you were earning a high salary or thought you could get no other job?

LOOKING AT STRUCTURE AND STYLE

5. How does Hawken's description of his "audit" of Ben and Jerry's in his opening paragraphs lead into his topic and thesis? Does it draw your interest? Why or why not?
6. What passages help develop Hawken's attitude and tone? Are they appropriate for his subject? Explain.
7. To whom is Hawken writing? Do you think Hawken is convincing enough to sway many heads of large corporations or stockholders in companies such as R. J. Reynolds, Lockheed, and General Electric to accept all or part of his plan? Why or why not?

EXPLORING DISCUSSION AND WRITING TOPICS

8. Respond to Hawken's plan by reacting to one of his twelve steps. Is it a feasible idea? What do you like or dislike about the step? What would it take to make it work?
9. Discuss in an essay what you think a particular company or corporation

could do to be more socially responsible. What would those changes do
to the company's profits?

10. In the mid-1990s Congress, under the guise of strengthening the economy,
    pushed hard "to get government out of business" by reducing corporate
    taxes, restrictions, and laws that reduced profits. Hawken says, "The
    reality is that business is preventing the economy from evolving" (19).
    Explain why you agree or disagree with him.

During the 1992 presidential election campaign, much rhetoric was heard about the need for personal responsibility. Since then, both liberals and conservatives have infused their political agendas with talk of morality and responsibility. In the following essay, which appeared in the November 29, 1993, issue of *In These Times,* David Futrelle argues that "progressives need to realize that vague talk of responsibility is not enough to counter the moralistic onslaught from the right." In Futrelle's view, "Conservatives have seized upon the notion of responsibility with an opportunistic fervor. But liberals and leftists have fared poorly in their attempts to incorporate the notion into a broader communitarian politics." Futrelle attempts to show what needs to be done if liberals are going "to articulate a vision of social responsibility that goes beyond cliché."

Surplus Values

Conservatives talk about values with a certain assurance. When Dan Quayle attacked Murphy Brown's "lifestyle choice," with a straight face and a sonorous tone, he did so in the name of "family, hard work, integrity and personal responsibility." When in the heat of the culture war Rep. William Dannemeyer (R-CA) attacked "obscene" art, he did so, he said, to protect "the Judeo-Christian ethic" from "Hollywood, homosexuals, abortionists, family planners, the sexually promiscuous, failed spouses, failed parents, failed kids" and all other such outgrowths of secular humanism. And when Rush Limbaugh assails the left (and the liberals he takes to be the left) he does so in the name of "those corny old traditional values."

Those on the left are more circumspect in their moralizing. And there are good reasons for the left to look upon talk of values with suspicion. Talk of morality is divisive; it often has been (and still is) used to stigmatize those who deviate (for good reason or bad) from the confines of convention. Too often, talk of morality and responsibility takes the form of veiled accusation: I am responsible, you are not; I am moral, you are immoral. Such accusations are an affront to the liberal value of tolerance.

While conservatives hesitate not a moment before invoking the   3
gods of decency, responsibility and the like, the left hedges its language,
speaking instead of abstract, seemingly objective qualities like justice
and equality. But these terms are less abstract and objective than they
appear: to speak of justice (and its opposite partner, injustice) we have
to have at first made a value judgment, or, rather, a series of value
judgments as to what is good and what is bad, what is acceptable and
what is unacceptable. The left, no less than the right, engages in a
politics of morality (and often, of moralism); but it is a politics that
in many ways, and in most cases, hides and denies its moral content.
(Generally, only those whose progressive politics stem from religious
conviction are willing to talk explicitly about morality.)

It is no wonder, then, that so many liberals respond with a guilty   4
defensiveness when the subject of "values" comes up. When prominent
citizens announce that our society is coming apart at the seams, we
can hardly disagree. Yet while we agree with the diagnosis, we look
upon the individualistic, symbolic solutions of the moralistic right with
a certain dismay. We don't want to stigmatize anyone, to make, say,
gays and women the scapegoats for family "decay." And we can hardly,
all by ourselves, "rush about revitalizing the family and renewing
respect for the law," as historian Robert Wiebe has observed. We're
stuck in a bind. "If we respond, we have difficulty knowing where to
begin," Wiebe notes. "Yet if we shrug and hide, we invite society to
go bankrupt around us."

Given such a distressing possibility, it is hardly a surprise that some   5
liberals (and a few vaguely on the left) have attempted to recapture the
language of morality—and, in particular, the language of responsibility—from the right. Some have done so with a notable opportunism—
like Bill Clinton, whose appeals to "personal responsibility" during
the campaign seemed less an attempt to infuse morality into the political realm as a coded message to white voters that he would be tough
with the "underclass."

Others have attempted to work the language of responsibility   6
into a broader, and explicitly progressive, morality. Michael Lerner,
the editor of the Jewish left-liberal journal *Tikkun*, argues that
progressives need to overcome their resistance to talking the language
of moral values. "It is pure self-delusion to think that moral values
can be kept out of politics," he writes. Indeed, "values [have] already
. . . entered the public sphere." During the Reagan-Bush years, in
fact, "right-wing values were triumphing because liberals refused to
enter the debate." Denouncing the Reaganite excesses of individualism
and greed, Lerner calls for liberals to "challenge the ethos of

selfishness and replace it with an ethos of caring, social responsibility, trust and mutual aid."

This notion of *social* responsibility is, at least in theory, a challenge   7
to the traditional American notion of *individual* responsibility. Yet liberals have not had a notable success in pushing the debate on responsibility to the left, away from individualism and toward the notion of "mutual aid." In attempting both to adapt to and to challenge the ideological constructs of the right, liberals have found themselves listing considerably (and increasingly) to the right. The notions of social or corporate responsibility—however laudable as ideas—have degenerated into public relations ploys on the part of businesses eager to convince customers that their products and procedures are ecologically and socially "responsible." And when liberals speak, as they increasingly do, of individual responsibility, it is often impossible to distinguish their version from that of the right.

The notion of responsibility is, indeed, burdened with a consider-   8
able historical and ideological weight. American popular philosophy has long been rooted in the country's myth of rugged individualism, the ideology of choice for a frontier capitalism. "Every man and woman in society has one big duty. That is, to take care of his or her own self," wrote William Graham Sumner, the economist and Social Darwinist philosopher, in 1883.

The notion of social responsibility, to Sumner, was a contradiction   9
in terms; the redistribution of money from the "fit" to the "unfit," Sumner argued, could only result in disaster. Every dollar given to a beggar, to "a shiftless and inefficient member of society," was one stolen, in effect, from the hands of the "productive laborer" who would have benefited directly from the dollar's wise investment.

Few these days would put their argument as starkly as Sumner—   10
and few would argue, as he did, that "a drunkard in the gutter is just where he ought to be," on the receiving end of Nature's just retribution. But much of the contemporary discussion of "responsibility"—among the right and even among many liberals—has a distinctly Victorian ring, combining an old-style moralism (and an equally old-fashioned faith in upward mobility) with the latest in psychological jargon. Discussions of responsibility today, just as they did in Victorian times, tend to turn quickly to the subject of the allegedly "irresponsible" poor.

Well-fed experts on the "underclass" laud each other in the pages   11
of prominent magazines for their supposed courage in restating what has now, once again, become the conventional wisdom: those who are poor are somehow deficient, dysfunctional, different, "undeserving"—in short, irresponsible.

This argument, as historian Jacqueline Jones has suggested, "serves   12
a larger political purpose, for it encourages some people to believe
that the poor positively revel in their own misery, that they shun
stable marriages and steady employment almost as a matter of perverse
principle. According to this view, the poor live in a different country,
living a life that is as incomprehensible as it is self-destructive."

We can read, in any number of recent books and articles, exquisite   13
explorations of the supposed "pathologies" of the poor, relying on
long-distance psychoanalysis of their "dysfunctions" and "dependency." Taking refuge in a reductive misreading of psychology, the
poverty experts present draconian welfare "reforms" as tough love for
childlike welfare "dependents." The problem with the poor, in this
model, is that we give them too much money; we coddle them and
make them weak. If we were to cut off their benefits, they would be
able to learn discipline and good character; thus cured of the psychic
wounds of "dependency," they too could climb (or claw) their way to
the top.

The political implications of the underclass model are apparent   14
enough. *The New Republic,* for example, in its editorial response
to the L.A. riots, fell into the classic language of blame-the-victim
neoliberalism. "The black underclass perpetuates racial division in this
country," the editors confidently announced. "It has helped weaken
the American city, speeding up white flight to the suburbs and decreasing the level of black-white geographic contact. When black-white
mixing does occur, the powerful image of the black underclass . . .
has served to stigmatize the vast majority of middle-class blacks, and
to powerfully perpetuate the racism of whites." The editors, warming
up to the task, called sternly for politicians to "break underclass culture," to "break through this culture of idleness, poverty, illegitimacy,
and crime" by tearing down the welfare system, "the critical sustaining
element in the life of the underclass."

This approach has its own internal logic; if you buy its central   15
assumptions these draconian policy suggestions make a certain sense.
But since much of the conventional wisdom about the underclass is
based less on facts than myths, the stern moralism of *The New Republic*
editors (like that of most of those who pontificate most confidently
on the subject) is at best irrelevant to the problems of the poor, and
in many ways actively harmful.

In reality, the poor suffer not from their own deficient natures,   16
but from a lack of good jobs; from segregation and governmental
neglect; from an educational system riddled with savage inequalities.
Indeed, poverty today is less the result of "idleness" or "illegitimacy"
than of poor wages. In contemporary America, Jones observes, "much

of the widening gap between the rich and the poor result[s] not from the growing ranks of the unemployed, but from the worsening relative position of two-parent families that [cannot] earn a living wage."

Few who have adopted the term "underclass"—as a generic reference for the demonized urban black poor—have gone to the trouble of defining the term with any precision. Not surprisingly, there is no real consensus over what, if anything, the term denotes. Some define virtually *all* urban poor people as part of the underclass; others reserve the term for the "deviant" minority of drug sellers, criminals and so on. Journalist Ken Auletta, whose 1982 book *The Underclass* popularized the term, defines the group by its "behavioral deficiencies," as a collection of misfits "operating outside the generally accepted boundaries of society . . . set apart by their 'deviant' or anti-social behavior, by their bad habits, not just their poverty." Academic Isabel Sawhill offers a simpler, if somewhat inexact, definition: the underclass consists of "people who engage in bad behavior or a set of bad behaviors."

Aside from the obvious candidates for "bad behavior"—drug dealing, mugging and the like—it has been the putatively deviant family structure of the underclass that has received the most attention from the think-tankers. We have been assured, over and over again for the last decade or so, that black fathers are "irresponsible" deserters, that similarly "irresponsible" black single mothers produce children at whim (or to increase their AFDC allotment), and that the instability of the black family has led to the social instability of the urban core.

In fact, many of the commonly asserted (and accepted) "facts" about the underclass are at best misleading, and at worst deliberate distortions. Most poor people are white, and poverty is as much rural as urban. Many among the urban poor fit few of the stereotypical characteristics ascribed to the underclass, such as single motherhood and persistent (if not willful) unemployment. As historian Stephanie Coontz points out, the majority of "the persistently poor urban black population . . . have one or more of the characteristics usually associated with the 'deserving poor': they are elderly, seriously disabled, or employed for a substantial portion of the year."

Black single mothers have been singled out for special opprobrium, denounced as opportunistic welfare chiselers producing babies for profit. In fact, though the percentage of black households headed by single women is high, and growing, the birthrates for black teenagers, far from spiraling out of control, have actually been *dropping* for the last few decades. And, though poverty pundits are convinced that AFDC payments are a major incentive to out-of-wedlock births, there is no real evidence of this; some researchers have found what appears to be an opposite effect. States with meager welfare benefits (like

17

18

19

20

Mississippi) have high rates of illegitimate births, while those with
relatively more generous benefits have lower rates. In fact, as sociologist Mark Rank reports, "welfare mothers" tend to have low fertility
rates during the times when they are receiving benefits.

The common remedy proposed by the poverty pundits is simple   21
discipline. In his notorious 1967 report on the "negro family," Daniel
Patrick Moynihan suggested that the "utterly masculine world" of
military service would provide black men an escape route of sorts from
the "disorganized and matrifocal family life in which so many negro
youths come of age . . . a world run by strong men of unquestioned
authority, where discipline, if harsh, is nonetheless orderly and predict-
able." Aside from the punitive condescension of Moynihan's language—not to mention his sexism—there are a few technical problems
with his solution to underclass pathology: studies have shown that
military families have higher rates of divorce, drug abuse and family
violence than other families.

More generally, poverty pundits turn to work as the salve for   22
underclass indiscipline. Any kind of work will do. Sawhill, for example,
sees the unwillingness of the urban poor "to take a low-paid job" as
a key example of underclass pathology. *New Republic* senior editor
Mickey Kaus, in his book *The End of Equality,* suggests that we
simply get rid of welfare, replacing the "underclass culture's life support
system" with the offer of sub-minimum wage jobs for all who are
"able" and willing to work—including single mothers with children.
Those who *aren't* willing to work will just have to survive without
money, relying on soup kitchens and homeless shelters; their children
will end up in orphanages. (Kaus assures us, like some latter-day
Herbert Hoover, that "nobody would starve.")

What Kaus forgets is that work (if it is of a sufficiently menial   23
sort, as so much of it is) can be as destructive to dignity as idleness.
It is true that the central problem of the underclass is the lack of
jobs—that the inner cities have been left stranded, over the last several
decades, as jobs have fled to the suburbs. But not *any* job will do.
Kaus, like many among the more comfortable members of society,
may find satisfaction and fulfillment in his work; single mothers flip-
ping burgers at McDonald's may not be quite so fulfilled. When "underclass" youths denounce the low pay of the degrading jobs available
to them as "chump change"—the poverty pundits never tire of repeating this phrase, for them the ultimate indication of a willful indolence—they are, in fact, in their own way, asserting a certain dignity.

It goes without saying that such an impulse, unless channelled in   24
a properly political way, may simply lead (as it does too often today)
to a self-defeating nihilism—to drugs, gangs and crime, to all the

familiar curses of the poor. Such behavior is rightly condemned. But the impulse behind such behavior does not itself flow from nihilism; in the refusal to accept the confines of the status quo we should see, rather, the potential for hope.

The conservatives are right about one thing: we on the left need   25 to speak more, and more explicitly, about dignity. Glenn C. Loury, the black neocon, is right when he argues that "the pride and self-respect valued by aspiring peoples throughout the world cannot be the gift of outsiders," and that "neither the guilt nor the pity of one's oppressor is a sufficient basis upon which to construct a sense of self-worth."

But Loury is wrong to argue that anyone—black, white, or what-   26 ever—should simply ignore the effects of past (and present) discrimination, and even more wrong to assume that "if we are to be a truly free people, we must accept responsibility for our fate even when it does not lie wholly in our hands." Why? It is not improper for someone who has faced injustice to demand redress; such a demand hardly reflects a poor sense of self-worth or an abdication of responsibility.

Over the last few years, conservatives have expended considerable   27 energy (and have shown a certain crackpot creativity) in their attempts to redefine the notion of "victimhood" in such a way that no one but the most extravagantly oppressed (and most obviously "innocent," that is, quiescent) victims count as legitimate recipients of public sympathy (not to mention public funding). In *A Nation of Victims*, for example, conservative polemicist Charles Sykes argues that "genuine victims" face their greatest dangers not from oppression but from "bogus victims" moving in on their turf. Rather than attempting to honestly weigh the claims of those who have, indeed, been victimized, Sykes argues that we should instead just declare a "moratorium on blame"—a convenient way to simply avoid the subject altogether.

If conservative thinkers have seized upon the notion of responsibil-   28 ity with an opportunistic fervor, liberals and leftists have fared poorly, to say the least, in their attempts to incorporate the notion into a broader "communitarian" agenda. Amitai Etzioni, a leading communitarian thinker and the author of the recent manifesto *The Spirit of Community*, argues (like Sykes) that the discourse of rights needs to give way to a discourse of responsibilities.

The progressive side of Etzioni's critique is his denunciation of   29 Reaganite greed; beyond that, though, his critique is hard to distinguish from that of the moralists on his right. Like the conservatives, he believes that social justice derives, first and foremost, from the moral responsibility of individuals "to help themselves as best they can"; responsibility to family, and to the broader community, comes second.

And, as sociologist Charles Derber has pointed out, Etzioni's communitarian vision is strikingly blind to the question of power: "Etzioni . . . seems to suggest that if we simply resolve to recharge our moral sensibilities and reform our families, schools and political campaigns, we will not have to attend to the explosively divisive issues of economic transformation." Even worse, Etzioni's pleas for an inclusive politics are belied by his contempt for ordinary working people, whom he dismisses in large part as small-minded bigots, "less progressive than Ronald Reagan [and] only a bit more ready for communitarian economics than the Chamber of Commerce."

More broadly, and with a notable lack of personal modesty, Michael Lerner has attempted (in the pages of *Tikkun* and elsewhere) to promote a vague and vacuous ideological concoction of social and moral responsibility he calls the "Politics of Meaning." [See the essay by Michael Lerner on pages 121 to 131.] The goals of Lerner's movement are certainly ambitious enough: he hopes that "over the course of the next two decades" he will be able to insinuate his "values-oriented, psychologically and spiritually sensitive approach" into "every area of contemporary thought and activity." It's not clear, though, that anyone would notice if he did; there's precious little meaning to the Politics of Meaning. Lerner's philosophy—an attempt to "deeply address the human needs for love, connection, meaning and purpose in a humane way"—manages to be both trivial and pretentious at once, as if one could provide "meaning" to life by simply repeating the word like a mantra.   30

Like his rhetoric, Lerner's specific policy recommendations lean heavily on the power of symbolism, and range from the meaningless (he asks Clinton to "create a new public discourse of caring, social responsibility, idealism and commitment to ethical, spiritual and ecological sensitivity") to the silly (he suggests that every congressional district hold a yearly contest to determine the 20 families that have "produced children who were, by age 18, the most loving, caring, honest, responsible and supportive people in their communities"). Lerner supports workfare, and though he declares himself against "alienated labor," he derides those who "talk about workers' rights without talking about their responsibilities as well." When faced with the specter of "irresponsible" workers, Lerner (uncharacteristically) turns stern: "The economy is not a bottomless cookie jar for us to reach in and remove goodies whenever we want." Most of us figured that out a long time ago, thank you.   31

But if Lerner has had his problems with the philosophy, he's had a notable success with the promotion: in April, Hillary Rodham Clinton delivered a speech drawing heavily on Lerner's rhetorical invocations   32 of caring and community. But there was an interesting slip that took place during the transit of Lerner's ideas from the page to Hillary's lips: Lerner called, you may recall, for "an ethos of caring and social responsibility." Hillary called, instead, for "a new ethos of individual responsibility and caring."

It wasn't just the order of the phrases that Hillary reversed; she changed the adjective as well—and by extension the political meaning of her call for meaning. There's a world of difference between those two adjectives—*social* and *individual*—though Lerner (like most liberals) appears not to understand (or even to have noticed) the crucial shift.   33

This is a perfect example of why the liberal invocation of responsibility has been so unsuccessful. Unable to distinguish between individual and social responsibility (or unable to recognize that the difference is important), those on the left hope that vague talk of values will be enough to offset the moralistic onslaught on the right. Unless liberals (and, more properly, those on the left) are able to articulate a vision of social responsibility that goes beyond cliché, and to talk about personal dignity without giving in to the illusions of *laissez-faire* individualism, all the newly popular talk about responsibility will merely help to grease the further slide of liberalism to the right. *That* would be irresponsible.   34

THINKING ABOUT THE CONTENT

1. Futrelle says that there is good reason for the left to look upon talk of values with suspicion. What reasons does he give? Do you agree? Why or why not?

2. When you hear the phrase *traditional values,* what values come to mind? Are they concrete? Are they values all of society should follow? Explain.

3. What does Futrelle mean by his title, "Surplus Values"?

4. Why does Futrelle believe it is difficult for those on the left to make their definition of responsibility clear? Why is there a conflict between individual responsibility and social responsibility in the United States?

5. How does the author respond to what he says is the current "conventional wisdom: those who are poor are somehow deficient, dysfunctional, different, 'undeserving'—in short, irresponsible" (11)? Do you agree with the conventional wisdom? Explain.

6. What, according to Futrelle, is wrong with the term *underclass?* Why? What arguments does he present?

7. Futrelle argues that when so-called underclass youths rebel against low pay that "they are . . . in their own way, asserting a certain dignity" (23). Is he right, or do you think such a refusal is an excuse for indolence?

8. What must those on the left do if they are to offset the "moralistic onslaught of the right"?

LOOKING AT STRUCTURE AND STYLE

9. Scan the essay and count the number of other works Futrelle cites in his essay. Is this an advantage or disadvantage in supporting his argument? How are they used?
10. Describe the essay's tone. What are some phrases that contribute to the tone?
11. How effective is the last paragraph in clarifying where the author stands on responsibility.

EXPLORING DISCUSSION AND WRITING TOPICS

12. Read one of the works mentioned in Futrelle's essay. Does he interpret the work correctly? Is he fair in his appraisal?
13. Follow a current political event for a period of a few days. How frequently is the language of responsibility and morality used? Do these terms as used go beyond cliché?
14. Write a definition of *social responsibility* that you think Futrelle might accept.

ROBERT S. MCNAMARA

Robert S. McNamara was secretary of defense for Presidents John F. Kennedy and Lyndon B. Johnson in the 1960s. In 1995, almost thirty years later, McNamara published *In Retrospect,* his account of Vietnam War policymaking from the highest levels. His book discusses what he thinks Kennedy would have done regarding Vietnam had he lived. He reveals the agony Johnson went through and how it damaged his presidency. And he shares some of the arguments and secret meetings that occurred over the Vietnam policy.

McNamara, at first believing that fighting communism in Southeast Asia was necessary, helped lead the United States into a war with Vietnam. He believed in the domino effect, that if Vietnam fell under communist rule, more Asia countries would fall one by one. In his position, he was fully aware of all the events that led us into the war and its continual escalation of manpower, weapons, and casualties. Gradually, he came to believe the war was unwinnable but failed to make his position public because he felt it was his duty and responsibility to support his government's position.

The following selection comes from McNamara's book.

🥀

From In Retrospect

The wars we fight in the post–Cold War world are likely more often than not to be "limited wars," like Vietnam. General Westmoreland made a comment about Vietnam at an LBJ Library Conference in March 1991 that is relevant here. Referring to the constraints that kept the Vietnam War "limited," he said: "At the time I felt that our hands were tied," but "we have to give President Johnson credit for *not* allowing the war to expand geographically [emphasis in original]." Certainly Vietnam taught us how immensely difficult it is to fight limited wars leading to U.S. casualties over long periods of time. But circumstances will arise where limited war is far preferable to unlimited war. Before engaging in such conflicts, the American people must understand the difficulties we will face; the American military must know and accept the constraints under which they will operate; and our leaders—and our people—must be prepared to cut our losses and withdraw if it appears our limited objectives cannot be achieved at acceptable risks or costs.

We must learn from Vietnam how to manage limited wars effectively. A major cause of the debacle there lay in our failure to establish an organization of top civilian and military officials capable of directing the task. Over and over again, as my story of the decision-making process makes shockingly clear, we failed to address fundamental issues; our failure to identify them was not recognized; and deep-seated disagreements among the president's advisers about how to proceed were neither surfaced nor resolved.

As I have suggested, this resulted in part from our failure to organize properly. No senior person in Washington dealt *solely* with Vietnam. With the president, the secretaries of state and defense, the national security adviser, the chairman of the Joint Chiefs, and their associates dividing their attention over a host of complex and demanding issues, some of our shortcomings—in particular, our failure to debate systemically the most fundamental issues—could have been predicted. To avoid these, we should have established a full-time team at the highest level—what Churchill called a War Cabinet—focused on Vietnam and nothing else. At a minimum, it should have included deputies of the secretaries of state and defense, the national security adviser, the chairman of the Joint Chiefs, and the CIA director. It should have met weekly with the president at prescribed times for long, uninterrupted discussions. The weekly meetings should have been expanded monthly to include the U.S. ambassador and U.S. military commander in Vietnam. The meetings should have been characterized by the openness and candor of Executive Committee deliberations during the Cuban Missile Crisis—which contributed to the avoidance of a catastrophe. Similar organizational arrangements should be established to direct all future military operations.

Finally, we must recognize that the consequences of large-scale military operations—particularly in this age of highly sophisticated and destructive weapons—are inherently difficult to predict and to control. Therefore, they must be avoided, excepting only when our nation's security is clearly and directly threatened. These are the lessons of Vietnam. Pray God we learn them.

I want to add a final word on Vietnam.

Let me be simple and direct—I want to be clearly understood: the United States of America fought in Vietnam for eight years for what it believed to be good and honest reasons. By such action, administrations of both parties sought to protect our security, prevent the spread of totalitarian Communism, and promote individual freedom and political democracy. The Kennedy, Johnson, and Nixon administrations made their decisions and by those decisions demanded sacrifices and, yes, inflicted terrible suffering in light of those goals and values.

Their hindsight was better than their foresight. The adage echoes   7
down the corridors of time, applying to many individuals, in many situations, in many ages. People are human; they are fallible. I concede with painful candor and a heavy heart that the adage applies to me and to my generation of American leadership regarding Vietnam. Although we sought to do the right thing—and believed we were doing the right thing—in my judgment, hindsight proves us wrong. We both overestimated the effect of South Vietnam's loss on the security of the West and failed to adhere to the fundamental principle that, in the final analysis, if the South Vietnamese were to be saved, they had to win the war themselves. Straying from this central truth, we built a progressively more massive effort on an inherently unstable foundation. External military force cannot substitute for the political order and stability that must be forged *by* a people *for* themselves.

In the end, we must confront the fate of those Americans who   8
served in Vietnam and never returned. Does the unwisdom of our intervention nullify their effort and their loss? I think not. They did not make the decisions. They answered their nation's call to service. They went in harm's way on its behalf. And they gave their lives for their country and its ideals. That our effort in Vietnam proved unwise does not make their sacrifice less noble. It endures for all to see. Let us learn from their sacrifice and, by doing so, validate and honor it.

THINKING ABOUT THE CONTENT

1. McNamara admits that in hindsight the United States' involvement in Vietnam was wrong. Does he seem to be taking responsibility for his involvement in the war or making excuses?

2. Do you think during the escalation of the war effort in the 1960s that McNamara should have expressed his views to the public that he did not believe the war was winnable? Did he have a higher responsibility as secretary of state than to remain quiet and support his presidents?

3. McNamara says he now knows that "if the South Vietnamese were to be saved, they had to win the war themselves," placing the responsibility on the people of South Vietnam (7). Should this be a policy regarding our military involvement in the problems of other nations? Is there ever a

time when the United States should be responsible for sending military troops to another country to fight an internal war?

4. Based on the organization failures McNamara lists in paragraph 2, does it appear the Vietnam situation was handled responsibly? Do you think current or future administrations will learn from these past mistakes? Will his advice be heard by the powers that be?

LOOKING AT STRUCTURE AND STYLE

5. Describe McNamara's tone.
6. To whom is McNamara writing?

EXPLORING DISCUSSION AND WRITING TOPICS

7. Why do you think it took McNamara so long to make his views on Vietnam public? Does it matter? Is the way he chose to do it appropriate?
8. As a Vietnam veteran or family member of a veteran, respond to McNamara's statement, "Although we sought to do the right thing—and believed we were doing the right thing—in my judgment, hindsight proves us wrong" (7).
9. McNamara says, "Let us learn from their [servicemen and women] sacrifice and, by so doing, validate and honor it" (8). What was learned that can be validated and honored?

Upon publication of Robert McNamara's book *In Retrospect,* many magazines and newspapers chastised the author for taking so long to divulge his belief that the Vietnam War was mishandled by the Kennedy and Johnson Administrations and that actions taken were often based on deceit to different sections of the administration as well as to the public.

One of the newspapers that showed McNamara little mercy for his part in the Vietnam debacle was the *New York Times,* whose editorial follows.

☙

Thousands of Days of Error

Comes now Robert McNamara with the announcement that he has   1
in the fullness of time grasped realities that seemed readily apparent
to millions of Americans throughout the Vietnam War. At the time,
he appeared to be helping an obsessed president prosecute a war of
no real consequence to the security of the United States. Millions of
loyal citizens concluded that the war was a militarily unnecessary and
politically futile effort to prop up a corrupt government that could
neither reform nor defend itself.

Through all the bloody years, those were the facts as they appeared   2
on the surface. Therefore, only one argument could be advanced to
clear President Lyndon Johnson and Mr. McNamara, his secretary of
defense, of the charge of wasting lives atrociously. That was the theory
that they possessed superior knowledge, not available to the public,
that the collapse of South Vietnam would lead to regional and perhaps
world domination by the Communists; and moreover, that their superior knowledge was so compelling it rendered unreliable and untrue
the apparent facts available to even the most expert opponents of the
war.

With a few throwaway lines in his new book, "In Retrospect,"   3
Mr. McNamara admits that such knowledge never existed. Indeed, as
they made the fateful first steps toward heavier fighting in the late
1963 and 1964, Mr. Johnson and his cabinet "had not truly investigated
what was essentially at stake and important to us."

As for testing their public position that only a wider war would 4
avail in the circumstances, "We never stopped to explore fully whether
there were other routes to our destination." Such sentences break the
heart while making clear that Mr. McNamara must not escape the
lasting moral condemnation of his countrymen.

Mr. McNamara wants us to know that he, too, realized by 1967 5
that the dissidents were right, that the war had to be stopped to avoid
"a major national disaster." Even so, he wants us to grant that his
delicate sense of protocol excused him from any obligation to join the
national debate over whether American troops should continue to die
at the rate of hundreds per week in a war he knew to be futile. Mr.
McNamara believes that retired cabinet members should not criticize
the presidents they served no matter how much the American people
need to know the truth. In his view, the president can never become
so steeped in a misguided war that patriotic duty would compel a
statement.

Perhaps the only value of "In Retrospect" is to remind us never 6
to forget that these were men who in the full hubristic glow of their
power would not listen to logical warning or ethical appeal. When
senior figures talked sense to Mr. Johnson and Mr. McNamara, they
were ignored or dismissed from government. When young people in
the ranks brought that message, they were court-martialed. When
young people in the streets shouted it, they were hounded from the
country.

It is important to remember how fate dispensed rewards and 7
punishment for Mr. McNamara's thousands of days of error. Three
million Vietnamese died. Fifty-eight thousand Americans got to come
home in body bags. Mr. McNamara, while tormented by his role in
the war, got a sinecure at the World Bank and summers at Martha's
Vineyard.

So much has changed since those horrendous times. Americans 8
have belatedly recognized the heroism of the U.S. troops who served
in good faith because they, in their innocence, could not fathom the
mendacity of their elders. But another set of heroes—the thousands
of students who returned the nation to sanity by chanting. "Hell, no,
we won't go"—is under renewed attack from a band of politicians
who sat out the war on student or family deferments. In that sense
we are still living in the wreckage created by the cabinet on which Mr.
McNamara served.

His regret cannot be huge enough to balance the books for our 9
dead soldiers. The ghosts of those unlived lives circle close around Mr.
McNamara. Surely he must in every quiet and prosperous moment

hear the ceaseless whispers of those poor boys in the infantry, dying in the tall grass, platoon by platoon, for no purpose. What he took from them cannot be repaid by prime-time apology and stale tears, three decades late.

Mr. McNamara says he weeps easily and has strong feelings when   10
he visits the Vietnam Memorial. But he says he will not speak of those feelings. Yet someone must, for that black wall is wide with the names of people who died in a war that he did not, at first, carefully research nor, in the end, believe to be necessary.

THINKING ABOUT THE CONTENT

1. According to the editorial, what knowledge would have to be advanced to show that President Johnson and McNamara were correct in advancing the war in Vietnam? Does such knowledge exist?
2. The editorial holds McNamara responsible for his deceit while in office and states that, "Mr. McNamara must not escape the lasting moral condemnation of his countrymen" (4). Do you agree? Why or why not?
3. Reread paragraph 6. Those who took on personal and social responsibility to bring the war to an end often felt harmful results. Why did the administration ignore or persecute them? How does such conduct cause people to think twice before acting personally or socially responsible where government is concerned?
4. The editorial states that in McNamara's view "the president can never become so steeped in a misguided war that patriotic duty would compel a statement" (5). Is this an example of a conflict between personal responsibility and social responsibility? Explain.

LOOKING AT STRUCTURE AND STYLE

5. Discuss the tone of the essay. What are some passages that contribute to the tone?
6. The editorial makes itself clear on its reaction to McNamara's book and on him personally. Discuss its opinions of both and how they are revealed.

EXPLORING DISCUSSION AND WRITING TOPICS

7. How should one react to reports of government deceit? Should we be cynical and accept it as a part of the way government works? Do we have a responsibility to try to change such behavior? Can anything be done?

8. Assume you were one of the anti-Vietnam protesters who were "hounded from the country" (6). What would you have to say to McNamara after reading reports of his book?

9. Do you think McNamara's book will have any effect on present-day politics? Why or why not? Have any lessons been learned from *In Retrospect*, and if so by whom?

ANDREW FERGUSON

Andrew Ferguson is a senior editor at the *Weekly Standard*. Like the editors at the *New York Times* in the previous reading selection ("Thousands of Days of Error"), Ferguson is not about to forgive Robert McNamara for his part in the Vietnam war policymaking establishment. But Ferguson goes beyond what he sees as McNamara's irresponsibility, claiming that McNamara is "spiritual father" to all the "Washington people who fail up."

Amidst all of Ferguson's displeasure with McNamara is the unstated question: Why do we seem to honor or award irresponsible people in politics?

The following essay is from the July 10, 1995, issue of *National Review*.

McNamara's Brand

I'm a little bit worried. As I write this, in early June, it's been a full month since I've read a nationally published article trashing Robert McNamara. All spring, immediately preceding the publication of McNamara's memoirs and then for a luscious period thereafter, you couldn't pick up a magazine or a reputable newspaper without exposing yourself to a shower of bile, all of it directed at our diminutive and bespectacled former secretary of defense. *NR* and *The American Spectator* pitched in, of course, but so did the *New York Times* and the *Boston Globe*, and *Time* and *Newsweek,* and *The New Yorker* and *The New Republic*—even *The Nation!* For a while there, many of us McNamara-despisers thought we'd died and gone to heaven (a fate, incidentally, that McNamara himself is unlikely to enjoy).

And then—silence. What gives? Apparently the scribes have moved on; never has the press's short attention span been so criminally obvious. I feel like a guy at a college beer bust who senses the buzz just starting to kick in and wants to *part-ay down,* only to discover that everybody has gone off to the library to cram for a chem final. But for all that, I am an optimist; I am one of those who believe the keg is half full rather than half empty. And speaking only for myself, I'm ready for another draft.

My interest in McNamara is intensified because he exemplifies a   3
peculiar Washington phenomenon. In Washington people fail up. The
city is exempt from the laws of professional gravity. No other city is
so accommodating of failure, so friendly to the people who fail. Large
awards await the bunglers and bobblers, the has-beens and wannabees-
who-never-could. Our present mayor, to cite an obvious example,
destroyed the city's finances, smoked crack on TV, went to prison—and
then got reelected. Other failures have shown greater artfulness. You
can see them cruising K Street in chauffeured Town Cars, cashing large
checks for their "consulting" businesses, digging into filets at the Palm.
Here's the Iran–Contra bungler, awarded a popular radio show for his
work destroying the Reagan Administration. Over there is the manager
of the 1992 Bush campaign, mulling offers from candidates to work
his magic again in 1996. And over here is the chief strategist for Jimmy
Carter during the Iranian hostage crisis—why, he's the secretary of
state!

McNamara is spiritual father to them all. He is the architect of a   4
career breathtaking in the scope of its screw-ups, a clockwork progres-
sion of failure and reward, error and advancement. Imagine a friend
who comes to visit. The first night he cooks you dinner and sets fire
to the kitchen. The next morning he accidentally electrocutes the cat.
He blows his nose in the curtains and never flushes the toilet. He
borrows your car and drives through the garage door, then spreads a
rare contagion to your kids. By the third day you make the decision:
You ask him to move in with you.

This is the pattern of McNamara's career. At Ford Motors, in the   5
late 1950s, he designed the sclerotic top-down management system
that almost sank the American automobile industry; for good measure,
he oversaw the production of the Edsel. Accordingly, JFK handed him
the Pentagon. There McNamara got the idea for the Vietnam War—the
Edsel of American foreign policy. So awed was the Washington establishment that it placed him at the head of the World Bank, in hopes
that he might do for the international economy what he had done
for the American military. And he did! Within ten years he had doubled
the amount of money loaned, and lost, to Third World kleptocracies
like Brazil and the Central African Empire. He was Midas in reverse.
Wherever he draped his hand, industries wilted, economies collapsed,
corpses piled up.

No one should have been surprised, then, that when McNamara   6
chose to write the story of his life, it should have turned out to be a
disaster by every literary measure: mendacious, sentimental, shameless
in its exculpation, oily in its tone, a book so badly written that no

one would ever really want to buy it. And of course it has been a rousing bestseller.

How does one explain a life thus charmed? His good looks? They   7 may indeed have dazzled back in the days when no one minded goofy wire rims and the stink of Brylcreem. His sensitivity? It's true he cried often, and still does—the one time I met him, at a think-tank luncheon, he teared up over the Cuban Missile Crisis—and in the pre–Alan Alda Sixties a man's capacity to cry could still disarm unwary companions. But none of this is sufficient. Washington's inverted culture, where failure propels a man ever upward, bespeaks a kind of masochism. Of course, the actual pain is dispersed to the country at large. But for the professional failure Washington remains safe harbor. Within weeks of the publication of the book, McNamara had been called "evil," a "liar," and a "hypocrite." Out in the heartland, a few Vietnam vets even sued him. Here in Washington Katharine Graham threw him a book party. Everybody who's anybody was there.

THINKING ABOUT THE CONTENT

1. What does Ferguson add to your knowledge regarding McNamara? Is what he says important in evaluating McNamara's role in Vietnam War policymaking? Why or why not?

2. Why do you think Ferguson feels the "press's short attention span" regarding McNamara and his book is "criminally obvious" (2)? What does he seem to want? Do you agree with him? Why or why not?

3. How well does Ferguson support his indictment of McNamara? Are his examples valid? Is his essay a "responsible" piece of journalism? Explain.

LOOKING AT STRUCTURE AND STYLE

4. Ferguson's title carries dual meanings. How well does it fit the content of the essay?

5. Ferguson doesn't name names in paragraph 3. What does this tell you about his audience? What group of people would know who he is talking about?

6. What are some words or phrases that develop Ferguson's tone and attitude?

EXPLORING DISCUSSION AND WRITING TOPICS

7. React to Ferguson's statement that "Washington's inverted culture, where failure propels a man ever upward, bespeaks a kind of masochism" (7). Who is the masochist? What examples are there to support his statement?

8. Write an evaluation or critique of Ferguson's essay.
9. Read some or all of McNamara's book *In Retrospect* and write your own review. Is it, as Ferguson says, "a disaster by every literary measure: mendacious, sentimental, shameless in it exculpation" (6)?

SOME RESEARCH SOURCES ON THE ISSUE OF RESPONSIBILITY

The following sources may be useful if you choose to do more reading or pursue a research project dealing with issues prompted by the reading selections in this unit.

Bellah, Robert N., et al. *Habits of the Heart.* New York: Harper, 1985.

Chavez, Linda. *Out of the Barrio.* New York: HarperCollins, 1991.

Corwin, Norman. *Trivializing America.* Secaucus, NJ.: Lyle Stuart, 1986.

Derber, Charles. *Money, Murder, and the American Dream.* Winchester, MA: Faber, 1992.

Edelman, Marian Wright. *The Measure of Our Success.* Boston: Beacon Press, 1992.

Fallows, Deborah. *A Mother's Work.* Boston: Houghton Mifflin, 1985.

Goldsmith, Suzanne. *A City Year: On the Streets and in the Neighborhoods with Twelve Young Community Service Volunteers.* New York: New Press, 1993.

Krishnamurti, J. *The First and Last Freedom.* New York, Harper, 1954.

Lasch, Christopher. *The Minimal Self.* New York: Norton, 1984.

McNamara, Robert. *In Retrospect.* New York: Random House, 1995.

Moyers, Bill, ed. "Sissela Bok," *A World of Ideas.* New York: Doubleday, 1989. 236–248.

Piller, Charles. *The Fail-Safe Society: Community Defiance and the End of American Technological Optimism.* New York: HarperCollins, 1991.

Robin, Peggy. *Saving the Neighborhood: You Can Fight Development and Win.* New York: Woodbine, 1992.

Schrank, Jeffrey. *Snap, Crackle, and Popular Taste.* New York: Dell, 1977.

Sevy, Grace, ed. *The American Experience in Vietnam.* Norman: University of Oklahoma Press, 1989.

Steele, Shelby. *The Content of Our Character.* New York: St. Martin's, 1990.

Utne Reader. September/October 1993 issue.

Zaller, John R. *The Nature and Origins of Mass Opinion.* New York: Cambridge, 1992.

Media

Were it left to me to decide whether we should have a government without newspapers or newspapers without government, I should not hesitate a moment to prefer the latter.

—THOMAS JEFFERSON

Newspapers are the world's mirrors.

—JAMES ELLIS

From the American newspapers you'd think America was populated solely by naked women and cinema stars.

—LADY ASTOR

Journalists do not live by words alone, although sometimes they have to eat them.

—ADLAI E. STEVENSON

Damn all expurgated books; the dirtiest book of all is the expurgated book.

—WALT WHITMAN

Only the suppressed word is dangerous.

—LUDWIG BÖRNE

Every burned book enlightens the world.

—RALPH WALDO EMERSON

He is always the severest censor of the merit of others who has the least worth of his own.

—ELIAS LYMAN MAGGON

Censorship reflects a society's lack of confidence in itself.

—POTTER STEWART

Television is a corporate vulgarity.

—JOHN LEONARD

Time has convinced me of one thing: Television is for appearing on—not for looking at.

—NOEL COWARD

I hate television. I hate it as much as peanuts. But I can't stop eating peanuts.

—ORSON WELLES

IT IS DIFFICULT TO ESCAPE FROM THE MEDIA. BESIDES AROUND-THE-clock radio and television providing nonstop information and entertainment, we can chose from four or five movies playing at the cineplex, or rent movies and documentaries at our local video store, or pick from dozens of magazine titles displayed in bookstores and newsstands, or just pick up the daily newspaper delivered to our home. As cable television continues to provide us with more and more outlets, national and international publications compete for more readers, and with some movies and television programs portraying graphic violence and sex, many people worry about the influence of mass media on society. Along with this, parental concerns over what books students should and should not read frequently flair up in the schools.

"The media's power is seen in its degrading influence not only on the nation's morals, but on everything else: national defense, the environment, nuclear power, economics, and virtually every area of life," writes Tim LaHaye in *The Hidden Censors*. According to David S. Barry in an article for *Media & Values*, the average American child will have watched 100,000 acts of media violence by the time he or she leaves elementary school. Says Barry, "Study after study shows a direct causal link between screen violence and violent criminal behavior." In "Television," a *USA Today* piece, Larry Woiwode concludes that television reduces people's ability to think critically: "TV teaches people *not* to read. It renders them incapable of engaging in an activity that now is perceived as strenuous, because it is not a passive hypnotized state." Nor do MTV and rock and rap videos escape criticism. The MTV show "Beavis and Butthead" was blamed for giving a five-year-old boy the idea for setting fire to his family's trailer in which his babysitter was burned to death. In Rob Lamp's article, "The World of 'Dark Rock' " in *The New American*, Dr. David Guttman claims, "Rock has so often been involved in these things [e.g., violence, teen suicide] many of us in psychiatry have had to take it more seriously." Carl Jensen, founder of Project Censored and author of the yearbook *Censored: The News that Didn't Make the News—and Why*, says, "Despite the surfeit of news and information, you and 250 million other Americans aren't being told everything you need—and have a right—to know. The fact is, we are victims of subtle but pervasive forms of censorship." Thus, many people are convinced that there are bad elements in what we read, hear, and watch which need to be monitored, boycotted, censored, or even "uncensored."

On the other hand, other commentators disagree that media has much negative influence on our behavior. For instance, Mike Males argues in his "Public Enemy Number One?" from *In These Times* that research into the effects of media violence is unreliable and that, "The best evidence shows that media violence is a small, derivative influence compared to the real-life violence . . . that our children face." The same article quotes columnist Carl T. Rowan saying, "The politicians won't or can't, deal with the real-life social problems that promote violence in America . . . so they try to make TV programs and movies the scapegoats!" In his book *Teleliteracy*, David Bianculli, a television critic reminds those who complain about the ill effects of television: "People who complain about TV's constant availability, like those who complain about its profane and violent content, seem to forget that every set comes equipped with both a channel changer and an on-off switch." Patricia Marks Greenfield in *Mind and Media* argues that "Television and film can . . . be used to enhance the comprehension and enjoyment of literature." And Leo N. Miletich, in an article for *Reason* magazine, writes that for centuries music has been attacked as dangerous to good morals and warns against those who want to censor what they don't like: "Thinking for yourself *is* dangerous. It carries with it the possibility of error as well as the weight of personal responsibility. For some people, that's too heavy a burden. They certainly have the right to denounce anything they don't like. But when they move to take what they don't like away from you, away from me, that's un-American. That's censorship."

All forms of the media seem to be held up to scrutiny. The readings in this unit will put you into contact with several of the current controversies that surround various aspect of the media.

BEN H. BAGDIKIAN

We like to think that the United States has a free press, that the news we receive is unbiased and uncensored. But is it? For several years now, Carl Jensen, founder and director of Project Censored, has been publishing a yearbook containing major stories that were censored or rejected by the mainstream media. According to Jensen in *Censored: The News that Didn't Make the News—and Why,* "The press is keeping a closely guarded secret from you and other Americans: despite your constitutional rights to free speech and a free press, you're only getting part of the information you need to be well informed about the world around you."

Ben H. Bagdikian, author of *The Media Monopoly* and former assistant managing editor of the *Washington Post,* reveals that in 1990 a mere twenty-three corporations owned and controlled all the media outlets in the United States. In the following essay from *Mother Jones,* Bagdikian believes the media has "sold out" to big business.

🌿

Journalism of Joy

In a roundup of the 1991 recession, an intriguing article in the *New*   1
York Times contained this paragraph: "There is little mystery about what caused the economic problems. The country is suffering a hangover from the mergers, rampant speculation, overbuilding, heavy borrowing and irresponsible government fiscal policy in the 1980s."

It's true. There is little mystery about how the 1980s caused our   2
economic (and social) problems. But if you watched television and read the daily papers during that era, you did not receive a picture of the accumulating wreckage produced by Reaganism. You were fed a steady diet of positive news about the "miracle" of the 1980s, the brilliant achievements of the "Reagan Revolution."

If it's all so unmysterious now, where was our news establishment   3
at the time? Did it sell out?

In a word, yes. And it's clear why it did. The great majority of   4
big media owners have always been happier with conservative Republicans, but in the 1980s they had reason to be ecstatic; as they were dispensing their relentlessly positive news about Reaganism, they were

being allowed by the government to create giant, monopolistic media empires.

During the 1980s, for example, the three big news networks were taken over by corporations that might have been deemed unqualified under earlier standards set by the Federal Communications Commission. ABC went to Capital Cities, a large newspaper chain whose acquisition increased cross-media domination. NBC was taken over by General Electric, which not only has a major stake in the news as a leading defense contractor and maker of nuclear reactors but has a remarkable history of convictions for fraud and antitrust violations. And a big real-estate operator, Laurence Tisch, took over CBS and decimated what used to be the best news and documentary operation in the United States.

The FCC also relieved broadcasters of traditional requirements for public service, made it almost impossible for citizen groups to challenge renewal of station licenses, and lifted limits on the number of stations that a single corporation can acquire.

The owners of the daily print press got their share of special government treatment too. The daily-news business was already controlled by monopolies in 98 percent of U.S cities, but in the 1980s the administration further sedated the antitrust laws to permit the biggest newspaper chains to sweep up these local monopolies. In addition, the National Labor Relations Board became stacked with pro-management members, and the media giants went on a ten-year spree of union busting.

Like all of big business, the broadcasters and print publishers benefited from Reagan's shift of corporate taxes onto the middle class and poor, but Americans did not see much coverage of that on television or in the printed news. Ditto with unemployment. To this day, joblessness continues to be reported as though it were a mysterious plague falling unbidden from heaven rather than a natural result of the speculative corporate debt, financial manipulations that rewarded big investors but weakened the products, and fabulous rake-offs by the merger artists of the 1980s.

When, for example, Time, Inc., and Warner Communications were permitted to merge into the world's largest media firm, the descriptions in the news were like those of all big mergers. It was an exciting battle between empire builders; it would produce more efficiency and creative "synergy." As in other cases, when citing "winners" and "losers" in the takeover battles, the news mentioned only the Wall Street adventurers, not the workers and consumers. Only in 1990 did we learn that one of the merger operators who manipulated the Time-Warner deal,

Steven Ross, received an annual compensation of seventy-eight million
dollars. The next year he laid off six hundred Time, Inc., employees.

It is clear why owners were happy to delude themselves and the   10
public about Reaganism. But what about the 100,000 print and broadcast journalists who did the actual reporting and editing? Did they,
too, sell out the American public?

Unlike their bosses, the majority of working journalists certainly   11
did not acquire more money or power during the 1980s. Like the rest
of the middle class, they experienced a decline in real purchasing power.

Journalists as a class are hardly exempt from the sins of vanity,   12
sloth, or greed, but this does not explain the misrepresentation of
reality that they helped create. For one thing, during the 1980s, local
print and broadcast news outlets periodically produced serious stories
about the growing economic and social problems in their own communities. The same was true from time to time at the national level.
Though major network documentaries practically disappeared, an occasional mini-documentary produced powerful evidence of the social
dislocations caused by Washington policies; daily newspapers occasionally reported the underside of the 1980s, as well.

But for every story of that kind there were dozens of the cheerlead-   13
ing variety, which quickly wiped out the impact of the critical stories.
Isolated reports seldom frame the citizen's view of the world; rather,
news items that are treated briefly and not pursued soon become
forgotten bits of flotsam and jetsam in the great tides of information
that hourly and daily inundate the public. It is the *pattern* of coverage
that creates the dominant impression.

Nevertheless, even the occasional bits of realistic news were   14
enough to bring White House complaints to media owners and executives. Any negative story was in danger of official condemnation.
Meanwhile, the president's spin doctors were orchestrating daily photo
ops and sound bites, which were meant to brush aside any notion that
all was not well at 1600 Pennsylvania Avenue or in the country.

Media owners and managers openly spread the idea in U.S. news-   15
rooms that the news needed to be upbeat. Allen Neuharth, then chief
of Gannett, the country's largest newspaper chain, announced that it was
time for reporters to practice what he called the "journalism of hope."

Soon, the normal restraint exercised by most media owners over   16
inserting corporate propaganda into the news crumbled. For twenty
years, neoconservative intellectuals had been hammering U.S. journalists as liberal ideologues who tilted the news against business and
conservatives, often against the reporters' own bosses. It was an absurd
claim, given the similarity of voting patterns between journalists and

all professionals with college educations in the liberal arts. Even so, the campaign bore spectacular fruit. There has always been pressure in newsrooms to "prove you are not being unfair to conservatives." In the 1980s, it simply reached new levels of mandated blindness.

Systematically, David Gergen and other White House "communications" operatives complained to news executives that stories exposing gross consequences of Reagan policies—growing hunger, unemployment, poverty—were "unfair" and "unbalanced," invoking the magic words of the twenty-year campaign against independent journalism. These complaints found sympathetic ears among owners and top editors.   17

If, in the field, a correspondent showed the White House to be lying, as did the *New York Times'* Ray Bonner in El Salvador, that reporter was pulled back in favor of more congenial correspondents. Eventually, this process led to reporters such as Shirley Christian covering the area. Her stories, it would be fair to say, seemed closer to those that people like Elliott Abrams and Oliver North would favor. It is no surprise that the Iran-contra operation was disclosed by an obscure magazine in Beirut and not by any of the three thousand U.S. correspondents in Washington.   18

When reporters tried to penetrate the propaganda barricade at the White House, their own managements blocked their efforts. One example involved coverage of the president himself. The White House wanted to project an image of the titular leader of the "Reagan Revolution" as a shrewdly insightful, compelling visionary of policy, a natural genius in command of his administration.   19

The truth was that, left on his own with reporters, Reagan would have revealed himself to be one of the most ignorant men ever elected president, beating out even Calvin Coolidge, whose picture Reagan proudly remounted in the White House. He was subject to alarming fantasies about himself, slept through crucial meetings, and, even when awake, was easily confused by his own three-by-five cue cards.   20

What Reagan was really good at was B-movie acting—the cocky toss of the head, the gee-whiz smile of the guy next door, and the John Wayne posture on horseback. So the White House media staff came up with the ideal strategy: no words, just pictures, pictures, pictures. As reported by journalist Mark Hertsgaard, the president's media managers ordered Washington news bureaus to stop sending reporters to cover daily events like visits by foreign leaders. Only TV cameras and still photographers would be permitted. The reporters rebelled, but their home offices ordered them to obey. The result was the constant countrywide repetition on TV and front pages of the image of a masterful policy chief.   21

The owners' abandonment of their reporters gave White House   22
propaganda a free ticket into the nation's news. During his administration, the media regularly referred to Reagan as the most popular president in the history of U.S. public-opinion polling, even though basic
Gallup survey data showed he was not. Franklin Roosevelt, Eisenhower, Kennedy, and Johnson had higher peaks; all except Johnson
had higher averages. But the White Houses's spin doctors got away
with their own version.

The eagerness of media owners to accept the propaganda is what   23
did the trick. And the false image of the most popular president in
history intimidated his opponents. After Reagan left office, Michael
Deaver, coordinator of White House image making, admitted that
"Reagan enjoyed the most generous treatment by the press of any
president in the postwar era."

The mechanism by which owners control the news succeeds be-   24
cause it is invisible to the public. All owners carefully select their top
editor or producer with their corporate needs in mind. In turn, this news
executive assigns reporters and camerapeople and decides whether the
stories and footage that come back will be used or thrown out, whether
they will lead the news report emphatically or be relegated to brevity
and obscurity, whether they will be pursued as a theme in future stories
or dropped at once. No owner hires a top news executive who is expected
to spoil the owner's breakfast too often, nor keeps one who does.

Top editors have always been meticulously screened to make sure   25
that they will not be inclined to offend corporate desires. But during
the 1980s, a new twist was added: top editors were made part of the
business-management team, responsible for keeping up ad linage and
often sent to business schools for special training to make them think
more like corporate executives.

To intensify corporate control over top editors, most newspapers   26
now grant annual bonuses and stock options for those who remain in
the good graces of the business side. One example, though more grandi-
ose than for most newspapers, involves the managing editors of Time,
Inc.'s, publications. They receive about $250,000 in annual salary, plus
bonuses of from 50 to 75 percent of this figure—all at the discretion of
corporate bosses. In addition, many *Time*'s editors have options letting
them buy stock that in the past has sold for as high as $182. They,
like many newspaper editors, can, if they continue to please the corporation, retire as millionaires. It is not surprising that these editors start
thinking more like stockbrokers and less like journalists.

Owners and media companies vary in the latitude they permit   27
editors and news staffs. But even firms with the best journalistic reputations will eject esteemed editors and producers if they do not sufficiently

conform to corporate wishes. Gene Roberts is probably the most respected news editor of this generation. More than anyone else, he personally fashioned and operated the strategy that converted the old *Philadelphia Inquirer* from a national joke to one of the most respected (and prosperous) newspapers in the country. The result was a daily that swept the field in its city and region. Then, last year, Roberts unexpectedly "resigned." As with most such disappearances, the victim said little in public to condemn his old paper and bosses, but his closest associates made it plain that the reason for his departure was his refusal to accept new conditions laid down by the parent firm, Knight-Ridder. The same thing happened to Bill Kovach, the editor who reversed the downward slide of the *Atlanta Journal & Constitution* and reestablished it as a respectable force in its area. He had reported important news that too often embarrassed powerful friends of the owners.

28   Editors learn from these emblematic events. The result is deep and widespread self-censorship from the top down in U.S. journalism. The internalized censorship can continue for years or decades after a single, dramatic demonstration by an owner shows that serious punishment will follow if independent news judgments offend that owner's politics or friends.

29   The same conditioning and self-censorship occur even more readily among reporters. Like their editors, reporters do not need constant reminders of the penalty for defying censorship imposed from the top. In 1982, a time when such stories, if reported nationally, might have prevented the current banking disasters, Earl Golz, a reporter with thirteen years of experience at the *Dallas Morning News,* wrote that federal bank examiners were alarmed about a local bank with unannounced bad loans. After the bank chairman told the paper's owners that Golz's report was a lie, Golz was fired, as was the editor who had approved the story. The bank failed two weeks later, and the examiners forced the dismissal of the chairman who had indignantly denied everything. But neither the reporter nor his editor was rehired. For a long time thereafter, no reporter or editor needed to be told that stories that anger influential bankers may end your career.

30   Even the most courageous reporter stops wasting time on stories that won't get on the air or into the paper. Self-censorship becomes epidemic. But it is an invisible epidemic, and all the harder to counter because the public never finds out about it.

31   Most censorship remains invisible for an ironic reason. Journalistic ethics among working reporters have risen enough to make it embarrassing if the censoring hand of the corporation leaves telltale fingerprints on the news. A frank statement by an editor to a reporter

that a story was killed for corporate reasons could end up in one of the country's journalism reviews, or even at another news outlet. For example, when Golz and his editor were fired because of the Dallas bank affair, the *Wall Street Journal* carried the whole embarrassing story.

Owners, like their journalists, have egos. And they prefer to avoid   32
negative publicity that could also affect favorability of the medium for advertising. So most owners have learned not to post embarrassing memoranda. Except for a few crude operations, editors no longer tell reporters, "The boss wants no more stories like this." Instead, reporters are given professionally acceptable reasons. These include decisions that could be legitimate editing judgments, like "No one's interested in that" or "We did that once." When the real reason involves orders from above or corporate anger at the truth, it is never stated.

Lawrence Grossman, former head of NBC News, revealed recently   33
that, following the stock-market crash in 1987, Jack Welch, CEO of NBC's owner, General Electric, called to say that he did not want the network's newscasts to use language that might depress GE stock. Grossman says he did not tell his staff about the call. He has not disclosed whether the private pressure from the top affected his decisions over what to allow on the news.

There is another management practice that may deeply diminish   34
good journalism for a long time. More than ever before, major news corporations are conducting systematic screenings of new reporters to keep out journalists who might not readily comply with corporate wishes or who might join newsroom unions. Some major news companies, including the nation's second-largest newspaper chain, Knight-Ridder, do the screening through mandatory, lengthy psychological questionnaires of all potential new reporters. Others, including some papers in the largest newspaper chain, Gannett, order editors to be deliberately blunt in interviews so that the applicants know the company wants only "team players" who will not rock the boat and are not in favor of unions. Hiring reporters who are not inclined to question authority is one way to guarantee bad journalism.

While there is widespread cynicism about such procedures, they   35
seem to have had real consequences. Ben Bradlee, former editor of the *Washington Post,* says that, today, "reporters are more conservative than the previous generation." Older correspondents in the gulf war, for instance, were appalled by the number of younger war correspondents who reported transparent military propaganda as if it were fact.

It is not simple to change trends like these. Strictly for profit   36
reasons, the news monopolies tend to hew closely to overwhelming public sentiment. Consequently, it will take a real alteration of the country's political and social atmosphere to force the media to work

harder to serve the public more and its owners' favorite political and economic causes less.

But viewers and readers are not powerless. Protests to the media   37
can produce some change. Clear and individually composed letters and phone calls seldom fail to make an internal impact, even if news organizations pretend they do not. Without such audience response, complaints from the organized right-wing and the powerful will dominate pressure on the news. In the end, the media needs the audience to stay in business.

Within journalism, professional news staffs in corporate media   38
should be permitted to elect their own top editor and have a substantial voice in long-range journalistic policies, as is done at some of the most prestigious newspapers in Europe. This would decrease the invisible corporate influence over the news But such a reform will not come until media owners recognize that the public is losing confidence in increasingly monopolistic and arrogant industry.

During the degradations of the 1980s, government lying was too   39
willingly supported by the media; high crimes and misdemeanors by the president of the United States became an accepted public boast; looting the public treasury and cheating the citizens were treated by most editors as necessary for liberation of the marketplace. For almost ten years, the media remained silent on the obvious—that Reaganite politics were taking a frightful toll in human suffering and crippling the economy.

The mass media gave the country a dismal demonstration of what   40
George Orwell saw forty years ago: ". . . political chaos is connected with the decay of the language. . . . Political language is designed to make lies sound truthful and murder respectable, and to give an appearance of solidity to pure wind."

From that kind of public morality neither the country nor journal-   41
ism will soon recover.

THINKING ABOUT THE CONTENT

1. What, according to the author, are the mechanisms by which the media owners control the news? How do editors and reporters fit into this mechanism? Do these accusations seem plausible? Why or why not?

2. What does Bagdikian mean by "self-censorship among reporters"? Why does he call self-censorship "an invisible epidemic" (30)? What did such approach to providing the news in the 1980s cover up, according to Bagdikian?

3. What does Bagdikian recommend viewers and readers of the news do to combat what he calls "journalism of joy"? Why will it be difficult to

change the course of news media trends? Are you concerned enough to be more alert regarding news reporting? Why or why not?

4. According to Carl Jensen's 1993 Project Censored yearbook, this article was suppressed by major news media outlets in 1992. Why do you think it was?

LOOKING AT STRUCTURE AND STYLE

5. How well does Bagdikian support his thesis? What kind of support does he provide? Is it convincing? Why or why not?

EXPLORING DISCUSSION AND WRITING TOPICS

6. Have other media takeovers occurred since Bagdikian wrote this article? Who owns the major television networks? Who controls the print news media? Does it matter? Why or why not?

7. Since news media outlets are in business to make a profit for their owners, is it possible for us to receive well-balanced news? What power does the media have? What dangers are there to society when news media outlets are controlled by so few?

Reprinted by permission. Courtesy of Dan Perkins.

PATRICIA J. WILLIAMS

Patricia J. Williams is a professor of law at Columbia University and author of *The Alchemy of Race and Rights*. In the following selection from the March/April 1994 issue of *Ms.* magazine, Williams examines the growing acceptance of *hate radio*, a term she uses for the likes of Rush Limbaugh, Howard Stern, and Bob Grant. Although the First Amendment allows freedom of speech, Williams worries that what she is listening to on the radio is "a large segment of white America think[ing] aloud," and that viewpoint "is a crude demagoguery that makes me heartsick." Since media can provoke violence, Williams wonders why "the very powerful leadership of the Republican party, from Ronald Reagan to Robert Dole to William Bennett," are "giving advice, counsel, and friendship to Rush Limbaugh's passionate divisiveness."

🌿

Hate Radio

Three years ago I stood at my sink, washing the dishes and listening 1 to the radio. I was tuned to rock and roll so I could avoid thinking about the big news from the day before—George Bush had just nominated Clarence Thomas to replace Thurgood Marshall on the Supreme Court. I was squeezing a dot of lemon Joy into each of the wineglasses when I realized that two smoothly radio-cultured voices, a man's and a woman's, had replaced the music.

"I think it's a stroke of genius on the president's part," said the 2 female voice.

"Yeah," said the male voice. "Then those blacks, those African 3 Americans, those Negroes—hey 'Negro' is good enough for Thurgood Marshall—whatever, they can't make up their minds [what] they want to be called. I'm gonna call them Blafricans. Black Africans. Yeah, I like it. Blafricans. Then they can get all upset because now the president appointed a Blafrican."

"Yeah, well, that's the way those liberals think. It's just crazy." 4

"And then after they turn down his nomination the president can 5 say he tried to please 'em, and then he can appoint someone with some intelligence."

Back then, this conversation seemed so horrendously unusual, so   6
singularly hateful, that I picked up a pencil and wrote it down. I was
certain that a firestorm of protest was going to engulf the station and
purge those foul radio mouths with the good clean soap of social
outrage.

I am so naive. When I finally turned on the radio and rolled my   7
dial to where everyone else had been tuned while I was busy watching
Cosby reruns, it took me a while to understand that there's a firestorm
all right, but not of protest. In the two and a half years since Thomas has
assumed his post on the Supreme Court, the underlying assumptions of
the conversation I heard as uniquely outrageous have become commonplace, popularly expressed, and louder in volume. I hear the style of
that snide polemicism everywhere, among acquaintances, on the street,
on television in toned-down versions. It is a crude demagoguery that
makes me heartsick. I feel more and more surrounded by that point
of view, the assumptions of being without intelligence, the coded epithets, the "Blafrican"-like stand-ins for "nigger," the mocking angry
glee, the endless tirades filled with nonspecific, nonempirically based
slurs against "these people" or "those minorities" or "feminazis" or
"liberals" or "scumbags" or "pansies" or "jerks" or "sleazeballs" or
"loonies" or "animals" or "foreigners."

At the same time I am not so naive as to suppose that this is   8
something new. In clearheaded moments I realize I am not listening
to the radio anymore, I am listening to a large segment of white America
think aloud in ever louder resurgent thoughts that have generations of
historical precedent. It's as though the radio has split open like an egg,
Morton Downey, Jr.'s clones and Joe McCarthy's ghost spilling out,
broken yolks, a great collective of sometimes clever, sometimes small,
but uniformly threatened brains—they have all come gushing out. Just
as they were about to pass into oblivion, Jack Benny and his humble
black sidekick Rochester get resurrected in the ungainly bodies of
Howard Stern and his faithful black henchwoman, Robin Quivers.
The culture of Amos and Andy has been revived and reassembled
in Bob Grant's radio minstrelsy and radio newcomer Daryl Gates's
sanctimonious imprecations on behalf of decent white people. And in
striking imitation of Jesse Helms's nearly forgotten days as a radio
host, the far Right has found its undisputed king in the personage of
Rush Limbaugh—a polished demagogue with a weekly radio audience
of at least 20 million, a television show that vies for ratings with the
likes of Jay Leno, a newsletter with a circulation of 380,000, and two
best-selling books whose combined sales are closing in on six million
copies.

From Churchill to Hitler to the old Soviet Union, it's clear that   9
radio and television have the power to change the course of history,
to proselytize, and to coalesce not merely the good and the noble, but
the very worst in human nature as well. Likewise, when Orson Welles
made his famous radio broadcast "witnessing" the landing of a space-
ship full of hostile Martians, the United States ought to have learned
a lesson about the power of radio to appeal to mass instincts and
incite mass hysteria. Radio remains a peculiarly powerful medium even
today, its visual emptiness in a world of six trillion flashing images
allowing one of the few remaining playgrounds for the aural subcon-
scious. Perhaps its power is attributable to our need for an oral tradition
after all, some conveying of stories, feelings, myths of ancestors, epics
of alienation, and the need to rejoin ancestral roots, even ignorant
bigoted roots. Perhaps the visual quiescence of radio is related to the
popularity of E-mail or electronic networking. Only the voice is made
manifest, unmasking worlds that cannot—or dare not?—be seen. Just
yet. Nostalgia crystallizing into a dangerous future. The preconscious
voice erupting into the expressed, the prime time.

What comes out of the modern radio mouth could be the *Iliad,*   10
the *Rubaiyat,* the griot's song of our times. If indeed radio is a vessel
for the American "Song of Songs," then what does it mean that a
manic, adolescent Howard Stern is so popular among radio listeners,
that Rush Limbaugh's wittily smooth sadism has gone the way of
prime-time television, and that both vie for the number one slot on
all the best-selling book lists? What to make of the stories being told
by our modern radio evangelists and their tragic unloved chorus of
callers? Is it really just a collapsing economy that spawns this drama
of grown people sitting around scaring themselves to death with fantasies of black feminist Mexican able-bodied gay soldiers earning
$100,000 a year on welfare who are so criminally depraved that Hillary
Clinton or the Antichrist-of-the-moment had no choice but to invite
them onto the government payroll so they can run the country? The
panicky exaggeration reminds me of a child's fear. . . . *And then,
and then, a huge lion jumped out of the shadows and was about to
gobble me up, and I can't ever sleep again for a whole week.*

As I spin the dial on my radio, I can't help thinking that this stuff   11
must be related to that most poignant of fiber-optic phenomena, phone
sex. Aural Sex. Radio Racism with a touch of S & M. High-priest
hosts with the power and run-amok ego to discipline listeners, to
smack with the verbal back of the hand, to smash the button that
shuts you up once and for all. "Idiot!" shouts New York City radio

demagogue Bob Grant and then the sound of droning telephone emptiness, the voice of dissent dumped out some trapdoor in aural space.

As I listened to a range of such programs what struck me as the   12
most unifying theme was not merely the specific intolerance on such
hot topics as race and gender, but a much more general contempt for the
world, a verbal stoning of anything different. It is like some unusually
violent game of "Simon Says," this mockery and shouting down of
callers, this roar of incantations, the insistence on agreement.

But, ah, if you *will* but only agree, what sweet and safe reward,   13
what soft enfolding by a stern and angry radio god. And as an added
bonus, the invisible shield of an AM community, a family of fans who
are Exactly Like You, to whom you can express, in anonymity, all the
filthy stuff you imagine "them" doing to you. The comfort and relief
of being able to ejaculate, to those who understand, about the dark
imagined excess overtaking, robbing, needing to be held down and
taught a good lesson, needing to put it in its place before the ravenous
demon enervates all that is true and good and pure in this life.

The audience for this genre of radio flagellation is mostly young,   14
white, and male. Two-thirds of Rush Limbaugh's audience is male.
According to *Time* magazine, 75 percent of Howard Stern's listeners
are white men. Most of the callers have spent their lives walling themselves off from any real experience with blacks, feminists, lesbians, or
gays. In this regard, it is probably true, as former Secretary of Education
William Bennett says, that Rush Limbaugh "tells his audience that
what you believe inside, you can talk about in the marketplace." Unfortunately, what's "inside" is then mistaken for what's "outside," treated as
empirical and political reality. The *National Review* extols Limbaugh's
conservative leadership as no less than that of Ronald Reagan, and
the Republican party provides Limbaugh with books to discuss, stories,
angles, and public support. "People were afraid of censure by gay
activists, feminists, environmentalists—now they are not because Rush
takes them on," says Bennett.

U.S. history has been marked by cycles in which brands of this   15
or that hatred come into fashion and go out, are unleashed and then
restrained. If racism, homophobia, jingoism, and woman-hating have
been features of national life in pretty much all of modern history, it
rather begs the question to spend a lot of time wondering if right-wing
radio is a symptom or a cause. For at least 400 years, prevailing
attitudes in the West have considered African Americans less intelligent.
Recent statistics show that 53 percent of people in the U.S. agree that
blacks and Latinos are less intelligent than whites, and a majority

believe that blacks are lazy, violent, welfare-dependent, and unpatriotic.

I think that what has made life more or less tolerable for "out" 16
groups have been those moments in history when those "inside" feelings were relatively restrained. In fact, if I could believe that right-wing radio were only about idiosyncratic, singular, rough-hewn individuals thinking those inside thoughts, I'd be much more inclined to agree with Columbia University media expert Everette Dennis, who says that Stern's and Limbaugh's popularity represents the "triumph of the individual" or with *Time* magazine's bottom line that "the fact that either is seriously considered a threat . . . is more worrisome than Stern or Limbaugh will ever be." If what I were hearing had even a tad more to do with real oppressions, with real white *and* black levels of joblessness and homelessness, or with the real problems of real white men, then I wouldn't have bothered to slog my way through hours of Howard Stern's miserable obsessions.

Yet at the heart of my anxiety is the worry that Stern, Limbaugh, 17
Grant, et al. represent the very antithesis of individualism's triumph. As the *National Review* said of Limbaugh's ascent, "It was a feat not only of the loudest voice but also of a keen political brain to round up, as Rush did, the media herd and drive them into the conservative corral." When asked about his political aspirations, Bob Grant gloated to the Washington *Post,* "I think I would make rather a good dictator."

The polemics of right-wing radio are putting nothing less than 18
hate onto the airwaves, into the marketplace, electing it to office, teaching it in schools, and exalting it as freedom. What worries me is the increasing-to-constant commerce of retribution, control, and lashing out, fed not by fact but fantasy. What worries me is the reemergence, more powerfully than at any time since the institution of Jim Crow, of a socio-centered self that excludes "the likes of," well, me for example, from the civic circle, and that would rob me of my worth and claim and identity as a citizen. As the *Economist* rightly observes, "Mr. Limbaugh takes a mass market—white, mainly male, middle-class, ordinary America—and talks to it as an endangered minority."

I worry about this identity whose external reference is a set of 19
beliefs, ethics, and practices that excludes, restricts, and acts in the world on me, or mine, as the perceived if not real enemy. I am acutely aware of losing *my* mythic individualism to the surface shapes of my mythic group fearsomeness as black, as female, as left wing. "I" merge not fluidly but irretrievably into a category of "them." I become a suspect self, a moving target of loathsome properties, not merely different but dangerous. And that worries me a lot.

What happens in my life with all this translated license, this permis- 20
sion to be uncivil? What happens to the social space that was supposedly at the sweet mountaintop of the civil rights movement's trail?
Can I get a seat on the bus without having to be reminded that I
should be standing? Did the civil rights movement guarantee us nothing
more than to use public accommodations while surrounded by raving
lunatic bigots? "They didn't beat this idiot [Rodney King] enough,"
says Howard Stern.

Not long ago I had the misfortune to hail a taxicab in which the 21
driver was listening to Howard Stern undress some woman. After some
blocks, I had to get out. I was, frankly, afraid to ask the driver to turn
it off—not because I was afraid of "censoring" him, which seems to
be the only thing people will talk about anymore, but because the
driver was stripping me too, as he leered through the rearview mirror.
"Something the matter?" he demanded, as I asked him to pull over
and let me out well short of my destination. (I'll spare you the full
story of what happened from there—trying to get another cab, as the
cabbies stopped for all the white businessmen who so much as
scratched their heads near the curb; a nice young white man, seeing
my plight, giving me his cab, having to thank him, he hero, me saved-
but-humiliated, cabdriver pissed and surly. I fight my way to my destination, finally arriving in bad mood, militant black woman, cranky
feminazi.)

When Yeltsin blared rock music at his opponents holed up in the 22
parliament building in Moscow, in imitation of the U.S. Marines trying
to torture Manual Noriega in Panama, all I could think of was that
it must be like being trapped in a crowded subway car when all the
portable stereos are tuned to Bob Grant or Howard Stern. With Howard Stern's voice a tinny, screeching backdrop, with all the faces growing dreamily mean as though some soporifically evil hallucinogen were
gushing into their bloodstreams, I'd start begging to surrender.

Surrender to what? Surrender to the laissez-faire resegregation 23
that is the metaphoric significance of the hundreds of "Rush rooms"
that have cropped up in restaurants around the country; rooms broadcasting Limbaugh's words, rooms for your listening pleasure, rooms
where bigots can capture the purity of a Rush-only lunch counter,
rooms where all those unpleasant others just "choose" not to eat?
Surrender to the naughty luxury of a room in which a Ku Klux Klan
meeting could take place in orderly, First Amendment fashion? Everyone's "free" to come in (and a few of you outsiders do), but mostly
the undesirable nonconformists are gently repulsed away. It's a high-
tech world of enhanced choice. Whites choose mostly to sit in the

Rush room. Feminists, blacks, lesbians, and gays "choose" to sit else-where. No need to buy black votes, you just pay them not to vote; no need to insist on white-only schools, you just sell the desirability of black-only schools. Just sit back and watch it work, like those invisible shock shields that keep dogs cowering in their own backyards.

How real is the driving perception behind all the Sturm und Drang   24
of this genre of radio-harangue—the perception that white men are an oppressed minority, with no power and no opportunity in the land that they made great? While it is true that power and opportunity are shrinking for all but the very wealthy in this country (and would that Limbaugh would take that issue on), the fact remains that white men are still this country's most privileged citizens and market actors. To give just a small example, according to the *Wall Street Journal,* blacks were the only racial group to suffer a net job loss during the 1990–91 economic downturn at the companies reporting to the Equal Employment Opportunity Commission. Whites, Latinos, and Asians, mean-while, gained thousands of jobs. While whites gained 71,144 jobs at these companies, Latinos gained 60,040, Asians gained 55,104, and blacks lost 59,479. If every black were hired in the United States tomorrow, the numbers would not be sufficient to account for white men's expanding balloon of fear that they have been specifically dispos-sessed by African Americans.

Given deep patterns of social segregation and general ignorance   25
of history, particularly racial history, media remain the principal source of most Americans' knowledge of each other. Media can provoke violence or induce passivity. In San Francisco, for example, a radio show on KMEL called "Street Soldiers" has taken this power as a responsibility with great consequence: "Unquestionably," writes Ken Auletta in the *New Yorker,* "the show has helped avert violence. When a Samoan teenager was slain, apparently by Filipino gang members, in a drive-by shooting, the phones lit up with calls from Samoans wanting to tell [the hosts] they would not rest until they had exacted revenge. Threats filled the air for a couple of weeks. Then the dead Samoan's father called in, and, in a poignant exchange, the father said he couldn't tolerate the thought of more young men senselessly slaughtered. There would be no retaliation, he vowed. And there was none." In contrast, we must wonder at the phenomenon of the very powerful leadership of the Republican party, from Ronald Reagan to Robert Dole to William Bennett, giving advice, counsel, and friendship to Rush Limbaugh's passionate divisiveness.

The outright denial of the material crisis at every level of U.S.   26
society, most urgently in black inner-city neighborhoods but facing us

all, is a kind of political circus, dissembling as it feeds the frustrations of the moment. We as a nation can no longer afford to deal with such crises by *imagining* an excess of bodies, of babies, of jobstealers, of welfare mothers, of overreaching immigrants, of too-powerful (Jewish, in whispers) liberal Hollywood, of lesbians and gays, of gang members ("gangsters" remain white, and no matter what the atrocity, less vilified than "gang members," who are black), of Arab terrorists, and uppity women. The reality of our social poverty far exceeds these scapegoats. This right-wing backlash resembles, in form if not substance, phenomena like anti-Semitism in Poland: there aren't but a handful of Jews left in that whole country, but the giant balloon of heated anti-Semitism flourishes apace, Jews blamed for the world's evils.

The overwhelming response to right-wing excesses in the United States has been to seek an odd sort of comfort in the fact that the First Amendment is working so well that you can't suppress this sort of thing. Look what's happened in Eastern Europe. Granted. So let's not talk about censorship or the First Amendment for the next ten minutes. But in Western Europe, where fascism is rising at an appalling rate, suppression is hardly the problem. In Eastern and Western Europe as well as the United States, we must begin to think just a little bit about the fiercely coalescing power of media to spark mistrust, to fan it into forest fires of fear and revenge. We must begin to think about the levels of national and social complacence in the face of such resolute ignorance. We must ask ourselves what the expected result is, not of censorship or suppression, but of so much encouragement, so much support, so much investment in the fashionability of hate. What future is it that we are designing with the devotion of such tremendous resources to the disgraceful propaganda of bigotry? 27

THINKING ABOUT THE CONTENT

1. Do you think Williams should be concerned about the popularity of personalities such as Rush Limbaugh and Howard Stern? Why would these talk shows be particularly offensive to or fearful for her? Should she be concerned? Why or why not?

2. Do you think the Limbaughs, Sterns, and Grants have the power to stir up people and bring out "the very worst in human nature" (9), or is it good that "the very worst in human nature" has an outlet for its venom?

3. Williams says, "The polemics of right-wing radio are putting nothing less than hate onto the airwaves, into the marketplace, electing it to office, teaching it in schools, and exalting it as freedom . . . fed not by fact but fantasy" (18). Is this true? Are there radio shows that counter the Limbaughs and Sterns? If so, are they as popular? Why or why not?

4. Williams believes that "hate radio" audiences reveal a fear and "general contempt for the world" (12). What do you think is the appeal of what Williams calls "hate radio"? Do you or have you listened to such programs? Why or why not?

5. Williams states, "We must ask ourselves what the expected result is, not of censorship or suppression, but of so much encouragement, so much support, so much investment in the fashionability of hate" (27). What do you think is or will be "the expected result"?

LOOKING AT STRUCTURE AND STYLE

6. Discuss the way Williams begins her essay and the way she introduces the reader into her topic and thesis. Is this effective in getting us interested in what she has to say? Why or why not?

7. What passages are particularly effective in establishing attitude and tone?

8. What facts does Williams provide to show that the white male audience of hate radio is not an oppressed minority? Is she convincing? Why or Why not?

EXPLORING DISCUSSION AND WRITING TOPICS

9. Discuss why we should or shouldn't tune into the Limbaughs and Sterns. What might we learn if we do? Is it important to know what is being said? Why?

10. Research one of the examples Williams uses in paragraph 9 to show the power of the media to change the course of history. How was the media used? What effect did it have? Are these examples reason for giving a second thought to the power of "hate radio"?

JEANNE ALBRONDA HEATON AND
NONA LEIGH WILSON

More than twenty daytime talk shows are now aired on television. Early on, most of them, such as "The Phil Donahue Show" (1967), dealt with a wide range of political and social issues with the intent of enlightening and empowering their mainly female audience. Viewers were urged to rise up and challenge the status quo. When "The Oprah Winfrey Show" aired nationally in 1985, it set off not only competition with Donahue, but a string of other talk shows: Sally Jessy Raphael, Richard Bey, Geraldo Rivera, Jenny Jones, Maury Povich, and Montel Williams, to name a few. With the increase in the ratings war, the shows no longer deal much with politics or social issues, but rather use class, race, and gender sensationalism to pull in an audience. In 1996, Donahue cancelled his show presumably because of the popularity of the trash-TV talk shows.

The following essay appeared in the September/October 1995 issue of *Ms.* magazine and was adapted from *Tuning In Trouble: Talk TV's Destructive Impact on Mental Health* by Jeanne Albronda Heaton and Nona Leigh Wilson. Heaton is a practicing psychologist and a teacher at Ohio University; Wilson is an assistant professor in counseling and human resources development at South Dakota State University. The authors argue that the "shows support the mistaken notion that the only power women have is to complain and that they cannot effect real changes."

ٱ

Tuning into Trouble

In 1967, *The Phil Donahue Show* aired in Dayton, Ohio, as a new daytime talk alternative. Donahue did not offer the customary "women's fare." On Monday of his first week he interviewed atheist Madalyn Murray O'Hair. Tuesday he featured single men talking about what they looked for in women. Wednesday he showed a film of a baby being born from the obstetrician's point of view. Thursday he sat in a coffin and interviewed a funeral director. And on Friday he held up "Little Brother," an anatomically correct doll without his diaper. When Donahue asked viewers to call in response, phone lines jammed.

For 18 years daytime talk *was* Donahue. His early guests reflected   2
the issues of the time and included Ralph Nader on consumer rights,
Bella Abzug on feminism, and Jerry Rubin on free speech. Never before
had such socially and personally relevant issues been discussed in
such a democratic way with daytime women viewers. But his most
revolutionary contribution was in making the audience an integral
part of the show's format. The women watching Donahue finally had
a place in the conversation, and they were determined to be heard.
The show provided useful information and dialogue that had largely
been unavailable to house-bound women, affording them the opportunity to voice their opinions about everything from politics to sex—and
even the politics of sex.

No real competition emerged until 1985, when *The Oprah Win-*   3
frey Show went national. Her appeal for more intimacy was a ratings
winner. She did the same topics Donahue had done but with a more
therapeutic tone. Donahue seemed driven to uncover and explore.
Winfrey came to share and understand. In 1987, Winfrey's show sur-
passed Donahue's by being ranked among the top 20 syndicated shows.
Phil and Oprah made it easier for those who followed; their successors
were able to move much more quickly to the top.

At their best, the shows "treated the opinions of women of all   4
classes, races, and educational levels as if they mattered," says Naomi
Wolf in her book *Fire with Fire:* "That daily act of listening, whatever
its shortcomings, made for a revolution in what women were willing
to ask for; the shows daily conditioned otherwise unheard women into
the belief that they were entitled to a voice." Both Donahue and Winfrey deserve enormous credit for providing a platform for the voices
of so many who needed to be heard, and for raising the nation's
consciousness on many important topics, including domestic violence,
child abuse, and other crucial problems. But those pioneering days are
over. As the number of shows increased and the ratings wars intensified,
the manner in which issues are presented has changed. Shows now
encourage conflict, name-calling, and fights. Producers set up under-
handed tricks and secret revelations. Hosts instruct guests to reveal
all. The more dramatic and bizarre the problems the better.

While more air time is given to the problems that women face,   5
the topics are presented in ways that are not likely to yield change.
The very same stereotypes that have plagued both women and men
for centuries are in full force. Instead of encouraging changes in sex
roles, the shows actually solidify them. Women viewers are given a
constant supply of the worst images of men, all the way from garden-
variety liars, cheats, and con artists to rapists and murderers.

If there is a man for every offense, there is certainly a woman for
every trauma. Most women on talk TV are perpetual victims presented
as having so little power that not only do they have to contend with real
dangers such as sexual or physical abuse, but they are also overcome by
bad hair, big thighs, and beautiful but predatory "other" women. The
women of talk are almost always upset and in need. The bonding that
occurs invariably centers around complaints about men or the worst
stereotypes about women. In order to be a part of the "sisterhood,"
women are required to be angry with men and dissatisfied with themselves. We need look no further than at some of the program titles to
recognize the message. Shows about men bring us a steady stream of
stalkers, adulterers, chauvinistic sons, abusive fathers, and men who
won't commit to women.

The shows provide a forum for women to complain, confront,
and cajole, but because there is never any change as a result of the letting
loose, this supports the mistaken notion that women's complaints have
"no weight," that the only power women have is to complain, and
that they cannot effect real changes. By bringing on offensive male
guests who do nothing but verify the grounds for complaint, the shows
are reinforcing some self-defeating propositions. The idea that women
should direct their energies toward men rather than look for solutions
in themselves is portrayed daily. And even when the audience chastises
such behavior, nothing changes, because only arguments and justifications follow.

On *The Jenny Jones Show* a woman was introduced as someone
who no longer had sex with her husband because she saw him with
a stripper. Viewers got to hear how the stripper "put her boobs in his
face" and then kissed him. The husband predictably defended his
actions: "At least I didn't tongue her." The next few minutes proceeded
with insult upon insult, to which the audience "oohed" and "aahed"
and applauded. To top it all off, viewers were informed that the offense
in question occurred at the husband's birthday party, which his wife
arranged, *stripper and all.* Then in the last few minutes a psychologist
pointed out the couple weren't wearing rings and didn't seem committed. She suggested that their fighting might be related to some other
problem. Her comments seemed reasonable enough until she suggested
that the wife might really be trying to get her husband to rape her.
That comment called up some of the most absurd and destructive ideas
imaginable about male and female relationships—yet there was no
explanation or discussion.

It is not that women and men don't find lots of ways to disappoint
each other, or that some women and some men don't act and think

like the women and men on the shows. The problem is talk TV's fixation on gender war, with endless portrayals of vicious acts, overboard retaliations, and outrageous justifications. As a result, viewers are pumped full of the ugliest, nastiest news from the front.

When issues affecting people of color are dealt with, the stereotypes about gender are layered on top of the stereotypes about race. Since most of the shows revolve around issues related to sex, violence, and relationships, they tend to feature people of color who reflect stereotypical images—in a steady stream of guests who have children out of wedlock, live on welfare, fight viciously, and have complicated unsolvable problems. While there are less-than-flattering depictions of white people on these shows, white viewers have the luxury of belonging to the dominant group, and therefore are more often presented in the media in positive ways. 10

On a *Ricki Lake* show about women who sleep with their friends' boyfriends, the majority of the guests were African American and Hispanic women who put on a flamboyant display of screaming and fighting. The profanity was so bad that many of the words had to be deleted. The segment had to be stopped because one guest yanked another's wig off. For many white viewers these are the images that form their beliefs about "minority" populations. 11

The shows set themselves up as reliable sources of information about what's really going on in the nation. And they often cover what sounds like common problems with work, love, and sex, but the information presented is skewed and confusing. Work problems become "fatal office feuds" and "backstabbing coworkers." Problems concerning love, sex, or romance become "marriage with a 14-year-old," "women in love with the men who shoot them," or "man-stealing sisters." TV talk shows suggest that "marrying a rapist" or having a "defiant teen" are catastrophes about to happen to everyone. 12

Day in and day out, the shows parade all the myriad traumas, betrayals, and afflictions that could possibly befall us. They suggest that certain issues are more common than they actually are, and embellish the symptoms and outcomes. In actuality, relatively few people are likely to be abducted as children, join a Satanic cult in adolescence, fall in love with serial rapists, marry their cousins, hate their own race, or get sex changes in midlife, but when presented over and over again the suggestion is that they are quite likely to occur. 13

With their incessant focus on individual problems, television talk shows are a major contributor to the recent trend of elevating personal concerns to the level of personal rights and then affording those "rights" more attention than their accompanying responsibilities. 14

Guests are brought on who have committed villainous acts (most often against other guests). The host and audience gratuitously "confront" the offenders about their wrongdoing and responsibilities. The alleged offenders almost always refute their accountability with revelations that they too were "victimized." On *Sally Jessy Raphael,* a man appeared with roses for the daughter he had sexually molested. He then revealed that he had been molested when he was five, and summed it up with "I'm on this show too! I need help, I'll go through therapy."

His sudden turnabout was not unusual. Viewers rarely see guests admit error early in the show, but a reversal often occurs with just a few minutes remaining. This works well for the shows because they need the conflict to move steadily to a crescendo before the final "go to therapy" resolution. But before that viewers are treated to lots of conflict and a heavy dose of pseudo-psychological explanations that are really nothing more than excuses, and often lame ones at that. The guests present their problems, the hosts encourage them to do so with concerned questions and occasional self-disclosures, and the audience frequently get in on the act with their own testimonies. Anything and everything goes.

The reigning motto is "Secrets keep you sick." On a *Jerry Springer* show about confronting secrets, a husband revealed to his wife that he had been having an affair. Not only was the unsuspecting wife humiliated and speechless, but Springer upped the ante by bringing out the mistress, who kissed the husband and informed the wife that she loved them both. Conflict predictably ensued, and viewers were told this was a good idea because now the problem was out in the open. When Ricki Lake did a similar show, a man explained to his very surprised roommate that he had "finally" informed the roommate's mother that her son was gay, a secret the roommate had been hiding from his family.

Referring to these premeditated catastrophes as simply "disclosures" softens their edges and affords them a kind of legitimacy they do not deserve. On a program about bigamy, Sally Jessy Raphael invited two women who had been married to the same man at the same time to appear on the show. The man was also on, via satellite and in disguise. His 19-year-old daughter by one of the wives sat on the stage while these women and her father tore each other apart. Sally and the audience encouraged the fight with "oohs" and "aahs" and rounds of applause at the ever-increasing accusations. A "relationship therapist" was brought on to do the postmortem. Her most notable warning was that all this turmoil could turn the daughter "to women," presumably meaning that she could become a lesbian. The scenario was almost too absurd for words, but it was just one more show like so many others: founded on stereotypes and capped off with clichés. From the "catfight" to the "no-good father" to archaic explanations of homosexuality—cheap thrills and bad advice are dressed up like information and expertise.

These scenarios are often legitimized by the use of pseudo-psycho- 18 logical explanations, otherwise known as psychobabble. This is regularly used as a "disclaimer," or as a prelude to nasty revelations, or as a new and more sophisticated way of reinforcing old stereotypes: "men are cognitive, not emotional," or "abused women draw abusive men to them." This not only leaves viewers with nothing more than platitudes to explain problems and clichés to resolve them, but it fails to offer guests with enormous conflicts and long histories of resentment and betrayals practical methods for changing their circumstances. The "four steps to get rid of your anger" may sound easy enough to implement, but what this kind of ready-made solution fails to acknowledge is that not all anger is the same, and certainly not everyone's anger needs the same treatment. Sometimes anger is a signal to people that they are being hurt, exploited, or taken advantage of, and it can motivate change.

Rather than encouraging discussion, exploration, or further under- 19 standing, psychobabble shuts it off. With only a phrase or two, we can believe that we understand all the related "issues." Guests confess that they are "codependents" or "enablers." Hosts encourage "healing," "empowerment," and "reclaiming of the inner spirit." In turn, viewers can nod knowingly without really knowing at all.

Talk TV initially had great potential as a vehicle for disseminating 20 accurate information and as a forum for public debate, although it would be hard to know it from what currently remains. Because most of these talk shows have come to rely on sensational entertainment as the means of increasing ratings, their potential has been lost. We are left with cheap shots, cheap thrills, and sound-bite stereotypes. Taken on its own, this combination is troubling enough, but when considered against the original opportunity for positive outcomes, what talk TV delivers is truly disturbing.

THINKING ABOUT THE CONTENT

1. The authors believe that television talk shows bring out the worst stereotypes of both gender and race. What are some of the stereotypes mentioned? How are these stereotypes fostered on talk shows, according to the authors?

2. Why are the authors opposed to talk shows' "incessant focus on individual

problems" (13)? What is the harm they create among participants and viewers? What potential do talk shows have if done correctly and not for sensationalism and ratings?

3. What is *psychobabble?* What are some examples provided by the authors? Why is psychobabble harmful?

4. Why do you think television talk shows are so popular? Who watches them? Do you watch any? What is your opinion of such shows?

LOOKING AT STRUCTURE AND STYLE

5. Discuss the attitude and tone of the authors. What words or phrases develop both?

6. To what audience are the authors writing? Why do you think so?

7. What kind of evidence do the authors use to support their conclusion? Is it valid evidence? Why or why not?

EXPLORING DISCUSSION AND WRITING TOPICS

8. Watch, if you don't already, one or more of the television talk shows mentioned in the article. Write an evaluation of the program's value. Is it harmful? What is its point? What do the programmers stress? What effect do you think the program has on the audience? Who is the audience?

9. More than 98 percent of homes in the United States have at least one television, and the majority of those televisions are on for more than seven hours a day. With that much exposure, how powerful is television in shaping our thoughts and lifestyles? Are we viewers being manipulated at many levels? Could television be used to better effect than it is currently? Does television programming need government regulating?

The real problem with prolonged television viewing is the same as the problem with any form of human isolation: it cuts the person off from those social relationships on which our moral nature in large part depends. As the psychiatrist George Ainslie writes, "the mass media [in heavy doses] impoverish a society in the same way as drugs and other addictions, by draining away more attention than they return." Passive, individual entertainment, whether in a drugged stupor, in a video arcade, or before an endlessly running TV screen, leads to self-absorption, and self-absorption in extreme doses is the enemy of moral competence, especially that form of competence that depends on our controlling our impulses.

—James Q. Wilson

With the concern over the "moral decline of modern society," fingers of blame point in many directions. Violent books, television shows, and films are all pointed to as a big part of the problem, thus raising the call for censorship. Andrew Klavan, author of thrillers *Don't Say a Word* and *The Animal Hour*, argues against censorship, claiming that he and many others actually love violence in fiction, and that reading or watching fictional violence may even be good for our mental health. Klavan believes "the relationship between fiction and humanity's unconscious is so complex, so resonant, that it is impossible to isolate one from the other in terms of cause and effect."

The following reading selection, excerpted from *Boston Review,* appeared in the November/December 1994 issue of *Utne Reader.*

In Praise of Gore

I love the sound of people screaming. Women screaming—with their clothes torn—as they run down endless hallways with some bogeyman in hot pursuit. Men, in their priapic cars, screaming as the road ends, as the fender plummets toward fiery oblivion under their wild eyes. Children? I'm a little squeamish about children, but okay, sure, I'll take screaming children too. And I get off on gunshots—machine gun shots goading a corpse into a posthumous jitterbug; and the coital jerk and plunge of a butcher knife, and axes; even claws, if you happen to have them. 1

Yes, yes, yes, only in stories. Of course; in fictions only: novels, TV shows, films. I've loved the scary, gooey stuff since I was a child. I've loved monsters, shootouts, bluddy murther; women in jeopardy (as they say in Hollywood); the slasher in the closet; the intruder's shadow that spreads up the bedroom wall like a stain. And now, having grown to man's estate, I make a very good living writing these things: thriller novels like *Don't Say a Word*, which begins with a nice old lady getting dusted and ends with an assault on a child, and *The Animal Hour*, which features a woman's head being severed and stuffed into a commode. 2

Is it vicious? Disgusting? Sexist? Sick? Tough luck, it's my imagina-   3
tion—sometimes it is—and it's my readers' too—always, for all I know.
And when they and I get together, when we dodge down that electric
alleyway of the human skull where only murder is delight—well then,
my friend, it's showtime.

But enough about me, let's talk about death. Cruel death, sexy death,   4
exciting death: death, that is, on the page and on the screen. Because
this is not a defense of violence in fiction; it's a celebration of it. And
not a moment too soon either.

Hard as it is for a sane man to believe, fictional violence is under   5
attack. Again. This year's list of would-be censors trying to shoulder
their way to the trough of celebrity is hardly worth enumerating: Their
15 minutes might be up by the time I'm done. Film critic Michael
Medved says cinematic violence is part of a pop culture "war on
traditional values"; Congressman Edward Markey says television violence should be reduced or regulated; some of our less thoughtful
feminists tried to quash the novel *American Psycho* because of its
descriptions of violence toward women and even some of the more
thoughtful, like Catharine MacKinnon, have fought for censorship
in law, claiming that written descriptions of "penises slamming into
vaginas" deprive actual human beings of their civil rights.

It's nonsense mostly, but it has the appeal of glamour, of flash.   6
Instead of trying to understand the sad, banal, ignorant souls who
generally pull the trigger in our society, we get to discuss the urbane
cannibal Hannibal Lecter from *The Silence of the Lambs,* Ice-T, penises,
vaginas. It makes for good sound bites, anyway—the all-American
diet of 15-second thoughts.

But Britain—where I've come to live because I loathe real guns   7
and political correctness—is far from exempt. Indeed, perhaps nowhere
has there been a more telling or emblematic attack on fictional violence
than is going on here right now. It is a textbook example of how easily
pundits and politicians can channel honest grief and rage at a true
crime into a senseless assault on the innocent tellers of tales.

It began here this time with the killing of a child by two other children.   8
On February 12, Jamie Bulger, a 2-year-old toddler, was led out of a
Merseyside shopping mall by two 10-year-olds—two little boys. The
boys prodded and carried and tugged the increasingly distraught baby
past dozens of witnesses who did not understand what they were
seeing. When they reached a deserted railroad embankment, the two

boys tortured, mutilated, and finally killed their captive for no reasons that anyone has been able to explain.

The nation's effort to understand, its grief and disgust, its sense   9
of social despair, did not resolve themselves upon a single issue until the trial judge pronounced sentence. "It is not for me to pass judgment on their upbringing," Mr. Justice Morland said of the boys. "But I suspect exposure to violent video films may in part be an explanation."

No one knew why he said such a thing. There had been speculation   10
in some of the papers that *Child's Play 3* (with its devil doll, Chucky), which had been rented by one of the killers' fathers, had given the son ideas. But there was no testimony at the trial, no evidence presented showing that the boy had seen it or that it had had a contributing effect. It didn't matter. As far as journalists were concerned, as far as public debate was concerned, "video nasties," as they are called here, became the central issue of the case.

We finally know what we are seeing when we look upon the   11
rampaging fire of violence in our society: We are seeing the effects of fiction on us. Got it? Our moral verities are crumbling by the hour. Our families are shattering. Our gods are dead. The best lack all conviction while the worst are full of passionate intensity.

And it's all Chucky's fault.   12

The instinct to censor is the tragic flaw of utopian minds. "Our first   13
job," said Plato in his classic attack on the democratic system, "is to oversee the work of the story writers, and to accept any good stories they write, but reject the others." Because the perfectibility of human society is a fiction itself, it comes under threat from other, more believable fictions, especially those that document and imply the cruel, the chaotic, the Dionysian for their thrills.

For me to engage the latter-day Platos on their own materialist,   14
political terms would be to be sucked in to a form of dialogue that does not reflect the reality I know—and know I know. Because personally, I understand the world not through language but through an unfathomable spirit and an infinite mind. With language as a rude tool I try to convey a shadow of the world my imagination makes of the world at large. I do this for money and pleasure and to win the admiration of women. And when, in an uncertain hour, I crave the palliative of meaning, I remind myself that people's souls run opposite to their bodies and grow more childlike as they mature—and so I have built, in my work, little places where those souls can go to play.

The proper response to anyone who would shut these playgrounds   15
down for any reason—to anyone who confuses these playgrounds with

the real world—is not the specious language of theory or logic or even the law. It's the language of the spirit, of celebration and screed, of jeremiad and hallelujah. Of this.

Now, I would not say that my fictions—any fictions—have no effect on real life. Or that books, movies, and TV are mere regurgitations of what's going on in the society around them. These arguments strike me as disingenuous and self-defeating. Rather, the relationship between fiction and humanity's unconscious is so complex, so resonant, that it is impossible to isolate one from the other in terms of cause and effect. Fiction and reality do interact, but we don't know how, not at all. And since we don't understand the effect of one upon the other—whence arises this magical certainty that violence in fiction begets violence in real life? [16]

The answer seems to come straight out of Psychology 1A, but that doesn't negate the truth of it. Pleasure that is unknowingly repressed is outwardly condemned. The censor always attacks the images that secretly appeal to him or her the most. The assault on violent fiction is not really an attempt to root out the causes of violence—no one can seriously believe that. The attempt to censor fictional violence is a guilt-ridden slap at ourselves, in the guise of a mythical *them,* for taking such pleasure in make-believe acts that, in real life, would be reprehensible. How—we seem to be asking ourselves—how, in a world in which Jamie Bulger dies so young, can we kick back with a beer at night and enjoy a couple of hours of *Child's Play 3*? [17]

How can we enjoy this stuff so much? So very much. [18]

Not all of us, perhaps. I'm forever being told that there are people who'd rather not take violence with their fiction—although I wonder how many would say so if you included the delicate violence of an Agatha Christie or the "literary" violence of, say, Hemingway and Faulkner. But even if we accept the exceptions, even if we limit the field to real gore, it does seem to me that the numbers are incredible, the attraction truly profound. [19]

Once I picked out what looked like a cheap horror novel by an author I'd never heard of. For months afterward, I asked the readers I knew if they had heard of the book, *Salem's Lot,* or its author, Stephen King. None of them had. Later, the movie *Carrie* helped launch what has to be one of the most successful novelistic careers since Dickens. But even before that, readers were steadily discovering the nausea and mayhem and terror of the man's vision. [20]

The moral, I mean, is this: To construct a bloodsoaked nightmare   21
of unrelenting horror is not an easy thing. But if you build it, they
will come. And so the maker of violent fiction—ho, ho—he walks
among us in Nietzschean glee. He has bottled the Dionysian whirlwind
and is selling it as a soft drink. Like deep-browed Homer, when he
told of a spear protruding from a man's head with an eyeball fixed to
the point, the violent storyteller knows that that gape of disgust on
your respectable mug is really the look of love. You may denounce
him, you may even censor him. You may just wrinkle your nose and
walk away. But sooner or later, in one form or another, he knows
you'll show up to see and listen to him. Fiction lives or dies not on
its messages, but on the depth and power of the emotional experience
it provides. An enormous amount of intellectual energy seems to have
been expended in a failed attempt to suppress the central, disturbing,
and irreducible fact of this experience: It's fun. Like sex: it's lots of
fun. We watch fictional people love and die and screw and suffer and
weep for our pleasure. It gives us joy.

And we watch them kill too. And this seems to give us as much   22
joy as anything.

All right, I suppose you can talk about the catharsis of terror, or the   23
harmless release of our violent impulses. Those are plausible excuses, I
guess. It doesn't take a genius to notice how often—practically always—it's the villain of a successful piece of violent art who becomes
its icon. Hannibal Lecter and Leatherface, Freddy Krueger and Dracula—these are the posters that go up on the wall, the characters that
we remember.

So I suppose, if you must, you could say these creatures represent   24
our buried feelings. Whether it's Medea or Jason (from *Friday the
13th*), the character who commits acts of savage violence always has
the appeal of a Caliban: that thing of darkness that must be acknowledged as our own. Not that people are essentially violent, but that
they are violent among other things and the violence has to be repressed. Some emotions must be repressed, and repressed emotions
return via the imagination in distorted and inflated forms: That's the
law of benevolent hypocrisy, the law of civilized life. It is an unstated
underpinning of utopian thought that the repressed can be eliminated
completely or denied or happily freed or remolded with the proper
education. It can't. Forget about it. Cross it off your list of things to
do. The monsters are always there in their cages. As Stephen King
says, with engaging simplicity, his job is to take them out for a walk
every now and then.

But again, this business of violent fiction as therapy—it's a defense, 25
isn't it, as if these stories needed a reason for being. In order to celebrate
violent fiction—I mean, *celebrate* it—it's the joy you've got to talk
about. The joy of cruelty, the thrill of terror, the adrenaline of the
hunter, the heartbeat of the deer—all reproduced in the safe playground
of art. A joy indeed.

When it comes to our messier, unseemly pleasures like fictional 26
gore, we are downright embarrassed by our delight. But delight it is.
Nubile teens caught out in flagrante by a nutcase in a hockey mask?
You bet it's erotic. Whole families tortured to death by a madman who's
traced them through their vacation photos? Ee-yewwww. Goblins who
jump out of the toilet to devour you ass first? Delightful stuff.

And we've always been that way. The myths of our ancient gods, 27
the lives of our medieval saints, the entertainments of our most civilized
cultures have always included healthy doses of rape, cannibalism,
evisceration, and general mayhem. Critics like Michael Medved complain that never before has it all been quite so graphic, especially on
screen. We are becoming "desensitized" to bloodshed, he claims, and
require more and more gore to excite our feelings. But when have
human beings ever been particularly "sensitized" to fictional violence?
The technology to create the illusion of bloodshed has certainly improved, but read *Titus Andronicus* with its wonderful stage direction,
"Enter a messenger with two heads and a hand," read the orgasmic
staking of Lucy in *Dracula,* read de Sade, for crying out loud. There
were always some pretty good indications of which way we'd go once
we got our hands on the machinery.

Because we love it. It makes us do a little inner dance of excitement, 28
tension, and release. Violent fiction with its graver purposes, if any,
concealed—fiction unadorned with overt message or historical significance—rubs our noses in the fact that narratives of horror, murder,
and gore are a blast, a gas. When knife-fingered Freddy Krueger of
the *Nightmare on Elm Street* movies disembowels someone in a geyser
of blood, when Hannibal Lecter washes down his victim with a nice
Chianti—the only possible reason for this nonreal, nonmeaningful
event to occur is that it's going to afford us pleasure. Which leaves
that pleasure obvious, exposed. It's the exposure, not the thrill, the
censors want to get rid of. Again: Celebration is the only defense.

And yet—I know—while I celebrate, the new, not-very-much- 29
improved Rome is burning.

Last year sometime, I had a conversation with a highly intelligent   30
Scottish filmmaker who had just returned from New York. Both of
us had recently seen Sylvester Stallone's mountaineering action picture
Cliffhanger. I'd seen it in a placid upper-class London neighborhood;
he'd seen it in a theater in Times Square. I had been thrilled by the
movie's special effects and found the hilariously dopey script sweetly
reminiscent of the comic books I'd read as a child. My friend had
found the picture grimly disturbing. The Times Square theater had
been filled with rowdy youths. Every time the bad guys killed someone,
the youths cheered—and when a woman was murdered, they howled
with delight.

I freely confess that I would have been unable to enjoy the movie   31
under those circumstances. Too damned noisy, for one thing. And, all
right, yes, as a repression fan, I could only get off on the cruelty of
the villains insofar as it fired my anticipation of the moment when Sly
would cut those suckers down. Another audience could just as easily
have been cheering the murder of Jews in *Schindler's List* or of blacks
in *Mississippi Burning*. I understand that, and it would be upsetting
and frightening to be surrounded by a crowd that seemed to have
abandoned the nonnegotiable values.

Michael Medved believes—not that one film produces one vicious   32
act—but that a ceaseless barrage of anti-religion, anti-family, slap-
happy-gore films and fictions has contributed to the erosion of values
so evident on 42nd Street. I don't know whether this is true or not—
neither does he—but, as with the judge's remarks in the Bulger case,
it strikes me as a very suspicious place to start. Surely, the Scotsman's
story illustrates that the problem lies not on the screen but in the seats,
in the lives that have produced that audience. Fiction cannot make of
people what life has not, good or evil.

But more to the point: Though the Times Square crowd's reaction   33
was scary—rude, too—it was not necessarily harmful in itself, either
to them or to me. For all I know, it was a beneficial release of energy
and hostility, good for the mental health. And in any case, it took
place in the context of their experience of a fiction and so (outside of
the unmannerly noise they made) was beyond my right to judge, approve, or condemn. Nobody has to explain his private pleasures
to me.

Because fiction and reality are different. It seems appalling that   34
anyone should have to say it, but it does need to be said. Fiction is
not subject to the same moral restrictions as real life. It should remain
absolutely free because, at whatever level, it is, like sex, a deeply
personal experience engaged in by consent in the hope of anything

from momentary release to satori. Like sex, it is available to fools and creeps and monsters, and that's life; that's tough. Because fiction is, like sex, at the core of our individual humanity. Stories are the basic building blocks of spiritual maturity. No one has any business messing with them. No one at all.

Reality, on the other hand, needs its limits, maintained by force   35
if necessary, for the simple reason that there are actions that directly harm the safety and liberty of other people. They don't merely offend them; they don't just threaten their delicate sense of themselves; they *hurt* them—really, painfully, a lot. Again, it seems wildly improbable that this should be forgotten, but Americans' current cultural discussions show every evidence that it has been. Just as fictions are being discussed as if they were actions, actual crimes and atrocities are being discussed as if they were cultural events, subject to aesthetic considerations. Trial lawyers won a lesser conviction for lady-killer Robert Chambers by claiming his victim was promiscuous; columnists defended dick-chopper Lorena Bobbitt, saying it might be all right to mutilate a man in his sleep, provided he was a really nasty guy. The fellows who savaged Reginald Denny during the Los Angeles riots claim they were just part of the psychology of the mob. And the Menendez brothers based much of their defense on a portrayal of themselves as victims, a portrayal of their victims as abusers. These are all arguments appropriate to fiction only. Only in fiction are crimes mitigated by symbolism and individuals judged not for what they've done but because of what they represent. To say that the reaction to fiction and the reaction to reality are on a continuum is moral nonsense.

Fiction and real life must be distinguished from one another. The   36
radical presumption of fiction is play, the radical presumption of real life is what Martin Amis called "the gentleness of human flesh." If we have lost the will to defend that gentleness, then God help us, because consigning Chucky to the flames is not going to bring it back.

One of the very best works of violent fiction to come along in the   37
past few years is Thomas Harris' novel *The Silence of the Lambs.* The story, inspired, like *Psycho,* by the real-life case of murderer Ed Gein, concerns the hunt for the serial killer Jame Gumb, a failed transsexual who strips his female victims' flesh in order to create a woman costume in which he can clothe himself.

When Harris introduces the killer's next victim—Catherine Mar-   38
tin—he presents us with a character we aren't meant to like very much. Rich, spoiled, arrogant, dissolute, Catherine is admirable only for the desperate cleverness she shows in her battle to stay alive. But for the rest of the novel—the attempt to rescue Catherine before it's too

late—Harris depends on our fear for her, our identification with her, our deep desire to see her get out of this in one piece. He relies on our irrational—spiritual—conviction that Catherine, irritating though she may be, must not be killed because . . . for no good reason: because she Must Not. Harris knowingly taps in to the purely emotional imperative we share with the book's heroine, Clarice Starling, the FBI agent who's trying to crack the case: Like her, we won't be able to sleep until the screaming of innocent lambs is stopped. Harris makes pretty well sure of it.

At the end, in the only injection of auctorial opinion in the book, Harris wryly notes that the scholarly journals' articles on the Gumb case never use the words *crazy* or *evil* in their discussions of the killer. The intellectual world is uncomfortable with the inherent Must Not, the instinctive absolute, and the individual responsibility those words ultimately suggest. Harris, I think, is trying to argue that if we don't trust our mindless belief in the sanctity of human life, we produce monsters that the sleep of reason never dreamed of. *The Silence of the Lambs,* as the title suggests, is a dramatization of a world in which the spirit has lost its power to speak. [39]

We live in that world, no question. With our culture atomizing, we think we can make up enough rules, impose enough restrictions, inject enough emptiness into our language to replace the shared moral conviction that's plainly gone. I think all stories—along with being fun—have the potential to humanize precisely because the richest fun of them is dependent on our identification with their characters. But stories can't do for us what experience hasn't. They're just not that powerful. And if some people are living lives in our society that make them unfit for even the most shallow thrills of fiction, you can't solve that problem by eliminating the fiction. By allowing politicians and pundits to turn our attention to "the problem of fictional violence," we are really allowing them to make us turn our backs on the problems of reality. [40]

After a crime like the Jamie Bulger murder, we should be asking ourselves a million questions: about our abandonment of family life, about our approach to poverty and unemployment, about the failures of our educational systems—about who and what we are and the ways we treat each other, the things we do and omit to do. These are hard, sometimes boring questions. But when instead we let our discussions devolve, as they have, into this glamour-rotten debate on whether people should be able to enjoy whatever fiction they please, then we make meaningless the taking of an individual's life. And that's no fun at all. [41]

THINKING ABOUT THE CONTENT

1. Do you agree with Klavan or the film critic Michael Medved and others who believe that cinematic violence is part of a pop culture "war on traditional values" (5)? Will censorship of violence stop or retard violence? Does fictional violence cause real violence? Why do you believe as you do?

2. Do you enjoy gory and violent fiction and films? Are they fun and entertaining? Do you feel that seeing films such as *Child's Play* and the *Friday the 13th* series, or reading Stephen King's works is harmful to you psychologically? Why or why not?

3. Klavan says, "The censor always attacks the images that secretly appeal to him or her the most" (17). Is he right? What do you think is the real reason behind those who want to censor violence? Do you or have you wanted to see something censored? If so, what and why?

4. How does Klavan distinguish between fiction and reality? How does he use his definitions to counter those who want to censor works like his? How well does he argue his case? With what do you agree and disagree?

LOOKING AT STRUCTURE AND STYLE

5. How effective is the opening paragraph? What is your reaction to it? How does it establish attitude and tone?

6. Several paragraphs are very short (e.g., 12, 18, 22). What is their effect?

7. How well does Klavan anticipate arguments from those who disagree with him? Do you think he is convincing, especially the statements in his two concluding paragraphs? Why or why not?

EXPLORING DISCUSSION AND WRITING TOPICS

8. If you have recently seen a gory or violent film or read a book of that category, defend your position on whether it should be censored. What effect did the work have on you? Did you enjoy seeing the gore or watching the violence? Will you continue to see or read such works?

9. Research information on studies that deal with the connection between violent fiction and violence in reality. Is there evidence to show a connection? Is the evidence reliable?

The following selection from the August 1995 issue of *Reed Magazine* is a talk Sallie Tisdale delivered to Reed College alumni that year as the keynote presentation for a reunion program titled "Pimps, Panderers, and Uncle Toms: The Limits of Expression and the Myth of Social Consensus." Tisdale is the author of several books, among them, *Talk Dirty to Me: An Intimate Philosophy of Sex* and *Stepping Westward*.

Tisdale lists a chronicle of contemporary censorship of books and discusses the dangers of attempts to limit freedom of expression.

※

The Myth of Social Consensus

I was the kind of child who loved libraries; they seemed radical places, dreams almost. I began going alone to the little Carnegie Library down the street from my house when I was about six years old. The library was a free place in which to roam, to be left alone, to think and imagine without constraint. My mother was a school-teacher and a great reader, and she believed in letting me have whatever I wanted to read. Her rule was that if I could figure out how to find it, I could read it. Then one day, when I was about thirteen, I found *The Joy of Sex*. When I tried to check it out, the librarian—who knew me and my mother, as everyone knew just about everyone else in that little town—called my mother at home and asked if it was all right.

Almost 25 years later, in Napa, California, a children's book by Norma Klein called *Naomi in the Middle* was challenged by a city councilor. It was inappropriate for schoolchildren, he said. The book, he explained, "could spark some thoughts and some creative adventures that they shouldn't have at this point in their lives."

I waited impatiently by that long-ago librarian's desk until my mother said I could have my book. I took it home and read it with no apparent harm. That was one more day in my lifelong affair with writing and books and libraries, with the idea of books and libraries, with the act of reading itself. Walt Whitman called reading "an exercise, a gymnast's struggle." To me it is creation, a lovemaking made of small discoveries, hidden treasures, big dreams.

I've just finished a book that took me three years to write. The   4
book is about sex—gender, desire, sexual acts, the importance of sexuality to human experience. And in the course of these three years I've
been forced to examine my own writerly commitment to honesty. I've
had to think long and carefully about the way a writer chooses what
to say and what not to say, and how the world influences a writer's
choices. I can't separate my external experience in this society, as an
American of a certain age and a certain time, from my internal experience as a writer and reader. I've had to think about my role as a parent,
and I've become—not coincidentally—actively involved in the politics
of free expression and censorship. I am saddened almost beyond words
when I think of what's being lost—what's already been destroyed—by
people who are afraid of books. I want to address what happens to
us as readers and as writers when we face the kind of censure so
common today, and why it counts.

There are many legitimate questions to be asked about the limits   5
of free expression, the role of education, and individual responsibility.
Unfortunately, very few of these questions are being asked in public
discourse, and little genuine dialogue is taking place. Instead I see
people of all political and social stripes engaged in a battle over books
and words, a war that takes place in a kind of no-man's-land devoid
of irony.

Louis Brandeis once said, "It is the function of speech to free men   6
from the bondage of irrational fears." But those irrational fears are
what drive people to silence certain kinds of speech. I consider prud-
ery—and I don't specifically mean sexual prudishness at all—to be a
great insult against life. The kind of prudishness I mean, the kind of
prudishness that leads to the banning of a book, is a squeamishness
about everything Other, everything different, disturbing, new. Of
course, those people who spend hours and weeks trying to ban a book
they fear will incite teen suicide—a book like *Romeo and Juliet*—could
spend those hours and weeks volunteering as tutors or suicide hotline
counselors or foster parents. But prevention of teen suicide itself is not
really their point. Their point is to prevent a polyglot and free-ranging
society, and teen suicide is just the convenient hook to hang that fear
upon.

Books are potent things; I could never honestly calm a person's   7
fear of a book by telling him or her that books don't matter. Just look
what Martin Luther accomplished with a list tacked up on a door.
Books and stories and reading are the meat of revolution and change;
they can be dangerous and unpredictable. But no matter how repugnant
or grotesque, or how apparently unimportant a book may be, to

remove it from examination is to take a position against change, against the possibility of change. So Aristophanes' classic play, *Lysistrata,* was banned from a Florida school because it "promotes women's lib." A book called *Myths and Their Meanings* was challenged in Colorado because, one citizen believed, stories about Zeus and Apollo might undermine teachings on Western civilization. To ban any one book is to ban, in essence, the idea of books themselves—it means to close the marketplace of imagination, the free exchange of ourselves.

We sometimes delude ourselves into thinking we live in a wildly   8
free society. Again and again in the last few years, I've been asked to respond to a person's concern about the rampant promiscuity of 1990s America. Isn't this a terribly sexual time? I am asked. But I don't think so. I think it's a terribly *lewd* time; I think we live in a world awash with shallow sexual images precisely because we *are* so prudish about sex. And in the same way, I think we are so bombarded with information itself, with a proliferation of all kinds of media, data, pictures, plots, statistics, stories, and consumer campaigns that we can be lulled into thinking this is a time of free information and Socratic conversation.

Sometimes I read book-banning anecdotes and laugh; a few do seem   9
to illustrate an epidemic of nuttiness. But I have to remind myself that it's *real,* that it happens, that these are real books and writers and real readers being hurt.

There are more formal challenges against books in schools and   10
public libraries than ever before. They have occurred in almost every state. Oregon has repeatedly been in the top five states in terms of the number of challenges; in 1992 and 1993, Oregon was second only behind California. That's not necessarily bad; I think the number of challenges reflects the heterogeneous nature of these states, and the fact that we read a lot of books around here. And people have as much right to complain about a book as they do to read one. But almost half of the attempts nationwide to remove or restrict school and library materials are successful.

What has been challenged, placed on a restricted shelf, or simply   11
banned in recent years? *Snow White. Hansel and Gretel. Sleeping Beauty. The Clan of the Cave Bear. The Adventures of Huckleberry Finn. Tom Sawyer.* In Sandy, Oregon, *All Quiet on the Western Front.* Pearl Buck's *The Good Earth. Tarzan of the Apes. Of Mice and Men. A Wrinkle in Time. Little House on the Prairie. The Bible. Newsweek.* This is a most incomplete short list, and please bear in mind that most

of these books have been challenged not once in one place, but again and again, in one town after the other.

The most common reason given in objection to a book is religion. 12 The second most common reason is that the work is sexually offensive or immoral. The third is simply that it contains profanity. The explanations given often seem illogical and confused. The single most challenged school material in the country is a self-esteem program called Pumsy, which uses puppets to help children act out socially problematic events. Pumsy has been accused of fomenting everything from New Age humanism, group therapy, hypnosis and mental illness to hallucinations. In one case, the objector complained that Pumsy was a kind of "mind control." Another said it was a form of Hinduism.

But with a careful reading, an agenda is frequently clear. Religious 13 objection or sexual offense often reveals itself to be at one and the same time religious and sexual propaganda; the objection is not just that something is contained in the book, but that something opposite is not. Almost every year the Multnomah County Library receives challenges to its books about the heretic religion of Roman Catholicism.

Jerry Falwell, in the same essay and almost in the same paragraph, 14 bemoans the loss of active Christian teaching in the public schools— "We were taught," he writes, "to reverence God, the Bible, and prayer"—and then accuses secular humanists of taking over the schools in order to indoctrinate children. Stephen King, who has seen every one of his novels banned in one place or another, said it best when he said, "What censorship is at bottom is about who's on top."

Many of the books banned, challenged, or restricted are guilty 15 only of being original. They are attacked for being too gruesome or dark, too occult, too questioning of Christianity or too respectful of other religions. Some books are banned simply because they have information *about* other religions—again here in Oregon, a book on stress management was banned from the Eagle Point high school library because it discussed yoga and meditation. These books are "unpatriotic" or "unconventional" or they "promote critical thinking." Some books are too honest about the angst of the modern teenager, about depression, suicide, drug use; they are seen to be disrespectful of the status quo, the elderly, wealth, power, or authority. Others speak to ordinary life in an uncomfortably realistic way, with profanity and intense emotion.

A certain amount of censorship is about protecting children from 16 a painful history and the painful realities of the present day. It is about trying to fix the real world to fit one's ideal, and this is one of the easiest kinds of censorship for me as a parent to practice. It is remarkably easy to rationalize not telling a child something, to not answer a question directly, and to go from there to making sure the child doesn't get hold of the information somewhere else. But where do we stop? *Night,* a memoir of living in a Nazi concentration camp, was challenged in Illinois for being too "negative." In Waukesha, Wisconsin, a novel by Tim O'Brien about Vietnam was banned, when the school board decided that the Vietnam War was too sensitive a topic for high school students to study. In Columbus, Indiana, a challenge has not yet been resolved that would restrict any text which used the word "nigger" in any context. In Auburn, Washington, the use of the word "Halloween" is no longer allowed. Trying to cover all the possible bases of discomfort, the Arts Council of Fairfax County, Virginia, refuses to allow the depiction of anything showing "nudes, weaponry, drug paraphernalia . . . violence, religious scenes, political expression or unpatriotic subjects."

Even when we are ostensibly trying to protect children, this kind   17
of censorship acts largely to protect each other and ultimately, ourselves, from the facts of life. There are people who would have us rewrite Homer, Shakespeare, and other works of history to fix the politically incorrect errors of the past. *Huckleberry Finn, The Learning Tree, Tom Sawyer,* and *Little House on the Prairie* have all been banned because of their purportedly racist content. In California, a local NAACP chapter challenged the book *The Cay.* The book is now being reviewed statewide. One NAACP official involved said, "Any book that offends any group should be taken out of the public libraries and schools."

His remark illustrates precisely the kind of limited vision censor-   18
ship requires. Surely he doesn't mean that if a biography of Martin Luther King, Jr. offended a member of the Aryan Nation, that book should be removed from circulation? But that is what he said. Physical censorship and physical repression leads to a psychic censorship, a repression of thought. Anyone who has ever written a memoir knows what it means to practice hindsight about our individual pasts. To practice hindsight about our communal history is to perform a frontal lobotomy on the culture.

To deny people, especially children, any reflection of their ordinary   19
lives, is to dislocate them. What happens to a child's sense of intellectual curiosity and social identity when every question is met with a stark glare? Or, worse, the black marker blotting out the answer, the example, the illustration? Dian Fossey's book, *Gorillas in the Mist,* was

allowed in a Pennsylvania high school class only after the passages describing gorilla mating habits were deleted. Quite recently, the California State Board of Education banned a short story by Alice Walker from an English-language competency test because it was "anti-meat eating." At the same time, they removed an excerpt from Annie Dillard's *An American Childhood,* because the scene of a snowball fight was "too violent." In Wellsville, Kansas, a student production of *Dracula* was allowed to continue only after most references to blood were removed.

Part of the problem we are facing now is the confusion between whether   20
books are or are not effective tools at transmitting ideas. When this confusion collides with the myth of a social consensus—with the idea that we actually agree in this country on what is good and not good—all hell breaks loose. Then the *Webster's Ninth Collegiate Dictionary* is banned because it contains a definition of the word "fuck." Perhaps we would all agree on the idea that *dictionaries,* as a concept, are good. But could we ever all agree on what a dictionary should do, what it should be, what it is for?

The idea that books should *not* be powerful, should not change   21
the reader, is a new idea. Thoreau said, "How many a man has dated a new era in his life from the reading of a book." Throughout history, literacy was considered a weapon. That's one reason it was withheld from the masses, from the poor, from women, and kept as an almost-exclusive tool of the wealthy and powerful men who ran society. They claimed that reading and writing distracted and bewildered these supposedly weak-minded members of society, who, anyway, had better things to do. But those in charge also knew what could happen. A few hundred years ago, anyone caught in England with written material criticizing the crown could have their hands amputated, and in some cases, their heads.

What happens today? A library aide in Kalispell, Montana, helped   22
two students research a project on witchcraft. The project was approved, but the school library lacked enough information, so the aide loaned the students two of her own books. For this she was fired.

In Riverside, California, members of the Eagle Forum, founded   23
by Phyllis Schlafly, protested a work about Rosa Parks because it "questions authority."

In Lake County, Florida, a newly elected school board began their   24
tenure by refusing to allow a Head Start program to open. They then tried, without success, to ban federally funded breakfasts for poor students. The head of the school board, who identifies herself as a

conservative Christian, speaks no foreign languages and has never traveled outside of the United States, managed to pass a new policy requiring school teachers to identify the United States as an inherently superior culture to that of any other country or period in history.

Such acts are little more than a kind of magical thinking. If we believe certain books will cause men to commit rape, then by banning the books, we can bring rape to an end. And we all know rapists stop at the library first. If we believe certain books and stories and ideas cause people to criticize authority, then by banning the ideas a utopian state of respect for authority will appear. If that hasn't happened yet, it's just a sign of how much more needs to be done, that not enough books have been banned yet. [25]

It hardly seems fair to move into the really juicy territory of nudity and sexual material now, but move I must. I've spent several years now talking to people about sex, and it took time for me to learn how to do so frankly. I know how difficult a confrontation with sexuality can be for people. But nudity? Sometimes I despair. In Oshkosh, Wisconsin, a formal challenge was made against the high school yearbook because of its "disgusting" nudity. The cover showed a detail from Michelangelo's Sistine Chapel—that of God creating Adam. Said one upset parent, "It surprises me what passes in the name of culture." [26]

One of the most pervasive modern American fears is that of the ordinary human body. We suffer a kind of physical dysphoria in this country. The "breast" and the "penis" evoke shame. The fact that just about every one in the world either has a penis or breasts is irrelevant. The very idea of penises and breasts haunts people. We fear their loss, we count the loss of either as unadulterated tragedy, but the depiction of a healthy breast or penis is condemned. [27]

A desperate effort is made to protect childhood innocence by sparing children the sight of the naked human body as long as possible. The sadness is that such efforts destroy their real innocence—the simple belief children have that their bodies are good. What do children learn from having the book *Where's Waldo?* snatched from the classroom shelves? This hugely popular book has been banned repeatedly because, in one crowded beach scene, the tiny profile of a woman's breast is visible. In Columbus, Ohio, the school librarian took it upon herself to paint clothes on the naked babies in Maurice Sendak's *In the Night Kitchen* and *Outside Over There*. [28]

Again, the breast, with irony. *A Woman's Worth*, a book by Marianne Williamson about the painfully low self-esteem many American women experience, was refused distribution by wholesalers in the Midwest and the South because the woman on the cover has half a [29] breast exposed. Since we women have breasts, what does this tell us about self-esteem? About shame? And about what we do and don't agree upon?

This "sex panic," like everything else, is really about being right,   30
presuming consensus instead of working toward it. The conservative feminist lawyer, Catharine MacKinnon, is fond of calling women like me "Uncle Toms." Because Catharine MacKinnon believes that pornography hurts women, she flatly states that any woman who disagrees is a traitor and cannot be considered a feminist. I have found myself over the last few years in the position of defending pornography as a feminist. As far as MacKinnon is concerned, I need only refuse to fight pornography—I need only defend free speech—to be one of her enemies. She calls us "Oreos." MacKinnon's colleagues, Andrea Dworkin and John Stoltenberg, call feminists who oppose censorship "pimps."

In October of 1992, law students at the University of Michigan,   31
where Catharine MacKinnon teaches, sponsored a conference on prostitution. As part of the conference, a local artist named Carol Jacobsen was hired to curate an art show.

Jacobsen's approach was to present art made by prostitutes about   32
their lives. Before the conference opened, a part of the show, an autobiographical videotape by a woman named Veronica Vera, was removed by John Stoltenberg, one of the conference speakers. He said it was "dangerous to women." When Carol Jacobsen found out, she chose to shut down her entire exhibit rather than show only parts of it.

I know Veronica Vera, and I've seen her videotape. I believe that   33
Vera's offense was that she doesn't bemoan her varied sexual experience. She celebrates it. She tells her story with humor and intelligence and a sensual joy in life. She credits her Catholic upbringing with turning her kinky, and credits her brief experiences as a sex worker with improving her self-esteem, her social life, and her savings account. This is not the vision of prostitution that MacKinnon's theories describe. There is no doubt in my mind that if the art show had featured tragic stories by miserable ex-prostitutes, no censorship would have taken place; the show would instead have been applauded for its honesty and raw power.

There is a particular irony here that almost escapes view. Jacobsen's   34
show was deliberately created as a forum for an almost completely silent and repressed class of women. That forum was shut down—silenced by a kind of scorched-earth politics. In the name of promoting one point of view, another point of view (and all debate between the

points of view) was cut off. MacKinnon herself, speaking to journalists about the ensuing controversy, dismissed the removal of the art as "a made-up sort of nothing incident." It wasn't to Carol Jacobsen, and it wasn't to Veronica Vera, and it wasn't to me. Such things should never be dismissed by anyone with an investment in social dialogue. In 1970, the English novelist Brigid Brophy said it quite neatly: "To defend society from sex is no one's business. To defend it from officiousness is the duty of everyone who values freedom—or sex."

I belong to something called the Working Group, a committee of   35
women formed by the National Coalition Against Censorship specifically to work on pornography issues. A lot of my time defending pornography's right to exist, and the right of any consenting adult to buy and make pornography without interference, has in the last few years centered around a proposed law called the Pornography Victim's Compensation Act. This bill came very close to passing into federal law last year, and was defeated only after a lengthy and expensive campaign by a coalition of writers, publishers, and anti-censorship groups. The Act would have created a "private right of action," that is, a civil law, in which the "producers, distributors, exhibitors, and sellers" of a work judged "obscene" could be sued by the victim of an act influenced by the work. (I will only mention in passing that such cause-and-effect relationships are extraordinarily hard to prove, and that if we were to look at the literary influences on violence and sexual crimes, the Bible would have to be considered carefully.)

The act as written is a masterpiece of circular thinking. The victim   36
in question needs to prove that the work in question is "obscene"—also an extraordinarily difficult thing to prove, and by Supreme Court definition, a local and therefore relative concept—and that the writer or bookseller involved should have "foreseen" that the violent act would occur. So if a nut reads a book which describes rape, and then rapes someone, the author and publisher and distributor and independent bookseller could all be sued for damages—that is, if the book was proven to be obscene rather than artistic in nature, and if the author *et al.* could have known that someone would imitate the rape. Of course, this is very bad law, and probably unusable in a court, but a great deal of money and time was spent promoting and fighting its tenets. It has already risen again in different forms. The Violence Against Women Act was written with a provision that judges would have to be trained in the causal relationship between violence and pornography, though such a relationship has never been proven to exist. And what happens to women who live with violence, if rape is never described, if they are taught not to tell the story, not to explain?

I've come to believe that it isn't enough to respond to sexual   37
censorship by saying something like, "Well, pornography is bad, but
censorship is worse." We have to go a step further into our world of
differences, and admit that plenty of thoughtful and good-hearted
people think pornography is a good thing. Just like art, we *don't* know
it when we see it. What's bread-and-butter to you might be poison to
me, or a big yawn. And vice versa.

Don Wildmon scares me; Jesse Helms scares me. But I'm also   38
genuinely worried by my liberal acquaintance who wants to eliminate
"brutality" from Hollywood films. I'm worried by my poet friend who
believes artists have a duty to produce only "positive and nourishing"
art. I'm worried just as much by all the socially involved, politically
concerned people who want to restrict—and punish—racist slang or
images of violence against women. Each of these people has a specific
example, a particular word or image, one book or movie, one incident
or picture, that exemplifies what they think goes too far.

If we agree—and I know we don't—that images "subordinating   39
women" should be illegal, what happens next? Using language adopted
from the works of Catharine MacKinnon and Andrea Dworkin, the
Canadian Supreme Court passed *Regina* v. *Butler* in 1992. Butler states
that "protecting" women against "harm" and "degradation" is a higher
value than protecting the freedom of speech.

I wish Andrea Dworkin and Catharine MacKinnon would just   40
wise up. I wish they could see how quaint and Victorian their rhetoric
is, how dangerously allied they are with a conservative position that
is no friend to female equality. Dworkin is, like me, a member of PEN,
which has a venerable reputation for protecting freedom of speech.
She fails to see to the dark heart of book banning. Only those who
already have power have an interest in censorship. Those who have
trouble being heard and seen in the first place, whose voices are quiet-
est, have the most to lose. Minorities, all women, the poor, the disenfranchised and politically incorrect—these are the people censorship
hurts first.

Since the Butler decision, more than a fourth of all Canadian   41
feminist bookstores have had material seized, and books by people
such as David Leavitt, Kathy Acker, and bell hooks have not been
allowed past the border. Andrea Dworkin's own book, titled *Woman
Hating*, was seized at the Canadian border because of its title alone.

All these things weaken us—as a society, as a nation. They weaken the   42
body of our culture. By bringing our children up in isolation—isolation

from history, new ideas, their own experiences—and by keeping ourselves in isolation, we are like people without antibodies, vulnerable
to the slightest germ. We lose touch with the ground on which this
country was built; we become afraid of freedom.

The Bill of Rights almost didn't get written, partly because the   43
leaders of the time—far-thinking men like Noah Webster and Alexander Hamilton—thought the rights in question were so obviously natural and worthy they would never be restricted. (Just as an aside, I have
to point that they were also writing laws to protect the world they
had made. A less rights-laden group, like Jefferson's personal slaves,
or the wives and daughters of any one of them, would likely have
suggested the Bill of Rights seemed like a good idea.) In the end it was
James Madison who prevailed, reciting again and again his fear of the
tyranny of the majority, his desire to protect the rights of a minority
even if it consisted of a single person. Words and pictures and ideas
that don't bother anyone don't need protection.

Now there is a ballot proposal in Anchorage that would create a   44
new tyranny of the majority—by allowing local citizens to vote, case
by case, on whether any given book in the elementary school library
should be available to students.

In Oklahoma, a program of environmental education was repeat-   45
edly challenged for being Satanic, "eastern," "psychological," and
"anti-Christian." One woman objecting explained that all environmental education is "Satanic," because the Bible says that the Earth will
burn. Do we want to go to the polls on this?

In Bloomington, Indiana, the book *The Bridge to Terabithia* by   46
Katherine Patterson was challenged by a group of fifth-graders' parents
because, the parents explained, the book teaches that people are innately good. And "God's word teaches us that we are all sinners," they
explained. How do we vote on that?

Catcher in the Rye by J.D. Salinger is perhaps the most publicly   47
and repeatedly challenged novel for young people. When it was challenged in Illinois not long ago for its "underlying hostility toward
Christianity," the complainant added that "respect for God's name
overrides the separation of church and state." To some, it also overrides
the Bill of Rights. The social scientist Marcia Pally called democracy
"a contact sport," and she was right.

When Ray Bradbury's classic work on censorship, *Fahrenheit 451*,   48
was taught in an Irvine, California public school not long ago, the
students were given copies with all the obscenities blacked out. In a
recent essay, Bradbury described his dismay over the years as teachers
and school librarians had committed similar crimes against his work.

But he had only just then found out that his own publisher had done the same: over the years since *Fahrenheit 451* was first published, one editor after the other had snipped offensive passages out of the work when new editions were being printed, until 75 separate sections of Bradbury's original writing were gone.

Such patronizing behavior makes us not only weak, but infantile. 49 In Georgia, the Heritage Education and Review Organization, which calls itself HERO, circulated a test for parents to use to determine if their children have been infected by "humanism." One of the questions on the test was, "Do your teachers ask you to make decisions about what is right and wrong?" Do these parents prefer their children to go out into the world unfinished—*untried?* This is what we get from censored thinking. This is what happens when people don't read books.

My good friend Karen Karbo wrote an essay last year about her 50 experiences with a publisher's lawyer. She had written a novel, *The Diamond Lane,* in which a character is injured by a falling ceiling fan in a fancy Los Angeles restaurant. This accident is a minor but critical turning point in the plot. The publisher's lawyer worried that any of the dozens of trendy restaurants in that neighborhood of L.A. might sue, though for what was not clear. Karen was reminded that her book contract, as do almost all book contracts, stipulates that if she is sued, and wins, she splits court costs 50:50 with her publisher. If she is sued and loses, she pays all the court costs herself. In Karen's words, "A cop sitting on your back bumper can make you nervous. He may only be on his way to Dunkin' Donuts, but the knowledge that he is sitting back there, watching, makes you slow down even if you aren't speeding."

Of course, we who work against censorship have our own agendas. 51 I have my reader's agenda, and I have my parent's agenda, and I have my writer's agenda, which is two-fold: I want, of course, to be able to write what I want, without interference. I want to decide for myself, for better and for worse, what to say and how to say it. But deeper, and with more of a chill, I worry about what happens to me as a writer when I am faced with censure of any kind.

When I finished my new book, my publishers decided to have the 52 company lawyer read it. She had a number of questions, most of them about whether or not I was quoting people with their permission, and so on. It was the usual stuff, except for my reference to one of Andrea Dworkin's books. Though my comment was nothing more than a bit of literary criticism, the lawyer wanted me to edit it out. Why? Because Dworkin and MacKinnon are litigious, because they have sued my publisher before, because, as the lawyer pointed out, the "opinion defense" isn't as strong as it used to be. And, she added, even an obvious nuisance suit could cost me a bundle.

A lot of harm has been done in this world and to this world by do-gooders, people who are, above all else, sure of themselves. We live in what is arguably the most heterogeneous society of all time, and we live here with an unfinished and immature ethic, without a whole foundation. Such a foundation may be impossible. And for all this, each of us has to act, has to choose how to act, every day.   53

Creativity is fundamentally amoral. In the making of creative work, anything goes, everything is material. Then the mature artist decides what works and what doesn't, what serves the story and what distracts. I write for a lot of reasons, to express ideas, to challenge ideas, to tell stories, but mostly I write because of an irrational addiction to language. I love prosody, the sound of words, their layered uses, the feel of a good sentence in my mouth. Does some writing cause harm? Of course it does. Writing couldn't cause good if it didn't cause harm. But I don't write to cause harm or to create good particularly. I write just to write, for writing's sake. To do so wholeheartedly means coming to terms with ambivalence. It means sometimes being a little pushy, a little demanding, if the story needs it. In my work, my duty is to the work. Maturity, I believe, means not only tolerating ambivalence and discomfort, but to some extent encouraging it.   54

This talk is supposed to be on the limits of expression. I cannot tell you what I think the limits are. I can tell you what my limits are, but they are just for me. The idea of defining it, finding words to describe and write into law what should not be allowed to be written—I can't. As for social consensus, there never has been much that was black and white in the world. There are few issues in which a thoughtful person couldn't find more than one side, see the wisdom or at least the motivation for the conflict. The most useful, important and difficult practice for us as citizens is to practice that—practice not just solving problems, but understanding why social problems are so hard to solve, why so many good people, reasonable people, fail to agree. I can't find five like-minded people, in this room, on this campus, this city, five people who seem to think about the world in similar ways, and gather them around a table and get them to agree on a definition of almost anything. Pluralism is one of this country's great conundrums, but it's also one of our glories. I want to keep slugging away, digging out a position of tolerance toward the intolerant. I want to make clear my willingness to put up with people who don't want to put up with me, because that is all I ask from them.   55

Courage is required. It's that simple. In Grand Saline, Texas, a   56
group of parents accused a teacher of Satanic practices. She was seen
to have committed several sins. She had used a reader which contained
a story about Islam. She had discussed African folk tales. She had a
picture of Santa Claus on the wall. The protesters pointed out that
the letters in Santa can be arranged to spell Satan. After an extensive
hate campaign, the teacher resigned.

Where, in all this, was the school principal? Why was the district   57
superintendent so craven as to allow such a campaign to destroy a
woman? Where were the other teachers, the other parents? Why such
cowardice in the face of argument? Where is the courage of those who,
above and beyond all of us, should be vigorously defending our right,
and our children's right, to critical thinking?

It's only by going a little way toward another person, toward the   58
confusing beliefs of another person, that we can go a little way into
another, and find compassion. Nancy Garden's young adult book,
Annie On My Mind, won an American Library Association Best Book
award in 1982. In 1993 it was burned on the steps of the Kansas City
School District, by a group of citizens led by two ministers. In writing
about her experience this spring, Garden chose to quote her own
fictional character: "Don't let ignorance win. Let love."

LOOKING AT THE CONTENT

1. What is meant by "the myth of social consensus"? Can you think of
   anything or any idea that might achieve true "social consensus"? What
   has social consensus to do with censorship?
2. What are the most common reasons for wanting a book banned or censored, according to Tisdale? Do you agree with Tisdale that these are not
   good reasons for censoring or banning a work? Why or why not?
3. Have you read any of the books listed by Tisdale that have been banned
   or called objectionable? If so, do you believe any one of them should be
   considered objectionable? Explain.
4. Several of the instances Tisdale discusses where books were banned seem
   rather silly reasons to her. Why do you agree or disagree with her? How
   many of the books she mentions have you read? Are you qualified to
   judge on the validity of some of these "objectionable" books? Do you
   need to have read them in order to discuss why they should or should
   not be banned? Explain.

LOOKING AT STRUCTURE AND STYLE

5. How effective is the use of a personal anecdote in opening Tisdale's
   comments? How does it help lead into her subject and thesis?

6. What passages provide author attitude and tone? Do you think her tone helps sway readers who reject her views? Why or why not? Do you think it matters to her?

7. What are some of the examples that Tisdale uses to support her views that many books are censored or banned because of someone's or some group's fear? What do these people fear?

EXPLORING DISCUSSION AND WRITING TOPICS

8. Research a recent incident where a book was banned or an attempt was made to ban it. What were the objections to the book? Who objected? Was the objection reasonable? Was the outcome fitting? Why or why not?

9. Why do you think that a vocal *minority* is often given such power over what should and should not be in school books? Should a vocal *majority* be given the right to censor? Who should decide what books are fit for students to read? Should young people, as Tisdale was, be allowed to read whatever they want?

10. Respond to Tisdale's statement, "The most useful, important and difficult practice for us as citizens is to practice . . . not just solving problems, but understanding why social problems are so hard to solve, why so many good people, reasonable people, fail to agree" (55).

ANDREA DWORKIN

What is pornography, what is obscene? What should be allowed in the media, what should not? Are today's sexual materials an expression of human freedom, or are they another unacceptable example of male attempts at subjugating women? Even the U.S. Supreme Court has difficulty answering those questions. But perhaps nowhere is there a more vocal disagreement over pornography than within the feminist movement. The next two essays present two differing feminist views.

Law professor Catherine MacKinnon and author Andrea Dworkin in *Pornography and Civil Rights* argue for censoring works they define as demeaning to women. Together they wrote for the city of Minneapolis an amendment to the city's civil rights law that attempts to recognize pornography as a violation of the civil rights of women, as a form of sex discrimination, and an abuse of human rights. Several cities have also adopted the law, but not without resistance. The following selection is taken from Andrea Dworkin's introduction to her book *Pornography: Men Possessing Women.*

❦

Pornography: Men Possessing Women

> *The burden of proof will be on those of us who have been victimized. If I [any woman] am able to prove that the picture you are holding, the one where the knife is stuffed up my vagina, was taken when my pimp forced me at gunpoint and photographed it without my consent, if my existence is proved real, I am coming to take what is mine. If I can prove that the movie you are looking at called* Black Bondage, *the one where my black skin is synonymous with filth and my bondage and my slavery is encouraged, caused me harm and discrimination, if my existence is proved real, I am coming to take what is mine. Whether you like it or not, the time is coming when you will have to get your fantasy off my ass.*
> —THERESE STANTON, *"Fighting for Our Existence"*
> *in* Changing Men 15 *(fall 1985)*

In the fall of 1983, something changed. The speech of women hurt by pornography became public and real. It, they, began to exist in the sphere of public reality. Constitutional lawyer Catharine A.

1

543

MacKinnon and I were hired by the City of Minneapolis to draft an
amendment to the city's civil rights law: an amendment that would
recognize pornography as a violation of the civil rights of women, as
a form of sex discrimination, an abuse of human rights. We were also
asked to organize hearings that would provide a legislative record
showing the need for such a law. Essentially, the legislators needed
to know that these violations were systematic and pervasive in the
population they represented, not rare, peculiar anomalies.

The years of listening to the private stories had been years of   2
despair for me. It was hopeless. I could not help. There was no help.
I listened; I went on my way; nothing changed. Now, all the years
of listening were knowledge, real knowledge that could be mined: a
resource, not a burden and a curse. I knew how women were hurt by
pornography. My knowledge was concrete, not abstract: I knew the
ways it was used; I knew how it was made; I knew the scenes of
exploitation and abuse in real life—the lives of prostitutes, daughters,
girlfriends, wives; I knew the words the women said when they dared
to whisper what had happened to them; I could hear their voices in
my mind, in my heart. I didn't know that there were such women all
around me, everywhere, in Minneapolis that fall. I was heartbroken
as women I knew came forward to testify: though I listened with an
outer detachment to the stories of rape, incest, prostitution, battery,
and torture, each in the service of pornography, inside I wanted
to die.

The women who came forward to testify at the hearings held by   3
the Minneapolis City Council on December 12 and 13, 1983, gave
their names and specified the area of the city in which they lived. They
spoke on the record before a governmental body in the city where
they lived; there they were, for family, neighbors, friends, employers,
teachers, and strangers to see, to remember. They described in detail
sexual abuse through pornography as it had happened to them. They
were questioned on their testimony by Catharine MacKinnon and
myself and also by members of the city council and sometimes the city
attorney. There were photographers and television cameras. There
were a couple of hundred people in the room. There was no safety,
no privacy, no retreat, no protection; only a net of validation provided
by the testimony of experts—clinical psychologists, prosecutors, experimental psychologists, social scientists, experts in sexual abuse from
rape crisis centers and battered women's shelters, and those who
worked with sex offenders. The testimony of these experts was not
abstract or theoretical; it brought the lives of more women, more

children, into the room: more rape, more violation through pornography. They too were talking about real people who had been hurt, sometimes killed; they had seen, known, treated, interviewed, numbers of them. A new social truth emerged, one that had been buried in fear, shame, and the silence of the socially powerless: no woman hurt by pornography was alone—she never had been; no woman hurt by pornography would ever be alone again because each was—truly—a "living remnant of the general struggle." What the survivors said was speech; the pornography had been, throughout their lives, a means of actively suppressing their speech. They had been turned into pornography in life and made mute; terrorized by it and made mute. Now, the mute spoke; the socially invisible were seen; the women were real; they mattered. This speech—their speech—was new in the world of public discourse, and it was made possible by the development of a law that some called censorship. The women came forward because they thought that the new civil rights law recognized what had happened to them, gave them recourse and redress, enhanced their civil dignity and human worth. The law itself gave them *existence:* I am real; they believed me; I count; social policy at last will take my life into account, validate my worth—me, the woman who was forced to fuck a dog; me, the woman he urinated on; me, the woman he tied up for his friends to use; me, the woman he masturbated in; me, the woman he branded or maimed; me, the woman he prostituted; me, the woman they gang-raped.

The law was passed twice in Minneapolis in 1983 and 1984 by two different city councils; it was vetoed each time by the same mayor, a man active in Amnesty International, opposing torture outside of Minneapolis. The law was passed in 1984 in Indianapolis with a redrafted definition that targeted violent pornography—the kind "everyone" opposes. The city was sued for passing it; the courts found it unconstitutional. The appeals judge said that pornography did all the harm we claimed—it promoted insult and injury, rape and assault, even caused women to have lower wages—and that these effects proved its power as speech; therefore, it had to be protected. In 1985, the law was put on the ballot by popular petition in Cambridge, Massachusetts. The city council refused to allow it on the ballot; we had to sue for ballot access; the civil liberties people opposed our having that access; we won the court case and the city was ordered to put the law on the ballot. We got 42 percent of the vote, a higher percentage than feminists got on the first women's suffrage referendum. In 1988, the law was on the ballot in Bellingham, Washington, in the presidential election;

we got 62 percent of the vote. The city had tried to keep us off the ballot; again we had to get a court order to gain ballot access. The City of Bellingham was sued by the ACLU in federal court for having the law, however unwillingly; a federal district judge found the law unconstitutional, simply reiterating the previous appeals court decision in the Indianapolis case—indeed, there was a statement that the harms of pornography were recognized and not in dispute.

We have not been able to get the courts to confront a real woman   5
plaintiff suing a real pornographer for depriving her of real rights through sexual exploitation or sexual abuse. This is because the challenges to the civil rights law have been abstract arguments about speech, as if women's lives are abstract, as if the harms are abstract, conceded but not real. The women trapped in the pictures continue to be perceived as the free speech of the pimps who exploit them. No judge seems willing to look such a woman, three-dimensional and breathing, in the face and tell her that the pimp's use of her is his constitutionally protected right of speech; that he has a right to express himself by violating her. The women on whom the pornography is used in assault remain invisible and speechless in these court cases. No judge has had to try to sleep at night having heard a real woman's voice describing what happened to her, the incest, the rape, the gang rape, the battery, the forced prostitution. Keeping these women silent in courts of law is the main strategy of the free speech lawyers who defend the pornography industry. Hey, they love literature; they deplore sexism. If some women get hurt, that's the price we pay for freedom. Who are the "we"? What is the "freedom"? These speech-loving law-yers keep the women from speaking in court so that no judge will actually be able to listen to them.

Women continue speaking out in public forums, even though we   6
are formally and purposefully silenced in actual courts of law. Hearings were held by a subcommittee of the Senate Judiciary Committee on the effects of pornography on women and children; the Attorney General's Commission on Pornography listened to the testimony of women hurt by pornography; women are demanding to speak at conferences, de-bates, on television, radio. This civil rights law is taught in law schools all over the country; it is written about in law journals, often favorably; increasingly, it has academic support; and its passage has been cited as precedent in at least one judicial decision finding that pornography in the workplace can be legally recognized as sexual harassment. The time of silence—at least the time of absolute silence—is over. And the civil rights law developed in Minneapolis has had an impact around the world. It is on the agenda of legislators in England, Ireland, West

Germany, New Zealand, Tasmania, and Canada; it is on the agenda
of political activists all over the world.

The law itself is civil, not criminal. It allows people who have   7
been hurt by pornography to sue for sex discrimination. Under this
law, it is sex discrimination to coerce, intimidate, or fraudulently induce
anyone into pornography; it is sex discrimination to force pornography
on a person in any place of employment, education, home, or any
public place; it is sex discrimination to assault, physically attack, or
injure any person in a way that is directly caused by a specific piece
of pornography—the pornographers share responsibility for the assault; in the Bellingham version, it is also sex discrimination to defame
any person through the unauthorized use in pornography of their
name, image, and/or recognizable personal likeness; and it is sex discrimination to produce, sell, exhibit, or distribute pornography—to
traffic in the exploitation of women, to traffic in material that provably
causes aggression against and lower civil status for women in society.

The law's definition of pornography is concrete, not abstract.   8
Pornography is defined as the graphic, sexually explicit subordination
of women in pictures and/or words that also includes women presented
dehumanized as sexual objects, things, or commodities; or women
presented as sexual objects who enjoy pain or humiliation; or women
presented as sexual objects who experience sexual pleasure in being
raped; or women presented as sexual objects tied up or cut up or
mutilated or bruised or physically hurt; or women presented in postures
or positions of sexual submission, servility, or display; or women's
body parts—including but not limited to vaginas, breasts, buttocks—
exhibited such that women are reduced to those parts; or women
presented as whores by nature; or women presented being penetrated
by objects or animals; or women presented in scenarios of degradation,
injury, torture, shown as filthy or inferior, bleeding, bruised, or hurt
in a context that makes these conditions sexual. If men, children, or
transsexuals are used in any of the same ways, the material also meets
the definition of pornography.

For women hurt by pornography, this law simply describes reality;   9
it is a map of a real world. Because the law allows them to sue those
who have imposed this reality on them—especially the makers, sellers,
exhibitors, and distributors of pornography—they have a way of re-
drawing the map. The courts now protect the pornography; they recognize the harm to women in judicial decisions—or they use words that
say they recognize the harm—and then tell women that the Constitution protects the harm; profit is real to them and they make sure the
pimps stay rich, even as women and their children are this country's

poor. The civil rights law is designed to confront both the courts and the pornographers with a demand for substantive, not theoretical, equality. This law says: we have the right to stop them from doing this to us because we are human beings. "If my existence is proved real, I am coming to take what is mine," Therese Stanton wrote for every woman who wants to use this law. How terrifying that thought must be to those who have been using women with impunity.

Initially an amendment to a city ordinance, this law has had a global impact because: (1) it tells the truth about what pornography is and does; (2) it tells the truth about how women are exploited and hurt by the use of pornography; (3) it seeks to expand the speech of women by taking the pornographers' gags out of our mouths; (4) it seeks to expand the speech and enhance the civil status of women by giving us the courts as a forum in which we will have standing and authority; (5) it is a mechanism for redistributing power, taking it from pimps, giving it to those they have been exploiting for profit, injuring for pleasure; (6) it says that women matter, including the women in the pornography. This law and the political vision and experience that inform it are not going to go away. We are going to stop the pornographers. We are going to claim our human dignity under law. One ex-prostitute, who is an organizer for the passage of this civil rights law, wrote: "Confronting how I've been hurt is the hardest thing that I've ever had to do in my life. A hard life, if I may say so." She is right. Confronting the pornographers is easier—their threats, their violence, their power. Confronting the courts is easier—their indifference, their contempt for women, their plain stupidity. Confronting the status quo is easier. Patience is easier and so is every form of political activism, however dangerous. Beaver is real, all right. A serious woman—formidable even—she is coming to take what is hers.

THINKING ABOUT THE CONTENT

1. Dworkin wants laws that "recognize pornography as a violation of the civil rights of women, as a form of sex discrimination, an abuse of human rights" (1). How does Dworkin define *pornography*? How does the law define *pornography*? Does Dworkin disagree with the law's definition?

2. Who were the women who came forward to testify at the hearings held in Minneapolis before the city council (3)? How were they involved in pornography? Does Dworkin imply that pornography is behind all sexual abuse to women or that sexual abuse is pornography?

3. For what reasons have some courts been unwilling to pass the law or cities sued for passing it? What affect has this had on women who have been sexually abused?

4. According to Dworkin, "The courts now protect the pornography; they recognize the harm to women in judicial decisions—or they use words that say they recognize the harm—and then tell women that the Constitution protects the harm" (9). What evidence does she cite that shows a relationship between pornography and sexual abuse?

LOOKING AT STRUCTURE AND STYLE

5. What words or passages help develop Dworkin's attitude and tone? Is it fitting for her topic and thesis? Why or why not?
6. How persuasive is Dworkin? Does reference to the women who testified before the city council about their abusive treatment supply enough support for her thesis? Why or why not?

EXPLORING DISCUSSION AND WRITING TOPICS

Read the following essay ("The Perils of Pornophobia" by Nadine Strossen) before exploring possible essay topics.

Worried over the pro-censorship movement among some feminists, Nadine Strossen feels the McKinnons and the Dworkins threaten "to impair the very women's rights movement it professes to serve." She feels there is a difference between seeking freedom *within* our culture and seeking freedom *from* it. Strossen warns of the dangers to freedom posed by using censorship as a tool for social change and argues against the point made in the previous reading selection (Andrea Dworkin's "Pornography: Men Possessing Women").

Nadine Strossen is a constitutional law professor at New York Law School and president of the American Civil Liberties Union. The following essay from the May/June 1995 issue of the *Humanist* is adapted from her book, *Defending Pornography: Free Speech, Sex, and the Fight for Woman's Rights*.

෴

The Perils of Pornophobia

In 1992, in response to a complaint, officials at Pennsylvania State University unceremoniously removed Francisco de Goya's masterpiece, *The Nude Maja*, from a classroom wall. The complaint had not been lodged by Jesse Helms or some irate member of the Christian Coalition. Instead, the complainant was a feminist English professor who protested that the eighteenth-century painting of a recumbent nude woman made her and her female students "uncomfortable."

This was not an isolated incident. At the University of Arizona at Tucson, feminist students physically attacked a graduate student's exhibit of photographic self-portraits. Why? The artist had photographed *herself* in her *underwear*. And at the University of Michigan Law School, feminist students who had organized a conference on "Prostitution: From Academia to Activism" removed a feminist-curated art exhibition held in conjunction with the conference. Their reason? Conference speakers had complained that a composite videotape containing interviews of working prostitutes was "pornographic" and therefore unacceptable.

What is wrong with this picture? Where have they come from—these feminists who behave like religious conservatives, who censor works of art because they deal with sexual themes? Have not feminists long known that censorship is a dangerous weapon which, if permitted, would inevitably be turned against them? Certainly that was the irrefutable lesson of the early women's rights movement, when Margaret Sanger, Mary Ware Dennett, and other activists were arrested, charged with "obscenity," and prosecuted for distributing educational pamphlets about sex and birth control. Theirs was a struggle for freedom of sexual expression and full gender equality, which they understood to be mutually reinforcing.

Theirs was also a lesson well understood by the second wave of   4
feminism in the 1970s, when writers such as Germaine Greer, Betty Friedan, and Betty Dodson boldly asserted that women had the right to be free from discrimination not only in the workplace and in the classroom but in the bedroom as well. Freedom from limiting, conventional stereotypes concerning female sexuality was an essential aspect of what we then called "women's liberation." Women should not be seen as victims in their sexual relations with men but as equally assertive partners, just as capable of experiencing sexual pleasure.

But it is a lesson that, alas, many feminists have now forgotten.   5
Today, an increasingly influential feminist pro-censorship movement threatens to impair the very women's rights movement it professes to serve. Led by law professor Catharine MacKinnon and writer Andrea Dworkin, this faction of the feminist movement maintains that sexually oriented *expression*—not sex-segregated labor markets, sexist concepts of marriage and family, or pent-up rage—is the preeminent cause of discrimination and violence against women. Their solution is seemingly simple: suppress all "pornography."

Censorship, however, is never a simple matter. First, the offense   6
must be described. And how does one define something so infinitely variable, so deeply personal, so uniquely individualized as the image, the word, and the fantasy that cause sexual arousal? For decades, the U.S. Supreme Court has engaged in a Sisyphean struggle to craft a definition of *obscenity* that the lower courts can apply with some fairness and consistency. Their dilemma was best summed up in former Justice Potter Stewart's now famous statement: "I shall not today attempt further to define [obscenity]; and perhaps I could never succeed in intelligibly doing so. But I know it when I see it."

The censorious feminists are not so modest as Justice Stewart.   7
They have fashioned an elaborate definition of *pornography* that encompasses vastly more material than does the currently recognized law of *obscenity.* As set out in their model law (which has been considered in more than a dozen jurisdictions in the United States and overseas, and

which has been substantially adopted in Canada), pornography is "the sexually explicit subordination of women through pictures and/ or words." The model law lists eight different criteria that attempt to illustrate their concept of "subordination," such as depictions in which "women are presented in postures or positions of sexual submission, servility, or display" or "women are presented in scenarios of degradation, humiliation, injury, torture . . . in a context that makes these conditions sexual." This linguistic driftnet can ensnare anything from religious imagery and documentary footage about the mass rapes in the Balkans to self-help books about women's health. Indeed, the Boston Women's Health Book Collective, publisher of the now-classic book on women's health and sexuality, *Our Bodies, Ourselves*, actively campaigned against the MacKinnon-Dworkin model law when it was proposed in Cambridge, Massachusetts, in 1985, recognizing that the book's explicit text and pictures could be targeted as pornographic under the law.

Although the "MacDworkinite" approach to pornography has an   8 intuitive appeal to many feminists, it is *itself* based on subordinating and demeaning stereotypes about women. Central to the pornophobic feminists—and to many traditional conservatives and right-wing fundamentalists, as well—is the notion that *sex* is inherently degrading to women (although not to men). Not just sexual expression but sex itself—even consensual, nonviolent sex—is an evil from which women, like children, must be protected.

MacKinnon puts it this way: "Compare victims' reports of rape   9 with women's reports of sex. They look a lot alike. . . . The major distinction between intercourse (normal) and rape (abnormal) is that the normal happens so often that one cannot get anyone to see anything wrong with it." And from Dworkin: "Intercourse remains a means or the means of physiologically making a woman inferior." Given society's pervasive sexism, she believes, women cannot freely consent to sexual relations with men; those who do consent are, in Dworkin's words, "collaborators . . . experiencing pleasure in their own inferiority."

These ideas are hardly radical. Rather, they are a reincarnation   10 of disempowering puritanical, Victorian notions that feminists have long tried to consign to the dustbin of history: woman as sexual victim; man as voracious satyr. The MacDworkinite approach to sexual expression is a throwback to the archaic stereotypes that formed the basis for nineteenth-century laws which prohibited "vulgar" or sexually suggestive language from being used in the presence of women and girls.

In those days, women were barred from practicing law and serving   11 as jurors lest they be exposed to such language. Such "protective" laws have historically functioned to bar women from full legal equality. Paternalism always leads to exclusion, discrimination, and the loss of freedom and autonomy. And in its most extreme form, it leads to purdah, in which women are completely shrouded from public view.

The pro-censorship feminists are not fighting alone. Although they try   12
to distance themselves from such traditional "family-values" conservatives as Jesse Helms, Phyllis Schlafly, and Donald Wildmon, who are less interested in protecting women than in preserving male dominance, a common hatred of sexual expression and fondness for censorship unite the two camps. For example, the Indianapolis City Council adopted the MacKinnon-Dworkin model law in 1984 thanks to the hard work of former council member Beulah Coughenour, a leader of the Indiana Stop ERA movement. (Federal courts later declared the law unconstitutional.) And when Phyllis Schlafly's Eagle Forum and Beverly LaHaye's Concerned Women for America launched their "Enough Is Enough" anti-pornography campaign, they trumpeted the words of Andrea Dworkin in promotional materials.

This mutually reinforcing relationship does a serious disservice to   13
the fight for women's equality. It lends credibility to and strengthens the right wing and its anti-feminist, anti-choice, homophobic agenda. This is particularly damaging in light of the growing influence of the religious right in the Republican Party and the recent Republican sweep of both Congress and many state governments. If anyone doubts that the newly empowered GOP intends to forge ahead with anti-woman agendas, they need only read the party's "Contract with America" which, among other things, reintroduces the recently repealed "gag rule" forbidding government-funded family-planning clinics from even discussing abortion with their patients.

The pro-censorship feminists base their efforts on the largely unex-   14
amined assumption that ridding society of pornography would reduce sexism and violence against women. If there were any evidence that this were true, anti-censorship feminists—myself included—would be compelled at least to reexamine our opposition to censorship. But there is no such evidence to be found.

A causal connection between exposure to pornography and the   15
commission of sexual violence has never been established. The National Research Council's Panel on Understanding and Preventing Violence concluded in a 1993 survey of laboratory studies that "demonstrated empirical links between pornography and sex crimes in general are weak or absent." Even according to another research literature survey that former U.S. Surgeon General C. Everett Koop conducted at the behest of the staunchly anti-pornography Meese Commission,

only two reliable generalizations could be made about the impact of "degrading" sexual material on its viewers: it caused them to think that a variety of sexual practices was more common than they had previously believed, and to more accurately estimate the prevalence of varied sexual practices.

Correlational studies are similarly unsupportive of the pro-censor- 16 ship cause. There are no consistent correlations between the availability of pornography in various communities, states, and countries and their rates of sexual offenses. If anything, studies suggest an inverse relationship: a greater availability of sexually explicit material seems to correlate not with higher rates of sexual violence but, rather, with higher indices of gender equality. For example, Singapore, with its tight restrictions on pornography, has experienced a much greater increase in rape rates than has Sweden, with its liberalized obscenity laws.

There *is* mounting evidence, however, that MacDworkinite-type 17 laws will be used against the very people they are supposed to protect— namely, women. In 1992, for example, the Canadian Supreme Court incorporated the MacKinnon-Dworkin concept of pornography into Canadian obscenity law. Since that ruling, in *Butler* v. *The Queen*— which MacKinnon enthusiastically hailed as "a stunning victory for women"—well over half of all feminist bookstores in Canada have had materials confiscated or detained by customs. According to the *Feminist Bookstore News,* a Canadian publication, "The *Butler* decision has been used . . . only to seize lesbian, gay, and feminist material."

Ironically but predictably, one of the victims of Canada's new law 18 is Andrea Dworkin herself. Two of her books, *Pornography: Men Possessing Women* and *Women Hating,* were seized, customs officials said, because they "illegally eroticized pain and bondage." Like the MacKinnon-Dworkin model law, the *Butler* decision makes no exceptions for material that is part of a feminist critique of pornography or other feminist presentation. And this inevitably overbroad sweep is precisely why censorship is antithetical to the fight for women's rights.

The pornophobia that grips MacKinnon, Dworkin, and their fol- 19 lowers has had further counterproductive impacts on the fight for women's rights. Censorship factionalism within the feminist movement has led to an enormously wasteful diversion of energy from the real cause of and solutions to the ongoing problems of discrimination and violence against women. Moreover, the "porn-made-me-do-it" defense, whereby convicted rapists cite MacKinnon and Dworkin in seeking to reduce their sentences, actually impedes the aggressive enforcement of criminal laws against sexual violence.

A return to the basic principles of women's liberation would put   20
the feminist movement back on course. We women are entitled to
freedom of expression—to read, think, speak, sing, write, paint, dance,
dream, photograph, film, and fantasize as we wish. We are also entitled
to our dignity, autonomy, and equality. Fortunately, we can—and
will—have both.

THINKING ABOUT THE CONTENT

1. For what reasons does Strossen feel that the "feminist pro-censorship
   movement threatens to impair the very women's rights movement it professes to serve" (5)? Strossen feels an antipornography movement makes
   women look like victims and gives the impression "that sex is inherently
   degrading to women," the very image the feminist movement has wanted
   to avoid in their quest for equality. Why do you agree or not agree with
   her?
2. How has the MacKinnon-Dworkin definition of *pornography* created in
   Strossen's words, a "linguistic driftnet" (7)? What does she mean? How
   did the law "backfire" on Dworkin?
3. According to Strossen, no causal connection exists between exposure to
   pornography and the act of perpetrating sexual violence (15). What is
   her evidence? Does this mean there is no connection between the two?
   Why or why not?

LOOKING AT STRUCTURE AND STYLE

4. Strossen uses examples in her first two paragraphs. How are they used
   to support her topic and thesis? Are these useful examples? Why or why
   not?
5. How well does Strossen explain her opponents' viewpoints regarding
   pornography and censorship? How well does she explain why she disagrees with those views?
6. Which article do you think is the stronger in style and argument, Andrea
   Dworkin's or Nadine Strossen's? Why?

EXPLORING DISCUSSION AND WRITING TOPICS

7. Research the U.S. Supreme Court's definition of *obscenity* and *pornography*. Why do you think the Supreme Court has had such difficulty formu-
   lating definitions? How do you define the two? Do you think the First
   Amendment should include freedom to use obscenity or pornography in
   the media? Why or why not?
8. Will ridding the availability of pornography reduce sexual violence and
   provide men with a more equal view of women? Do you think men see

women as sexual objects to be used? Are there other ways this image of women is portrayed in our society that are not pornographic but suggestive, such as advertisements, television programs, movies, and so on?

9. Read more from Andrea Dworkin's book, *Pornography: Men Possessing Women.* Why would it be confiscated in Canada as "illegally eroticized pain and bondage" (18)? Under Dworkin's own definition, is her book pornographic? Should it be censored?

10. Research books or movies that have been banned or censored in the United States. For what reasons have books such as Mark Twain's *Adventures of Huckleberry Finn,* J. D. Salinger's *Catcher in the Rye,* James Joyce's *Ulysses,* D. H. Lawrence's *Lady Chatterly's Lover,* Laura Ingalls Wilder's, *Little House on the Prairie,* and The Brothers Grimm's *Snow White,* to name a few, been banned or censored?

BARBARA DORITY

Barbara Dority is president of the Humanists of Washington, executive director of the Washington Coalition Against Censorship, cochair of the Northwest Feminist Anti-Censorship Taskforce, and vice-president and newsletter editor of the Hemlock Society of Washington State, a nonprofit organization promoting the right of people who are terminally ill to take their own lives.

In her following essay from the May/June 1995 issue of the *Humanist* magazine, Dority cautions against being too quick in the censorship of "objectionable" music. Once certain censorship steps have been accomplished by the offended, what form of censorship would come next? For Dority, rap music represents the voice of certain young people whose reality of "drug use, sexual activity, and violence" is a reality that needs to be confronted, not silenced.

ꙮ

The War on Rock and Rap Music

All music lovers, including those who prefer classical music and opera to more modern sounds, should be vitally concerned about the censorship of rock and rap music. As a long-time anti-censorship activist, I am alarmed by recent events which make a mockery of our Bill of Rights. I am convinced that we must take a stand against this strong-arm suppression of intellectual freedom and free speech. 1

A nationwide movement to restrict access to music began in 1985 with the founding of the Parents' Music Resource Center by Susan Baker, wife of Secretary of State James Baker, and Tipper Gore, wife of Senator Albert Gore. After a series of sensational congressional hearings failed to convince Congress to pass legislation mandating government labeling of "objectionable" music, the PMRC shifted its pressure tactics to the record companies. Insisting that rock and rap lyrics cause violence and sexual irresponsibility, the PMRC demanded that record producers institute a system of "voluntary" labeling. 2

Persistence pays off. On May 9, 1990, the Recording Industry Association of America announced the coming of a uniform warning label system on "all possibly objectionable materials" beginning in July. 3

This alarming concession, however, still falls woefully short of   4
what pro-censorship activists really want. Many states are considering
repressive legislation that would ban the sale of recordings containing
lyrics about adultery, incest, illicit drug or alcohol use, murder, or
suicide. Opera lovers will note that such works as *Madame Butterfly,
Tosca, Carmen, La Traviata,* and many others would fall victim to
these standards.

In Missouri, Representative Jean Dixon, with help from Phyllis   5
Schlafly's Eagle Forum, has fashioned a model anti-rock-and-rap bill
that would make labeling mandatory for music containing "unsuitable"
lyrics. Proposed measures in 20 other states would prohibit the sale
of stickered recordings to those under 18. Some would prohibit minors
from attending live concerts by the targeted groups. Many would
provide for awarding damages to persons injured by someone "motivated" by a recording.

Such proposals have frightened retailers into requiring proof of   6
age for purchases, pulling labeled recordings altogether, or applying
their own stickers. (Meyer Music Markets have gone so far as to apply
a warning label to Frank Zappa's *Jazz from Hell,* an all-instrumental
album.)

This year [1990] we witnessed the first two music obscenity trials   7
ever held in the United States. In February, an Alabama retailer was
arrested and charged for selling a purportedly obscene rap album by
the group 2 Live Crew to a police officer. An Alabama jury acquitted
him after a four-day trial in which experts traced the musical and
cultural developments of rap music. The high cost of defending against
such prosecutions has, of course, created a chilling effect on the content
of creative works.

After a grand jury in Volusia County, Florida, declared 2 Live   8
Crew's best-selling *As Nasty As They Wanna Be* obscene, another
record store clerk in Sarasota was arrested for selling the album to a
minor. He faces up to five years in prison and a $5,000 fine. At least
six other Florida counties have banned 2 Live Crew's recordings.

In June, a U.S. district court judge in Fort Lauderdale ruled that   9
a second 2 Live Crew album was obscene. The ruling was followed
within days by the arrest of a record shop owner and the Gestapo-
style arrest of two members of the band. That picture is engraved
forever behind my eyes: two young black musicians being led away
in handcuffs in the middle of the night. As Frank Zappa says, "Is this
really the Land of the Free and the Home of the Brave? Then where
the hell are we, Wanda?"

Meanwhile, the Federal Communications Commission is cracking 10
down on what it calls "indecency" in broadcast music. Last October,
KLUC in Las Vegas was fined $2,000 for playing Prince's "Erotic
City"; WTZA in Miami was fined $2,000 for playing "Penis Envy"
by the folk group Uncle Bonsai; and WIOD in Miami was fined
$10,000 for various broadcast music infractions.

Late last year, the FBI became a formidable rock critic when its 11
chief spokesperson, Milt Ahlerich, sent a letter on Department of
Justice stationery to the president of Priority Records, which had just
released the million-selling album *Straight Outta Compton* by the rap
group N.W.A. [niggers with attitude]. The letter, referring to a song
from the album called "——tha police" (dashes in the official title),
states that the song "encourages violence against and disrespect for
law enforcement officers. I wanted you to be aware of the FBI's position. . . . I believe my views reflect the opinion of the entire law
enforcement community."

The FBI's letter is historic; the bureau has never before taken an 12
official position on a work of art. Although direct FBI action wasn't
specifically threatened, it was hardly necessary. Local police departments faxed a version of the song from city to city. When N.W.A.
attempted to perform the song at a concert in Detroit, police moved
toward the stage and ended the set.

Rap music is a powerful force for young people. This new form 13
of communication and protest is the voice of the disenfranchised.
N.W.A. and other rap groups—almost exclusively young black musicians—are deliberately provocative. These people are expressing the
reality of their lives and their culture, which includes drug use, sexual
activity, and violence. In today's climate of hostility and violence between police and the black community, these songs illuminate a harsh
reality—a reality we must confront. This cannot be accomplished by
silencing bands. In fact, this draconian suppression will only further
enflame the situation.

"——the police" is part of a long tradition of literature and art 14
that question authority. So far, the FBI seems concerned only when
those expressing anti-authority sentiments are young, black, and ampli-
fied. Certainly this music from the streets and ghettos of America
makes many people uncomfortable. That's what it's supposed to do.
The First Amendment itself makes many people uncomfortable. But
it doesn't exist to promote comfort. It exists to promote freedom.

Rockers, rappers, and free speech advocates are organizing to 15
fight back. Music in Action, a coalition of artists, retailers, fans, and

concerned citizens, is forming local affiliates and has held several rallies in Washington, D.C. At one rally, rock critic and journalist Dave Marsh told the crowd, "It's shameful that on this day we live in a climate of fear. We are here to serve notice that free speech is for everyone, not just the elite." You can contact MA at 705 President Street, Brooklyn, NY 11215. Rock & Roll Confidential, another group keeping members informed and fighting music censorship, can be contacted at Box 15052, Long Beach, CA 90815.

16   If the state is given license to require producers and retailers to label and restrict access to commercial recordings, it's a small step to requiring publishers and booksellers to label and restrict access to books. New forms of music have always served as the cutting-edge voice of youth and have long been attacked due to sex, drugs, and obscenity. But the current campaign goes beyond past efforts and involves many powerful people. Why? I believe, along with Dave Marsh, that suppression tactics have increased because of the explosion of social and political comment in pop music and the growing social and political involvement of musicians and their audiences.

17   These heavy-handed attacks on the freedom of expression of young musicians are direct assaults on everyone's First Amendment rights of free speech and political dissent. We *must not tolerate* government censorship. We must stand together against this tyranny!

THINKING ABOUT THE CONTENT

1. Who does Dority believe is responsible for the push to censor music that some people find offensive? What does Dority imply is the real reason behind the drive to censor certain lyrics? Is she correct?
2. Do you find some rap music, such as the lyrics of 2 Live Crew, N.W.A., and Ice-T, offensive? Why or why not? What makes something offensive? Is offensive speech protected by the First Amendment?
3. Do you agree with Dority? Why or why not? What are her arguments against censorship? What are your arguments for or against censorship? Are they valid?

LOOKING AT STRUCTURE AND STYLE

4. Describe the effectiveness of her opening and closing paragraphs. To whom is she writing?
5. Dority names names and supplies numerous examples of arrests and fines for selling or broadcasting banned music. How does this help support her conclusion regarding censorship of music? Could this information be used to support an opposite thesis?

EXPLORING DISCUSSION AND WRITING TOPICS

6. Dority wrote her essay in 1990. What changes have taken place since then regarding efforts to ban or censor certain rap music? Who seems to be winning the war on rap music?
7. Evaluate the lyrics of one of the groups whose music is considered objectionable. Do you find the lyrics offensive? Are the roots of rap, as some defenders believe, a youth rebellion against an attempt to control black masculinity? Is there a social message that politicians and certain members of society don't want to hear at a deeper level than the objectionable words? Would you allow your teenager to hear these lyrics? Do you like to listen to rap music?
8. What exactly does *freedom of speech* mean? Are there limits to what people should be free to say? Where is the line drawn, if any? Who suffers when items are censored? Is more gained or lost by censorship? Who should determine what should or should not be censored?

SOME RESEARCH SOURCES ON MEDIA ISSUES

The following sources may be useful if you choose to do more reading or pursue a research project dealing with issues prompted by the reading selections in this unit.

Auletta, Ken. *Three Blind Mice: How the Networks Lost Their Way.* New York: Random House, 1991.

Bagdikian, Ben H. *The Media Monopoly.* Boston: Beacon Press, 1987.

Bosmajian, Haig, ed. *The First Amendment in the Classroom* Series. New York: Neal-Schuman, various dates.

Davis, Douglas. *The Five Myths of the Power of Television: Or, Why the Medium Is Not the Message.* New York: Simon & Schuster, 1993.

Fallows, James. *Breaking the News: How the Media Undermine American Democracy.* New York: Pantheon, 1996.

Franken, Al. *Rush Limbaugh Is a Big Fat Idiot and Other Observations.* New York: Delacorte, 1996.

Fuller, Jack. *News Values.* Chicago: University of Chicago Press, 1996.

Gans, Herbert. *Deciding What's News.* New York: Vintage, 1980.

Halberstam, David. *The Powers That Be.* New York: Dell, 1979.

Heaton, Jeanne A., and Nora Leigh Wilson. *Tuning in Trouble.* San Francisco: Jossey-Bass, 1995.

Hentoff, Nat. *Free Speech for Me—But Not for Thee.* New York: HarperCollins, 1992.

Iyengar, Shanto. *Is Anyone Responsible?* Chicago: University of Chicago Press, 1991.

Jensen, Carl. *Censored: The News that Didn't Make the News—and Why.* Chapel Hill, NC: Shelburne Press, published annually.

Lodziak, Conrad. *The Power of Television: A Critical Appraisal.* New York: St. Martin's, 1986.

Parenti, Michael. *Inventing Reality: The Politics of News Media,* 2nd edition. New York: St. Martin's Press, 1992.

Postman, Neil, and Steve Powers. *How to Watch TV News.* New York: Penguin, 1992.

Rosenblum, Mort. *Who Stole the News?* New York: John Wiley & Sons, 1993.

Winn, Marie. *The Plug-In Drug: Television, Children and the Family.* New York: Penguin, 1977.

Zeller, John R. *The Nature and Origins of Mass Opinion.* New York: Cambridge, 1992.

APPENDIX A

Essay Format and Proofreading Guide

Essay Format

If your instructor does not mandate what form your final essay should take, follow these standard rules.

If you type or use a word processor

1. Use standard 8½″ × 11″ bond typing paper. Don't use erasable bond paper because it smears too easily. Make certain that your typewriter or computer printer ribbon makes a clear, dark imprint. Don't use script or unusual type, especially if you print out your paper on a dot matrix printer. Make certain all letters are distinguishable (for instance, some printers don't make clear p's or d's).

2. Double space your paper to provide room for your instructor to make comments and corrections. This also leaves enough space for you to correct any typing, spelling, or punctuation errors you notice when proofreading your typed copy. (See proofreading correction symbols on page 574.) If your paper is very messy, retype it.

3. Leave at least 1″ margins all around your page.

4. Your name, your instructor's name, the course number, and the date should appear in the upper left- or right-hand corner on the first page. Double space, then center your title, capitalizing the first letter of each word unless it is an article, conjunction, or preposition. Don't underline, italicize, or place quotation marks around your title. (If other writers refer to your essay by title in their writing, then they should place quotation marks around your title to identify it as such.)

5. Indent the first line of each paragraph five spaces.

6. Leave two spaces after every period, question mark, or exclamation mark; use only one space after commas, semicolons, or colons.

7. Use quotation marks around short quotations that run fewer than five lines of your own manuscript. If the quote runs longer, then

indent ten spaces from the left and right to set it off from your own writing; no quotation marks are needed, but the quotation should be followed by the source cited in parentheses (see Appendix C, "Quoting and Documenting Sources"). When the quotation is completed, return to your regular margins.

8. Number all pages consecutively in the upper right-hand corner about ½″ from the top. You may want to place your last name next to the page number. No page number is needed for the first page unless your instructor wants a title page. In that case, ask the instructor for more details on format. Title pages are generally used for lengthy research papers, which require outlines and footnote and bibliography pages.

9. Staple your pages together in order at the upper left-hand corner only. Don't use paper clips; they fall off or get caught in other students' essays when stacked in a pile. Don't bend the corners together with a little tear—it doesn't work.

10. Don't use binders or folders unless your instructor requests them.

11. Make a copy in case something happens to the original. If you use a word processor, be sure to make a backup copy on disk.

If your essay is handwritten

It's generally not a good idea to submit handwritten papers. If your instructor does permit it, you should follow the rules above for typed papers, with these differences:

1. Use white, wide-lined paper, no smaller than 8 ½″ × 11″.

2. If you write on paper from a spiral notebook, cut off the ragged edges before you submit it.

3. Write on every other line, using only one side of a page.

4. Use only black or dark blue ink.

5. If your handwriting is poor, print. If you can't write or print neatly, pay a typist. An instructor has many papers to grade and has little patience with papers that are difficult to read.

Following these essay format rules is fairly safe, but it is always a good idea to ask any instructors who allow handwritten essays what format they want you to use.

First Page of Manuscript without a Title Page

↑
1"
↓

←1"→ Kate Brody
English 110
Dr. Mythe
March 25, 1996

2 spaces ↕

Bilingual Education Needs Fixing

4 spaces ↕

Indent ⎯⎯⎯→ Started twenty-seven years ago to help poor
5 spaces

Mexican Americans, bilingual education programs

were begun with good intentions, but today they

have grown out of proportion into a $10-billion

bureaucracy annually. . . .

Numbering Subsequent Pages

Brody 2
↑
1"
↓

Bilingual education was intended to give help to new

immigrants. During earlier waves of immigration, children

who . . .

Proofreading Guide

Correction Symbols

Once you have finished typing your paper, be certain that you or someone else proofreads it carefully. Read it aloud or have it read aloud to you. If you notice many mistakes, you should type it over. If there are only a few errors, you can correct them by hand using the following symbols. Just be neat and use dark ink.

a.	to inset an apostrophe or double quotation marks	Is this Gingrich's book?
b.	to insert a word, letter, or comma	insert word, leter or comma
c.	to insert a period	Insert a period
d.	to delete	delete
e.	to indicate a new paragraph	. . . end a sentence. The next point . . .
f.	to indicate no new paragraph	. . . end of a sentence. The next point . . .
g.	to insert a space	insert space
h.	to close up space	close up space
i.	to transpose letters or words	reverse
j.	to indicate a capital letter	september
k.	to indicate a lowercase letter	Small Letters

Proofreading for Mechanics

The following brief summary of some mechanical rules may be of help before you finalize your paper.

Underlining

In typing, underlining is reserved for the following:

a. to identify books, magazines, newspapers, films, or recordings (e.g., tapes, CDs)

Gerald Graff's <u>Beyond the Culture Wars</u>
<u>Time</u> magazine (Notice that *magazine* is not underlined.)
<u>Los Angeles Times</u> (Quotation marks are used around titles
   of chapters, articles, essays, or poems that appear in books,
   magazines, or newspapers.)
Oliver Stone's <u>Truman</u>
The Beatles' <u>Sergeant Pepper's Lonely Hearts Club Band</u>
   (Quotation marks are used around titles of songs in an
   album.)

  b. to identify foreign words not found in a standard U.S. dictionary
     or not in everyday use

     The Welsh call themselves <u>cymry</u>.

  c. to call attention to a particular word

     The word <u>run</u> has more than twenty definitions.
     The student used <u>affect</u> when she meant <u>effect</u>.

  d. to denote sounds

     With a <u>plunk,</u> the penny slowly dropped to the bottom of the
     well.

Note: If your word processor has italic fonts, you can use italics in
place of underlining.

Numbers

In general, these rules apply to writing numbers and figures:

  a. Spell out numbers that can be written in one or two words.
       twenty
       twenty-two (hyphenated numbers are considered one word)
       twenty-two thousand

  b. Use numerals for numbers that require more than two words.
       275 (two hundred seventy-five)
       22,645 (twenty-two thousand, six hundred forty-five)

  c. Numerals are almost always used for money: $35; occasionally
     they're written out: one dollar. There are times when the use of
     figures is more impressive looking. For instance, *one trillion*
     doesn't have the visual snap that seeing the figure
     $1,000,000,000,000 has.

  d. When starting a sentence, it's better to spell out numbers. Forty-
     three people attended the lecture.

e. When referring to page numbers, prices, or scores, use figures.
    From page 16 of <u>Newsweek,</u> he learned that the tickets were
    $15.
    The Giants beat the Cardinals 10–4.

Capital Letters

Use capital letters:

a. to refer to persons, places, and brand names
    Albert Einstein
    Yellowstone National Park
    Porsche
    Harvard University

b. to refer to title or rank
    Mayor Lodge
    Bishop Tutu
    Princess Diana

c. to refer to names of religions and members of them
    Buddhism, Unitarians, Jewish

d. to refer to titles of written works
    Bloom's <u>The Lexington Reader</u> (book)
    Smith's "<u>What Will Become</u> of the Latchkey Kids?" (essay)
    Frost's "Stopping by the Woods" (poem)
    Notice that the phrases *of the* and *by the* in the titles are not
    capitalized. Unless they begin the title, articles (a, an, the), preposi-
    tions (of, on, by, in, to), and conjunctions (and, or) are not capi-
    talized.

e. for the names of the days and months
    This year March has four Sundays.

Manuscript style manuals vary, but unless your instructor requires a
particular style manual, these rules should be acceptable.

APPENDIX B

Quoting and Documenting Sources

Quoting Sources

Quotations from other sources are basically used for one of three reasons: (1) they contain authoritative information or ideas that support or help explain your thesis, (2) they contain ideas you want to argue against or prove wrong, or (3) they are so well-written that they make your point better than your own explanation could. However, before you use any quotations, ask yourself what purpose they serve. Too many quotations can be confusing and distracting to a reader. Quotations should not be used as a substitute for your own writing.

There are several ways of quoting your source material. One way is to quote an entire sentence, such as:

> In her article, "The State of American Values," Susanna McBee claims, "The recent U.S. News & World Report survey findings show that the questions of morality are troubling ordinary people."

Notice that the title and author of the quotation are provided before the quotation is given. Never use a quotation without providing a lead into it. Usually, verbs such as *says, explains, states,* and *writes,* are used to lead into a quotation. In this case, it is *claims*. Notice, too, the placement of punctuation marks, especially the comma after *claims* and the closing quotation marks after the period.

Another way to quote sources is to incorporate part of a quotation into your own writing:

> In her article, "The State of American Values," Susanna McBee claims that a recent survey conducted by U.S. News & World Report shows that "the questions of morality are troubling ordinary people."

Quotation marks are only placed around McBee's exact words. Because her words are used as part of the writer's sentence, the first word from McBee's quotation is not capitalized. Notice the way the quotation marks are placed at the beginning and end of the quotation being used.

At times, you may want to make an indirect quotation. Indirect quotations do not require the use of quotation marks because you are

paraphrasing, that is, rewriting the information using your own words.
Notice how the McBee quotation is paraphrased here:

> In her article, "The State of American Values," Susanna
> McBee states that according to a recent survey conducted
> by U.S. News & World Report, the average person is both-
> ered by what is and isn't moral.

When the exact wording of a quotation is not vital, it is better to
paraphrase the quotation. However, be sure not to change the meaning
of the quotation or to imply something not stated there. When paraphrasing, you must still provide the reader with the source of the
information you paraphrase.

When quotations run more than five lines, don't use quotation
marks. Instead, indent the quoted material ten spaces from the left
and right margins and skip a line. This is called a *block quote* and it
shows that the quotation is not part of your own writing:

> In her article, "The State of American Values," Susanna
> McBee concludes by stating:

> > Where individuals should be cautious, warn social scien-
> > tists and theologians, is in forcing their standards upon
> > others. In the words of the Rev. McKinley Young of Big
> > Bethal AME Church of Atlanta: "When you find some-
> > body waving all those flags and banners, watch closely.
> > Morality, if you're not careful, carries a sense of self-
> > righteousness. Whenever you pat yourself on the back,
> > it creates all kinds of cramps."

Here, quotation marks are not needed for the McBee quotation. But
because McBee's quoted statement contains a quotation by someone
else, those quotation marks must be included in the block quote. This
is a quotation within a quotation.

Try to avoid quotations within quotations that are shorter than
five lines. They are awkward to follow. But if you do need to, here is
the way:

> McBee concludes by saying, "In the words of Rev. McKinley
> Young of Big Bethal AME Church of Atlanta: 'Morality
> . . . carries a sense of self-righteousness. Whenever you pat
> yourself on the back, it creates all kinds of cramps.' "

Notice the position of the first set of quotation marks (")—just before
the beginning of the McBee quotation. Then, when McBee begins

quoting Young's words, a single quotation mark (') is used. Because the entire quotation ends with a quote within a quote, a single quotation mark must be used to show the end of Young's words, followed by a double quotation mark to show the end of McBee's words. You can see why it's best to avoid this structure if possible.

Look in the example above at the use of what looks like three periods (. . .) between the words *Morality* and *carries*. This is called an *ellipsis*, which is used to indicate that part of the quotation is left out. When part of a quote is not important to your point, you may use an ellipsis to shorten the quoted material. Be sure, however, that you haven't changed the meaning of the original quotation. Furthermore, always make certain that the remaining quoted material is a complete thought or sentence, as in the example.

Documenting Sources

Most English instructors require that you document your sources by following the guidelines of the Modern Language Association (MLA). The following examples show how to document most of the sources you would probably use. However, it is not complete, so you may want to consult the *MLA Handbook for Writers of Research Papers* for further information.

When you use quotations, you must identify your sources. Documenting your sources lets your readers know that the information and ideas of others are not your own. It also lets readers know where more information on your subject can be found in case they choose to read your sources for themselves. You cite your sources in two places: in your paper after the quotation, and at the end of your paper under a heading entitled *Works Cited.*

Citing within the Paper

Here's how you would show where the examples above came from.

> In her article, "The State of American Values," Susanna McBee claims, "The recent U.S. News & World Report survey findings show that the questions of morality are troubling ordinary people" (54).

The number in parentheses (54) refers to the page number in the McBee article where the quotation can be found. Because the author and article title are provided in the lead-in to the quote, only the page number is needed at the end. Readers can consult the *Works Cited* at the end of your paper to learn where and when the article appeared. Notice that when the source ends with a quotation the parentheses and page number go *after* the quotation marks and *before* the period.

When paraphrasing a quotation, use the following citation form:

> In her article, "The State of American Values," Susanna McBee states that according to a recent survey conducted by U.S. News & World Report, the average person is both- ered by what is and isn't moral (54).

Here the parentheses and page number go after the last word and before the period.

If the quote is not identified by author, the author's name and page number should be included in the parentheses.

> A recent survey shows that the average person is bothered by what should be considered moral (McBee 54).

By including the author's name and page number, you let the reader know where to look in the *Works Cited* for the complete documenta- tion information.

Works Cited

All the sources used for writing the paper should be listed alphabetically by the author's last name in the *Works Cited*. If no author's name appears on the work, then alphabetize it using the first letter of the first word of the title, unless it begins with an article *(a, an, the)*. Here are the proper forms for the more basic sources. Note especially the punctuation and spacing.

Books by one author

> Bloom, Alan. The Closing of the American Mind. New York: Simon, 1987.

As usual, two spaces are used after periods; single spacing is used elsewhere. A colon is used after the name of the city where the publisher is located, followed by the publisher's name. Book publishers' names can be shortened to conserve space. For instance, the full name of the publisher in the example above is *Simon and Schuster.* A comma is used before the date and a period after it.

If two or more books by the same author are listed, you do not need to provide the name again. Use three hyphens instead. For example:

> ---. Shakespeare's Politics. Chicago: University of Chicago Press, 1972.

Books by two or three authors

> Postman, Neil, and Steve Powers. How to Watch TV News. New York: Penguin, 1992.

The same punctuation and spacing are used, but only the name of the first author listed on the book's title page is inverted. The authors' names are separated by a comma.

Books by more than three authors

> Gundersen, Joan R., et al. America Changing Times, 2nd ed. New York: Wiley, 1993.

The Latin phrase *et al.,* which means *and others,* is used in place of all but the name of the first author listed on the book's title page. Notice its placement and the use of punctuation before and after.

Books that are edited

> Dupuis, Maw M., ed. Reading in the Content Areas. Newark, N.J.: International Reading Association, 1994.

The citing is the same as for authored books except for the insertion of *ed.* to signify that it is edited rather than authored by the person named. If there is more than one editor, follow the same form as for authors, inserting *eds.* after the last editor's name.

Magazine articles

> McBee, Susanna. "The State of American Values." U.S. News & World Report (9 Dec. 1995): 54–58.

When citing magazine articles, use abbreviations for the month. The order of the listing is (1) author, (2) article title, (2) magazine title, (3) date, and (4) page number(s) of the article. Note carefully how and where the punctuation is used.

Newspaper articles

> D'Souza, Dinesh. "The Need for Black Investment." Los Angeles Times (24 September 1995): M2.

The citing is basically the same as that for a magazine article. The difference here is that you include the letter of the newspaper section with the page number ("M2" in the sample).

Scholarly journal articles

> Clair, Linda H. "Teaching Students to Think." Journal of College Reading
> and Learning 26 (1995): 65–74.

Citation for a scholarly journal article is similar as for a magazine
article except that the journal volume number (26 in the example) and
the date (only the year in parentheses) are cited differently. Volume
numbers for journals can usually be found on the cover or on the table
of contents page.

Encyclopedia article

> "Television." Encyclopedia Americana. 1985 ed.

Encyclopedias are written by many staff authors, so no one author
can be cited. Begin with the title of the section you read, then the
name of the encyclopedia, and the date of the edition you used. No
page numbers are needed. Notice the position of the punctuation
marks.

Interview that you conducted yourself

> Stone, James. Personal interview. 9 Jan. 1996.

Lecture

> Dunn, Harold. "Poverty of the Arts in an Affluent Society." Santa Barbara
> City College. 3 May 1996.

If a lecture has no title, substitute the word *Lecture.*

Movies and Videos

> Jules and Jim. Dir. Francois Truffaut. With Jeanne Moreau, Oscar Werner,
> and Henri Serre. Carrose Films, 1962.

The listing order is title, director, actors, distributor, and year the film
was made.

Television shows

> ABC Nightly News. With Peter Jennings. KABC, Los Angeles. 2 May
> 1996.

CD-ROM (original printed source)

> West, Cornel. "The Dilemma of the Black Intellectual." *Critical Quarterly*
> 29 (1987):39–52. *MLA International Biography.* CD-ROM. SilverPlat-
> ter. Feb. 1995.

The listing order for material that has a printed version is the same as it is for the printed source with the addition of the database title (underlined), the publication medium, the name of the vendor (if available), and the publication date of the database.

CD-ROM (no printed source):

> Reemy, Paul. "Company Disclosures." 13 October 1995. *Compact Disclosure.* CD-ROM. Disclosure Inc. 6 June 1996.

The listing order for material that has no printed source is the author's name (if provided), title of the material (placed in quotation marks), the date of the material, then the database information as in the example for database material with a printed version (shown above).

CD-ROM (nonperiodical publication):

> *Mozart: String Quartet in C Major.* CD-ROM. Santa Monica: Voyager. 1991.

Online Database (printed source):

> Mooney, Christopher. "Who is Responsible?" *Christian Science Monitor* 6 July 1995: 9. On-line. Dialog. 12 Jan 1996.

The listing order includes what you would provide for a printed source, plus the medium (such as On-line), the name of the computer service (such as Dialog, CompuServe or America Online) or network (such as Internet), and the date of access.

APPENDIX C

Library Research Sources

There are two types of library sources, *primary* and *secondary*. *Primary sources* are original sources, such as literary works (novels, poems, stories), autobiographies, journals, diaries, letters, or firsthand accounts of events. *Secondary sources* are works that explain or interpret primary sources, such as a literary critic's explanation of a literary work, a biography, an interpretation of a U.S. Supreme Court decision, or an analysis of data based on a scientific study or survey. Secondary sources are often helpful in research because they pull together other information on your topic. However, they are generally opinions or interpretations of others. Primary sources, on the other hand, require your own analysis and interpretation.

Let's say you are assigned to do research on what critics have said about Dinesh D'Souza's *The End of Racism*. In such a case secondary sources will be called for in your paper. If, on the other hand, the assignment calls for your analysis of the book, you will need to stick to the primary source, D'Souza's book. Reading secondary sources on the book, however, may provide you with ideas and arguments that could be useful in supporting your own analysis. The assignment itself will determine which sources are the most useful.

In addition to the usual starting places—the library card catalogue or computer database, which catalogues works in the library under subject and title, and the *Reader's Guide to Periodical Literature,* which indexes current articles from popular magazines such as *Time, Newsweek, Harper's,* and *Ladies' Home Journal*—here are some other sources. Look over the list now to get an idea of what is available in various subject areas.

Encyclopedias

General

Encyclopedia Americana
Encyclopaedia Britannica
Collier's Encyclopedia
New Columbia Encyclopedia
Random House Encyclopedia

Specialized

Bibliography of the Negro in Africa and America
Encyclopedia of World Art
Encyclopedia of the Biological Sciences
Encyclopedia of Management
Encyclopedia of Chemistry
Encyclopedia of Education
Engineering Encyclopedia
Dictionary of American History
Oxford Companion to American History
Oxford Companion to American Literature
Oxford Companion to English Literature
Oxford Companion to the Theatre
Literary History of the United States
Grove's Dictionary of Music and Musicians
Encyclopedia of Pop, Rock, and Soul
World's Encyclopedia of Recorded Music
American Political Dictionary
Encyclopedia of Modern World Politics
Encyclopedia of Psychology
Encyclopedia of Philosophy
Concise Encyclopedia of Western Philosophy
Dictionary of Anthropology
Encyclopedia of Science Fiction and Fantasy
Encyclopedia of the Social Sciences
Encyclopedia of Social Work
Complete Encyclopedia of Television Programs, 1947–1979
New York Times Encyclopedia of Television
Oxford Companion to Sports and Games

Biographical References

Current Biography
Contemporary Authors
Dictionary of American Biography
Twentieth-Century Authors
Who's Who in America
Who's Who Among Black Americans
Who's Who and Where in Women's Studies
Who's Who in Education
Who's Who in American Politics
Who's Who in Rock

Indexes

Social Science and Humanities Index
Humanities Index
Social Sciences Index
Essay and General Literature Index
Art Index
Music Index
Book Review Index
Business Periodical Index
Education Index
American Statistics Index
Applied Science and Technology Index
Biological and Agricultural Index
Computer Literature Index
Engineering Index

Your Librarian

Most librarians enjoy helping students discover what materials are available on a subject and where to locate them in the library. Of course they won't do your research for you, but librarians can save you time when you need to find something. Don't overlook this vital resource, especially if you're unfamiliar with using a library.

Index

Acknowledgments

AKBAR S. AHMED "Terror and Tolerance," by Akbar S. Ahmed, *New Perspectives Quarterly*, Summer 1993. Reprinted by permission of Blackwell Publishers.

GORDON ALLPORT G. Allport, *The Nature of Prejudice*, (pages 178–188), © 1979 by Addison Wesley Publishing Company, Inc. Reprinted by permission of Addison-Wesley Longman Publishing Company, Inc.

KAREN ARMSTRONG "Introduction" from *Muhammad: A Biography of the Prophet* by Karen Armstrong. Copyright © 1992 by Karen Armstrong. Reprinted by permission of HarperCollins Publishers, Inc., and Victor Gollancz Limited.

BEN H. BAGDIKIAN Reprinted with permission from *Mother Jones* Magazine, © 1992. Foundation for National Progress.

DOUG BANDOW "Social Responsibility: A Conservative View," by Doug Bandow, *Business and Society Review*, Spring 1992. Reprinted by permission of the author.

DAVE BARRY From *Dave Barry's Complete Guide to Guys* by Dave Barry. Copyright © 1995 by Dave Barry. Reprinted by permission of Random House, Inc.

BRUCE BRAWER Reprinted with the permission of Simon & Schuster from *A Place at the Table* by Bruce Brawer. Copyright © 1993 by Bruce Brawer.

MARY KAY BLAKELY From *American Mom* by Mary Kay Blakely. Copyright © 1994 by the author. Reprinted by permission of Algonquin Books of Chapel Hill, a division of Workman Publishing.

ROSEMARY BRAY Copyright © 1992 K-III Magazine Corporation. All rights reserved. Reprinted with permission of *New York* Magazine.

JUAN CADENA "It's My Country Too," by Juan Cadena, from *Making Voices/American Dreams: An Oral History of Mexican Immigration to the United States* edited by Marilyn P. Davis, © 1990 by Marilyn P. Davis. Reprinted by permission of Henry Holt and Co., Inc.

JOSEPH CAMPBELL From *Myths to Live By* by Joseph Campbell. Copyright © 1972 by Joseph Campbell. Used by permission of Viking Penguin, a division of Penguin Books USA Inc.

LINDA CHAVEZ "Out of the Barrio," from *Out of the Barrio* by Linda Chavez. Copyright © 1991 by BasicBooks, a division of HarperCollins Publishers Inc. Reprinted by permission of BasicBooks, a division of HarperCollins Publishers, Inc.

CHRISTIAN COALITION From *Contract with the American Family* by Christian Coalition. Copyright © 1995 by Christian Coalition. Reprinted by permission of Ballantine Books, a division of Random House, Inc.

WARD CHURCHILL "The Indian Chant and the Tomahawk Chop," by Ward Churchill, from "Crimes Against Humanity," *Z Magazine*, March 1993.

Acknowledgments

589

NORMAN CORWIN From *Trivializing America* by Norman Corwin. Copyright © 1986 by Norman Corwin. Published by arrangement with Carol Publishing Group.

CATHY CRIMMINS AND TOM NAEDER From *Newt Gingrich's Bedtime Stories for Orphans* by Cathy Crimmins and Tom Naeder. Copyright © 1995. Reprinted by permission of Dove Books.

COUNTEE CULLEN Reprinted by permission of GRM Associates, Inc., Agents for the Estate of Ida M. Cullen. Excerpt from the poem "Heritage" from the book *Color* by Countee Cullen. Copyright © 1925 by Harper & Brothers; copyright renewed 1953 by Ida M. Cullen.

DINESH D'SOUZA Reprinted with the permission of The Free Press, a division of Simon & Schuster from *The End of Racism* by Dinesh D'Souza. Copyright © 1995 by Dinesh D'Souza.

CHARLES DERBER Copyright © 1996 by Charles Derber. From *The Wilding of America: How Greed and Violence are Eroding Our Nation's Character* by Charles Derber. Reprinted by permission of St. Martin's Press Incorporated.

BARBARA DORITY "The War on Rock and Rap Music," by Barbara Dority, *The Humanist*, September/October 1990. Reprinted by permission of the author.

ANDREA DWORKIN From *Pornography* by Andrea Dworkin. Copyright © 1979, 1980, 1981 by Andrea Dworkin. Used by permission of Dutton Signet, a division of Penguin Books USA Inc.

GERALD EARLY Source: "Understanding Afrocentrism," by Gerald Early, *Civilization*, July/August 1995, pp. 31–39. Reprinted by permission of the author.

DEBORAH FALLOWS Reprinted with permission from *The Washington Monthly*. Copyright by The Washington Monthly Company, 1611 Connecticut Ave., N.W., Washington, D.C. 20009 (202) 462-0128.

FARRAKHAN/MONROE " 'They Suck the Life from You'," an interview between Louis Farrakhan and Sylvester Monroe, *Time*, February 28, 1994, pp. 24–25. © 1994 Time Inc. Reprinted by permission.

ANDREW FERGUSON "McNamara's Brand," © 1995 by *National Review*, Inc., 150 East 35th Street, New York, NY 10016. Reprinted by permission.

DAVID FUTRELLE Source: "Surplus Values," by David Futrelle, *In These Times*, November 29, 1993, pp. 14–18. Reprinted by permission.

SUSAN GARVER AND PAULA MCGUIRE "America for the Americans" by Susan Garver and Paula McGuire, from *Coming to North America from Mexico, Cuba and Puerto Rico*. Copyright © 1981 by Visual Education Corporation. Reprinted by permission of Visual Education Corporation.

ANDREW HACKER Reprinted with the permission of Scribner, a Division of Simon & Schuster from *Two Nations: Black and White, Separate, Hostile, Unequal* by Andrew Hacker. Copyright © 1992 by Andrew Hacker.

THICH NHAT HANH Reprinted by permission of The Putnam Publishing Group/Riverhead Books from *Living Buddha, Living Christ* by Thich Nhat Hanh. Copyright © 1995 by Thich Nhat Hanh.

PAUL HAWKEN "A Declaration of Sustainability: 12 Steps Society Can Take to Save the Whole Enchilada," by Paul Hawken, Special to *Utne Reader*, September/October 1993, pp. 54–61. Reprinted by permission.